Microsoft® Official Academic Course

Microsoft® SQL Server® 2005 Implementation and Maintenance (70-431)

Joseph L. Jorden
Dandy Weyn
Dave Owen

WILEY

Credits

EXECUTIVE EDITOR	John Kane
DIRECTOR OF MARKETING AND SALES	Mitchell Beaton
MICROSOFT STRATEGIC RELATIONSHIPS MANAGER	Merrick Van Dongen of Microsoft Learning
EDITORIAL ASSISTANT	Jennifer Lartz
PRODUCTION MANAGER	Micheline Frederick
CREATIVE DIRECTOR/COVER DESIGNER	Harry Nolan
TECHNOLOGY AND MEDIA	Lauren Sapira/Elena Santa Maria
TECHNICAL EDITOR	Steve Strom, Butler Community College

Content in Appendix A from Hellerstein, Joseph M., and Michael Stonebraker, eds., *Readings in Database Systems*, Fourth Edition. 15,000 word excerpt from pages 44–89, © 2005 Massachusetts Institute of Technology, by permission of The MIT Press.

This book was set in Garamond by Aptara, Inc. and printed and bound by Bind Rite Graphics. The covers were printed by Phoenix Color.

ISBN 978-0-470-11596-1

Printed in the United States of America

10 9 8 7 6 5 4 3 2 1

Foreword from the Publisher

Wiley's publishing vision for the Microsoft Official Academic Course series is to provide students and instructors with the skills and knowledge they need to use Microsoft technology effectively in all aspects of their personal and professional lives. Quality instruction is required to help both educators and students get the most from Microsoft's software tools and to become more productive. Thus our mission is to make our instructional programs trusted educational companions for life.

To accomplish this mission, Wiley and Microsoft have partnered to develop the highest quality educational programs for Information Workers, IT Professionals, and Developers. Materials created by this partnership carry the brand name "Microsoft Official Academic Course," assuring instructors and students alike that the content of these textbooks is fully endorsed by Microsoft, and that they provide the highest quality information and instruction on Microsoft products. The Microsoft Official Academic Course textbooks are "Official" in still one more way—they are the officially sanctioned courseware for Microsoft IT Academy members.

The Microsoft Official Academic Course series focuses on *workforce development*. These programs are aimed at those students seeking to enter the workforce, change jobs, or embark on new careers as information workers, IT professionals, and developers. Microsoft Official Academic Course programs address their needs by emphasizing authentic workplace scenarios with an abundance of projects, exercises, cases, and assessments.

The Microsoft Official Academic Courses are mapped to Microsoft's extensive research and job-task analysis, the same research and analysis used to create the Microsoft Certified Technology Specialist (MCTS) exam. The textbooks focus on real skills for real jobs. As students work through the projects and exercises in the textbooks they enhance their level of knowledge and their ability to apply the latest Microsoft technology to everyday tasks. These students also gain resume-building credentials that can assist them in finding a job, keeping their current job, or in furthering their education.

The concept of life-long learning is today an utmost necessity. Job roles, and even whole job categories, are changing so quickly that none of us can stay competitive and productive without continuously updating our skills and capabilities. The Microsoft Official Academic Course offerings, and their focus on Microsoft certification exam preparation, provide a means for people to acquire and effectively update their skills and knowledge. Wiley supports students in this endeavor through the development and distribution of these courses as Microsoft's official academic publisher.

Today educational publishing requires attention to providing quality print and robust electronic content. By integrating Microsoft Official Academic Course products, and Microsoft certifications, we are better able to deliver efficient learning solutions for students and teachers alike.

Bonnie Lieberman
General Manager and Senior Vice President

Welcome to the Microsoft Official Academic Course (MOAC) program for Microsoft SQL Server 2005. MOAC represents the collaboration between Microsoft Learning and John Wiley & Sons, Inc. publishing company. Microsoft and Wiley teamed up to produce a series of textbooks that deliver compelling and innovative teaching solutions to instructors and superior learning experiences for students. Infused and informed by in-depth knowledge from the creators of Microsoft products, and crafted by a publisher known worldwide for the pedagogical quality of its products these textbooks maximize skills transfer in minimum time. Students are challenged to reach their potential by using their new technical skills as highly productive members of the workforce.

Because this knowledgebase comes directly from Microsoft, architect of Microsoft SQL Server 2005 and creator of the Microsoft Certified Technology Specialist (MCTS) exams (www.microsoft.com/learning/mcp/mcts), you are sure to receive the topical coverage that is most relevant to students' personal and professional success. Microsoft's direct participation not only assures you that MOAC textbook content is accurate and current; it also means that students will receive the best instruction possible to enable their success on certification exams and in the workplace.

■ The Microsoft Official Academic Course Program

The *Microsoft Official Academic Course* series is a complete program for instructors and institutions to prepare and deliver great courses on Microsoft software technologies. With MOAC, we recognize that, because of the rapid pace of change in the technology and curriculum developed by Microsoft, there is an ongoing set of needs beyond classroom instruction tools for an instructor to be ready to teach the course. The MOAC program endeavors to provide solutions for all these needs in a systematic manner in order to ensure a successful and rewarding course experience for both instructor and student—technical and curriculum training for instructor readiness with new software releases; the software itself for student use at home for building hands-on skills, assessment, and validation of skill development; and a great set of tools for delivering instruction in the classroom and lab. All are important to the smooth delivery of an interesting course on Microsoft software, and all are provided with the MOAC program. We think about the model below as a gauge for ensuring that we completely support you in your goal of teaching a great course. As you evaluate your instructional materials options, you may wish to use the model for comparison purposes with available products.

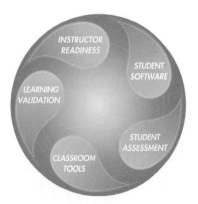

■ Pedagogical Features

The MOAC textbook for Microsoft SQL Server 2005 is designed to cover all the learning objectives for that MCTS exam, which is referred to as its "objective domain." The Microsoft Certified Technology Specialist (MCTS) exam objectives are highlighted throughout the textbook. Many pedagogical features have been developed specifically for *Microsoft Official Academic Course* programs.

Presenting the extensive procedural information and technical concepts woven throughout the textbook raises challenges for the student and instructor alike. The Illustrated Book Tour that follows provides a guide to the rich features contributing to *Microsoft Official Academic Course* program's pedagogical plan. Following is a list of key features in each lesson designed to prepare students for success on the certification exams and in the workplace:

- Each lesson begins with a **Lesson Skill Matrix.** More than a standard list of learning objectives, the Domain Matrix correlates each software skill covered in the lesson to the specific MCTS objective domain.3

- Concise and frequent **Step-by-Step** instructions teach students new features and provide an opportunity for hands-on practice. Numbered steps give detailed, step-by-step instructions to help students learn software skills.

- **Key Terms:** Important technical vocabulary is listed with definitions at the beginning of the lesson. When these terms are used later in the lesson, they appear in bold italic type and are defined. The Glossary contains all of the key terms and their definitions.

- Engaging point-of-use **Reader Aids,** located throughout the lessons, tell students why this topic is relevant (*The Bottom Line*), provide students with helpful hints (*Take Note*), or show alternate ways to accomplish tasks (*Another Way*). Reader Aids also provide additional relevant or background information that adds value to the lesson.

- **Certification Ready?** features throughout the text signal students where a specific certification objective is covered. They provide students with a chance to check their understanding of that particular MCTS objective and, if necessary, review the section of the lesson where it is covered. MOAC offers complete preparation for MCTS certification.

- **Knowledge Assessments** provide multiple-choice questions and Case Scenarios.

- **Student CD:** The companion CD contains files necessary for completing exercises and six complete practice exams that correspond to the MCTS exam in a special testing package.

■ Lesson Features

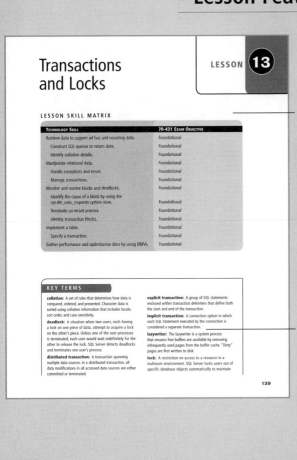

Lesson Skill Matrix

X Ref
Reader Aid

Key Terms

The Bottom
Line Reader
Aid

Transactions and Locks

LESSON 13

LESSON SKILL MATRIX

TECHNOLOGY SKILL	70-431 EXAM OBJECTIVE
Retrieve data to support ad hoc and recurring data.	Foundational
Construct SQL queries to return data.	Foundational
Identify collation details.	Foundational
Manipulate relational data.	Foundational
Handle exceptions and errors.	Foundational
Manage transactions.	Foundational
Monitor and resolve blocks and deadlocks.	Foundational
Identify the cause of a block by using the sys.dm_exec_requests system view.	Foundational
Terminate an errant process.	Foundational
Identify transaction blocks.	Foundational
Implement a table.	Foundational
Specify a transaction.	Foundational
Gather performance and optimization data by using DMVs.	Foundational

KEY TERMS

collation: A set of rules that determines how data is compared, ordered, and presented. Character data is sorted using collation information that includes locale, sort order, and case sensitivity.

deadlock: A situation when two users, each having a lock on one piece of data, attempt to acquire a lock on the other's piece. Unless one of the user processes is terminated, each user would wait indefinitely for the other to release the lock. SQL Server detects deadlocks and terminates one user's process.

distributed transaction: A transaction spanning multiple data sources. In a distributed transaction, all data modifications in all accessed data sources are either committed or terminated.

explicit transaction: A group of SQL statements enclosed within transaction delimiters that define both the start and end of the transaction.

implicit transaction: A connection option in which each SQL Statement executed by the connection is considered a separate transaction.

lazywriter: The lazywriter is a system process that ensures free buffers are available by removing infrequently used pages from the buffer cache. "Dirty" pages are first written to disk.

lock: A restriction on access to a resource in a multiuser environment. SQL Server locks users out of specific database objects automatically to maintain

139

---

140 | Lesson 13

security or prevent concurrent data modification problems.

transaction: A group of database operations combined into a logical unit of work that is either wholly committed or totally rolled back.

transaction log: A database file in which all changes to the database are recorded. SQL Server

uses transaction logs during recovery to assure data integrity.

transaction rollback: Recovery of a user-specified transaction to the last savepoint inside a transaction or to the beginning of transaction; used to restore data to a known and correct state.

■ Using Transactions

THE BOTTOM LINE

A *transaction* is a series of steps that perform a logical unit of work. Transactions must adhere to ACID properties, that is:

1. **Atomicity:** Either all of the steps must succeed or none of them may succeed.
2. **Consistency:** The data must be left in a predictable and usable state.
3. **Isolation:** Changes made must not be influenced by other concurrent transactions.
4. **Durability:** The changes made must be permanent in the database and survive even system failures.

Understanding Transactions

To help you understand how SQL Server handles and works with transactions to perform data manipulations (via DML), this section will cover how data is inserted and allocated in memory before the data is written into the *transaction log*, and then how it is applied to the database data files. When performing data manipulations, SQL Server records all changes made in the transaction log to allow any changes to be undone (rolled back) or redone (rolled forward) in case of a system failure.

When updating or inserting a record into a database, the record is first allocated in buffer memory, and the buffer manager guarantees that the transaction log is written before the changes to the database file are written. It does this by keeping track of a log position using a log sequence number (LSN).

At certain intervals, SQL Server issues a checkpoint in the transaction log that issues a write from the transaction log to the data file. Depending on the setting of the transaction log defined in the database recovery model, the transaction log will keep the committed and written records in the transaction log or truncate the log.

This process of working with the transaction log and recording actions in the transaction log before applying them to the actual data files allows SQL Server to recover from failures in case of an unexpected shutdown; this is known as *autorecovery*.

The autorecovery process will check the database to see what the last-issued checkpoint and written LSN were and will then write all committed records from the transaction log that were not recorded yet in the data file to the data file. This process is a rollforward. Different from other database systems such as Oracle, SQL Server automatically issues a transaction (autocommitted) on every statement, so you don't need to explicitly commit these transactions.

UNDERSTANDING THE TRANSACTION LOG

SQL Server 2005 uses a buffer cache, which is an in-memory structure, into which it retrieves data pages from disk for use by applications and users. Each modification to a data page is made to the copy of the page in the buffer cache. A modified buffer page in the

---

150 | Lesson 13

PRESENTING DATA IN A DIFFERENT FORMAT

To format data, you have several functions you can apply to a query. For example, you can apply the CONVERT function to convert between datatypes; or you can format datetime options, as shown here:

```
- This example will display a string with
- the current date displayed as: Today is mm/dd/yyyy
SELECT 'Today is ' + CONVERT(varchar,getdate(),101) as 'Current Date'
```

Notice that only the SELECT keyword is required; all others are optional.

PRESENTING DATA IN A DIFFERENT ORDER

The ORDER BY clause provides the primary means of organizing data, and it has two major keywords: ASC and DESC. Specifying ASC (the default) causes the resultset to begin with the minimum value and end with the maximum value, as in these two short examples:

```
1            A
2            B
3            C
```

Specifying DESC causes the resultset to begin with the maximum value and end with the minimum value, as in these two short examples:

```
3            C
2            B
1            A
```

PRESENTING DATA IN DIFFERENT COLLATIONS

Collations are used within databases to display and store an international character set, based on business requirements. When returning data, you have the ability to retrieve the data in a collation type different from how it was stored. When working with these multiple collations, you can invoke the COLLATE keyword and then specify the collation type you prefer to use. You can use the COLLATE keyword in various ways and at several levels:

COLLATE on database creation: You can use the COLLATE clause of the CREATE DATABASE or ALTER DATABASE statement to specify the default collation of the database. You can also specify a collation when you create a database using SQL Server Management Studio. If you do not specify a collation, the database is assigned the default collation of the instance of SQL Server.

COLLATE on table creation: You can specify collations for each varchar or char column using the COLLATE clause in the CREATE TABLE or ALTER TABLE statement. You can also specify a collation when you create a table using SQL Server Management Studio. If you do not specify a collation, the column is assigned the default collation of the database.

COLLATE by casting or expression: You can use the COLLATE clause to cast an expression to a certain collation. You can assign the COLLATE clause to any ORDER BY or comparison statement, as listed in the example here:

```
USE AdventureWorks
SELECT FirstName, LastName from Person.Contact
ORDER BY LastName COLLATE Latin1_General_BIN
```

Collations supported by SQL 2005 SQL Server 2005 supports more than 1,000 collation types, so it is important to know whether the data you want to retrieve needs to match a certain collation.

To view an overview of existing collation types, since you have to reference them by name in SQL Server 2005, use SQL Server Books Online and the fn_ HelpCollations( ) function, as in:

```
SELECT * from fn_HelpCollations().
```

X REF

For a list and explanation of the built-in functions for presenting data, see Lesson 12.

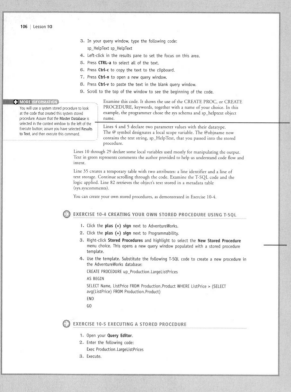

More Information Reader Aid

Hands-on Practice

Easy-to-Read Tables

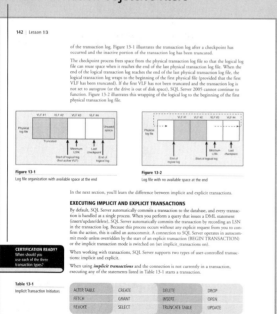

MCTS Certification Objective Alert

Take Note Reader Aid

SQL Server 2005 Stored Procedures | 109

- ERROR_SEVERITY( )
- ERROR_STATE( )

CHANGING STORED PROCEDURES

You may DROP (the syntax is DROP PROC *Name*) at any time and CREATE a replacement. This also drops any associated permissions.

When changing something about the stored procedure, consider using the ALTER PROC syntax. This retains the established security context.

Introducing CLR Procedures

A common language runtime (CLR) procedure is a reference to a method that supports parameters and is cataloged as a procedure in SQL Server. CLR procedures are written in a .NET CLR interpretable language such as Visual Basic .NET or C#. A .NET Framework CLR method is exposed to SQL as a method defined in a .NET assembly. Before you can use a CLR procedure, the assembly needs to be cataloged in SQL Server (CREATE ASSEMBLY), and the method within the assembly needs to be exposed as a SQL Server stored procedure (CREATE PROCEDURE).

Using Visual Studio, you can automatically deploy the stored procedure from within an SQL Server project. Within SQL Server, the user who references or calls the CLR procedure won't see any difference between a CLR procedure call and a T-SQL procedure call; it is called, just like a T-SQL stored procedure, using the EXEC keyword.

The scope and functionality of a CLR procedure is huge. You can create a procedure that uses the entire .NET Framework, meaning it will allow you to gain access to external objects outside SQL Server.

Since a SQL Server CLR procedure runs and is hosted within the .NET Framework, it is common to use CLR or managed procedures for complex calculations and for access to objects such as the network or file system.

CREATING CLR STORED PROCEDURES

To create a CLR stored procedure, you will use a development tool such as Visual Studio. The actual syntax in Visual Studio will then depend on the language in which you program (coverage of the syntax to create managed stored procedures is beyond the scope of this text for the exam certification).

Creating and Deploying a CLR Procedure

You write a CLR or managed code procedure in a CLR-supported language such as Visual Basic .NET or C#. From within Visual Studio 2005, you can create a SQL Server project.

When a project is deployed to SQL Server, the assembly or DLL file will be cataloged in the SQL database. These objects are displayable by querying the sys.assemblies system view.

However, it is possible to deploy a solution from within Visual Studio 2005. It is common for a database administrator to catalog the assembly and then create procedures from the methods exposed within the library (DLL or assembly).

ENABLING THE SERVER FOR CLR SUPPORT

Before you can use CLR-managed objects, you first need to enable the server for CLR support. The CLR integration is a feature; it can be enabled or disabled. You do this by executing the following syntax:

```
sp_configure 'clr_enabled', 1
reconfigure
```

ANOTHER WAY

Open **SQL Server 2005 Surface Area Configuration → Surface Area Configuration for Features → Database Engine → CLR Integration → Enable CLR Integration.**

Another Way Reader Aid

Skill Summary

SQL Server 2005 Transactions and Locks | 155

Remember that all INSERT, UPDATE, and DELETE actions are logged in the transaction file. Should you need to audit what happens on the network or in the transaction file, third-party tools can capture and read all activities, allowing you to prove data changes prior to being stored in the database.

SKILL SUMMARY

IN THIS LESSON YOU LEARNED:

Working with transactions allows you to roll back or cancel a transaction to execute in case of a certain event or condition, or even roll back multiple grouped statements in a distributed environment.

SQL Server 2005 supports various recovery models. The most common—but also the one with the biggest transaction log size—is the Full recovery model. However, if you perform large amounts of batch and bulk inserts, it might be useful not to set the recovery model to Full and instead use the Bulk-Logged recovery model.

The error handling in SQL Server 2005 is one of the best error-handling capabilities so far in the SQL language because it implements a TRY...CATCH block, just as it does in programming languages such as VisualBasic and C#. Since the release of SQL Server 2005, you can now easily retrieve the error message, which was a bit more difficult in SQL Server 2000.

For the certification examination:

- Understand and be able to use transactions. You need to truly understand how transactions work and how you can enforce an explicit transaction within a SQL batch. It is also important to understand how distributed transactions work and how you can implement error handling within the transactional processing.

- Know how to identify collations. You need to understand that SQL Server uses collations to play around with different sort orders and character sets within the database. Collations can be designed on a database level, but they also are implemented with the table creation—or even enforced by explicitly casting or converting to a different collation type. Understand how to handle exceptions and errors. The main focus on error handling should be on how to implement a TRY...CATCH block and roll back transactions within the error handling. You need to be familiar with the new methods in error handling and how to use their syntax.

- Understand how to configure database recovery models. When configuring database recovery models, you need to fully understand that a BULK INSERT statement has a huge impact on the size of your transaction log when defined in a Full recovery model. Therefore, you must be able to identify when to use a Bulk-Logged recovery model to minimize the impact on the transaction log and transaction log performance.

- Know how to format query results. When working with queries, it is important to understand datatype conversion and the various functions that can be used within T-SQL to format a query layout.

■ **Knowledge Assessment**

Multiple Choice

Circle the letter or letters that correspond to the best answer or answers.

1. You are designing two order-processing SQL Server 2000 client applications. Application A will be used by the sales representatives for taking orders. Application B will be used by the shipping employees when fulfilling orders. Both applications

Case Scenarios

SQL Server 2005 Transactions and Locks | 157

you obtain an error. How can you make the stored procedure work with a minimum amount of effort?
   a. Use the COLLATE keyword to convert one of the columns to the collation of the other column.
   b. Alter one of the tables, and use the same collations as for the other column.
   c. Alter both tables, and choose a common collation for both columns.
   d. Use a temporary table.

8. Which of the following operators and functions are collation-sensitive? (Select all that apply.)
   a. The MAX operator
   b. UNION ALL
   c. CHARINDEX
   d. REPLACE

9. Which options are available in SQL Server 2005 to limit the number of rows returned by a query? (Select all that apply.)
   a. The TOP operator
   b. The TABLESAMPLE clause
   c. The SET ROWCOUNT statement
   d. The @@ROWCOUNT function

10. What options to retrieve metadata are available in SQL Server? (Select all that apply.)
   a. Catalog views
   b. Dynamic management views
   c. Dynamic management functions
   d. Information schema views

11. You have a query that displays a list of products. You want to make the results more readable for the product names. Which code can help you?
   a. SELECT CAST(ProdName AS char(32)) AS ProductName FROM Sales.Products
   b. SELECT CAST(ProdName AS varchar(32)) AS ProductName FROM Sales.Products
   c. SELECT CAST(ProdName AS nvarchar(32)) AS ProductName FROM Sales.Products
   d. SELECT ProdName FROM Sales.Products

■ **Case Scenarios**

Scenario 13-1: Avoiding Performance Snags

You have been promoted to program manager. Your job is to see that the application programmers and database administrators work together to achieve the milestones laid out by upper management. Initial testing has shown really poor response. Each query appears to halt briefly, and they don't all return resultsets. As a classroom discussion, what is probably going on? What are the likely solutions?

Knowledge Assessment Questions

www.wiley.com/college/microsoft or call the MOAC Toll-Free Number: 1+(888) 764-7001 (U.S. & Canada only)

Conventions and Features Used in This Book

This book uses particular fonts, symbols, and heading conventions to highlight important information or to call your attention to special steps. For more information about the features in each lesson, refer to the Illustrated Book Tour section.

CONVENTION	MEANING
↓ THE BOTTOM LINE	This feature provides a brief summary of the material to be covered in the section that follows.
CERTIFICATION READY?	This feature signals the point in the text where a specific certification objective is covered. It provides you with a chance to check your understanding of that particular MCTS objective and, if necessary, review the section of the lesson where it is covered.
TAKE NOTE	Reader aids appear in shaded boxes found in your text. *Take Note* provides helpful hints related to particular tasks or topics.
◆ ANOTHER WAY	*Another Way* provides an alternative procedure for accomplishing a particular task.
X REF	These notes provide pointers to information discussed elsewhere in the textbook or describe interesting features of SQL Server that are not directly addressed in the current topic or exercise.
A *check constraint* is a T-SQL statment that is linked to a field.	Key terms appear in bold italic.
Key **My Name is**.	Any text you are asked to key appears in bold.
Click **OK**.	Any button on the screen you are supposed to click on or select will also appear in bold.

■ Beginning the Course

This course has three prerequisites as outlined in Lesson 1. If you take the Readiness Test in Lesson 1 and then lack confidence in successfully completing this course, start with the Database Concepts presented in Appendix A and Data Manipulation Language material covered in Appendix B.

Appendix A provides guidance in developing an enterprise database; a historical background to help you understand what developments led to the creation of a relational database management system (RDBMS); several architectural differences in the design of competing RDBMSs; and objects you must manage in your RDBMS as a SQL Server Administrator.

Appendix B offers an introduction to the Structured Query Language. SQL Server 2005, more than any previous edition, requires knowledge of code structures—both Transact-SQL and Common Language Runtime options. Many of the configuration wizards prompt for Transact-SQL entries prior to completion. Checking for data in Dynamic Management Views is best done with queries.

■ Student CD

The CD-ROM included with this book contains six complete practice exams that will help you hone your knowledge before you take the MCTS: SQL Server 2005 (Exam 70-431) certification examination. Each exam has between 50 and 60 questions and is timed for 90 minutes. The exams are meant to simulate the testing environment you will encounter as you take the certification examination; as well, they are good practice and reinforcement of the material covered in the course.

The enclosed Student CD will run automatically. Upon accepting the licensing agreement, you will proceed directly to the exams. The exams also can be accessed through the Assets folder located within the CD files.

■ Technical Support

If you have trouble with the CD-ROM, please call the Wiley Product Technical Support phone number: (800) 762-2974. Outside the United States, call 1(317) 572-3994. You can also contact Wiley Product Technical Support through the internet at: http://support.wiley.com. Wiley Publishing will provide technical support only for installation and other general quality control items; for technical support on the applications themselves, consult the program's vendor or author.

Instructor Support Program

The *Microsoft Official Academic Course* programs are accompanied by a rich array of resources that incorporate the extensive textbook visuals to form a pedagogically cohesive package. These resources provide all the materials instructors need to deploy and deliver their courses. Resources available online for download include:

- The **MSDN Academic Alliance** is designed to provide the easiest and most inexpensive developer tools, products, and technologies available to faculty and students in labs, classrooms, and on student PCs. A free 3-year membership is available to qualified MOAC adopters.

  Note: Microsoft SQL Server 2005 can be downloaded from MSDN AA for use by students in this course

- The **Instructor's Guide** contains Solutions to all the textbook exercises and Syllabi for various term lengths. The Instructor's Guide also includes chapter summaries and lecture notes. The Instructor's Guide is available from the Book Companion site (http://www.wiley.com/college/microsoft).

- **PowerPoint Presentations and Images.** A complete set of PowerPoint presentations is available on the Instructor's Book Companion site (http://www.wiley.com/college/microsoft). Approximately 50 PowerPoint slides are provided for each lesson. Tailored to the text's topical coverage and Skills Matrix, these presentations are designed to convey key SQL Server concepts addressed in the text.

  All figures from the text are on the Instructor's Book Companion site (http://www.wiley.com/college/microsoft). You can incorporate them into your PowerPoint presentations, or create your own overhead transparencies and handouts.

  By using these visuals in class discussions, you can help focus students' attention on key elements of SQL Server and help them understand how to use it effectively in the workplace.

- **The Wiley Faculty Network** lets you tap into a large community of your peers effortlessly. Wiley Faculty Network mentors are faculty like you, from educational institutions around the country, who are passionate about enhancing instructional efficiency and effectiveness through best practices. Faculty Network activities include technology training and tutorials, virtual seminars, peer-to-peer exchanges of experience and ideas, personal consulting, and sharing of resources. To register for a seminar, go to www.wherefacultyconnect.com or phone 1-866-4FACULTY (U.S. and Canada only).

MSDN ACADEMIC ALLIANCE—FREE 3-YEAR MEMBERSHIP AVAILABLE TO QUALIFIED ADOPTERS!

MSDN Academic Alliance (MSDN AA) is designed to provide the easiest and most inexpensive way for universities to make the latest Microsoft developer tools, products, and technologies available in labs, classrooms, and on student PCs. MSDN AA is an annual membership program for departments teaching Science, Technology, Engineering, and Mathematics (STEM) courses. The membership provides a complete solution to keep academic labs, faculty, and students on the leading edge of technology.

Software available in the MSDN AA program is provided at no charge to adopting departments through the Wiley and Microsoft publishing partnership.

As a bonus to this free offer, faculty will be introduced to Microsoft's Faculty Connection and Academic Resource Center. It takes time and preparation to keep students engaged while giving them a fundamental understanding of theory, and the Microsoft Faculty Connection is designed to help STEM professors with this preparation by providing articles, curriculum, and tools that professors can use to engage and inspire today's technology students.

* Contact your Wiley rep for details.

For more information about the MSDN Academic Alliance program, go to:

http://msdn.microsoft.com/academic/

Note: Microsoft SQL Server 2005 can be downloaded from MSDN AA for use by students in this course.

Important Web Addresses and Phone Numbers

To locate the Wiley Higher Education Rep in your area, go to the following Web address and click on the "*Who's My Rep?*" link at the top of the page.

http://www.wiley.com/college

Or Call the MOAC Toll Free Number: 1 + (888) 764-7001 (U.S. & Canada only).

To learn more about becoming a Microsoft Certified Technology Specialist and exam availability, visit www.microsoft.com/learning/mcp/mcts.

Book Companion Website (www.wiley.com/college/microsoft)

The book companion site for the MOAC series includes the Instructor Resources, the student course files, and Web links to important information for students and instructors.

Wiley Desktop Editions

> **ANOTHER WAY**
>
> You can use the Search function in the Open dialog box to quickly find the specific file for which you are looking.

Wiley MOAC Desktop Editions are innovative, electronic versions of printed textbooks. Students buy the desktop version for 50% off the U.S. price of the printed text, and get the added value of permanence and portability. Wiley Desktop Editions provide students with numerous additional benefits that are not available with other e-text solutions.

Wiley Desktop Editions are NOT subscriptions; students download the Wiley Desktop Edition to their computer desktops. Students own the content they buy to keep for as long as they want. Once a Wiley Desktop Edition is downloaded to the computer desktop, students have instant access to all of the content without being online. Students can also print out the sections they prefer to read in hard copy. Students also have access to fully integrated resources within their Wiley Desktop Edition. From highlighting their e-text to taking and sharing notes, students can easily personalize their Wiley Desktop Edition as they are reading or following along in class.

Preparing to Take the Microsoft Certified Technology Specialist (MCTS) Exam

The Microsoft Certified Technology Specialist program is part of the new and enhanced Microsoft Business Certifications. It is easily attainable through a series of verifications that provide a simple and convenient framework for skills assessment and validation.

For organizations, the new certification program provides better skills verification tools that help with assessing not only in-demand skills on Microsoft SQL Server 2005, but also the ability to quickly complete on-the-job tasks. Individuals will find it easier to identify and work towards the certification credential that meets their personal and professional goals.

Obtaining this certificate for SQL Server 2005 has only one examination requirement, 70-431TS: Microsoft SQL Server 2005—Implementation and Maintenance. Your book gives you the information you need to prepare for this exam. But don't put the book away after you pass and you have advanced at work; it will serve as a valuable reference during your career as a SQL Server 2005 professional.

Introducing the Microsoft Certification Program

Since the inception of its certification program, Microsoft has certified millions of people. Over the years, Microsoft has learned what it takes to help people show their skills through certification. Based on that experience, Microsoft has introduced a new generation of certifications:

- Microsoft Certified Technology Specialist (MCTS)
- Microsoft Certified IT Professional (MCITP)

- Microsoft Certified Professional Developer (MCPD)
- Microsoft Certified Architect (MCA)

TAKE NOTE *

For more details about the new generation of Microsoft Certifications visit: www.microsoft.com/learning/mcp.

The *MCTS certification program* is designed to validate core technology and product skills for a specific product. It helps you prove you are capable of implementing, building, troubleshooting, and debugging that product.

The new generation of exams offers a shorter certification path than previous iterations. For example, to become a Microsoft Certified Database Administrator (applicable to SQL Server 2000), you have to pass four exams. To obtain an MCTS certification, you need to pass only one exam.

Having achieved your MCTS, you may aspire to achieve recognized competency in one or more of three additional Microsoft certification tracks leading to becoming a Microsoft Certified Information Technology Professional:

- Database Developer, exam 70–441 and exam 70–442
- Database Administrator, exam 70–443 and exam 70–444
- Business Intelligence Developer, exam 70–445 and exam 70–446

Becoming Certified on SQL Server 2005

As mentioned, you have to pass only one test to gain certification, but attaining a Microsoft certification has always been a challenge. In the past, students have been able to acquire detailed exam information—even most of the exam questions—from online "brain dumps" and third party "cram" books or software products. No longer.

To ensure that a Microsoft certification really means something, Microsoft has taken strong steps to protect the security and integrity of its certification tracks. Now prospective candidates must complete a course of study that develops detailed knowledge about a wide range of topics. The training supplies them with the true skills needed, derived from working with SQL Server 2005.

The SQL Server 2005 certification programs are heavily weighted toward hands-on skills and experience. Microsoft has stated that "nearly half of the core required exam's content demands that the candidate have troubleshooting skills acquired through hands-on experience and working knowledge."

Fortunately, if you are willing to dedicate the time and effort to learn SQL Server 2005, you can prepare yourself well for the exams by using the proper tools. By working through this book, you can successfully meet the exam requirements to pass the SQL Server 2005—Implementation and Maintenance exam.

Registering for the Exam

You may take the Microsoft exams at any Authorized Prometric Testing Center (APTC). For the location of a testing center near you, call Prometric at 800-755-EXAM (755-3926). Outside the United States and Canada, contact your local Prometric registration center.

Find out the number of the exam you want to take (70-431 for the SQL Server 2005—Implementation and Maintenance exam), and then register with Prometric. At this point, you will be asked for advance payment for the exam. The exams vary in price depending on the country in which you take them. You can schedule exams up to six weeks in advance or as late as one working day prior to the date of the exam. You can cancel or reschedule your exam if you contact the center at least two working days prior to the exam. Same-day registration is available in some locations, subject to space availability. Where same-day registration is available, you must register a minimum of two hours before test time.

You may also register for your exams online at www.prometric.com.

When you schedule the exam, you will be provided with instructions regarding appointment and cancellation procedures, information about ID requirements, and information about the testing center location. In addition, you will receive a registration and payment confirmation letter from Prometric.

Microsoft requires certification candidates to accept the terms of a nondisclosure agreement before taking certification exams.

Understanding the Types of Exam Questions

In an effort to both refine the testing process and protect the quality of its certifications, Microsoft has focused its exams on real experience and hands-on proficiency. The test places greater emphasis on your past working environments and responsibilities and less emphasis on how well you can memorize. In fact, Microsoft says an MCTS candidate should have at least one year of hands-on experience.

Microsoft will accomplish its goal of protecting the exams' integrity by regularly adding and removing exam questions, limiting the number of questions that any individual sees in a beta exam, and adding new exam elements.

The 70–431 exam covers a set of precise objectives. This book is based on these objectives and requirements for the Microsoft exam. When you take the exam, you will see approximately 52 questions, although the number of questions might be subject to change. At the end of an exam, you will get your exam score, pointing out your level of knowledge on each topic and your exam score total with a pass or a fail.

Exam questions may be in a variety of formats. Depending on which exam you take, you'll see:

- Simulations
- Multiple-choice questions
- Select-and-place questions
- Prioritize-a-list questions

TAKE NOTE*

Microsoft publishes the objectives at www.microsoft.com/learning/exams/70-431.mspx.

Answering Simulation Questions

Simulations require you to actually execute tasks, rather than simply answering questions about it in order to assess working skill levels. The focus is on results, not the path taken to achieve the correct result.

Answering Multiple-choice Questions

Multiple-choice questions come in two main forms. One is a straightforward question followed by several possible answers, of which one or more is correct. The other type of multiple-choice question is more complex and based on a specific scenario. The scenario may focus on several areas or objectives.

Answering Select-and-place Questions

Select-and-place exam questions involve graphical elements that you must manipulate to successfully answer the question. A typical diagram will show computers and other components next to boxes that contain the text "Place here." The labels for the boxes represent various computer roles on a network, such as a print server and a file server. Based on information given for each computer, you are asked to select each label and place it in the correct box. You need to place all the labels correctly. No credit is given for the question if you correctly label only some of the boxes.

Answering Prioritize-a-list Questions

In the prioritize-a-list questions, you might be asked to put a series of steps in order by dragging items from boxes on the left to boxes on the right and placing them in the correct order. One other type requires that you drag an item from the left and place it under an item in a column on the right.

Microsoft will regularly add and remove questions from the exams. This is called item seeding. It is part of the effort to make it more difficult for individuals to merely memorize exam questions that previous test takers gave them.

Taking the Exam

Here are some general tips for achieving success on your certification exam:

- Arrive early at the exam center so you can relax and review your study materials. During this final review, you can look over tables and lists of exam-related information.
- Read the questions carefully. Don't be tempted to jump to an early conclusion. Make sure you know exactly what the question is asking.
- For questions you're not sure about, use a process of elimination to get rid of the obviously incorrect answers first. This improves your odds of selecting the correct answer when you need to make an educated guess.

CERTIFICATION READY?
For more information on the various exam question types, go to www.microsoft.com/learning.

Acknowledgments

We thank the hundreds of instructors who participated in our focus groups and surveys to ensure that the Microsoft Official Academic Courses best met the needs of our customers.

Jean Aguilar, Mt. Hood Community College
Konrad Akens, Zane State College
Michael Albers, University of Memphis
Diana Anderson, Big Sandy Community & Technical College
Phyllis Anderson, Delaware County Community College
Judith Andrews, Feather River College
Damon Antos, American River College
Bridget Archer, Oakton Community College
Linda Arnold, Harrisburg Area Community College–
   Lebanon Campus
Neha Arya, Fullerton College
Mohammad Bajwa, Katharine Gibbs School–New York
Virginia Baker, University of Alaska Fairbanks
Carla Bannick, Pima Community College
Rita Barkley, Northeast Alabama Community College
Elsa Barr, Central Community College–Hastings
Ronald W. Barry, Ventura County Community College
   District
Elizabeth Bastedo, Central Carolina Technical College
Karen Baston, Waubonsee Community College
Karen Bean, Blinn College
Scott Beckstrand, Community College of Southern Nevada
Paulette Bell, Santa Rosa Junior College
Liz Bennett, Southeast Technical Institute
Nancy Bermea, Olympic College
Lucy Betz, Milwaukee Area Technical College
Meral Binbasioglu, Hofstra University
Catherine Binder, Strayer University & Katharine Gibbs
   School–Philadelphia
Terrel Blair, El Centro College
Ruth Blalock, Alamance Community College
Beverly Bohner, Reading Area Community College
Henry Bojack, Farmingdale State University
Matthew Bowie, Luna Community College
Julie Boyles, Portland Community College
Karen Brandt, College of the Albemarle
Stephen Brown, College of San Mateo
Jared Bruckner, Southern Adventist University
Pam Brune, Chattanooga State Technical
   Community College
Sue Buchholz, Georgia Perimeter College
Roberta Buczyna, Edison College

Angela Butler, Mississippi Gulf Coast Community College
Rebecca Byrd, Augusta Technical College
Kristen Callahan, Mercer County Community College
Judy Cameron, Spokane Community College
Dianne Campbell, Athens Technical College
Gena Casas, Florida Community College at Jacksonville
Jesus Castrejon, Latin Technologies
Gail Chambers, Southwest Tennessee Community College
Jacques Chansavang, Indiana University–Purdue University
   Fort Wayne
Nancy Chapko, Milwaukee Area Technical College
Rebecca Chavez, Yavapai College
Sanjiv Chopra, Thomas Nelson Community College
Greg Clements, Midland Lutheran College
Dayna Coker, Southwestern Oklahoma State University–
   Sayre Campus
Tamra Collins, Otero Junior College
Janet Conrey, Gavilan Community College
Carol Cornforth, West Virginia Northern
   Community College
Gary Cotton, American River College
Edie Cox, Chattahoochee Technical College
Rollie Cox, Madison Area Technical College
David Crawford, Northwestern Michigan College
J.K. Crowley, Victor Valley College
Rosalyn Culver, Washtenaw Community College
Sharon Custer, Huntington University
Sandra Daniels, New River Community College
Anila Das, Cedar Valley College
Brad Davis, Santa Rosa Junior College
Susan Davis, Green River Community College
Mark Dawdy, Lincoln Land Community College
Jennifer Day, Sinclair Community College
Carol Deane, Eastern Idaho Technical College
Julie DeBuhr, Lewis-Clark State College
Janis DeHaven, Central Community College
Drew Dekreon, University of Alaska–Anchorage
Joy DePover, Central Lakes College
Salli DiBartolo, Brevard Community College
Melissa Diegnau, Riverland Community College
Al Dillard, Lansdale School of Business
Marjorie Duffy, Cosumnes River College
Sarah Dunn, Southwest Tennessee Community College
Shahla Durany, Tarrant County College–South Campus
Kay Durden, University of Tennessee at Martin
Dineen Ebert, St. Louis Community College–Meramec
Donna Ehrhart, State University of New York–Brockport

Larry Elias, Montgomery County Community College
Glenda Elser, New Mexico State University at Alamogordo
Angela Evangelinos, Monroe County Community College
Angie Evans, Ivy Tech Community College of Indiana
Linda Farrington, Indian Hills Community College
Dana Fladhammer, Phoenix College
Richard Flores, Citrus College
Connie Fox, Community and Technical College at Institute of Technology West Virginia University
Wanda Freeman, Okefenokee Technical College
Brenda Freeman, Augusta Technical College
Susan Fry, Boise State University
Roger Fulk, Wright State University–Lake Campus
Sue Furnas, Collin County Community College District
Sandy Gabel, Vernon College
Laura Galvan, Fayetteville Technical Community College
Candace Garrod, Red Rocks Community College
Sherrie Geitgey, Northwest State Community College
Chris Gerig, Chattahoochee Technical College
Barb Gillespie, Cuyamaca College
Jessica Gilmore, Highline Community College
Pamela Gilmore, Reedley College
Debbie Glinert, Queensborough Community College
Steven Goldman, Polk Community College
Bettie Goodman, C.S. Mott Community College
Mike Grabill, Katharine Gibbs School–Philadelphia
Francis Green, Penn State University
Walter Griffin, Blinn College
Fillmore Guinn, Odessa College
Helen Haasch, Milwaukee Area Technical College
John Habal, Ventura College
Joy Haerens, Chaffey College
Norman Hahn, Thomas Nelson Community College
Kathy Hall, Alamance Community College
Teri Harbacheck, Boise State University
Linda Harper, Richland Community College
Maureen Harper, Indian Hills Community College
Steve Harris, Katharine Gibbs School–New York
Robyn Hart, Fresno City College
Darien Hartman, Boise State University
Gina Hatcher, Tacoma Community College
Winona T. Hatcher, Aiken Technical College
BJ Hathaway, Northeast Wisconsin Tech College
Cynthia Hauki, West Hills College – Coalinga
Mary L. Haynes, Wayne County Community College
Marcie Hawkins, Zane State College
Steve Hebrock, Ohio State University Agricultural Technical Institute
Sue Heistand, Iowa Central Community College
Heith Hennel, Valencia Community College
Donna Hendricks, South Arkansas Community College
Judy Hendrix, Dyersburg State Community College
Gloria Hensel, Matanuska-Susitna College University of Alaska Anchorage

Gwendolyn Hester, Richland College
Tammarra Holmes, Laramie County Community College
Dee Hobson, Richland College
Keith Hoell, Katharine Gibbs School–New York
Pashia Hogan, Northeast State Technical Community College
Susan Hoggard, Tulsa Community College
Kathleen Holliman, Wallace Community College Selma
Chastity Honchul, Brown Mackie College/Wright State University
Christie Hovey, Lincoln Land Community College
Peggy Hughes, Allegany College of Maryland
Sandra Hume, Chippewa Valley Technical College
John Hutson, Aims Community College
Celia Ing, Sacramento City College
Joan Ivey, Lanier Technical College
Barbara Jaffari, College of the Redwoods
Penny Jakes, University of Montana College of Technology
Eduardo Jaramillo, Peninsula College
Barbara Jauken, Southeast Community College
Susan Jennings, Stephen F. Austin State University
Leslie Jernberg, Eastern Idaho Technical College
Linda Johns, Georgia Perimeter College
Brent Johnson, Okefenokee Technical College
Mary Johnson, Mt. San Antonio College
Shirley Johnson, Trinidad State Junior College–Valley Campus
Sandra M. Jolley, Tarrant County College
Teresa Jolly, South Georgia Technical College
Dr. Deborah Jones, South Georgia Technical College
Margie Jones, Central Virginia Community College
Randall Jones, Marshall Community and Technical College
Diane Karlsbraaten, Lake Region State College
Teresa Keller, Ivy Tech Community College of Indiana
Charles Kemnitz, Pennsylvania College of Technology
Sandra Kinghorn, Ventura College
Bill Klein, Katharine Gibbs School–Philadelphia
Bea Knaapen, Fresno City College
Kit Kofoed, Western Wyoming Community College
Maria Kolatis, County College of Morris
Barry Kolb, Ocean County College
Karen Kuralt, University of Arkansas at Little Rock
Belva-Carole Lamb, Rogue Community College
Betty Lambert, Des Moines Area Community College
Anita Lande, Cabrillo College
Junnae Landry, Pratt Community College
Karen Lankisch, UC Clermont
David Lanzilla, Central Florida Community College
Nora Laredo, Cerritos Community College
Jennifer Larrabee, Chippewa Valley Technical College
Debra Larson, Idaho State University
Barb Lave, Portland Community College
Audrey Lawrence, Tidewater Community College
Deborah Layton, Eastern Oklahoma State College

Larry LeBlanc, Owen Graduate School–
 Vanderbilt University
Philip Lee, Nashville State Community College
Michael Lehrfeld, Brevard Community College
Vasant Limaye, Southwest Collegiate Institute for the
 Deaf – Howard College
Anne C. Lewis, Edgecombe Community College
Stephen Linkin, Houston Community College
Peggy Linston, Athens Technical College
Hugh Lofton, Moultrie Technical College
Donna Lohn, Lakeland Community College
Jackie Lou, Lake Tahoe Community College
Donna Love, Gaston College
Curt Lynch, Ozarks Technical Community College
Sheilah Lynn, Florida Community College–Jacksonville
Pat R. Lyon, Tomball College
Bill Madden, Bergen Community College
Heather Madden, Delaware Technical &
 Community College
Donna Madsen, Kirkwood Community College
Jane Maringer-Cantu, Gavilan College
Suzanne Marks, Bellevue Community College
Carol Martin, Louisiana State University–Alexandria
Cheryl Martucci, Diablo Valley College
Roberta Marvel, Eastern Wyoming College
Tom Mason, Brookdale Community College
Mindy Mass, Santa Barbara City College
Dixie Massaro, Irvine Valley College
Rebekah May, Ashland Community
 & Technical College
Emma Mays-Reynolds, Dyersburg State
 Community College
Timothy Mayes, Metropolitan State College of Denver
Reggie McCarthy, Central Lakes College
Matt McCaskill, Brevard Community College
Kevin McFarlane, Front Range Community College
Donna McGill, Yuba Community College
Terri McKeever, Ozarks Technical Community College
Patricia McMahon, South Suburban College
Sally McMillin, Katharine Gibbs School–Philadelphia
Charles McNerney, Bergen Community College
Lisa Mears, Palm Beach Community College
Imran Mehmood, ITT Technical Institute–King of
 Prussia Campus
Virginia Melvin, Southwest Tennessee Community College
Jeanne Mercer, Texas State Technical College
Denise Merrell, Jefferson Community & Technical College
Catherine Merrikin, Pearl River Community College
Diane D. Mickey, Northern Virginia Community College
Darrelyn Miller, Grays Harbor College
Sue Mitchell, Calhoun Community College
Jacquie Moldenhauer, Front Range Community College
Linda Motonaga, Los Angeles City College
Sam Mryyan, Allen County Community College

Cindy Murphy, Southeastern Community College
Ryan Murphy, Sinclair Community College
Sharon E. Nastav, Johnson County Community College
Christine Naylor, Kent State University Ashtabula
Haji Nazarian, Seattle Central Community College
Nancy Noe, Linn-Benton Community College
Jennie Noriega, San Joaquin Delta College
Linda Nutter, Peninsula College
Thomas Omerza, Middle Bucks Institute of Technology
Edith Orozco, St. Philip's College
Dona Orr, Boise State University
Joanne Osgood, Chaffey College
Janice Owens, Kishwaukee College
Tatyana Pashnyak, Bainbridge College
John Partacz, College of DuPage
Tim Paul, Montana State University–Great Falls
Joseph Perez, South Texas College
Mike Peterson, Chemeketa Community College
Dr. Karen R. Petitto, West Virginia Wesleyan College
Terry Pierce, Onandaga Community College
Ashlee Pieris, Raritan Valley Community College
Jamie Pinchot, Thiel College
Michelle Poertner, Northwestern Michigan College
Betty Posta, University of Toledo
Deborah Powell, West Central Technical College
Mark Pranger, Rogers State University
Carolyn Rainey, Southeast Missouri State University
Linda Raskovich, Hibbing Community College
Leslie Ratliff, Griffin Technical College
Mar-Sue Ratzke, Rio Hondo Community College
Roxy Reissen, Southeastern Community College
Silvio Reyes, Technical Career Institutes
Patricia Rishavy, Anoka Technical College
Jean Robbins, Southeast Technical Institute
Carol Roberts, Eastern Maine Community College
 and University of Maine
Teresa Roberts, Wilson Technical Community College
Vicki Robertson, Southwest Tennessee Community College
Betty Rogge, Ohio State Agricultural Technical Institute
Lynne Rusley, Missouri Southern State University
Claude Russo, Brevard Community College
Ginger Sabine, Northwestern Technical College
Steven Sachs, Los Angeles Valley College
Joanne Salas, Olympic College
Lloyd Sandmann, Pima Community College–Desert
 Vista Campus
Beverly Santillo, Georgia Perimeter College
Theresa Savarese, San Diego City College
Sharolyn Sayers, Milwaukee Area Technical College
Judith Scheeren, Westmoreland County
 Community College
Adolph Scheiwe, Joliet Junior College
Marilyn Schmid, Asheville-Buncombe Technical
 Community College

Janet Sebesy, Cuyahoga Community College
Phyllis T. Shafer, Brookdale Community College
Ralph Shafer, Truckee Meadows Community College
Anne Marie Shanley, County College of Morris
Shelia Shelton, Surry Community College
Merilyn Shepherd, Danville Area Community College
Susan Sinele, Aims Community College
Beth Sindt, Hawkeye Community College
Andrew Smith, Marian College
Brenda Smith, Southwest Tennessee Community College
Lynne Smith, State University of New York–Delhi
Rob Smith, Katharine Gibbs School–Philadelphia
Tonya Smith, Arkansas State University–Mountain Home
Del Spencer – Trinity Valley Community College
Jeri Spinner, Idaho State University
Eric Stadnik, Santa Rosa Junior College
Karen Stanton, Los Medanos College
Meg Stoner, Santa Rosa Junior College
Beverly Stowers, Ivy Tech Community College of Indiana
Marcia Stranix, Yuba College
Kim Styles, Tri-County Technical College
Sylvia Summers, Tacoma Community College
Beverly Swann, Delaware Technical & Community College
Ann Taff, Tulsa Community College
Mike Theiss, University of Wisconsin–Marathon Campus
Romy Thiele, Cañada College
Sharron Thompson, Portland Community College
Ingrid Thompson-Sellers, Georgia Perimeter College
Barbara Tietsort, University of Cincinnati–Raymond
    Walters College
Janine Tiffany, Reading Area Community College
Denise Tillery, University of Nevada Las Vegas
Susan Trebelhorn, Normandale Community College
Noel Trout, Santiago Canyon College
Cheryl Turgeon, Asnuntuck Community College
Steve Turner, Ventura College
Sylvia Unwin, Bellevue Community College

Lilly Vigil, Colorado Mountain College
Sabrina Vincent, College of the Mainland
Mary Vitrano, Palm Beach Community College
Brad Vogt, Northeast Community College
Cozell Wagner, Southeastern Community College
Carolyn Walker, Tri-County Technical College
Sherry Walker, Tulsa Community College
Qi Wang, Tacoma Community College
Betty Wanielista, Valencia Community College
Marge Warber, Lanier Technical College–Forsyth Campus
Marjorie Webster, Bergen Community College
Linda Wenn, Central Community College
Mark Westlund, Olympic College
Carolyn Whited, Roane State Community College
Winona Whited, Richland College
Jerry Wilkerson, Scott Community College
Joel Willenbring, Fullerton College
Barbara Williams, WITC Superior
Charlotte Williams, Jones County Junior College
Bonnie Willy, Ivy Tech Community College of Indiana
Diane Wilson, J. Sargeant Reynolds Community College
James Wolfe, Metropolitan Community College
Marjory Wooten, Lanier Technical College
Mark Yanko, Hocking College
Alexis Yusov, Pace University
Naeem Zaman, San Joaquin Delta College
Kathleen Zimmerman, Des Moines Area
    Community College

We also thank Lutz Ziob, Sanjay Advani, Jim DiIanni,
Merrick Van Dongen, Jim LeValley, Bruce Curling,
Joe Wilson, and Naman Khan at Microsoft for their
encouragement and support in making the Microsoft
Official Academic Course programs the finest instructional
materials for mastering the newest Microsoft technologies
for both students and instructors.

Brief Contents

Contents

Introduction

LESSON SKILL MATRIX

TECHNOLOGY SKILL	70-431 EXAM OBJECTIVE
Preparing for the course.	Supplemental
Retrieve data to support ad hoc and recurring queries.	Foundational
Construct SQL queries to return data.	Foundational
Manipulate relational data.	Foundational
Insert, update and delete data.	Foundational
Diagnose and resolve database server errors.	Foundational
Review error messages in event logs.	Foundational

KEY TERMS

RDBMS: Relational database management system; a system that organizes data into related rows and columns; distinguished from flat-file database systems; SQL Server is a relational database management system (RDBMS); Oracle, DB2, MySQL, Sybase, and many, many others are RDBMSs.

SQL: Structured Query Language; a means of defining, controlling, and manipulating RDBMS data.

VPC: Virtual Personal Computer; an application that runs an operating system on your host operating system; a means of isolating one computer environment from another running in the same operating system.

■ Preparing for the Microsoft SQL Server 2005: Implementation and Maintenance Course

↓ THE BOTTOM LINE

Learning the many aspects of Microsoft SQL Server requires both preparation and study.

- Preparation means you understand database concepts, as this is a how-to course rather than a theory class; preparation means you understand the basics of the Windows Server operating system, as this is the only environment in which SQL Server will meet production criteria; and preparation means you understand the Structure Query Language constructs, as SQL Server 2005, more than in previous editions, requires programmatic skills.

- Study means you must practice and understand each facet of SQL Server. You must gain hands-on experience, which can only be done by establishing a practice configuration and then actually using it. If you can't do this at home, be sure your school has a laboratory you can use on your own time. Work through both the textbook exercises and the laboratory manual projects multiple times.

Starting Your Adventure

Welcome. You have already begun a lifetime journey in information technology. This course provides another milestone in achieving your career goals. One accomplishment will be the recognition by Microsoft that you understand and can manage the core concepts of SQL Server 2005. Doing this means passing a competency test covering six elements of *relational database management system (RDBMS)* server implementation and maintenance:

- Installing and configuring SQL Server 2005.
- Implementing high availability and disaster recovery.
- Supporting data consumers.
- Maintaining databases.
- Monitoring and troubleshooting SQL Server performance.
- Creating and implementing database objects.

This exam tests your knowledge of many facets of SQL Server 2005 implementation and maintenance, including tuning and configuring, creating databases and objects, backing up and restoring databases, managing security, and supporting end users. To pass the test, you need to fully understand these topics. Careful study of this book, along with hands-on training included here in the classroom and in your workplace, will help you prepare for this exam.

Preparing for This Course

Are you ready to take this course? Consider three prerequisites: understanding database concepts, understanding Structured Query Language constructs, and having proficiency in Windows Server 2003.

UNDERSTANDING DATABASE CONCEPTS

This book provides information on using Microsoft SQL Server 2005 and learning the skills needed to implement and maintain this particular RDBMS. This course teaches the mechanics of how to create and manage your database. Consider taking an introductory information systems course first if you are unfamiliar with why you need to:

- Create a table.
- Normalize to the third level.
- Diagram entity relationships.
- Create parent-child links.
- Design an analysis services solution.

UNDERSTANDING STRUCTURED QUERY LANGUAGE CONSTRUCTS

This course presumes a working knowledge of the *Structured Query Language (SQL)*. It presents Transact-SQL code, and you must be able to modify syntax appropriately to meet your specific business needs. Consider taking an introductory SQL programming course first if you are unfamiliar with how to code solutions for the following requirements:

- Return all rows and all columns from two or more tables.
- Change the table data based on a given attribute condition.
- Prepare an annual report from data stored in 12 unique monthly tables.
- Change the date format from 21 July 2008 to 7/21/08.
- Create a query when an important test value is unknowable prior to runtime.

HAVING PROFICIENCY IN WINDOWS SERVER 2003

SQL Server executes only in a Windows operating system environment. Consider taking an introductory course to Windows XP, Vista, or Windows Server 2003 (or newer) if you are unfamiliar with how to:

- Create a new user or group and apply appropriate permissions.
- Change a user password and add the user to a specified group.
- Read the contents of the Event Viewer.

CERTIFICATION READY?
Be sure you know the basic syntax rules for the select, insert, update, and delete statements. You'll find it helpful to also understand joins, subqueries, DDL, and DCL rules.

- Test for and set an alert for approaching low disk space.
- Create a shared printer and set permissions allowing only one remote connection at a time.

PASSING THE READINESS TEST

Take the knowledge assessment multiple choice quiz at the end of this section. There are 10 questions for each of these three prerequisites. Confirm your abilities to succeed in this course.

Creating a Practice Environment for Independent Study

To enable all features usually available in SQL Server 2005, load Windows Server 2003 and VisualStudio 2005 to create common language runtime routines in C# or Visual Basic. Some capabilities won't work in Windows 2000 Server. Still fewer features function in Windows XP or Vista. The use of Windows 98 is not recommended, as Integration Services, Analysis Management Objects, and ADOMD.NET interfaces are not supported. The same is true for earlier versions of Visual Studio.

You have four options for building your personal learning setup.

- Dedicated standalone or domain controller server
- Dual boot server installation
- Virtual PC emulation environment
- Using Developer Edition

BUILDING A DESKTOP SERVER

The first option involves locating an available PC computer with a CPU clock speed of 733 MHz or faster, 1 GB or more of RAM, at least 3 GB of available disk space, and a DVD reader for the installing code from your distribution disks.

Download or purchase from Microsoft trial or licensed versions of each product: Microsoft Server 2003 (180-day trial), Microsoft Visual Studio 2005 (90-day trial), and Microsoft SQL Server 2005 (180-day trial).

Allow a full day to perform a fresh install. Obtain all Microsoft Update hot patches, fixes, and service packs. Stop occasionally to perform a disk defragmentation operation. You may make this machine a domain controller if you wish. If you do so, be aware the operating system will consume another 250 MB.

You must reformat at the end of the 180-day evaluation period.

INSTALLING A SECOND OPERATING SYSTEM

Dual booting permits loading a choice of two or more operating systems on a single machine. Each operates totally independently, although files can be accessed from nonsystem drives. To dual boot, you need multiple partitions or hard drives.

After that, the procedure follows the same steps as for a desktop server.

UNDERSTANDING VIRTUAL PC

Microsoft makes available as a free download ***Virtual PC 2007*** (***VPC***). You may delete the Virtual PC hard drive files at the end of the trial period of your included disks and erase all evidence of the additional software. There is no further need to clean up files or the operating system.

Virtual PC, however, requires *lots* of memory. Let's assume your host operating system is Windows XP or Vista. They both require memory to manage their own business needs. Let's further assume you have an integrated video system displaying high definition for your 16:10 aspect monitor, and that you have 4 GB of memory installed. You have 3 GB available (after display requirements). The operating system (Vista) wants 1 GB. This leaves you with but 2 gibibytes for your Windows Server 2003/SQL Server 2005 installation. This provides acceptable practice performance levels for all exercises in this textbook. You will notice a slow response if you provide only 1 gibibyte.

TAKE NOTE*

The National Institute of Science and Technology (NIST), managed by the U.S. Department of Commerce, establishes standards for use in the United States. Kilo, as used in the United States, is a Base 10 unit and therefore equals 1000. Computers use Base 2 arithmetic, which means $2^{10} = 1024$. Marketers of disk drives advertise their capacity in gigabytes, which is far larger than your computer reports the capacity—which is in gibibytes. Go to *http://physics.nist.gov/cuu/Units/binary.html* for full details.

DOWNLOADING VIRTUAL PC

Connect to *www.Microsoft.com/Downloads* and search for "Virtual PC 2007." Follow the download and installation instructions. After a successful load you will find an icon on the Desktop labeled "Virtual PC." Click on it. A dialog box labeled "Virtual PC Console" opens. Start by clicking **Settings**. Look at each setting and make it appropriate for your environment. Choose a **File Name**; perhaps SQL Server 2005. Allocate **Memory**; perhaps 1536 MB. Enable your CD/DVD drive by clicking in the checkbox. Do you want to print from your VPC? Configure LPT1. You definitely want networking capability so you can download and install hot fixes and service packs. Make the Networking option match your conditions.

You are now ready to install Windows Server 2003. Click on the **New Button** in the Virtual PC Console. You probably want to *Create a virtual machine*. Follow the wizard through the rest of the steps. Once installed, Click **Start** → **All Programs** → **Windows Update**, to obtain and install all hot fixes and service packs. Stop and click **Start** → **Accessories** → **System Tools** → **Disk Defragmentor** between each step.

Now that Windows Server 2003 functions, make sure your CD is set to **Use Physical Drive** [as appropriate]. Then insert your SQL Server 2005 disk. It should autostart. If not, find setup.exe to start the installation. At this point follow the on-screen guidance.

USING VIRTUAL PC

The single most important rule: right-alt. Instead of using Ctrl-Alt-Delete—use Right-Alt-Delete. To change between full screen view and a window view, use Right-Alt-Enter.

DELETING VIRTUAL PC

Your trial period for the applications has ended. Using Add or Remove Programs, delete Virtual PC, if you wish. Note the file location listed in the Settings option of your Virtual PC Console first so you can delete it and, thereby, remove all traces of your practice environment.

USING THE DEVELOPER EDITION

You don't want your SQL Server installation to expire? You don't want to use Virtual PC? Consider buying the Developer's edition. The list price is $50. Educational discounts can be as much as 20 percent. See if your classmates want to pool their purchases to obtain the best discount.

 APPROACHING YOUR STUDIES

Each lesson introduces a core concept. Each concept is presented in isolation of other concepts. At the end of each lesson, think about the new concept and how it might apply to other topics. For example, after learning about functions in Lesson 12 you should think about how, when, and why to use functions in stored procedures introduced to you in Lesson 10.

Try to avoid using this text to cram; rather, use it as the foundation for learning skills to apply in your workplace. You will be introduced to concepts that have no immediate application in your corporation. Focus and learn them anyway. An opportunity for applying these concepts will surely arise. When you follow these precepts, the examination knowledge will result in a bonus benefit.

Each lesson ends with review questions and unguided exercises you can use to check the knowledge you've gained and to place the concept firmly in your mind. The questions often expose interesting special situations.

This book provides a solid foundation for the serious effort of preparing for the exam. To best benefit from this book, you may want to use the following study method:

1. Read each lesson carefully. Do your best to fully understand the information.

2. Complete all hands-on exercises in each lesson, referring to the text as necessary so you understand each step you take. Install the evaluation version of SQL Server, and get some experience with the product. Use an evaluation version of SQL Server Enterprise Edition (which can be downloaded from *www.microsoft.com/sql*) instead of Express Edition, because Express Edition does not have all the features discussed in this book.

3. Answer the review questions at the end of each chapter. If you prefer to answer the questions in a timed and graded format, install the Edge Tests from the CD that accompanies this book and answer the chapter questions there, in addition to those in the book.

4. Note which questions you did not understand, and study the corresponding sections of the book again.

5. Make sure you complete the entire book.

6. Before taking the exam, go through the review questions, bonus exams, flash cards, and so on, included on the CD that accompanies this book.

To learn all the material covered in this book, you will need to study regularly and with discipline. Try to set aside the same time every day to study, and select a comfortable and quiet place in which to do it. If you work hard, you will be surprised at how quickly you learn this material. Earn success!

SKILL SUMMARY

IN THIS LESSON YOU LEARNED:

You are embarking on an adventure. Learning SQL Server 2005 core concepts requires dedication and commitment. It's time to begin!

■ Knowledge Assessment

Multiple Choice

Circle the letter or letters that correspond to the best answer or answers.

1. You support a bookstore. They need an in-store kiosk customer support system so clients can easily find what they desire. You create a Books table and an Authors table. Then you realize one book can have many authors and one author can write many books. This is known as a many-to-many relationship. What do you do to enable searches for all books by one author and all authors by one book?

   a. Do nothing; modern RDBMSs accommodate many-to-many relationships.

   b. Create a junction table named BooksAuthors with a Foreign Key relationship to the Primary Key in the Books and Authors tables.

    c. Write a SELECT statement that also checks for additional authors for a specific book.

    d. Write a SELECT statement that also checks for additional books for a specific author.

2. You are the administrator for a college campus. You suspect the database design created by students in the Computer Science Department fails to meet the third normal form. What are the criteria failures for this requirement?

    a. All tables lack a primary key.

    b. Addresses for students and faculty are stored in different tables.

    c. A composite key fails to uniquely identify records.

    d. Aggregate values are stored in tables.

3. You teach an introductory information systems course at a community college. You offer examples of databases. Which of these qualify?

    a. Dictionary

    b. Telephone directory

    c. Rolodex

    d. Textbook index

4. You are engaged in affinity analysis. What does this mean?

    a. Grouping entities and attributes in logically organized table structures.

    b. Looking for data that logically attracts interest.

    c. Capturing all relevant information about a topic in a single interview with subject matter experts.

    d. Searching for pattern matches.

5. You are an application service provider (ASP) offering database support to small companies in your community. Each, however, competes with the other and wants to prevent the other from gaining knowledge about the business activities you store in your information stores. What can you do to assure data privacy for each client?

    a. Create a separate database on a separate server with a separate IP address for each client.

    b. Create a separate database instance on a shared server with a shared IP address.

    c. Load a separate copy of SQL Server 2005 on one server sharing one IP address among all. Set permissions to allow only appropriate clients to gain access to each database.

    d. Load one copy of SQL Server 2005. A modern RDBMS accommodates building multiple databases in isolation from each other.

6. An index purports to speed data retrieval. You, therefore, index every attribute in each table. What is the consequence?

    a. Data retrieval is optimized, providing you use a WHERE statement in your SELECT query.

    b. Data entry is slowed as every INSERT, UPDATE or DELETE statement must also update every index.

    c. Data retrieval on the Gender column is optimized.

    d. This technique eliminates the need for a Primary Key.

7. You have normalized your database. Data is stored but once. You need to delete data in a parent table (Customer) that has a relationship with another table (Address). Which technique can change the data appropriately in both tables?

    a. Use a stored procedure.

    b. Use a user-defined function.

    c. Use a DML trigger.

    d. Use a DDL trigger.

8. What is a relational database?

    a. Data is stored in a table.

    b. Data is stored in multiple tables each with a relationship to each other.

    c. Data is arranged in a table as rows and columns so data can be extracted at an intersection rather than reading the whole table from beginning to end.

    d. Database design follows the 12 principles proffered by Dr. Edgar F. Codd.

9. You have heard the term "object" in discussions among your classmates. What is a database object?
   a. A data value at the intersection of a column and row; a field.
   b. An ancillary tool in database design, such as ERStudio (Embarcadaro Technologies) or ERWIN (Computer Associates).
   c. An RDBMS structure that must be named such as an index, stored procedure, table, and function.
   d. The subject of a table; the characteristic values needed to describe what is stored.

10. You have decided to accept the new position as database administrator in your company. Congratulations. What is your most important function?
    a. Convince your boss that a new client application is required so users will have a more intuitive sense of how to collect and enter needed data.
    b. Convince your boss that the infrastructure requires upgrading so users will experience a database response time of two to three seconds, instead of four or five minutes.
    c. Provide training to users to optimize the data collection and reporting functions.
    d. Maintain data integrity.

11. You need to offload database information into small text files for use by financial analysts using Excel spreadsheets. After due analysis, you choose to save a COMPUTE BY statement as text. Will this work?
    a. Yes; Excel can import a text file whether comma- or tab-delimited.
    b. No; embedded nonnumeric characters will cause a failure.
    c. No; modern RDBMSs no longer support COMPUTE BY.
    d. Yes; Excel has a wizard designed to accept COMPUTE BY text files.

12. You need to extract data from the system your predecessor created. You discover tables have been created according to the third normal form. You find the needed data in three different tables. What SQL syntax allows you to garner this data?
    a. Union
    b. Join
    c. Select
    d. Having

13. You have an unknown or unknowable data value (such as the maximum entry in the table) that you need for mathematical manipulation or for comparison purposes. Which SQL structure is the most likely solution?
    a. The WHERE clause
    b. Functions; for example, MIN, MAX, AVG
    c. Subquery
    d. AGGREGATION statement

14. You are the administrator supporting a client application developer. She submits a specification suggesting the need for back-end processing for her front-end consumption. This suggests that you create a:
    a. Function
    b. Trigger
    c. Query
    d. Stored procedure

15. You write a query that involves a simple mathematical calculation involving adding a column value times another column value minus a third column value. You get unexpected results. What should you consider to resolve the issue?
    a. Aggregation
    b. Precedence
    c. Column order
    d. Bad data types

16. You write a query:

USE AdventureWorks

SELECT *

```
FROM Person.Contact
WHERE LastName = 'Smith'
HAVING FirstName = 'Adam'
GROUP BY LastName, FirstName
ORDER BY LastName
```

You experience an error. Why?
   a. There is no such table as Person.Contact; tables can be referenced only by dbo.
   b. There is no entry for Smith in the database.
   c. The syntax requires GROUP BY prior to ORDER BY.
   d. The syntax requires the HAVING clause follow the GROUP BY clause.

17. You write a query:

    `SELECT ALL LName, FName FROM Personnel WHERE LName = 'BROWN'.`

    Why did you include the key word ALL?
       a. You wanted all columns returned, not just LName and FName.
       b. You wanted every instance of Brown, not just the first one found.
       c. You wanted to include Brown and BROWN and brown in the results.
       d. You wanted to override the DISTINCT keyword default.

18. You decided to write your query in VI. You saved your file where it is available to the SQL Server server. You want to execute it. What are your options?
       a. ISQL
       b. OSQL
       c. SQLCMD
       d. sp_executesql

19. Users want to find all instances for the data in the column Description ending with "café." You therefore create a stored procedure that uses a query such as:

    `SELECT * FROM Eateries WHERE Description LIKE '%cafe'.`

    Users start complaining about slow query response times. Why?
       a. There are too many restaurants with their name ending with café.
       b. Too many users are invoking this stored procedure at essentially the same time.
       c. The syntax forces a table scan, which is inherently the slowest of all execution plan options.
       d. The network is slow; let everyone know so the boss will allow you to upgrade the infrastructure.

20. You want to present the last name followed by the first name from a table named Customers in a database named Sales. Which query best meets that goal?
       a. USE Sales

          `SELECT LName + ', ' + Fname FROM Customers.`
       b. PRINT LName && FName WHERE DATABASE 5 'Sales'
       c. SELECT LName & FName FROM Customers WHERE DATABASE = 'Sales'
       d. PRINT LName, FName WHEN TABLE Customers AND DATABASE Sales.

21. You are the administrator for your member server hosting the RDBMS. Your server experiences CPU failures and replacements can't be delivered for several days. A second server is available but has insufficient disk space. First you install the disk drives from the database server into the available server but the disks do not appear in Disk Management. What actions should you perform?
       a. Install the disks in the available server; initialize the disks.
       b. Install the disks in the available server; rescan the disks.
       c. In Disk Management, select each replaced disk. Then select the option to import foreign disks.
       d. In Disk Management, select each replaced disk. Then select the option to repair the volume.
       e. On the new server, run the mountvol /p command from the command prompt.
       f. On the new server, convert the dynamic disks to basic disks.

22. You are the database administrator. Users report that SQL Server is no longer available. You determine the MSSQL service has stopped. The Windows administrator reports that the password of the service account had expired and was changed. He resets the password on the service to match the new password of the service account. You attempt to restart the service but are unsuccessful. What should you do? Tell the administrator to:
    a. Set User cannot change password.
    b. Set Password never expires.
    c. Store passwords using reversible encryption.
    d. Uncheck Account is disabled.

23. You are the network administrator. You use your nonadministrative account named Bill to log on to a client computer. You need to change the password for a domain user account name Melissa. You open the Active Directory Users and Computers console. When you attempt to change Melissa's password, you receive the following error message: "Access is denied." What should you do?
    a. Add the nonadministrative domain user account to the local administrators group.
    b. Use the runas command to run Active Directory Users and Computers with domain administrative credentials.
    c. From a command prompt, run the net user Melissa /add /passwordreq:yes command.
    d. From a command prompt, run the net accounts /uniquepw: /domain command.

24. You are the network administrator for the Windows Server 2003 installation that consists of a single active directory domain. A new management directive states that users can log on to the domain only during business hours. Users who try to remain logged on after business hours must be automatically disconnected from network resources. What should you do?
    a. Configure the Default Domain Group Policy object to increase scheduling priority for all users.
    b. Configure the Default Domain Group Policy object to force users to log off when their logon hours expire.
    c. Select all user accounts. Modify the account properties to restrict logon hours to business hours.
    d. Create a domain user account named Trial. Configure the account properties to restrict logon hours to business hours.
    e. Modify the DACL on the Default Domain Policy Group Policy object to assign the Allow–Read permissions to the Users group.

25. You are the Windows Server administrator. You add a Windows Server 2003 computer to the domain to support SQL Server 2005. You create server local accounts on the server to manage the application. Some users report they are having difficulty accessing SQL Server through a local account in order to gather more information. What should you do?
    a. In Group Policy, audit account login events.
    b. In Group Policy, audit account management.
    c. In Group Policy, audit directory service access.
    d. In Group Policy, audit login events.

26. Users in the Marketing Department use a printer named MarketingPrinter. A user named Bill in the Marketing Department is responsible for pausing documents that are submitted to the Marketing printer when required. Bill reports that he cannot pause documents submitted by other users. What should you do?
    a. Assign Bill the Allow–Manage Documents for MarketingPrinter.
    b. Remove the Allow–Manage Printers permission assigned to Bill.
    c. Assign Bill the Allow–Modify permission for the C:\Windows\System32\Spool\ Printers folder.
    d. Assign Bill the Deny–Full Control permission for the C:\Windows\System32\Spool\ Printers folder.

27. You are the operating system administrator for your database member server, which is joined to an Active Directory Domain Controller. Your manager requires that you set an alert that will inform you when the D:\ drive reaches 80 percent capacity. Which performance counter should you add to the Performance Logs and Alerts File?

    a. Object: _____

    b. Counter: _____

    c. Instance: _____

28. You are the network administrator supporting SQL Server 2005. The network consists of a single Active Directory domain. All servers run Windows Server 2003. Your database server has a locally attached tape drive. You need to back up all data at least once a week. Every day, you need to back up the data that was changed after the last backup. You need to minimize the amount of data that must be backed up every day. Which backup types should you use?

    a. Copy

    b. Full

    c. Incremental

    d. Differential

29. You are the database administrator. Sally is the operating system administrator. You want to minimize your work as employees are hired and quit. You should cleverly ask Sally to establish groups in Windows Server 2003 and add and subtract users when needed. What do you have to do?

    a. Make sure Sally creates groups that map to database access requirements from your perspective.

    b. Make sure Sally removes users promptly when they are fired or quit.

    c. Make sure Sally adds users promptly when they are hired.

    d. Make sure Sally moves users from one group to the new appropriate group when a user is transferred, promoted, or demoted.

30. Mabel was just fired and told to clean out her desk and be out of the building by noon. You just found out she has administrative functions within the database and the operating system. What should you do?

    a. Assign someone to watch Mabel. You don't want her to damage the operating system or database in any way.

    b. Disable Mabel's OS User Account immediately.

    c. Invite Mabel to lunch quickly. Have everybody join you in offering Mabel a farewell tribute.

    d. Do nothing; you have a recent backup. What damage can she do that you haven't prepared for?

■ Case Scenarios

Scenario 1-1: Discussing the Prevalence of Databases

Partner with several classmates. Discuss your mutual understanding of how many businesses and individuals use databases.

- Stamp collectors
- Telephone companies
- Campus bookstore
- Point-of-sale cash registers
- Gas pumps
- Credit unions

Scenario 1-2: Discussing the Importance of Databases

As a class, discuss the importance of databases in today's economy. Look specifically at Amazon.com. Ask each other how Amazon could manage their business model without a database. What aspects of their business depend on data storage: inventory, shipping, accounts receivable, customer habits?

Scenario 1-3: Discussing the Uses of Databases

Consider what you can do with a database. Which actions are possible only because of a database? Which decisions can best be made because information is stored in a database?

Installing Microsoft SQL Server 2005

LESSON SKILL MATRIX

TECHNOLOGY SKILL	70-431 EXAM OBJECTIVE
Install SQL Server 2005.	Foundational
Verify prerequisites.	Foundational
Upgrade from an earlier version of SQL Server.	Foundational
Create an instance.	Foundational
Diagnose and resolve database server errors.	Foundational
Review SQL Server startup logs.	Foundational

KEY TERMS

code page: For character data, a definition of the bit patterns that represent specific letters, numbers, or symbols. ASCII characters use 1 byte per character; each byte can have 1 to 256 bit patterns. Unicode data uses 2 bytes per character and have 1 to 65,536 bit patterns.

code point: The Universal Character Set (UCS) encodes characters. The UCS contains more than 100,000 abstract characters, each identified by an unambiguous name and an integer number called its *code point.* The UCS facilitates ordering and keeping localities such as Japan and China distinct in sorted results.

domain: A centrally managed server to which users must authenticate (log on with an identification phrase and password) that applies uniform security rules to everyone.

forest: Domains that share a common Active Directory database schema; that is, the Active Directory components are the same; are in common with every domain.

RDBMS: Relational database management system; a system that organizes data into related rows and columns; distinguished from flat-file database systems; SQL Server is a relational database management system, as are Oracle, DB2, MySQL, Sybase, and many, many others.

sort order: The set of rules in a collation that define how characters are evaluated in comparison operations and the sequence in which they are sorted.

tree: Contiguous name space in a network. MSN.COM and MICROSOFT.COM must necessarily be two trees even though in the same forest, as they represent different names. Research.Microsoft.Com and Marketing.Microsoft.com, in contrast, are in the same tree.

workgroup: An arrangement of clients that each stands alone; each must be administered individually; there is no central domain controller.

■ Installing SQL Server 2005

 THE BOTTOM LINE — Installing SQL Server 2005 involves a few simple steps. But before you take them, you have two decisions to make: Should this installation be in a domain as part of the tree and forest? Should this be a standalone server in a workgroup?

Examining Your Environment

Examine your business plan. Which edition of SQL Server 2005 do you need? Examine your network both for intranet and remote requirements. Do you need more bandwidth? Examine your available servers. Do they meet the hardware and user load requisites? Examine your user's workstations. Are you planning a thin client, Web-browser-based application, or something more robust? Create a total solution.

MEETING THE PREREQUISITES

You will need a few pieces in place on your machine before you can install SQL Server 2005. The first is Internet Explorer (IE) 6.0 Service Pack 1 (SP1) or newer. Many people see this requirement and instantly think SQL Server requires IE to serve data. That is not the case. The only parts of SQL Server 2005 that require IE are the Microsoft Management Console and Books Online (BOL).

You must also be certain your machine meets the minimum hardware requirements before you can install SQL Server 2005. Otherwise, SQL Server may run very slowly, or not at all. Each edition of SQL Server has a different set of hardware requirements. Table 2-1 lists the hardware requirements for the Express Edition; Table 2-2 lists the Workgroup Edition requirements; and Table 2-3 lists the Standard Edition Developer Edition and Enterprise Edition requirements.

> **CERTIFICATION READY?**
> After reading this section, close your eyes. What are the requirements for each scenario?

Table 2-1

Express Edition Requirements

COMPONENT	32-BIT
Processor	600 megahertz (MHz) Pentium III-compatible or faster processor; 1 gigahertz (GHz) or faster processor recommended
Memory	192 megabytes (MB) of random access memory (RAM) or more; 512 MB or more recommended
Disk drive	CD or DVD drive
Hard disk space	Approximately 350 MB of available hard disk space for the recommended installation, with approximately 425 MB of additional space for SQL Server BOL, SQL Server Mobile BOL, and sample databases
Operating system	Windows XP with SP2 or newer; Vista; Windows 2000 Server with SP4 or newer; Windows Server 2003 Standard Edition, Enterprise Edition, or Datacenter Edition with SP1 or newer; Windows Small Business Server 2003 with SP1 or newer

Table 2-2

Workgroup Edition Requirements

COMPONENT	32-BIT
Processor	600 MHz Pentium III-compatible or faster processor; 1 GHz or faster processor recommended
Memory	512 MB of RAM or more; 1 GB or more recommended
Disk drive	CD or DVD drive
Hard disk space	Approximately 350 MB of available hard disk space for the recommended installation, with approximately 425 MB of additional space for SQL Server BOL, SQL Server Mobile BOL, and sample databases
Operating system	Microsoft Windows 2000 Server with SP4 or newer; Windows 2000 Professional Edition with SP4 or newer; Windows XP with SP2 or newer; Vista; Windows Server 2003 Enterprise Edition, Standard Edition, or Datacenter Edition with SP1 or newer; Windows Small Business Server 2003 with SP1 or newer

Table 2-3

Developer, Standard, and Enterprise Edition Requirements

COMPONENT	32-BIT	x64	ITANIUM
Processor	600 MHz Pentium III–compatible or faster processor; 1 GHz or faster processor recommended	1 GHz AMD Opteron, AMD Athlon 64, Intel Xeon with Intel EM64T support, Intel Pentium IV with EM64T support processor	1 GHz Itanium or faster processor
Memory	512 MB of RAM or more; 1 GB or more recommended	512 MB of RAM or more; 1 GB or more recommended	512 MB of RAM or more; 1 GB or more recommended
Disk drive	CD or DVD drive	CD or DVD drive	CD or DVD drive
Hard disk space	Approximately 350 MB of available hard disk space for the recommended installation, with approximately 425 MB of additional space for SQL Server BOL, SQL Server Mobile BOL, and sample databases	Approximately 350 MB of available hard disk space for the recommended installation, with approximately 425 MB of additional space for SQL Server BOL, SQL Server Mobile BOL, and sample databases	Approximately 350 MB of available hard disk space for the recommended installation, with approximately 425 MB of additional space for SQL Server BOL, SQL Server Mobile BOL, and sample databases
Operating system	Microsoft Windows 2000 Server with SP4 or newer; Windows 2000 Professional Edition with SP4 or newer; Windows XP with SP2 or newer; Vista; Windows Server 2003 Enterprise Edition, Standard Edition, or Datacenter Edition with SP1 or newer; Windows Small Business Server 2003 with SP1 or newer	Microsoft Windows Server 2003 Standard x64 Edition, Enterprise x64 Edition, or Datacenter x64 Edition with SP1 or newer; Windows XP Professional x64 Edition or newer; Vista	Microsoft Windows Server 2003 Enterprise Edition or Datacenter Edition for Itanium-based systems with SP1 or newer

At this point you are probably wondering why there are so many versions of SQL Server 2005 and which one is right for you. The following discussion compares the versions and tells you what each edition does:

- **Compact Edition:** The Compact Edition can be deployed on desktop computers, smart devices, and Tablet PCs. Compact Edition provides relational database functionality in a small footprint; it is a robust data store and an optimizing query processor; and it provides reliable, scalable connectivity.
- **Express Edition/Express Edition with Advanced Services:** The Express Edition supports one central processing unit (CPU) and up to 1 GB of RAM, and has a maximum database size of 4 GB. It does not have full 64-bit support, but it will run on 64-bit operating systems using the Windows-on-Windows (WOW) technology. The Advanced Services adds Management Studio Express, full-text catalogs, and support for viewing reports.
- **Workgroup Edition:** The Workgroup Edition supports two CPUs and up to 3 GB of RAM; it has no maximum database size limit. It does not have full 64-bit support, but it will run on 64-bit operating systems using the WOW technology. In addition, this edition provides backup log-shipping, full-text search, the SQL Server Agent scheduling service, and the Report Builder.
- **Standard Edition:** Standard Edition supports four CPUs and as much RAM as the operating system (OS) can support; it has no maximum database size limit. It offers full 64-bit support. In addition to all the features that Workgroup Edition provides,

Standard Edition has database mirroring, failover clustering, the Database Tuning Advisor, Notification Services, Integration Services with basic transforms, and Hypertext Transfer Protocol (HTTP) endpoints.

- **Enterprise Edition/Developer Edition/Evaluation Edition:** These three editions support as many CPUs as the OS allows and as much RAM as the OS can support; they have no maximum database size limit, although the Developer Edition is licensed for a single user and the Evaluation Edition expires after 180 days. They offer full 64-bit support. In addition to all the features that the Standard Edition and Workgroup Edition provide, these editions offer partitioning, parallel index operations, indexed views, online indexing and restoration, fast recovery, Integration Services advanced transforms, Oracle replication, the scale-out of report servers, and data-driven subscriptions (for Reporting Services).

- **Runtime Edition:** This edition is offered through the Microsoft Independent Software Vendor Royalty Program. Under the end-user license agreement, the edition may be embedded into a software solution, provided the end user can't use the runtime outside of the application.

Now you have the hardware and OS in place, but you have still more to consider before you can install SQL Server.

Preparing to Install

Before you actually install SQL Server, which you'll do in Exercise 2-1, you'll need to understand a few topics, so in this section you'll examine some decisions you need to make before installing.

LOCATING IN A DOMAIN OR WORKGROUP

You may place SQL Server, which is an example of a relational database management system (RDBMS), in a domain or a workgroup.

A *domain* sets a security boundary within a *tree*, which is a branch of your enterprise topography with contiguous name space for included domains, and within a *forest*, which uses a common schema for all active directory instances. Your database may be placed on the domain controller, as with Small Business Server, or may be installed on a member server. Servers are generally administered centrally in your organization.

A *workgroup* operates without an active directory, and each server and workstation within the local network requires individual administrative attention. The SQL Server installation within a workgroup is installed on a standalone server.

CHOOSING DEFAULT INSTANCES OR NAMED INSTANCES

One of the first choices you need to make is whether this SQL Server will be the default instance or a named instance. That may seem a bit confusing if you are new to SQL Server, so here's the distinction:

- Named instances are essentially like running multiple SQL Servers on one machine. The most common time to run multiple instances is when you need to run multiple versions of SQL Server but you have limited hardware resources. By using this method you can have SQL Server 2005 running as a named instance and SQL Server 7.0 or 2000 running as the default instance. Your client machines will see two distinct SQL Servers on the network, even though they are both running on the same machine.

- The default instance is automatically selected and should be left that way for the first installation of SQL Server on a machine. Subsequent installations on the same machine can be given installation names of up to 16 characters. Clients will then use this new name to refer to the new instance.

CERTIFICATION READY?
Do you understand all aspects? If in doubt, check Books Online (introduced in the next lesson). Search for "Hardware and Software Requirements for Installing SQL Server 2005."

CERTIFICATION READY?
SQL Server 2005 works only in the Windows environment. Make sure you know the difference between domain server, member server, and standalone server.

CHOOSING SERVICE ACCOUNTS

When you first turn on your Windows machine and try to use it, you are presented with a dialog box that asks you for a username and password. That username and password give you access to the machine (and the network) with whatever privileges your administrator has seen fit to assign. Many services, such as programs running in the background, require a user account, just like you do. This special user account, called a *service account*, gives the service access to the machine and network with the privileges it requires to get its work done.

The SQL Server services require a user account to run, so you need to pick one of three types, from those shown in Table 2-4.

Table 2-4

Service Account Comparison

Type	Limitations	Advantages
Built-in system account	You will not be able to communicate with other SQL Servers over the network.	Easy to set up, since you don't need to create a user account.
Local user account	You will not be able to communicate with other SQL Servers over the network.	Allows you to control the service permissions without allowing network access.
Domain user account	None, but slightly more difficult to configure than the other two because a network administrator must create and configure the accounts.	Allows you to communicate fully with other network machines, including SQL Servers and e-mail servers.

If you opt to use a user account (local or domain), you must first create it using the appropriate tool for your operating system. If you create only one account to be used by both SQL Server and SQL Server Agent services, then you must add the user account to the Administrators local group; otherwise, replication (discussed in Lesson 23) will not function properly. If you decide you want greater control over the security on your network, then you can add two separate accounts, one for the SQL Server service and one for the SQL Server Agent service. A good reason to do this is that only the SQL Server Agent service really requires administrative authority; the other can get by just fine as a standard user.

SELECTING AN AUTHENTICATION MODE

Another important decision is which authentication mode to use. Lesson 16 discusses authentication modes in more detail, but it helps to know a little about them for setup purposes. To access SQL Server, your users need to log in to the server, and to log in to the server, they need an account. The type of account they use depends on the authentication mode that you set. If you select Windows Authentication Mode, then only clients that have a Windows operating system account will be able to access the system. If you have other clients (like Novell or Unix), then you should select Mixed Mode. You can change the authentication mode at any time after installation; in other words, if you choose the wrong one for your needs, it is okay.

CHOOSING A COLLATION SETTING

In versions of SQL Server prior to SQL Server 2000, it was necessary to choose a character set, a *sort order*, and a Unicode collation setting. In SQL Server 2005, these three entities have been combined to form the collation setting. You can choose from two collation settings: SQL Collation and Windows Collation.

SQL Collation is for backward compatibility with older versions of SQL Server and does not control Unicode character storage. If you need to replicate with older versions of SQL Server, or you will be switching between SQL Server 2005 and SQL Server 7.0 and older, you should use SQL Collation. If you are installing SQL Server 2005 on a machine with an older version of SQL installed, then the setup program will detect the necessary collation for you; otherwise, you need to select the proper collation. Windows Collation uses the collation (***code page***, sort order, and so on) of the underlying operating system, and controls Unicode and non-Unicode sorting and storage. If you choose Windows Collation, then you have two more issues to address: the collation designator and the sort order.

SELECTING A COLLATION DESIGNATOR

As you read this book, you see the characters as lines, curves, and various shapes. If you read Cyrillic, you see different shapes for the characters than someone reading German or English. Computers need to read and interpret characters just like you do; the only problem is that computers don't see them as various shapes—they see them as different combinations of 1s and 0s. It makes sense then that if your computer is storing German data, it must store different characters, or combinations of 1s and 0s, than an English server stores. How these characters are stored is controlled by the collation designator. If you decide to use Windows Collation, then it is best to use the collation of the underlying operating system; for example, if you are running a German server, then you will most likely choose a German collation designator. The easiest way to find your collation designator is to look in the Control Panel under the Regional and Language Options; you should use the locale displayed there as your collation designator. The most common selection in North America is Latin1_General.

SELECTING A SORT ORDER

All the data you are storing on your server must be sorted from time to time, usually during queries or indexing (discussed in Lessons 7 and 13). You sort data because looking at a mass of it in unsorted form is hard on the brain, whereas looking at a nicely sequenced report of data is pleasing to the eye. The sort order defines how SQL sorts and compares your data during queries or indexing. This sort order is the second part of the collation setting.

Several sort options are available. The default sort order is case, accent, kana, and width-insensitive. This means SQL Server will not pay attention to case or special character marks when sorting, when indexing, or when performing queries. Some options can change this behavior, and if you are familiar with previous versions of SQL Server, then you will want to pay attention because they have changed:

- **Binary:** Using the default sort order, SQL Server will view characters as characters; by using binary, SQL Server will view characters as byte representations. This is the fastest sort order available, but it is case-, accent-, and kana-sensitive.

- **Binary code point:** This works much the same as binary sorting but has some additional functionality. This sort order uses Unicode ***code points*** when sorting, which allows SQL Server to sort on the locale as well as the data. This means English data would be sorted separately from Japanese data stored as Unicode. This order, too, is case-, accent-, and kana-sensitive.

- **Case-sensitive:** This simply tells SQL Server to use dictionary sort order and pay attention to case.

- **Accent-sensitive:** This tells SQL Server to use dictionary order and pay attention to accent marks.

- **Kana-sensitive:** This tells SQL Server to use dictionary order and pay attention to kana marks, which are used in many Asian languages.

- **Width-sensitive:** This tells SQL Server to treat single-byte characters and double-byte characters as different characters.

Here's the catch: Once you have installed SQL Server, you cannot change the collation setting. To change it, you must reinstall SQL Server and rebuild all your databases. So, choose wisely. It is usually best to use the default sort setting of case insensitivity, then build sensitivity into your applications if you need it.

Upgrading from a Previous Version

You can directly upgrade to SQL Server 2005 from SQL Server 2000 SP3 or SQL Server 7.0 SP4. Most of the upgrade operations are handled during setup, so you don't need to run any special wizard or installation program. To make sure you are completely prepared, though, you need to run the Upgrade Advisor.

To use the Upgrade Advisor, you first need to install .NET Framework 2.0 and then install the Upgrade Advisor. The first time you run the Upgrade Advisor, you should run the Analysis Wizard, which will analyze various parts of your existing SQL Server installation and let you know whether they are ready for upgrade. Specifically, the Analysis Wizard checks the following:

- Database engine
- Analysis Services
- Notification Services
- Reporting Services
- SQL Server Integration Services

The wizard generates a report based on its findings, which you can view using the Upgrade Advisor Report Viewer. Anything marked with a green icon is ready to upgrade. A yellow icon indicates a potential problem that can usually be fixed after the upgrade is complete. Anything marked with a red icon needs to be fixed before an upgrade can take place.

Once you have made sure your system meets all the requirements, and have made all the necessary decisions about setup, you are ready to install SQL Server 2005.

Installing SQL Server 2005

Now you are ready to install SQL Server 2005 on your own machine. Follow the steps in Exercise 2-1 to do so. (Note: These steps are for installing the Standard Edition, but the steps are similar for all editions.)

EXERCISE 2-1 INSTALLING SQL SERVER 2005

1. Create a user account named SqlServer with a password of Pa$$w0rd, and make it a member of the Administrators local group. You can perform this task using one of these tools: on a Windows member server or on Windows XP, use Computer Management (right-click **My Computer** → **Manage**); on a Windows domain controller, use **Active Directory Users** and **Computers** (click **Start** → **Administrative Tools**).

2. Insert the **SQL Server CD**, and wait for the automenu to open.

3. Under Install, click **Server Components, Tools, Books Online,** and **Samples.**

4. You then will be asked to read and agree with the end-user license agreement (EULA); check the box to agree, and click **Next.**

5. If your machine does not have all the prerequisites installed, the setup will install them for you at this time. Click **Install** if you are asked to do so. When complete, click **Next.**

6. Next you will see a screen telling you that the setup is inspecting your system's configuration again, after which the Welcome screen appears. Click **Next** to continue.

7. Another, more in-depth, system configuration screen appears letting you know whether any configuration settings will prevent SQL Server from being installed.

Errors (marked with a red icon) need to be repaired before you can continue. Warnings (yellow icon) can optionally be repaired and will not prevent SQL Server from installing. Once you have made any needed changes, click **Next**.

8. After a few configuration setting screens appear, you will be asked for your product key. Enter it, and click **Next**.

9. On the next screen, you need to select the components you want to install. Click the **Advanced** button to view the advanced options for the setup. For training, be sure to select the **AdventureWorks** database and all training tools.

10. Click the **Back** button to return to the basic options screen, and check the boxes next to SQL Server Database Services, Integration Services, and Workstation Components, Books Online, and Development Tools. Then click **Next**.

11. On the Instance Name screen, choose **Default Instance**, and click **Next** (you'll install a named instance in the next exercise).

12. On the next screen, enter the account information for the service account you created in step 1. You will be using the same account for each service in this exercise. When finished, click **Next**.

13. On the Authentication Mode screen, select **Mixed Mode**, enter a password of Pa$$w0rd for the sa account, and click **Next**.

14. Select the **Latin1_General** collation designator on the next screen, and click **Next**.

15. On the following screen, you can select to send error and feature usage information directly to Microsoft. This setting is entirely up to you, but you will not be checking it here. So, leave the defaults, and click **Next**.

16. On the Ready to Install screen, you can review your settings, and then click **Install**.

17. The setup progress appears during the install process. When the setup is finished (which may take several minutes), click **Next**.

18. The final screen gives you an installation report, letting you know whether any errors occurred and reminding you of any postinstallation steps to take. Click **Finish** to complete your install.

19. Reboot your system if requested to do so.

Now that you have SQL installed, you should make sure it is running. Go to **Start → All Programs → Microsoft SQL Server 2005 → Configuration Tools → SQL Server Configuration Manager**. Select **SQL Server 2005 Services** and check the icons. If the icon next to SQL Server (MSSQLServer) service is green, your installation is a success. You did succeed, right? If not, refer to the last section in this chapter for troubleshooting hints.

INSTALLING A SECOND INSTANCE

Because SQL Server 2005 has the capability of running multiple instances of itself on the same machine, it is a good idea to try installing more than one instance. In Exercise 2-2, you will create a second instance of SQL Server on the same machine using a different sort order.

⊙→ EXERCISE 2-2 INSTALLING A NAMED INSTANCE OF SQL SERVER 2005

1. Insert the SQL Server 2005 CD and wait for the automenu to open.

2. Under Install, click **Server Components, Tools, Books Online**, and **Samples**.

3. You then will be asked to read and agree with the EULA; check the box to agree, and click **Next**.

4. Next you should see a screen telling you that the setup is inspecting your system's configuration again, and then the Welcome screen appears. Click **Next** to continue.

5. Another, more in-depth, system configuration screen appears letting you know whether any configuration settings will prevent SQL Server from being installed. Errors (marked with a red icon) need to be repaired before you can continue. Warnings (yellow icon) can optionally be repaired and will not prevent SQL Server from installing. Once you have made any needed changes, click **Next**.

6. Check the box next to SQL Server Database Services, and click **Next**.

7. On the **Instance Name** screen, choose **Named Instance**, enter **Instance1** in the text box, and click **Next**.

8. On the next screen, enter the account information for the service account you created in step 1 of Exercise 2-1. You will use the same account for each service in this exercise. When finished, click **Next**.

9. On the Authentication Mode screen, select **Mixed Mode**, enter a password for the sa account, and click **Next**.

10. Select the **Dictionary Order, Case-Insensitive, for Use with 1252 Character Set** option in the SQL Collations list, and click **Next**.

11. On the following screen, you can select to send error and feature usage information directly to Microsoft. This setting is entirely up to you, but you will not be checking it here. So, leave the defaults, and click **Next**.

12. On the Ready to Install screen, you can review your settings and then click **Install**.

13. The setup progress appears during the install process. When the setup is finished (which may take several minutes), click **Next**.

14. The final screen gives you an installation report, letting you know whether any errors occurred and reminding you of any postinstallation steps to take. Click **Finish** to complete your install.

15. Reboot your system if requested to do so.

CERTIFICATION READY?
Where can you find information about installation failures?

You can now test the second instance of SQL Server using the same method for testing the default instance. Go to **Start** → **All Programs** → **Microsoft SQL Server 2005** → **Configuration Tools** → **SQL Server Configuration Manager**. Select **SQL Server 2005 Services** and refer to the icons. If the icon next to SQL Server (Second) instance is green, your installation is a success.

Troubleshooting the Installation

If it turns out that your install failed, there are a few steps you can take to troubleshoot it. The first place to look when you have problems is in the Windows *Event Viewer*. SQL will log any problems it encounters in the Application log, so check there first. If you find a problem, write down the error number and some of the text of the message and look them up in TechNet or on the Microsoft support Web site (*http://support.microsoft.com*).

If you do not find the source of your problems in the Event Viewer, navigate to X:\ Program Files\Microsoft SQL Server\90\Setup Bootstrap\LOG, open the Summary.txt file, and check for error messages. If that doesn't help, open the SQLSetupxxxx.cab file. If that CAB file does not exist, open the SQLSetupxxxx_ComputerName_Core.log file. Or, if you saw an error during the graphical portion of the setup process, you can also check the SQLSetupxxxx_ ComputerName_WI.log file. And you can check the SQLSetupxxxx_ ComputerName_SQL.log file. In any of these SQLSetupxxxx files, you can perform a search for the phrase "UE 3," which is short for Return Value 3, which means an error occurred.

SKILL SUMMARY

This lesson explained the ins and outs of the installation process. First you learned the prerequisites of each of the editions of SQL Server. Those editions are:

- Compact Edition
- Express/Express with Advanced Services
- Workgroup
- Standard
- Enterprise/Enterprise Evaluation
- Developer
- Runtime Edition

After learning the prerequisites, you discovered there are some decisions to make before you can run the installation. First you need to decide whether to install a named instance or a default instance. If you already have a default instance of SQL Server installed on the machine, then you must install a named instance.

Next you learned that you need to choose the right service accounts for the services to run under. Service accounts allow services to log on as a Windows user and inherit all of that user's permissions on the machine and the network.

You also discovered that you need to choose the right authentication mode, which dictates how users log in to the SQL Server instance. Windows Only mode only allows users with Windows accounts to access SQL Server, whereas Mixed Mode allows access to users with Windows accounts and SQL Server standard accounts.

You also learned about choosing the right collation setting. The collation setting tells SQL Server how to store characters in tables. Each language has a collation setting that works best.

Next you installed a default instance and a second instance of SQL Server 2005 on your system. Finally, you learned how to troubleshoot setup if anything goes awry.

For the certification examination:

- Know the prerequisites: Know the system prerequisites, how much memory you need, how fast a processor you need, and which operating system version is best.
- Understand the Upgrade Advisor: Know how to use the Upgrade Advisor and how to read the report it produces. In particular, you need to know when an upgrade is going to fail based on the Upgrade Advisor's report.

■ Knowledge Assessment

Multiple Choice

Circle the letter or letters that correspond to the best answer or answers.

1. You have a machine that has an 800 MHz Pentium III processor with 256 MB of RAM, and a 400 GB hard drive running Windows Server 2000 SP4. Which editions of SQL Server 2005 can you install? (Choose all that apply.)
   a. Express Edition
   b. Workgroup Edition
   c. Standard Edition
   d. Enterprise Edition
   e. Developer Edition

2. One of your third-party applications has been certified to run on SQL Server 2000 but not 2005. Your company has just bought a new application that requires SQL Server 2005 to run. How can you run both of these applications with minimal overhead?
   a. Buy a second server and install SQL Server 2005 on the new machine.
   b. You can't run both applications; you will have to wait until the older application is certified to run on SQL Server 2005.
   c. Install SQL Server 2005 as a named instance, and configure your new application to use the new instance.
   d. Install SQL Server 2005 as the default instance, and configure your new application to use the new instance.

3. You are installing a new SQL Server 2005 instance on a machine in a small peer-to-peer network. You will not be performing replication, so SQL Server will not need to communicate with other servers over the network. You need to be able to change the service account's password every six months per company policy. Which service account type should you use?
   a. Built-in system account
   b. Local system account
   c. Domain account

4. One of the databases you will be using on your new SQL Server holds data in several different languages, including U.S. English, German, and Italian. When your users search the data, they may be looking for information in any of the available languages. You want to be able to sort through data as quickly as possible, and you are not concerned with sensitivity. Which sort order is best?
   a. Binary
   b. Binary code point
   c. Binary without the case-sensitivity option
   d. Binary code point without the case-sensitivity option

5. You have a machine that has a 3.2 GHz Pentium Xeon processor with 4 GB of RAM, and a 320 GB hard drive running Windows Server 2003 Enterprise Edition. Which editions of SQL Server 2005 can you install? (Choose all that apply.)
   a. Express Edition
   b. Workgroup Edition
   c. Standard Edition
   d. Enterprise Edition
   e. Developer Edition

6. Your company has decided it is time to upgrade to SQL Server 2005. You currently run SQL Server 7.0 SP3. What do you need to do before you can upgrade?
   a. Nothing; you can upgrade directly to SQL Server 2005.
   b. Upgrade to SQL Server 2000, and then you can upgrade to SQL Server 2005.
   c. Upgrade to SQL Server 2000, install SQL Server 2000 SP3, and then upgrade to SQL Server 2005.
   d. Install SQL Server 7.0 SP4, and then upgrade to SQL Server 2005.

7. When you run the Upgrade Advisor, you get a report with a warning telling you "Full-Text Search Word Breakers and Filters Significantly Improved in SQL 2005." What do you need to do before upgrading?
   a. Uninstall full-text search on your machine, and rerun the Upgrade Advisor.
   b. Nothing; you can install without modification.
   c. Uninstall full-text search, and do not rerun the Upgrade Advisor.
   d. Run the Upgrade Advisor with the /NoFTSCheck option.

8. You are installing a new SQL Server 2005 instance on a machine in a large network with several Active Directory domains across the country. You need to replicate data between several SQL Servers. Which service account type should you use?
   a. Built-in system account
   b. Local system account
   c. Domain account

9. You have a wide variety of clients on your network that need access to SQL Server. Many of these run Unix with Samba, which allows them to use an Active Directory account to access resources on the Windows domain. Several others use Mac clients with the AppleTalk protocol for accessing the network. The remaining clients are Windows 98 and XP Professional clients. Which authentication mode setting should you select when installing SQL Server?
   a. Windows Authentication Mode
   b. Mixed Mode

10. You have a machine that has a 1 GHz AMD Opteron processor with 512 MB of RAM, and a 400 GB hard drive running Windows 2003 Standard x64 Edition. Management wants to make sure the new software will take full advantage of the hardware. Which editions of SQL Server 2005 can you install? (Choose all that apply.)
   a. Express Edition
   b. Workgroup Edition
   c. Standard Edition
   d. Enterprise Edition

11. You are going to upgrade to SQL Server 2005 and you want to employ a two-node failover cluster for high availability. Which version of SQL Server can you use? (Choose all that apply.)
   a. Express Edition
   b. Workgroup Edition
   c. Standard Edition
   d. Enterprise Edition

12. You are going to upgrade to SQL Server 2005. Your company has several Oracle servers and you need to be able to synchronize the data between your SQL Server and Oracle databases using replication. Which version of SQL Server can you use? (Choose all that apply.)
   a. Express Edition
   b. Workgroup Edition
   c. Standard Edition
   d. Enterprise Edition

13. One of the databases you will be using on your new SQL Server holds data in several different languages, including U.S. English, German, and Italian. Users will primarily search for data in their own language but occasionally search for data in other languages. You want to be able to sort through data as quickly as possible, and you are not concerned with sensitivity. Which sort order is best?
   a. Binary
   b. Binary code point
   c. Binary without the case-sensitivity option
   d. Binary code point without the case-sensitivity option

14. Your company has an Active Directory domain with primarily Windows XP and Windows 2000 Professional clients, all of which have Active Directory accounts, but you also have a few Unix clients that do not have Active Directory accounts. Only your Windows-based clients will need access to your SQL Server. Which authentication mode setting should you select when installing SQL Server?
   a. Windows Authentication Mode
   b. Mixed Mode

15. When installing SQL Server 2005, you meant to use the default SQL Collation setting (the Dictionary Order, Case-Insensitive, for Use with 1252 Character Set option); instead, you chose the case-sensitive version by accident. What should you do to switch to the correct character set?
   a. Change the character set using SQL Server Configuration Manager.
   b. Run the sp_change_collation system stored procedure.
   c. Reinstall SQL Server 2005 with the correct sort order and collation.
   d. Run the sp_change_sort system stored procedure.

16. Your installation of SQL Server 2005 has failed. Where is the first place you should look to find clues about the cause?
   a. The System log in the Event Viewer
   b. The Summary.txt file
   c. The SQLSetupxxxx_ComputerName_Core.log file
   d. The Application log in the Event Viewer

17. You are going to upgrade to SQL Server 2005 and you want to use full-text search for many of your applications. Which version of SQL Server can you use? (Choose all that apply.)
   a. Express Edition
   b. Workgroup Edition
   c. Standard Edition
   d. Enterprise Edition

18. You are installing a new SQL Server 2005 instance on a machine in a small network. This is the only SQL Server on the network and you want to make administration as simple as possible. Which service account type should you use?
   a. Built-in system account
   b. Local system account
   c. Domain account

19. You are installing a new server with SQL Server 2005. Your sister company runs SQL Server 7.0 SP4. You need to replicate data between the two servers regularly. What collation setting should you use?
   a. Windows Collation
   b. SQL Collation

20. Your installation of SQL Server has failed, giving you a graphical error message, which you wrote down and misplaced. Can you find the error message again?
   a. Graphical error messages are not recorded during setup.
   b. Graphical error messages are recorded in the Summary.txt file.
   c. Graphical error messages are recorded in the SQLSetupxxxx_ComputerName_Core.log file.
   d. Graphical error messages are recorded in the SQLSetupxxxx_ComputerName_WI.log file.

■ Case Scenario

Scenario 2-1: Installing a Third Instance

You are the administrator for your group. You have decided to test Database Mirroring. To do it, you installed a default and an instance on your local computer (in this lesson). Now, add a third instance named Instance2. At this point, you will have a default instance using your server name, a secondary named Instance1, and a third named Instance2. The exercise for Database Mirroring uses all three databases.

3 LESSON

Navigating SQL Server 2005

LESSON SKILL MATRIX

TECHNOLOGY SKILL	70-431 EXAM OBJECTIVE
General capabilities.	Supplemental
Navigating user interface tools.	Supplemental

KEY TERMS

SQL Server Management Studio: The primary tool for managing objects in your database.

SQL Server Books Online: The reference required for all aspects of SQL Server. BOL includes T-SQL syntax, tutorials, and how-to's; it is the definitive guide to solving SQL Server issues.

SQL Server Surface Area Configuration: Enable or disable various features you need or

don't need specifically. Reduce your hacker attack vulnerability by presenting the minimum features possible.

SQL Server Configuration Manager: Enable or disable services and protocols, again, to minimize your vulnerability to attack.

■ Using SQL Server Tools

THE BOTTOM LINE All relational database management systems require maintenance and management. Microsoft supplies very capable tools to assist you in these tasks.

Understanding SQL Server Tools

Now that you have loaded SQL Server 2005, it's time to introduce you to the four main *graphical user interface (GUI)* management tools:

- SQL Server Management Studio
- SQL Server Configuration Manager
- SQL Server Surface Area Configuration
- SQL Server Books Online

You will find these four applications by Clicking **Start → All Programs → Microsoft SQL Server 2005**, and looking in the first pop-out menu or in the submenus *Configuration Tools* and *Documentation and Tutorials*.

For your convenience, right-click each in turn, select **Send To** and **Desktop**. This will place a shortcut on your desktop for easier access in the future.

The last section introduces you to nongraphical methods you might find useful.

Introducing SQL Server Management Studio (SSMS)

SQL Server Management Studio, new in SQL Server 2005, is an integrated environment for accessing, configuring, managing, administering, and developing all components of the RDBMS. Management Studio combines a broad group of graphical tools with a number of rich script editors to provide access to SQL Server to developers and administrators of all skill levels.

Double left-click your **SSMS** desktop item to launch the program. A splash screen appears alerting you to having chosen *Management Studio*. You are then invited to Connect. Click the down arrow in each of the selection boxes to discover you can connect to other than the Database Engine. Note the options of Analysis Services, Reporting Services, and more. This is an integrated work environment for many of SQL Server's features. Clicking the **Server** name and, perhaps, **<Browse for More>** allows you to connect to other RDBMS instances on your server or other servers on your network. And, finally, you have the option to connect to your network server as a trusted user (Windows Authentication) or standard user (SQL Server Authentication). You also have the option of cancelling and directly starting a New Query.

USING THE OBJECT BROWSER

The tree view in the left-hand pane contains an expandable view of the objects currently configured in SQL Server. Click the plus signs adjacent to major objects and discover how deeply you can drill down. Start with databases.

 EXERCISE 3-1 INVESTIGATING A DATABASE DIAGRAM

1. Click the **plus sign** next to Databases.
2. Click the **plus sign** next to AdventureWorks.
3. Right-click **Database Diagrams** and select **New Database Diagram**.
4. Select **ALL** by highlighting the first table and then scrolling to the last table. Holding down the **Shift** key, click on the **last entry**. Assure that all tables have been highlighted in blue.
5. When the wizard finishes, click **Close**. You will probably have to change the scale to 10% to see all of the objects.
6. Grab a table by pressing the **left mouse key** and move it. Eventually, you will have tables organized well enough that you can increase the scale to 25%.
7. Right-click a table and from the menu choose **Table View** to see the various display options. Start with **Standard**. Then select **Column Names**.
8. Continue down the menu. You see all of the management aspects pertaining to a table presented. You can totally manage a database in this diagrammatic view.
9. Right-click any empty space. Note that the menu changes. Now you can create a new table.

Click the **plus sign** next to Tables. You will now see a list of tables included in the AdventureWorks Database. Click a **plus sign** next to any table and then just keep going. Drill down to examine the details of any specific table. It has columns. It has datatypes.

Do the same thing for Views, Synonyms, Programmability, Service Broker, Storage, and Security. Examine what is included in each category.

USING THE QUERY EDITOR

Start a New Query by clicking the button near the upper left corner of your screen. You will be asked for your authentication credentials, as you are making another connection to the database engine.

As you work, notice the editor presents your text in colors. If you type in the keyword "USE" correctly, the letters turn blue, while AdventureWorks remains black—"USE" is an SQL keyword; "AdventureWorks" is not.

EXERCISE 3-2 EXECUTE A QUERY

1. In the query window, type the following code:
   USE AdventureWorks
   SELECT * FROM

2. At this point, open **Databases** → **AdventureWorks** → **Tables**, and with your left mouse button drag **Person.Contact** from the list onto the query pane immediately behind the FROM keyword separated with a space. It should look like this:

   use adventureworks

   select * from person.contact

3. Click the **Execute** box, press the **F5** key or press the combination of **Ctrl** and **e** (**Ctrl-e** because uppercase E doesn't work). Congratulations! You've executed your first query.

4. Let your mouse point hover over the buttons across the top in turn. Discover whether Results to Grid or Results to Text is selected. Whichever has the black border, change to the other one and execute again. The display is quite different. The desired option depends on the data you retrieve.

5. Try:
   SELECT @@VERSION

6. Again switch the Results to Grid and Results to Text back and forth executing the query after each switch. Decide which proves easier to read.

7. Add a new Query window by pressing **Ctrl-n** (Ctrl-Shift-N starts a new project). Note that you now have multiple query windows open. SQL Server now supports multiple active result sets. Click the black **X** to the immediate right of the query tabs. Decide whether you want to save your query and finish closing it.

USING THE SOLUTION EXPLORER

SQL Server now supports a development platform for Transact-SQL. Either press the **Ctrl-Shift-N** keys or click on the **File** drop-down menu and select **New** and **Project**. After you assure that SQL Server Scripts is highlighted, change the name to Practice and specify a more convenient location than My Documents—how about C:\? Assure that the Create directory for solution is selected. Click **OK**.

The Solution Explorer opens, displaying your Practice project. Although you can perform all administrative tasks by executing Transact-SQL statements, it is often easier to use SSMS. However, you should generate the corresponding Transact-SQL scripts and save them in the project for future reference.

 EXERCISE 3-3 SCRIPT STORAGE

1. Right-click on **Queries** in the Practice submenu and make a **New Query.**

2. Right-click the new query and **Rename** it as Config1.

3. Connect to your server instance.

4. In the Object Browser, right-click your server and select **Properties**.

5. Select the **Security** page.

6. In the Login auditing section of the right-hand pane, click the **Both failed and successful logins**.

7. Click the **down arrow** adjacent to the Script box in the upper left-hand corner of the Properties box and copy the internally generated script to the clipboard.

8. Right-click in the **Config1 Query window** and paste in the results.

9. Click **OK** in the server property box to effect the change.

10. Click the query window closed; save the change.

11. Finally, double-click your **Config1** to verify the change was stored.

Introducing Books Online

No one can know everything about SQL Server. That is why *SQL Server Books Online*, the authoritative reference guide, comes with your distribution disk. You might avoid placing it on your production service, but be sure it is loaded to your development workstation.

Microsoft Corporation updates this documentation regularly. Check occasionally for a newer file. At the time of this writing, the current version was dated September 15, 2007.

You may already know that SQL Server Express Edition is free. Before you install it at home for learning purposes, click on the **Books Online** icon now on your desktop.

 EXERCISE 3-4 SEARCHING BOOKS ONLINE

1. Once open, click the **Magnifying** button.
2. Enter this string in the **Search** text box: "Features Supported by Editions of SQL Server 2005."
3. Double left-click the article of interest from the search results list.
4. Scroll the article to verify the features you need to learn are included.
5. Click the **Sync with Table of Contents** button. Look in the contents window for other articles to browse.
6. Look up the details about @@VERSION that you executed in the Query window.
7. Notice that usage examples appear near the end of most syntax pages.

Introducing SQL Server Configuration Manager

You may not be the Windows Server 2003 Administrator. To start and stop Windows services, and to enable and disable network protocols, Microsoft gives you a special access tool called the *SQL Server Configuration Manager*.

 EXERCISE 3-5 USING CONFIGURATION MANAGER

1. Double-click the icon shortcut you placed on your desktop. This opens the Microsoft Management Console for managing network connections.
2. Click on **SQL Server 2005 Services** in the tree view.
3. Right-click **SQL Server Agent**. Select **Restart** from the context menu. This stops and starts the service that an operating system administrator would otherwise have to do for you.
4. Click the **plus sign** in from of SQL Server 2005 Network Configuration and then left-click the **Protocols** for your listed service.
5. Right-click **TCP/IP** and choose **Properties** from the menu. Explore the options on the two tabs to understand the controls you can set.
6. Similarly, explore SQL Native Client Configuration.
7. Close the tool when you are done.

> **CERTIFICATION READY?**
> Be sure to note the duplication of functionality in these last two tools. Both, for example, allow you to stop and start services.

Introducing SQL Server Surface Area Configuration

SQL Server Surface Area Configuration is a management application that lets you start, stop, and disable unused components. Surface area reduction helps to improve security by providing fewer avenues for potential attacks on your system.

EXERCISE 3-6 USING SURFACE AREA CONFIGURATION

1. Start the tool.
2. Begin your tour by clicking on the **Surface Area Configuration for Services and Connections** link. Now ask yourself, "Do I need the Reporting Services service running?" If not, turn it off. If you don't need to allow remote connections, deny access.
3. Also click the **Surface Area Configuration for Features** link. Browse this list. If you don't need SQL Mail, leave the Enable SQL Mail stored procedures unchecked.
4. Close the tool after you have explored all options.

Introducing Nongraphical Support Tools

Not all support tools are built into the various graphical user interface (GUI) tools.

USING CATALOG VIEWS

Catalog views enable you to query metadata about SQL Server database objects. A few of the catalog views list serverwide information, but the majority is database-specific. There are more than 200 catalog views. In the next exercise you will investigate one.

 EXERCISE 3-7 CATALOG VIEW

1. Open **Management Studio**. Navigate to **Databases** → **AdventureWorks** → **Views** → **System Views**, and scroll through the list.
2. Start a **New Query**. Use the following code:

   USE AdventureWorks

   SELECT * FROM sys.databases
3. Execute the query.
4. Examine the output. This is an example of the detail available about your database.
5. Try a few others.

USING METADATA FUNCTIONS

SQL Server 2005 defines several categories of functions that return information about the database and database objects. Whereas catalog views return multiple rows of information, these functions return only a single value; they are known as *scalar functions*.

EXERCISE 3-8 METADATA FUNCTIONS

1. Open **Management Studio**. Navigate to **Databases** → **AdventureWorks** → **Programmability** → **Functions** → **System Functions** → **Metadata Functions**, and scroll through the list.
2. Start a **New Query**. Use the following code:

   USE AdventureWorks

   SELECT DB_ID( )
3. Execute the query.
4. Examine the output. This is an example of the detail available about your database.
5. Try a few others.

USING SYSTEM STORED PROCEDURES

SQL Server 2005 defines several categories of system stored procedures that return information about the database and database objects. Some stored procedures accept passed arguments to be selective about the output and are an alternative way to query information the catalog views also provide.

EXERCISE 3-9 STORED PROCEDURES

1. Open **Management Studio**. Navigate to **Databases** → **AdventureWorks** → **Programmability** → **Stored Procedures** → **System Stored Procedures**, and scroll through the list.

2. Start a **New Query**. Use the following code:

   USE AdventureWorks

   EXEC sp_databases

3. Execute the query.

4. Examine the output. This is an example of the detail available about your database.

5. Try a few others. Try sp_HelpDB.

USING DATABASE CONSOLE CHECKERS

SQL Server 2005 defines many DBCC routines to help you maintain your database.

 EXERCISE 3-10 CHECK THE CURRENT DATABASE

1. Open **Management Studio**.

2. Start a **New Query**. Use the following code:

   USE AdventureWorks

   DBCC CheckDB

3. Execute the query. This will take a few minutes.

4. Examine the output. This is an example of the detail available about your database.

5. Find **DBCC CheckDB** in BOL. Sync with **Table of Contents**. Scroll through the list.

6. Try a few others.

SKILL SUMMARY

IN THIS LESSON YOU LEARNED:

SQL Server 2005 comes with all of the management tools need to implement, configure, and maintain an enterprise database. You will use these tools extensively in the coming lessons.

Knowledge Assessment

Multiple Choice

Circle the letter or letters that correspond to the best answer or answers.

1. You need to restart SQL Server service. Where can you do this?
   a. In SQL Server Management Studio
   b. In SQL Server Configuration Manager
   c. In SQL Server Surface Area Configuration
   d. In Services, located in Administrative Tools

2. In case of a disaster, you want to create a script to reproduce all database objects. In previous editions of SQL Server, you would have to create a script. In SQL Server Management Studio, though, you can create a:
   a. Project
   b. Script
   c. Solution
   d. Program

3. The Query Editor now recognizes the syntax requirements of:
   a. Database engine queries
   b. Analysis Services MDX queries
   c. Analysis Services DMX queries
   d. Analysis Services XMLA queries
   e. SQL Server Compact Edition queries

■ Case Scenarios

Scenario 3-1: Supporting Non-Windows Clients

You have Macintosh and Novell users on your network who require access to your database. Add one or more additional standard SQL logins to your default instance.

Datatypes

LESSON SKILL MATRIX

TECHNOLOGY SKILL	70-431 EXAM OBJECTIVE
Create user-defined types.	Foundational
Create a Transact-SQL user-defined type.	Foundational
Specify details in the data type.	Foundational
Create a CLR user-defined type.	Foundational

KEY TERMS

alias datatype: A user-defined datatype based on existing built-in datatypes—for example, ZipCode based on Char(5). Formerly known as *user-defined datatypes*.

built-in datatype: Microsoft-supplied options for storing data in a table; in the table creation, the datatype for an attribute must always be specified.

CLR: Common language runtime; database objects created in Visual Basic, C#, Python, Perl, and many other procedural languages.

datatype: A specification for the way SQL Server stores data in a table; data formats failing the enumerated requirement will fail to be loaded into the table and generate an error.

page: A unit of storage and processing; in SQL Server, this is fixed as 8 KB in size, or 8,192 bytes. Page sizes vary in other RDBMSs, and are selectable in some.

Unicode: Unicode defines a set of letters, numbers, and symbols that SQL Server recognizes in the nchar, navarchar, and ntext datatypes. It is related to but separate from character sets. Unicode has 65,536 possible values, compared to the ASCII character set's 256, and takes twice as much space to store. Unicode includes characters for most languages.

user-defined datatype: The terminology used to describe a named object for use as a datatype in a table; now known as an *alias datatype*.

■ Introducing Datatypes

 THE BOTTOM LINE Every attribute in every table must have an associated datatype. SQL Server uses datatypes to enforce consistent data entry to maintain data integrity. This lesson introduces you to built-in, alias, and trusted-code datatypes.

Introducing Built-in Datatypes

A *datatype* is an attribute that specifies the kind of information that can be stored in a column, parameter, or variable. System-supplied datatypes are provided by SQL Server. *Alias datatypes* (formerly known as *user-defined datatypes*) can be created by any database user.

Each field in a table has a specific datatype, which causes the RDBMS to restrict the type of data that can be inserted. SQL Server provides ***built-in datatypes*** for this purpose. For example, if you create a field with a datatype of int (short for integer, which is a whole number [a number with no decimal point]), you won't be able to store characters (A–Z) or symbols (such as %, *, or #) in that field because SQL Server allows only whole numbers to be stored in int fields. Char or varchar (short for character and variable character, respectively) means you can store characters in these fields, as well as symbols. A number can be represented as either an integer or a character; so if it is stored as a character, it is treated just like a letter, such as "A." However, if numbers are stored in these fields, you won't be able to perform mathematical functions on them directly because SQL Server sees them as characters, not numbers. Several of these datatypes deal with ***Unicode*** data (indicated by the prepended letter "n," which stands for "national"), which is used to store up to 65,536 different characters, as opposed to the standard ANSI character set, which stores 256 characters.

The following is a list of the SQL Server built-in datatypes:

Bigint: This datatype includes integer data from -2^{63} ($-9{,}223{,}372{,}036{,}854{,}775{,}808$) through $2^{63} - 1$ ($9{,}223{,}372{,}036{,}854{,}775{,}807$). It takes 8 bytes of hard disk space to store and is useful for extremely large whole numbers that won't fit in an int field.

Binary: This datatype includes fixed-length binary data with a maximum length of 8,000 bytes. It's interpreted as a string of bits (e.g., 11011001011) and is useful for storing anything that looks better in binary or hexadecimal shorthand, such as a security identifier or a photograph.

Bit: This can contain only a 1 or a 0 as a value (or null, which is no value). It's useful as a status bit—on/off, yes/no, or true/false, for example. SQL Server can allocate no less than a byte. The first bit consumes a byte, while the second bit fits in that byte. The ninth bit requires the addition of a new byte.

Char: This datatype includes fixed-length non-Unicode character data with a maximum length of 8,000 characters. It's useful for character data that will always be the same length, such as a State field, which will contain only two characters in every record. This uses the same amount of space on disk no matter how many characters are actually stored in the field. For example, char(5) always uses 5 bytes of space, even if only two characters are stored in the field.

Datetime: This datatype includes date and time data from January 1, 1753, through December 31, 9999, with values rounded to increments of .000, .003, or .007 seconds. This takes 8 bytes of space on the hard disk and should be used when you need to track specific dates and times.

Decimal: This datatype includes fixed-precision and scale-numeric data from $-10^{38} - 1$ through $10^{38} - 1$ (for comparison, this is a 1 with 38 zeros following it). It uses two parameters: *precision* and *scale*. Precision is the total count of digits that can be stored in the field, and scale is the number of digits that can be stored to the right of the decimal point. Thus, if you have a precision of 5 and a scale of 2, your field has the format 111.22. You should use this type when you're storing partial numbers (numbers with a decimal point).

Float: This datatype includes floating-precision number data from $-1.79E + 308$ through $1.79E + 308$. Some numbers don't end after the decimal point—pi is an example. For such numbers, you must approximate the end, which is what float does. For example, if you set a datatype of float(2), pi will be stored as 3.14, with only two numbers after the decimal point.

Int: This can contain integer (or whole number) data from -2^{31}($-2{,}147{,}483{,}648$) through $2^{31} - 1$ ($2{,}147{,}483{,}647$). It takes 4 bytes of hard disk space to store and is useful for storing large numbers that you'll use in mathematical functions.

Money: This datatype includes monetary data values from -2^{63} ($-922{,}337{,}203{,}685{,}477.580$ 8) through $2^{63} - 1$ ($922{,}337{,}203{,}685{,}477.5807$), with accuracy to a ten-thousandth of a monetary unit. It takes 8 bytes of hard disk space to store and is useful for storing sums of money larger than 214,748.3647.

TAKE NOTE*

Microsoft SQL Server performs implicit conversions, which means an integer can be added to a character. This behavior can cause unexpected results.

Nchar: This datatype includes fixed-length Unicode data with a maximum length of 4,000 characters. Like all Unicode datatypes, it's useful for storing small amounts of text that will be read by clients that use different languages (i.e., some using Japanese Katana and some using German).

Numeric: This is a synonym for decimal—they're one and the same.

Nvarchar: This datatype includes variable-length Unicode data with a maximum length of 4,000 characters. It's the same as nchar except that nvarchar uses less disk space when there are fewer characters.

Nvarchar(max): This is just like nvarchar; but when the (max) size is specified, the datatype holds $2^{31}-1$ (2,147,483,647) bytes of data.

Real: This datatype includes floating precision number data from $-3.40E + 38$ through $3.40E+ 38$. This is a quick way of saying float(24)—it's a floating type with 24 numbers represented after the decimal point.

Smalldatetime: This datatype includes date and time data from January 1, 1900, through June 6, 2079, with an accuracy of one minute. It takes only 4 bytes of disk space and should be used for less specific dates and times than would be stored in datetime.

Smallint: This datatype includes integer data from $-2^{15}(-32,768)$ through $2^{15}-1$ (32,767). It takes 2 bytes of hard disk space to store and is useful for slightly smaller numbers than you would store in an int field, because smallint takes less space than int.

Smallmoney: This datatype includes monetary data values from $-214,748.3648$ through 214,748.3647, with accuracy to a ten-thousandth of a monetary unit. It takes 4 bytes of space and is useful for storing smaller sums of money than would be stored in a money field.

Sql_variant: This isn't an actual datatype per se; it lets you store values of different datatypes. The only values it cannot store are varchar(max), nvarchar(max), text, image, sql_variant, varbinary(max), xml, ntext, timestamp, and user-defined datatypes. The text, ntext, and image datatypes have been deprecated in this version of SQL Server. You should replace these with varchar(max), nvarchar(max), and varbinary(max).

Timestamp: This is used to stamp a record with the time it is inserted and every time it's updated thereafter. This datatype is useful for tracking changes to your data. Note that this isn't actually time; it is a counter that increments by 1 each time it's used and requires 8 bytes of storage space.

Tinyint: This datatype includes integer data from 0 through 255. It takes 1 byte of space on the disk and is limited in usefulness since it stores values only up to 255. Tinyint may be useful for something like a product code when you have fewer than 256 products.

Uniqueidentifier: The NEWID( ) function is used to create globally unique identifiers that might appear as follows: 6F9619FF–8B86–D011–B42D–00C04FC964FF in hexadecimal. These unique numbers can be stored in the unique identifier type field; they may be useful for creating tracking numbers or serial numbers that have no possible way of being duplicated. It requires 16 bytes of storage space.

Varbinary: This datatype includes variable-length binary data with a maximum length of 8,000 bytes. It's just like binary, except that varbinary uses less hard disk space when fewer bits are stored in the field.

Varbinary(max): This has the same attributes as the varbinary datatype; but when the (max) size is declared, the datatype can hold $2^{31}-1$ (2,147,483,647) bytes of data. This is useful for storing binary objects such as JPEG image files or Microsoft Word documents.

Varchar: This datatype includes variable-length non-Unicode data with a maximum of 8,000 characters. It's useful when the data won't always be the same length, such as in a first-name field where each name has a different number of characters. This uses less disk space when fewer characters appear in the field. For example, if you have a field of varchar(20) but you're storing a name with only 10 characters, the field will take up only 10 bytes of space, not 20. This field will accept a maximum of 20 characters.

Varchar(max): This is just like the varchar datatype; but with a size of (max) specified, the datatype can hold $2^{31}-1$ (2,147,483,647) bytes of data.

Xml: This datatype stores entire Extensible Markup Language (XML) documents or fragments (a document that is missing the top-level element).

Here are some special cases:

Identity: This isn't actually a datatype, but it serves an important role. It's a property, usually used in conjunction with the int datatype, and it's used to increment the value of the column each time a new record is inserted. For example, the first record in the table would have an identity value of 1, and the next would be 2, then 3, and so on. The beginning number is the *seed* and the number added for each new instance is the *increment*. These are specified as: identity (10, 2).

Ntext, Text, and **Image:** These datatypes will be removed from future versions of Microsoft SQL Server. Therefore, avoid using these datatypes in new development work and plan to modify applications that currently use them.

You can't assign two other datatypes to a column: cursor and table. You can use these two datatypes only as variables:

- **Cursor:** Queries in SQL Server return a complete set of rows for an application to use. Sometimes the application can't work with the resulting set of rows as a whole, so it requests a cursor that is a subset of the original recordset, with some added features (such as the ability to move back and forth between records or to position on a specific row). The cursor datatype allows you to return a cursor from a stored procedure. You can also store a cursor in a variable. However, you can't store a cursor in a table using this datatype.
- **Table:** This datatype returns datasets (rows and columns) from stored procedures or functions, or stores tables in variables for later processing. You can't use this datatype to store a table in a column of another table, however.

CERTIFICATION READY?
Pause, go back, and ask yourself: What distinguishes a tinyint, smallint, int, and bigint? A nvarchar and char? A smalldatetime and datetime?

Just because the list proved too short, SQL Server 2005 Service Pack 2 inaugurates a new data storage format option available only in Enterprise Edition:

VarDecimal: Uses from 5 to 22 bytes of storage when expressing decimal values of widely varying sizes.

When you're adding these datatypes, you must specify any required parameters. For example, if you're creating a field to hold state abbreviations, you need to specify char(2) and then the appropriate constraints (discussed in Lesson 9) to ensure that users enter only valid state abbreviations. Finally, you include a default that will add data to the fields if your users forget.

UNDERSTANDING DATATYPE PRECEDENCE

As already mentioned, datatypes have a certain order, or *precedence*. This means when combining datatypes, implicit data conversion will occur, and the datatype with the highest rank will be given priority.

When working with datatypes and returning query results, it is important to understand the datatype precedence, which is displayed in order here:

1. User-defined data types (highest)
2. Sql_variant
3. Xml
4. Datetime
5. Smalldatetime

6. Float

7. Real

8. Decimal

9. Money

10. Smallmoney

11. Bigint

12. Int

13. Smallint

14. Tinyint

15. Bit

16. Ntext

17. Text

18. Image

19. Timestamp

20. Uniqueidentifier

21. Nvarchar/Nvarchar(max)

22. Nchar

23. Varchar/Varchar(max)

24. Char

25. Varbinary/Varbinary(max)

26. Binary (lowest)

Datatype precedence is often forgotten in application code, which, of course, could cause more unexpected results.

 EXERCISE 4-1 SUMMING DIFFERENT DATATYPES

1. Open **Management Studio.** Start a **New Query.** Enter the following code:
   SELECT 2 Result
2. Execute. You should see a resultset of 2. Add a character 2 like this:
   SELECT 2 + '2' Result
3. Execute. You should see a resultset of 4. This might be an unexpected result, and certainly something of which to be keenly aware.
4. Continue this by adding a floating-point value, like this:
   SELECT 2 + '2' + 2.0 Result
5. Execute. You should see a resultset of 6.0. SQL Server converted all of the previous datatypes to floating-point. Is that what you expected?

> **TAKE NOTE***
> In VisualStudio, you have the ability to set OPTION EXPLICIT, which guards against these consequences. There is no OPTION EXPLICIT equivalent in Transact-SQL.

Formatting and Converting Data

You'll often need to convert and modify data. SQL Server offers an extensive set of functions you can use to perform conversions and formatting. You can categorize these functions into groups, as delineated in the following sections.

CASTING AND CONVERTING

When working with data, often you'll want to represent data in a different format, or explicitly convert data to a different datatype.

In the following example, you have two integers that you want to calculate with—say you want to divide 5 by 2. What should this result in? Well, that depends. A logical answer is that 5 divided by 2 returns 2.5, right? But what happens if you run the following example in a query?

```
Declare @col1 int
Declare @col2 int
Declare @result decimal (9, 2)
Set @col1 = 5
Set @col2 = 2
Set @result = @col1 / @col2
print @result
```

Something happens that you probably didn't expect: your resultset is 2.0.

What is the story behind this? This is an example of the aforementioned datatype precedence. As explained, every datatype in SQL Server gets a certain ranking or priority. So, if you combine two integers together in a calculation, your resultset will be an integer as well.

In the previous example, the @result variable is declared as a decimal. So the calculation with the integer will take place and then it will be stored in a decimal column, which is why the resultset gives 2.0 instead of the expected 2.5.

To do the conversion appropriately, you need to first cast or convert one of the integer datatypes to a decimal. The CAST and CONVERT functions will basically return the same result but have different notation.

This is the CAST syntax:

```
CAST ( expression AS data_type [ (length ) ])
```

This is the CONVERT syntax:

```
CONVERT ( data_type [ ( length ) ], expression [, style ] )
```

This means that if you want to modify the statement from the previous example to get the required resultset, you can use CAST or CONVERT. The following example shows you the CAST function:

```
Declare @col1 int
Declare @col2 int
Declare @result decimal (9,2)
Set @col1 = 5
Set @col2 = 2
Set @result = cast(@col1 as decimal(9,2)) / @col2
print @result
```

Of course, you can also write this using CONVERT:

```
Declare @col1 int
Declare @col2 int
Declare @result decimal (9,2)
Set @col1 = 5
Set @col2 = 2
Set @result = convert (decimal(9, 2),@col1) / @col2
print @result
```

You might find CAST preferable; some find it more readable. There is initially no difference. That said, you should use CONVERT when playing around with dates, because with this function you can specify the style in which you want to present a date. Table 4-1 shows the most common styles used with the CONVERT function.

So if you want to represent the current date as a varchar with only the date part, your statement will look like this:

```
SELECT CONVERT(varchar, getdate( ), 101)
```

When converting datatypes, you can use the CAST function or the CONVERT function. This will allow you to explicitly convert two datatypes. CONVERT and CAST provide the same features, but with CONVERT you have the ability to return a date in a certain format by specifying the style.

Table 4-1

Common Styles Used with the CONVERT Function

STYLE	EXAMPLE
101	mm/dd/yyyy
102	yy.mm.dd
103	dd/mm/yy
104	dd.mm.yy
105	dd-mm-yy
106	dd mon yy
107	Mon dd, yy
108	hh:mm:ss

→ **EXERCISE 4-2 CONVERTING A DATE FORMAT**

1. Open **SQL Server Management Studio.** Start a **New Query.** Enter this code:
   SELECT CONVERT(nvarchar(30), GETDATE(), 102) Date
2. Execute this code. You should get back a date in a format that looks like 2008.02.13.
3. Change the 102 to 111 and execute again. You should get back a date in a format that looks like 2008/02/18.
4. Change the nvarchar(30) to nvarchar(3) and execute again. You should get back a date in a format that looks like 200. SQL Server truncated the output to fit the desired field length.
5. Change the nvarchar(3) to just nvarchar (no parentheses) and execute again. You should get back a date in a format that looks like 2008/02/18. You just learned that the default length for an undefined nvarchar is 30.
6. Close the **Query Editor.**

TAKE NOTE*

Other RDBMSs use different default values. This could lead to unexpected results if your code is run on cross platforms.

Introducing Alias Datatypes

Sometimes it's useful to create your own datatypes in order to streamline your business environment and use a common method for referring to specific data. You might want to create, for example, a zip datatype. This is far more descriptive when reviewing your table definition than would be char(5).

A major benefit of using managed code, as you already learned by creating managed procedures and *CLR* (common language runtime) functions, is that it will also give you the ability to create a complex datatype and define its methods and properties.

CREATING T-SQL ALIAS TYPES

You define an *alias datatype* in SQL Server 2005 by using the CREATE TYPE or the sp_addtype syntax.

The type you create always needs to match with a system-defined type, and you have the ability to set the length and NOT NULL option.

CREATE TYPE proves to be the preferred syntax in SQL Server 2005, and must be the method if you are importing CLR code.

Here is an example of using the CREATE TYPE syntax:

```
CREATE TYPE Zip FROM char(5) NOT NULL
```

The syntax of sp_addtype has changed from SQL Server 2000 (the owner option is no longer supported):

```
sp_addtype [ @typename = ] type,
[ @phystype = ] system_data_type
[, [ @nulltype = ] 'null_type' ]
```

Here's an example:

```
EXEC sp_addtype ssn, 'VARCHAR(11)', 'NOT NULL'
```

EXERCISE 4-3 CREATING A T-SQL USER-DEFINED TYPE

1. Open a new database query window on the AdventureWorks database.
2. Create a user-defined type by using the following syntax:
   ```
   CREATE TYPE ssn FROM varchar(11) NOT NULL
   ```
3. Use the defined type in a CREATE TABLE statement:

   ```
   USE AdventureWorks
   CREATE TABLE HumanResources.Employees
   (EmployeeID int identity (1,1),
   Employeename nvarchar(200),DepartmentID int,
   EmployeeSSN ssn)
   ```
4. Delete the **HumanResources.Employees** table you just created. In Management Studio, highlight the table in the Object Browser and press the **Delete** key on your keyboard.

Because a T-SQL datatype always maps to an existing system datatype, it is often referred to as an *alias type*. Historically, it's been user-defined type; you'll see both terminologies in the literature.

Creating CLR User-Defined Types

Working with managed code datatypes or CLR alias types adds a new dimension to how you will work with SQL Server 2005. A user-defined type is a CLR class that will have reference types and value types.

Alias types contain multiple elements and are useful in environments to indicate geospatial data, to indicate date and time functionality, or even to perform data encryption or object-oriented storage.

You will learn that you first need to catalog the assembly (CREATE ASSEMBLY) and create the datatype by using a CREATE TYPE statement, in which you reference the assembly:

```
CREATE TYPE [ schema_name. ] type_name
{
FROM base_type
[ ( precision [, scale ] ) ]
[ NULL | NOT NULL ]
| EXTERNAL NAME assembly_name [.class_name ]
} [; ]
```

Here's a code example:

```
CREATE TYPE Distance
EXTERNAL NAME
Distances.[Samples.UserDefinedTypes.Distance];
```

GETTING MORE CLR FUNCTIONALITY

Besides creating a CLR function, you also can create user-defined aggregates. This gives you the ability to group and summarize functions using managed code, which then can be used within an SQL view or query.

Just like being able to create managed stored procedures and functions, you also can create a managed code trigger. This is, however, used only to perform complex trigger code on the data for the given trigger action.

Understanding How SQL Server Organizes Data in Rows

A data row consists of a row header (4 bytes) followed by a data portion. The data portion can contain:

- Fixed-length data
- Null block
- Variable block
- Variable-length data

The fixed-length data is entered into a slot on a *page* before variable-length data. An empty fixed-length data entry takes as much space as a populated entry. A table with only fixed-length columns always stores the same number of rows on a page.

The null block is a variable-length set of bytes—never fewer than the allocation unit of 1 byte. It consists of 2 bytes that store the number of columns, followed by a null bitmap indicating whether each individual column is null. With 8 bits per bit map byte, the ninth null requires the allocation of another byte, the seventeenth null yet another byte.

The variable block consists of 2 bytes that describe how many variable-length columns are present in the table. An additional 2 bytes per column point to the end of each variable-length column. The variable block is omitted if there are no variable-length columns.

Variable-length data is entered into the slot on the page after the variable block. An empty variable-length data row takes up no space.

Use this information to calculate your table storage requirements. You must perform trade-offs: an integer can count higher than a Tinyint datatype but takes up four times the space on your hard drive. Character datatypes may waste storage space if the entry length varies widely, but varchar datatypes require many bytes of overhead.

Assume you manage the database for a bicycle store chain. Initially, you set the StoreID attribute to Tinyint. You never dreamed of more than 255 stores. Now your boss bought a competitor's chain. He asks you to merge its data into your database. Tinyint no longer meets the data requirement.

There is no one right answer. The next section gives you the tools to estimate ultimate database size based on your current assumptions.

ESTIMATING TABLE STORAGE REQUIREMENTS

Tables are really nothing more than templates specifying how data is to be stored. All data stored in a table must adhere to a datatype. You can follow a specific process to estimate the space required by a table:

1. Calculate the space used by a single row of the table.
2. Calculate the number of rows that will fit on one page.
3. Estimate the number of rows the table will hold.
4. Calculate the total number of pages that will be required to hold these rows.

CALCULATING ROW SIZE

Datatypes have various shapes and sizes and give you incredible control over how your data is stored. Table 4-2 lists some of the most common (but not all available) datatypes.

Table 4-2

Datatypes and Sizes

DATATYPE NAME	DESCRIPTION	SIZE
Tinyint	Integer from 0 to 255	1 byte
Smallint	Integer from −32,768 to 32,767	2 bytes
Int	Integer from −2,147,483,648 to 2,147,483,647	4 bytes
Real	1- to 7-digit precision, floating-point	4 bytes
Float	8- to15-digit precision, floating-point	8 bytes
Smalldatetime	1/1/1900 to 6/6/2079, with accuracy to the minute	4 bytes
Datetime	1/1/100 to 12/31/9999, with accuracy to 3.33 milliseconds	8 bytes
Smallmoney	4-byte integer with 4-digit scale	4 bytes
Money	8-byte integer with 4-digit scale	8 bytes
Char	Character data 1	Byte per character

When calculating storage requirements for a table, you simply add the storage requirements for each datatype in the table, plus the additional overhead. This will give you the total space that is occupied by a single row. For example, if a table in a database has five columns defined as char(10), varchar(20), varchar(10), int, and money, you could calculate the storage space required for each row as follows:

Overhead = 9 bytes (header + null block + null bit map + variable block)

Char(10) = 10 bytes

Varchar(20) = 22 bytes

Varchar(10) = 12 bytes

Int = 4 bytes

Money = 8 bytes

This totals 65 bytes. Looking at it again:

- Each row also has a small amount of overhead, called the *null bitmap* (because it is used to maintain nullable data). Here is the calculation to find the size of the null bitmap:

  null_bitmap = ((number of nullable columns + 7) ÷ 8)

  To find the amount of overhead for this table, the calculation is 2 + ((4 + 7) ÷ 8) = 3.375. Throwing out the remainder, you get 3 bytes of overhead for the table.

- Now you need to know how much space to allocate for the variable-length columns. Here is the formula:

  variable_datasize = 2 + (num_variable_columns × 2) + max_varchar_size

  To calculate the space for the variable-length columns, you use this equation: 2 + (2 × 2) + 30 = 36. So, the variable-length columns should take 36 bytes out of the table (not 30 as you might expect from the sizes of the columns).

- The last step is to figure out the total row size, which you can do using this calculation:

  Row_Size = Fixed_Data_Size + Variable_Data_Size + Null Block + Null_Bitmap + Row_Header. Because the row header is always 4, you can use this to calculate the table size: 22 + 36 + 3 + 4 = 65. Therefore, each row in the table takes 65 bytes.

CALCULATING ROWS PER PAGE

Once you have a number indicating the total bytes used per row, you can easily calculate the number of rows that will fit on a single page. Because every page is 8 KB in size, and has a header, about 8,096 bytes are free for storing data. You can calculate the total number of rows per page as follows:

8096 ÷ (RowSize + 2)

The resulting value is truncated to an integer.

In this example, each row requires 65 bytes of space to store. Therefore, you can calculate the rows per page as 8,096 ÷ (65 + 2) = 120.

As you did here, you'll need to round down to the nearest whole number when performing these calculations because a row cannot be split between two pages.

TAKE NOTE*

SQL Server 2005 introduces multiple-page rows under certain and limited conditions.

CONSIDERING SPECIAL FACTORS

When calculating rows per page, you will need to consider some additional factors. Remember that rows can rarely cross pages. If a page does not have enough space to complete the row, the entire row will be placed on the next page. This is why you had to round down the result of your calculation.

In addition, the number of rows that can fit on one page may also depend on a *fill factor* that is used for the clustered index. Fill factor is a way of keeping the page from becoming 100 percent full when the index is created. Using a fill factor may reduce the amount of space used on a page when the index is built, but since fill factor is not maintained, the space will be eventually used.

As an example, if a clustered index were built on the example table with a fill factor of 75 percent, the data would be reorganized such that the data pages would be only 75 percent full. This means that instead of 8,096 bytes free on each page, you could use only 6,072 bytes.

ESTIMATING THE NUMBER OF ROWS FOR THE TABLE

There is no secret formula for estimating the number of rows used in your table. You have to know your data to estimate how many rows your table will eventually hold. When you make this estimate, try to consider—as accurately as possible—how large you expect your table to grow. If you do not allow for this growth in your estimates, you will need to expand the database at some point in the future. Make that as far in the future as you can.

CALCULATING THE NUMBER OF PAGES NEEDED

Calculating the number of pages needed is another simple calculation, as long as you have reliable figures for the number of rows per page and the number of rows you expect the table to hold. The calculation is the number of rows in the table divided by the number of rows per page. Here, the result will be rounded up to the nearest whole number (again, this is because a row cannot usually span pages).

In the previous example, you saw that 120 rows would fit in a single page of the table. If you expected this table to eventually hold 1,000,000 records, the calculation would be as follows:

1. $1,000,000 \div 120 = 8,333.33$.
2. Round the value up to 8,334 pages.

Now multiply the number of pages by the actual size of a page (8,192 bytes) and divide by a 1024 twice, and you get 65,109,375 bytes, or about 65 MB. Add a little bit of space for possible unexpected growth (in other words, maybe you end up with 1,100,000 rows), and you are ready to proceed to the next step.

ESTIMATING INDEX STORAGE REQUIREMENTS

Indexes in SQL Server are stored in a balanced-tree (B-tree) format; that is, you can think of an index as a large tree. You can also think of an index as a table with a pyramid on top of it. The ultimate concept here is that every index has a single entry point: the root of the inverted tree or the apex of the pyramid.

When estimating storage requirements, you can think of the base of this pyramid as a table. You go through a similar process in estimating the "leaf" level of an index as you would in estimating the storage requirements of a table. Although the process is similar, a few issues are important to consider:

- You are adding the datatypes of the index keys, not the data rows.
- Clustered indexes use the data page as the leaf level. You do not need to add storage requirements for a clustered-index leaf level.

The most difficult part of estimating the size of an index is estimating the size and number of levels you will have in your index. Although you can use a fairly long and complex series of calculations to determine this exactly, it is usually sufficient to add 35 percent of the leaf-level space estimated for the other levels of the index.

Finally, your index fill factor can be set to less than 100 percent. If so, multiply the estimated size by the inverse of the fill factor. If your fill factor is, for example, 50 percent multiply by 2.

SKILL SUMMARY

IN THIS LESSON YOU LEARNED:

You already know you must sit down with subject matter experts and plan data requirements prior to creating database objects. Consider using the techniques espoused by Business Process Reengineering, Joint Application Design, or Service-Oriented Architecture techniques to help you. You need to decide what tables will contain, and make the tables as specific as possible. Consider using automated tools such as ERStudio (Embarcadaro Systems) or ERWIN (Computer Associates) to help you with such tasks as affinity analysis (the grouping of related items appropriate to a single table).

You also know that tables consist of columns and rows (entities and instances) and that each of the fields in the table has a specific datatype that restricts the form of data it can hold. Here you have learned how to apply this knowledge with actual practice.

Then you learned you can create your own datatypes that are just system datatypes with all the required parameters presupplied and labeled in a more obvious way; for example, zip instead of char(5).

For the certification examination:

- Know your datatypes. Be familiar with the built-in datatypes and know when to use each one. For example, it might be obvious to you when you should use varchar instead of float, but it might not be as obvious when you need to use smallmoney versus money. Designing databases is all about trade-offs and balances. The certification examination will pose a question requiring the best solution.

- Know the difference between CAST and CONVERT. Both can do most functions. CONVERT adds date formatting capabilities.

Knowledge Assessment

Multiple Choice

Circle the letter or letters that correspond to the best answer or answers.

1. You add a character datatype to an integer datatype like so: SELECT '1' + 1. Which datatype holds the resultset?
   a. Character
   b. Integer
   c. Floating point
   d. Decimal

2. Which datatype is best suited for storing large images (greater than 8 KB)?
   a. Varchar(max)
   b. Varbinary(max)
   c. Binary
   d. Image

3. You try to add a last name to a field defined as an integer. What happens?
   a. SQL Server does an implicit conversion and updates the value.
   b. SQL Server rejects the operation and declares an error.
   c. SQL Server accepts the value because you originally defined the datatype as sql_variant.
   d. SQL Server doesn't care; it just does it.

4. You have created a table with the columns shown in Table 4-3. Approximately how much space will this table require on disk if it has 1,000,000 rows?
   a. 150 MB
   b. 162 MB
   c. 144 MB
   d. 207 MB

Table 4-3

Table Specification

NAME	DATATYPE
ID	Int
FirstName	Char(25)
Lastname	Char(25)
Address	Char(50)
City	Char(20)
State	Char(2)
ZipCode	Char(5)

5. You are creating a new database for your accounting department that will have the tables as shown in Tables 4-4, 4-5, and 4-6. Each table has a clustered index in the ID column. The Vendors table has a nonclustered index on the Name column. The accounting department expects to have about 2,000,000 rows in the Vendors table, 5,000 rows in the Receivables table, and 2,500 rows in the Payables table at any given time. How much space will the Receivables table take?
   a. 15 MB
   b. 150 MB
   c. 15 KB
   d. 150 KB

6. In the scenario from Tables 4-4, 4-5, and 4-6, how much space will the Payables table take?
   a. 21 MB
   b. 21 KB
   c. 112 MB
   d. 112 KB

7. In the scenario from Tables 4-4, 4-5, and 4-6, how much space will the Vendors table take?
   a. 167 MB
   b. 185 KB
   c. 200 MB
   d. 156 MB

8. In the scenario from Tables 4-4, 4-5, and 4-6, how big should you make the Accounting data file?
   a. 300 MB
   b. 230 MB
   c. 180 MB
   d. 150 MB

9. In the scenario from Tables 4-4, 4-5, and 4-6, how big should you make the Accounting transaction log?
   a. 36 MB
   b. 60 MB
   c. 100 MB
   d. 57 MB

Table 4-4

Receivables Table

NAME	DATATYPE
ID	Int
VendorID	Int
BalanceDue	Money
DateDue	Datetime

Table 4-5

Payables Table

NAME	DATATYPE
ID	Int
VendorID	Int
BalanceDue	Money
DateDue	Datetime
Terms	Char(50)
PrevBalance	Float

Table 4-6

Vendors Table

NAME	DATATYPE
ID	Int
Name	Varchar(50)
Address	Varchar(50)
City	Varchar(20)
State	Char(2)
PostalCode	Char(9)

10. You have created a table with the columns shown in Table 4-7. Approximately how much space will this table require on disk if it has 100,000 rows?
    a. 150 MB
    b. 162 MB
    c. 144 MB
    d. 207 MB

11. You have created a table with a fill factor of 80 percent. How many bytes per page are reserved for future input?
    a. 6,476
    b. 1,620
    c. 2,640
    d. 3,126

Table 4-7

Table Specification

NAME	DATATYPE
ID	Int
Description	Varchar(27)
Price	Money
Instock	Bit
VendorID	Int

■ Case Scenarios

Scenario 4-1: Creating Alias Datatypes

You have been assigned to the Joint Application Design team. The programmers have asked you to create two custom datatypes that they need. Create a ZipCode datatype and a State datatype.

Scenario 4-2: Design a Database

You work in the IT department of your organization. Your boss wants you to track IT assets of all types throughout the organization. She wants to know the acquisition cost, the acquisition date, software installed on each user and server machine, licenses owned and actually used, user assignment, and other details. What do you need to do first? Discuss the solution to this scenario as a classroom idea exchange.

Databases

LESSON SKILL MATRIX

TECHNOLOGY SKILL	70-431 EXAM OBJECTIVE
Configure SQL Server 2005 instances and databases.	Foundational
Configuring log files and data files.	Foundational
Choosing a recovery model for the database.	Foundational
Implement a table.	Foundational
Specify a filegroup.	Foundational

KEY TERMS

catalog: The ANSI-compliant term for a database; fully synonymous with database.

database: A catalog of tables and entities describing a solution for collecting and reporting data and information.

extent: Eight pages; 64 KB of data; the physical disk input/output unit of transfer.

page: 8 KB; the basic storage unit of SQL Server 2005. Except under special circumstances, a row in a database cannot exceed 8,096 bytes in size.

RAID: Redundant Array of Independent Disks; in the original paper presented before the ACM, this was entitled "Redundant Array of Inexpensive Disks." Both terms are in use today, although to most people "inexpensive" is relative.

spindle: A physical disk drive; distinct from partition, which may be one or more per spindle.

VLDB: A very large database—many gibibytes or tebibytes.

■ Using Databases

THE BOTTOM LINE

A database, also known as a *catalog*, provides a framework for housing all the necessary objects (such as tables, indexes, stored procedures, and many more) to efficiently store and retrieve data. A *database* is a securable; that is, the RDBMS controls access to only those with the proper credentials.

Using SQL Server 2005

You can use SQL Server to perform transaction processing, store and analyze data, and build new database applications.

SQL Server is a family of products and technologies that meets the data storage needs of online transaction processing (OLTP) and online analytical processing (OLAP) environments. OLTP specializes in getting the data into the database, while OLAP focuses on getting the information out of the database.

SQL Server is a relational database management system (RDBMS) that:

- Manages data storage for transactions and analysis.
- Stores data in a wide array of datatypes, including text, numeric, XML, and large objects (CLOBS, character large objects, and BLOBS, binary large objects).
- Responds to requests from client applications.
- Uses Transact-SQL, XML, or other SQL commands to send requests between the client application and SQL Server.

The RDBMS component of SQL Server is responsible for:

- Maintaining the relationships among data in a database.
- Ensuring that data is stored correctly and the rules defining the relationships among data are not violated.
- Recovering data to a point of known consistency in the event of an infrastructure failure.

You've chosen Microsoft SQL Server 2005. You've loaded it on your server. You know about datatypes and how to estimate your spindle storage needs. It's time to get started; it's time to create a database.

Planning Your Database

SQL Server 2005 uses two types of files to store your database information: one or more database files and one or more transaction log files. As an administrator, it is your responsibility to create and maintain these files. As part of your role as a database creator, you must decide how large to make these database files and what type of growth characteristics they should have, as well as their physical placement on your system.

Before you create a database, you need to know some important facts. First you need to know how large to make the database and how much growth to expect. Then you need to think about the physical location for the database files. To make an informed decision in these matters, it is helpful to understand how memory is allocated in SQL Server. In this section, we will talk about how you will create your database, where you should place the database, and what the different internal memory management structures are.

INTRODUCING DATABASE FILES

In SQL Server 2005, a new user database is really a copy of the Model database. Everything in the Model database will show up in your newly created database. Once the copy of the database has been made, it expands to the requested size. When you create a database in SQL Server 2005, you must specify at least one file to store the data and hold your system tables and another file to hold the transaction log.

Databases can comprise up to three file types. Primary data files have a default extension of .mdf. If you create a database that spans multiple data files, then secondary data files are used, which have a default filename extension of .ndf. The transaction log is stored in one or more files, with a default .ldf extension. Additional transaction log files, however, don't change their extensions. You should remember several important facts about your data and log files:

- It is recommended that you create the data and log files on a storage area network (SAN), iSCSI-based network, or locally attached drive.
- Only one database is allowed per data file, but a single database can span multiple data files.
- Transaction logs must reside in their own file; they can also span multiple log files.
- SQL Server fills the database files in a filegroup proportionally. (Filegroups are discussed at length shortly.) This means if you have two data files, one with 100 MB free and one with 200 MB free, SQL Server will allocate one extent from the first file and two extents from the second file when writing data. In this manner, you can eliminate "hot spots" and reduce contention in high-volume online transaction processing (OLTP) environments.

- Transaction log files are not filled proportionally; instead, they fill each log file to capacity before continuing to the next log file.
- When you create a database and don't specify a transaction log size, the transaction log will be resized to 25 percent of the size of your data file request.

It is suggested that you place your transaction logs on separate physical hard drives (also known as *spindles*). Doing so enables you to recover your data up to the moment in the event of a data storage media failure.

Why have multiple data files? This technique, as opposed to just enlarging your current database files, has certain advantages and disadvantages. The main disadvantage of multiple database files is administration. You need to be aware of these different files, their locations, and their use. The main advantage is that you can place these files on separate physical hard disks (if you are not using striping, which is RAID 0 and is discussed in the next section), avoiding the creation of hot spots and thereby improving performance. When you use database files, you can back up individual database files rather than the whole database in one session. If you also take advantage of filegroups, you can improve performance by explicitly placing tables on one filegroup and the indexes for those tables on a separate filegroup. A filegroup is a logical grouping of database files used for performance and to improve administration on very large databases (*VLDB*s)—usually in the hundreds of gigabyte or terabyte range. You will learn more about filegroups in the next section.

When you create a database, you are allocating hard disk space for both the data and the transaction log.

INTRODUCING FILEGROUPS

X REF

For a discussion of indexes, please refer to Lesson 7.

You can logically group database files into a filegroup. Using filegroups, you can explicitly place database objects into a particular set of database files. For example, you can separate tables and their nonclustered indexes (you'll learn about indexes in Lesson 7) into separate filegroups. This can improve performance, because modifications to the table can be written to both the table and the index at the same time. Another advantage of filegroups is the ability to back up only a single filegroup at a time. This can be extremely useful for a VLDB, because the sheer size of the database could make backing up an extremely time-consuming process. Yet another advantage is the ability to mark the filegroup and all data in the files that are part of it as either read-only or read-write.

There are really only two disadvantages to using filegroups. The first is the administration involved in keeping track of the files in the filegroup and the database objects that are placed in them. The second is that if you are working with a smaller database and have RAID-5 implemented, you may not be improving performance.

The two basic filegroups in SQL Server 2005 are the primary, or default, filegroup, which is created with every database, and the user-defined filegroups, which are created for a particular database. The primary filegroup will always contain the primary data file and any other files that are not specifically created in a user-defined filegroup. You can create additional filegroups using the ALTER DATABASE command or Management Studio.

When working with filegroups you must follow several rules:

- The first (or primary) data file must reside in the primary filegroup.
- All system files must be placed in the primary filegroup.
- A file cannot be a member of more than one filegroup at a time.
- Filegroups can be allocated indexes, tables, text, ntext, and image data.
- New data pages are not automatically allocated to user-defined filegroups if the primary filegroup runs out of space.

If you place tables in one filegroup and their corresponding indexes in a different filegroup, you must back up the two filegroups as a single unit—they cannot be backed up separately.

CERTIFICATION READY?
Why have filegroups?

DECIDING ON DATABASE FILE PLACEMENT

Placing database files in the appropriate location is highly dependent on your available hardware and software. There are few hard-and-fast rules when it comes to databases; that is, administration is about deciding between good choices or creating a balance between competing concepts. In fact, the only definite rule is that of design; specifically, the more thoroughly you plan and design your system, the less work it will be later, which is why it is so important to develop a good capacity plan and, prior to that, a great entity relationship diagram.

When you are attempting to decide where to place your database files, you should keep several issues in mind. These include planning for growth, communication, fault tolerance, reliability, and speed.

Among the several measures you can take to ensure the reliability and consistency of your database—each with its own features and drawbacks—are the different levels of Redundant Array of Independent Disks (**_RAID_**). RAID exists in many configurations. Microsoft Server 2003 supports RAID 1 (striping), RAID 1 (mirroring) and RAID 5 (parity) in software. Hardware solutions are typically much faster, and offload the responsibility to the specialized equipment. Hardware solutions also include RAID 2 (which uses the Hamming code to recover from two disk drive failures in an array); RAID 3 (which uses a single check disk per group); and RAID 4 (which supports independent reads and writes). Other RAID options also exist for specific purposes such as video streaming. For database purposes, though, focus on RAID 0, 1, and 5.

➕ MORE INFORMATION

See BOL, Create Database.

Unlike previous versions of SQL Server, it is possible to create network-based files (files stored on another server or network-attached storage) by using trace flag 1807.

INTRODUCING RAID-0

RAID-0 uses disk striping; that is, it writes data across multiple hard disk partitions in what is called a _stripe set_. This can greatly improve speed because multiple hard disks are working at the same time. You can implement RAID-0 through the use of Windows Server software or third-party hardware. Although RAID-0 gives you the best speed, it does not provide any fault tolerance. That means, if one of the hard disks in the stripe set is damaged, you lose all of your data. Because of the lack of fault tolerance, Microsoft doesn't recommend storing any of your SQL Server data on RAID-0 volumes.

INTRODUCING RAID-1

RAID-1 uses _disk mirroring_. Disk mirroring actually writes your information to disk twice: once to the primary spindle and once to the mirrored drive. This gives you excellent fault tolerance, but it is fairly slow, because you must write to disk twice. Windows Server allows you to implement RAID-1 with a single controller; or you can use a controller for each drive in the mirror, commonly referred to as _disk duplexing_. This is the recommended place for storing your transaction logs because RAID-1 gives fast sequential write speed (writing data in sequence on the disk rather than jumping from one empty spot to the next), a requirement for transaction logs.

INTRODUCING RAID-5

RAID-5—_striping with parity_—writes data to the hard disk in stripe sets. Parity checksums will be written across all disks in the stripe set. This gives you excellent fault tolerance, as well as excellent speed with a reasonable amount of overhead. You can use the parity checksums to re-create information lost if a single disk in the stripe set fails. If more than one disk in the stripe set fails, however, you will lose all your data. Although Windows Server supports RAID-5 in a software implementation, a hardware implementation is faster and more reliable, thus we suggest you use it if you can afford it. Microsoft recommends storing your data files on this type of RAID because data files require fast read speed, as opposed to transaction logs, which need fast write speed.

INTRODUCING RAID-10

You should use RAID-10 (sometimes referred to as RAID 1 + 0) in mission-critical systems that require 24/7 uptime and the fastest possible access. RAID-10 implements striping and then mirrors the stripe sets. So, you get the incredible speed and fault tolerance; but RAID-10 has a drawback. With this type of RAID you get the added expense of using more than twice the disk space of RAID-1. Then again, you are in a situation where you can afford no SQL Server downtime.

Unless you can afford a RAID-10 array, Microsoft suggests a combination of RAID-5 and RAID-1. In this scenario, you place your data files on the RAID-5 array for speed and redundancy, and you place your transaction log files on the RAID-1 drives so they can be mirrored.

Creating Data Storage Structures

SQL Server 2005 has two main types of storage structures: extents and pages.

INTRODUCING EXTENTS

An *extent* is a block of eight pages totaling 64 KB in size. Because the extent is the basic unit of allocation for tables and indexes, and all objects are saved in a table of some kind, all objects are stored in extents. SQL Server has two types of extents:

Uniform: In uniform extents, all eight pages are used by the same object.

Mixed: Mixed extents are used by objects that are too small to take up eight pages, so more than one object is stored in the extent.

When a table or an index needs additional storage space, another extent is allocated to that object. A new extent will generally not be allocated for a table or index until all pages on that extent have been used. This process of allocating extents, rather than individual pages to objects, serves two useful purposes:

- First, the time-consuming process of allocation takes place in one batch rather than forcing each allocation to occur whenever a new page is needed.
- Second, it forces the pages allocated to an object to be at least somewhat contiguous.

If pages were allocated directly, on an as-needed basis, then pages belonging to a single object would not be next to each other in the data file. Page 1 might belong to table 1, page 2 might belong to index 3, page 3 might belong to table 5, and so on. This is called *fragmentation* (which we will discuss more fully later in this book). Fragmentation can have a significant negative impact on performance. When pages for a single object are contiguous, though, reads and writes can occur much more quickly.

INTRODUCING PAGES

At the most fundamental level, everything in SQL Server is stored on an 8 KB page. The page is the one common denominator for all objects in SQL Server. Many types of pages exist, but every page has some factors in common. Pages are always 8 KB in size and always have a header, leaving about 8,060 bytes of usable space on every page.

SQL Server has eight primary types of pages:

Data pages: Data pages hold the actual database records. The data page is 8,192 bytes, but only 8,060 of those bytes are available for data storage because a header at the beginning of each data page contains information about the page itself. Rows are not usually allowed to span more than one page, but if you have variable-length columns (varchar, nvarchar, varbinary or sql_variant datatypes) that exceed this limit, you can move them to a page in the ROW_OVERFLOW_DATA allocation unit.

Index pages: Index pages store the index keys and levels making up the entire index tree. Unlike data pages, you have no limit for the total number of entries you can make on an index page.

Text/image pages: Text and image pages hold the actual data associated with text, ntext, and image datatypes. When a text field is saved, the record will contain a 16-byte pointer to a linked list of text pages that hold the actual text data. Only the 16-byte pointer inside the record is counted against the 8,060-byte record-size limit.

Global Allocation Map pages: The Global Allocation Map (GAM) page type keeps track of which extents in a data file have been allocated and which are still available.

Index Allocation Map pages: Index Allocation Map (IAM) pages keep track of what an extent is being used for—specifically, to which table or index the extent has been allocated.

Page Free Space pages: This is not an empty page; rather, it is a special type of page that keeps track of free space on all the other pages in the database. Each Page Free Space page can keep track of the amount of free space of up to 8,000 other pages.

Bulk Changed Map pages: This page contains information about other pages that have been modified by bulk operations (such as BULK INSERT) since the last BACKUP LOG statement.

Differential Changed Map pages: This page contains information about other pages that have changed since the last BACKUP DATABASE statement.

In previous versions of SQL Server, you were limited to a hard 8,096-byte length limit for data rows. In SQL Server 2005, this limit has been relaxed for variable-length columns by the introduction of ROW_OVERFLOW_DATA. This means if you have a table with variable-length columns whose length exceeds the 8,096-byte limit, the variable-length columns will be moved from the page that contains the table to the ROW_OVERFLOW_DATA area, leaving behind only a 24-byte pointer. This happens when an insert or update is performed that increases the record past the 8,096-byte limit. If a subsequent update is performed that decreases the row size, then the data is returned to the original page.

The 8,096-byte restriction does not apply to the large object datatypes—varchar(max), nvarchar(max), varbinary(max), text, image, and xml—because they are stored separately from the table, leaving behind a 16-byte pointer. The multiple-page storage applies only to varchar, nvarchar, varbinary, sql_variant, or common language runtime (CLR) user-defined datatypes.

The page is the smallest unit of input/output (I/O) in SQL Server. Every time data is either read from or written to a database, this occurs in page units. Most of the time this reading and writing is actually going back and forth between the data cache and disk. The data cache is divided into 8 KB buffers, intended solely for the purpose of holding 8 KB pages. This is an important part of database capacity planning.

Creating and Configuring Databases

In this section, you will learn how to create and configure databases.

CREATING A DATABASE

You can create a database in SQL Server in two ways. You can use the CREATE DATABASE statement in a Transact-SQL (T-SQL) query, or you can use the graphical tools in Management Studio. In Exercise 5-1, you will create a database named MyFirstDB using the Query Editor; and in Exercise 5-2, you will create MSSQL_Training using Management Studio. You will have two data files, each 3 MB in size, with a FILEGROWTH of 1 MB and a maximum size of 20 MB. You will also create a transaction log with a size of 1 MB, a FILEGROWTH of 1 MB, and no maximum size.

 EXERCISE 5-1 CREATING A DATABASE USING QUERY EDITOR

1. In Query Editor, type:

   CREATE DATABASE MyFirstDB
2. Execute.

Congratulations! Three little words are all it takes.

TAKE NOTE*

You may need to refresh the display. Do this by highlighting **Database** in Object Explorer and pressing **F5**, or by right-clicking and selecting **Refresh** from the context menu.

Return to Object Explorer. Open your new database named "MyFirstDB" by clicking the **plus sign** to the left of its name.

As you drill down into your new database, you discover a lot of objects are included—such is the power of three little words. SQL Server used the Model Database as a template in creating your database. Anything not specifically included in your Transact-SQL code is copied into each new database you create.

This also means that anything you want included as a routine can be added to the template—the Model Database—for subsequent inclusion in your new databases.

EXERCISE 5-2 CREATING A DATABASE USING MANAGEMENT STUDIO

1. Start Management Studio by selecting **Start → Programs → Microsoft SQL Server 2005 → Management Studio.**
2. Connect to your SQL Server.
3. Click the **plus sign** next to Databases to expand your Databases folder.
4. Right-click either the **Databases** folder in the console tree or the white space in the right pane, and choose **New Database** from the context menu.
5. You should now see the General page of the Database properties sheet. Enter the database name, MSSQL_Training, and leave the owner as <default>.
6. In the data files grid, in the Logical Name column, change the name of the primary data file to MSSQL_Training_data. Use the default location for the file, and make sure the initial size is 3.
7. Click the **ellipsis** button (the one with three periods) in the Autogrowth column for the MSSQL_Training_data file; then, in the dialog box that pops up, select the **Restricted File Growth (MB)** radio button, and restrict the file growth to 20 MB; then click **OK.**
8. To add the secondary data file, click the **Add** button, and change the logical name of the new file to MSSQL_Training_Data2. Here, too, use the default location for the file, and make sure the initial size is 3.
9. Restrict the file growth to a maximum of 20 MB for MSSQL_Training_Data2 by clicking the **ellipsis** button in the Autogrowth column.
10. Leave all of the defaults for the MSSQL_Training_log file.
11. Click **OK** when you are finished. You should now have a new MSSQL_Training database.

CERTIFICATION READY?
Where is the log file created by default?

CERTIFICATION READY?
Examine the CREATE DATABASE syntax in Books Online to understand configuration options and how these are expressed or missing in SQL Server Management Studio.

GATHERING INFORMATION ABOUT YOUR DATABASE

Using Management Studio, you can gather a wealth of information about your database. This includes the size of the database, its current capacity, any options currently set, and so on.

When you select a database in Management Studio, right-click and choose **Reports.** You will see a variety of reports that you can use to gather information.

You can also use system stored procedures to gather information about your database. The sp_helpdb stored procedure (more about this in Lesson 10) used by itself will give you information about all databases in your SQL Server. You can gather information about a particular database by using the database name as a parameter

Notice that the MSSQL_Training database is 7 MB in size; this is the size of both of the data files and the log file combined.

If you switch to the MSSQL_Training database (by selecting it from the available databases drop-down list on the toolbar) and run the sp_HelpFile stored procedure, you can gather information about the data and log files that are used for the MSSQL_Training database.

You can gather information about file sizes and locations, the filegroups they are members of, and the database file usage (either data or log).

EXERCISE 5-3 CREATING A REPORT

1. From the last exercise, you should still be in Management Studio. Click the **plus sign** next to Databases → Right-click **AdventureWorks,** and from the menu choose **Reports** → **Choose Standard Reports.** Finally, choose **Disk Usage.**

2. Examine other report options.

SETTING DATABASE OPTIONS

Database options allow you to specify how your database will behave in given situations. You can view and modify database options using Management Studio or the ALTER DATABASE statement.

Look at the database options currently set on the MSSQL_Training database you created earlier. Start **Management Studio,** and move down through the console tree until you see your database. Right-click **your database,** and choose **Properties.** From the Database Properties sheet, click the **Options** page.

You can set a number of options on this page:

Collation: This is the collation designator for the database, which you learned about in Lesson 2. As a reminder, essentially, this tells SQL Server which language the data uses in this database, and whether it is case-sensitive.

Recovery Model: You can choose from three recovery models, which requires more attention later in this lesson.

Compatibility Level: This option will change the way a database behaves so it is compatible with previous versions of SQL Server. The three levels of compatibility are SQL Server 7.0 (70), SQL Server 2000 (80), and SQL Server 2005 (90).

Auto Close: This option safely closes your database when the last user has exited from it. This can be a useful option for optimization on databases that are infrequently accessed, because it decreases the amount of resources that SQL Server needs to consume in order to maintain user information and locks. This should not be set on databases that are accessed on a frequent basis because the overhead of opening the database can outweigh the benefits of closing the database in the first place.

Auto Create Statistics: This option automatically generates statistics on the distribution of values found in your columns. The SQL Server Query Optimizer uses these statistics to determine the best method to run a particular query.

Auto Shrink: This option automatically shrinks both data and log files. Log files will be shrunk after a backup of the log has been made. Data files will be shrunk when a periodic check of the database finds that the database has more than 25 percent of its assigned space free. Your database will then be shrunk to a size that leaves 25 percent free.

Auto Update Statistics: This option works with the Auto Create Statistics option. As you make changes to the data in your database, the statistics will be less and less accurate. This option periodically updates those statistics.

Auto Update Statistics Asynchronously: This option works with the Auto Create Statistics option. As you make changes to the data in your database, the statistics will be less and less accurate. This option periodically updates those statistics.

Close Cursor on Commit Enabled: When this option is set to true, any cursor that is open will be closed when the transaction that opened it is committed or rolled back. When false, the cursor will stay open when the transaction is committed, and will be closed only when the transaction is rolled back.

Default Cursor: This specifies whether cursors are global or local by default.

ANSI NULL Default: This option specifies the default setting for ANSI NULL comparisons. When this is on, any query that compares a value with a null returns a 0. When off, any query that compares a value with a null returns a null value.

ANSI NULLS Enabled: This specifies whether ANSI NULLS are on or off for the database.

ANSI Padding Enabled: When this option is set to true, if you store data in a column that is less than the column width, then the remaining data is filled in with trailing blanks. When set to false, any remaining data is trimmed off.

ANSI Warnings Enabled: When set to true, a warning is generated when a null value is used in an aggregate function (like SUM( ) or AVG( )). When false, no warning is generated.

Arithmetic Abort Enabled: When this is set to on, a divide-by-zero error will cause a query to terminate. If this is off, the query will continue and a message will be displayed.

Concatenate Null Yields Null: This option specifies that anything you concatenate to a null value will return a null value.

Cross-Database Ownership Chaining: This server option allows you to control cross-database ownership chaining at the database level or to allow cross-database ownership chaining for all databases.

Date Correlation Optimization Enabled: When this option is set to on, SQL Server maintains statistics between any two tables in the database that are linked by a FOREIGN KEY constraint and have datetime columns. When it is set to off, correlation statistics are not maintained.

Numeric Round-Abort: When this is on, a loss of precision will generate an error message. When it is off, a message will not be generated.

Parameterization: When this is set to Simple, SQL Server may choose to replace some of the literal values in a query with a parameter, but you have no control over what is changed into a parameter. When set to Forced, all literal values are replaced with a parameter.

Quoted Identifiers Enabled: This option allows you to use double quotation marks as part of a SQL Server identifier (object name). This can be useful in situations in which you have identifiers that are also SQL Server reserved words or when you must pass values to other RDBMSs.

Recursive Triggers Enabled: This option allows recursive triggers to fire. Recursive triggers occur when one trigger fires a trigger on another table, which in turn fires another trigger on the originating table.

Trustworthy: Database modules (for example, user-defined functions or stored procedures) that use an impersonation context can access resources outside the database.

Page Verify: This option controls how SQL Server verifies the validity of each page in the database. This setting has three options:

- **None:** No verification takes place.
- **Checksum:** A mathematical calculation is run against all of the data on the page, and the value (called the checksum) is stored in the header. When the mathematical calculation is run again, if the result does not match the checksum value, then the page is determined to be damaged.
- **Torn Page Detection:** The smallest unit of data SQL Server works with is 8 KB, but the smallest unit of data that is written to disk is 512 bytes. This means parts of a page may not be written to disk, a condition known as a *torn page*. This option allows SQL Server to detect when this problem occurs. It is not as accurate as checksum, but it can be faster.

Database Read-Only: When true, this option marks the database as read-only. No changes to the database will be allowed. This is usually set to speed up access to archival data that will never be written to.

Database State: This option has three possible settings:

- **Offline:** The database is closed, shut down cleanly, and marked offline. The database cannot be modified while it is offline.

- **Online:** The database is open and available for use.
- **Emergency:** The database is marked read-only, logging is disabled, and access is limited to members of the sysadmin fixed server role. Emergency is primarily used for trouble-shooting purposes. For example, a database marked as suspect due to a corrupted log file can be set to the emergency state. This could enable the system administrator read-only access to the database. Only members of the sysadmin fixed server role can set a database to the emergency state.

Restrict Access: This option has three possible settings:

- **Multiple:** Everyone with permissions can access the database. This is the default setting.
- **Single:** Only one user at a time can access the database and with only a single connection. This is used primarily when you are restoring or renaming databases, because only one person, you, should be in the database during these activities. Make sure no one is using the database when you set this option.
- **Restricted:** Only members of db_owner, dbcreator, and sysadmin security roles have access to this database when this option is selected. This option is used during development or when you need to change the structure of one of the objects in the database and do not want anyone to access the new objects until you are done.

These are a lot of options, but one in particular requires special attention: Recovery Model. This is because the model you choose affects how fast your backups complete and how effectively you can restore data after a crash. You can choose from three models:

- **Simple:** The transaction log is used for very little in this recovery model. In fact, almost nothing is recorded in the log. This means any database set to use this model can be recovered only up to the last backup. Any changes made to your database after the last backup was performed will be lost because they do not remain recorded in the transaction log. This model is a good choice for development databases where most data is test data that does not need to be restored after a crash. It is also a good choice for databases that are not changed often, such as an OLAP database.

- **Bulk-Logged:** This model records much more information in the transaction log than the Simple model. Bulk operations such as SELECT INTO, BCP, BULK INSERT, CREATE INDEX, and text and ntext operations are the only information not recorded. This means you can recover most of the data in the event of a crash; only bulk operations may be lost. You can set this option just before performing a bulk-insert operation to speed up the bulk insert. You need to back up your database immediately after performing bulk operations if this option is selected because everything that is inserted during this time is not in the transaction log, so it will all be lost if the database crashes before the next backup.

CERTIFICATION READY?
These three models dictate how backup and restores operate. Look also at Lesson 17 to understand how they interrelate.

- **Full:** This is the default option, which records every operation against the database in the transaction log. Using this model, you will be able to recover your database up to the moment of a crash. This is a good option for most production databases because it offers the highest level of protection.

SKILL SUMMARY

IN THIS LESSON YOU LEARNED:

There is much more to data storage in SQL Server than meets the eye. The SQL Server data storage structure is more than just a file or a collection of files. It is an entire internal architecture designed for one purpose alone: to input and store your data as quickly and efficiently as possible. This lesson covered many aspects of data storage. Databases and the files they are made of include the following:

- The primary data file has an .mdf extension and is used to hold data.

- Secondary data files have an .ndf extension and are used to hold data.

- Log files have an .ldf extension and are used to store transactions before they are written to the database so that the database can be recovered in the event of an emergency.

You were introduced to the various RAID levels you can use for fault tolerance and performance:

- RAID-1 is used primarily for transaction logs.
- RAID-5 should be used for your data files.
- RAID-10 (also called RAID 0 + 1) can be used for either data or logs, but it is more expensive and available only as a third-party hardware solution.

You learned how to estimate the size of a data file before creating it.

You learned how to create databases using Management Studio and T-SQL.

You learned about the recovery models, what they do, and when to use each one.

For the certification examination:

- Know how to create databases. This is what SQL Server is all about: storing and retrieving data in databases.
- Understand your files. Know how big to make your files and where those files should be placed.
- Know your recovery models. Know how each recovery model functions and what they allow you to restore.

■ Knowledge Assessment

Multiple Choice

Circle the letter or letters that correspond to the best answer or answers.

Table 5-1

Server Configuration

SCSI RAID Adapter RAID-5 Disk Array	SCSI Adapter Physical Disk 0
40 GB Physical Disk	90 GB
40 GB Physical Disk	
40 GB Physical Disk	
40 GB Physical Disk	

1. You are a SQL Server 2005 administrator. You have a server with a database named Commerce that will be used to store sales transactions. The database must be available at all times and must be as fast as possible. Your server is configured according to Table 5-1. Where should you place your database and transaction logs for maximum speed and fault tolerance?
   a. Place the transaction log on physical disk 0 and the data file on the RAID-5 disk array.
   b. Place the transaction log on the RAID-5 disk array and the data file on physical disk 0.
   c. Place the transaction log and the data file on physical disk 0.
   d. Place the transaction log and the data file on the RAID-5 disk array.

2. You have just installed two new 40 GB hard disks in your server that you are going to use to hold a database named Inventory. You need to add, update, and delete data as fast as possible. How should you configure these hard disks? (Choose two.)
   a. Configure the hard disks as a RAID-1 array.
   b. Configure the hard disks as a RAID-0 array.
   c. Configure the hard disks as a RAID-5 array.
   d. Configure the hard disks as two independent drives.
   e. Place the data files and log files on the same volume.
   f. Place the data file on the first volume and the log file on the second volume.

3. You are about to bring a new server online, and you want the most efficient disk configuration possible for your new system. Select the proper RAID array on which to place your files for optimum performance and fault tolerance. Choose from RAID-1, RAID-2, RAID-0, and RAID-5:
   - OS/Binaries
   - Data files
   - Transaction

   a. RAID 0 _____

   b. RAID 1 _____

   c. RAID 2 _____

   d. RAID 5 _____

Table 5-2

Spindle Configuration

PHYSICAL DISK 0	PHYSICAL DISK 1
Drive C: 4.5 GB	Drive E: 4.5 GB
Drive D: 4.5 GB	Drive F: 4.5 GB

4. You are creating an Inventory database that requires 6 GB of data space and 2 GB of log space. Your servers' hard disks are configured as shown in Table 5-2. Your OS files are on the C drive. You want to maximize performance. What should you do?
   a. Add a 1 GB log to drive C, a 1 GB log to drive D, a 3 GB data file to drive E, and a 3 GB data file to drive F.
   b. Add a 1 GB log to drive E, a 1 GB log to drive F, a 3 GB data file to drive E, and a 3 GB data file to drive F.
   c. Add a 2 GB log to drive D, a 3 GB data file to drive E, and a 3 GB data file to drive F.
   d. Add a 2 GB log to drive F, a 3 GB data file to drive D, and a 3 GB data file to drive E.

5. You are the administrator of a SQL Server 2005 server that contains a development database. Your developers are not concerned with recovering any of the data in the database in the event of an emergency, and they want to keep the transaction log from accidentally filling up. Which recovery model should you use?
   a. Simple
   b. Bulk-Logged
   c. Full

6. You need to configure your system for optimum access to a 1.5 TB database. Approximately half of the tables are used primarily for writing; the rest are used primarily for reading and generating reports. How can you optimize this database for the fastest access?
   a. Place the log file and data file on the same disk so the system has to work from only one disk.
   b. Create two log files and place each on a separate disk while leaving the data file on a single disk array.

   c. Place the files that are used for reading in one filegroup and the files that are used primarily for writing in a second filegroup on another disk array.

   d. Limit the number of users who can access the database at once.

7. Which statement about placing tables and indexes in filegroups is true?

   a. Tables and their corresponding indexes must be placed in the same filegroup.

   b. Tables and their corresponding indexes must be placed in separate filegroups.

   c. Tables and indexes that are placed in separate filegroups must be backed up together.

   d. Tables and indexes that are placed in separate filegroups cannot be backed up together.

8. Your company has just installed a new storage area network, and you have been asked for the best RAID model to use for your databases. You need optimum speed and reliability. How should you configure these hard disks?

   a. Configure the hard disks as a RAID-1 array for data and a RAID-5 array for logs.

   b. Configure the hard disks as a RAID-0 array for data and a RAID-5 array for logs.

   c. Configure the hard disks as a RAID-5 array for both data and logs.

   d. Configure the hard disks as two RAID-10 arrays for both data and logs.

9. You need to import a large amount of data into a table in one of your production databases using a BULK INSERT statement. Put these steps in the correct order for optimum speed and reliability.

   a. Set the database to use the Full recovery model.

   b. Set the database to use the Bulk-Logged recovery model.

   c. Set the database to use the Simple recovery model.

   d. Back up the database.

   e. Run the BULK INSERT statement.

10. Your servers' hard disks are filling to capacity, and your database is running out of space. You do not have money in the budget for more disk space right now, but you do have plenty of disk space on one of your file servers. Can SQL Server use this disk space for database files?

   a. Yes, just create secondary data files on the remote server using the UNC filename convention (\\server\share\filename.ext); no other configuration is necessary.

   b. Yes, just turn on trace flag 1807, and then create secondary data files on the remote server using the UNC filename convention (\\server\share\filename.ext).

   c. Yes, just turn on trace flag 3205, and then create secondary data files on the remote server using the UNC filename convention (\\server\share\filename.ext).

   d. No, SQL Server cannot use remote drives for database file storage.

11. You have just created a database with a 500 MB data file. How big will the transaction log be by default?

   a. 130 MB

   b. 120 MB

   c. 125 MB

   d. 225 MB

12. Which of these page types is used to store information about changes to the database since the last BACKUP DATABASE statement was executed?

   a. Index Allocation Map page

   b. Global Allocation Map page

   c. Differential Changed Map page

   d. Data page

   e. Page Free Space page

   f. Index page

   g. Bulk Changed Map page

   h. Text/image page

■ Case Scenarios

Scenario 5-1: Creating a Database

You had another meeting with the programmers on the Joint Application Design team. They ask you to create a prototype database with a name of your choice that they can play with; change the log growth size; change recovery to Bulk-logged. Delete this database. Determine whether the physical files were also removed.

Scenario 5-2: Creating the IT Asset Database

Create the database for the IT Asset inventory and reporting system introduced in the previous lesson. What is a good name? Discuss this with your classmates.

Tables

LESSON SKILL MATRIX

TECHNOLOGY SKILL	70-431 EXAM OBJECTIVE
Implement a table.	Foundational
Specify column details.	Foundational
Specify a partition scheme when creating a table.	Foundational
Implement partitions.	Foundational

KEY TERMS

partition: A unit of a partitioned table, index or view; a part of a total dataset that may be across multiple servers; a mechanism allowing federated servers.

partition function: A tool to define how the rows of a partitioned table or index are spread across a set of partitions based on the values of specific columns.

partition scheme: A database object that maps the partitions of a partition function to a set of filegroups.

table: A two-dimensional database object that consists of rows and columns and stores data about an entity modeled in a relational database.

■ Using Tables

THE BOTTOM LINE

Tables store data. Tables are relational; that is, they store data organized as row and columns. Data can be retrieved efficiently because the RDBMS can locate a specific field (the intersection of a row and column) without having the read the entire table (as in a flat-file database system).

Creating Tables

CERTIFICATION READY?
How many properties can be specified for each row? Check BOL "Create Table (Transact-SQL)".

In Lesson 5, you created a database named MSSQL_Training. In this section, you'll create three tables in that MSSQL_Training database, in Exercises 6-1, 6-2, 6-3, and 6-4. The first table, imaginatively named Customers, stores customer information such as name, address, customer ID, and so on. The next table, which you'll call Orders, contains order detail information such as an order number, product ID, and quantity ordered. Finally, the Products table will contain such product information as the name of the product, the product ID, and whether the product is in stock. Table 6-1, Table 6-2, and Table 6-3 list the properties of the three tables.

Table 6-1

Products Table Attributes

ATTRIBUTE NAME	DATATYPE	CONTAINS
ProdID	Int, identity	A unique ID number for each product that can be referenced in other tables to avoid data duplication
Description	Nvarchar(100)	A brief text description of the product
InStock	Int	The amount of product in stock

Table 6-2

Customers Table Attributes

ATTRIBUTE NAME	DATATYPE	CONTAINS
CustID	Int, identity	A unique number for each customer that can be referenced in other tables
Fname	Nvarchar(20)	The customer's first name
Lname	Nvarchar(20)	The customer's last name
Address	Nvarchar(50)	The customer's street address
City	Nvarchar(20)	The city where the customer lives
State	Nchar(2)	The state where the customer lives
Zip	Nchar(5)	The customer's zip code
Phone	Nchar(10)	The customer's phone number without hyphens or parentheses (to save space, these will be displayed but not stored)

Table 6-3

Orders Table Attributes

ATTRIBUTE NAME	NAME DATATYPE	CONTAINS
CustID	Int	References the customer number stored in the Customers table so you don't need to duplicate the customer information for each order placed
ProdID	Int	References the Products table so you don't need to duplicate product information
Qty	Int	The amount of products sold for an order
OrdDate	Smalldatetime	The date and time the order was placed

EXERCISE 6-1 CREATING THE PRODUCTS TABLE IN QUERY EDITOR

1. Open a new query.
2. Enter the following Transact-SQL code:

```
USE MSSQL_Training
CREATE TABLE Products
(
ProdID          Int       NOT NULL      IDENTITY(1,1),
[Description]    nvarchar(100)           NOT NULL,
InStock         Int                     NOT NULL
)
```

3. Execute the query.
4. Open and refresh Object Explorer.
5. Verify the new table's creation.

Review, but don't create, the table, in the next exercise. This process creates exactly the same object.

EXERCISE 6-2 CREATING THE PRODUCTS TABLE IN MANAGEMENT STUDIO

1. Open **SQL Server Management Studio.** In Object Explorer, expand **Server —> Databases —> MSSQL_Training.**
2. Right-click the **Tables** icon, and select **New Table** to open the Table Designer.
3. In the first row, under Column Name, enter **ProdID.**
4. Just to the right of that, under Data Type, select **Int.**
5. Make certain Allow Nulls isn't checked. The field can be completely void of data if this option is checked, and you don't want that here.
6. In the bottom half of the screen, under Column Properties and in the Table Designer section, expand **Identity Specification,** and then change (**Is Identity**) to **Yes.**
7. Just under ProdID, in the second row under Column Name, enter **Description.**
8. Just to the right of that, under Data Type, enter **nvarchar(100).**
9. Make certain Allow Nulls is cleared.
10. Under Column Name in the third row, enter **InStock.**
11. Under Data Type, select **Int.**
12. Uncheck **Allow Nulls.**
13. Click the **Save** button on the left side of the toolbar (it looks like a floppy disk).
14. In the Choose Name box that pops up, enter **Products.**
15. Close the Table Designer by clicking the **X** in the upper-right corner of the window.

If you did try to create this object, you received an error that the object already exists. This is expected as you already created this object in Exercise 6-1.

Now create the second and third tables using Management Studio.

EXERCISE 6-3 CREATING THE CUSTOMERS TABLE

1. Right-click the **Tables** icon, and select **New Table** to open the Table Designer.
2. In the first row, under Column Name, enter **CustID.**
3. Under Data Type, select **Int.**
4. Make certain Allow Nulls isn't checked.
5. Under Column Properties and in the Table Designer section, expand **Identity Specification**, and then change (**Is Identity**) to **Yes.**
6. Just under CustID, in the second row under Column Name, enter **Fname.**
7. Just to the right of that, under Data Type, enter **nvarchar(20).**
8. Make certain Allow Nulls is unchecked.
9. Using the parameters displayed earlier, fill in the information for the remaining columns. Don't allow nulls in any of the fields.
10. Click the **Save** button.
11. In the Choose Name box that pops up, enter **Customers**.
12. Close the **Table Designer.**

EXERCISE 6-4 CREATING THE ORDERS TABLE

1. Right-click the **Tables** icon, and select **New Table** to open the Table Designer.
2. In the first row, under Column Name, enter **CustID**.
3. Under Data Type, select **Int**.
4. Make certain Allow Nulls isn't checked.
5. This won't be an identity column as it was in the Customers table, so don't make any changes to the Identity Specification settings.
6. Just under CustID and in the second row under Column Name, enter **ProdID** with a datatype of **int**. Don't change the Identity Specification settings. Don't allow null values.
7. Just below ProdID, create a field named **Qty** with a datatype of **int** that doesn't allow nulls.
8. Create a column named **OrdDate** with a datatype of **smalldatetime**. Don't allow null values.
9. Click the **Save** button.
10. In the Choose Name box that pops up, enter **Orders**.
11. Close the Table Designer.

To verify that all three of your tables exist, expand **Tables** under the MSSQL_Training database; you should see the three tables you created (you may need to right-click the **Tables** icon and select **Refresh** to see the tables).

Partitioning Tables

Tables in SQL Server can range from small, having only a single record, to huge, with millions of records. These large tables can be difficult for users to work with simply because of their size. To make them smaller without losing any data, you can *partition* your tables.

CERTIFICATION READY?
Partitioning tables and views (see Lesson 8) across multiple servers results in a federation of servers.

Partitioning tables works just like it sounds: you cut tables into multiple sections that can be stored and accessed independently without the users' knowledge. Suppose you have a table that contains order information, and the table has about 50 million rows. That may seem like a big table, but such a size isn't uncommon. To partition this table, you first need to decide on a partition column and a range of values for the column. In a table of order data, you probably have an order date column, which is an excellent candidate. The range can be any value you like; but since you want to make the most current orders easily accessible, you may want to set the range at anything older than a year. Now you can use the partition column and range to create a *partition function*, which SQL Server will use to allocate the data across the partitions.

You create partition functions using the CREATE PARTITION FUNCTION statement. You can use this to create two types of ranges: LEFT and RIGHT. The difference is simple really; take this code, for example:

```
CREATE PARTITION FUNCTION pfQty (int)

AS RANGE LEFT FOR VALUES (50, 100)
```

This code creates three partitions that divide a table based on integer values of a column. Here is how it divides:

PARTITION 1	PARTITION 2	PARTITION 3
COL <= 50	COL > 50 AND <= 100	COL > 100

To create a right range, just use this code:

```
CREATE PARTITION FUNCTION pfQty (int)

AS RANGE RIGHT FOR VALUES (50, 100)
```

This divides the table in this way:

PARTITION 1	PARTITION 2	PARTITION 3
COL < 50	COL >= 50 AND < 100	COL >= 100

After you figure out how to divvy up the table, you need to decide where to keep the partitioned data physically; this is called the ***partition scheme***. You can keep archived data on one hard disk and current data on another disk by storing the partitions in separate filegroups, which can be assigned to different disks.

If you are going to divide current data from archive data, you will want to put the current data on the fastest disks you have because it is accessed more frequently. Also, you may want to mark the archive filegroup as read-only. This will speed up access because SQL Server does not place write locks on a read-only filegroup.

Once you have planned your partitions, you can create partitioned tables using the methods already discussed in this lesson.

In Exercise 6-5, you will create a partition function and scheme for the Orders table. The partition will be based on the OrdDate column and will separate current orders from archive orders. Anything in the last 30 days will be considered current.

Some good examples are the TransactionHistory and TransactionHistory–Archive tables in the AdventureWorks database, which are partitioned on the ModifiedDate field.

 EXERCISE 6-5 CREATING A PARTITION FUNCTION AND SCHEME

1. In SQL Server Management Studio, right-click the **MSSQL_Training** database, and click **Properties**.
2. On the **Filegroups** page, click the **Add** button.
3. In the Name box, enter **TestPF1**.
4. Click **Add** again, and in the Name box, enter **TestPF2**.
5. Click **Add** again, and in the Name Box, enter **TestPF3**.
6. Click **OK**.
7. Select **MSSQL_Training** from the drop-down list on the toolbar.
8. Open a new query window, and execute the following code to create the partition function:

```
CREATE PARTITION FUNCTION pfOrders (smalldatetime) AS RANGE LEFT FOR VALUES ((Getdate() - 30)
```

9. To create a partition scheme based on this function, execute this code:

```
CREATE PARTITION SCHEME pfOrders AS PARTITION pfOrders TO (TestPF1, TestPF2, TestPF3);
```

SKILL SUMMARY

IN THIS LESSON YOU LEARNED:

- **Planning tables:** You learned you must sit down with a pencil and paper to draw the tables before you create them. You need to decide what the tables will contain, making them as specific as possible. You also learned that tables consist of entities (which contain a specific type of data) and rows (an entity in the table that spans all columns). Each of the columns in the table has a specific datatype that restricts the data it can hold.
- **Creating tables:** You learned the mechanics of creating tables in the database using both Transact-SQL and Management Studio.
- **Partitioning tables:** You then learned you can spread the contents of a table over multiple resources, creating ultimately a federation of servers.

For the certification examination:

- **Understand table partitions:** Partitioning tables allows you to break a table into multiple pieces stored in separate files on multiple disks across multiple servers. To partition a table, you need to select a column, create a partition function, and then create a partition scheme. The partition function can be a LEFT or RIGHT range, so make sure you know how and why to choose.
- **Understand tables:** A table is a collection of records and attributes (rows and columns) that SQL Server uses to store and organize data.

■ Knowledge Assessment

Multiple Choice

Circle the letter or letters that correspond to the best answer or answers.

Table 6-4

Table Specification

PRODUCTNAME	DESCRIPTION	QUANTITY	INSTOCK	VENDORID
Datatype: varchar(50)	Datatype: varchar(100)	Datatype: int	Datatype: bit	Datatype: uniqueidentifier
Screwdriver	Use with screws	500	1	AD5A83CD-AB64-CA25-B23E-A1C54DF584A1
Hammer	Use with nails	350	1	7D1A87FC-7D2A-20FC-A52C-10F2B1C38F2C
Wrench	Use with bolts	0	0	6F9619FF-8B86-D011-B42D-00C04FC964FF

1. You have data in your database that looks like Table 6-4. What is the ProductName object?
   a. A record
   b. An entity
   c. A datatype
   d. A view

2. In Table 6-4, which object contains all the data about screwdrivers?
   a. A record
   b. A field
   c. A datatype
   d. A view

3. In Table 6-4, which values can be used in the InStock field?
   a. Dates
   b. Numbers
   c. Text
   d. 0s and 1s

4. Suppose you want to add a column to Table 6-4 that contains the price of the product. None of your products will cost more than $300. Which datatype should you use?
   a. Int
   b. Money
   c. Smallmoney
   d. Float
   e. Real

Table 6-5

Table Specification

EMPID	FIRSTNAME	LASTNAME	ADDRESS	CITY	STATE	ZIPCODE	PHONE	SSN	PAY
Datatype: int, identity not nullable	Datatype: varchar (20) not nullable	Datatype: varchar (20) not nullable	Datatype: varchar (50) not nullable	Datatype: varchar (20) not nullable	Datatype: char(2) not nullable	Datatype: char(5) not nullable	Datatype: char(10) not nullable	Datatype: char(9) not nullable	Datatype Money nullable
1	John	Jackson	20 N. 2nd	Oakland	CA	94905	111 5551212	111223333	50,000.00
2	Jane	Samuels	37 S. Elm	Springfield	IL	65201	222 5551212	444556666	65,000.00
3	Tom	Johnson	256 Park	Quahog	RI	05102	333 5551212	777889999	45,000.00

5. Using the data from Table 6-5, you need to partition the table into three divisions, one for employees who make less than 50,000, one for employees who make 50,001 to 70,000, and one for employees who make 70,0001 and higher. Place the following steps in order to create a partition for this table.

   a. Create a partition scheme.

   b. Create a partition function.

   c. Add filegroups to the database.

   d. Choose a partition column and value.

6. Using the data from Table 6-5, you need to partition the table into three divisions, one for employees who make less than 50,000, one for employees who make 50,001 to 70,000, and one for employees who make 70,0001 and higher. Which function should you use?

   a. Use the following:

   CREATE PARTITION FUNCTION pfSalary (money) AS RANGE LEFT FOR VALUES (50000, 70000);

   b. Use the following:

   CREATE PARTITION FUNCTION pfSalary (money) AS RANGE LEFT FOR VALUES (50001, 70001);

   c. Use the following:

   CREATE PARTITION FUNCTION pfSalary (money) AS RANGE RIGHT FOR VALUES (50000, 70000);

   d. Use the following:

   CREATE PARTITION FUNCTION pfSalary (money) AS RANGE RIGHT FOR VALUES (50001, 70001);

7. Using the data from Table 6-5, you need to partition the table into three divisions, one for employees who make less than 49,999 one for employees who make 50,000 to 69,999, and one for employees who make 70,0000 and higher. Which function should you use?

   a. Use the following:

   CREATE PARTITION FUNCTION pfSalary (money) AS RANGE LEFT FOR VALUES (50000, 70000);

   b. Use the following:

   CREATE PARTITION FUNCTION pfSalary (money) AS RANGE LEFT FOR VALUES (50001, 70001);

c. Use the following:

```
CREATE PARTITION FUNCTION pfSalary (money) AS RANGE RIGHT FOR VALUES
(50000, 70000);
```

d. Use the following:

```
CREATE PARTITION FUNCTION pfSalary (money) AS RANGE RIGHT FOR VALUES
(50001, 70001);
```

■ Case Scenarios

Scenario 6-1: Creating a New Table

The programmers just keep meeting and meeting. This time they want you to create another table in the MSSQL_Training database—call it MailingList. What should go in this table? Which datatypes? (Note: Don't delete the table. You will use it in the next lesson.)

Scenario 6-2: Creating Tables for the IT Asset Database

Create the tables for the ITAssets database. How many did you decide you needed? You may have seen a many-to-many relationship that might call for creating a junction table. Discuss this among your peers and with your instructor. What's the issue you must solve?

Performing Indexing and Full-Text Searching

LESSON SKILL MATRIX

TECHNOLOGY SKILL	70-431 EXAM OBJECTIVE
Implement indexes.	Foundational
Specify the filegroup.	Foundational
Specify the index type.	Foundational
Specify relational index options.	Foundational
Specify columns.	Foundational
Specify a partition scheme when creating an index.	Foundational
Disable an index.	Foundational
Create an online index by using an ONLINE Argument.	Foundational
Implement a full-text search.	Foundational
Create a catalog.	Foundational
Create an index.	Foundational
Specify a full-text population method.	Foundational

KEY TERMS

clustered index: An index that physically arranges the records in ascending order and stores the records in the leaf level of the index.

extent: Eight 8 KB pages; the unit of disk I/O.

fill factor: The percentage to which index pages are filled on initial creation or rebuild; they are not maintained at this level. You must perform regular maintenance on indexes to recover the desired fill factor.

heap: A data store without an index.

index allocation map: A means by which SQL Server finds all database pages; SQL Server walks the map;

the output order is unpredictable—not necessarily the order in which entered.

nonclustered index: An index in which the logical order of the index key values is different from the physical order of the corresponding rows in a table. The index contains row locators that point to the storage location of the table data.

selectivity: The uniqueness of data entries. The gender column has low selectivity—approximately 50 percent are male and 50 percent are female. The Query Optimizer may not use an index unless the selectivity is in the 5 to 7 percent range.

Using Indexes

↓
THE BOTTOM LINE

Indexes can potentially speed resultset creation during a query, but only when a WHERE clause specifies an effective search argument. Indexes always slow data entry. You must balance these competing goals to keep your database performing optimally.

Understanding Index Architecture

In Lesson 4, you learned that SQL Server stores data on the hard disk in 8 KB pages inside the database files. By default, these pages and the data they contain aren't organized in any way. To bring order to this chaos, you can create an index. Once you've done so, you have index pages as well as data pages. The data pages contain the information that users have inserted in the tables, and the index pages store a list of all the values in an indexed column (called *key values*), along with pointers to the locations of the records that contain those values in the indexed table. For example, if you have an index on a LastName column, a key value might be Smith 520617: this indicates that the first record with a value of Smith in the LastName field is on extent 52, page 6, record number 17 (an ***extent*** is a collection of eight contiguous pages in a data file).

But first you must decide whether you should create an index at all. During data entry in an OLTP, the data also must be indexed, thus slowing processing. During data reporting, if no WHERE clause is used, or no index exists, SQL Server must perform a table scan, thus slowing processing. Data entry and data recovery optimization are mutually exclusive goals.

For data entry, the desired number of indexes is unambiguously zero. If you must normalize—and many organizations (the federal government, for example) require it—you must create a primary key, as shown in Table 7-1. A primary key is enforced with an index. This justifies one index. Then if, for some reason, you need to enforce uniqueness in a column, a second index is justified. After that, you should consider the need for another index with skepticism. Each additional index will cost you in overhead processing time.

For data reporting, consider moving your data (usually with an overnight job) into an OLAP structure: relational online analytical processing (ROLAP), multidimensional online analytical processing (MOLAP or cube), or hybrid online analytical process (HOLAP). The ROLAP is built with a denormalized star schema structure and highly indexed for optimum report generation.

You can create two types of indexes on a table: clustered and nonclustered. Which type should you use and where? To answer that question accurately, you need to understand how SQL Server stores and accesses data when no index exists—this type of table is called a heap.

UNDERSTANDING HEAPS

Tables with no clustered index in place are called ***heaps***. SQL Server stores tables on disk by allocating one extent (eight contiguous 8 KB pages) at a time in the database file. When one extent fills with data, another is allotted. These extents, however, aren't physically next to each other in the database file; they're scattered about. That is part of what makes data access on a heap so slow: SQL Server needs to access an ***index allocation map (IAM)*** to find various extents for the table it's searching.

Suppose, for instance, that you're searching for a record named Adams in a Customers table. The Customers table may be quite sizable, so SQL Server needs to find all the extents that belong to that table in the database file before it can begin to search for Adams. To find those extents, SQL Server must query the sys.sysindexes table.

Table 7-1

Database Normalization

TABLE CREATION:
Attributes (columns) and instances (rows) should describe one and only one entity (together, a *table*).
All rows must be unique, and there must be a primary key.
The column and row order must not matter.

FIRST NORMAL FORM:
An attribute cannot have two (or more) values at one time for the same entity instance.
A database complies with the first normal form if no table has columns that define similar attributes, and if no column contains multiple values in a single row.
Look for the possibility of a field value in multiple rows (the same data occurring in different rows) and for the possibility of multiple field values in any column for a single row (multiple data entries).

SECOND NORMAL FORM:
The model must be in the first normal form, and determining the values of the nonkey attributes is dependent on knowing the values of the entire primary key.
A database complies with the second normal form if it complies with the first normal form and if each column that is not part of a primary key depends on all of the columns that are covered by the primary key in that table and not on a subset of the columns that are covered by the primary key.
Look for aggregate keys to see whether some attributes (columns) can be completely described by a single-column primary key.

THIRD NORMAL FORM:
The model must be in the second normal form, and nonkey attributes must be dependent only on the key.
A database complies with the third normal form if it complies with the second normal form and if, in each table, columns that are not covered by the primary key do not depend on each other.
Look for attributes that can be described by a column that *is not* defined as a key, and remove any derived data columns

This system table is used to store index information: every table in your database has an entry in the sysindexes table whether or not the particular table has an index in place. If your table is a heap (such as this Customers table), it has a record in the sysindexes table with a value of 0 in the indid (index identifier) column. Once SQL Server finds the record for the Customers table in the sysindexes table and reads a 0 in the indid column, SQL Server looks specifically at the FirstIAM column.

The FirstIAM column tells SQL Server exactly where to find the first ***index allocation map (IAM)*** page in the database. Much like the street map you use to find various sections of a street, the IAM is what SQL Server must use to find various extents of a heap. This IAM is the only thing that links pages together in a heap; without the IAM page, SQL Server would need to scan every page in the database file to find one table—just as you would have to drive every street in town to find a single address if you had no street map.

Even with this IAM page, data access is generally slower than if your table were indexed. SQL Server must constantly refer to the IAM page to find the next extent of a table to continue searching for data. This process of scanning the IAM page, and then scanning each extent of the table for the record needed, is called a *table scan*. You can see what a table scan looks like by completing Exercise 7-1.

⊕ **EXERCISE 7-1 GENERATING A TABLE SCAN**

1. Open **SQL Server Management Studio,** and connect using **Windows Authentication.**

2. To force SQL Server to perform a table scan, you need to delete an index (which you'll re-create later in this lesson). In Object Explorer, expand **Server** ⟶ **Databases** ⟶ **AdventureWorks** ⟶ **Tables.**

3. Right-click **HumanResources.EmployeePayHistory,** and select **Modify.**

4. Right-click the **EmployeeID** column, and click **Remove Primary Key.**

5. Click the **Save** button on the toolbar.

6. Open a new query and enter, but do not execute, the following code:

   USE AdventureWorks

   SELECT * FROM HumanResources.EmployeePayHistory

7. On the Query menu, click **Display Estimated Execution Plan** (third to the right of the Execute button). This will show you how SQL Server goes about finding your data.

8. Scroll down to the bottom of the results pane, and hover your mouse pointer over the Table Scan icon to view the cost of the scan—this tells you how much CPU time the scan should take (in milliseconds).

To find all the pages associated with a table, SQL Server must reference the IAM page.

Table scans can slow your system, but they don't always. In fact, table scans can be faster than indexed access if your table is small (about one extent in size). If you create an index on such a small table, SQL Server must read the index pages and then the table pages. It would be faster just to scan the table and be done with it. So, on small tables, a heap is preferable. On larger tables, though, you need to avoid table scans; to do that, you must include a WHERE clause. To prepare an effective SARG (search argument), you should understand indexes, starting with clustered indexes.

UNDERSTANDING CLUSTERED INDEXES

Clustered indexes physically rearrange the data that users insert in your tables. The arrangement of a clustered index on disk can be compared to that in a dictionary, because they both use the same storage paradigm. If you needed to look up a word in the dictionary—for example, "satellite"—how would you do it? You would turn right to the S section of the dictionary and continue through the alphabetically arranged list until you found the word "satellite." The process is similar with a clustered index: a clustered index on a LastName column would place Adams physically before Burns in the database file. This way, SQL Server can more easily pinpoint the exact data pages it wants.

It might help to visualize an index in SQL Server as an upside-down tree. In fact, the index structure is called a B-tree (balanced-tree) structure. At the top of the B-tree structure, you find the root page; it contains information about the location of other pages, called intermediate-level pages, further down the line. These intermediate-level pages contain yet more key values that can point to still other intermediate-level pages or data pages. The pages at the bottom of a clustered index, the leaf pages, contain the actual data, which is physically arranged on disk to conform to the constraints of the index. Data access on a clustered index is a little more complex than just looking for letters or numbers in the data pages, though.

You can have only one clustered index per table because clustered indexes physically rearrange the data in the indexed table.

ACCESSING DATA WITH A CLUSTERED INDEX

The beginning point of an index traversal is the root page of the clustered index. Each intermediate level of the clustered index grows initially from the root, to two pages, to four pages, to eight pages, and so on. Because an index is organized as a balanced inverted tree, each move from one index page eliminates half of the data to be scanned.

When you perform a query on a column that is part of a clustered index (by using a SELECT statement), SQL Server must refer to the sysindexes table, where every table has a record. Tables with a clustered index have a value of 1 in the indid column (unlike heaps, which have a value of 0). Once the record has been located, SQL Server looks at the root column, which contains the location of the root page of the clustered index.

When SQL Server locates the root page of the index, it begins to search for your data. If you're searching for Smith, for example, SQL Server searches through the entire root page looking for an entry for Smith. Since the data you're seeking is toward the bottom of the table, SQL Server most likely won't find Smith in the root page. What it will find at the bottom of the root page is a link to the next intermediate-level page in the chain.

Each page in the clustered index has pointers, or links, to the index page just before it and the index page just after it. Having these links built into the index pages eliminates the need for the IAM pages that heaps require. This speeds up data access because you don't need to keep referring to the IAM pages—you move right to the next index page in the chain.

SQL Server then looks through each intermediate-level page, where it may be redirected to another intermediate-level page or, finally, to the leaf level. The leaf level in a clustered index is the end destination—the data you requested in your SELECT query. If you've requested one record, that single record found at the leaf level will be displayed.

Suppose, though, that you've requested a range of data (for example, Quincy through to Smith). Because the data has been physically rearranged, as soon as SQL Server has located the first value in the search, it can read each subsequent record until it reaches Smith. SQL Server has no need to keep referring to the root and intermediate-level pages to find subsequent data. This makes a clustered index an excellent choice for columns where you're constantly searching for ranges of data or columns with low selectivity. *Selectivity* is the number of duplicate values in a column; low selectivity means a column has many duplicate values. For example, a LastName column may contain several hundred records with a value of Smith, which means it has low selectivity, whereas a PhoneNumber column should have few records with duplicate values, meaning it has high selectivity. The data in a table with a clustered index is physically rearranged for ease of location.

You now know how SQL Server accesses data via a clustered index, but there is more to it than that. Next you need to understand how that data gets there in the first place, and what happens if it changes.

MODIFYING DATA WITH A CLUSTERED INDEX

To access data on a table with a clustered index, you use a standard SELECT statement—there is nothing special about it. Modifying data with a clustered index is the same—you use standard INSERT, UPDATE, and DELETE statements. What makes this process intriguing is the way SQL Server has to store your data: it must be physically rearranged to conform to the clustered index parameters.

On a heap, the data is inserted at the end of the table, which is the bottom of the last data page. If there is no room on any of the data pages, SQL Server allocates a new extent and starts filling it with data. Because you've told SQL Server to physically rearrange your data by creating a clustered index, SQL Server no longer has the freedom to stuff data wherever room exists. The data must be placed in order physically. To help SQL Server accomplish this task efficiently, you need to leave a little room at the end of each data page on a clustered index. This blank space is referred to as the *fill factor*.

Setting the fill factor on a clustered index tells SQL Server to leave blank space at the end of each data page so it has room to insert new data. For example, suppose you have a clustered index on a LastName column, and you want to add a new customer with a last name of Chen, which needs to be placed on one of the data pages containing the C data. SQL Server must put this record on the C page; with a fill factor specified, you'll have room at the end of the page to insert this new data. Without a fill factor, the C page may fill entirely, leaving no room for Chen.

You specify the fill factor when you create the clustered index; you can change it later if you want. A higher fill factor gives less room, and a lower fill factor gives more room. If you specify a fill factor of 70, for example, the data page is filled with 70 percent data and 30 percent blank space. If you specify 100, the data page is filled to nearly 100 percent, with room for only one record at the bottom of the page (it seems strange, but that's how SQL Server views 100 percent full).

SQL Server doesn't automatically maintain the fill factor, though. This means your data pages can and will fill to capacity, eventually. What happens when a data page fills completely?

When you need to insert data into a page that has become completely full, SQL Server performs a page split. This means SQL Server takes approximately half the data from the full page and moves it to an empty page, thus creating two half-full pages (or two half-empty pages, depending on how you look at it). Now you have plenty of room for the new data, but you have to contend with a new problem. This clustered index is a doubly linked list, with each page having a link to the page before it and a link to the page after it. So, when SQL Server splits a page, it must also update the headers at the top of each page to reflect the new location of the data that has been moved. Because this new page can be anywhere in the database file, the links on the pages don't necessarily point to the next physical page on the disk. A link may point to a different extent altogether, which can slow the system.

For example, if you have inserted a new record named Chen into the database, but your C page is full, SQL Server will perform a page split. Half the data will be moved to a new page to make room for the Chen record, but the new page for the data that has been moved won't be in line anymore.

Notice that before the page split, all the pages were neatly lined up—page 99 pointed to page 100, page 100 pointed to page 101, and so on. After the page split, some of the data had to be moved from page 100 to page 102. Now page 102 comes directly after 100 in the linked list. This means that when you search for data, SQL Server will need to jump from page 99 to page 100, from page 100 to page 102, from page 102 back to page 101, and then from page 101 to page 103. You can see how that might slow down the system, so you may wish to configure the fill factor to avoid excessive page splits.

The term "excessive" is subjective when discussing page splits, however. In an environment where data is used primarily for reading, such as a decision support services environment, you'll want to use a high fill factor (less free space). This high fill factor will ensure that data is read from fewer pages in the database file. You should use a lower fill factor (more free space) in environments that have a lot of INSERT traffic. This lower fill factor will cut down on page splits and increase write performance, but at the expense of using more hard drive space.

Now that you have a better understanding of the inner workings of a clustered index, you're probably ready to create one for each column of your table. But please don't try to do that just yet (even if you want to, you're limited to one clustered index per table), because before you find out where and how to create indexes, you need to learn about nonclustered indexes.

UNDERSTANDING NONCLUSTERED INDEXES

Like its clustered cousin, the ***nonclustered index*** is a B-tree structure having a root page, intermediate levels, and a leaf level. However, two major differences separate the index types. The first is that the leaf level of the nonclustered index doesn't contain the actual data; it contains pointers to the data that is stored in data pages. The second big difference is that the nonclustered index doesn't physically rearrange the data. You can think of it as the difference between a dictionary and an index at the back of a topically arranged book.

A clustered index is much like a dictionary in that the data it contains is physically arranged to meet the constraints of the index. So if you wanted to find "triggers" in a dictionary, you would turn to the T section and find your way from there. A nonclustered index is more like the index at the back of a book. If you wanted to find "triggers" in this book, you couldn't turn to the T section of the book because there is no T section to turn to, as there is in a dictionary. Instead, you would turn to the back of the book and refer to the index, which does have a T section. Once you located "triggers" in the index, you would turn to the page number listed to find the information you needed. If you were searching for a range of data, you would have to repeatedly refer to the index to find the data you needed, because most of the data is contained on different pages.

ACCESSING DATA WITH A NONCLUSTERED INDEX

When you search for data on a table with a nonclustered index, SQL Server first queries the sysindexes table, looking for a record that contains your table name and a value in the indid column from 2 to 251 (0 denotes a heap, and 1 is for a clustered index). Once SQL Server finds this record, it looks at the root column to find the root page of the index (just like it did with a clustered index). Once SQL Server has the location of the root page, it can begin searching for your data.

If you're searching for Smith, for example, SQL Server looks through the root page to find Smith; if it isn't there, the server finds the highest value in the root page and follows that pointer to the next intermediate-level page. SQL Server keeps following the intermediate-level links until it finds Smith in the leaf level. This is another difference between clustered and nonclustered indexes: the leaf level in a nonclustered index doesn't contain the actual data you seek; it contains a pointer to the data, which is contained in a separate data page—much like the index at the back of a book doesn't have a description of what you're looking for but refers you to a particular page of the book that does.

If you're searching for a single value, SQL Server needs to search the index only once because the pointer at the leaf level directs SQL Server directly to the data. If you're looking for a range of values, though, SQL Server must refer to the index repeatedly to locate the key value for each record in the range you're trying to find. This means you should use nonclustered indexes on columns in which you seldom search for ranges of data, or columns with high selectivity. As mentioned previously in this lesson, selectivity refers to the number of duplicate values in a column; low selectivity means a column contains many duplicate values, and high selectivity means a column contains few duplicate values.

Once SQL Server finds the leaf level it needs, it can use the pointer to find the data page that contains Smith; how SQL Server finds the data page depends on whether you have a clustered index in place yet.

If you're searching a nonclustered index that is based on a heap (a table with no clustered index in place), SQL Server uses the pointer in the leaf-level page to jump right to the data page and return your data.

If your table has a clustered index in place, the nonclustered index leaf level doesn't contain a pointer directly to the data; rather, it contains a pointer to the clustered index key value. This means once SQL Server is done searching your nonclustered index, it has to traverse your clustered index as well. Why on earth would you want to search two indexes to come up with a single value? Wouldn't one index be faster? Not necessarily—the secret lies in updating the data.

MODIFYING DATA WITH A NONCLUSTERED INDEX

The commands used to modify data here aren't anything special: you use the standard T-SQL statements—INSERT, UPDATE, and DELETE—to accomplish these tasks. The interesting part is how SQL Server stores the data.

When inserting data using a nonclustered index on a heap, SQL Server doesn't have much work to do. It stuffs the data wherever it finds room and adds a new key value that points to the new record of the associated index pages. The process becomes a bit more complex when you throw a clustered index into the equation.

When you insert data into a table with both a nonclustered and a clustered index in place, SQL Server physically inserts the data where it belongs in the order of the clustered index, and updates the key values of the nonclustered index to point to the key values of the clustered index. When one of the data pages becomes full and you still have more data to insert, a page split occurs: half the records on the full page are moved to a new page to make room for more data. This process of page splitting is why the key values of the nonclustered index point to the clustered index instead of the data pages themselves.

When you're using a nonclustered index without a clustered index in place, each index page contains key values that point to the data. This pointer contains the location of the extent and the page and record number of the data being sought. If a page split occurred and the nonclustered index didn't use clustered index key values, then all the key values for the data that had been moved would be incorrect because all the pointers would be wrong. The entire nonclustered index would need to be rebuilt to reflect the changes. However, because the nonclustered index references the clustered index key values (not the actual data), all the pointers in the nonclustered index will be correct even after a page split has occurred, and the nonclustered index won't need to be rebuilt. That is why you reference the key values of a clustered index in a nonclustered index.

Table 7-2 summarizes the differences between clustered and nonclustered indexes.

Table 7-2

Differences between Clustered and Nonclustered Indexes

CLUSTERED	NONCLUSTERED
Only 1 allowed per table	Up to 249 allowed per table
Physically rearranges the data in the table to conform to the index constraints	Creates a separate list of key values with pointers to the location of the data in the data pages
For use on columns that are frequently searched for ranges of data	For use on columns that are searched for single values
For use on columns with low selectivity	For use on columns with high selectivity

If the Query Optimizer finds that a query, let's say,

SELECT LName, FName FROM Products.Contacts

has both columns requested in the index, the Query Optimizer will pull the data directly from the index—never looking in the table itself. This is known as a *covered index*. This, as you might imagine, results in highly efficient data retrieval. It's so efficient that many programmers purposely add columns to make a larger composite key to realize these benefits.

In SQL Server 2005, you can extend nonclustered indexes to include nonkey columns. This is referred to as an index with *included columns*. Including nonkey columns in a nonclustered index can significantly improve performance in queries where all the columns are included in the index and, therefore, all data fields are covered without having to be a primary key. When using nonkey columns, you need to keep a few guidelines in mind:

- Nonkey columns can be included only in nonclustered indexes.
- Columns can't be defined in both the key column and the INCLUDE list.
- Column names can't be repeated in the INCLUDE list.
- At least one key column must be defined.
- Nonkey columns can't be dropped from a table unless the index is dropped first.
- A column can't be both a key column and an included column.
- You must have at least one key column defined with a maximum of 16 key columns.
- You can have only up to a maximum of 1,023 included columns.
- The only changes allowed to nonkey columns are to nullability (from NULL to NOT NULL, and vice versa), and increasing the length of varbinary, varchar, or nvarchar columns.

Both types of indexes have several options in common that can change the way the index functions. The following section describes what those options are.

SETTING RELATIONAL OPTIONS

Clustered and nonclustered indexes share common options that can change the way the index works:

PAD_INDEX: When the PAD_INDEX option is set to ON, the percentage of free space that is specified by the fill factor is applied to the intermediate-level pages of the index. When this is OFF, the intermediate-level pages are filled to the point at which there is room for one new record.

FILLFACTOR: FILLFACTOR specifies how full the database engine should make each page during index creation or rebuild. Valid values are from 0 to 100. Values of 0 and 100 are the same in that they both tell the database engine to fill the page to capacity, leaving room for only one new record. Any other value specifies the amount of space to use for data; for instance, a fill factor of 70 tells the database engine to fill the page to 70 percent full with 30 percent free space.

Partitioned Indexes

As discussed in Lesson 6, tables can be partitioned for performance and storage reasons; well, so can indexes. It's usually best to partition a table and then create an index on the table so that SQL Server can partition the index for you based on the partition function and schema of the table. However, you can partition indexes separately. This is useful in the following cases:

- The base table isn't partitioned.
- Your index key is unique but doesn't contain the partition column of the table.
- You want the base table to participate in collocated JOINs with other tables using different JOIN columns.

If you decide you need to partition your index separately, then you need to keep the following in mind:

- The arguments of the partition function for the table and index must have the same datatype. For example, if your table is partitioned on a datetime column, your index must be partitioned on a datetime column.
- Your table and index must define the same number of partitions.
- The table and index must have the same partition boundaries.

SORT_IN_TEMPDB: When SQL Server builds an index, it must perform a sort on the table during the build. Setting this option to ON tells SQL Server to store the results of this intermediate sort in TempDB. This can speed up index creation if TempDB is on a different set of hard disks, but it also takes more disk space than OFF. Setting this option to OFF tells SQL Server to store the intermediate sort results in the same database as the table being indexed.

IGNORE_DUP_KEY: This option tells SQL Server what to do when it encounters a duplicate value while creating a unique index. OFF tells SQL Server to issue an error message and stop building the entire index. ON tells SQL Server to issue a warning message and that only the record with the duplicate value will fail. This can't be set to ON for XML indexes or indexes created on a view.

STATISTICS_NORECOMPUTE: For the Query Optimizer to work correctly, it must know which indexes are available and what data those indexes cover. That information is referred to as *statistics*. By default, this option is OFF, which means SQL Server will automatically recompute statistics to keep them up to date. Setting this option to ON tells SQL Server not to update statistics, in which case you must do it yourself. You can turn this on when you want to schedule recomputation after-hours so it does not interfere with normal read-write operations.

DROP_EXISTING: Setting this option to ON allows you to create a new index with the same name as an existing index. If this option is OFF and you try to create a new index with the same name as an existing index, you will get an error. This is useful after making a large amount of changes (perhaps after a BULK INSERT operation) that may require you to re-create your index to reflect the changes to the underlying data.

ONLINE: In SQL Server 2005 Enterprise Edition, this option states whether the underlying tables and indexes are available for queries and data modification while indexing operations are taking place. This has two available settings:

- **OFF:** Table locks are applied for the duration of the index operation. Clustered index operations acquire a schema lock, which prevents all user access to the underlying table for the duration of the index operation. Nonclustered operations acquire a shared lock on the table that allows for read operations but prevents data modification.

- **ON:** Long-term table locks are not held for the duration of the index operation with this setting. During the main phase of the operation, SQL Server will first acquire an intent share lock, which allows queries and data modifications. Then SQL Server acquires a shared lock at the start of the index operation and quickly releases it. If a nonclustered index is being created, SQL Server will acquire a shared lock again at the end of the operation. If a clustered index is being created or dropped, or a nonclustered index is being rebuilt, SQL Server acquires a schema modification lock at the end of the operation. ONLINE can't be set to ON for indexes created on local temporary tables (tables whose names start with the # character).

ALLOW_ROW_LOCKS: Setting this to ON allows SQL Server to use row locks on an index. OFF does not allow row locks to be used.

ALLOW_PAGE_LOCKS: Setting this to ON allows SQL Server to use page locks on an index. OFF does not allow page locks to be used.

MAXDOP: SQL Server is capable of using multiple processors when executing a query. This option tells SQL Server how many processors it is allowed to use; or, rather, it sets the maximum degree of parallelism. Setting this to 1 prevents parallel plan execution, so only one processor is used. Anything greater than 1 sets the number of processors that SQL Server can use (in other words, 5 tells SQL Server to use as many as five processors). A setting of 0 tells SQL Server that it can use all available processors when querying this index; this is the default setting.

Now that you know when and where to create both types of indexes, all that's left is to learn how to create them. In the next section, we'll cover the mechanics of creating indexes.

Creating Indexes

After all the work of planning your indexes, creating them will seem like a breeze. You'll create a simple index on the HumanResources.EmployeePayHistory table of the AdventureWorks database in Exercise 7-2. You can see how easy it is to create an index this way. If you want to make this a nonclustered index, all you need to do is leave the Create as Clustered box unchecked. There's nothing to it—the hard part is deciding what to index, as discussed earlier. Now you are ready for a more advanced use of indexes. The next section covers how to work with primary keys.

USING PRIMARY KEYS

A primary key ensures that each of the records in your table is unique in some way. It does this by creating a special type of index called a *unique index*. An index is ordinarily used to speed up access to data by reading all of the values in a column and keeping an organized list of where the record that contains that value is located in the table. A unique index not only generates that list, but it also prohibits duplicate values from being stored in the index. If a user tries to enter a duplicate value in the indexed field, the unique index will return an error, and the data modification will fail.

 EXERCISE 7-2 CREATING AN INDEX

1. Open **SQL Server Management Studio**, and connect using **Windows Authentication**.
2. Expand your server in Object Explorer, and then choose **Databases** → **Adventure-Works** → **Tables** → **HumanResources.EmployeePayHistory.**
3. Right-click **Indexes,** and select **New Index.**
4. Limber up your typing fingers, and in the Index Name box, enter **idx_Modified-Date.**
5. Select **Nonclustered** for the Index Type option.
6. Click the **Add** button next to the Index Key Columns grid.
7. Select the boxes next to the ModifiedDate column.
8. Click **OK** to return to the New Index dialog box.
9. Click **OK** to create the index.

Suppose, for instance, you have defined the custid field in the Customers table as a primary key, and that you have a customer with ID 1 already in the table. If one of your users tried to create another customer with ID 1, he or she would receive an error, and the update would be rejected because custid 1 already exists in the primary key's unique index. Of course, this is just an example, because your custid field has the identity property set, which automatically assigns a number with each new record inserted and will not allow you to enter a number of your own choosing.

When a column can be used as a unique identifier for a row (such as an identity column), it is referred to as a *surrogate* or *candidate key*.

The primary key should consist of a column (or columns) that contains unique values. This makes an identity column the perfect candidate for becoming a primary key, because the values contained therein are unique by definition. If you do not have an identity column, make sure to choose a column, or combination of columns, in which each value is unique. The choice here is easy; in Exercise 7-1, you deleted the primary key for the HumanResources. EmployeePay–History table of the AdventureWorks database. In Exercise 7-3, you'll re-create that index using Management Studio.

 EXERCISE 7-3 CREATING A PRIMARY KEY

1. Open **SQL Server Management Studio** by selecting it from the SQL Server 2005 group in Programs on your Start menu, and connect using **Windows Authentication**.
2. In Object Explorer, expand **Databases** → **AdventureWorks** → **Tables.**
3. Right-click the **HumanResources.EmployeePayHistory** table, and select **Modify.**
4. Hold down the **Shift** key, and click the **EmployeeID** and **RateChangeDate** columns.
5. Right-click **EmployeeID** under Column Name, and select **Set Primary Key.** Notice that just to the left of both fields a small key icon now denotes that this is the primary key.
6. When you click the **Save** icon on the toolbar, SQL Server will create a new unique index, which ensures that no duplicate values can be entered in the custid field.
7. Close the **Table Designer**.

You can use primary keys with foreign keys to relate two tables on a common column. The two column names are unimportant, but the datatypes must be the same. If this relationship is used often for joins, consider indexing the foreign key, as it will speed performance.

The index types discussed so far are fine for most types of data, but not all. For larger datatypes, you can use full-text search.

Using Full-Text Searching

People generally stored small amounts of data in their tables when databases first came into use. As time went on, however, people figured out that databases are excellent containers for all sorts of data, including massive amounts of text. Many companies, in fact, have entire libraries of corporate documents stored in their databases. To store such large amounts of text in a database, the text datatype was formulated. When this datatype first came out, everybody was still using standard SELECT queries to pull the data out of the text columns, but SELECT wasn't designed to handle such large amounts of text. For instance, if you wanted to find a phrase somewhere in the text column, SELECT couldn't do it efficiently. Or if you wanted to find two words that were close to each other in the text, SELECT fell short. That is why something else had to be devised, something more robust. Enter full-text searching.

You perform full-text searching through a completely separate program that runs as a service, called the SQL Server FullText Search service, or msftesq, and that can be used to index all sorts of information from most of the BackOffice (or even non-Microsoft) products. For example, FullText Search can index an entire mailbox in Microsoft Exchange to make it easier to find text in your mail messages. To accomplish this task, FullText Search runs as a separate service in the background, from which the BackOffice products can request data. Thus, when you perform one of these full-text searches, you are telling SQL Server to make a request of the FullText Search service. To perform a full-text search, you need to use only the CONTAINS, CONTAINSTABLE, FREETEXT, or FREETEXTTABLE clause in your SELECT query.

Before you can start to use this powerful tool, you need to configure it. The first step is to create a full-text index. Full-text indexes are created using SQL Server tools, such as Management Studio, but they are maintained by the FullText Search service and stored on disk as files separate from the database. To keep the full-text indexes organized, they are stored in catalogs in the database. You can create as many catalogs in your databases as you like to organize your indexes, but these catalogs cannot span databases. You will create a catalog and index in the AdventureWorks database in Exercise 7-4.

 EXERCISE 7-4 CREATING A FULL-TEXT CATALOG AND INDEX

1. Open **SQL Server Management Studio**, and in Object Explorer expand **Databases** → **AdventureWorks** → **Tables**.

2. Right-click **Production.Document,** move to **Full-Text Index,** and click **Define Full-Text Index.**

3. On the first screen of the Full-Text Indexing Wizard, click **Next.**

4. For full-text searching to work, each table on which you create a full-text index must already have a unique index associated with it. In this instance, select the default **PK_Document_DocumentID** index, and click **Next.**

5. On the next screen, you are asked which column you want to full-text index. Document-Summary is the only nvarchar(max) column in the table, so it is the best candidate; select it here by checking the box next to it, and click **Next.**

6. On the next screen, you are asked when you want changes to the full-text index applied. These are your options:

   • **Automatically:** Means that the full-text index is updated with every change made to the table. This is the easiest way to keep full-text indexes up to date, but it can tax the server because it means changes to the table and index and the associated overhead take place all at once.

   • **Manually:** Means changes to the underlying data are maintained, but you will have to schedule index population yourself. This is a slightly slower way to update the index, but it is not as taxing on the server because changes to the data are maintained but the index is not updated immediately.

- **Do Not Track Changes:** Means changes to the underlying data are not tracked. This is the least taxing, and slowest, way to update the full-text index. Changes are not maintained, so when the index is updated, the FullText Search service must read the entire table for changes before updating the index.

7. Choose **Automatically,** and click **Next.**

8. The next screen asks you to select a catalog. You'll need to create a new one here, because there are none available. In the Name field, enter **AdventureWorks Catalog.** You can also select a filegroup to place the catalog on; leave this as default, and click **Next.**

9. On the next screen, you are asked to create a schedule for automatically repopulating the full-text index. If your data is frequently updated, you will want to do this more often, maybe once a day. If it is read more often than it is changed, you should repopulate less frequently. You can schedule population for a single table or an entire catalog at a time. Here, you will set repopulation to happen just once for the entire catalog by clicking the **New Catalog Schedule** button.

10. On the New Schedule Properties screen, enter **Populate AdventureWorks,** and click **OK.**

11. When you are taken back to the Full-Text Indexing Wizard, click Next.

12. On the final screen of the wizard, you are given a summary of the choices you have made. Click Finish to create the index.

13. To see your new catalog and index, in Object Explorer expand the **AdventureWorks** → **Storage** → **Full-Text Catalogs.**

14. Double-click the AdventureWorks catalog to open its properties.

15. Click **Cancel** to close the Properties window.

Now that you have a fully populated full-text index, you will be able to start querying it using full-text clauses.

ADDING FULL-TEXT CLAUSES

Full-text query clauses include:

- CONTAINS
- FREETEXT
- CONTAINSTABLE
- FREETEXTTABLE

Here are two quick examples:

```
USE AdventureWorks
Select Comments
FROM Production.ProductReview
WHERE CONTAINS (Comments, ' "learning curve" ')
```

This returns all text in the Comments column containing the phrase "learning curve."

```
USE AdventureWorks
SELECT AddressLine1, KEY_TBL.RANK
FROM Person.Address AS Address INNER JOIN
CONTAINSTABLE (Person.Address, AddressLine1, 'ISABOUT
("Bay*", Street WEIGHT (0.9), View WEIGHT (0.1)) ' )
```

AS KEY_TBL ON Address.AddressID = KEY_TBL.[KEY]

ORDER BY KEY_TBL.RANK

This returns all text in the AddressLine1 column ranking (and ordering by highest rank) containing the letters "Bay" with a street weight far more important than the view weight.

You have probably seen this form in Web search returns that rank the relevance for you.

SKILL SUMMARY

IN THIS LESSON YOU LEARNED:

In this lesson, you first learned how SQL Server accesses and stores data when no index is in place. Without a clustered index, the table is called a heap, and the data is stored on a first-come, first-served basis. When accessing this data, SQL Server must perform a table scan, which means SQL Server must read every record in the table to find the data you're seeking. This can make data access slow on larger tables; but on smaller tables that are about one extent in size, table scans can be faster than indexing.

Next you learned how to accelerate data access by using indexes. The first index you looked at was the clustered index. This type of index physically rearranges the data in the database file. This property makes the clustered index ideal for columns that are constantly being searched for ranges of data and that have low selectivity, meaning several duplicate values.

Next came nonclustered indexes. These indexes don't physically rearrange the data in the database but rather create pointers to the actual data. This type of index is best suited to high-selectivity tables (few duplicate values) where single records are desired rather than ranges. Then you learned how to create indexes using SQL Server Management Studio.

Finally, you found that full-text searching could greatly enhance SELECT queries by allowing you to find words or phrases in your text fields.

With this newfound knowledge about indexing, you'll be able to speed up data access for your users.

For the certification examination:

- Know the difference between clustered and nonclustered indexes. Clustered indexes physically rearrange the data in a table to match the definition of the index. Nonclustered indexes are separate objects in the database that refer to the original table, without rearranging the table in any way.

- Understand full-text indexing. Understand what full-text indexing is for and how to manage it. Full-text indexing runs as a separate service and is used to search columns of text for phrases, instead of just single words. You have to repopulate the index occasionally to keep it up to date with the underlying table. SQL Server can do this for you automatically if you want.

- Know the relational options for creating indexes. In the "Setting Relational Options" section, you learned about the different relational options and what they do. Familiarize yourself with these options for the exam.

■ Knowledge Assessment

Multiple Choice

Circle the letter or letters that correspond to the best answer or answers.

Table 7-3

Customer Table

ID	FNAME	LNAME	CITY	STATE	ZIP
1	John	Smith	San Jose	CA	94602
2	Bob	Brown	Fresno	CA	96105
3	Bill	Jones	Los Angeles	CA	90028
4	Jim	White	Fairfield	CA	94533

1. Which of the columns in Table 7-3 has the lowest selectivity?
   a. State
   b. Phone
   c. FName
   d. LName

2. In Table 7-3, your users frequently query the database for zip codes based on the customer's last name. For example, the query to find the zip code for the customer with the last name of Smith would look like this:

   SELECT FName, LName, ZIP FROM Customers WHERE LName = 'Smith'

   You are going to create an index on the LName column, and there are no existing indexes in place on the table. Which type of index should it be, and why?
   a. Clustered, because the LName column has low selectivity.
   b. Nonclustered, because the LName column has low selectivity.
   c. Clustered, because the LName column has high selectivity.
   d. Nonclustered, because the LName column has high selectivity.

3. You need to create a nonclustered index on one of your tables. You want to make certain that 30 percent of each index page is left open so there is enough room to insert new leaf nodes in the index when new records are inserted into the table. How should you create the index?
   a. Create the index with a 30 percent fill factor.
   b. Create the index with a 70 percent fill factor.
   c. Create the index using the OPENSPACE(30) function.
   d. Do nothing; SQL Server leaves 30 percent of each index page open by default.

4. You have a large table that is in use 24/7. You need to be able to perform maintenance on the indexes on this table, but you can't take the table offline to perform the maintenance. What can you do to make the table available while performing index operations?
   a. Create the index with UPDATEABLE = ON.
   b. Create the index with ONLINE = ON.
   c. Create the index with MAXDOP = 0.
   d. You can't do anything; the table will not be available during index operations.

5. You have a SQL Server 2005 that houses a busy database containing your company's product catalog. This table is being queried all the time, and although your server can handle the current load, you are not sure if it can handle the load of a full-text index population. You need to create a full-text index on the table, but you want to populate it

manually, off-hours. You do not want any impact on performance during working hours. What should you do?

    a. When creating the full-text index, tell SQL Server to automatically apply changes to the index.

    b. When creating the full-text index, tell SQL Server to manually apply changes to the index.

    c. When creating the full-text index, tell SQL Server not to track changes on the table.

    d. Do nothing; SQL Server populates full-text indexes off-hours by default.

6. Which versions of SQL Server allow you to create an ONLINE index? (Choose all that apply.)

    a. Express Edition

    b. Workgroup Edition

    c. Standard Edition

    d. Enterprise Edition

7. You have a table that contains information about books you sell. One of the columns is a varchar(max) column that contains a large amount of text describing each book. You want to be able to query the data in this column for phrases instead of just single words. What can you do?

    a. Create a clustered index on the column.

    b. Create a nonclustered index on the column.

    c. Create a full-text index on the column.

    d. Create an ONLINE index on the column.

8. You have a server with several hard disk sets; all of your system databases, including TempDB, Master, and Model, are on one disk set, and a user database that you will be updating is on a disk set of its own. You need to create an index on a large table, and you want to make it as fast as possible. You are not worried about system resources such as disk space, processor time, or memory used. What can you do to create this index as fast as possible?

    a. Create the index with MAXDOP = 0.

    b. Create the index with STATISTICS_NORECOMPUTE = ON.

    c. Create the index with SORT_IN_TEMPDB = ON.

    d. Create the index with PAD_INDEX = ON.

9. You have a table containing product information that your users query frequently. They specifically use this query most often:

SELECT Name, Description, Vendor, InStock, Price FROM Products where Name = 'name'

You have a nonclustered index on this table on the Name column, but your users are complaining that the query is still too slow. What can you do to speed it up?

    a. Modify the index to include the Description, Vendor, InStock, and Price columns as nonkey columns.

    b. Create a new nonclustered index on the Description, Vendor, InStock, and Price columns.

    c. Create a new clustered index on the Description, Vendor, InStock, and Price columns.

    d. You can't do anything to speed up this query.

10. You have a SQL Server 2005 that houses a busy database containing your company's product catalog. This table is being queried all the time, and although your server can handle the current load, you are not sure if it can handle the extra load of recalculating index statistics. What can you do to minimize the overhead required to recalculate index statistics?

    a. Create the index with ALLOW_ROW_LOCKS = ON.

    b. Create the index with ALLOW_PAGE_LOCKS = ON.

    c. Create the index with STATISTICS_NORECOMPUTE = ON.

    d. Create the index with SORT_IN_TEMPDB = ON.

11. You have a table containing employee information that your users query frequently. They specifically use this query most often:

    SELECT FirstName, LastName, Address, Phone FROM Employees WHERE SSN = 'ssn'

    You have a clustered index on this table on the SSN column, but your users are complaining that the query is still too slow. What can you do to speed it up?
    a. Modify the index to include the FirstName, LastName, Address, and Phone columns as nonkey columns.
    b. Create a new nonclustered index on the FirstName, LastName, Address, and Phone columns.
    c. Create a new clustered index on the FirstName, LastName, Address, and Phone columns.
    d. You can't do anything to speed up this query.

12. You have a machine with eight processors, 12 GB of RAM, and a RAID-5 hard disk array. You want SQL Server to query indexes as fast as possible, so you decide to let SQL Server use all available processors when querying data. What setting do you need to use to configure this?
    a. MAXDOP = 0.
    b. MAXDOP = 1.
    c. MAXDOP = ALL.
    d. None; SQL Server will use all processors by default.

13. You work for a small company that has a limited budget for servers. One of your main servers has eight processors. To conserve hardware resources, you decide to run SQL Server and SharePoint Services on this machine, which means you need to limit the resources SQL Server uses while running queries. What can you do to configure SQL Server to use only four of the available processors when querying an index?
    a. Set MAXDOP = 4.
    b. Set MAXDOP = 0.
    c. Set MAXDOP = 1.
    d. You can't do anything; SQL Server uses all available processors for every query.

14. You have a SQL Server 2005 that houses your company's product catalog database. You need to create and maintain a full-text index on the table. The server has more than enough system resources, and you want to make this index as easy as possible to maintain. What should you do?
    a. When creating the full-text index, tell SQL Server to automatically apply changes to the index.
    b. When creating the full-text index, tell SQL Server to manually apply changes to the index.
    c. When creating the full-text index, tell SQL Server not to track changes on the table.
    d. Do nothing; SQL Server automatically populates full-text by default.

15. You have created a clustered index on a table with a fill factor of 72 percent. When a data page in this index fills to capacity, what happens?
    a. SQL Server moves 25 percent of the data to a new data page to maintain the fill factor and make room for new data.
    b. SQL Server moves 75 percent of the data to a new data page to maintain the fill factor and make room for new data.
    c. SQL Server moves 50 percent of the data to a new data page to make room for new data.
    d. SQL Server starts filling a new page and leaves the current pages intact.

16. You have a large table with several thousand rows of product data. You have just imported a whole new catalog of seasonal data that has changed most of the data in the Products table. You have a nonclustered index on the table that is now out of date. You need to bring it back up to date quickly. What can you do?

   a. Re-create the index using STATISTICS_NORECOMPUTE = ON.

   b. Re-create the index using DROP_EXISTING = ON.

   c. Drop the existing index manually and re-create it.

   d. Do nothing; SQL Server will bring the index back up to date automatically.

17. You have a table with customer information that is updated frequently. You need to create an index on this table, but you need to make sure there is enough room at every level of the index for the constant influx of new records. What can you do to accomplish this goal? (Choose all that apply.)

   a. Create the index with FILLFACTOR = 0.

   b. Create the index with FILLFACTOR = 70.

   c. Create the index with PAD_INDEX = ON.

   d. Create the index with PAD_INDEX = OFF.

18. You have a table that contains employee information. Human Resources frequently queries this table using a query similar to the following:

   SELECT FirstName, LastName, Address, Phone FROM Employees WHERE SSN = 'ssn'

   You need to create an index to speed up this query. Which type should you create?

   a. Create a clustered index on the SSN column.

   b. Create a nonclustered index on the SSN column.

   c. Create a full-text index on the SSN column.

19. You have a table that contains product data. The table has a column that contains the product ID, but because of some data entry problems, several of the products have been entered more than once. You need to create a clustered unique index on the Products table. How can you do this with duplicate data in the column?

   a. Create the index with ONERROR=CONTINUE.

   b. Create the index with IGNORE_DUP_KEY = ON.

   c. Create the index with IGNORE_DUP_KEY = OFF.

   d. You will have to manually remove the duplicate values before creating the index.

20. When monitoring SQL Server using Profiler, you find many table scans are being performed on the Orders table in your sales database. What should you do?

   a. Create a clustered or nonclustered index on the table.

   b. Create a clustered or nonclustered index with IGNORE_DUP_KEY = ON.

   c. Create a full-text index on the table.

   d. Do nothing; table scans are normal on heavily used tables.

■ Case Scenarios

Scenario 7-1: Creating an Index

Those pesky programmers. Now they want you to create an index on something in the MailingList table. Write a query using that index (include a WHERE clause). Prove the index was used by checking the actual execution plan displayed in the Query Editor. The programmers also want to test their application code interface to a retrieve the results of a full-text search. Follow the example steps in the article "Getting Started with Full-Text Search" in Books Online to establish this capability.

Scenario 7-2: Creating Indexes for the ITAssets Database

You continue to develop the ITAssets database introduced in Lesson 5. Now create a nonclustered index on the LName column in the Employees table in the ITAssets database.

Views

LESSON SKILL MATRIX

TECHNOLOGY SKILL	70-431 EXAM OBJECTIVE
Implement a view.	Foundational
Create an indexed view.	Foundational
Create an updateable view.	Foundational
Implement partitions.	Foundational

KEY TERMS

view: A filter through which one or more columns from one or more base tables are displayed.

indexed view: An arrangement of rows and column in which data from one or more columns from one or more base tables are materialized; that is, data is stored in a clustered indexed view.

partitioned view: A view whose base tables may be from one or more servers; a technique for implementing federated servers.

■ Using Views

THE BOTTOM LINE

A *view* can be queried just like a table. A view reveals data from one or more columns from one or more base tables, usually for limiting user data access to the totality of the base table. An indexed view calculates aggregated data and is used when the cost of materializing the view is less than the cost of aggregating data in a standard view.

Understanding Views

Microsoft describes a view as either a virtual table or a stored SELECT query, but you might prefer to think of it as similar to a filter. Views represent the data that is stored in one or more columns in one or more base tables. Of course, a view has more advantages than just looking at the data stored in a table. For instance, you may want to see only a subset of records in a large table, or you may want to see data from multiple tables in a single query. Both of these are good reasons to use a view.

Yet another great reason has to do with security. Permissions can be established on the view, which are independent of the base table(s) permissions. For example, you may wish to create a view called TelephoneDirectory on the PersonnelTable. This is good; you don't have to maintain the data—Human Resources does. You allow SELECT permissions on the view to the Public Role and, thus, everyone can look up telephone numbers without even knowing the PersonnelTable is the actual data source.

In Exercise 8-1, you will create a view that displays only those records in a table that have 398 as the first three characters of the phone number. Because you do not have many records in the MSSQL_Training database, you will use the AdventureWorks sample database.

CERTIFICATION READY?
Views come in several forms: simple, indexed, and partitioned. Understand the differences and where to use each.

EXERCISE 8-1 CREATING THE CONTACTS_IN_398 VIEW

1. Open **SQL Server Management Studio** by selecting it from the SQL Server 2005 group under Programs on your Start menu; connect with **Windows Authentication** if requested.

2. In Object Explorer, expand your **Server** → **Databases** → **AdventureWorks**; then right-click **Views**, and select **New View.**

3. In the Add Table dialog box, select **Contact (Person)**, and click **Add.**

4. Click **Close**, which opens the View Designer.

5. In the T-SQL syntax editor text box, under the column grid, enter the following:

   SELECT LastName, FirstName, Phone FROM Person.Contact WHERE (Phone LIKE '398%')

6. Click the **Execute** button (the red exclamation point) on the toolbar to test the query.

7. Choose **File** → **Save View** → **dbo.View_1.**

8. In the Choose Name dialog box, enter **Contacts_in_398**, and click **OK.**

9. To test the view, click the **New Query** button, and execute the following code:

   USE AdventureWorks

   SELECT * FROM Person.Contacts_in_398

10. To verify that the results are accurate, open a new query and execute the code used to create the view:

    USE AdventureWorks

    SELECT lastname, firstname, phone from Person.Contact WHERE phone LIKE '398%'

Notice that the view and the SELECT query in Exercise 3-9 returned the same results. But which was easier to query? The view, because it took less code. However, the requirements for your view may change over time, so you may need to modify the view to reflect those requirements. You can see the power and flexibility that a view can give you. But there is more: You can use views to modify your data, as well.

Other advantages: your client programmers can't see the base table details—privacy and confidentiality are assured; any complexities are hidden—the user or programmer sees only a simple tablelike structure; and security can be better managed, as the view is a completely separate object that can have its own unique permissions.

Modifying Data through a View

Not only can you use views to retrieve data, but you can also modify data through them—inserting, updating, and deleting records. If you decide to use views to make changes to your data, keep these points in mind:

- If you use a view to modify data, the modification can affect only one base table at a time. This means if a view presents data from two tables, you can write a statement that will update only one of those tables. If your statement tries to update both tables, you'll get an error message.

- You can't modify data in a view that uses aggregate functions. Aggregates are functions that return a summary value of some kind, such as SUM( ) or AVG( ). If you try to modify such a view, you'll get an error.

- You saw earlier that views don't necessarily present all the fields in a table; you may see only a few. If you try to insert a record into a view that doesn't show all fields, you could run into a problem. Some of the fields that aren't shown in the view may not accept null values, but you can't insert a value into those fields if they aren't represented in the view. Because you can't insert values in those fields, and they don't allow null values, your insert will fail. You can still use such a view for UPDATEs and DELETEs, however.

To overcome these limitations, you need to use INSTEAD OF triggers, which are discussed in Lesson 11.

To modify data through a view, you need to create a view that will allow you to modify data. You don't have one yet, because the view you've been working on thus far doesn't contain enough columns from any of its base tables to allow modifications; so, you need to create a simpler view, which you will do in Exercise 8-2.

EXERCISE 8-2 CREATING AN UPDATEABLE VIEW

1. Open **SQL Server Management Studio** by selecting it from the SQL Server 2005 group under Programs on your Start menu; connect with **Windows Authentication** if requested.

2. In Object Explorer, expand your **Server** → **Databases** → **AdventureWorks**; right-click **Views**, and select **New View.**

3. In the Add Table dialog box, select **Location (Production)**, and click **Add.**

4. Click **Close** to open the View Designer.

5. In the Transact-SQL syntax editor text box, enter the following:

   SELECT Name, CostRate, Availability

   FROM Production.Location

6. Choose **File** → **Save View** → **dbo.View_1**.

7. In the Choose Name box, enter **Update_Product_Location**.

8. To test your view, open a new query and execute the following code:

   USE AdventureWorks

   SELECT * FROM dbo.Update_Product_Location

9. Now that you're sure the view is working the way you want, you'll create a new record. Open a new SQL Server query, then enter and execute the following code:

   USE AdventureWorks

   INSERT dbo.Update_Product_Location

   VALUES ('Update Test Tool', 55.00, 10)

10. To verify that the record was inserted, and that you can see it in the view, execute the following code in the query window:

    USE AdventureWorks

    SELECT * FROM dbo.Update_Product_Location

    WHERE Name = 'Update Test Tool'

11. To view the data as it was inserted into the base table, enter and execute the following code in the query window:

    USE AdventureWorks

    SELECT * FROM Production.Location WHERE Name 5 'Update Test Tool'

When you look at the resultset from the dbo.Update_Product_Location view, you should see only three columns, all filled in. When you look at the base table, though, you'll see five columns, all filled in. When you modified the view, you inserted values for only the three columns that were available—SQL Server populated the remaining two columns in the base table because they have default constraints applied. The views you've created so far have returned fairly simple resultsets; in the real world, your views will be more complex and will require a lot of resources to return a resultset. To optimize this process, particularly when lots of aggregated values are needed, you may want to consider using indexed views.

Working with Indexed Views

The views you've created thus far in this lesson have returned simple resultsets that haven't taxed system resources. In reality, you'll use queries that require a lot of calculation and data manipulation; such complex queries can take a toll on your system resources and thus slow it. One way around this bottleneck is to use *indexed views*. Doing so does, however, slow data entry, as both the data itself and the materialized view must be updated.

As you saw in the previous lesson, an index is a list of all the values in a specific column of one of your tables that SQL Server can reference to speed up data queries. One type of index is called a clustered index; it physically arranges the data in a table so that the data conforms to the parameters of the index. A clustered index works a great deal like a dictionary, which physically arranges words so you can go right to them. To make data access faster on a complex view, you can create a clustered index on the view.

When you create a clustered index on a view, the resultset returned by the view is stored in the database the same way a table with a clustered index is stored, meaning the resultset of the view is stored as an entirely separate object in the database and doesn't have to be regenerated (or materialized) every time someone runs a SELECT query against it. However, don't jump in and start creating clustered indexes on all your views just yet, as you need to consider a few things first.

Using indexes on complex views has its benefits, the first being performance. Every time a view is queried, SQL Server must *materialize* the view. Materialization is the process of performing all the JOINs and calculations necessary to return a resultset to the user. If the view is complex (requiring a large number of calculations and JOINs), indexing it can speed up access because the resultset will never need to be materialized—it will exist in the database as a separate object, and SQL Server can call it whenever it's queried.

Another advantage to indexing a view is the way the Query Optimizer treats indexed views. The Query Optimizer is the component in SQL Server that analyzes your queries, compares them with available indexes, and decides which index will return a resultset the fastest. Once you've indexed a view, the Query Optimizer considers this view in all future queries no matter what you're querying. This means queries on other tables may benefit from the index you create on the view.

The disadvantage of indexing a view is the overhead it incurs on the system. First, indexed views take up disk space because they're stored as separate objects in the database that look just like tables with a clustered index. Because clustered indexes store the actual data rather than just a pointer to the data in the base tables, they require extra disk space. For example, if you create a view that displays the Firstname, Lastname, and Extension columns from an Employees table, and subsequently place a clustered index on that view, the FirstName, LastName, and Extension columns will be duplicated in the database.

Another consideration is the way the indexed view is updated. When you first create an indexed view, it's based on the data that exists at the time of the indexing. When you update the tables the view is based on, however, the indexed view is immediately updated to reflect the changes to the base table. This means if you create an indexed view on a table and then make changes to the records in that table, SQL Server will automatically update the view at the same time. So, if you have an indexed view on a table, the modifications are doubled, and so is the system overhead.

If you decide your database would benefit from an indexed view, the tables and view itself must adhere to a few restrictions:

- The ANSI_NULLS and QUOTED_IDENTIFIER options must be turned on when the view is created. To do this, use the ALTER DATABASE T-SQL statement:

```
SET ANSI_NULLS ON
SET QUOTED_IDENTIFIER ON
```

X REF

For a discussion of indexes, please refer to Lesson 7.

TAKE NOTE*

The Query Optimizer in Standard Edition ignores indexed views unless you add a query hint.

TAKE NOTE*

Access Creating Indexed Views in BOL for a complete list of restrictions.

- The view can't reference other views, only tables.
- Any user-defined function's data access property must be NO SQL, and external access property must be NO.
- All the tables referenced by the view must be in the same database as the view and must have the same owner as the view.
- The view must be created with the SCHEMABINDING option. This option prohibits the schema of the base tables from being changed (adding or dropping a column, for instance). If the tables can be changed, the indexed view may be rendered useless. To change the tables, you must first drop the indexed view.
- Any user-defined functions referenced in the view must have been created with the SCHEMABINDING option as well.
- All objects in the view must be referenced by their two-part names; for example, schema. object. No one-, three-, or four-part names are allowed.
- SQL Server has two types of functions: *deterministic* functions return the same value each time they're invoked with the same arguments; *nondeterministic* functions return different values when they're invoked with the same arguments. DATEADD( ), for example, returns the same result each time you execute it with the same arguments. GETDATE( ), however, returns a different value each time you execute it with the same arguments, making it nondeterministic. Any functions referenced in an indexed view must be deterministic.
- The SELECT statement that is used to create the view must follow these restrictions:
  - Column names must be explicitly stated in the SELECT statement; you can't use * or tablename.* to access columns.
  - You may not reference a column twice in the SELECT statement unless all references, or all but one reference, to the column are made in a complex expression. For example, the following is illegal:

    SELECT qty, orderid, qty

    However, the following is legal:

    SELECT qty, orderid, SUM(qty)

- You may not use a derived table that comes from using a SELECT statement encased in parentheses in the FROM clause of a SELECT statement.
- You can't use ROWSET, UNION, TOP, ORDER BY, DISTINCT, COUNT(*), COMPUTE, or COMPUTE BY.
- Subqueries and outer or self JOINs can't be used.
- The AVG( ), MAX( ), MIN( ), STDEV( ), STDEVP( ), VAR( ), and VARP( ) aggregate functions aren't allowed in the SELECT statement. If you need the functionality they provide, consider replacing them with either SUM( ) or COUNT_BIG( ).
- A SUM( ) that references a nullable expression isn't allowed.
- A Common Language Specification (CLS) user-defined function can appear only in the SELECT list of the view; it can't be used in WHERE or JOIN clauses.
- CONTAINS and FREETEXT aren't allowed in the SELECT statement.
- If you use GROUP BY, you can't use HAVING, ROLLUP, or CUBE; and you must use COUNT_ BIG( ) in the select list.

All the aggregate and string functions in SQL Server 2005 are considered deterministic.

That is an abundance of restrictions, but each one is necessary to keep the indexed view functioning. With all the considerations out of the way, you can create your own indexed view in Exercise 8-3.

EXERCISE 8-3 CREATING AN INDEXED VIEW

1. Open **SQL Server Management Studio;** connect using **Windows Authentication** if requested.
2. Click the **New Query** button, and select **New SQL Server Query**. Connect using **Windows Authentication** if requested.
3. Create a view similar to dbo.Contacts_in_398 but without the XML column and ORDER BY and TOP clauses. Add the **ContactID** field and **SCHEMABINDING** so that the view can be indexed on the ContactID field, which is unique. To do all this, enter and execute the following code:

   SET QUOTED_IDENTIFIER ON

   GO

   CREATE VIEW [Person].[Indexed_Contacts_in_398] WITH SCHEMABINDING

   AS

   SELECT c.ContactID, title as [Title], lastname AS

   [Last Name], firstname as [First Name], phone AS [Phone Number], c3.cardtype as [Card Type] FROM Person.Contact c JOIN Sales.ContactCreditCard c2 ON c.ContactID = c2.ContactID JOIN Sales.CreditCard c3 ON c2.CreditCardID = c3.CreditCardID WHERE phone LIKE '398%'

4. To test the Person.Indexed_Contacts_in_398 view, enter and execute the following query:

   USE [AdventureWorks]

   SELECT * FROM Person.Indexed_Contacts_in_398

5. Now you'll create an index on the ContactID column, because it's unique. To do that, open a new query window and execute this code:

   USE [AdventureWorks]

   CREATE UNIQUE CLUSTERED INDEX CI_Indexed_View

   ON Person.Indexed_Contacts_in_398(ContactID)

6. To make sure your index has been created, right-click **Views** under **AdventureWorks** in Object Explorer, and click **Refresh.**
7. Next, expand **Views → Person.Indexed_Contacts_in_398 → Indexes**. You should see the new CI_Indexed_View index listed.
8. To test the indexed view, execute this code:

   USE [AdventureWorks]

   SELECT * FROM Person.Indexed_Contacts_in_398

This query obviously isn't too complex, but it does give a simple method for demonstrating the mechanics of creating a clustered index on a view. In the real world, this process will be much more complex, so weigh the benefits carefully before implementing this solution.

Making a Partitioned View

A *partitioned view* displays horizontally divided data from a set of member tables across one or more servers, making the data appear as it is from one table. The partitioned view uses the UNION ALL clause to combine the results of SELECT statements on all the member tables in a single resultset. SQL Server distinguishes between:

- Local partitioned views
- Distributed partitioned views

In a local partitioned view, all participating tables and the view itself reside on the same instance of SQL Server. The preferred method for partitioning data locally is by using partitioned tables—not partitioned views.

In a distributed partitioned view, at least one of the participating tables resides on a different (remote) server.

CERTIFICATION READY?
Review the differences between a partitioned table and a view. When should you use one over the other?

Because each base table can be scanned in parallel, performance can be enhanced. Since the base tables are distributed, rebuilding indexes and backing up tables can each be quicker.

Partitioned views implement a federation of database servers. Federated servers are each administered independently but cooperate to share the processing load of a total system.

SKILL SUMMARY

IN THIS LESSON YOU LEARNED:

You learned your view doesn't actually contain any data—it's just a filter through which you see the data in underlying tables. After that, you actually created a simple view based on a single table.

Next you learned how to use a view to modify data. Don't forget that modifying data through a view has a few caveats:

- You can't modify more than one table at a time through a view.

- If your view is based on aggregate functions, you can't use it to modify data.

- If your view is based on a table that contains fields that don't allow null values, yet your view doesn't display those fields, then you won't be able to insert new data. You can, however, update and delete data.

Then you discovered you can index views. Doing so is particularly useful if your view is complex; but be aware indexing can take a while to materialize. If you create an index on a view, SQL Server won't need to populate the view every time someone queries it because the resultset is stored in the database the same way a table with a clustered index is stored. Just remember that creating and maintaining indexed views has many caveats, so be absolutely sure you need them, and check the restrictions listed in Books Online.

For the certification examination:

- Understand views. It sounds basic but you should know what views are. Views do not actually contain data; they are used to display the data stored in one or more columns in one or more base tables in a different format with different security controls.

- Know how to index a view. Views can be indexed to speed up query times, but they have a large number of restrictions. Review the list of considerations for indexing a view and make sure you are familiar with them.

- Know how to make an updateable view. You can update the values in an underlying table used to create a view, but you need to consider a few issues. If you use a view to modify data, the modification can affect only one base table at a time. You can't modify data in a view that uses aggregate functions such as SUM( ) or AVG( ). If you try to insert a record into a view that doesn't show all fields, and if any of those missing fields do not accept null values, the insert will fail. You can still use such a view for UPDATEs and DELETEs, though.

■ Knowledge Assessment

Multiple Choice

Circle the letter or letters that correspond to the best answer or answers.

1. You need to create a clustered index on a view. Which functions can be used inside the view definition? (Choose all that apply.)
   a. AVG( )
   b. RAND( )
   c. RAND(1000)
   d. GETDATE( )

Table 8-1

Table Layout

CustID	FirstName	LastName	Address	City	State	ZipCode	Phone
Datatype: int, identity	Datatype: varchar(20)	Datatype: varchar(20)	Datatype: varchar(50)	Datatype: varchar(20)	Datatype: char(2)	Datatype: char(5)	Datatype: char(10)
1	Bob	Jones	500 N. Main	Fresno	CA	94905	1115551212
2	Sally	Smith	205 E. 3rd	Chicago	IL	65201	2225551212
3	Andy	Thompson	718 Oak	Portland	OR	98716	3335551212

2. In Table 8-1, your users need an easy way to display only the first name, last name, and phone number for customers in the 222 area code. What should you have them do?

   a. Use this query on the table:

      SELECT * FROM customers WHERE phone LIKE '222%'

   b. Use this query on the table:

      SELECT firstname, lastname, phone FROM customers
      WHERE phone like '222%'

   c. Create a view based on the table using this query:

      SELECT * FROM customers WHERE phone LIKE '222%'

      Then have users query the view.

   d. Create a view based on the table using this query:

      SELECT firstname, lastname, phone FROM customers
      WHERE phone like '222%'

      Then have users query the view.

3. You need to create a new view, and you are planning on using this code:

   CREATE VIEW Contacts_in_222 AS SELECT c.ContactID, title as [Title], lastname as [Last Name], firstname as [First Name], phone as [Phone Number], c3.cardtype as [Card Type] FROM Person.Contact c JOIN Sales.ContactCreditCard c2 on c.ContactID = c2.ContactID JOIN Sales.CreditCard c3 on c2.CreditCardID = c3.CreditCardID WHERE phone LIKE '222%'

   You may need to index this view later to improve performance. What changes, if any, do you need to make to this code to be able to index the view later?

   a. No changes are necessary.

   b. Change the code to this:

      CREATE VIEW Contacts_in_222 WITH SCHEMABINDING AS SELECT c.ContactID, title as [Title], lastname as [Last Name], firstname as [First Name], phone as [Phone Number], c3.cardtype as [Card Type] FROM Person.Contact c JOIN Sales.ContactCreditCard c2 on c.ContactID = c2.ContactID JOIN Sales.CreditCard c3 on c2.CreditCardID = c3.CreditCardID WHERE phone LIKE '222%'

   c. Change the code to this:

      CREATE VIEW Contacts_in_222 WITH INDEXABLE AS SELECT c.ContactID, title as [Title], lastname as [Last Name], firstname as [First Name], phone as [Phone Number], c3.cardtype as [Card Type] FROM Person.Contact c JOIN Sales.ContactCreditCard c2 on c.ContactID = c2.ContactID JOIN Sales.CreditCard c3 on c2.CreditCardID = c3.CreditCardID WHERE phone LIKE '222%'

d. Change the code to this:

```
CREATE VIEW Contacts_in_222 WITH TABLEBINDING AS SELECT c.ContactID, title as
[Title], lastname as [Last Name], firstname as [First Name], phone as [Phone Num-
ber], c3.cardtype as [Card Type] FROM Person.Contact c JOIN Sales.ContactCredit-
Card c2 on c.ContactID 5 c2.ContactID JOIN Sales.CreditCard c3 on c2.CreditCardID
5 c3.CreditCardID WHERE phone LIKE '222%'
```

4. You need to create a new view, and you are planning on using this code:

```
CREATE VIEW Contacts_in_222 WITH SCHEMABINDING AS SELECT c.ContactID, title as
[Title], lastname as [Last Name], firstname as [First Name], phone as [Phone Number],
c3.* FROM Person.Contact c JOIN Sales.ContactCreditCard c2 on c.ContactID = c2.ContactID
JOIN Sales.CreditCard c3 on c2.CreditCardID = c3.CreditCardID WHERE phone LIKE '222%'
```

You may need to index this view later to improve performance. What changes, if any, do you need to make to this code to be able to index the view later?

a. No changes are necessary.

b. Change the code to this:

```
CREATE VIEW Contacts_in_222 WITH SCHEMABINDING, SELECTALL AS SELECT
c.ContactID, title as [Title], lastname as [Last Name], firstname as [First Name],
phone as [Phone Number], c3.* FROM Person.Contact c JOIN Sales.ContactCredit-
Card c2 on c.ContactID = c2.ContactID JOIN Sales.CreditCard c3 on c2.CreditCardID
= c3.CreditCardID WHERE phone LIKE '222%'
```

c. Change the code to this:

```
CREATE VIEW Contacts_in_222 WITH SCHEMABINDING AS SELECT c.ContactID,
title as [Title], lastname as [Last Name], firstname as [First Name], phone as
[Phone Number], c3.[*] FROM Person.Contact c JOIN Sales.ContactCreditCard c2
on c.ContactID = c2.ContactID JOIN Sales.CreditCard c3 on c2.CreditCardID =
c3.CreditCardID WHERE phone LIKE '222%'
```

d. Change the code to this:

```
CREATE VIEW Contacts_in_222 WITH SCHEMABINDING AS SELECT c.ContactID, title
as [Title], lastname as [Last Name], firstname as [First Name], phone as [Phone
Number], c3.CreditCardType as [Card Type] FROM Person.Contact c JOIN Sales.
ContactCreditCard c2 on c.ContactID = c2.ContactID JOIN Sales.CreditCard c3 on
c2.CreditCardID = c3.CreditCardID WHERE phone LIKE '222%'
```

Table 8-2

Table Definition

EmpID	FirstName	LastName	Address	City	State	ZipCode	Phone	SSN	Pay
Datatype: int, identity not nullable	Datatype: varchar(20) not nullable	Datatype: varchar(20) not nullable	Datatype: varchar(50) not nullable	Datatype: varchar(20) not nullable	Datatype: char(2) not nullable	Datatype: char(5) not nullable	Datatype: char(10) not nullable	Datatype: char(9) not nullable	Datatype: Money nullable
1	John	Jackson	20 N. 2nd	Oakland	CA	94905	1115551212	111223333	50,000.00
2	Jane	Samuels	37 S. Elm	Springfield	IL	65201	2225551212	444556666	65,000.00
3	Tom	Johnson	256 Park	Quahog	RI	05102	3335551212	777889999	45,000.00

5. Using the data from Table 8-2, you need to create a view that allows users to add new employees. You want them to be able to add all the information except the pay rate. What changes do you need to make to the table to accomplish this?

a. Add a default constraint to the Pay column with a value of 0.00.

b. Change the Pay column so it is not nullable, and add a default constraint with a value of 0.00.

      c. Change all the columns to nullable.

      d. Do nothing; the table is fine as is.

6. Using the data from Table 8-2, you need to create a view that allows users to update the FirstName, LastName, Phone, and Pay columns. The code to create the view looks like this:

   ```
   CREATE VIEW Update_Pay WITH SCHEMABINDING AS SELECT FirstName, LastName,
   Phone, Pay FROM HumanResources.Employees
   ```

   Users complain they cannot use the new view to add new employees. Why does this fail?

   a. Some columns in the table are not nullable, so the view can't be used to insert new records.

   b. The EmpID column was not included in the view, so the view can't be used to insert new records.

   c. WITH SCHEMABINDING can't be used on an updateable view, so the view can't be used to insert new records.

   d. Columns with the money datatype, such as the Pay column, can't be used in updateable views, so the view can't be used to insert new records.

7. You have created a view that your users need to use to update records in one of your tables. The code to create the view looks like this:

   ```
   CREATE VIEW ProductCost WITH SCHEMABINDING AS SELECT ProdID, Cost, Qty,
   SUM(qty * cost) FROM Products
   ```

   What do you need to change on this view to make it updateable?

   a. Nothing, the view is updateable as is.

   b. Change the code to look like this:

   ```
   CREATE VIEW ProductCost AS SELECT ProdID, Cost, Qty, SUM(qty * cost) FROM
   Products
   ```

   c. Change the code to look like this:

   ```
   CREATE VIEW ProductCost WITH ALLOWAGREGATES AS

   SELECT ProdID, Cost, Qty, SUM(qty * cost) FROM Products
   ```

   d. Change the code to look like this:

   ```
   CREATE VIEW ProductCost WITH SCHEMABINDING AS SELECT ProdID, Cost, Qty FROM
   Products
   ```

8. You have created a view with the following code:

   ```
   CREATE VIEW Update_Pay WITH SCHEMABINDING AS SELECT FirstName, LastName,
   Phone, Pay FROM HumanResources.dbo.Employees
   ```

   What changes do you need to make to this code to make this view indexable?

   a. No changes are needed; the view is already indexable.

   b. Change the code to look like this:

   ```
   CREATE VIEW Update_Pay WITH SCHEMABINDING AS SELECT FirstName, LastName,
   Phone, Pay FROM HumanResources.dbo.Employees
   ```

   c. Change the code to look like this:

   ```
   CREATE VIEW Update_Pay WITH SCHEMABINDING AS SELECT FirstName, LastName,
   Phone, Pay FROM HumanResources.dbo.Employees
   ```

   d. Change the code to look like this:

   ```
   CREATE VIEW Update_Pay AS SELECT FirstName, LastName, Phone, Pay FROM
   HumanResources.Employees
   ```

9. You have created a view with the following code:

   ```
   CREATE VIEW Get_Pay WITH SCHEMABINDING AS SELECT FirstName, LastName, Phone,
   Pay, GetDate() FROM HumanResources.Employees
   ```

What changes do you need to make to this code to make this view indexable?

a. Change the code to look like this:

```
CREATE VIEW Get_Pay WITH SCHEMABINDING AS SELECT FirstName, LastName,
Phone, Pay FROM HumanResources.Employees
```

b. Change the code to look like this:

```
CREATE VIEW Get_Pay AS SELECT FirstName, LastName, Phone, Pay, GetDate() FROM
HumanResources.Employees
```

c. Change the code to look like this:

```
CREATE VIEW Get_Pay WITH SCHEMABINDING AS SELECT FirstName, LastName,
Phone, Pay, GetDate() FROM HumanResources.dbo.Employees
```

d. No changes are needed; the view is already indexable.

■ Case Scenarios

Scenario 8-1: Creating a View

The Joint Application Design team continues to need your support. This time they need a view. Use AdventureWorks. Create a view on the Person.Contact table that lists the first and last name of the contact, plus the telephone number.

Scenario 8-2: Creating an ITAssets View

Use ITAssets. Create a view that shows the hostname assigned to each person. Assign permissions to the view limiting it to read-only for everyone.

9 LESSON

Constraints

LESSON SKILL MATRIX

TECHNOLOGY SKILL	70-431 EXAM OBJECTIVE
Implement constraints.	Foundational
Specify the scope of a constraint.	Foundational
Create a new constraint.	Foundational

KEY TERMS

check constraint: Specifies data values that are acceptable in a column; it can be based on columns in other tables or columns in the same table.

default constraint: Specifies the value for the column when an INSERT statement does not provide a value.

foreign key constraint: Specifies the data values that are acceptable to update, based on values in another column or table.

NULL: Specifies whether the column value may be void or the column must have a value (NOT NULL).

primary key constraint: Identifies each row uniquely. Null values are not allowed.

rule: A constraint defined once and applied to potentially many tables; not encouraged for use in SQL Server 2005.

trigger: A stored procedure implemented to fire automatically during an insert, update, and/or delete action against a table.

unique constraint: Prevents duplication of alternative (not primary key) values in columns. Null values are allowed.

▪ Restricting the Data

THE BOTTOM LINE

When you first create a table, it's nearly wide open to your users. It's true they can't violate datatype restrictions by entering characters in an int type field and the like, but that is really the only restriction. It's safe to say you probably want more restrictions than that. For example, you probably don't want your users to enter "XZ" for a state abbreviation in a State field (because "XZ" isn't a valid abbreviation), and you don't want them entering numbers for someone's first name. You also don't want a male reported as pregnant, or a female listed as dead before she was born. Therefore, you need to restrict what your users can enter in your fields, and you do this by using constraints.

Introducing Constraints

SQL Server supports:

- **Domain Integrity:** A domain refers to a column in a table. Domain integrity includes datatypes, *rules*, and defaults, constraints, *triggers*, and XML schema as applied to a column.

CERTIFICATION READY?
Be sure to understand the different constraints and when to apply them. Remember, you can still use rules but they are no longer recommended. Rules have the advantage of being defined once and used many times on multiple tables. See BOL Rules for more details.

- **Entity Integrity:** Entity integrity applies to rows and includes rules, *NULLs*, defaults, constraints, and triggers.
- **Referential Integrity:** Referential integrity applies between tables or columns of the same table, and includes constraints and triggers.

USING CHECK CONSTRAINTS

A *check constraint* is a T-SQL statement that is linked to a field. Check constraints restrict the data that is accepted in the field even if the data is of the correct datatype. For example, the Zip field in the Customers table is the nchar datatype, which means it could technically accept letters. This can be a problem, because in the United States no zip codes contain letters (zip codes with letters are generally referred to as postal codes), so you need to keep users from entering letters in the Zip field. In Exercise 9-1, you will create the check constraint that will accomplish this.

 EXERCISE 9-1 CREATING THE VALID ZIP CODE CONSTRAINT

1. In Object Explorer, expand the **MSSQL_Training** database → **Tables** → **dbo.Customers**.
2. Right-click **Constraints**, and click **New Constraint**.
3. In the Check Constraint dialog box, enter **CK_Zip** in the (Name) text box.
4. In the Description text box, enter **Check** for valid zip codes.
5. To create a constraint that will accept only five characters that can be 0 through 9, enter the following code in the Expression text box:

   (zip like '[0-9][0-9][0-9][0-9][0-9]')
6. Click **Close**.
7. Click the **Save** button at the top left of the toolbar.
8. Close the **Table Designer** (which was opened when you started to create the constraint).

X REF

For a discussion about INSERT statements, please refer to Lesson 13.

To test the new constraint you just created, let's enter some new records into the table by using the INSERT statement, which you will learn more about in Lesson 13. You will test your constraint in Exercise 9-2.

EXERCISE 9-2 TESTING YOUR CONSTRAINT

1. In SQL Server Management Studio, click the **New Query** button.
2. Enter the following code into the query window:

   USE MSSQL_Training

   INSERT customers VALUES ('Gary', 'McKee', '111 Main', 'Palm Springs', 'CA', '94312', '7605551212')
3. Click the **Execute** button just above the query window to execute the query, and notice the successful results.
4. To see the new record, click the **New Query** button and execute the following code:

   SELECT * FROM Customers
5. Notice that the record now exists with a CustID of 1 (because of the identity property discussed earlier, which automatically added the number for you).
6. To test the check constraint by adding characters in the Zip field, click the **New Query** button and execute the following code (note the letters in the Zip field):

   USE MSSQL_Training

   INSERT customers VALUES ('Amanda', 'Smith', '817 3rd', 'Chicago', 'IL', 'AAB1C', '8015551212')
7. Notice in the results pane that the query violated a constraint, and so failed.

You may have used *rules* in the past to do the work of check constraints. Rules are slated to be removed from future versions of SQL Server, so you should convert all your existing rules to check constraints.

It's easy to see how the check constraint can be a powerful ally against entering wrong data; all you need to do is figure out what data belongs in your column and create a constraint instructing SQL Server not to accept anything else. Check constraints serve no purpose if your users simply forget to enter data in a column, however—that is why default constraints exist.

USING DEFAULT CONSTRAINTS

If users leave fields blank by not including them in the INSERT or UPDATE statement that they use to add or modify a record, *default constraints* fill in those fields. This can be a big timesaver in a data-entry department—if you use it correctly.

For example, suppose most of your clientele live in California and your data-entry people must enter "CA" for every new customer they enter. That may not seem like much work, but if you have a sizable customer base, those two characters can add up to a lot of typing. By using a default constraint, your users can leave the State field intentionally blank, and SQL Server will fill it in.

You can't use default constraints in a few places, though:

- Defaults can't be used on columns with the timestamp datatype.
- Defaults can't be used on IDENTITY columns. IDENTITY columns contain a number that is automatically incremented with each new record.
- Defaults can't be used on columns with the ROWGUIDCOL property set. ROWGUIDCOL indicates that the column is a globally unique identifier (GUID) column for the table.

To demonstrate the capabilities of default constraints, let's create one on the Customers table in Exercise 9-3.

 EXERCISE 9-3 CREATING A DEFAULT CONSTRAINT

1. Open **SQL Server Management Studio**. In Object Explorer, expand **Server → Databases → MSSQL_Training → Tables → dbo.Customers → Columns**.
2. Right-click the **State** column, and click **Modify**.
3. In the bottom half of the screen, in the Default Value or Binding text box, type **'CA'** (with single quote marks).
4. Click the **Save** button, and exit the Table Designer.
5. To test the default, click the **New Query** button in SQL Server Management Studio. Select **New SQL Server Query**; connect with **Windows Authentication** if requested.
6. Enter and execute the following code:

   USE MSSQL_Training

   INSERT customers (fname, lname, address, city, zip, phone) VALUES ('Tom', 'Smith', '609 Georgia', 'Fresno', '33405', '5105551212')
7. To verify that CA was entered in the State field, select **Query → New Query with Current Connection**.
8. Enter and execute the following code:

   SELECT * FROM customers
9. Notice that the Tom Smith record has CA in the State field.

 **ANOTHER WAY**

You may leave off the column names if you supply values in the correct column order and number. In this case, insert the keyword DEFAULT between Fresno and 33405.

USING UNIQUE CONSTRAINTS

You should use a ***unique constraint*** when you need to ensure that no duplicate values can be added to a field. A bad example of a field that might require a unique constraint is a Social Security number field, because duplicates and alpha characters both legitimately exist. Good candidates include employee badge number and parking space assignments.

Because you don't have a perfect candidate for a unique constraint in your tables, you'll come as close as you can by creating a unique constraint on the Phone field in Exercise 9-4.

EXERCISE 9-4 CREATING A UNIQUE CONSTRAINT

1. In SQL Server Management Studio, click the **New Query** button.
2. Select **MSSQL_Training** in the database drop-down list on the toolbar.
3. Enter and execute the following code:

   ALTER TABLE customers

   ADD CONSTRAINT CK_Phone UNIQUE (Phone)
4. To test your new constraint, click the **New Query** button, and execute the following code to add a new record to the Customers table:

   USE MSSQL_Training

   INSERT customers VALUES ('Shane', 'Travis', '806 Star', 'Phoenix', 'AZ', '85202', '6021112222')
5. Click the **New Query** button, and try entering another customer with the same phone number by entering and executing the following:

   USE MSSQL_Training

   INSERT customers VALUES ('Janet', 'McBroom', '5403 Western', 'Tempe', 'AZ', '85103', '6021112222')
6. Notice that this fails, with a message that the UNIQUE_KEY constraint was violated by the duplicate phone number.

You now know how to protect the data that is entered in your tables by enforcing domain and entity integrity, but you still have one more area of integrity to consider. You need to know how to protect related data that is stored in separate tables by enforcing referential integrity

Introducing Primary and Foreign Keys

A ***primary key constraint*** uses one or more columns in a table. When using two or more columns, it's called a *composite primary key*. The primary key uniquely identifies a row in a table. Some considerations include:

* You may have but one primary key per table.
* The value of the column, or composite of two or more columns, is ensured to be unique. A duplicate value will be denied by the RDBMS.
* Null values are not allowed.

Primary keys can be defined in the CREATE TABLE or ALTER TABLE statements. Here's an example from a CREATE TABLE statement:

```
CONSTRAINT [PK_Department_DepartmentID] PRIMARY KEY CLUSTERED
([DepartmentID] ASC) WITH (IGNORE_DUP_KEY = OFF) ON [PRIMARY]
```

A foreign key is a column or combination of columns that is used to establish and enforce a link between the data in two tables or columns in one table. Some considerations include:

* The ***foreign key*** must reference a primary key or unique constraint.
* A user must have REFERENCES permission on a referenced table.

- A foreign key constraint that uses only the REFERENCES clause without the FOREIGN KEY clause refers to a column in the same table.
- Foreign keys do not create indexes automatically.
- The datatype of the foreign key and the datatype of the column to which it points must match. The names do not need to match.
- You may declare multiple foreign keys in a single table.

Foreign keys can be defined in the CREATE TABLE or ALTER TABLE statements. Here's an example using the ALTER TABLE statement:

```
ALTER TABLE [Sales].[SalesOrderHeader] WITH CHECK ADD CONSTRAINT
[FK_SalesOrderHeader_Customer_CustomerID] FOREIGN KEY ([CustomerID])
REFERENCES [Sales].[Customer] ([CustomerID])
```

The foreign key constraint includes a CASCADE option that allows any change to a column value that defines a UNIQUE or PRIMARY KEY constraint to propagate the change to any foreign key values that reference it. This is called *cascading referential integrity*.

The REFERENCES clause of the CREATE TABLE or ALTER TABLE statements supports ON DELETE and ON UPDATE clauses. These clauses allow you to specify the behavior of the cascading referential integrity. Possible options include NO ACTION (the default), CASCADE, SET NULL, and SET DEFAULT.

SKILL SUMMARY

IN THIS LESSON YOU LEARNED:

You learned that tables are wide open to just about any kind of data when they're first created. The only restriction is that users can't violate the datatype of an attribute; other than that, the table will accept anything, including the illogical. Guard against a data-entry person making an appointment for a date in the past, for example.

To restrict the data your users can enter in a text box in the client application, you learned to create default, check, and unique constraints.

Primary key and unique constraints guard against duplicate data entry.

For the certification examination:

- Know your constraints. Understand the constraints discussed in this lesson. Check constraints restrict the data a user is allowed to enter in a column, even through the datatype does not restrict the data. Default constraints fill in data for you automatically when you do not specify a value while inserting a new record. Unique constraints prevent users from accidentally inserting repetitive values.

■ Knowledge Assessment

Multiple Choice

Circle the letter or letters that correspond to the best answer or answers.

1. You need to make sure the users entering new employee names do not accidentally enter the same employee twice. What can you do?
    a. Create a unique constraint on the FirstName and LastName fields.
    b. Create a unique constraint on the EmpID field.
    c. Create a unique constraint on the SSN field.
    d. Create a unique constraint on the phone field.
    e. Do nothing; nothing is unique.

Table 9-1

Table Layout

EMPID	FIRSTNAME	LASTNAME	ADDRESS	CITY	STATE	ZIPCODE	PHONE	SSN	PAY
Datatype: int, identity not nullable	Datatype: varchar(20) not nullable	Datatype: varchar(20) not nullable	Datatype: varchar(50) not nullable	Datatype: varchar(20) not nullable	Datatype: char(2) not nullable	Datatype: char(5) not nullable	Datatype: char(10) not nullable	Datatype: char(9) not nullable	Datatype: Money nullable
1	John	Jackson	20 N. 2nd	Oakland	CA	94905	1115551212	111223333	50,000.00
2	Jane	Samuels	37 S. Elm	Springfield	IL	65201	2225551212	444556666	65,000.00
3	Tom	Johnson	256 Park	Quahog	RI	05102	3335551212	777889999	45,000.00

Table 9-2

Table Specification

CUSTID	FIRSTNAME	LASTNAME	ADDRESS	CITY	STATE	ZIPCODE	PHONE
Datatype: int, identity	Datatype: varchar(20)	Datatype: varchar(20)	Datatype: varchar(50)	Datatype: varchar(20)	Datatype: char(2)	Datatype: char(5)	Datatype: char(10)
1	Bob	Jones	500 N. Main	Fresno	CA	94905	1115551212
2	Sally	Smith	205 E. 3rd	Chicago	IL	65201	2225551212
3	Andy	Thompson	718 Oak	Portland	OR	98716	3335551212

2. You have data in your database that looks like Table 9-2. How can you prevent your users from entering invalid state abbreviations (like XZ) in the State field?
   a. Create a default constraint.
   b. Create a unique constraint.
   c. Create a check constraint.
   d. There is no way to prevent this.

■ Case Scenarios

Scenario 9-1: Creating a Constraint

Imagine a client database for a governmental organization—say, Workforce Development Division of your local county. As a classroom exercise, write constraints that will prevent a counselor from entering:

- A death date preceding a birth date.
- A pregnancy flag for a male.
- Authority for welfare to minors granted to senior citizens.
- Authority for family subsistence payments for wealthy residents.
- Aid to unmarried females when a boyfriend or father shares expenses.

10 LESSON

Stored Procedures

LESSON SKILL MATRIX

TECHNOLOGY SKILL	70-431 EXAM OBJECTIVE
Implement stored procedures.	Foundational
Create a stored procedure.	Foundational
Recompile a stored procedure.	Foundational

KEY TERMS

cache: An allocated section of system memory (RAM); commonly used to hold the compiled code of a stored procedure for fast, efficient processing.

compile: The act of converting high-level code (such as T-SQL) to machine language code by the Query Optimizer.

recompile: Conditions always change; when statistics become out of date, a recompile may improve performance

by giving the Query Optimizer a chance to reoptimize the execution plan.

stored procedure: A precompiled collection of Transact-SQL or managed code statements that are stored under a name and processed as a unit.

◼ Using Stored Procedures

THE BOTTOM LINE

Stored procedures in SQL Server are similar to the procedures you write in other programming languages. Specifically, a *stored procedure* is a predefined batch of code that is stored as an object in the database to do work.

Introducing Stored Procedures

A stored procedure has the ability to accept parameters, but it doesn't necessarily need to use parameters. Within a stored procedure, you can use almost all T-SQL statements, except another CREATE PROCEDURE statement.

SQL Server 2005 supports several types of procedures:

- System stored procedures that start with an "sp_" (e.g., sp_help) and are stored in the Master and MSDB databases
- User stored procedures that can be written with either Transact-SQL or common language runtime code
- Extended stored procedures that historically started with an "xp_" and are implemented as dynamic linked libraries

Microsoft supplies a large number of stored procedures for your use. How many? Work through Exercise 10-1 to find the answer.

 EXERCISE 10-1 NUMBER OF SQL SERVER INCLUDED STORED PROCEDURES

1. Start SQL Server Management Studio.
2. Click the **plus (+) sign** next to Databases.
3. Click the **plus (+) sign** next to Master.
4. Click the **plus (+) sign** next to Stored Procedures.
5. Click the **plus (+) sign** next to System Stored Procedures.
6. Scroll down the list to appreciate how many stored procedures Microsoft makes available to you.
7. Do the same thing for the MSDB database.
8. Execute this query just for fun:

   USE Master

   SELECT [Name] FROM Sys.SysObjects

   WHERE [Name] LIKE 'sp_%' ORDER BY [Name]

The resultset is larger than 1,300 rows of objects named sp_*something*! What do all of these stored procedures accomplish? Look in Books Online for an explanation. Follow the steps of Exercise 10-2.

 EXERCISE 10-2 EXAMINING BOOKS ONLINE FOR SP EXPLANATIONS

1. Launch **Books Online**.
2. Click the **search icon** (it looks like a magnifying glass).
3. Enter sp_Help in the search field and press **Enter**.
4. Double left-click the **sp_help** (Transact-SQL) article summary in Local Help.
5. Press the **Sync with Table of Contents** button (to the left of Ask a Question).
6. Scroll through the list in the Contents pane. Stop every once in a while, double-click an article, and discover its functionality.

You should familiarize yourself with at least this list:

- sp_Add_Job
- sp_DBOption
- sp_ExecuteSQL
- sp_Help
- sp_HelpDB
- sp_Configure
- sp_Who
- sp_Xml_PrepareDocument
- xp_CmdShell
- xp_SendMail

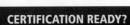
CERTIFICATION READY?
Your test might refer to one specific stored procedure and ask you to identify the correct option. Look through enough of these to grasp the consistent pattern, if not the specifics of each. For example: Does it require single quotes? Does it require parentheses?

Exercise 10-3 shows you what a stored procedure looks like.

 EXERCISE 10-3 UNDERSTANDING SP_HELPTEXT

1. Go to the Query Editor by clicking the **New Query** button on the upper left of Management Studio.
2. Click **Connect**.

3. In your query window, type the following code:

sp_HelpText sp_HelpText

4. Left-click in the results pane to set the focus on this area.
5. Press **Ctrl-a** to select all of the text.
6. Press **Ctrl-c** to copy the text to the clipboard.
7. Press **Ctrl-n** to open a new query window.
8. Press **Ctrl-v** to paste the text in the blank query window.
9. Scroll to the top of the window to see the beginning of the code.

➕ MORE INFORMATION

You will use a system stored procedure to look at the code that created this system stored procedure. Assure that the **Master Database** is selected in the context window to the left of the Execute button; assure you have selected **Results to Text**, and then execute this command.

Examine this code. It shows the use of the CREATE PROC, or CREATE PROCEDURE, keywords, together with a name of your choice. In this example, the programmer chose the sys schema and sp_helptext object name.

Lines 4 and 5 declare two parameter values with their datatype. The @ symbol designates a local scope variable. The @objname now contains the text string, sp_HelpText, that you passed into the stored procedure.

Lines 10 through 29 declare some local variables used mostly for manipulating the output. Text in green represents comments the author provided to help us understand code flow and intent.

Line 35 creates a temporary table with two attributes: a line identifier and a line of text storage. Continue scrolling through the code. Examine the T-SQL code and the logic applied. Line 82 retrieves the object's text stored in a metadata table (sys.syscomments).

You can create your own stored procedures, as demonstrated in Exercise 10-4.

EXERCISE 10-4 CREATING YOUR OWN STORED PROCEDURE USING T-SQL

1. Click the **plus (+) sign** next to AdventureWorks.
2. Click the **plus (+) sign** next to Programmability.
3. Right-click **Stored Procedures** and highlight to select the **New Stored Procedure** menu choice. This opens a new query window populated with a stored procedure template.
4. Use the template. Substitute the following T-SQL code to create a new procedure in the AdventureWorks database:

CREATE PROCEDURE up_Production.LargeListPrices

AS BEGIN

SELECT Name, ListPrice FROM Production.Product WHERE ListPrice > (SELECT avg(ListPrice) FROM Production.Product)

END

GO

EXERCISE 10-5 EXECUTING A STORED PROCEDURE

1. Open your **Query Editor**.
2. Enter the following code:

Exec Production.LargeListPrices

3. Execute.

You create stored procedures by using the CREATE PROCEDURE syntax:

```
CREATE { PROC | PROCEDURE }
[schema_name.] procedure_name [; number ]
[ { @parameter [ type_schema_name> ] data_type }
[ VARYING ] [ = default ] [ [ OUT [ PUT ]
] [,...n ]
[ WITH <procedure_option> [,...n ]
[ FOR REPLICATION ]
AS { <sql_statement> [;][...n ] | <method_specifier> }
[;]
<procedure_option>::=
[ ENCRYPTION ]
[ RECOMPILE ]
[ EXECUTE_AS_Clause ]
<sql_statement>::=
{ [ BEGIN ] statements [ END ] }
<method_specifier>::=
EXTERNAL NAME assembly_name.class_name.method_name
```

USING PROCEDURE OPTION STATEMENTS

You learned that SQL Server stores the text used to create an object, and that anyone may run the sp_HelpText system stored procedure and view it. If you are a vendor and you wish to guard your intellectual property, consider adding the WITH ENCRYPTION option. This hides the text from copycats.

The WITH RECOMPILE option indicates you don't want the execution plan cached in memory and that you want it *recompiled* each time it is called.

The WITH EXECUTE AS clause permits the stored procedure to be run under any designated user's security context. Permission must be granted only on the stored procedure itself, without having to grant explicit permissions on underlying or referenced objects. See the discussion in Lesson 12 for details.

ADDING INPUT PARAMETERS

When creating attributes in a table, you must follow naming convention guidelines, define a datatype, and perhaps set a default value.

Examine this example:

```
ALTER PROC Schema.Name
@MinLength int = -1
-- Sets a default value of negative one.
```

ADDING OUTPUT AND HANDLING ERRORS

Output parameters allow any changes to the parameter that result from the execution of the stored procedure to be retained, even after the stored procedure completes execution.

To use an output parameter, you must specify the OUTPUT keyword in both the CREATE PROCEDURE and the EXECUTE statements. If the OUTPUT keyword is omitted when the stored procedure is executed, the stored procedure still completes but does not return the modified value.

Here's a code snippet showing how to use OUTPUT:

```
CREATE PROC HumanResources.AddDepartment
@Name nvarchar(30), @GroupName nvarchar(30),
@DeptID smallint OUTPUT
AS
...
```

X REF

For a discussion of functions, please refer to Lesson 12.

Check values before major processing. Discover early that someone forgot to pass a parameter, or passed an invalid parameter. For example:

```
...
IF (@MinLength < 1) -Validate
  BEGIN
    RAISERROR ('Invalid value', 12, 1)
    RETURN
  END
...
```

Specifying a return value or a variable response requires adding the OUTPUT keyword and postpending a number on the RETURN keyword. This number is displayed and lets you know the failed code section. For example:

```
ALTER PROC Schema.Name
@MinLength int = -1 - Sets a default value of negative one.
@Report text(max) OUTPUT
IF (@MinLength < 1) - Validate
  BEGIN
    RAISERROR ('Invalid value', 12, 1)
    RETURN 1
  END
...
```

Structured exception handing has been added to the SQL Server 2005 edition. Examine this code snippet:

```
CREATE PROCEDURE Test.Object
@x int, @y int
AS
BEGIN TRY
  INSERT INTO Table VALUES (@x, @y)
END TRY
BEGIN CATCH
  SELECT ERROR_NUMBER() ErrorNumber, ERROR_MESSAGE() [Message]
END CATCH
```

Consider these rules and guidelines when using structured exception handing.

- The CATCH block must immediately follow the TRY block.
- If a transaction is specified in the TRY block (BEGIN TRAN and COMMIT TRAN), and an error happens, a jump to the CATCH block occurs, skipping the COMMIT TRAN statement. You probably need to put a ROLLBACK TRAN in the CATCH block to maintain data integrity.
- If a SET XACT_ABORT ON statement has been executed, the transaction is automatically rolled back, *except* in the CATCH block. Here it changes status to uncommittable. Check for this condition using the XACT_STATE( ) function:

```
BEGIN CATCH
  IF (XACT_STATE()) = -1 ROLLBACK TRAN
  -- Uncommittable
  ELSE IF (XACT_STATE()) = 1 COMMIT TRAN
END CATCH
```

Capture error information with one or more system functions:

- ERROR_LINE( )
- ERROR_MESSAGE( )
- ERROR_NUMBER( )
- ERROR_PROCEDURE( )

See Lesson 13 for the details of error handling.

- ERROR_SEVERITY( )
- ERROR_STATE( )

CHANGING STORED PROCEDURES

You may DROP (the syntax is DROP PROC *Name*) at any time and CREATE a replacement. This also drops any associated permissions.

When changing something about the stored procedure, consider using the ALTER PROC syntax. This retains the established security context.

Introducing CLR Procedures

A common language runtime (CLR) procedure is a reference to a method that supports parameters and is cataloged as a procedure in SQL Server. CLR procedures are written in a .NET CLR interpretable language such as Visual Basic. NET or C#. A .NET Framework CLR method is exposed to SQL as a method defined in a .NET assembly. Before you can use a CLR procedure, the assembly needs to be cataloged in SQL Server (CREATE ASSEMBLY), and the method within the assembly needs to be exposed as a SQL Server stored procedure (CREATE PROCEDURE).

Using Visual Studio, you can automatically deploy the stored procedure from within an SQL Server project. Within SQL Server, the user who references or calls the CLR procedure won't see any difference between a CLR procedure call and a T-SQL procedure call; it is called, just like a T-SQL stored procedure, using the EXEC keyword.

The scope and functionality of a CLR procedure is huge. You can create a procedure that uses the entire .NET Framework, meaning it will allow you to gain access to external objects outside SQL Server.

Since a SQL Server CLR procedure runs and is hosted within the .NET CLR, it is common to use CLR or managed procedures for complex calculations and for access to objects such as the network or file system.

CREATING CLR STORED PROCEDURES

To create a CLR stored procedure, you will use a development tool such as Visual Studio. The actual syntax in Visual Studio will then depend on the language in which you program (coverage of the syntax to create managed stored procedures is beyond the scope of this text for the exam certification).

CREATING AND DEPLOYING A CLR PROCEDURE

You write a CLR or managed code procedure in a CLR-supported language such as Visual Basic .NET or C#. From within Visual Studio 2005, you can create a SQL Server project.

When a project is deployed to SQL Server, the assembly or DLL file will be cataloged in the SQL database. These objects are displayable by querying the sys.assemblies system view.

However, it is possible to deploy a solution from within Visual Studio 2005. It is common for a database administrator to catalog the assembly and then create procedures from the methods exposed within the library (DLL or assembly).

ENABLING THE SERVER FOR CLR SUPPORT

Before you can use CLR-managed objects, you first need to enable the server for CLR support. The CLR integration is a feature; it can be enabled or disabled. You do this by executing the following syntax:

```
sp_configure 'clr_enabled', 1
reconfigure
```

⬥ ANOTHER WAY

Open **SQL Server 2005 Surface Area Configuration** → **Surface Area Configuration for Features** → **Database Engine** → **CLR Integration** → **Enable CLR Integration**.

When a call to a CLR procedure is made without the CLR enabled, an error message that says the .NET Framework is not enabled will appear.

In Exercise 10-6, you will deploy a procedure written in Visual Basic to create a new directory on your hard drive.

EXERCISE 10-6 CREATING AND DEPLOYING A CLR PROCEDURE

1. Create a new directory at the root of your C: drive named **Practice**. Copy **Lesson10.ddl** and **Lesson10.sql** to it.

2. Open a database query window in the Mssql_Training database.

3. Configure the server to allow the usage of CLR code that accesses objects stored outside of SQL Server and accesses the file system or network:

   USE Master

   ALTER DATABASE Mssql_Training SET TRUSTWORTHY ON

4. Catalog the assembly:

   USE Mssql_Training

   CREATE ASSEMBLY Lesson10 FROM C:\Practice\Lesson10.dll WITH PERMISSION_SET = EXTERNAL_ACCESS

5. After you have cataloged the assembly, create a stored procedure that references the assembly and the method:

   CREATE PROCEDURE [dbo].[up_CreateFolder] @foldername [navarchar](200) OUTPUT WITH EXECUTE AS CALLER AS EXTERNAL NAME [Lesson10]. [Chapter5].[StoredProcedures].[Createfolder]

6. Enable clr:

   sp_configure 'clr_enabled', 1

   reconfigure

7. Test the stored procedure:

   EXEC up_CreateFolder 'c:\Practice\Lesson10'

8. Verify, through Windows Explorer, that the new folder was created.

TAKE NOTE*

The external name references are case-sensitive.

Reviewing Development Guidance

Rules and considerations to keep in mind when developing stored procedures:

- Temporary stored procedures use the resources of TEMPDB. Minimize their use.
- SQL Server saves the connection string parameters specified during stored procedure creation. These settings override any client settings during execution.
- Use a naming convention other than "sp_" for your procedures. Consider using "up_" standing for "user procedure."
- Create, test, and troubleshoot your stored procedure code on your development workstation. Move it to your production environment during a minimal-use period when you can best afford some glitches. Test it from the client application using normal client permissions.
- Design each stored procedure to accomplish a single unit of work. Build a second or a third procedure rather than building one, hard-to-troubleshoot module.
- Qualify object names internal to the stored procedure by their two-part naming convention. This ensures other objects with different schemas remain accessible.

Processing Stored Procedures

When SQL Server processes a stored procedure, the Query Optimizer first checks the procedure cache for an already in-memory execution plan. If it finds one, it uses that plan to complete the execution request. Otherwise, it takes the time needed to *compile* and *cache* a new execution plan prior to executing the query.

If the same stored procedure exists under different schemas, they will each individually cache and, thus, waste memory space. Take care to create just one unique instance and provide an appropriate EXECUTE AS security context.

The compilation process consists of four stages:

- **Parsing:** SQL Server checks for syntax errors and prepares it for optimization.
- **Normalization:** SQL Server verifies that all object and column names in the query are correct.
- **Compilation:** SQL Server builds the execution plan for the stored procedure, creating query graphs for use by the Query Optimizer.
- **Optimization:** A cost-based approach decides the expense of different possible processing options.

ADDING RECOMPILE HINTS

Sometimes, SQL Server needs to recompile (reoptimize) stored procedure execution plans; for example, when your WHERE clause changes with each new query. When you examine the Execution Plan in Query Manager or suspect performance deficiency, you have three options:

- The sp_Recompile system stored procedure forces a recompile next time it is run. Use code similar to this example:

```
USE AdventureWorks
EXECUTE sp_Recompile Production.LargestListPrice
```

- Use the WITH RECOMPILE option in the CREATE PROCEDURE statement.
- Use the WITH RECOMPILE option with the EXECUTE statement:

```
USE AdventureWorks
EXEC Production.LargestListPrice WITH RECOMPILE
```

SKILL SUMMARY

IN THIS LESSON YOU LEARNED:

You learned that stored procedures:

- Provide a more secure method of accessing data than do direct calls from the client application.
- Reduce network traffic by processing on the server and delivering only the resultset to the client application or user.
- Are compiled and stored in cache memory for rapid and efficient execution.
- Require recompilation when the code, parameters, or conditions change in your environment.
- Package business functionality and create reusable application logic.
- Shield users from the details of the tables and other objects in the database.
- Provide additional security mechanisms.
- Reduce vulnerability to SQL injection attacks.
- Improve performance.

> For the certification examination:
>
> - Be able to decide between various solutions. Is the stored procedure the best solution in a given situation? Consider the alternatives of a trigger, function, and client code in your analysis. As emphasized throughout this book, there is no one way or one right answer. Administration is about balancing competing alternatives.

■ Knowledge Assessment

Multiple Choice

Circle the letter or letters that correspond to the best answer or answers.

1. You created a complex stored procedure for a tax application. Monitoring the performance of your stored procedure, you have noticed that it is recompiled on each execution. The cause of recompilation is a simple query statement. How can you optimize the performance of your stored procedure with minimum effort?
   a. Create an additional stored procedure, and include the query that causes the recompilation. Call the new stored procedure from the old one.
   b. Use the sp_recompile system stored procedure to force the recompilation of your stored procedure the next time it runs.
   c. Modify your stored procedure, and include the WITH RECOMPILE option in its definition.
   d. Add the RECOMPILE query hint to the query statement that causes the recompilation.

2. You need to recompile one of your stored procedures each time it is running. How can you achieve that? (Choose all that apply.)
   a. Use the sp_recompile system stored procedure.
   b. Modify your stored procedure, and include the WITH RECOMPILE option in its definition.
   c. Specify the WITH RECOMPILE option when you execute the stored procedure.
   d. Add the RECOMPILE query hint to one of the stored procedure statements.

3. You need to create a stored procedure that inserts a square value of a given integer. What is the best way to accomplish this?
   a. Create a CLR-managed code procedure.
   b. Use a built-in function inside a T-SQL stored procedure.
   c. Use a managed code function inside a T-SQL stored procedure.
   d. Create a user-defined datatype.

4. When executing a stored procedure, you get the error message, "Execution of user code in the .NET Framework is disabled. Enable 'clr enabled' configuration option." What statement do you need to execute to get the stored procedure to execute?
   a. sp_configure 'clr_enabled', 1
   b. sp_configure 'clr_enabled', 0
   c. sp_dboption 'clr_enabled', 0
   d. sp_dboption 'clr_enabled', 1

■ Case Scenarios

Scenario 10-1: Creating a Stored Procedure

Are those programmers you are supporting ever satisfied? Create a stored procedure for them that returns only the specified employee when the first and last names are supplied together with his or her title and his or her department. Use AdventureWorks.

Examine this code:

```
CREATE PROC HumanResources.up_GetEmployees
@LastName nvarchar(50)
@FirstName nvarchar(50)
AS
SELECT FirstName, LastName, JobTitle, Department
FROM HumanResources.vEmployeeDepartment
WHERE FirstName=@FirstName AND LastName=@LastName;
GO
```

Start a classroom discussion. Investigate what you see and what each aspect of this code means. Execute it to see if it returns what you anticipated.

11 LESSON

Triggers

LESSON SKILL MATRIX

TECHNOLOGY SKILL	70-431 EXAM OBJECTIVE
Implement triggers.	Foundational
Create a trigger.	Foundational
Create DDL triggers for responding to database structure changes.	Foundational
Identify recursive triggers.	Foundational
Identify nested triggers.	Foundational
Identify transaction triggers.	Foundational

KEY TERMS

direct recursion: Direct recursion occurs when a trigger fires and performs an action on the same table that causes the same trigger to fire again.

DML: Data Manipulation Language; SELECT, INSERT, UPDATE, and/or DELETE actions against data in tables.

DDL: Data Definition Language; CREATE, ALTER, and/or DROP statements that change the architecture (the schema) of the database.

event notification: A method of monitoring events using the Service Broker to reliably deliver the message.

indirect recursion: Indirect recursion occurs when a trigger fires and performs an action that causes

another trigger in the same or a different table to fire, and, subsequently, causes an update to occur on the original table. This then causes the original trigger to fire again.

nesting: Any trigger can contain an INSERT, UPDATE, and/or DELETE statement that affects another table. Triggers are nested when a trigger performs an action that initiates another trigger.

trigger: A collection of Transact-SQL or common language runtime code that automatically executes when an INSERT, UPDATE, and/or DELETE statement is run.

■ Using Triggers

THE BOTTOM LINE

SQL code permits you to access only one table for an INSERT, UPDATE, or DELETE statement. The trigger was invented to change related tables at the same time. If a parent table requires a change that must also be reflected in a child table, a trigger must be created.

Introducing Triggers

SQL Server has different options to implement business logic and data integrity. You have the option to implement constraints, or you can meet your requirements by implementing triggers.

A *trigger* has the same functionality as a stored procedure; it consists of a predefined set of T-SQL code that will execute on demand. A stored procedure is called by using an EXECUTE statement; in contrast, a trigger fires automatically when the event where it is defined occurs—it can never be called directly.

When combining triggers and constraints on a table, the constraint fires before the trigger does. If a constraint violation occurs, the trigger won't fire. The constraint is proactive, whereas the trigger is reactive.

In SQL Server 2005 you have two types of triggers:

- *Data Manipulation Language (DML)* triggers, which use INSERT, UPDATE, and DELETE SQL statements.
- *Data Definition Language (DDL)* triggers, which use CREATE, ALTER, and DROP SQL statements.

DML triggers existed in previous editions of SQL Server, but they are one of the key new features that will ease your work when logging, or even when manipulating DDL instructions.

In the following sections, you'll take a look at each of these trigger types.

Understanding DML Triggers

DML triggers execute automatically when a DML action (insert, delete, and/or update) is executed against a table or a view. Within a trigger you have the ability to work with the data affected by the DML statement, along with the original data.

By default, triggers in SQL Server are AFTER triggers, which means they execute after the statement that triggered it completes. The alternative is INSTEAD OF.

On a table, you can create multiple triggers for the same action. The sp_settriggerorder stored procedure permits you to specify which trigger fires first and which trigger fires last for AFTER triggers. Any additional triggers fire in an unpredictable order.

A recursive trigger performs an action that causes the same trigger to fire again, either directly or indirectly. For this to happen, you must set the database option Recursive Triggers Enabled to true or false. If the trigger recurses without good programmatic behavior, SQL Server will terminate it once the 32-level (trigger within a trigger within a trigger within a trigger, up to 32 times) *nesting* limit is exceeded and roll back the entire transaction.

UNDERSTANDING HOW A DML TRIGGER WORKS

When performing a trigger action, two special tables are used within the trigger action: the inserted and the deleted tables. These tables are managed by SQL Server and will be used to affect the DML statement. You will use these tables in various situations when you want to look at the rows affected by an INSERT, DELETE, or UPDATE statement.

UNDERSTANDING HOW AN INSERT TRIGGER WORKS

During a transaction, the inserted data will be available in an in-memory structure called *inserted*. Within the trigger action, you have the ability to retrieve and manipulate values inside the inserted table.

The inserted table will have a copy of all the affected rows during an INSERT statement. This is where you have the ability to interfere or interact with the records inserted.

Since the default behavior of a trigger is an AFTER action, you need to perform a rollback of the transaction if you don't want to perform the insert action.

UNDERSTANDING HOW A DELETE TRIGGER WORKS

In the case of a DELETE statement, the deleted table will have a copy of all the affected rows during that action. Again, if you don't want to perform the actual delete, you need to roll back the transaction.

UNDERSTANDING HOW AN UPDATE TRIGGER WORKS

You probably would assume for an UPDATE trigger there would be an updated table, but there isn't.

The UPDATE statement will use the deleted and inserted tables to keep track of the records that have been modified. The OLD status will be loaded in the deleted table, and the NEW status will be held in the inserted table.

Often, these tables are joined to provide you with a resultset of the old and new value of an update action.

USING THE INSERTED AND DELETED TABLES

Showing an audit trail has become increasingly important—especially since the Sarbanes-Oxley Act became law. Showing the change history has always been relevant, and executed as a trigger. The data entered or removed can be captured because both exist in the inserted and deleted tables for the life of the transaction the trigger starts. The data, plus the user, the action (insert, update or delete), and the date, are copied to a history table as a permanent record of change.

USING INSTEAD OF TRIGGERS

As explained, an AFTER trigger works after the actual action takes place, so if you want to avoid or revert this, you will need to roll back the transaction. Since the release of SQL Server 2000, you also have the ability to work more or less proactively by performing INSTEAD OF triggers.

As you can assume from its name, you perform a different task with INSTEAD OF performing the actual DML statement. Most likely, that new task will be to check some condition and then branch to an appropriate action.

 CREATING A DML TRIGGER

The following shows how to create a DML trigger:

```
CREATE TRIGGER [ schema_name. ]trigger_name
ON { table | view }
[ WITH <dml_trigger_option> [,...n ] ]
{ FOR | AFTER | INSTEAD OF }
{ [ INSERT ] [, ] [ UPDATE ] [, ] [ DELETE ] }
[ WITH APPEND ]
[ NOT FOR REPLICATION ]
AS { sql_statement [; ] [...n ] | EXTERNAL NAME <method
  specifier [; ] > }
<dml_trigger_option>::=
[ ENCRYPTION ]
[ EXECUTE AS Clause ]
<method_specifier>::=
assembly_name.class_name.method_name
```

The following trigger example will block records from being deleted from the products table if more than one record is deleted at the same time:

```
CREATE TRIGGER trg_delete on products FOR DELETE
AS
BEGIN
If (select count(*) from deleted) > 1
RAISERROR ('You can not delete more than one record at the
  same time', 16, 1)
ROLLBACK TRANSACTION
END
```

RAISERROR is a statement that will raise an error message that consists of an error severity level and a state identifier. Severity levels from 0 through 18 can be specified by any user. Severity levels from 19 through 25 can only be specified by members of the sysadmin fixed server role.

Understanding DDL Triggers

In SQL Server 2005, you also have the ability to create **DDL triggers**. The cool feature of DDL triggers is that you can now log every DROP TABLE and any other type of DDL event. This means you have the ability to allow the execution of DDL only under special conditions or circumstances; furthermore, it is in your power to roll back the DDL statement.

This means you can guard your table that recorded the user who illegally changed the data and whose identity was captured in the history record. If the user also tries to DROP the history table, your trigger will just as quickly replace it.

UNDERSTANDING HOW A DDL TRIGGER WORKS

A DDL trigger executes automatically, like any other trigger, and it fires when a certain action occurs—in this case, a DDL statement. DDL triggers are often used to protect your production environment from the effects of issuing certain DDL statements, and they can provide auditing and logging of specific DDL statements in a database.

CREATING A DDL TRIGGER

To create a DDL trigger, you use the CREATE TRIGGER statement, which is the same as when adding a DML trigger. The difference will be for the object you specify it on, which could be the database or the server. Here's the syntax:

> **TAKE NOTE** *
>
> DDL triggers are always AFTER triggers. This means the action completes; for example, the table was dropped and then recovered. Sometimes, this recovery process can slow the production system noticeably.

```
CREATE TRIGGER trigger_name
ON { ALL SERVER | DATABASE }
[ WITH <ddl_trigger_option> [,...n ] ]
{ FOR | AFTER } { event_type | event_group } [,...n
]
AS { sql_statement [; ] [...n ] |
EXTERNAL NAME < method specifier > [; ] }
<ddl_trigger_option>::=
[ ENCRYPTION ]
[ EXECUTE AS Clause ]
<method_specifier>::=
assembly_name.class_name.method_name
```

The following trigger will allow you to recover after someone executes a CREATE or DROP table statement. It will fire only within the database it is protecting.

```
CREATE TRIGGER trg_block_droptable_altertable
ON DATABASE
FOR DROP_TABLE, ALTER_TABLE
AS
PRINT 'You can not drop or alter tables'
ROLLBACK
```

DDL triggers generally have their scope inside the database; however, you can create them on the server level as well. This allows you to fire triggers on server events, such as the creation of databases.

UNDERSTANDING DDL TRIGGER EVENTS AND SCOPE

Since DDL triggers are new to SQL Server, it is important to understand their scope. DDL events can be categorized into two different scopes: a database scope or a server scope. This means that in the CREATE TRIGGER statement ON DATABASE | SERVER, you can specify the event only if it is declared within the scope.

It is important to have a clear understanding of the capabilities of DDL triggers. In Exercise 11-1, you will create and test the functionality of a DDL trigger, and log the actual statement in a log table.

 EXERCISE 11-1 CREATING A DDL TRIGGER

1. Open a new database query window in the MSSQL_Training database.
2. Create a trigger on the database that will roll back every DDL event:
   ```
   CREATE TRIGGER trg_block_ddl ON DATABASE
   FOR DDL_DATABASE_LEVEL_EVENTS AS RAISERROR ('Database
     locked for DDL events', 16, 1)
   ROLLBACK TRANSACTION
   ```
3. Test the trigger functionality by creating a table:
   ```
   USE MSSQL_Training
   CREATE TABLE Test (testid int)
   ```
4. Drop the existing trigger:
   ```
   DROP TRIGGER trg_block_ddl ON DATABASE
   ```

Understanding Trigger Recursion and Nesting

When working with triggers, you can force one trigger to execute a trigger event on another or on the same table. This means these trigger events will be fired within another trigger action and will thus nest them.

Nested triggers: SQL Server supports the nesting of triggers up to a maximum of 32 levels. Nesting means that when a trigger is fired, it will also cause another trigger to be fired; thus, each incorporates the prior as part of the transaction.

If a trigger creates an infinite loop, the nesting level of 32 will be exceeded and the trigger will cancel with an error message. You can disable trigger nesting by using a system stored procedure with the nested trigger option. For example:

```
SP_CONFIGURE 'nested_triggers',0
RECONFIGURE
```

This statement will block trigger nesting, but it also blocks indirect recursion.

Recursive triggers: When a trigger fires and performs a statement that will cause the same trigger to fire, recursion will occur. SQL Server has two types of recursion:

- **Direct recursion:** Direct recursion occurs when the trigger TRIGGER1 fires on a table, which will perform a statement in the trigger that will cause the same trigger, TRIGGER1, to fire again.
- **Indirect recursion:** Indirect recursion occurs when the trigger TRIGGER1 fires on a table and performs a statement inside the trigger that will cause another trigger, TRIGGER2, to fire on a different table. TRIGGER2 causes TRIGGER1 to fire again.

This is like playing tennis: you hit the ball and your opponent hits the ball back.

Blocking recursion: You can block direct recursion only by issuing the RECURSIVE_TRIGGERS option. You can block indirect recursion only by blocking nested triggers.

By default, recursion is disabled; you can enable recursion by using an ALTER DATABASE statement or by specifying the options on the database configuration page. For example:

```
ALTER DATABASE databasename
SET RECURSIVE_TRIGGERS ON | OFF
```

Understanding Disabling Triggers

To prevent a trigger from firing, you can use DISABLE to disable it. In the case of a DML trigger, you have two options to disable a trigger: you can use an ALTER TABLE statement or a DISABLE TRIGGER statement. For example:

```
DISABLE TRIGGER { [ schema. ] trigger_name
[,...n ] | ALL }
ON { object_name | DATABASE | ALL SERVER } [; ]
```

Understanding Event Notifications

Another way of implementing event monitoring, instead of using DDL triggers, is by creating *event notifications*. Event notifications use SQL Server Broker architecture, which is covered later in this book. Event notifications issue the event to an SQL Server Service Broker service by submitting it to a queue.

To better understand the difference between event notifications and triggers, see Table 11-1.

Table 11-1

Trigger and Event Notifications Comparison

TRIGGERS	EVENT NOTIFICATIONS
Executes on DDL or DML statements	Notifies on DDL or DML statements as well as trace events
Contains the execution code in the trigger	Submits to an SQL Server Broker architecture
Has fewer options on the server level	Allows most of the database scope events to also be defined on the server level

For a discussion of SQL Server Service Broker architecture, please refer to Lesson 20.

The syntax for creating event notifications looks similar to creating a DDL trigger, but directly logs to a broker service. Therefore, the first step when configuring event notification is to set up a SQL Server Service Broker architecture. Lesson 20 covers this in detail.

UNDERSTANDING EVENT NOTIFICATIONS DDL EVENTS AND SCOPE

The DDL events that can occur in a SQL Server environment can be logged by event notifications at both the database and server levels. Different from DDL triggers, event notifications can also manage trace events and log them to a broker server.

Event notifications certainly have more capabilities in terms of monitoring than DDL triggers have. You can also put most of the DDL events on both the server and the database scope.

CREATING AN EVENT NOTIFICATION

To create an event notification, you use the CREATE EVENT NOTIFICATION syntax. In the following example, an event notification is generated for a login event on the server level.

Here's the code syntax:

```
CREATE EVENT NOTIFICATION event_notification_name
ON { SERVER | DATABASE | QUEUE queue_name }
[ WITH FAN_IN ]
FOR { event_type | event_group } [,...n ]
TO SERVICE 'broker_service',
{ 'broker_instance_specifier' | 'current database' }
[; ]
```

For example:

```
CREATE EVENT NOTIFICATION Evt_logins
ON SERVER
FOR AUDIT_LOGIN TO SERVICE 'EVENTLOGSERVICE'
```

For a discussion of SQL Server Broker Service, please refer to Lesson 20.

Before event notifications services can be logged to a Service Broker, the broker service has to be configured. This means that the necessary contracts, queues, and message types have to be created. To find out more about SQL Server Broker Service, see Lesson 20.

INTRODUCING EVENTDATA COLLECTION

The EVENTDATA( ) function gives you access to all the information that is gathered in a DDL trigger or during event notifications. This function is extremely useful to perform tracing and monitoring on the actual event or the DDL trigger that executed. The EVENTDATA( ) function has two methods: value and query. The EVENTDATA( ) value function returns an Extensible Markup Language (XML) resultset in the following structure:

```
<EVENT_INSTANCE>
<EventType>type</EventType>
<PostTime>date-time</PostTime>
<SPID>spid</SPID>
<ServerName>name</ServerName>
<LoginName>name</LoginName>
<UserName>name</UserName>
<DatabaseName>name</DatabaseName>
<SchemaName>name</SchemaName>
<ObjectName>name</ObjectName>
<ObjectType>type</ObjectType>
<TSQLCommand>command</TSQLCommand>
</EVENT_INSTANCE>
```

To retrieve a scalar datatype, you need to decompose the XML resultset into relational data. In Lesson 15, you will learn how to work with XML data in SQL Server 2005, and how you can return XML data in T-SQL and scalar data.

SKILL SUMMARY

IN THIS LESSON YOU LEARNED:

Triggers provide the capability to automatically execute code when an event occurs; this can be a DDL event, such as CREATE TABLE and UPDATE_STATISTICS, or a DML event, such as the insertion of records in a table.

For the certification examination:

- Understand DDL triggers and DML triggers. Understand the functional difference between these triggers and when to use DDL triggers. Familiarize yourself with the syntax of creating DDL and DML triggers; know how triggers are executed; and be able to determine their scope. It's also important to know how triggers can be nested and how recursion can be blocked or enabled.

■ Knowledge Assessment

Multiple Choice

Circle the letter or letters that correspond to the best answer or answers.

1. You need to create a trigger for auditing the creation of new tables in a database named Test. You need to record the login name, the username, the command text, and the time. Which code can you use?

a. Use the following:

```
USE Test GO
CREATE TRIGGER audit_CREATE_TABLE ON DATABASE FOR CREATE_TABLE
AS
INSERT tblAudit( PostTime,LoginName,UserName, QLText)
VALUES (GETDATE(), SYSTEM_USER, CURRENT_USER,
EVENTDATA().value ('(/EVENT_INSTANCE/TSQLCommand)[1]', 'nvarchar(2000)'))
RETURN;
GO
```

b. Use the following:

```
USE Test GO
CREATE TRIGGER audit_CREATE_TABLE ON DATABASE FOR CREATE_TABLE
AS
INSERT tblAudit( PostTime,LoginName,UserName,SQLText)
VALUES (GETDATE(), SYSTEM_USER, CURRENT_USER,
EVENTDATA().value ('(/EVENT_INSTANCE/EventType)[1]', 'nvarchar(2000)'))
RETURN;
GO
```

c. Use the following:

```
USE Test GO
CREATE TRIGGER audit_CREATE_TABLE ON DATABASE FOR CREATE_TABLE
AS
INSERT tblAudit( PostTime,LoginName,UserName,SQLText)
VALUES (GETDATE(), SYSTEM_USER, CURRENT_USER,
EVENTDATA().query ('(/EVENT_INSTANCE/TSQLCommand)[1]', 'nvarchar(2000)'))
RETURN;
GO
```

d. Use the following:

```
USE Test GO
CREATE TRIGGER audit_CREATE_TABLE ON DATABASE FOR DDL_DATABASE_LEVEL_
EVENTS AS
INSERT tblAudit( PostTime,LoginName,UserName,SQLText)
VALUES (GETDATE(), SYSTEM_USER, CURRENT_USER,
EVENTDATA().value ('(/EVENT_INSTANCE/EventType)[1]', 'nvarchar(2000)'))
RETURN;
GO
```

2. You need to disable all modifications for a reporting database named CompanyReports. Which code can you use?

a. Use the following:

```
CREATE TRIGGER PreventModifications
ON DATABASE FOR DDL_DATABASE_LEVEL_EVENTS
AS
INSERT tblAudit(PostTime, LoginName, UserName, SQLText)
VALUES (GETDATE(), SYSTEM_USER, CURRENT_USER,
EVENTDATA().value ('(/EVENT_INSTANCE/EventType)[1]', 'nvarchar(2000)'))
RETURN;
GO
```

b. Use the following:

```
CREATE TRIGGER PreventModifications
ON DATABASE FOR CREATE_TABLE
AS
RAISERROR ('You are not allowed to modify this
    production database.', 16, -1)
ROLLBACK
RETURN;
GO
```

c. Use the following:

```
CREATE TRIGGER PreventModifications
ON DATABASE FOR DDL_DATABASE_LEVEL_EVENTS
AS
RAISERROR ('You are not allowed to modify this
    production database.', 16, -1)
ROLLBACK
RETURN;
GO
```

3. You need to determine the nesting level of a DDL trigger named AuditUpdates. Which code can you use?

a. Use the following:

```
 SELECT TRIGGER_NESTLEVEL (OBJECT_ID ('AuditUpdates'), 'AFTER', 'DML');
GO
```

b. Use the following:

```
SELECT TRIGGER_NESTLEVEL(( SELECT object_id FROM sys.triggers WHERE name =
'AuditUpdates'), 'AFTER', 'DML' );
GO
```

c. Use the following:

```
SELECT TRIGGER_NESTLEVEL (OBJECT_ID('AuditUpdates'), 'AFTER', 'DDL' );
GO
```

d. Use the following:

```
SELECT TRIGGER_NESTLEVEL((SELECT object_id FROM sys.triggers WHERE name =
'AuditUpdates'), 'AFTER', 'DDL' );
GO
```

4. You create a DML trigger to audit the updates of a table. You need to prevent the trigger from nesting more than three levels. How can you accomplish that?

a. Using sp_configure, set the nested triggers server option to 0.

b. Using ALTER DATABASE, disable the RECURSIVE_TRIGGERS option.

c. Use the following code inside your trigger:

```
IF ((SELECT TRIGGER_NESTLEVEL()) > 3 ) RETURN
```

d. Use the following code inside your trigger:

```
IF ((SELECT TRIGGER_NESTLEVEL()) > 2 ) RETURN
```

5. Your database server is configured using the default settings, and the user databases have the default options. One of your applications updates a table named tblCustomers. The update fires a trigger named UpdateCustomerDetails that will modify the tblCustomerDetails table. The modification of table tblCustomerDetails fires a trigger

named UpdateCustomer that will modify the tblCustomers table. This behavior generates recursion. Which option allows this behavior?

    a. The RECURSIVE_TRIGGERS database option set to ON.

    b. The RECURSIVE_TRIGGERS database option set to OFF.

    c. The nested triggers' server configuration option set to 0.

    d. The nested triggers' server configuration option set to 1.

6. One of your applications updates a table named tblOrders. The update fires a trigger named UpdateOrderDate that will modify the tblOrders table by setting a date column. The modification of table tblOrders will fire the UpdateOrderDate trigger again. How can you prevent the UpdateOrderDate trigger from firing again? (Choose all that apply.)

    a. Use sp_configure to set the nested triggers' server option to 0.

    b. Use ALTER DATABASE, and disable the RECURSIVE_TRIGGERS option.

    c. Insert the following code as the beginning of your trigger:

```
IF ((SELECT TRIGGER_NESTLEVEL()) > 1 ) RETURN
```

    d. Insert the following code as the beginning of your trigger:

```
IF ((SELECT TRIGGER_NESTLEVEL()) = 1 ) RETURN
```

7. You implemented a trigger that blocks and restricts the creation of tables in the production database. To create an additional table, you need to temporarily remove the DDL trigger. How can you perform this with the least administrative effort?

    a. ALTER TABLE

    b. DISABLE TRIGGER

    c. SP_CONFIGURE 'block_triggers',0

    d. DROP TRIGGER

8. You are required to log every change to the customer data in a separate table named customer_ history. How can you achieve this?

    a. Create a DML trigger on the customer table.

    b. Create a DDL trigger on the customer table.

    c. Use database snapshots.

    d. Use database mirroring.

9. After creating some triggers on a table, you realize that they execute in the wrong order. What can you do to cause the triggers execute in the right order?

    a. Drop the triggers, and re-create them in the corresponding order.

    b. Use the sp_settriggerorder system stored procedure.

    c. Execute an ALTER TABLE statement with ALTER TRIGGER to change the trigger order.

    d. Create the triggers with _x, where *x* is the trigger order number.

10. You are the database administrator of your company. One of your company's applications should maintain data integrity and return custom error messages when the entry data is incorrect. How can you achieve that with minimum effort?

    a. Add check constraints to necessary columns.

    b. Use a DDL trigger.

    c. Use a CLR trigger.

    d. Use a DML trigger.

11. Your company has a CRM application. Some contacts are imported directly from e-mail messages, and sometimes the import fails. You investigate the problem and find out that the cause is a check constraint that validates a column called PhoneNumber. The constraint rejects all phone numbers that contain dashes or parentheses. How can you solve the problem without modifying the check constraint?

    a. Create an additional check constraint that would remove nonnumeric characters.

    b. Create a DML AFTER trigger to remove nonnumeric characters.

    c. Create a DML INSTEAD OF trigger to remove nonnumeric characters.

    d. Create a DML FOR trigger to remove nonnumeric characters.

Case Scenarios

Scenario 11-1: Examining Triggers

Look at the following code. Discuss with your fellow students what it does.

```
CREATE TRIGGER Reminder1
ON Sales.Customer AFTER INSERT, UPDATE
AS RAISERROR ('Notify Sales Clerk'), 15, 10
GO
```

Functions

LESSON SKILL MATRIX

TECHNOLOGY SKILL	70-431 EXAM OBJECTIVE
Implement functions.	Foundational
Create a function.	Foundational
Identify deterministic versus nondeterministic functions.	Foundational
Retrieve data to support ad hoc and recurring queries.	Foundational
Format the results of SQL queries.	Foundational

KEY TERMS

computed column: When you use the CREATE TABLE syntax, you may create a column that is derived from other columns in the table. For example, the Unit Sales column times the Unit Price column provides the Total Sales column. Normalization techniques prohibit storing aggregated values (total sales), yet such a column can reduce the need for JOINs and thus decrease overhead processing when delivering a resultset. Values are stored in the index—not in the data column itself.

deterministic function: A deterministic process returns the same value each time it is invoked. The square root of 4 is 2, every time.

inline table-valued function: An inline routine returns a dataset (rows and columns) based on internal Transact-SQL logic between BEGIN and END statements.

nondeterministic function: A nondeterministic process returns a different value each time it is run. The system time changes with each check.

OLTP: Online transaction processing; as distinct from OLAP, which stands for online analytical processing. OLTP is optimized for data entry, whereas OLAP is optimized for data analysis.

scalar function: A scalar code segment returns a single data value as defined by the RETURN statement.

multistatement table-valued function: A table-valued routine returns a data set (row and columns) based on an included SELECT statement.

■ Introducing Functions

THE BOTTOM LINE — A function is a piece of code or routine that accepts parameters and is stored as an object in SQL Server. The function always returns a result or resultset from invocation.

Understanding Functions

A function can be called within a SELECT statement or even a WHERE clause, whereas a stored procedure is called using an EXECUTE procedure statement.

SQL Server supports several types of functions:

- Built-in functions
- Scalar functions
- Inline table-valued functions
- Multistatement table-valued functions
- CLR functions

Using Built-in Functions

You need to become familiar with a large number of functions provided to you by Microsoft.

 EXERCISE 12-1 EXAMINING BUILT-IN FUNCTIONS

1. Click **Start** → **All Programs** → **Microsoft SQL Server 2005** → **SQL Server Management Studio**. Click **Connect**.
2. Click the **plus (+) sign** next to databases. → Click the **plus (+) sign** next to AdventureWorks → Click the **plus (+) sign** next to Programmability. → Click the **plus (+) sign** next to Functions. → Click the **plus (+) sign** next to System Functions. → Click the **plus (+) sign** next to Aggregate Functions.

Aggregate functions perform operations that combine multiple values into one value by grouping, summarizing, or averaging the values. The aggregate functions are shown in Table 12-1.

Table 12-1

Aggregate Functions

Avg( )	Min( )	Checksum( )	Stdev( )
Checksum_Agg( )	Stdevp( )	Count( )	Sum( )
Count_Big( )	Var( )	Grouping( )	Varp( )
Binary_Checksum( )	Max( )		

Examine the system functions provided by hovering your mouse pointer over each supplied routine in turn. Notice that avg( ) returns the average of the values in a group; count(*) returns the number of records in the table; and min( ) returns the least value in the table.

 EXERCISE 12-2 MAX() FUNCTION

1. You are already in Management Studio. Start a **New Query**.
2. Enter this code example in your query editor:
   USE AdventureWorks
   SELECT MAX(ListPrice) from Production.Product
3. Execute the query.

ANOTHER WAY

Press **F5** or **Ctrl-e;** click **Execute.**

From this you learn the highest-priced bicycle is $3,578.27.

Data values that are unknown and unknowable must be derived in a subquery. In the next example, the average list price is first calculated in the WHERE clause.

➡ EXERCISE 12-3 AVG() FUNCTION

1. Enter this code example in your query editor:

   USE AdventureWorks
   SELECT Name, ListPrice FROM Production.Product
   WHERE ListPrice > (SELECT avg(ListPrice)
   FROM Production.Product)
   ORDER BY ListPrice

2. Execute the query.

From this you view all the products exceeding the average cost of all products.

Configuration scalar functions return information about system settings.

Cryptographic functions support encryption, decryption, digital signing, and the validation of digital signatures. Be sure to hover your mouse pointer over each function supplied in SQL Server to learn its capabilities. SQL Server 2005 supports the encryption and decryption of data using the EncryptByKey( ) and DecryptByKey( ) functions. SQL Server Books Online gives you a full overview of the functionality of these resources.

Configuration functions include server_name( ) and db_name( ), which will give you information about server and database configurations, respectively. Be sure to hover your mouse pointer over each function supplied in SQL Server to learn its capabilities.

➡ EXERCISE 12-4 VERSION SYSTEM FUNCTION

1. Now click the **plus (+) sign** next to Configuration Functions. Again, hover your mouse pointer over each in turn. You learn that @@Max_Precision returns the precision level used by decimal and numeric datatypes currently set in the server.

2. Return to your Query Editor.

3. Type **USE AdventureWorks**; press **ENTER,** then **SELECT**, and a space.

4. Using your left mouse button, capture and drag **@@Version** from the Object Explorer to the Query window, so that it looks like this:

   USE AdventureWorks

   SELECT @@Version

5. Execute the query.

6. This is difficult to read in the Results to Grid mode, so if this is your setting, change it by clicking on the **Results to Text** button on the same row as the AdventureWorks database context display.

7. Execute your query again.

Cursor functions return information about the status of a cursor. Notice that @@Cursor_Rows returns the number of qualifying rows currently in the last cursor opened in the connection.

➡ EXERCISE 12-5 CURSOR_ROWS SYSTEM FUNCTION

1. Now click the **plus (+) sign** next to Cursor Functions in the Object Browser.

2. Return to your Query Editor pane.

3. Type **SELECT** plus a space, and drag **@@Cursor_Rows** from the browser.

4. The code should look like this:

   SELECT @@Cursor_Rows

5. Click **Execute** or press **F5.**

The value returned should be 0, as you don't have a cursor opened.

Date and time functions provide you with the capability to manipulate and calculate with dates and time values. Date functions prove to be widely used. For example, you might want to archive anything in your **OLTP (online transaction processing)** database prior to six month ago. Table 12-2 describes the date and time functions.

Table 12-2

Date and Time Functions

FUNCTION	DESCRIPTION
Dateadd( )	Returns a new datetime value based on adding an interval to the specified date.
Datediff( )	Returns the number of date and time boundaries crossed between two specified dates.
Datename( )	Returns a character string representing the specified date name of the specified date.
Datepart( )	Returns an integer that represents the specified date part of the specified date.
Day( )	Returns an integer representing the day part of the specified date.
Getdate( )	Returns the current system date and time in the SQL Server 2005 standard internal format for datetime values.
Getutcdate( )	Returns the datetime value representing the current UTC (Coordinated Universal Time). The current UTC is derived from the current local time and the time zone setting in the operating system of the computer on which the instance of Microsoft SQL Server is running.
Month( )	Returns an integer that represents the month part of a specified date.
Year( )	Returns an integer that represents the year part of a specified date.

EXERCISE 12-6 DATEDIFF() AND GETDATE() FUNCTIONS

1. Click the **plus (+) sign** next to Date and Time Functions. And yet again, hover your mouse pointer over each function in turn.
2. Enter the following code in Query Manager:

   USE AdventureWorks

   SELECT DATEDIFF(Day, OrderDate, GETDATE()) as 'Number of Days' FROM Sales.SalesOrderHeader
3. Execute.

This displays the number of days since the last order was placed in AdventureWorks.

Mathematical functions perform trigonometric, geometric, and other numeric operations. These functions are listed in Table 12-3.

Table 12-3

Mathematical Functions

ABS( )	LOG10( )	ACOS( )	PI( )
Asin( )	Power( )	Atan( )	Radians( )
Atn2( )	Rand( )	Ceiling( )	Round( )
Cos( )	Sign( )	Cot( )	Sin( )
Degrees( )	Sqrt( )	Exp( )	Square( )
Floor( )	Tan( )	Log( )	

Metadata functions return information about the attributes of databases and database objects.

Other functions return information about your system's performance. A list is provided in Table 12-4.

Table 12-4

Other Functions

FUNCTION	DESCRIPTION
App_Name( )	Returns the application name for the current session if set by the application.
Caseexpression( )	Evaluates the expression in a multivalued IF statement.
Cast( ) and Convert( )	Explicitly converts an expression of one datatype to another.
Coalesce( )	Returns the first nonnull expression among its arguments.
Collationproperty( )	Returns the property of a specified collation.
Columns_Updated( )	Returns a varbinary bit pattern that indicates the columns in a table or view that were inserted or updated. COLUMNS_UPDATED is used anywhere inside the body of a T-SQL INSERT or UPDATE trigger to test whether the trigger should execute certain actions.
Current_Timestamp	Returns the current date and time.
Current_User	Returns the name of the current user.
Datalength( )	Returns the number of bytes used to represent any expression.
@@Error	Returns the error number for the last T-SQL statement executed.
Error_Line( )	Returns the line number at which an error occurred that caused the CATCH block of a TRY...CATCH construct to be run.
Error_Message( )	Returns the message text of the error that caused the CATCH block of a TRY...CATCH construct to be run.
Error_Number( )	Returns the error number of the error that caused the CATCH block of a TRY...CATCH construct to be run.
Error_State ( )	Returns the state number of the error that caused the CATCH block of a TRY...CATCH construct to be run.
Fn_Helpcollations( )	Returns a list of all the collations supported by Microsoft SQL Server 2005.
Fn_Servershareddrives( )	Returns the names of shared drives used by the clustered server.
Fn_Virtualfilestats( )	Returns I/O statistics for database files, including log files.
Getansinull( )	Returns the default nullability for the database for this session.
Host_Id( )	Returns the workstation identification number.
Host_Name( )	Returns the workstation name.
Ident_Curren( )t	Returns the last identity value generated for a specified table or view in any session and any scope.
Ident_Incr( )	Returns the increment value of an identity.
Ident_Seed( )	Returns the seed value that was specified on an identity column
@@Identity	Returns the last-inserted identity value.
Identity( )	Used only in a SELECT statement with an INTO table clause to insert an identity column into a new table.
Isdate( )	Determines whether an input expression is a valid date.
Isnull( )	Determines whether an input value is null.
Isnumeric( )	Determines whether an input value is numeric.
Newid( )	Generates a new GUID.
Nullif( )	Returns null if two expressions are equal.
Parsename( )	Returns the specified part of an object name.
@@Trancount	Counts the currently opened transactions.
Update( )	Validates to true if a column is updated.
User_Name( )	Returns the username.

Ranking functions are nondeterministic functions that return a ranking value for each row in a partition. Ranking functions are new to SQL Server 2005 and allow you to use a rank or a row number within a resultset. Table 12-5 describes the ranking functions.

Table 12-5

Ranking Functions

FUNCTION	DESCRIPTION
Dense_Rank( )	Returns the rank of rows within the partition of a resultset, without any gaps in the ranking. The rank of a row is 1 plus the number of distinct ranks that come before the row in question.
Ntile( )	Distributes the rows in an ordered partition into a specified number of groups. The groups are numbered, starting at 1. For each row, NTILE returns the number of the group to which the row belongs.
Rank( )	Returns the rank of each row within the partition of a resultset. The rank of a row is 1 plus the number of ranks that come before the row in question.
Row_Number( )	Returns the sequential number of a row within a partition of a resultset, starting at 1 for the first row in each partition.

 EXERCISE 12-7 RANK() FUNCTION

1. Examine and enter this code:

   USE AdventureWorks

   GO

   SELECT i.ProductID, p.Name, i.LocationID, i.Quantity, RANK() OVER

   (PARTITION BY i.LocationID ORDERBY i.Quantity DESC) as 'Rank'

   FROM Production.ProductInventory i INNER JOIN Production.Product p ON i.ProductID = p.ProductID

   ORDER BY p.Name;

   GO

2. Execute.

Rowset functions return the rowsets that can be used in place of a table referenced in a T-SQL statement; security functions return information about users and roles.

String functions manipulate character text. Once again, examine each function in turn. String manipulations might be the single most used feature of SQL Server functions. You need to display results to users in a format useful to them. The string functions are listed in Table 12-6.

Let's say you store data in your table as char(50) but you entered a last name simply as "Smith". You retrieve that data as 50 characters but you want to display only 5 of them. Consider RTRIM. This function removes any trailing spaces inserted by SQL Server when the data was originally stored.

 EXERCISE 12-8 RTRIM() FUNCTION

1. Click the **plus (+) sign** adjoining String Functions. Hover your mouse pointer over each function to learn its purpose.

2. Enter the following code in your Query Editor:

   USE AdventureWorks

   SELECT RTRIM(LastName) FROM Person.Contact

3. Execute.

As another example, perhaps you need to display only the first initial of someone's first name. Consider using SUBSTRING, as delineated in Exercise 12-9.

Table 12-6

String Functions

FUNCTION	DESCRIPTION
Ascii( )	Returns the ASCII value of a character.
Char( )	Returns the character value of an integer.
Charindex( )	Returns the position where a character appears in the provided string set.
Difference( )	Returns an integer value that indicates the difference between the SOUNDEX values of two character expressions.
Left( )	Returns the left part of a character string with the specified number of characters.
Len( )	Returns the number of characters of the specified string expression, excluding trailing blanks.
Lower( )	Returns the lowercase value of a given string.
Ltrim( )	Returns the string value, without leading blanks.
Nchar( )	Returns the Unicode character with the specified integer code, as defined by the Unicode standard.
Patindex( )	Returns the starting position of the first occurrence of a pattern in a specified expression.
Quotename( )	Puts the string value in a given quoted notation.
Replace( )	Replaces the first occurrence in the string value.
Replicate( )	Replicates a character set a given number of times.
Reverse( )	Reverses the string.
Right( )	Returns an *x* number of rightmost values of a string.
Rtrim( )	Returns the string value, excluding trailing blanks.
Soundex( )	Returns a four-character (SOUNDEX) code to evaluate the similarity of two strings.
Space( )	Returns the number of spaces provided.
Str( )	Converts the provided datatype in a string value.
Stuff( )	Deletes a specified length of characters and inserts another set of characters at a specified starting point.
Substring( )	Returns a subset of the string value.
Unicode( )	Returns the integer value, as defined by the Unicode standard, for the first character of the input expression.
Upper( )	Returns the uppercase value of a given string.

EXERCISE 12-9 SUBSTRING() FUNCTION

1. Type the code shown below into your query window:

```
USE AdventureWorks
SELECT SUBSTRING(FirstName, 1, 1) Initial
FROM Person.Contact
WHERE LastName LIKE 'Barl%'
ORDER BY Last Name
```

2. Execute by pressing **Ctrl-e.**

Your resultset should include an R and B.

And don't ignore STUFF. This function deletes a specified length of characters and inserts another set of characters at a specified starting point. Exercise 12-10 shows how.

 EXERCISE 12-10 STUFF() FUNCTION

1. Enter this code:
   SELECT STUFF('abcdef', 2, 3, 'ijklmn')
2. Execute by pressing **F5**.

This results in "aijklmnef."

Finish by clicking the **plus (+) sign** next to System Statistical Functions and Text and Image Functions. As before, hover your mouse pointer over each function to discover the functionality provided by these built-in functions.

System statistical functions return information about the performance of SQL Server; text and image functions change text and image data values.

Creating Functions

Before you learn the specifics of the three function types, you need to understand execution context. Execution context establishes the identity against which permissions are checked. Without specifying the execution context, the user or login calling the module, such as a stored procedure or function, usually determines the permissions invoked.

Using this short example:

CREATE FUNCTION GetNames RETURNS TABLE WITH EXECUTE AS 'Jim' AS RETURN (SELECT * FROM Person.Contact)

If Frank owns the table Person.Contact, and he GRANTS SELECT permissions only to user Jim, then Mary can't access this table.

If Jim owns a user-defined function named GetNames that reads data from the Person.Contact table, Jim can execute this function without any security problems because Jim has SELECT permission on the table.

If Jim GRANTS EXECUTE permission on the table to Mary, this would result in an error when Mary tries to run the procedure because, by default, the function executes as Mary, and Mary does not have SELECT permission on the Person.Contact table.

To allow Mary to gain access to the underlying table, the execution context must be set to someone such as Jim, who has access.

The general syntax is:

WITH EXECUTE AS { CALLER | SELF | OWNER | User_Name }

When you use the EXECUTE AS clause, the code is said to "impersonate" the alternative user. By default, the scope of impersonation is limited to the current database. To communicate with another instance on the same or a remote server, the calling database must be marked as trustworthy. This is an option of the properties for a database: SET TRUSTWORTHY true or false. The user must also have a login for the target instance and have the AUTHENTICATE permission set.

CREATING SCALAR FUNCTIONS

A *scalar function* passes and/or returns a single value. This simple example totals all of the sales quantity for a particular product and returns the total as an int datatype.

CERTIFICATION READY?
Functions can be used or included in: (1) the select list of a query that uses a SELECT statement to return a value; (2) a WHERE clause search condition of a SELECT or data modification (SELECT, INSERT, DELETE, or UPDATE) statement to limit the rows that qualify for the query; (3) the search condition WHERE clause of a view, to make the view dynamically comply with the user or environment at runtime; (4) any expression; (5) a CHECK constraint or trigger, to look for specified values when data is inserted; or (6) a DEFAULT constraint or trigger, to supply a value in case one is not specified by an INSERT.

TAKE NOTE *
This example demonstrates a broken ownership chain.

```
CREATE FUNCTION Sales.SumSold(@ProductID in) RETURNS int AS
BEGIN DECLARE @ret int
  SELECT @ret = SUM(OrderQTY FROM Sales.SalesOrderDetail WHERE
  ProductID = @ProductID
  IF (@ret IS NULL) SET @ret = 0 RETURN @ret
END
```

CREATING MULTISTATEMENT TABLE-VALUED FUNCTIONS

A *multistatement table-valued function* is a combination of a view and a stored procedure. You can use user-defined functions that return a table (rows and columns) to replace stored procedures or views.

This function is characterized by having:

- A BEGIN and END statement to delimit the body of the function; that is, to bound the start and completion of the code logic.
- The RETURNS clause specifies TABLE as the datatype returned; that is, this function returns a dataset—columns and rows.
- The RETURNS clause defines a name for the table and defines the format of the table. The scope of the return variable name is local to the function.

EXERCISE 12-11 MULTISTATEMENT TABLE-VALUED FUNCTION

1. Examine and enter this code:

```
USE AdventureWorks
GO
CREATE FUNCTION dbo.fn_Contacts
(@Length nvarchar(5))
RETURNS @tbl_Employees TABLE — Note the datatype
(ContactID int PRIMARY KEY NOT NULL,
[Contact Name] nvarchar(50) NOT NULL)
AS
BEGIN
IF @Length = 'Short'
INSERT @tbl_Contacts SELECT ContactID, LastName
FROM Person.Contact
ELSE IF @Length = 'Long'
INSERT @tbl_Contacts SELECT ContactID,
(FirstName + ' '
+ Lastname) FROM Person.Contact
RETURN
END
```

2. Execute. This creates the function.
3. Use this function in the FROM clause of your query instead of using a table or a view.

```
SELECT * FROM dbo.fn_Contacts('Short')
```
or
```
SELECT * FROM dbo.fn_Contacts('Long')
```

CREATING INLINE TABLE-VALUED FUNCTIONS

Inline table-valued functions return a table and are referenced in the FROM clause, just like a view.

When using inline user-defined functions, consider the following characteristics:

- The RETURN clause contains a single SELECT statement in parentheses. The resultset forms the table that the function returns. The SELECT statement use is subject to the same restrictions as SELECT statements used in views.
- The SELECT statement cannot:
  - Include COMPUTE or COMPUTE BY clauses. Remember, the text "sum" gets in the way.
  - Include an ORDER BY clause unless there is also a TOP clause in the select list of the SELECT statement.
  - Include the INTO keyword, as dropping the results into another table is not logical.
  - Reference a temporary table or a table variable.
- BEGIN and END do *not* delimit the body of the function.
- RETURNS specifies TABLE as the datatype returned.

You do not have to define the format of a return variable because it is set by the format of the resultset of the SELECT statement in the RETURN clause.

 EXERCISE 12-12 INLINE TABLE-VALUED FUNCTION

1. Enter the following code in your Query Editor:
   ```
   USE AdventureWorks
   GO
   CREATE FUNCTION fn_CustomerNamesInStates
   (@RegionParameter nvarchar(30))
   RETURNS Table
   AS
   RETURN (
   SELECT CustomerID, LastName
   FROM Person.Contact
   WHERE ModifiedDate > '01/01/2005')
   ```
2. Execute the statement.

Introducing CLR Functions

In the same way you can write managed code procedures, you now can also write a user-defined function in any .NET programming language. Also, as with the scalar functions or a table-valued Transact-SQL function, a managed code (CLR) function can be scalar or table-valued. An example of the implementation of a CLR scalar-valued functions is a real-time currency conversion. It is possible within the managed procedure to gain access to a Web service, get the most recent conversion data, and use that within the scalar-valued CLR function.

Before you can use a managed function, you first need to enable CLR support on the server. You can do this by executing the following syntax in the Query Editor:

```
sp_configure 'clr_enabled', 1
reconfigure
```

When a call to a CLR function is made without having the CLR enabled, an error message will appear, saying that the .NET Framework is not enabled.

A CLR function is also useful in an environment where you want to have access to the operating system. The following example, written in VB.NET, performs an operating system call to determine the current computer's IP address:

```
Imports System
Imports System.Data
Imports System.Data.SqlClient
Imports System.Data.SqlTypes
Imports Microsoft.SqlServer.Server
Imports System.Net
Imports System.Runtime.InteropServices
Partial Public Class UserDefinedFunctions
<Microsoft.SqlServer.Server.SqlFunction
(name:="GetIP", fillrowmethodname:="FillIpRow",
tabledefinition:="ipaddress
nvarchar(20)")> _
Public Shared Function GetIP(ByVal servername As
SqlString) As IEnumerable
Dim hostname As IPHostEntry
hostname = Dns.GetHostEntry(servername.Value)
' Resolve is obsolete
Return hostname.AddressList
End Function
Public Shared Sub FillIpRow(ByVal o As Object, <Out()> ByRef ip
As
SqlString)
ip = o.ToString
End Sub
End Class
```

The resulting intermediate file must be imported into SQL Server by using the CREATE ASSEMBLY Transact-SQL statement. You must then use the CREATE FUNCTION statement to generate the new CLR function.

Understanding Deterministic and Nondeterministic Functions

SQL Server marks a function as deterministic or nondeterministic. A **deterministic function** always returns the same result, given a specific input value. For example, a conversion function that transforms a temperature from Fahrenheit to Celsius is deterministic because given an input value, it will always return the same resultset. A **nondeterministric function** always returns a different value each time it is invoked.

You can create an index on a **computed column** if a function is deterministic. This means whenever the row is updated, the index will also be updated, and you could gain a lot of query performance when using the function in a query expression.

User-defined functions are deterministic when they are:

- Schema-bound
- Defined with only deterministic user-defined or built-in functions

EXERCISE 12-13 IS THE FUNCTION DETERMINISTIC?

1. Enter this code:

    USE AdventureWorks

    IF ObjectProperty (Object_ID ('dbo.ufnGetProductDealerPrice'), 'IsDeterministic') = 0
    PRINT 'This function is not deterministic'

2. Execute.

The result shows the function is not deterministic.

As with managed procedures, you use CLR functions to perform complex calculations or conversions that are outside the scope of a data-centric environment, or to create functionality that scopes outside of SQL Server and cannot be resolved within a T-SQL function. All functions are deterministic or nondeterministic:

- Deterministic functions always return the same result any time they are called with a specific set of input values.
- Nondeterministic functions may return different results each time they are called with a specific set of input values.

Whether a function is deterministic or nondeterministic is called the *determinism of the function*. A function needs to be deterministic in order to be able to create an index on the computed column or on the view definition where the function is used.

SQL Server 2005 permits the use of nondeterministic built-in functions within user-defined functions, with the exception of NEWID( ), RAND( ), NEWSEQUENTIALID( ), and TEXTPTR( ).

Using Schema Binding

SCHEMA BINDING connects the function to the object that it references. All attempts to drop the object referenced by a schema-bound function will fail. To create a function with the WITH SCHEMABINDING option, the following must be true:

- All views and user-defined functions referenced by the function must be schema-bound as well.
- All objects referenced by the function must be in the same database.

EXERCISE 12-14 CREATING A CLR USER-DEFINED FUNCTION

1. Copy **Lesson12.dll** and **Lesson12.sql** from your text CD to the Practice directory already created on the root of your C: drive.
2. Open a new database Query Editor instance on the MSSQL_Training database context.
3. Create a user-defined function by using the following syntax:
   USE MSSQL_Training
   CREATE ASSEMBLY Lesson12
   FROM 'C:\Practice\Lesson12.dll'
   WITH PERMISSION_SET = EXTERNAL_ACCESS
   If you processed the assembly in a previous exercise, you will get an error message that the assembly is already cataloged.
4. Create a function from the Visual Basic code supplied as a dynamic linked library:
   CREATE FUNCTION [dbo].[GetIP] (@servername [nvarchar](4000)) RETURNS TABLE ([IPaddress] [nvarchar](20)) AS EXTERNAL NAME [Lesson12].[Chapter5.UserDefinedFunctions].[GetIP]
5. Test the CLR user-defined function:
   SELECT * FROM [Mssql_Training].[dbo].[GetIP] ('localhost')

You don't want users to question you about resultsets from queries you run for them that include the word "null." Instead of answering the question: "What does null mean in the middle of a name?" you decide to write a scalar user-defined function.

⊙ **EXERCISE 12-15 CREATING A TRANSACT-SQL USER-DEFINED FUNCTION**

1. Use this example code:

```
CREATE FUNCTION FN_NMN
(@Null_Input nvarchar(30))
RETURNS char(30) —— Note the RETURNS with an S
BEGIN
IF @Null_Input IS NULL
SET @Null_Input = ' NMN '—— Abbreviation for No
—— Middle Name
RETURN @Null_Input —— Note the RETURN without an S
END
```

2. Execute.

3. You then use it as follows:

```
USE MyDateBase
SELECT FName, FN_NMI(MName), LName
FROM MyTable
```

4. The resultset then appears as:

Mary Tyler Moore
Sam NMN Snead

SKILL SUMMARY

IN THIS LESSON YOU LEARNED:

You learned that functions have three forms: scalar, multistatement table-valued, and inline table-valued. Scalar types return a single value; for example, GETDATE( ) returns the current day and time. Both forms of table-valued functions return a dataset; for example, rows and columns.

Built-in functions perform common tasks. They have been developed over the years, and their number keeps increasing as new situations warrant the inclusion of new solutions in SQL Server.

For the certification examination:

- Know the use of functions. Know when to apply any of the three forms to specific scenarios.

- Know, in general, the built-in functions. Know, in particular, Substring( ), Datediff( ), and Dateadd( ).

- Know the consequences of including nondeterministic functions and functions that reference alias datatypes.

■ Knowledge Assessment

Multiple Choice

Circle the letter or letters that correspond to the best answer or answers.

1. You need to determine whether a function named fnTest from the sales schema is deterministic. Which code can you use?

   a. SELECT OBJECTPROPERTY (OBJECT_ID ('sales.fnTest'),
      'IsDeterministic');
      GO

b. SELECT OBJECTPROPERTY (OBJECT_ID ('sales.fnTest'),
   'Deterministic');
   GO

c. SELECT TYPEPROPERTY (OBJECT_ID ('sales.fnTest')
   'IsDeterministic');
   GO

d. SELECT TYPEPROPERTY (OBJECT_ID ('sales.fnTest'),
   'Deterministic');
   GO

2. You need to create a clustered index on a view. Which functions can be used inside the view definition? (Choose all that apply.)
   a. AVG()
   b. RAND()
   c. RAND(1000)
   d. GETDATE()

3. You have a query that returns a list with employees. You want to add a column to your query that will display a sequential number for identification purposes. Which of the following functions can be used?
   a. The RANK function
   b. The DENSE_RANK function
   c. The ROW_NUMBER function
   d. The NTILE function

Case Scenarios

Scenario 12-1: Using Functions

You continue to support the Joint Application Design team. They have three more assignments. You have asked for help from your staff. Stand at the whiteboard and facilitate discussion of how to achieve these three assignments:

- You have stored your zip codes for United States of America addresses as datatype characters of length 9 (char(9)). Write a scalar function that will insert a hyphen after the fifth character position.

- You have stored your customers' first name, middle name, and last name in separate varchar(50) fields. Write a function that will combine the names with their middle initials, suitable for use on a mailing label.

- You have stored your sales data as UnitsOfSale in Integer datatype and UnitPrice in Money datatype. Write a function that will include the total dollar sales per record in the resultset.

Transactions and Locks

LESSON SKILL MATRIX

TECHNOLOGY SKILL	70-431 EXAM OBJECTIVE
Retrieve data to support ad hoc and recurring data.	Foundational
Construct SQL queries to return data.	Foundational
Identify collation details.	Foundational
Manipulate relational data.	Foundational
Handle exceptions and errors.	Foundational
Manage transactions.	Foundational
Monitor and resolve blocks and deadlocks.	Foundational
Identify the cause of a block by using the sys.dm_exec_requests system view.	Foundational
Terminate an errant process.	Foundational
Identify transaction blocks.	Foundational
Implement a table.	Foundational
Specify a transaction.	Foundational
Gather performance and optimization data by using DMVs.	Foundational

KEY TERMS

collation: A set of rules that determines how data is compared, ordered, and presented. Character data is sorted using collation information that includes locale, sort order, and case sensitivity.

deadlock: A situation when two users, each having a lock on one piece of data, attempt to acquire a lock on the other's piece. Unless one of the user processes is terminated, each user would wait indefinitely for the other to release the lock. SQL Server detects deadlocks and terminates one user's process.

distributed transaction: A transaction spanning multiple data sources. In a distributed transaction, all data modifications in all accessed data sources are either committed or terminated.

explicit transaction: A group of SQL statements enclosed within transaction delimiters that define both the start and end of the transaction.

implicit transaction: A connection option in which each SQL Statement executed by the connection is considered a separate transaction.

lazywriter: The lazywriter is a system process that ensures free buffers are available by removing infrequently used pages from the buffer cache. "Dirty" pages are first written to disk.

lock: A restriction on access to a resource in a multiuser environment. SQL Server locks users out of specific database objects automatically to maintain security or prevent concurrent data modification problems.

transaction: A group of database operations combined into a logical unit of work that is either wholly committed or totally rolled back.

transaction log: A database file in which all changes to the database are recorded. SQL Server uses transaction logs during recovery to assure data integrity.

transaction rollback: Recovery of a user-specified transaction to the last savepoint inside a transaction or to the beginning of transaction; used to restore data to a known and correct state.

Using Transactions

THE BOTTOM LINE

A *transaction* is a series of steps that perform a logical unit of work. Transactions must adhere to ACID properties, that is:

1. **Atomicity:** Either all of the steps must succeed or none of them may succeed.
2. **Consistency:** The data must be left in a predictable and usable state.
3. **Isolation:** Changes made must not be influenced by other concurrent transactions.
4. **Durability:** The changes made must be permanent in the database and survive even system failures.

Understanding Transactions

To help you understand how SQL Server handles and works with transactions to perform data manipulations (via DML), this section will cover how data is inserted and allocated in memory before the data is written into the *transaction log*, and then how it is applied to the database data files. When performing data manipulations, SQL Server records all changes made in the transaction log to allow any changes to be undone (rolled back) or redone (rolled forward) in case of a system failure.

When updating or inserting a record into a database, the record is first allocated in buffer memory, and the buffer manager guarantees that the transaction log is written before the changes to the database file are written. It does this by keeping track of a log position using a log sequence number (LSN).

At certain intervals, SQL Server issues a checkpoint in the transaction log that issues a write from the transaction log to the data file. Depending on the setting of the transaction log defined in the database recovery model, the transaction log will keep the committed and written records in the transaction log or truncate the log.

This process of working with the transaction log and recording actions in the transaction log before applying them to the actual data files allows SQL Server to recover from failures in case of an unexpected shutdown; this is known as *autorecovery*.

The autorecovery process will check the database to see what the last-issued checkpoint and written LSN were and will then write all committed records from the transaction log that were not recorded yet in the data file to the data file. This process is a rollforward. Different from other database systems such as Oracle, SQL Server automatically issues a transaction (autocommitted) on every statement, so you don't need to explicitly commit these transactions.

UNDERSTANDING THE TRANSACTION LOG

SQL Server 2005 uses a buffer cache, which is an in-memory structure, into which it retrieves data pages from disk for use by applications and users. Each modification to a data page is made to the copy of the page in the buffer cache. A modified buffer page in the cache that has not yet been written to disk is called a *dirty page*. The modification is recorded in the transaction log before it is written to disk. For this reason, the SQL Server 2005 transaction log is called a *write-ahead* transaction log. SQL Server 2005 has internal logic to ensure that a modification is recorded in the transaction log before the associated dirty page is written to disk. When SQL Server writes the dirty page in the cache to the disk, it is called *flushing the page*.

SQL Server 2005 periodically writes dirty pages to disk from the buffer cache. These writes occur either when a database checkpoint process occurs or when an operating system thread (either an individual worker thread or a **lazywriter** thread) scans for dirty pages, writes the dirty pages to disk, and then clears space in the buffer cache to hold new data pages. Operating system threads may write dirty pages to disk before SQL Server 2005 knows whether the transaction is complete. However, if a transaction rolls back or never completes, the transaction log ensures that modifications made to disk by transactions that did not complete will be rolled back either via a rollback command or when the server restarts in the case of a server failure.

The checkpoint process is designed to minimize the recovery time if the server fails by minimizing the number of pages in the buffer cache that have not been written to disk. Checkpoints occur whenever:

- A CHECKPOINT statement is issued.
- The ALTER DATABASE statement is used.
- An instance of SQL Server 2005 is stopped normally.
- An automatic checkpoint is issued.

Automatic checkpoints are generated periodically based on the number of records in the active portion of the transaction log, not on the amount of time that has elapsed since the last checkpoint

The checkpoint process records the lowest LSN (log sequence number) that must be present for a successful rollback of an incomplete transaction. This number is called the *minimum LSN* (MinLSN). The MinLSN is based on the lowest LSN of the oldest active transaction, the beginning of the oldest replication transaction that has not been replicated yet to all subscribers, or the start of the checkpoint. The portion of the transaction log from the MinLSN to the most recent transaction log record is the active portion of the transaction log and must be present to ensure a successful rollback, if necessary. Whenever SQL Server 2005 starts, a recovery process occurs on each database. The recovery process checks the transaction log for complete transactions that were not written to disk and rolls them forward. It also checks the transaction log for incomplete transactions and makes sure they were not written to disk. If they were written to disk, they are removed from the disk. The MinLSN from the most recent checkpoint identifies the earliest LSN that SQL Server 2005 must look at during this recovery process.

All transaction log records lower than the MinLSN are no longer active (the checkpoint ensures that records older then the MinLSN have been written to disk). To reuse this space, the transaction log records must be truncated (deleted) from the transaction log file. The smallest unit of truncation is an individual VLF (virtual log file). If any part of a VLF is part of the active log, that VLF cannot be truncated. If the simple recovery model is used, the checkpoint process simply truncates each VLF within the inactive portion of the transaction log (allowing these VLFs to be reused). If the Full recovery or Bulk-Logged recovery models are used, you must back up the transaction log to truncate the inactive portion

TAKE NOTE*

A VLF is an individual physical file. The database engine chooses the size of the virtual files dynamically. You want as few as possible, but you can't control this directly, so allocate as large a space as you can, initially. If the log file must grow, make each increment as large as possible.

of the transaction log. Figure 13-1 illustrates the transaction log after a checkpoint has occurred and the inactive portion of the transaction log has been truncated.

The checkpoint process frees space from the physical transaction log file so that the logical log file can reuse space when it reaches the end of the last physical transaction log file. When the end of the logical transaction log reaches the end of the last physical transaction log file, the logical transaction log wraps to the beginning of the first physical file (provided that the first VLF has been truncated). If the first VLF has not been truncated and the transaction log is not set to autogrow (or the drive is out of disk space), SQL Server 2005 cannot continue to function. Figure 13-2 illustrates this wrapping of the logical log to the beginning of the first physical transaction log file.

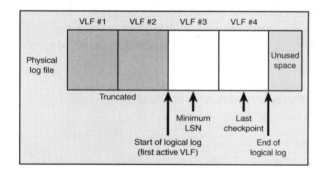

Figure 13-1

Log file organization with available space at the end

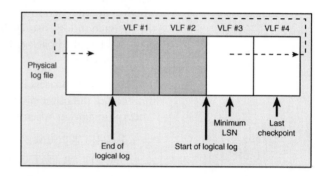

Figure 13-2

Log file with no available space at the end

In the next section, you'll learn the difference between implicit and explicit transactions.

EXECUTING IMPLICIT AND EXPLICIT TRANSACTIONS

By default, SQL Server automatically commits a transaction to the database, and every transaction is handled as a single process. When you perform a query that issues a DML statement (insert/update/delete), SQL Server automatically commits the transaction by recording an LSN in the transaction log. Because this process occurs without any explicit request from you to confirm the action, this is called an autocommit. A connection to SQL Server operates in autocommit mode unless overridden by the start of an explicit transaction (BEGIN TRANSACTION) or the implicit transaction mode is switched on (SET IMPLICIT_TRANSACTIONS ON).

CERTIFICATION READY?
When should you use each of the three transaction types?

When working with transactions, SQL Server supports two types of user-controlled transactions: implicit and explicit.

When using *implicit transactions* and the connection is not currently in a transaction, executing any of the statements listed in Table 13-1 starts a transaction.

Table 13-1

Implicit Transaction Initiators

ALTER TABLE	CREATE	DELETE	DROP
FETCH	GRANT	INSERT	OPEN
REVOKE	SELECT	TRUNCATE TABLE	UPDATE

If the connection is already in an open transaction, the statements are included in the current process and committed. Transactions started automatically must be explicitly committed or rolled back before you disconnect. The difference between an implicit transaction and auto-committed transactions is that you still need to COMMIT the implicit transaction by the end of the session.

In order to group actions together as one single unit, you must use *explicit transactions*. For example, when you transfer money from one bank account to another using a transaction, you want the action to take place on both of the accounts at the same time; to guarantee this happens, you have to perform an explicit transaction. When working with explicit transactions, you identify the Transact-SQL code to be included by using a BEGIN TRANSACTION and a COMMIT TRANSACTION or ROLLBACK TRANSACTION statement.

The following code demonstrates the process of grouping actions logically based on transactional consistency for the same banking example:

```
BEGIN TRANSACTION
-- Take $500 from the savings account
UPDATE Savings
SET Balance = Balance - 500
WHERE Account = 10401
-- Error check: make sure there's $500 available
-- Add $500 to the checking account
UPDATE Checking
Set Balance = Balance + 500
WHERE Account = 10401
-- Error check: make sure the checking account is active
COMMIT TRANSACTION
```

COMMITTING AND ROLLING BACK

TAKE NOTE*

Both actions (deducting from savings and adding to checking) must happen, or nothing must happen. The bank must not experience losing someone's money because a subtraction was made and then a power failure occurred.

When you want to confirm a transaction, you issue a COMMIT TRANSACTION statement. This will close the open statements and confirm the grouped DML statements. If you don't want a transaction to occur, that is, you want to cause a ***transaction rollback***, you issue a ROLLBACK TRANSACTION statement.

A typical transaction block looks like this:

```
BEGIN TRANSACTION
-- If failure or error
ROLLBACK TRANSACTION
-- Else
COMMIT TRANSACTION
```

For example, say you want to delete a customer in your Customers database; however, before you delete the customer, you want to insert the customer details into a history table and commit the deletion only if the insert into the temporary table succeeded. Your decision whether to roll back or commit a transaction depends on error handling (learn more in the "Introducing Error Handling" section).

SQL Server supports the nesting of transactions; in other words, within a transaction, another transaction can be called. When nesting transactions, the outer transaction will determine when the inner transaction is committed. This allows you to partially commit and roll back some of the transactions within an outer transaction block. You can, for example, roll back the inner statement or statements while committing the outer statement. The following code segment demonstrates the concept of a typical nested transaction process:

```
BEGIN TRANSACTION
-- Statements
  BEGIN TRANSACTION
  -- Statements
  COMMIT TRANSACTION
COMMIT TRANSACTION
```

You can monitor transactions in SQL Server using the @@TRANCOUNT variable, which will show you the number of open transactions.

EXECUTING DISTRIBUTED TRANSACTIONS

When executing a ***distributed transaction***, SQL Server doesn't really differ a lot from executing an explicit transaction. The transaction, however, will be considered to execute over a remote connection and will be managed and coordinated by the Microsoft Distributed Transaction Coordinator (DTC). In a distributed environment, you work over the network segment, so the execution of the transaction will take place using a two-phase commit.

The code looks similar to what you've seen so far:

```
BEGIN DISTRIBUTED TRANSACTION
  UPDATE DatabaseRemote.Checking.Accounts
  SET Balance = Balance + 500
  WHERE Account = 10401
  UPDATE DatabaseRemote.Savings.Accounts
  SET Balance = Balance - 500
  WHERE Account = 10401
COMMIT TRANSACTION
```

Understanding Locks

Consider the banking example of moving money from savings to checking. Assume a husband and wife each enter a different branch office where a teller performs the same action against their joint account. When the teller at Branch A performs the action, SQL Server issues a lock on the account to prevent the teller at Branch B from doing anything until Teller A has finished. Locks prevent users from reading or modifying data that other users are in the process of changing.

As another example, if you want to compute the average of all account values, you want assurance someone else is not changing the data you are using to compute the aggregate value. Locks, then, prevent conflicts.

Two main types of lock come into play:

- **Read locks:** Read locks ensure other users don't change the data you are retrieving but allow other users to read the data at the same time.
- **Write locks:** Write locks ensure no other users can examine or change the data you are updating.

Sometimes deadlocks can occur. Consider the banking example again:

BRANCH A	BRANCH B
UPDATE Savings	UPDATE Checking
SET Balance = Balance + 500	SET Balance = Balance − 500
WHERE Account = 10401	WHERE Account = 10401

Branch A needs to update Checking and Branch B needs to update Savings on the same account. Neither can complete the transactions as each has a hold on the row in the table the other needs. This is called a *deadlock*. So that the tellers don't have to wait forever, the SQL Server detects the deadlock and kills the transaction with the least cost invested and issues an Error 1205.

Application programmers must pay special heed to Error 1205, as it indicates the transaction was not completed and must be initiated again. This is one of the error checks discussed in the error handling section later in this lesson.

Locks permit the *serialization* of transactions, meaning only one person can change a data element at a time.

During a transaction, SQL Server controls and sets the appropriate level of locking. You can control how some locks are used by including locking hints in your query. Look at the SELECT statement in step 3 of Exercise 13-3 for an example.

Specific types of locks allow users to access and update data at the same time. A SELECT may be allowed at the same time as an UPDATE, but the UPDATE blocks a second UPDATE. This concept, known as *concurrency*, can increase response time from the user's perspective.

Concurrency control means changes made by one person do not adversely affect modifications other users make. There are two types of concurrency control:

- **Pessimistic:** Pessimistic concurrency control locks data when data is read in preparation for an update.
- **Optimistic:** Optimistic concurrency control does not lock data when data is initially read.

You have a number of control mechanisms to enforce the concurrency control you might need in your environment. The bottom line, again, is user response versus data consistency. Use pessimistic concurrency where high contention for data exists and the cost of protecting the data with locks is less than the cost of rolling back transactions if concurrency conflicts occur. Use optimistic concurrency when low contention for data exists and the cost of occasionally rolling back a transaction is less than the cost of locking data when it is read.

When users access data concurrently, a risk exists that one user's actions might affect the records another user is accessing. Locks can prevent the following situations that compromise transaction integrity:

- **Lost updates:** An update can be overwritten by a second update. The initial update is lost.
- **Uncommitted dependencies (dirty read):** A read operation captures data prior to the prior transaction completing. If other changes occur within the update or delete transaction, the read operation may have data that no longer exists.
- **Inconsistent analysis (nonrepeatable read):** When a transaction reads the same row more than one time, and between the two (or more) readings the data changes, different values are retrieved.
- **Phantom reads:** Mysterious data returns can occur when transactions are not isolated from each other. If you first read the data while another user inserts a new record to that table, the next time you read it an additional record is present.

To control these situations SQL Server locks resources, as shown in Table 13-2.

Table 13-2

Lockable Resources

ITEM	DESCRIPTION
RID	Row identifier
Key	Row lock within an index
Page	Data or index page
Extent	Group of pages
Table	Entire table
HOBT	A heap or B-tree
File	A database file
Application	An application-specified resource
Metadata	System table locks
Allocation unit	A set of pages that can be operated on as a whole
Database	Entire database

SQL Server uses different locking modes to control how resources can be accessed by concurrent transactions. These types of locks are:

- Shared
- Exclusive
- Intent
- Update
- Schema
- Bulk update

Shared locks are used for operations that don't change data. They are used for read-only operations.

Exclusive locks are used for write operations. Only one transaction can acquire an exclusive lock on a resource for an INSERT, UPDATE, and/or DELETE operation. A shared lock is blocked when an exclusive lock holds the resource.

Intent locks minimize locking conflicts by establishing a locking hierarchy, preventing transactions from gaining a more inclusive lock. If a transaction holds a row lock on a resource, another transaction can't gain a table lock that also includes the affected row.

Update locks hold a page available for change at a later point. Once ready, SQL Server promotes the update page lock to an exclusive page lock. This, like Intent locks, prevents locking conflicts.

Schema locks prevent an architectural change (e.g., a table or index being dropped or altered) at the same time it is referenced by another session.

Bulk update locks enable processes to bulk copy data concurrently into the same table while preventing other processes that are not mass copying data from accessing the table.

Locks must cooperate at yet another level. Table 13-3 shows the compatibility one lock has with another. Two users, for example, can hold shared locks on the same resource, but only one update lock can be issued for the included data at any one time.

Table 13-3

Lock Compatibility

	EXISTING GRANTED LOCK					
Requested Lock	*IS*	*S*	*U*	*IX*	*SIX*	*X*
Intent Shared (IS)	Yes	Yes	Yes	Yes	Yes	No
Shared (S)	Yes	Yes	Yes	No	No	No
Update (U)	Yes	Yes	No	No	No	No
Intent Exclusive (IX)	Yes	No	No	Yes	No	No
Shared with Intent Exclusive (SIX)	Yes	No	No	No	No	No
Exclusive (X)	No	No	No	No	No	No

SQL Server controls locking options at the session level with the transaction isolation level setting. The syntax is simple:

```
SET TRANSACTION ISOLATION LEVEL {READ UNCOMMITTED | READ
COMMITTED | REPEATABLE READ | SNAPSHOT | SERIALIZABLE}
```

CERTIFICATION READY?
The isolation level controls SQL Server behavior in conjunction with a SELECT statement.

The isolation level controls the locking and row-versioning behavior of Transact-SQL statements issued by a connection to SQL Server. All read operations performed within the transaction operate under the rules for the specified isolation level, unless a table hint in the FROM clause of a statement specifies different locking or versioning behavior for the table. Because this is a connection property, these controls occur at execute or runtime and not at parse time. Table 13-4 provides a brief description of each setting.

Table 13-4

Isolation Level Options

OPTION	DESCRIPTION
READ COMMITTED with READ_COMMITTED_SNAPSHOT OFF	Directs SQL Server to use shared locks while reading. At this level, you cannot experience dirty reads.
READ COMMITTED with READ_COMMITTED_SNAPSHOT ON	Directs SQL Server to use row versioning instead of locking. The data is not protected from updates made by other transactions.
READ UNCOMMITTED	Directs SQL Server not to issue shared locks and does not honor exclusive locks. You can experience dirty reads.
REPEATABLE READ	Indicates that dirty reads and nonrepeatable reads cannot occur. Shared locks are held until the end of the transaction.
SERIALIZABLE	Prevents other users from updating or inserting new rows that match the criteria in the WHERE clause of the transaction. Phantoms cannot occur.
SNAPSHOT	Directs SQL Server not to lock the data but to present a snapshot view of the data at the beginning of the transaction.

EXERCISE 13-1 EXAMINING USER OPTIONS

1. Migrate to a new **Query Editor** session.
2. In the Query Editor, enter the following code:

```
SET TRANSACTION ISOLATION LEVEL READ UNCOMMITTED
DBCC USEROPTIONS
```

3. Examine the output. Near the bottom of the 13 rows returned you should see confirmation of isolation level setting.

TAKE NOTE * To use the SNAPSHOT isolation level, the ALLOW_SNAPSHOT_ISOLATION database option must be set to ON.

You may set the maximum amount of time that SQL Server allows a transaction to wait for the release of a blocked resource (including deadlocks). Use the following syntax:

```
SET LOCK_TIMEOUT Length_of_time_in_milliseconds
```

This example sets the lock timeout period to three minutes:

```
SET LOCK_TIMEOUT 180000
```

The default value is −1 (wait forever). Any change lasts for as long as the connection exists. A value of 0 means no wait at all—return a message as soon as a lock is encountered.

You need to know what's going on with locks. Examine the following tools:

- Activity Monitor window in Management Studio
- sys.dm_tranlocks Dynamic Management View
- EnumLocks method
- SQL Server Profiler
- Windows 2003 System Monitor

Use the Activity Monitor in SQL Server Management Studio to display information about current locking activity. You can view server activity by user and locking information by process or object.

 EXERCISE 13-2 CURRENT ACTIVITY WINDOW

1. Open **Management Studio**.
2. Click the **plus (+) sign** next to Management in your Object Browser → double-left-click **Activity Monitor**.
3. Note that in the *Select a page view* you have three choices. Click on **Locks by Object**.
4. You are presented with a resultset identifying the Process ID in the first column and the Request Mode in the eighth column. Note the entries. Go back to Table 13-3, if necessary, and identify each lock type.
5. Change to **Locks by Process**. Examine the information. Note the Request Mode column is repeated, but the other entries give you slightly different information.
6. Click on **Process Info**. Let's say you detected a problem with Process ID 54. Right-click that row, and note that you can kill the process to remove the errant blockage from holding up the rest of your users. Note also that this display indicates the user owning the process. You might talk to him or her prior to bumping him or her off.

CERTIFICATION READY?
Dynamic management views are new to SQL Server 2005.

You can query the sys.dm_tran_lock view to retrieve information about the locks currently held by an instance of the database engine. Each row returned describes a currently granted lock or a requested lock.

 EXERCISE 13-3 QUERY A DYNAMIC MANAGEMENT VIEW

1. Return to **Management Studio**.
2. Start a **New Query**.
3. Set up some activity by entering and executing the following T-SQL code:

```
USE TempDB
GO
-- Create a test table and index
CREATE TABLE t_lock (c1 int, c2 int);
GO
CREATE INDEX t_lock_ci on t_lock(c1);
GO
-- Insert values into the test table
INSERT INTO t_lock VALUES (1, 1);
INSERT INTO t_lock VALUES (2, 2);
INSERT INTO t_lock VALUES (3, 3);
INSERT INTO t_lock VALUES (4, 4);
INSERT INTO t_lock VALUES (5, 5);
INSERT INTO t_lock VALUES (6, 6);
-- Session 1
SET TRANSACTION ISOLATION LEVEL READ COMMITTED;
BEGIN TRAN
-- The next line shows the use of query hints.
```

```
SELECT c1 FROM t_lock WITH (holdlock, rowlock);
-- Session 2
BEGIN TRAN
UPDATE t_lock SET c1 = 10;
-- Note that both transactions are held open
```

4. Get the identification of TempDB.

```
-- Get TempDB id
SELECT Name, Database_id FROM sys.databases WHERE Name = tempdb'
```

5. Query the dynamic management view.

```
-- Query for lock information.
-- In the query substitute the actual database id
-- you just received for ,dbid. in the WHERE
-- clause.
SELECT resource_type, resource_associated_entity_id, request_status, request_mode,
request_session_id, resource_description FROM sys.dm_tran_locks WHERE resource_
database_id = ,dbid.
```

6. Examine the output. Both transactions are held open; both must maintain their locks until complete.

7. Return to **Management Studio** and the **Current Activity** window. Kill the process listed in the request_session_id column.

An application that uses the SQL Management Objects (SMO) application programming interface can get a list of the active locks of the database engine or a database by using the EnumLocks method of the Server or Database class, respectively.

SQL Server Profiler monitors server activities. Use the Locks Event Category to capture locking information in a trace.

You can view SQL Server locking information by using Microsoft Windows Server 2003 System Monitor. Use the SQLServer:Locks objects to retrieve this information.

Using Data Manipulation Language Queries

The data manipulation language keywords SELECT, INSERT, UPDATE, and DELETE examine and change data in your tables.

USING THE SELECT STATEMENT

To retrieve data from one or more tables, use these keywords in this order:

```
SELECT
FROM
WHERE
GROUP BY
HAVING
ORDER BY
```

Check Books Online for the full syntax and all options for the SELECT statement.

When querying data, you sometimes need to return the data in a different manner than how you stored it. For instance, the data could be returned as follows:

- In a different format
- In a different order
- In a different collation

For a list and explanation of the built-in functions for presenting data, see Lesson 12.

PRESENTING DATA IN A DIFFERENT FORMAT

To format data, you have several functions you can apply to a query. For example, you can apply the CONVERT function to convert between datatypes; or you can format datetime options, as shown here:

```
-- This example will display a string with
-- the current date displayed as: Today is mm/dd/yyyy
SELECT 'Today is ' + CONVERT(varchar,getdate(),101) as 'Current Date'
```

Notice that only the SELECT keyword is required; all others are optional.

PRESENTING DATA IN A DIFFERENT ORDER

The ORDER BY clause provides the primary means of organizing data, and it has two major keywords: ASC and DESC. Specifying ASC (the default) causes the resultset to begin with the minimum value and end with the maximum value, as in these two short examples:

1	A
2	B
3	C

Specifying DESC causes the resultset to begin with the maximum value and end with the minimum value, as in these two short examples:

3	C
2	B
1	A

PRESENTING DATA IN DIFFERENT COLLATIONS

Collations are used within databases to display and store an international character set, based on business requirements. When returning data, you have the ability to retrieve the data in a collation type different from how it was stored. When working with these multiple collations, you can invoke the COLLATE keyword and then specify the collation type you prefer to use. You can use the COLLATE keyword in various ways and at several levels:

COLLATE on database creation: You can use the COLLATE clause of the CREATE DATABASE or ALTER DATABASE statement to specify the default collation of the database. You can also specify a collation when you create a database using SQL Server Management Studio. If you do not specify a collation, the database is assigned the default collation of the instance of SQL Server.

COLLATE on table creation: You can specify collations for each varchar or char column using the COLLATE clause in the CREATE TABLE or ALTER TABLE statement. You can also specify a collation when you create a table using SQL Server Management Studio. If you do not specify a collation, the column is assigned the default collation of the database.

COLLATE by casting or expression: You can use the COLLATE clause to cast an expression to a certain collation. You can assign the COLLATE clause to any ORDER BY or comparison statement, as listed in the example here:

```
USE AdventureWorks
SELECT FirstName, LastName from Person.Contact
ORDER BY LastName COLLATE Latin1_General_BIN
```

Collations supported by SQL 2005 SQL: Server 2005 supports more than 1,000 collation types, so it is important to know whether the data you want to retrieve needs to match a certain collation.

To view an overview of existing collation types, since you have to reference them by name in SQL Server 2005, use SQL Server Books Online or the fn_ HelpCollations( ) function, as in:

```
SELECT * from fn_HelpCollations().
```

Introducing Error Handling

SQL Server 2005 has greatly improved error-handling capabilities when compared to other database platforms. In the following sections, you will learn how to use various error-handling techniques and methods that are available within SQL Server. This includes everything from implementing a TRY…CATCH block as used within various programming languages such as VisualBasic and C# to creating user-defined error messages that can be raised from within a T-SQL batch.

SQL Server also uses various application variables that will provide you detailed information about the actual occurred error. It is important to understand how to create and work with error messages and how to suppress and handle potential errors within a T-SQL batch. You'll learn about the RAISERROR statement first.

USING RAISERROR

RAISERROR allows you to raise custom error messages, based on a predefined error or a user-defined error messages. You can use the RAISERROR statement in a T-SQL batch based on the error's severity level.

The code syntax for the RAISERROR statement is as follows:

```
RAISERROR ( { msg_id | msg_str | @local_variable }
{,severity,state }
[,argument [,...n ] ] )
[ WITH option [,...n ] ]
```

The message displayed can be a predefined error message that is called by the message_id or a message string that you pass to the statement, as shown here:

```
RAISERROR ('This is a message', 1, 1)
```

The severity level identifies the level of error. Any user can specify levels from 0 to 18, and only members of the sysadmin roles or users with the ALTER TRACE permission can execute levels from 19 to 25. When you specify a severity level from 19 to 25, you also need to set the WITH LOG option to log in the Application log. If you specify a severity level from 20 to 25, SQL Server will immediately stop executing code, and even close the client connection.

The values and settings that are generated by the RAISERROR statement are defined in the ERROR_ LINE, ERROR_MESSAGE, ERROR_NUMBER, ERROR_PROCEDURE, ERROR_MESSAGE, ERROR_SEVERITY, and ERROR_STATE system functions. The @@ERROR global variable contains the error number.

When RAISERROR is executed with a severity of 11 or greater, it will transfer control to the CATCH block when executed in a TRY block. You can find more information about how to use the TRY…CATCH block in the "Using TRY…CATCH Blocks" section of this lesson.

You can also use the RAISERROR statement to raise a user-defined error number, such as `RAISERROR (50001,10,1)`.

USING @@ERROR

The @@ERROR system variable returns an error number if the previously executed statement encountered an error. @@ERROR is cleared and reset on every executed statement, therefore it is important to check its value at the end of every statement.

The @@ERROR statement was a frequently used statement in SQL Server 2000; however, by using SQL Server 2005, you can now benefit from using the TRY…CATCH block, which provides enhanced error logging and error handling.

The @@ERROR is often used in the following context:

```
-- perform a certain action
If @@ERROR = 0
Begin
-- The previous statement executed successfully
End
```

When working with the @@ERROR variable, it is always better to first assign the error to a variable and work with the variable, since @@ERROR will be reset on every single statement (including an IF clause).

USING ERROR MESSAGES

Error messages and error handling have always been a problem in T-SQL; therefore, you will be pleased to learn that a number of changes have occurred to the way error handling takes place in SQL Server 2005. You can now benefit from additional system functions that provide detailed information about the occurred error. However, these will be available only within the TRY…CATCH block.

ERROR_LINE: Returns the line number at which an error occurred that caused the CATCH block of a TRY…CATCH construct to be run.

ERROR_MESSAGE: Returns the message text of the error that caused the CATCH block of a TRY…CATCH construct to be run.

ERROR_NUMBER: Returns the error number of the error that caused the CATCH block of a TRY…CATCH construct to be run.

ERROR_PROCEDURE: Returns the name of the stored procedure or trigger where an error occurred that caused the CATCH block of a TRY…CATCH construct to be run.

ERROR_SEVERITY: Returns the severity of the error that caused the CATCH block of a TRY…CATCH construct to be run.

ERROR_STATE: Returns the state number of the error that caused the CATCH block of a TRY…CATCH construct to be run.

So, in SQL Server 2005, error handling is something you do by using a TRY…CATCH block, and it really is a great way of handling errors because of its improved functionality. If you worked with @@ERROR, you will really like the way this is implemented.

USING TRY…CATCH BLOCKS

As mentioned, TRY…CATCH blocks are a great way to implement error handling in SQL Server 2005. These blocks work the same as (or very similar to) any programming language that uses a TRY…CATCH construct, and they will catch every error that has a severity level greater than 10, but not cause any termination in the database connection.

How do they work? You type the corresponding statements you want to execute in the TRY block, and you handle it in the CATCH block. A TRY…CATCH block looks like this:

```
BEGIN TRY
{ sql_statement | statement_block }
END TRY
BEGIN CATCH
{ sql_statement | statement_block }
END CATCH
[; ]
```

When the code in the CATCH block completes, the control is passed back to the actual statement after END CATCH. Any error that is caught in the CATCH block is not returned to the application, therefore you probably want to implement an error handler that uses a RAISERROR or PRINT statement within the block.

CERTIFICATION READY?
TRY…CATCH blocks can also be used in stored procedures and triggers.

Now you'll learn how to invoke a TRY...CATCH block. For this example, say you want to execute an easy calculation. To do that, you will create two variables and assign them a value:

```
Declare @var1 int
Declare @var2 int
Declare @result int
Set @var1 = 10
Set @var2 = 5
BEGIN TRY
Set @result = @var1 / @var2
Print @result
END TRY
BEGIN CATCH
Select error_number() as ErrorNumber,
error_message() as ErrorMessage
END CATCH
```

This example results in 2.

However, if you assign the variable var2 a value of 0, the statement will jump into the CATCH block because of a division-by-zero error and return the error number and message:

```
Declare @var1 int
Declare @var2 int
Declare @result int
Set @var1 = 10
Set @var2 = 0
BEGIN TRY
Set @result = @var1 / @var2
Print @result
END TRY
BEGIN CATCH
Select error_number() as ErrorNumber,
error_message() as ErrorMessage
END CATCH
```

It is considered a best practice to always include error handling within your SQL batches and stored procedures.

In Exercise 13-4 you will implement a TRY...CATCH error-handling method to prevent a logical application error—a division-by-zero error message.

EXERCISE 13-4 WORKING WITH A TRY...CATCH BLOCK

1. Type the following code in a new query window:

```
Declare @col1 int
Declare @col2 int
Declare @result decimal (9,2)
Set @col1 = 5
Set @col2 = 2
Set @result = convert(decimal(9,2),@col1) / @col2 print @result
```

2. When you execute the previous code, you get a result set of 2.5.

3. Modify the code as follows:

```
Declare @col1 int
Declare @col2 int
Declare @result decimal (9,2)
Set @col1 = 5
Set @col2 = 0
Set @result = convert(decimal(9,2),@col1) / @col2
print @result
```

4. When you execute the previous code, you will get an error message stating you cannot divide by zero. Your next step is to prevent this error message from occurring by adding a TRY...CATCH block. Modify the code to display this:

```
BEGIN TRY
Declare @col1 int
Declare @col2 int
Declare @result decimal (9,2)
Set @col1 = 5
Set @col2 = 0
Set @result = convert(decimal(9,2),@col1) / @col2
print @result
END TRY
BEGIN CATCH
Select error_message(), error_number()
END CATCH
```

You have now prevented the error.

Using Two Additional SQL Server Features

In Lesson 11, you learned that during an INSERT operation the inserted table is dynamically created, and that during a DELETE operation the deleted table is likewise created in memory for the life of the transaction. Now, instead of a trigger, you may use the OUTPUT clause to manipulate data.

You may need to keep a record of all deleted records in a history table. Consider something as conceptually simple as:

```
CREATE PROCEDURE up_AddToHistory
AS
DECLARE @HistoryTable TABLE (RowID int, RowValue varchar(100))
DELETE TOP (1) MainTable
OUTPUT deleted.* INTO @HistoryTable
```

You can then verify it works by using:

```
SELECT * from @HistoryTable
```

You learned in the Executing Implicit and Explicit Transactions section you can enclose a number of DML statements between a BEGIN TRANSACTION and a COMMIT TRANSACTION. You can also specify a mark that references the beginning of the transaction so you can later restore the log to the referenced point, like this:

```
BEGIN TRANSACTION CandidateDelete WITH MARK N'Deleting a
Job Candidate'
GO
USE AdventureWorks
GO
DELETE FROM AdventureWorks.HumanResources.JobCandidate
WHERE JobCandidateID = 13;
GO
COMMIT TRANSACTION CandidateDelete;
GO
```

Now presume something went wrong and you have determined it was this transaction. You may restore from database or log backups, stopping the restore prior to the execution of this transaction, like so:

```
RESTORE LOG AdventureWorks FROM AdventureWorksBackups WITH
FILE = 4, RECOVERY, STOPATMARK = 'Deleting a Job Candidate'
```

Remember that all INSERT, UPDATE, and DELETE actions are logged in the transaction file. Should you need to audit what happens on the network or in the transaction file, third-party tools can capture and read all activities, allowing you to prove data changes prior to being stored in the database.

SKILL SUMMARY

IN THIS LESSON YOU LEARNED:

Working with transactions allows you to roll back or cancel a transaction to execute in case of a certain event or condition, or even roll back multiple grouped statements in a distributed environment.

SQL Server 2005 supports various recovery models. The most common—but also the one with the biggest transaction log size—is the Full recovery model. However, if you perform large amounts of batch and bulk inserts, it might be useful not to set the recovery model to Full and instead use the Bulk-Logged recovery model.

The error handling in SQL Server 2005 is one of the best error-handling capabilities so far in the SQL language because it implements a TRY...CATCH block, just as it does in programming languages such as VisualBasic and C#. Since the release of SQL Server 2005, you can now easily retrieve the error message, which was a bit more difficult in SQL Server 2000.

For the certification examination:

- Understand and be able to use transactions. You need to truly understand how transactions work and how you can enforce an explicit transaction within a SQL batch. It is also important to understand how distributed transactions work and how you can implement error handling within the transactional processing.

- Know how to identify collations. You need to understand that SQL Server uses collations to play around with different sort orders and character sets within the database. Collations can be designed on a database level, but they also are implemented with the table creation—or even enforced by explicitly casting or converting to a different collation type. Understand how to handle exceptions and errors. The main focus on error handling should be on how to implement a TRY...CATCH block and roll back transactions within the error handling. You need to be familiar with the new methods in error handling and how to use their syntax.

- Understand how to configure database recovery models. When configuring database recovery models, you need to fully understand that a BULK INSERT statement has a huge impact on the size of your transaction log when defined in a Full recovery model. Therefore, you must be able to identify when to use a Bulk-Logged recovery model to minimize the impact on the transaction log and transaction log performance.

- Know how to format query results. When working with queries, it is important to understand datatype conversion and the various functions that can be used within T-SQL to format a query layout.

■ Knowledge Assessment

Multiple Choice

Circle the letter or letters that correspond to the best answer or answers.

1. You are designing two order-processing SQL Server 2000 client applications. Application A will be used by the sales representatives for taking orders. Application B will be used by the shipping employees when fulfilling orders. Both applications

will be used concurrently. Each application will modify the data in the PRODUCTS, ORDERS, and ORDER DETAILS tables in a single transaction. In what sequence should the applications access the tables to minimize the possibility of deadlocks?

a. **Application A**
   PRODUCTS
   ORDERS
   ORDER DETAILS
   Application B
   ORDER DETAILS
   ORDERS
   PRODUCTS

b. **Application A**
   ORDERS
   PRODUCTS
   ORDER DETAILS
   Application B
   PRODUCTS
   ORDERS
   ORDER DETAILS

c. **Application A**
   PRODUCTS
   ORDERS
   ORDER DETAILS
   Application B
   ORDERS
   PRODUCTS
   ORDER DETAILS

d. **Application A**
   PRODUCTS
   ORDERS
   ORDER DETAILS
   Application B
   PRODUCTS
   ORDERS
   ORDER DETAILS

2. You want to start a distributed transaction using MS DTC. Which statement can you use?
   a. BEGIN DISTRIBUTED TRAN
   b. BEGIN TRAN
   c. SAVE TRAN
   d. ROLLBACK TRAN

3. You want to use a TRY…CATCH block to capture error information. Which functions can be used to get information about the error? (Select all that apply.)
   a. ERROR_NUMBER()
   b. ERROR_MESSAGE()
   c. ERROR_SEVERITY()
   d. DERROR_PROCEDURE()

4. You are writing the code for a stored procedure. Inside your stored procedure you open an explicit transaction. You want to terminate the entire transaction if a T-SQL statement raises a runtime error. How can you do this automatically?
   a. Use SET XACT_ABORT ON inside your stored procedure.
   b. Use a TRY…CATCH block.
   c. Use RAISERROR.
   d. Use SET IMPLICIT_TRANSACTIONS OFF inside your stored procedure.

5. You are designing several DML queries. As a part of the testing process, you want to get more information about the rows affected by these queries. Which method can you use with minimum effort?
   a. Create DML triggers on affected tables.
   b. Create DDL triggers.
   c. Use the OUTPUT clause.
   d. Use the @@ROWCOUNT.

6. You have several large tables in your database. You want to delete all rows from these tables. How can you achieve that in the fastest way?
   a. Use a TRUNCATE TABLE statement.
   b. Use a DELETE statement.
   c. Change the recovery model of your database to Simple.
   d. Change the recovery model of your database to Full.

7. One of your stored procedures contains a JOIN statement between two nvarchar columns from two tables having different collations. When you run the stored procedure,

you obtain an error. How can you make the stored procedure work with a minimum amount of effort?

   a. Use the COLLATE keyword to convert one of the columns to the collation of the other column.

   b. Alter one of the tables, and use the same collations as for the other column.

   c. Alter both tables, and choose a common collation for both columns.

   d. Use a temporary table.

8. Which of the following operators and functions are collation-sensitive? (Select all that apply.)

   a. The MAX operator

   b. UNION ALL

   c. CHARINDEX

   d. REPLACE

9. Which options are available in SQL Server 2005 to limit the number of rows returned by a query? (Select all that apply.)

   a. The TOP operator

   b. The TABLESAMPLE clause

   c. The SET ROWCOUNT statement

   d. The @@ROWCOUNT function

10. What options to retrieve metadata are available in SQL Server? (Select all that apply.)

   a. Catalog views

   b. Dynamic management views

   c. Dynamic management functions

   d. Information schema views

11. You have a query that displays a list of products. You want to make the results more readable for the product names. Which code can help you?

   a. SELECT CAST(ProdName AS char(32)) AS ProductName FROM Sales.Products

   b. SELECT CAST(ProdName AS varchar(32)) AS ProductName FROM Sales. Products

   c. SELECT CAST(ProdName AS nvarchar(32)) AS ProductName FROM Sales. Products

   d. SELECT ProdName FROM Sales.Products

■ Case Scenarios

Scenario 13-1: Avoiding Performance Snags

You have been promoted to program manager. Your job is to see that the application programmers and database administrators work together to achieve the milestones laid out by upper management. Initial testing has shown really poor response. Each query appears to halt briefly, and they don't all return resultsets. As a classroom discussion, what is probably going on? What are the likely solutions?

LESSON 14

Moving Data

LESSON SKILL MATRIX

TECHNOLOGY SKILL	70-431 EXAM OBJECTIVE
Import and export data from a file.	Foundational
Set a database to the Bulk-Logged recovery model to avoid inflating the transaction log.	Foundational
Run the bcp utility.	Foundational
Perform a bulk-insert task.	Foundational
Import bulk XML data using the OPENROWSET function.	Foundational
Copy data from one table to another by using the SQL Server 2005 Integration Services (SSIS) Import and Export Wizard.	Foundational
Move a database between servers.	Foundational
Choose an appropriate method for moving a database.	

KEY TERMS

bulk export: To copy a large set of data rows from a SQL Server table into a data file.

bulk import: To load a large set of data rows from a data file into a SQL Server table. The database engine applies logging and locking optimizations when possible.

ETL: Extraction, transformation and loading; the complex process of copying and cleaning data from heterogeneous sources.

■ Moving Data

THE BOTTOM LINE

The data you need originates in a great number of disparate sources. You may need demographic data from the Census Bureau; you may need tract data from the County Assessor's Office; you may need to simply aggregate data collected and maintained in Access databases everywhere in your company. SQL Server provides the tools to move data from all of these (and more) sources.

At the same time, you probably have to supply data to others. Your suppliers may need order information; the Department of Labor (through state agencies) may need employment data; the Securities and Exchange Commission has its requirements. Again, SQL Server provides the tools to move data to all of these (and more) consumers.

Understanding the Tools Available

When populating tables by inserting data, you will discover that data can come from various sources. One of these sources could be an application where you would use INSERT, UPDATE, and DELETE statements to populate and manipulate the data you store in a SQL Server database, as demonstrated in Lesson 13. However, various options and data coming from heterogeneous environments can end up stored in SQL Server as their final storage destination. Therefore, it is important to identify the appropriate methods for inserting this data in the most common and preferable way.

One of these could be by using BULK INSERT statements to populate and load data from a file system; another might be the insertion of data using complex data transformations. You can import data using the following:

- BULK INSERT statements
- The bcp utility
- Data transformations using SSIS

We will cover the various options in the next sections.

CERTIFICATION READY?
What's the impact on the transaction log? Should the database be in Simple, Bulk-Logged, or Full mode? The answer is in the last section.

Importing Data Using Bulk Insert

A BULK INSERT statement loads a data file into the database using a user-specified format, without forcing the execution of the constraints defined on the destination object.

The key strength of a BULK INSERT statement is that you can also specify what will be the field terminator and the row terminator, because they are configured in the source file to perform the bulk inserts. However, when performing a BULK INSERT statement, you need to make sure the data retrieved from the source file matches the columns in the table into which you are inserting. The following code sample uses the pipe (|) as a field terminator and \n (newline) as a row terminator:

```
BULK INSERT MSSQL_Trianing.dbo.Airportcodes
FROM ',Location of this file.\Airportcodes.tbl'
WITH
(
FIELDTERMINATOR =' |',
ROWTERMINATOR =' \n'
)
The following is the full syntax of the BULK INSERT statement:
BULK INSERT
[ database_name. [ schema_name ].
| schema_name. ] [ table_name | view_name ]
FROM 'data_file'
[ WITH
(
[[, ] BATCHSIZE 5 batch_size ]
[[, ] CHECK_CONSTRAINTS ]
[[, ] CODEPAGE = { 'ACP' | 'OEM' | 'RAW' | 'code_page' } ]
[[, ] DATA FILETYPE =
{ 'char' | 'native'| 'widechar' | 'widenative' } ]
[[, ] FIELDTERMINATOR = 'field_terminator' ]
[[, ] FIRSTROW 5first_row ]
```

```
[[, ] FIRE_TRIGGERS ]
[[, ] FORMATFILE = 'format_file_path' ]
[[, ] KEEPIDENTITY ]
[[, ] KEEPNULLS ]
[[, ] KILOBYTES_PER_BATCH 5kilobytes_per_batch ]
[[, ] LASTROW = last_row ]
[[, ] MAXERRORS = max_errors ]
[[, ] ORDER ( { column [ ASC|DESC ] } [,...n ] ) ]
[[, ] ROWS_PER_BATCH = rows_per_batch ]
[[, ] ROWTERMINATOR = 'row_terminator' ]
[[, ] TABLOCK ]
[[, ] ERRORFILE = 'file_name' ] )]
```

Importing Data Using the bcp Utility

The bcp utility, a command-line tool, is commonly used for importing and exporting data by performing bulk imports/exports of text data. The utility allows you to do the following:

- You can **bulk export** data from a table to a file.
- You can bulk export data from a query to a file.
- You can **bulk import** data into SQL Server.
- You can create format files.

The bcp utility is a command prompt tool that requires the necessary switches to specify the datatype of the data file, and you can create a format file based on the questions that the bcp tool asks you when you don't specify a format file. Here's the syntax:

```
bcp {[[database_name.][owner].]
{table_name | view_name} | "query"}
{in | out | queryout | format} data_file
[-mmax_errors] [-fformat_file] [-x] [-eerr_file]
[-Ffirst_row] [-Llast_row] [-bbatch_size]
[-n] [-c] [-w] [-N] [-V (60 | 65 | 70 | 80)] [-6]
[-q] [-C { ACP | OEM | RAW | code_page } ]
[-tfield_term][-rrow_term] [-iinput_file]
[-ooutput_file] [-apacket_size]
[-Sserver_name[\instance_name]]
[-Ulogin_id] [-Ppassword]
[-T] [-v] [-R] [-k] [-E] [-h"hint [,...n]"]
```

To create a format file, you use the format argument in the bcp command. You use the in parameter to import data, and you use the out parameter to export from a table or view. However, when you want to export from a query, you need to use the queryout option.

In Exercise 14-1, you will learn how to import a list of countries into a country table in the MSSQL_Training database using the bcp utility.

EXERCISE 14-1 IMPORTING DATA FROM A TEXT FILE USING BCP

1. Open a new database query window in SQL Management Studio.
2. Type the following syntax to create the countries table:

```
USE MSSQL_Training
CREATE TABLE Countries
(CountryCode char(2), CountryName varchar(50))
```

3. After you execute the **CREATE TABLE** statement (by clicking the **Execute** button or pressing the **F5** function key), you may close SQL Management Studio.

4. Open a command prompt window, and change the directory location to your CD, and locate the countries.txt file.

5. You will now use the bcp utility to import data from a text file by typing the following command:

```
bcp MSSQL_Training.dbo.countries in countries.txt -f
countries.fmt -T
```

6. When you execute this command, you will get the following resultset:

```
Starting copy...
4 rows copied.
Network packet size (bytes): 4096
Clock Time (ms.): total 1
```

7. Now use the sqlcmd command to verify that the records have successfully been inserted using the bcp utility:

```
sqlcmd -E -Q "select * from
MSSQL_Training.dbo.countries"
```

8. This results in the following:

```
countrycode countryname
------------ ------------------------

BE Belgium
CA Canada
US USA
FR France
(4 rows affected)
```

9. Close the command prompt window.

Using SSIS

In SQL Server 2000 a commonly used tool to import and export data was the SQL Server 2000 DTS Wizard. SQL Server 2005 provides a new extract/transfer/load (**ETL**) platform: SSIS. With SSIS you have the ability to import and export data from heterogeneous sources to various destinations. The toolset provides you with extensive data transformations.

SSIS integrates with SQL Server Business Intelligence Development Studio and allows you to use a package designer or a wizard to import and export data while setting custom transformations. It works with data adapters that allow you to transfer data from any source to basically any destination. A package can connect to relational databases by using .NET and OLE DB providers and to many databases by using ODBC drivers. You can also connect to flat files, Excel files, and Analysis Services projects.

SSIS is a tool that is often used to populate data marts and data warehouses. Figure 14-1 shows you the SSIS window that consists of a Data Flow panel and a Control Flow panel, where the entire data transfer is specified.

With its extensive data transformation capabilities and record manipulations that can be performed inside an SSIS package, you should consider using SSIS as a high-performance ETL tool, which allows you to perform complex data transformations often required in an ETL process. The benefit of SSIS over bcp and bulk inserts is that you can work with transactions; in addition, you have many more options for transferring data and performing custom data mapping.

In Exercise 14-2, you will open an SSIS package to import data from an Excel spreadsheet to a SQL Server 2005 database.

Figure 14-1

SSIS interface

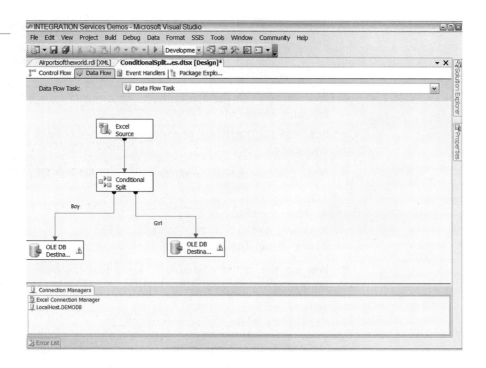

SSIS provides a graphical interface that allows you to transfer data from multiple sources to many destinations using complex manipulations. In this exercise, you will work with an SSIS package that will transfer data from a single Excel spreadsheet to SQL Server but that splits the source data into two tables. You'll manage this by using a conditional split, one of the new features of SSIS.

 EXERCISE 14-2 IMPORTING DATA

1. Open an existing package and review its content.
2. On your CD, double-click **DemoSolution.ssln**.
3. View the **Data Flow** panel; there, do the following:
   a. View the data coming from the Excel spreadsheet.
   b. View the two data sources going to SQL Server 2005.
4. Execute the SSIS package by deploying it and then executing it using **dtsexec**. You will only debug the package and check its execution, rather than compile it and run it using dtsexec or schedule it to run as a job.
5. To debug the package, hit the **F5** function key to execute it. You will see that the package executes successfully.
6. On the Data Flow panel, review the inserted number of records.

You have now successfully tested and executed an SSIS package.

USING THE IMPORT AND EXPORT WIZARD

The SQL Server Import and Export Wizard offers the simplest method to create the Microsoft Server 2005 Integration Services package that copies data from a source to a destination. The wizard can access a variety of data sources, including:

- SQL Server
- Flat files
- Access
- Excel
- Other OLE DB providers

In Exercise 14-3, you will export data to a file using the Import and Export Wizard.

EXERCISE 14-3 EXPORTING DATA

1. Click **Start**, point to **All Programs**, point to **Microsoft SQL Server 2005**, and then click **SQL Server Management Studio**.

2. In the Connect to Server dialog box, specify the values in the following table and then click **Connect**.

PROPERTY	VALUE
Server type	Database engine
Server name	<YourComputerName>
Authentication	Windows Authentication

3. If Object Explorer is not visible, click **Object Explorer** on the View menu.

4. In Object Explorer, expand **Databases**.

5. Right-click **AdventureWorks**, point to **Tasks**, and then click **Export Data**.

6. Click **Next** on the Welcome to SQL Server Import and Export Wizard page.

7. In the Choose a Data Source page, specify the values in the following table, and then click **Next**.

PROPERTY	VALUE
Data source	SQL Native Client
Server name	<YourComputerName>
Authentication	Windows Authentication
Database	AdventureWorks

8. In the Choose a Destination page, specify the values in the following table, and then click **Next**.

PROPERTY	VALUE
Destination	Flat-file destination
Filename	C:\Contacts.txt
Locale	English (United States)
Code page	1252 (ANSI Latin 1)
Format	Delimited
Text qualifier	<None>
Column names in the first data row	Select the check box

9. In the Specify Table Copy or Query page, select **Write a query** to specify the data to transfer, and then click **Next**.

10. In the Provide a Source Query page, type:

    SELECT Firstname, Lastname FROM Person.Contact WHERE
    ContactID < 10
    and then click **Next**.

11. In the Configure Flat File Destination page, accept the default file settings, and then click **Next**.

12. In the Save and Execute Package page, ensure **Execute immediately** is selected, and then click **Finish**.

13. In the Complete the Wizard page, click **Finish**. When execution has completed successfully, click **Close**.

14. Open **C:\Contacts.txt** in Notepad, and then ensure that that you have exported the correct data.

15. Close **Notepad** and **SQL Server Management Studio**.

Copying Databases

One of the handiest tools in the SQL Server arsenal is the Copy Database Wizard. You can use this wizard to copy or move a database and all of its associated objects to another server. Why would you want to do that? For a few reasons:

- If you are upgrading your server, the Copy Database Wizard is a quick way to move your data to the new system.

- You can use the wizard to create a backup copy of the database on another server, ready to use in case of emergency.

- Developers can copy an existing database and use the copy to make changes without endangering the live database.

The Copy Database Wizard will prove to be a valuable tool in your administrative functions, so you'll use it in Exercise 14-4 to make a copy of the MSSQL_Training database.

> **CERTIFICATION READY?**
> Do you understand why this tool was not listed as an import/export utility?

EXERCISE 14-4 RUNNING THE COPY DATABASE WIZARD

1. Open **Management Studio** by selecting it from the **Microsoft SQL Server** group under **Programs** on the **Start** menu; expand your server, and expand **Databases**.

2. Right-click the **MSSQL_Training database**, go to **Tasks**, and select **Copy Database**. You will see the welcome page.

3. Click **Next**.

4. On the second page, you are asked to select a source server. Select the default instance of your server and the proper authentication type (usually Windows Authentication), and click **Next**.

5. On the next page, you need to select a destination. Here you will choose the **(local) instance** of the server as the destination. Choose the appropriate security, and click **Next**.

6. Next you are asked which mode you would like to use. Attach/detach is useful for copying databases between servers that are in remote locations from each other and requires the database to be taken offline. The SQL Management Object transfer method allows you to keep the database online and gives you the flexibility to make a copy on the same server, so select the **SQL Management Object Method** option, and click **Next**.

7. Next you are asked which database you would like to move or copy. Check the **Copy** box next to MSSQL_Training, and click **Next**.

8. On the Database Destination page, you need to make a few changes:

   a. Change the destination database name to **MSSQL_Training_Copy**.

   b. Change MSSQL_Training.mdf to **MSSQL_Training_copy.mdf**.

   c. Change MSSQL_Training_log.ldf to **MSSQL_Training_log_copy.ldf**.

9. Click **Next**. You now have the option to change the name of the package that will be created; this matters only if you plan to save the package and execute it later. Accept the defaults, and click **Next.**

10. On the next page, you are asked when you would like to run the SSIS job created by the wizard. Select **Run Immediately**, and click **Next**.

11. The final page summarizes the choices you have made. Click **Finish** to copy the MSSQL_Training database.

12. You will see the Log Detail page, which shows you each section of the job as it executes. Clicking the **Report** button will show each step of the job and its outcome.

13. Click **Close** on the Performing Operation page to complete the wizard. The Copy Database Wizard is a simple tool that makes a complex task much easier.

Bulk-Inserting XML Data

You can bulk-insert data to import large amounts of data in SQL Server using T-SQL syntax. You can accomplish this by using an OPENROWSET function or a BULK INSERT statement.

OPENROWSET: Since you can have the XML datatype as a native datatype in SQL Server 2005, you can definitely benefit from performing bulk insert tasks to easily import or even update XML data. This is usually performed using an OPENROWSET statement. The following example inserts an order detail into the xmldata column of the table tbl_orders:

```
INSERT INTO Tbl_orders(Xmldata)
SELECT * FROM OPENROWSET(
BULK '<Location of this file>\OpenRowsetXmldata.xml',
SINGLE_BLOB) AS x
```

Of course, you also have the option to update existing data using the BULK INSERT statement, as shown here:

```
UPDATE tbl_orders
SET Xmldata =(
SELECT * FROM OPENROWSET(
BULK '<Location of this file>\OpenRowsetXMLdata.xml',
SINGLE_BLOB
) AS x
)
WHERE RowID = 1
GO
```

Besides being able to use the OPENROWSET to insert XML data, you can also use it to retrieve data from different OLE DB or ODBC providers using the full OPENROWSET syntax:

```
OPENROWSET
( { 'provider_name',
{ 'datasource'; 'user_id'; 'password'
| 'provider_string' }
, { [ catalog. ] [ schema. ] object
| 'query'
}
| BULK 'data_file',
{ FORMATFILE = 'format_file_path'
[ ,bulk_options. ]
| SINGLE_BLOB | SINGLE_CLOB | SINGLE_NCLOB }
} )
<bulk_options>::=
[, CODEPAGE = { 'ACP' | 'OEM'
```

```
 | 'RAW' | 'code_page' } ]
[, ERRORFILE = 'file_name' ]
[, FIRSTROW = first_row ]
[, LASTROW = last_row ]
[, MAXERRORS = maximum_errors ]
[, ROWS_PER_BATCH = rows_per_batch ]
```

BULK INSERT: Another option for inserting XML data is to use the BULK INSERT statement, covered earlier in this lesson; this allows you to specify that the format file be in an XML format.

Supporting the Bulk-Logged Recovery Model

Choosing a Full database recovery model would have a big impact on the transaction log when performing BULK INSERT statements. To have less impact on the transaction log, you can implement the Bulk-Logged recovery model.

In contrast to the Full recovery model, the Bulk-Logged model logs bulk operations in a minimal mode. This allows the Bulk-Logged model to protect against media failures, provide the best performance, and use the least log space.

When setting the Bulk-Logged recovery model, you can recover from a full backup only in total, that is, without performing a point-in-time recovery. When performing a log backup, you will also require access to the data files that contain the bulk-logged transactions, because the Bulk-Logged recovery model does not insert the actual transactions in the transaction log; it just keeps track of them. This means when data files in the Bulk-Logged recovery model are not accessible you will not be able to perform any log backup.

To set the Bulk-Logged recovery model, you can use the ALTER database statement, as shown here:

```
ALTER DATABASE MSSQL_Training SET RECOVERY BULK_LOGGED
```

Of course, you can also alter the database settings by using SQL Server Management Studio. Right-click your **database** and select **Properties** from the menu. Click on **Options**. Set the **Recovery Model** near the top of the page.

SKILL SUMMARY

IN THIS LESSON YOU LEARNED:

In this lesson you learned how to work with relational data in terms of importing and exporting data. An interesting capability of SQL Server is the various methods you can use to bulk-import or even export data to the file system using command-line utilities such as bcp or the BULK INSERT statement.

SSIS is the ETL tool you use to perform advanced data migrations and specify data workflows with custom scripting and transformations. The power of this tool is that you can use heterogeneous data sources and destinations.

For the certification examination:

- Be able to run the bcp utility. The bcp utility has several options, including creating a format file and specifying your input or output result based on a table or a query. It is important to be able to identify the correct syntax to use to perform various bcp statements.

- Know how to import and export data. You need to have a good understanding of how to import and export data by using BULK INSERT statements or even by using the OPENROWSET function. You also can use advanced ETL features with SSIS, and you need to be able to identify which tool to use for each purpose.

■ Knowledge Assessment

Multiple Choice

Circle the letter or letters that correspond to the best answer or answers.

1. You use the bcp utility to import data during nonworking hours. After importing data into the database, you execute a full backup statement. You need to ensure that the impact on the database during the insert is reduced to a minimum. Which of the following options can help you achieve that?
   a. Set the recovery model to Full.
   b. Set the recovery model to Simple.
   c. Set the recovery model to Bulk-Logged.
   d. Back up the transaction log while performing the inserts.

2. You import data periodically using the BULK INSERT statement for a database that is involved in log shipping. You need to minimize the time taken by the import operations. Which actions can you take?
   a. Set the recovery model to Bulk-Logged.
   b. Set the recovery model to Simple.
   c. Set the recovery model to Full.
   d. Do not import data in parallel.

3. Which of the following parameters of the bcp utility allows you to copy data from a query?
   a. in
   b. out
   c. queryout
   d. format

4. You need to bulk-import and bulk-export data from a SQL Server database. Which methods can you use? (Select all that apply.)
   a. Use the bcp utility.
   b. Use the BULK INSERT statement.
   c. Use the INSERT... SELECT * FROM OPENROWSET(BULK...) statement.
   d. Use SSIS.

5. Which of the following are true about the bulk insert task of SSIS? (Select all that apply.)
   a. You can use the bulk insert task to transfer data directly from other database management systems.
   b. The destination for the bulk insert task must be a table or view in a SQL Server database.
   c. You can use a format file in the bulk insert task.
   d. If the destination table or view already contains data, the new data will replace the existing data when the bulk insert task runs.

6. Which of the following is not a step for configuring a bulk insert task?
   a. Specify whether to check constraints or keep nulls when data is inserted.
   b. Specify the destination SQL Server database and the table or view.
   c. Define the format used by the bulk insert task.
   d. Set up an execute SQL task to delete existing data.

7. You want to create an SSIS package that copies data from a source to a destination. You want to run the package after you create it. Which is the simplest method to accomplish that?

    a. Use Business Intelligence Development Studio, and start the SQL Server Import and Export Wizard from an SSIS project.

    b. Use SQL Server Management Studio, and start the SQL Server Import and Export Wizard.

    c. Create the package in SSIS Designer.

    d. Use a bulk insert task.

8. Which of the following data sources can the SQL Server Import and Export Wizard use? (Select all that apply.)

    a. .NET providers

    b. SQL Server

    c. Flat files

    d. Excel

■ Case Scenarios

Scenario 14-1: Moving Data

It turns out that your remote office has all the data you need to populate your database to support those programmers. The remote office uses Oracle 8.1.5 (Oracle 8i). Many solutions exist to transfer the data. As a classroom discussion, see how many you can list on the board, together with the advantages and disadvantages to each.

XML Data

LESSON SKILL MATRIX

TECHNOLOGY SKILL	70-431 EXAM OBJECTIVE
Manage XML data.	Foundational
Identify the specific structure needed by a consumer.	Foundational
Retrieve XML data.	Foundational
Modify XML data.	Foundational
Convert between XML data and relational data.	Foundational
Create an XML index.	Foundational
Load an XML schema.	Foundational
Gather performance and optimization data by using DMVs.	Foundational

KEY TERMS

typed XML: XML that is validated by an XML schema.

untyped XML: Allows storing of any form of XML data inside the database without verifying it and matching the data with an XML schema.

XSD: XML Schema Definition Language. An XML schema defines the elements, attributes, and datatypes that conform to the World Wide Web Consortium (W3C) XML Schema Part 1: Structures Recommendation for the SML Schema Definition Language. The W3C XML Schema Part 2: Datatypes Recommendation is the guidance for defining datatypes used in XML schemas. The XML schema definition language enables you to define the structure and datatypes for XML messages.

XSL: Extensible Stylesheet Language; an XML vocabulary that is used to transform XML data to another form, such as HTML, by means of a style sheet that defines presentation rules.

XSLT: Extensible Stylesheet Language Transformations. This evolved from the early Extensible Stylesheet Language (XSL) standard. XSL specifies a language definition for XML data presentation and data transformations. Data presentation means displaying data in some format and/or medium, and concerns style. Data transformation refers to parsing an input XML document into a tree of nodes and then converting the source tree into a result tree; transformation concerns data exchange.

■ Introducing XML Data

THE BOTTOM LINE

The introduction of XML as a native datatype could be considered one of the truly significant changes to SQL Server. In previous versions of SQL Server, storing XML data and retrieving it were possible but not in the same way or as extensively as you can do it with SQL Server 2005.

Using XML

XML is an abbreviation for Extensible Markup Language. XML has been evolving since 1997 and has found widespread use as a standard for the structure of data and for its transmission across a variety of networks, most notably the World Wide Web. Related standards are being developed constantly, and hundreds of XML-related languages have proliferated through many organizations and industries around the world.

USING XML AS A METALANGUAGE

Whereas programming languages like VisualBasic, C#, or Java are used to create programs for conducting specific calculations, actions, and decisions, XML is used to create languages that are used to develop specific documents (or files) for use by developers, their organizations, or their industries.

XML allows developers to create their own specific, customized collections of components such as tags, elements, and attributes that accurately describe the physical contents of their documents. In this capacity, XML acts like an alphabet, combined with its punctuation and other semantic symbols.

XML doesn't make any sense alone; you have to create appropriate meaningful combinations with it and have a specific program that interacts with it.

USING XML AS A MARKUP LANGUAGE

XML is also a markup language and, as such, it is used to describe text. "Markup" refers to the insertion of characters or symbols to indicate how the information in a document should appear when it is printed or displayed, or to describe a document's logical structure. Marking up text is a way to add information about your data to the data itself.

The recipient of your file needs to be able to interpret the essence of the communication, whether it is in the format and content of database data, multimedia graphics, audio, credit card authorizations, or any of the other hundreds of document types.

USING XML SCHEMA DEFINITIONS

"Schema" is a term borrowed from database technology, where it is used to describe the structure of data in relational tables. In the context of XML, an *XSD* (XML Schema Definition) describes a model for a whole class of documents. The model describes the possible arrangement of elements, attributes, and text in a schema-valid document.

In schemas, models are described in terms of constraints. A constraint defines what can appear in a given language or documents. Consider two kinds of constraints: content model constraints and datatype constraints. Content model constraints define the elements that can appear and, in this way, the schema establishes the vocabulary. Datatype constraints describe the units of data that the schema considers valid.

USING THE EXTENSIBLE STYLESHEET LANGUAGE

XSL (Extensible Stylesheet Language) expresses formatting, just as cascading stylesheets are used with HTML documents. An XSL is a file that describes how to display an XML document of a given type. Today, XML documents and data can be formatted and rendered both for the World Wide Web and for print media.

XSL uses two additional XML-related languages:

- XPATH
- XSLT

XPATH (XML Path Language) is essential for those occasions when you want to prescribe exactly which parts of a document are to be transformed. XPATH allows you to specify, for example, to extract all paragraphs belonging to the chapter element, or use only the third list item.

XLST (XSL Transformations) is designed for changing an XML document into another, and uses its own kind of stylesheet to do so. XSLT stylesheets actually change the structure and type of an XML document as, for example, to automatically generate tables of contents, cross-references, and indexes. XSLT stylesheets can also transform an XML document into another XML document using a different vocabulary from the original.

Understanding XML Data

When storing XML data in your database, you can store the data as varchar or text data, you can decompose the data in relational data, or you can store the data as a native XML datatype:

- When storing XML as varchar or text data, you will lose most of its representation. You will not be able to perform schema validation on the XML data, and you won't be able to perform XML queries on the data.
- You can shred (reformat) the XML document into relational data and use a FOR XML clause with the SELECT statement to retrieve an XML structure from the relational data you store in the database. This way of storing XML and retrieving content in a database is how it was frequently done in SQL Server 2000. To support the retrieval of XML data from relational storage, SQL Server 2005 has made some enhancements to the FOR XML clause, which will be covered later in this lesson.
- Since SQL Server 2005 supports XML as a true datatype, you can now benefit from that by storing XML natively inside the database. Think about the big benefits you get from this: You have the ability to store and retrieve XML in a flexible way, and you have the opportunity to query inside the XML data using XQuery expressions, which gives you the benefits of indexes.

USING THE XML DATATYPE

You can use the XML datatype in many ways; it is comparable to using any other SQL Server datatype. For example, this is how you use it in variable declarations:

```
DECLARE @xmltype XML
SET @xmltype =
'<ROOT><Publisher>Wiley</Publisher></ROOT>'
```

And this is how you use it in table declarations:

```
CREATE Table Publishers

(PublisherID int, PublisherName varchar(50),
Publishercontactdetails XML)
```

Of course, you can also use XML datatypes in stored procedures as parameters and many other options. SQL Server is flexible in the way you work with the XML data; you have the ability to store both *typed XML* and *untyped XML* in the database.

In Exercise 15-1, you will create a table that contains an XML column. You will also insert some records into the table.

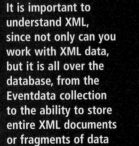

EXERCISE 15-1 CREATING A TABLE CONTAINING AN XML COLUMN

1. Create a table with an XML column:

   ```
   CREATE Table Publishers (PublisherID int,
   PublisherName varchar(50), Publishercontactdetails XML)
   ```

2. Insert valid XML in the table:

   ```
   insert into publishers
   values (1,'Wiley','<ROOT><Publisher>
   John Wiley & Sons</Publisher></ROOT> ')
   ```

3. Insert valid XML in the table:

```
insert into publishers values
(1,'Wiley','<invalid>Wrong Format>')
```

4. The previous INSERT statement will result in an error message:

```
Msg 102, Level 15, State 1, Line 2
Incorrect syntax near '<invalid>Wrong Format>'.
```

USING UNTYPED XML

When using untyped XML, you can store XML in the database in any form, as long as it is well-formed XML. This means that upon defining an XML column and inserting or assigning a value to the XML column, a check will occur to see whether the data you are about to insert matches the XML standard, without validating it against an XML schema.

A single XML column can take up to 2 GB of storage, so you have a robust datatype to work with, rather than storing the data in text or varchar data as you could do with previous editions of SQL Server. The danger, of course, is that instead of coming up with an organized relational database model, you might put whatever you can think of in an XML column. You have to be cautious in doing this; everything has its best practices.

Because of its structure, when using untyped XML, you can store any form of XML data inside the database without verifying it and matching the data with an XML schema.

■ Case Study: Working with the XML Datatype to Ease a Relational Model and Optimize Database Performance

A sports company runs a Web application that enables customers to buy sport items online. All the products the company sells have a different set of properties that need to be searchable by the customers.

If you want to buy a pair of sport shoes, for example, you want to be able to search by brand, size, color, or other properties. If you want to buy a tennis racket, you will want to search using different properties, and when you want to buy that nice sports outfit, you'll care about size, color, and so on. Finally, a box with tennis balls will have different properties than a pair of sport socks.

Now, how would you define all this in a relational database? It would definitely need a complex relational model and a lot of multiple table querying (think about that JOIN syntax) in order to represent or even retrieve the information. The solution to this will be XML data storage, because you can really benefit from the flexible structure you have with storing data in XML.

In this case, you would define one XML column that would be associated with the article or product, and that would contain all properties you can assign to a product.

The table definition from the real-life scenario might look like this:

```
CREATE TABLE articles

(articleID int, ArticleName varchar(50),
Articleproperties XML)
```

This will provide a much more flexible way to store this kind of data; and the key benefit is that if you need to query it, instead of just representing it, you can use one of the SQL Server XML methods to retrieve the data (as a scalar type or even as XML).

Of course, when storing data in XML, you need to have a good method to retrieve that information, as well. And that is something you will accomplish by using various query methods, where you will learn not only how to retrieve XML data but also how to *decompose* XML data into relational information.

USING TYPED XML

If you want to validate XML with an XML schema, you can specify an XML schema validation when creating or defining the XML datatype. You do this by referring to the XML schema, which you initially need to store and catalog in the SQL database. XML that is validated by an XML schema is called **typed XML**.

We often refer to XML *schema validation* as putting a check constraint on a scalar datatype, since it performs a check on the values you provide. In next section, you will learn how to work with XML Schema collections and how to store the schema in SQL Server 2005.

How do you create a datatype with schema validation? It's easy:

```
Declare @xmldata XML (schema.xmlschemacollection)
```

In the previous example, you will need to determine whether the XML schema has already been stored inside the database; otherwise, you need to "catalog" it first.

The XML datatype adds a new level of storing XML data inside SQL Server; it does this in a way whereby complex data structures can easily be converted to an XML datatype. You can think about using the XML datatype not only for storing XML for XML purposes but also to create undefined relational structures.

This would break down relational information in such a way that it would easily resolve real-world problems, such as when you are unable to create a nice relational model or come up with an optimized relational design.

Working with XML Schema

When an XML datatype is assigned to a Schema collection, you will not be able to insert any columns that don't match the schema definition. This can be useful in environments where the XML data you are providing and storing in the database has to match a strict definition, such as an invoice. And that is exactly where you would use the XML datatype, since on some of the structured data you would not perform heavy queries, but would just want to represent the data in its whole.

Storing Typed XML Data

A broker company provides highly skilled and qualified IT professionals to enterprise customers all over the world. To streamline and use a uniform set of résumés that the company can send out from the IT professionals, the company was originally using a Microsoft Word document as a template. The company asked all the IT professionals to provide their information and skills inside the résumé template.

One of the key problems the company had was that it also needed to create an entire structure of relational data to be able to search within the profiles/résumés. So within that company, initially a lot of data was stored twice and in two formats. When an IT professional submitted a new résumé, someone entered part of that information as keywords in a relational database application to support the search capabilities.

When the company switched to SQL Server 2005, it redesigned its approach of entering and providing this information. The key power the company has now is that it can store the résumé data in its native XML format directly in the database, without performing any manual action.

Because of the nature of the XML datatype and the query search capabilities, now data can easily be loaded, stored, and retrieved using XML-specific query methods.

To use XML Schema collections in the database and associate them with variables and columns of the XML datatype, SQL Server uses the CREATE XML SCHEMA statement:

```
CREATE XML SCHEMA COLLECTION ProductDetails AS
'<xsd:schema targetNamespace = "http://schemas.Wiley.com/sqlserv-
er/2008/01/70-431
/ProductDetails"

xmlns =
"http://schemas.Wiley.com/sqlserver/2008/01/70-431 /ProductDetails"
elementFormDefault="qualified"
xmlns:xsd="http://www.w3.org/2001/XMLSchema">
<xsd:element name="Packagetype"> <xsd:complexType>
<xsd:sequence> <xsd:element name="PackageUnit" type="xsd:string"/>
<xsd:element
name="PackageDescription" type="xsd:string"/>
</xsd:sequence> </xsd:complexType> </xsd:element>
</xsd:schema> ';
```

After the XML Schema collection is cataloged, you can retrieve information about it by using the XML_schema_namespace function, as shown in the following example. This example shows you the schema of the cataloged XML Schema collection called Productdetails as it was cataloged in the dbo schema:

```
SELECT xml_schema_namespace(N'dbo',N'ProductDetails')
```

TAKE NOTE*

Unicode strings have a format similar to character strings but are preceded by an N identifier (N stands for National Language). The N prefix, which must be uppercase, causes the string to be stored in a two-bytes-per-character format.

Once the schema is defined, you can use it and refer to it in a CREATE TABLE or even a DECLARE XML statement. The following is an example of how to define a variable as an XML datatype:

```
declare @Packagetype xml (Productdetails)
set @packagetype = '<Publisher>Wiley</Publisher>'
select @packagetype
```

TAKE NOTE*

The letter case for variables does not matter. This example uses the same variable with differing cases to make the point.

This results in an error message, as it does not validate the schema definition. It produces the following error:

```
Msg 6913, Level 16, State 1, Line 2
XML Validation:
Declaration not found for element 'Publisher'.
Location: /*:Publisher[1]
```

A better solution is to provide a value that matches the schema definition:

```
DECLARE @var XML(Productdetails)
SET @var =
'<Packagetype
xmlns="http://schemas.sybex.com/sqlserver
/2006/01/70-431/ProductDetails
<PackageUnit>Box</PackageUnit>
<PackageDescription>Carton Box</PackageDescription>
</Packagetype>'
```

The previous example used a unique name to identify the XML namespace. That is a best practice; but of course you can make the example easier by performing something like this:

```
CREATE XML SCHEMA COLLECTION Countries AS '
<schema xmlns="http://www.w3.org/2001/XMLSchema">
<element name="root">
<complexType>
```

```
<sequence>
<element name="Country" type="string"/>
<element name="Code" type="string"/>
</sequence>
</complexType>
</element>
</schema>'
declare @xml xml (Countries)
set @xml =
'<root><Country>Belgium</Country><Code>BEL</Code>
</root>'
```

And you can use this in a table definition as well:

```
CREATE table students
(studentid int identity(1,1), studentname
varchar(50), Country xml (countries))
```

An INSERT statement such as the following one would definitely succeed:

```
Insert into students (studentname, country)

values ('Joe', '<root><Country>United
States</Country><Code>USA</Code></root>')
```

To work with XML schemas, the schema needs to be loaded into the database before you can reference it. To catalog a schema inside the SQL Server database, you use the CREATE XML SCHEMA COLLECTION statement.

Querying XML Data

Because of the hierarchical structure inside XML data, you can use query methods to retrieve information and search for data in an XML datatype. The new datatype is an object that comes with its own methods that allow you to retrieve information from the XML data you stored in the database. The XML methods you can use to retrieve data from an XML datatype are as follows:

- **Query method:** Returns a fragment of untyped XML.
- **Value method:** Returns XML data as a scalar datatype.
- **Exists method:** Checks whether a certain node exists in the XML data.
- **Nodes method:** Returns a single column rowset of nodes from the XML column.

You will learn in the next sections about each method's functionality, with an example.

USING THE QUERY METHOD

On the XML column, you have to specify the query method in order to return a certain value from a table. The following example shows you how you can return a value from within an XML column:

```
SELECT country.query ('/root/Country') FROM Students
```

This will result in the following partial resultset, but will return a fragment of untyped XML:

```
<Country>Belgium</Country>
<Country>United States</Country>
```

If you want to retrieve only the values, you can also use the data function.

You will use this query method to retrieve fragments of XML data and return them as an XML value. If you want to return data in a scalar datatype, you will have to use the value method, as described in the next section.

To get just the value of the matching element, you can use the data function:

```
select country.query ('data(/root/Code)') from
students
```

In this case, the resultset will appear as follows:

```
BEL
USA
. . .
```

You use the query method to decompose XML data into a relational data resultset.

USING THE VALUE METHOD

The value method works much like the query method, and is invoked in the same way. The difference is that the value method will accept an additional parameter to determine the resulting scalar datatype. The value is returned as an instance of that type.

The following example will return a scalar int datatype, using the XML value method:

```
declare @myDoc xml
declare @ProdID int
set @myDoc = '<Root>
<ProductDescription ProductID="500"
ProductName="SQL Server 2005">
<Editions>
<Edition>Standard</Edition>
<MaximumCPU>4</MaximumCPU>
</Editions>
</ProductDescription>
</Root>'
select @mydoc.value
('(/Root/ProductDescription/@ProductID)[1]', 'int')
```

This results in:

```
500
```

Remember that you must declare the namespace of the document if the source column is a typed XML column.

TAKE NOTE *

The XML datatype is near the highest in the datatype precedence. This means when XML is used in expressions with other datatypes, implicit conversion to the XML datatype will occur.

To avoid implicit conversion and conversion errors, it is a best practice to use the CONVERT or CAST function to explicitly convert to the destination datatype.

USING THE EXIST METHOD

The exist method takes an expression that selects a single node within the XML document and returns either True (bit value 1), if the node exists, or False (bit value 0), if it does not. If the source column is a typed XML column, and the element contains null, the method returns NULL instead. Therefore, the following query will return True for all items where the student has country details:

```
SELECT country.exist ('/root/Country') FROM students
```

You can also use the exist method in the WHERE clause of a statement:

```
SELECT * FROM students WHERE
country.exist ('/root/Country') = 1
```

USING THE MODIFY METHOD

The modify method consists of three substatements:

- INSERT
- DELETE
- REPLACE

What makes these statements so useful? Instead of working with the entire XML structure, loading the document, and then performing updates or modifications, you can use the modify method to manipulate the current XML data stored in a table. This provides you with strong and powerful statements that give you the opportunity to manipulate XML data inside the XML column; for example, you could modify a specific value in an order line stored in an XML column.

Remember that in a typed XML column, the resulting XML document, after executing the XML/DML statement, must conform to the schema for the column. If not, the update will fail, and an error will be raised. As an example, the following code deletes the product node that has an attribute id="501" in an XML document:

```
UPDATE @xml
SET xmlcol.modify('delete /root/product[@id="501"]')
```

To insert a new node or fragment of XML, you use an INSERT statement. The syntax for this is as follows:

```
xml-column.modify('insert new-content
{as first | as last} into | before | after
xpath-expression')
```

USING THE NODES METHOD

The previous sections covered the query, value, exist, and modify methods, which are exposed by the new XML datatype in SQL Server 2005. Using the nodes method, you can extract data from an XML document and use that to generate subnodes that can be used for various purposes, such as to create new content or insert content into new tables.

If you have, for example, an XML document that contains a list of airport codes per country, you would be able to use the nodes method to create a new table where each rowset becomes a row in the table.

Suppose you have an XML document that looks like this:

```
DECLARE @x xml

SET @x='<Root> <row id="1"><Airportcode>EWR
</Airportcode>

<Airportname>Newark</Airportname></row>
<row id="2"><Airportcode>LGA</Airportcode></row>
<row id="3" />
</Root>'
```

When executing the following nodes query, you will return relational data to which you should apply the XML value method in order to truly decompose it into a relational value:

```
SELECT T.c.query('.') AS result
FROM @x.nodes('/Root/row') T(c)
go
```

This will result in the following:

```
Result
-----------

<row id="1"><Airportcode>EWR</Airportcode>
<Airportname>Newark</Airportname></row>

<row id="2"><Airportcode>LGA</Airportcode></row>
<row id="3" />
```

In the following example, you will apply the value method to the resultset returned by the nodes method:

```
SELECT T.c.value('@id','int') as id,
T.c.query('Airportcode') as Airportcode
FROM @x.nodes('/Root/row') T(c)
```

You will get the following resultset:

```
Id Airportcode
------------------------------------
1 <Airportcode>EWR</Airportcode>
2 <Airportcode>LGA</Airportcode>
```

In the previous resultset, however, you'll probably notice that ID 3 does not have an airport code. If you want to filter out these records, you can use the exists method to see whether a row exists, as mentioned earlier in this chapter:

```
SELECT T.c.value('@id','int') AS id,
T.c.query('Airportcode') as Airportcode
FROM @x.nodes('/Root/row') T(c)
WHERE T.c.exist('Airportcode') = 1;
```

In the XML methods we have covered, two methods, value and exists, will return a scalar resultset.

The XML method query will always return an XML fragment. The exists method checks whether a certain node exists inside the XML document you are querying and will, therefore, always return a bit datatype.

Decomposing XML Data

As database administrator, you can benefit from using XML in combination with the EVENTDATA( ) function.

If you have to write a trigger every time you want to use the Eventdata collection, and in that trigger decompose your XML data into a relational format to store it inside a log table, you would be wasting a lot of work rewriting or copying the code data that decomposes the Eventdata results in relational data.

You would definitely benefit by combining the decomposition of the XML Eventdata to a user-defined function. In Exercise 15-2, you will implement all these. You are basically able to copy and paste the definition of your user-defined functions into any database and extend its functionality for the valuable data you want to retrieve from an XML column.

What other benefits do you get from defining user-defined functions in which you decompose the XML data? Suppose a future version of SQL Server has a change in the Eventdata collection. You won't need to verify every single trigger you defined or every single procedure where you used the XML data collection.

In Exercise 15-2, you will create and use user-defined functions to decompose data gathered from the Eventdata collection that you executed in a DDL trigger.

EXERCISE 15-2 DECOMPOSING XML INTO RELATIONAL DATA

1. In SQL Server Management Studio, open a new query window, and connect to the **MSSQL_Training database**.

2. Type and execute the following syntax to create a new schema:

```
CREATE SCHEMA EventFunctions
GO
```

3. After you have created the schema, you will create a function that decomposes the Eventdata:

```
XML in relational data:
-- Create a function that decomposes the eventtype
-- out of Eventdata
```

```
CREATE FUNCTION EventFunctions.fn_Eventtype
(@eventdata xml)
RETURNS nvarchar(max)
AS
BEGIN
RETURN @eventdata.value
('(/EVENT_INSTANCE/EventType)[1]','nvarchar(max)')
END
GO
```

4. Type the following syntax to decompose the T-SQL statement from the XML collection:

```
- Create a function that decomposes the
TSQLstatement out of Eventdata
CREATE FUNCTION EventFunctions.fn_TSQLStatement
(@eventdata xml)
returns nvarchar(max)
AS
BEGIN
RETURN
@eventdata.value
('(/EVENT_INSTANCE/TSQLCommand/
CommandText)[1]','nvarchar(max)')
END
GO
```

5. Create a DDL trigger in which you will call the two functions you created:

```
- Create a ddl trigger to test the functionality
CREATE TRIGGER TRG_DDL_event ON DATABASE
FOR DDL_DATABASE_LEVEL_EVENTS
AS
declare @eventdata xml
set @eventdata = EVENTDATA()
select EventFunctions.fn_TSQLStatement
(@eventdata), EventFunctions.
fn_TSQLStatement (@eventdata)
```

6. Test the trigger's functionality by creating a table:

```
CREATE TABLE tbl_test (test int)
```

7. This will give you the following resultset:

```
CREATE TABLE tbl_test (test int)
```

8. Drop the trigger you created:

```
DROP TRIGGER TRG_DDL_event ON DATABASE
```

Creating XML Indexes

The XML column in its native datatype provides great capabilities in terms of retrieving data from within the XML column using various query methods. To support the querying of XML data, you can create indexes on these columns.

The start of an XML index is a *primary XML index,* and all other XML indexes will depend on the primary index. You have the ability to create the following XML indexes to support optimized XML querying:

Primary XML index: This is a shredded and persisted representation of the XML data in the XML datatype column. For each XML binary large object (BLOB) in the column, the index creates several rows of data. The number of rows in the index is approximately equal to the number of nodes in the XML binary large object. Each row stores the following node information:

- Tag name
- Node value
- Node type
- Order information
- Root path
- Primary key of the data row

Path XML index: This improves search capabilities for queries based on path instructions. A path index is a secondary XML index, which means a primary index needs to be created first.

Value XML index: This improves search capabilities for queries based on values. A *value index* is a secondary XML index, which means that a primary index needs to be created first.

Property XML index: Queries that retrieve one or more values from individual XML instances may benefit from this type of index. This scenario occurs when you retrieve object properties using the value method of the XML datatype, and when the primary key value of the object is known.

■ Case Study: Implementing XML in SQL 2005

A company ships orders from pharmaceutical companies to customers all over the world. The company has implemented SQL Server 2005 within its business environment. Some of the products the company ships require different preparations and are composed of several other products that are customized based on the required usage.

Some of the articles the company provides require special handling and have different package shipping requirements. In addition, the company receives prescriptions that require a combination of medicines. The usage of the medicines that are produced will depend on the patient's age, weight, and other factors that have to be considered when taking a variety of medicines in combination with one another. In this environment, the prescription for some of these medicines is simple (e.g., take three pills a day); and others are complex prescriptions that are a combination of medicines.

To be able to address the variety of different package units/product compositions and prescriptions, the company created a complex data model using relational storage. However, the query response when testing all the application functionality ended up performing poorly when large amounts of data were loaded and retrieved from the database.

After optimizing and reviewing the data model, the company decided to store any complex structure with unknown properties in an XML format. This allowed a less complex query method to retrieve the product information and prescriptions in general, while still allowing the retrieval of specific data that was initially decomposed in relational data.

One of the key benefits of using the XML datatype instead of a complex model of relational tables is that when the company needs to represent a prescription entered by a doctor, it can easily retrieve it in its entire structure. To allow the maximum flexibility, the company decided to store the data as untyped XML. To improve query response, it created a primary XML index on all XML columns. The company's DBA is using SQL Server Profiler to trace the most common XML queries that are sent to the database; it will later create supportive path queries to optimize query response.

By deciding to choose the XML datatype as a storage type, a lot of CPU-intensive relational processing has been resolved.

SKILL SUMMARY

IN THIS LESSON YOU LEARNED:

In this lesson, you learned about the XML datatype, which is a new and native datatype supported in SQL Server 2005. Using and storing XML data in SQL Server 2005 can be easy or complex, but it is important that you understand the benefits of using the XML datatype.

You also learned how SQL Server 2005 works with XML and how you can decompose XML into relational data. However, these are just basic components of the XML datatype and its associated methods.

To query XML data, you learned different methods to use. The nodes and value methods can convert XML data into relational data and, therefore, are probably the most commonly used methods.

SQL Server supports two types of XML: typed and untyped. When using typed XML, you first need to catalog the XML Schema inside SQL Server using a CREATE XML SCHEMA COLLECTION statement.

For the certification examination:

- Be able to identify the data structure. Understand when to use XML and when another datatype is preferable or usable.

- Know how to retrieve XML data. To retrieve XML data, you can use several methods. To be able to work with XML data, it is important to know the query, exist, nodes, value, and modify methods. You need to fully understand how to decompose to XML, as well as how to convert it.

- Know how to modify XML data. XML data can be modified in the XML column using the modify method, and you don't need to shred out and update the entire XML data in order to replace, insert, or even delete data in an XML column.

- Understand how to convert between XML data and relational data. Since the XML datatype is near the highest in the datatype precedence hierarchy, you will have conversion from and to the XML datatype. It is important to know how to use the CAST and CONVERT functions to support the XML datatype.

- Know how to create an XML index. When optimizing XML querying, you can create multiple indexes, which are the primary starting points for your XML optimization. To support the various types of XML queries, you will create secondary indexes.

- Know how to load an XML schema. SQL Server stores typed or untyped XML; when storing typed XML, you first will need to load an XML schema in the database before you can use it, and have schema validation in variables, columns, and expressions. It is important to be familiar with this syntax.

■ Knowledge Assessment

Multiple Choice

Circle the letter or letters that correspond to the best answer or answers.

1. You need to obtain a rowset from an XML document and avoid null results. Which code can you use? (Choose all that apply.)

   a. ```
      DECLARE @doc XML
      SET @doc = '<?xml version="1.0" ?>
      <Order OrderId="1">
      ```
      ```

```
        <Product ProductID="110" Quantity="50" />
        <Product ProductID="115" Quantity="40" />
        <Product ProductID="120" Quantity="70" />
        </Order>'
        DECLARE @idoc int
        EXEC sp_xml_preparedocument @idoc OUTPUT, @doc
        SELECT *
        FROM OPENXML (@idoc, '/Order/Product',1)
        WITH (ProductID int,
        Quantity int)
```

b.
```
        DECLARE @doc varchar(MAX)
        SET @doc = '<?xml version="1.0" ?>
        <Order OrderId="1">
        <Product ProductID="110" Quantity="50" />
        <Product ProductID="115" Quantity="40" />
        <Product ProductID="120" Quantity="70" />
        </Order>'
        DECLARE @idoc int
        EXEC sp_xml_preparedocument @idoc OUTPUT, @doc
        SELECT *
        FROM OPENXML (@idoc, '/Order/Product',0)
        WITH (ProductID int,
        Quantity int)
```

c.
```
        DECLARE @doc XML
        SET @doc = '<?xml version="1.0" ?>
        <Order OrderId="1">
        <Product ProductID="110" Quantity="50" />
        <Product ProductID="115" Quantity="40" />
        <Product ProductID="120" Quantity="70" />
        </Order>'
        DECLARE @idoc int
        EXEC sp_xml_preparedocument @idoc OUTPUT, @doc
        SELECT *
        FROM OPENXML (@idoc, '/Order/Product',2)
        WITH (ProductID int,
        Quantity int)
```

d.
```
        DECLARE @doc XML
        SET @doc = '<?xml version="1.0" ?>
        <Order OrderId="1">
        <Product ProductID="110" Quantity="50" />
        <Product ProductID="115" Quantity="40" />
        <Product ProductID="120" Quantity="70" />
        </Order>'
        DECLARE @idoc int
        EXEC sp_xml_preparedocument @idoc OUTPUT, @doc
        SELECT *
```

```
FROM OPENXML (@idoc, '/Order/Product',0)
WITH (ProductID int,
Quantity int)
```

2. You have an XML variable declared using the following code:

```
DECLARE @doc XML
SET @doc = '<?xml version="1.0" ?>
<Order OrderId="1">
<Product ProductID="110" Quantity="50" />
<Product ProductID="115" Quantity="40" />
<Product ProductID="120" Quantity="70" />
</Order>'
```

You want to insert the values of the ProductID and Quantity attributes in a table. Which code can you use? (Choose all that apply.)

a.
```
DECLARE @idoc int
EXEC sp_xml_preparedocument @idoc OUTPUT, @doc
INSERT INTO tblTempOrders(ProductId,Quantity)
SELECT *
FROM OPENXML (@idoc, '/Order/Product',0)
WITH (ProductID int,
Quantity int)
```

b.
```
DECLARE @idoc int
EXEC sp_xml_preparedocument @idoc OUTPUT, @doc
INSERT INTO tblTempOrders(ProductId,Quantity)
SELECT *
FROM OPENXML (@idoc, '/Order/Product',1)
WITH (ProductID int,
Quantity int)
```

c.
```
DECLARE @idoc int
EXEC sp_xml_preparedocument @idoc OUTPUT, @doc
INSERT INTO tblTempOrders(ProductId,Quantity)
SELECT *
FROM OPENXML (@idoc, '/Order/Product',0)
WITH (ProductID int '@ProductID',
Quantity int '@Quantity')
```

d.
```
INSERT INTO tblTempOrders(ProductId,Quantity)
SELECT
T.c.value('@ProductID','int') AS ProductID,
T.c.value('@Quantity','int') AS Quantity
FROM @doc.nodes('/Order/Product') T(c)
```

3. One of your tables has an XML column with a primary XML index defined on it. You want to improve the performance of several queries that specify complete path expressions without wildcards on the XML column. Which method is optimal?

a. Define an additional primary XML index.

b. Create a path secondary XML index.

c. Create a value secondary XML index.

d. Create a property secondary XML index.

4. Which of the following is not true regarding XML indexes? (Choose all that apply.)
   a. When you create a primary XML index, the table that contains the XML column (that will be indexed), which is the base table, must have a clustered index on the primary key.
   b. When you create a primary XML index, the table that contains the XML column (that will be indexed) must have a nonclustered index on the primary key.
   c. A primary XML index can be created on a multiple XML-type column.
   d. You can have an XML index and a non-XML index on the same table with the same name.

5. You want to import a UTF-8 encoded XML file. Which of the following options is recommended?
   a. `INSERT INTO tblImport(XmlCol)`
      `SELECT * FROM OPENROWSET(`
      `BULK 'C:\Import\XmlDataFile.txt',`
      `SINGLE_NCLOB) AS xmlResult`
   b. `INSERT INTO tblImport(XmlCol)`
      `SELECT * FROM OPENROWSET(`
      `BULK 'C:\Import\XmlDataFile.txt',`
      `SINGLE_CLOB) AS xmlResult`
   c. `INSERT INTO tblImport(XmlCol)`
      `SELECT * FROM OPENROWSET(`
      `BULK 'C:\Import\XmlDataFile.txt',`
      `SINGLE_BLOB) AS xmlResult`
   d. `INSERT INTO tblImport(XmlCol)`
      `SELECT BulkColumn FROM OPENROWSET(`
      `BULK 'C:\Import\XmlDataFile.txt',`
      `SINGLE_NCLOB) AS xmlResult`

6. You need to import data from a document that contains a Document Type Definition (DTD). Which of the following scripts can be used?
   a. `INSERT INTO tblImport(XmlCol)`
      `SELECT CONVERT(xml, BulkColumn, 2)`
      `FROM OPENROWSET(Bulk 'C:\Import\DataFile.xml',`
      `SINGLE_BLOB) AS xmlResult`
   b. `INSERT INTO tblImport(XmlCol)`
      `SELECT BulkColumn`
      `FROM OPENROWSET(Bulk 'C:\Import\DataFile.xml',`
      `SINGLE_BLOB) AS xmlResult`
   c. `INSERT INTO tblImport(XmlCol)`
      `SELECT *`
      `FROM OPENROWSET(Bulk 'C:\Import\DataFile.xml',`
      `SINGLE_BLOB) AS xmlResult`
   d. `INSERT INTO tblImport(XmlCol)`
      `SELECT CONVERT(xml, BulkColumn, 2)`
      `FROM OPENROWSET(Bulk 'C:\Import\DataFile.xml',`
      `SINGLE_BLOB) AS xmlResult`

7. You need to write a query that will return element-centric XML. Additionally, you want null columns to be included in the results. Which code can you use?
   a. `SELECT ProductId, Name, ListPrice, Color`
      `FROM Production.Product`
      `FOR XML RAW, ELEMENTS`

b. SELECT ProductId, Name, ListPrice, Color

   FROM Production.Product

   FOR XML RAW

c. SELECT ProductId, Name, ListPrice, Color

   FROM Production.Product

   FOR XML AUTO, ELEMENTS XSINIL

d. SELECT ProductId, Name, ListPrice, Color

   FROM Production.Product

   FOR XML AUTO

8. By default, FOR XML queries return XML fragments. You need to return a well-formed XML document. How can you accomplish this?
   a. Use the XMLSCHEMA directive.
   b. Use the EXPLICIT mode.
   c. Use the TYPE directive.
   d. Use the ROOT directive.

9. You have created an XML Schema collection named ContractSchemas. You want to associate it to an XML column for validation. Both documents and valid fragments should be allowed. Which code can you use? (Choose all that apply.)
   a. CREATE TABLE HR.Documents(

   DocumentId int,

   DocumentText xml (DOCUMENT ContractSchemas))

   b. CREATE TABLE HR.Documents(

   DocumentId int,

   DocumentText xml)

   c. CREATE TABLE HR.Documents(

   DocumentId int,

   DocumentText xml (ContractSchemas))

   d. CREATE TABLE HR.Documents(

   DocumentId int,

   DocumentText xml (CONTENT ContractSchemas))

10. You try to associate an XML schema collection to an XML column using the following code:

```
CREATE XML SCHEMA COLLECTION ContractSchemas AS '
<schema xmlns="http://www.w3.org/2001/XMLSchema">
<element name="contract" type="string"/>
</schema>
<schema xmlns="http://www.w3.org/2001/XMLSchema">
<element name="template" type="string"/>
</schema>'
CREATE TABLE HR.Contracts (
DocumentId int,
DocumentText xml (ContractSchemas)
)
GO
```

You obtained the following error:

```
"Collection specified does not exist in metadata:
'ContractSchemas'."
```

What is the cause of the error?

    a. The attribute targetNameSpace is not specified.

    b. You cannot define multiple XML schemas in a Schema collection.

    c. The XML declaration is missing.

    d. A Schema collection cannot be referenced in the same batch where it was created.

11. You have declared an XML document using the following code:

```
DECLARE @myDoc XML
SET @myDoc = '<?xml version="1.0" ?>
<booklist>
<book category="Programming">
<title>Beginning ASP.NET 2.0
E-Commerce in C# 2005</title>
<authors>
<author>Cristian Darie</author>
</authors>
<year>2005</year>
</book>
</booklist>'
```

You want to modify the XML document by adding another author after the existing one. Which code can you use? (Choose all that apply.)

    a.
```
SET @myDoc.modify('
insert <author>Karli Watson</author>
as last into (/booklist/book/authors)[1]')
```

    b.
```
SET @myDoc.modify('
insert element author {"Karli Watson"}
as first into (/booklist/book/authors)[1]')
```

    c.
```
SET @myDoc.modify('
insert element author {"Karli Watson"}
as last into (/booklist/book/authors)[1]')
```

    d.
```
SET @myDoc.modify('
insert <author>Karli Watson</author>
as first into (/booklist/book/authors)[1]')
```

12. You have declared the following XML document:

```
DECLARE @myDoc XML
SET @myDoc = '<?xml version="1.0" ?>
<booklist>
<book category="Programming">
<title>Beginning ASP.NET 2.0
E-Commerce in C# 2005</title>
<authors>
<author>Cristian Darie</author>
<author>Karli Watson</author>
</authors>
<year>2005</year>
</book>
</booklist>'
```

You want to replace the category attribute value with ASP.NET instead of Programming. How can you accomplish this?

a. SET @myDoc.modify('
```
   replace value of (/booklist/book/@category)[1]
   with "ASP.NET"')
```

b. SET @myDoc.modify('
```
   replace value of (/booklist/book/@category)[0]
   with "ASP.NET"')
```

c. SET @myDoc.modify('
```
   replace value of (/booklist/book/category)[1]
   with "ASP.NET"')
```

d. SET @myDoc.modify('
```
   replace value of (/booklist/book/category)[0]
   with "ASP.NET"')
```

13. You have declared the following XML document:
```
DECLARE @myDoc XML
SET @myDoc = '<?xml version="1.0" ?>
<booklist>
<book category="Programming">
<title>Beginning ASP.NET 2.0
E-Commerce in C# 2005</title>
<authors>
<author>Cristian Darie</author>
<author>Karli</author>
<author>Karli Watson</author>
</authors>
<year>2005</year>
</book>
</booklist>'
```

You want to delete the second author. Which code can you use?

a. SET @myDoc.modify(' delete
   /book/authors/author[2]')

b. SET @myDoc.modify(' delete
   /booklist/book/authors/author[2]')

c. SET @myDoc.modify(' delete /authors/author[2]')

d. SET @myDoc.modify(' delete
   /booklist/book/authors/author/[2]')

14. Which of the following is not an argument for using the native XML datatype? (Choose all that apply.)
   a. You want to modify the XML data.
   b. You need XML indexes for faster response time.
   c. You need to store exact copies of the XML data.
   d. You need to validate your XML data.

15. Which of the following is not a characteristic of XML Schema collections?
   a. Schema collections are scoped to the database where they are created.
   b. Schema collections can span databases or instances.
   c. You can assign more than one XML schema to an XML column.
   d. You can load an XML schema using the OPENROWSET function.

16. Which of the following is an argument for using relational storage instead of the native XML datatype?
    a. Your data is hierarchical.
    b. Your data consists of large documents frequently updated.
    c. Your data consists of large documents rarely updated.
    d. Your data is semistructured.

17. You want to store XML documents in SQL Server and you have to decide which format to use. Considering that you receive the information in XML format and that you need to validate, query, and modify the data, what's the best storage option using the minimum amount of work?
    a. Store the XML documents in tables using the relational model.
    b. Use the native XML datatype.
    c. Store the XML documents in an nvarchar(max) column.
    d. Store the XML documents in a varchar(max) column.

18. You need to retrieve a scalar value from an XML instance. Which method can you use?
    a. value
    b. query
    c. exist
    d. nodes

19. You want to obtain information about XML indexes including fragmentation. Which metadata views can be used? (Choose all that apply.)
    a. sys.xml_indexes
    b. sys.dm_db_index_physical_stats
    c. sys.indexes
    d. sys.system_objects

20. You want to convert a string to XML and preserve white spaces. Which code can you use?
    a. `SELECT CONVERT(xml, N'<root>`
       `<element></element> </root>', 1)`
    b. `DECLARE @x XML SET @x = '<root>`
       `<element></element> </root>'`
    c. `SELECT CONVERT(xml, N'<root>`
       `<element></element> </root>')`
    d. `SELECT CAST(N'<root> <element></element>`
       `</root>' AS XML)`

21. You want to convert a string to an XML datatype and remove insignificant spaces. Which code can you use? (Choose all that apply.)
    a. `SELECT CONVERT(XML, '<root> <element/>`
       `</root>')`
    b. `SELECT CONVERT(XML, '<root> <element/>`
       `</root>',1)`
    c. `SELECT CONVERT(XML, '<root> <element/>`
       `</root>',0)`
    d. `SELECT CAST('<root> <element/> </root>' AS XML)`

■ Case Scenarios

Scenario 15-1: Understanding XML

You have been around the world twice and through it once. You remember when everyone pooh-poohed GWBASIC because it interpreted text during processing, rather than being compiled. You also remember that Microsoft's Transaction Server and Sun Microsystems CORBUS accomplished essentially the same thing, but neither worked on all browsers. Why is everyone pushing so hard for a text-based solution again? What is it that XML offers that makes it so exciting? What has SOAP to do with anything? What does WSDL offer?

Permissions

LESSON SKILL MATRIX

TECHNOLOGY SKILL	70-431 EXAM OBJECTIVES
Configure SQL Server security.	Foundational
Configure server security principals.	Foundational
Configure database securables.	Foundational
Configure encryption.	Foundational
Configure linked servers by using SQL Server Management Studio (SSMS).	Foundational
Identify the external data source.	Foundational
Identify the characteristics of the data source.	Foundational
Identify the security model of the data source.	Foundational
Implement a table.	Foundational
Assign permissions to a role for tables.	Foundational
Implement a view.	Foundational
Assign permissions to a role or schema for a view.	Foundational
Implement stored procedures.	Foundational
Assign permissions to a role for a stored procedure.	Foundational

KEY TERMS

encryption: A method for keeping sensitive information confidential by changing data into an unreadable form.

linked server: A definition of an OLE DB data source used by SQL Server-distributed queries. The linked server definition specifies the OLE DB provider required to access the data and includes enough addressing information for the OLE DB provider to connect to the data. Any rowsets exposed by the OLEDB data source can then be referenced as tables, called *linked tables*, in SQL Server distributed queries.

permission: Any one of many access tokens created to enable a principal to access a securable.

principal: Any type of authenticated user logged in to SQL Server.

securable: An object that can have a security descriptor.

stored procedure: A precompiled collection of Transact-SQL statements or CLR code segments that are stored under a name and processed as a unit. SQL Server supplies stored procedures for managing SQL Server and displaying information about databases and users. SQL Server–supplied procedures are called system stored procedures.

table: A two-dimensional object that consists of rows and columns that stores data about an entity modeled in a relational database.

■ Guarding Your Data

THE BOTTOM LINE

Maintaining data integrity is your most important job, for information is a corporation's greatest asset. You can't allow just anyone access to your company's information. You must make sure that users assigned to do specific tasks can do *only* specific tasks. Applying permissions is one technique to protect your data.

Understanding Security Modes

An authentication mode is how SQL Server processes usernames and passwords. SQL Server 2005 provides two such modes: Windows Authentication and Mixed.

USING WINDOWS AUTHENTICATION MODE

With this mode, users can sit down at their computers, log in to the Windows domain, and gain access to SQL Server using the Kerberos security protocol. Here is a brief overview of how this protocol works:

1. When the user logs in, Windows performs a Domain Name System (DNS) lookup to locate a key distribution center (KDC).
2. The user's machine logs in to the domain.
3. The KDC issues a special security token, called a *ticket-granting ticket (TGT)*, to the user.
4. To access the SQL Server, the user's machine presents the TGT to SQL Server.
5. If the operating system security identifier (SID) matches that which is stored in the sys.server_principals metadata *table*, the user is allowed to access.

TAKE NOTE*

The SID was placed in the table when you first added the new user.

The main advantage of Windows Authentication mode is that users don't have to remember multiple usernames and passwords. This vastly increases security, because there is less danger of users writing down their passwords and storing them in an unsafe place (such as on a sticky note on their monitors). This mode also gives you tighter rein over security, because you can apply Windows password policies, which perform such tasks as expiring passwords, requiring a minimum length for passwords, keeping a history of passwords, and so on.

One of the disadvantages of this mode is that only users with Windows accounts can open a trusted connection to SQL Server. This means others, such as Novell clients, can't use Windows Authentication mode because they don't have a Windows account. If you have such clients, you'll need to implement Mixed mode.

USING MIXED MODE

Mixed mode allows both Windows Authentication and SQL Server Authentication (or Standard Authentication). SQL Server Authentication works as follows:

1. Users log in to their network, Windows or otherwise.
2. Users open a *nontrusted connection* to SQL Server using a username and password other than those used to gain network access. It's called a nontrusted connection because SQL Server doesn't trust the operating system to verify the users' passwords.
3. SQL Server matches the username and password entered by the user to an entry in the sys.sql_logins table.

TAKE NOTE*

The system table sys-logins is maintained as a view for backward compatibility with SQL Server 2000.

The primary advantage of Mixed mode is that anyone can gain access to SQL Server using it. Mac users, Novell users, Unix users, and the like, can gain access using SQL Server authentication. You might also consider this to be a second layer of security, because if someone hacks into your Windows Server network, and all database access requires SQL Server logins, the intruder won't be able to access your corporate data. To maximize security in this scenario, make the userID different from that for the network, be sure to set strong passwords, and manually change user passwords at regular intervals.

Be aware, however, that multiple passwords can be a problem as well as an advantage. Consider that users will have one username and password to log in to the network and a completely separate username and password to gain access to SQL Server. When users have to remember multiple sets of credentials, they tend to write them down and thus breach the security system you have worked so hard to set up.

SETTING THE AUTHENTICATION MODE

As an administrator, you'll probably set the authentication mode no more than once: at installation time. The only other time you might need to change the authentication mode would be if changes were made to your network. For example, if you set your SQL Server to Windows Authentication mode and later need to include Macintosh clients, you would need to change to Mixed mode.

It's interesting to note that although you can perform most tasks in SQL Server through either SQL Server Management Studio or T-SQL, setting the authentication mode is one of the rare tasks you can do only through SQL Server Management Studio. Exercise 16-1 takes you through setting the authentication mode.

Now that you've set the proper authentication mode, it's time to give your users access to your server with SQL Server logins.

 EXERCISE 16-1 SETTING THE AUTHENTICATION MODE

1. Click **Start** → **All Programs** → **Microsoft SQL Server 2005** → **SQL Server Management Studio**. Click **Connect**.

2. Right-click **your server** in Object Explorer and select **Properties** from the context menu. The dialog box that appears should be labeled Server Properties, followed by your server name. Select the **Security** page in the Select a page tree view.

3. In the Server Authentication section, select **SQL Server** and **Windows Authentication Mode**. SQL Server service must be restarted.

4. Click **Start** → **All Programs** → **Microsoft SQL Server 2005** → **Configuration Tools** launch **SQL Server Surface Area Configuration**.

5. Click the **Surface Area Configuration for Services and Connections** link near the bottom of the page.

6. After a moment, the View by Instance tab is populated.

7. Open, if necessary, the **Database Engine**. Make sure the black arrow points to Service, and in the dialog box press the **Stop** and then the **Start** buttons.

8. Click **OK** to close the Server Properties box.

Doing this sets you to Mixed mode for the rest of the exercises.

Understanding SQL Server Logins

A SQL Server key—a login—gives your users access to SQL Server as a whole, not to the resources (such as databases) inside. If you're a member of the sysadmin or securityadmin fixed server role (discussed later in this lesson), you can create one of two types of logins: standard logins and Windows logins.

USING STANDARD LOGINS

You learned earlier in this lesson that only clients with a Windows account can make trusted connections to SQL Server (where SQL Server trusts Windows to validate the user's password). If the user (such as a Macintosh or Novell client) for whom you're creating a login can't make a trusted connection, you must create a standard login for him or her. In Exercise 16-2, you'll create two standard logins that will be used later in the lesson.

Although you can create standard logins in Windows Authentication mode, you won't be able to use them. If you try, SQL Server will ignore you and use your Windows credentials instead.

EXERCISE 16-2 CREATING STANDARD LOGINS

1. Click **Start** → **All Programs** → **Microsoft SQL Server 2005** → **SQL Server Management Studio**. Click **Connect**.

2. Click the **plus (+) sign** next to your server in Object Explorer. Click the **plus (+) sign** next to Security. Click the **plus (+) sign** next to logins to view the current users. Right-click **Logins** and select **New Login** from the menu. Select the **SQL Server Authentication** radio button.

3. In the Login Name box, type **SmithB**.

4. In the Password text box, type **Pa$$w0rd** (remember, passwords are case-sensitive).

5. In the Confirm Password text box, type **Pa$$w0rd** again.

6. For the Default Database option, select **AdventureWorks** as the default database.

7. Uncheck the **User Must Change Password at Next Login** box.

8. Switch to the **User** mapping page by clicking "**User Mapping**" in the Select a Page view. On the User Mapping page, check the **Map** box next to AdventureWorks to give your user access to the default database.

9. Click **OK** to create your new login.

10. Repeat the process once more to add a second user, named GibsonH.

11. Test your registration success by clicking the **New Query** button located near the upper left in Management Studio.

12. Click the **Change Connection** button located just below the New Query button.

13. In the Connect to Database Engine dialog box, select **SQL Server Authentication** from the Authentication drop-down menu.

14. In the Login box, type **SmithB**.

15. In the Password box, type **Pa$$w0rd**.

16. Click **Connect** to connect to AdventureWorks.

USING WINDOWS LOGINS

Creating Windows logins isn't much different from creating standard logins. Although standard logins apply to only one user, a Windows login can be mapped to one of the following:

- A single user
- A Windows group that an administrator has created
- A Windows built-in group (for example, Administrators)

Before you create a Windows login, you must decide to which of these three you want to map it. Generally, you'll map to a group you've created. Doing so will help you a great deal in later administration. For example, suppose you have an Accounting database to which all 50 of your accountants require access. You could create a separate login for each of them, which would require you to manage 50 SQL Server logins. But if you create a Windows group for these 50 accountants and map your SQL Server login to this group, you'll have only one SQL Server login to manage. The Windows Administrator does most of the work.

The first step in creating Windows logins is to create user accounts in the operating system.

EXERCISE 16-3 CREATING WINDOWS ACCOUNTS

1. For a Domain Controller: Click **Start** → **Administrative Tools** → **Active Directory Users and Computers** → Right-click **Users**→Choose **New** from the menu and **User** from the drop-down menu.

2. For a Standalone or Member Server: Click **Start** → Right-click **My Computer** → Click **Manage** from the context menu → Click the **plus (+) sign** next to Local Users and Groups → Right-click **Users** and select **New User**.

3. Create six new users with the criteria from the list in Table 16-1.

Table 16-1

User Requirements

Username	Description	Password	Must Change	Never Expires
MorrisL	IT	Pa$$w0rd	Deselect	Select
RosmanD	Administration	Pa$$w0rd	Deselect	Select
JohnsonK	Accounting	Pa$$w0rd	Deselect	Select
JonesB	Accounting	Pa$$w0rd	Deselect	Select
ChenJ	Sales	Pa$$w0rd	Deselect	Select
SamuelsR	Sales	Pa$$w0rd	Deselect	Select

4. For a Domain Controller: Click **Start** → **Administrative Tools** → **Active Directory Users and Computers**. Right-click **Users**. Choose **New** from the menu and Group from the drop-down menu.

5. For a Standalone or Member Server: Click **Start**→ Right-click **My Computer** Choose **Manage** → Click the **plus (+) sign** next to Local Users and Groups→ Right-click **Groups** and select **New Group**.

6. Create a group called **Accounting.**

7. Add the new users you just created, whose Description value is Accounting.

8. While still in Computer Management or Active Directory Users and Computers, create a group named **Sales**.

9. Add all the users whose Description value is Sales.

10. Click **Start** → **Run** →Enter **MMC** and click **OK**. Click **File** → **Add/Remove Snap-in** → **Add** → **Group Policy Object Editor** → **Add.**

    a. For a Domain Controller: Click **Browse** → **Domain Controllers** for your domain name. Highlight the **Default Domain Controller Policy** and click **OK.**

    b. For a Standalone or Member Server: Make sure that **Local Computer** is listed in the Group Policy Object text box and click **Finish.**

11. Click **Finish** → Click **OK** → Click **Close** → Click **OK**. Click the **plus (+) sign** to expand your policy → Click the **plus (+) sign** next to Computer Configuration → Click the **plus (+) sign** next to Windows Settings → Click the **plus (+) sign** next to Security → Click the **plus (+) sign** next to Local Policies. Click **User Rights Assignment.**

12. Double-click the **Allow Log on Locally** right, and click **Add User or Group**. Select the **Everyone** group, click **OK**, then click **OK** again.

13. Close the **MMC**. Answer **No** to save console settings.

 TAKE NOTE✱

On a production machine, this is not a best practice; this is only for this exercise.

 EXERCISE 16-4 CREATING SQL SERVER LOGINS FOR WINDOWS ACCOUNTS

1. Click **Start** → **All Programs** → **Microsoft SQL Server 2005** → **SQL Server Management Studio**. Click **Connect.**

2. Click the **plus (+) sign** next to your server in Object Explorer. Click the **plus (+) sign** next to Security. Click the **plus (+) sign** next to Logins to view the current users. Right-click **Logins** and select **New Login** from the menu.

3. In the **Login Name** box, type **<Your Domain or Server Name>\Accounting**—which you created earlier. For the Default Database option, select **AdventureWorks**.

4. On the User Mapping page, check the **Map** box next to AdventureWorks to give your user access to the default database.

5. Click **OK** to create the login.

6. Right-click **Logins**, and select **New Login**.

7. In the Login name box, type **<Your Domain or Server Name>\Sales**—which you also created earlier.

8. For the Default Database option, select **AdventureWorks** as the default database.

9. On the User Mapping page, check the **Map** box next to AdventureWorks to give your user access to the default database.

10. Click **OK** to create the login.

11. Right-click **Logins**, and select **New Login**.

12. Fill in the Login Name field with **<YourServerName>\RosmanD**.

13. For the Default Database option, select **AdventureWorks** as the default database.

14. On the Database Access page, check the **Permit** box next to AdventureWorks to give your user access to the default database.

15. Click **OK** to create the login.

16. Right-click **Logins**, and select **New Login**.

17. Fill in the Login Name field with **<YourServerName>\MorrisL**.

18. For the Default Database option, select **AdventureWorks** as the default database.

19. On the Database Access page, check the **Permit** box next to AdventureWorks to give your user access to the default database.

20. Click **OK** to create the login.

Now that you have some Windows groups and user logins to work with, you'll test them. First you'll log in as a member of one of the groups you created, and then you'll log in as a specific user.

 EXERCISE 16-5 TESTING SQL SERVER LOGINS FOR WINDOWS ACCOUNTS

1. Log out of **Windows**, and log back in as **JonesB**.

2. Open a new **SQL Server query** in SQL Server Management Studio, and select **Windows Authentication** from the Authentication drop-down menu.

3. Close **SQL Server Management Studio**, log out of **Windows**, and log back in as **RosmanD**.

4. Open a new **SQL Server query** in SQL Server Management Studio, and select **Windows Authentication** from the Authentication drop-down list.

Understanding the Items Common to All Logins

You may have noticed that some features are common to all the logins you created.

The first is the default database. When users first log in to SQL Server, they connect to the default database. If you don't set the default database, users connect to Master, which isn't the best place for your users to get started. You should change that to a different database; for example, change it to the Accounting database if you're working with an accounting user. You can also set a default language, which won't need frequent changing, because the default is the server's language. You can set a different language here for users who require it.

In all types of logins, you can grant database access at create time. On the User Mapping page of the SQL Server Management Studio New Login dialog box, all you need to do is select the database to which this login requires access; doing so automatically creates a database user account, as you did for the AdventureWorks database in the previous set of exercises.

If you create a Windows login using sp_grantlogin, you can't set the default database or language.

In addition, you can add users to a fixed server role at the time you create them; you do this on the Server Roles tab in SQL Server Management Studio. The next section discusses fixed server roles—that is, limitations on access.

UNDERSTANDING FIXED SERVER ROLES

Fixed server roles are used to limit the amount of administrative access a user has once he or she has logged in to SQL Server. Some users may be allowed to do whatever they want, whereas others may be able only to manage security. You can assign users any of eight server roles. The following list starts at the highest level and describes the administrative access granted:

sysadmin: Members of the sysadmin role have the authority to perform any task in SQL Server. Be careful whom you assign to this role, because people who are unfamiliar with SQL Server can accidentally cause serious problems. This role is intended for the database administrators (DBAs).

serveradmin: These users can set serverwide configuration options, such as how much memory SQL Server can use or how much information to send over the network in a single frame. They can also shut down the server. If you make your assistant DBAs members of this role, you can relieve yourself of some of the administrative burden.

setupadmin: Members here can install replication and manage extended **stored procedures** (these can perform actions not native to SQL Server). Give this role to the assistant DBAs as well.

securityadmin: These users manage security issues such as creating and deleting logins, reading the audit logs, and granting users permission to create databases. This too is a good role for assistant DBAs.

processadmin: SQL Server is capable of multitasking; that is, SQL Server can perform more than one task at a time by executing multiple processes. For instance, SQL Server might spawn one process for writing to the cache and another for reading from the cache. A member of the processadmin group can end (or "kill," as it's called in SQL Server) a process. This is another good role for assistant DBAs and developers. Developers especially need to kill processes that may have been triggered by an improperly designed query or stored procedure.

dbcreator: These users can create and make changes to databases. This may be a good role for assistant DBAs as well as developers (who should be warned against creating unnecessary databases and wasting server space).

diskadmin: These users manage files on disk. They perform actions such as mirroring databases and adding backup devices. Assistant DBAs should be members of this role.

bulkadmin: Members of this role can execute the BULK INSERT statement, which allows them to import data into SQL Server databases from text files. Assistant DBAs should be members of this role.

Now you'll apply this knowledge by assigning some users to fixed server roles, thereby limiting their administrative authority.

If you don't want users to have any administrative authority, don't assign them to a server role. This limits them to being normal users.

EXERCISE 16-6 ADDING LOGINS TO FIXED SERVER ROLES

1. Click **Start** → **All Programs** → **Microsoft SQL Server 2005** → **SQL Server Management Studio**. Click **Connect**.

2. Click the **plus (+) sign** next to Security → Click the **plus (+) sign** next to Server Roles. This displays the built-in server roles. Double-click **Sysadmin** to open its properties. Assure that your dialog box title is "Server Role Properties—sysadmin."

3. Click **Add**, click **Browse**, check the **<YourServerName>\MorrisL** box, click **OK**, and click **OK** again.

4. MorrisL should now appear in the Role Members list.

5. Click **OK** to exit the Server Role Properties dialog box.

6. Double-click **Serveradmin Server Role Properties**.

7. Click **Add**, enter **GibsonH**, and click **OK**.

8. Click **OK** to exit the Server Role Properties dialog box.

BUILTIN\Administrators is automatically made a member of the sysadmin server role, giving SQL Server administrative rights to all of your Windows administrators. Because not all of your Windows administrators should have these rights, you may want to create a SQLAdmins group in Windows, add your SQL Server administrators to that group, and make the group a member of the sysadmin role. Afterward, you should remove BUILTIN\Administrators from the sysadmin role.

CREATING DATABASE USER ACCOUNTS

Now that your employees have access to your "building," as well as the proper administrative access once they're inside, they need access to other resources to do their work. For example, if you want to give your accounting department access to the accounting files, you need to give them a new key—one to the file cabinet. Your employees now have two keys, one for the front door and one for the file cabinet.

In much the same way, you need to give users access to databases once they have logged in to SQL Server. You do so by creating database user accounts and then assigning permissions to those user accounts (we discuss permissions later in this lesson). Once this process is complete, your SQL Server users also have more than one key: one for the front door (the login) and one for each file cabinet (database) to which they need access. In Exercise 16-7, you'll give users access to the AdventureWorks database by creating database user accounts.

 EXERCISE 16-7 CREATING USER ACCOUNTS IN ADVENTUREWORKS

1. Click **Start** → **All Programs** → **Microsoft SQL Server 2005** → **SQL Server Management Studio**. Click **Connect**.

2. Click the **plus (+) sign** next to Databases. Click the **plus (+) sign** next to AdventureWorks. Click the **plus (+) sign** next to Security. Click the **plus (+) sign** next to Users. Right-click **Users** and select **New User**. Make sure the dialog box title is "Database User—New."

3. Click the **ellipsis** button next to the Login Name box, and click **Browse**. View all the available names; note that only logins you've already created are available.

4. Check the **GibsonH** box, and click **OK** twice.

5. Enter **GibsonH** in the User Name box and **dbo** in the Default Schema box.

6. Click **OK** to create the GibsonH database user account.

You may have noticed that two user accounts already exist in your databases when they are first created: DBO and Guest. Members of the sysadmin fixed server role automatically become the database owner (DBO) user in every database on the system. In this way, they can perform all the necessary administrative functions in the databases, such as adding users and creating tables. All others who have a SQL Server login but not a user account in a database gain access to that database as Guest. These users can log in to the server as themselves and access any database where they don't have a user account. Because any permissions set for Guest become available to any user, the Guest account should be carefully limited in function.

Whenever a member of the sysadmin fixed server role creates an object (such as a table), it isn't owned by that login; it's owned by the DBO. If GibsonH created a table, the table wouldn't be referred to as GibsonH.table but as dbo.table.

Understanding SQL Server's Security Architecture

Principals are entities that can request SQL Server resources. Principals are arranged in a hierarchy. The scope of influence of a principal depends on the scope of the definition of the principal: Windows, Server, Database, or whether the principal is indivisible or a collection, as shown in Table 16-2. Every principal has a security identifier (SID).

Table 16-2

Principals

WINDOWS LEVEL	SQL SERVER LEVEL	DATABASE LEVEL
Windows domain login	SQL Server login	Database user
Windows local login		Database role
		Application role

Every object in a database has a unique fully qualified name in the form *ServerName.DatabaseName.SchemaName.ObjectName*. This implies a server level, database level, schema level, and object hierarchy. Within each of these four scopes exist ***securables***, as shown in Table 16-3.

Table 16-3

Securables

SERVER SCOPE	DATABASE SCOPE	SCHEMA SCOPE	OBJECT
Endpoint	User	Type	Aggregate
Login	Role	XML schema collection	Constraint
Database	Application role	Object	Function
	Assembly		Procedure
	Message type		Queue
	Route		Statistic
	Service		Synonym
	Remote service binding		Table
	Full-text catalog		View
	Asymmetric key		
	Symmetric key		
	Contract		
	Schema		

Within each of these scopes exist permissions. ***Permissions*** complete the security architecture model. The permissions available for data manipulation language securables are shown in Table 16-4.

Table 16-4

Permissions Applicable to DML Securables

SELECT	UPDATE	REFERENCES	INSERT
Delete	Execute	Receive	View definition
Alter	Take ownership	Control	

TAKE NOTE *

Other DDL and DCL permissions exist; for example: Impersonate, Create, Grant With, and many others.

The SQL Server security architecture consists of principals, securables, and permissions.

You secure all these objects by applying permissions at the appropriate scope. For example, applying a permission at the schema scope ripples down to the object level. To put it another way, anything a user is granted at the schema scope, he or she can do to objects within the schema scope.

 EXERCISE 16-8 EXAMINE THE BUILT-IN PERMISSIONS

1. Open your **Query Editor**. Type the following code:

   ```
   USE Master
   SELECT * FROM fn_builtin_permissions(default);
   ```

2. Execute.
3. Scroll through the list. You discover 186 built-in permissions!
4. Now try this code:

   ```
   USE AdventureWorks
   SELECT * FROM fn_my_permissions('person.address', 'object');
   ```

5. You now discover 35 permissions available for this specific table object.

Manageability is now your challenge. Start with permissions.

UNDERSTANDING PERMISSIONS

Now that you've created user accounts for everyone, you need to restrict what those users are allowed to do with the database. You do so by assigning permissions directly to the users or adding the users to a database role with a predefined set of permissions.

For example, not all your corporate users should be permitted to access the privacy or financial data in the accounting department or human resources department databases, because they contain sensitive information. Even users who are allowed in to these sensitive databases should not necessarily be given full access.

APPLYING STATEMENT PERMISSIONS

In SQL Server, you may also grant permission to use DDL statements. Statement permissions have nothing to do with the actual data; rather, they allow users to create the structures that hold the data. It's important not to grant these permissions haphazardly, because doing so can lead to such problems as broken ownership chains (discussed later) and wasted server resources. It's best to restrict statement permissions to DBAs, assistant DBAs, and developers. These permissions include

- Create Database
- Create Table
- Create View
- Create Procedure

TAKE NOTE*

Sysdatabases is retained as a view for backward compatibility with SQL Server 2000.

- Create Index
- Create Rule
- Create Default

When you create a new database, a record is added to the sys.databases system table, which is stored in the master database. Therefore, the CREATE DATABASE statement can be granted on the master database only.

 EXERCISE 16-9 APPLYING STATEMENT PERMISSIONS

1. Click **Start** → **All Programs** → **Microsoft SQL Server 2005** → **SQL Server Management Studio**. Click **Connect**.

2. Click the **New Query** button.

3. To prepare SQL Server for the following exercises, you need to remove permissions from the public role, because the existing permissions will interfere with your work. Open a new **Query Editor** window in SQL Server Management Studio, and execute the following query:

```
USE AdventureWorks
REVOKE ALL from public
```

TAKE NOTE* You may see a warning that says, "The ALL permission is deprecated and maintained only for compatibility. It DOES NOT imply ALL permissions defined on the entity." You can safely ignore this, as at the Database scope "ALL" means Backup Database, Backup Log, Create Database, Create Default, Create Function, Create Procedure, Create Rule, Create Table, and Create View.

4. Close the **Query window** without saving changes. In Object Explorer, click **your server** → Click the **plus (+) sign** next to Databases → Right-click **AdventureWorks** and select **Properties** from the menu. Assure that the dialog window title is "Database Properties—AdventureWorks." Select the **Permissions** page.

5. Grant RosmanD the Create Table permission by selecting **RosmanD** in the Users or Roles list and checking the **Grant** box next to Create Table.

6. Grant Accounting the permissions called **Backup Database and Backup Log**.

7. If the guest user has any permissions granted, remove them by unchecking the boxes. Click **OK** to apply your changes.

8. Log out of **Windows**, and log back in as **JonesB**.

9. Open a new **SQL Server query** in SQL Server Management Studio, connect using **Windows Authentication**, and type the following query:

```
USE AdventureWorks
CREATE TABLE Statement1
(column1 varchar(5) not null,
 column2 varchar(10) not null)
```

10. From the Query drop-down menu, select **Execute Query**. Notice that the query is unsuccessful because JonesB (a member of the Accounting group) doesn't have permission to create a table.

11. Close **SQL Server Management Studio**, log out of **Windows**, and log back in as **RosmanD**.

12. Open a new **SQL Server query** in SQL Server Management Studio, and enter and execute the code from step 10 again. This time it's successful, because RosmanD has permission to create tables.

APPLYING OBJECT PERMISSIONS

Once the structure exists to hold the data, you need to give users permission to start working with the data in the databases. This is accomplished by granting object permissions to your users. Using object permissions, you can control who is allowed to read from, write to, or otherwise manipulate your data. The 12 object permissions are as follows:

- **Control:** This permission gives the principal ownershiplike capabilities on the object and all objects under it in the hierarchy. For example, if you grant users Control permission on the database, they then have Control permission on all the objects in the database, such as tables and views.
- **Alter:** This permission allows users to create, alter, and drop the securable and any object under it in the hierarchy. The only property they can't change is ownership.
- **Take Ownership:** This allows users to take ownership of an object.
- **Impersonate:** This permission allows one login or user to impersonate another.
- **Create:** As the name implies, this permission lets users create objects.
- **View Definition:** This permission allows users to see the T-SQL syntax that was used to create the object being secured.
- **Select:** When granted, this permission allows users to read data from the table or view. When granted at the column level, it lets users read from a single column.
- **Insert:** This permission allows users to insert new rows into a table.
- **Update:** This permission lets users modify existing data in a table but not add new rows to or delete existing rows from a table. When this permission is granted on a column, users can modify data in that single column.
- **Delete:** This permission allows users to remove rows from a table.
- **References:** Tables can be linked together on a common column with a foreign key relationship, which is designed to protect data across tables. When two tables are linked with a foreign key, this permission allows the user to select data from the primary table without having the Select permission on the foreign table.
- **Execute:** This permission allows users to execute the stored procedure where the permission is applied.

EXERCISE 16-10 APPLYING AND TESTING OBJECT PERMISSIONS

1. Click **Start → All Programs → Microsoft SQL Server 2005 → SQL Server Management Studio**. Click **Connect**.
2. Expand your server. Click the **plus (+) sign** next to Databases → Click the **plus (+) sign** next to AdventureWorks → Click the **plus (+) sign** next to Tables. Right-click the table **Person.Address** and select **Properties**. Assure that the title of this dialog box is "Table Properties—Address."
3. On the Permissions page, add **<Your Domain or Server Name>\Sales** and **SmithB** under the Users or Roles list.
4. Select **<Your Domain or Server Name>\Sales** in the Users or Roles list, and grant Sales the Select permission by checking the **Grant** box next to Select.
5. Select **SmithB** in the Users or Roles list, and grant SmithB the Select permission by checking the **Grant** box next to Select.
6. If the guest user has any permissions granted, remove them by clicking each one until all check boxes are clear.
7. Click **OK**, and close **SQL Server Management Studio**.
8. Log out of **Windows**, and log back in as **JonesB**.
9. Open a new **SQL Server query** in SQL Server Management Studio, and connect using **Windows Authentication**.

10. Execute the following query (it fails because Accounting doesn't have Select permission):

    ```
    USE AdventureWorks
    SELECT * FROM Person.Contact
    ```

11. Close **SQL Server Management Studio**, and repeat steps 8 through 10, but for ChenJ. The query succeeds this time because Sales (of which ChenJ is a member) has Select permission.

12. Log out of **Windows**, and log back in as yourself.

Understanding Database Roles

Although granting permissions to single users is useful from time to time, it's better, faster, and easier to apply permissions en masse. This requires understanding database roles.

In SQL Server, when several users need permission to access a database, it's much easier to give them permissions as a group rather than try to manage each user separately. That is what database roles are for—granting permissions to groups of database users, rather than to each database user separately. You have three types of database roles to consider:

- Fixed
- Custom
- Application

USING FIXED DATABASE ROLES

Fixed database roles have permissions already applied; that is, all you have to do is add users to these roles and the users inherit the associated permissions. (This is different from custom database roles, as you'll see later.) You can use several fixed database roles in SQL Server to grant permissions:

- **db_owner:** Members of this role can do everything the members of the other roles can do, as well as some administrative functions.
- **db_accessadmin:** These users have the authority to say who gets access to the database, by adding or removing users.
- **db_datareader:** Members here can read data from any table in the database.
- **db_datawriter:** These users can add, change, and delete data from all the tables in the database.
- **db_ddladmin:** DDL administrators can issue all DDL commands; this allows them to create, modify, or change database objects without viewing the data inside.
- **db_securityadmin:** Members here can add and remove users from database roles, and they can manage statement and object permissions.
- **db_backupoperator:** These users can back up the database.
- **db_denydatareader:** Members can't read the data in the database, but they can make schema changes (for example, adding a column to a table).
- **db_denydatawriter:** These users can't make changes to the data in the database, but they're allowed to read the data.
- **public:** The purpose of this group is to grant users a default set of permissions in the database. All database users automatically join this group and can't be removed. Because all database users are automatically members of the public database role, you need to be cautious about the permissions assigned to this role.

CERTIFICATION READY?
System tables also have assigned roles. Take note of the additional roles provided in the MSDB database.

It's time to limit the administrative authority of your users once they gain access to the database by adding them to fixed database roles.

EXERCISE 16-11 ADDING USERS TO FIXED DATABASE ROLES

1. Click **Start** → **All Programs** → **Microsoft SQL Server 2005** → **SQL Server Management Studio**. Click **Connect**.

2. Click the **plus (+) sign** next to Databases → Click the **plus (+) sign** next to AdventureWorks → Click the **plus (+) sign** next to Security → Click the **plus (+) sign** next to Roles → Click the **plus (+) sign** next to Database Roles. Right-click **db_denydatawriter** and select **Properties**. Use the automatically selected **General** page. The Window should be entitled "Database Role Properties—db_denydatawriter."

3. Click **Add**.

4. Type **SmithB** in the Enter Object Names to Select box, and click **OK**.

5. Click **OK** again to return to SQL Server Management Studio.

6. Right-click **db_denydatareader**, and select **Properties**.

7. Click **Add**.

8. Type **GibsonH** in the Enter Object Names to Select box, and click **OK**.

9. Open a new **SQL Server query** in SQL Server Management Studio, and connect using **SQL Server Authentication**.

10. In the User Name box, type **SmithB**; in the Password box, type **Pa$$w0rd**.

11. The following query tries to update information in the HumanResources.Department table, but it fails because SmithB is a member of the db_denydatawriter role:

    ```
    INSERT INTO HumanResources.Department
    (DepartmentID, Name, GroupName, ModifiedDate)
    values (200, 'Test','TestGroup',GetDate())
    ```

12. Close the query window.

USING CUSTOM DATABASE ROLES

Fixed database roles cover many—but not all—of the situations that require permissions to be assigned to users. That is why you need to understand custom database roles.

Sometimes, of course, the fixed database roles don't meet your security needs. You may have several users who need Select, Update, and Execute permissions in your database and nothing more. Because none of the fixed database roles gives that set of permissions, you need to create a custom database role. When you create this new role, you assign permissions to it and then assign users to the role; the users inherit whatever permissions you assign to that role. This is different from the fixed database roles, where you don't need to assign permissions, but just add users.

You can make your custom database roles members of other database roles. This is referred to as *nesting roles.*

 EXERCISE 16-12 CREATING AND ADDING USERS TO CUSTOM DATABASE ROLES

1. Click **Start** → **All Programs** → **Microsoft SQL Server 2005** → **SQL Server Management Studio**. Click **Connect**.

2. Click the **plus (+) sign** next to Databases → Click the **plus (+) sign** next to AdventureWorks → Click the **plus (+) sign** next to Security → Click the **plus (+) sign** next to Roles →Right-click **Database Roles** and select **New Database Role**. Accept the selection of the General Page. The dialog box title should be "Database Role—New."

3. In the Role Name box, type **SelectOnly**, and enter **dbo** in the Owner box.

4. Add **<YourServerName>\RosmanD** to the Role Members list.

5. On the Securables page, click **Add** under the Securables list box, select the **Specific Objects** radio button, and click **OK**.

6. Click the **Objects Type** button, select Tables, and click **OK**.

7. Click **Browse**, check the **HumanResources.Department** box, and click **OK**, then click **OK** again.

8. In the Explicit Permissions for HumanResources.Department list, check the **Grant** box next to Select, and click **OK**.

9. Click **OK** to create the role and return to SQL Server Management Studio.

10. Close all programs, log off **Windows**, and log back in as **RosmanD**.

11. Open a new **SQL Server query** in SQL Server Management Studio, and connect using **Windows Authentication**.

12. Notice that the following query succeeds because RosmanD is a member of the new SelectOnly role:

   USE AdventureWorks

   SELECT * FROM HumanResources.Department

13. Now notice the failure of the next query because RosmanD is a member of a role that is allowed to select only:

   INSERT INTO HumanResources.Department

   (DepartmentID, Name, GroupName, ModifiedDate)

   values (200, 'Test','TestGroup',GetDate())

14. Close all programs, log out of **Windows**, and log back in as yourself.

USING APPLICATION ROLES

The final database role—the application role—grants you a great deal of authority over which applications can be used to work with the data in your databases.

Suppose your HR department uses a custom program to access its database and you don't want the HR employees using any other program, for fear they might damage the data. You can set this level of security by using an application role. With this special role, your users can't access data using just their SQL Server login and database account; they must use the proper application. Here is how it works:

1. Create an application role, and assign it permissions.

2. Users open the approved application and are logged in to SQL Server.

3. To enable the application role, the application executes the sp_setapprole stored procedure (which is written into the application at design time).

Once the application role has been enabled, SQL Server no longer sees users as themselves; it sees them as the application and grants them application role permissions.

EXERCISE 16-13 CREATING AND TESTING AN APPLICATION ROLE

1. Click **Start** → **All Programs** → **Microsoft SQL Server 2005** → **SQL Server Management Studio**. Click **Connect**.

2. Click the **plus (+) sign** next to Databases → Click the **plus (+) sign** next to AdventureWorks → Click the **plus (+) sign** next to Security → Click the **plus (+) sign** next to Roles. Right-click **Application Roles** and select **New Application Role**. Accept the selection of the General Page. The dialog box title should be "Application Role—New."

3. In the Role Name box, type **EntAppRole**.

4. Enter **dbo** in the Default Schema box.

5. In the Password and Confirm Password boxes, type **Pa$$w0rd**.

6. On the Securables page, click **Add** under the Securables list box, select the **Specific Objects** radio button, and click **OK**.

7. Click the **Objects Type** button, select **Tables**, and click **OK**.

8. Click **Browse**, check the **HumanResources.Department** box, and click **OK**, then click **OK** again.

9. In the Explicit Permissions for HumanResources.Department list, check the **Grant** box next to Select, and click **OK**.

10. Open a new **SQL Server query** in SQL Server Management Studio, and connect using **SQL Authentication** with **GibsonH** as the username and **Pa$$w0rd** as the password.

11. Notice that the following query fails because GibsonH has been denied Select permissions due to membership in the db_denydatareader database role:

    ```
    USE AdventureWorks
    SELECT * FROM HumanResources.Department
    ```

12. To activate the application role, execute the following query:

    ```
    sp_setapprole @rolename='EntAppRole',
    @password='Pa$$w0rd'
    ```

13. Clear the query window, and don't save the changes; repeat step 9 without opening a new query, and notice that the query is successful this time. This is because SQL Server now sees the user as EntAppRole, which has Select permission.

14. Close the query window.

Understanding Permission States

All the permissions in SQL Server can exist in one of three states:

- Granted
- Revoked
- Denied

GRANTING A PERMISSION

Granting allows users to use a specific permission. For instance, if you grant SmithB Select permission on a table, SmithB can read the table's data. You know a permission has been granted when the Allow check box is selected next to the permission in the Permissions list.

REVOKING A PERMISSION

A revoked permission isn't specifically granted, but a user can inherit the permission if it has been granted to another role of which he or she is a member. That is, if you revoke the Select permission from SmithB, SmithB can't use it. If, however, SmithB is a member of a role that has been granted Select permission, SmithB can read the data just as if he or she had the Select permission. A permission is revoked when neither the Allow nor Deny box is selected next to a permission.

DENYING A PERMISSION

If you deny a permission, the user doesn't get the permission, no matter what. If you deny SmithB Select permission on a table, even if he or she is a member of a role with Select permission, SmithB can't read the data. You know a permission has been denied when the Deny box is checked next to the permission in the Permissions list.

In Exercise 16-14, you'll get some hands-on experience with changing the states of permissions and witnessing the effects.

➔ **EXERCISE 16-14 TESTING PERMISSION STATES**

1. Click **Start** → **All Programs** → **Microsoft SQL Server 2005** → **SQL Server Management Studio**. Click **Connect**.

2. Click the **plus (+) sign** next to Databases → Click the **plus (+) sign** next to AdventureWorks → Click the **plus (+) sign** next to Security. Expand **Users**. Right-click **SmithB** and select **Properties**. Select the **Securables** page. The dialog box title should be "Database User—SmithB."

3. Click **Add** under the Securables list box, select the **Specific Objects** radio button, and click **OK**.

4. Click the **Objects Type** button, select **Tables**, and click **OK**.

5. Click **Browse**, check the **HumanResources.Department** box, and click **OK**.

6. In the Explicit Permissions for HumanResources.Department list, check the **Grant** box next to Select, and click **OK**.

7. Open a new **SQL Server query**, and connect as **SmithB** using **SQL Server Authentication**.

8. Execute the following query. It's successful because SmithB has Select permission on the HumanResources.Department table:

   USE AdventureWorks

   SELECT * FROM HumanResources.Department

9. Right-click **SmithB** under Users in the AdventureWorks database, and select **Properties**.

10. On the Securables page, click **Add** under the Securables list box, select the **Specific Objects** radio button, and click **OK**.

11. Click the **Objects Type** button, select **Tables**, and click **OK**.

12. Click **Browse**, check the **HumanResources.Department** box, and click **OK**.

13. In the Explicit Permissions for HumanResources.Department list, uncheck the **Grant** box next to Select, and click **OK**.

14. Return to the query window and execute the query in step 8. It fails because SmithB doesn't have explicit Select permission.

15. Right-click **SmithB** under Users in the AdventureWorks database, and select **Properties**.

16. Under Role Membership, check the box next to the db_datareader role.

17. Return to the query window, and rerun the query from step 8. Now it's successful, because SmithB has inherited the Select permission from the db_datareader role and doesn't need to have it explicitly applied.

18. Right-click **SmithB** under Users in the AdventureWorks database, and select **Properties**.

19. On the Securables page, click **Add** under the Securables list box, select the **Specific Objects** radio button, and click **OK**.

20. Click the **Objects Type** button, select **Tables**, and click **OK**.

21. Click **Browse**, check the **HumanResources.Department** box, and click **OK**.

22. In the Explicit Permissions for HumanResources.Department list, check the **Deny** box next to Select, and click **OK**.

23. Return to the query window, and again run the query from step 8. It fails this time because you've specifically denied SmithB access; therefore, SmithB can no longer inherit the Select permission from the db_datareader role.

24. Right-click **SmithB** under Users in the AdventureWorks database, and select **Properties**.

25. Under Role Membership, uncheck the box next to the db_datareader role.

26. On the Securables page, click **Add** under the Securables list box, select the **Specific Objects** radio button, and click **OK**.

27. Click the **Objects Type** button, select Tables, and click **OK**.

28. Click **Browse**, check the **HumanResources.Department** box, and click **OK**.

29. In the Explicit Permissions for HumanResources.Department list, uncheck the **Deny** box next to Select, and click **OK**.

CERTIFICATION READY?
SQL Server 2005 introduces schemas to help avoid ownership chain problems.

Introducing Ownership Chains

With a better understanding of how and where permissions are applied, we'll now look into one of the problems generated when permissions are applied improperly: the broken owner-ship chain.

In the physical world, people own objects, with which they can do as they please, including lending or giving them to others. SQL Server understands this concept of ownership. When users create an object, they own that object and can do whatever they want with it. For example, if RosmanD creates a table, RosmanD can assign permissions as needed, granting access only to those users deemed worthy. This is a good thing, until you consider what is known as an *ownership chain*.

An object that is on loan still belongs to the owner; the person who has borrowed it must ask the owner for permission before allowing another person to use it. Acting without such per-mission is an example of a *broken ownership chain*.

Suppose that RosmanD creates a table and grants permissions on that table to Accounting. Then one of the members of Accounting creates a view based on that table and grants Select permission to SmithB. Can SmithB select the data from that view? No, because the owner-ship chain has been broken. SQL Server checks permissions on an underlying object (in this case, the table) only when the owner changes. Therefore, if RosmanD had created both the table and the view, there would be no problem, because SQL Server would check only the permissions on the view. But because the owner changed from Accounting (who owned the view) to RosmanD (who owned the table), SQL Server needed to check the permissions on both the view and the table, and discovered they were different.

How can you avoid broken ownership chains? The first way that may come to mind is to make everyone who needs to create objects a member of the sysadmin fixed server role; then everything they create would be owned by the DBO user rather than by the login. For exam-ple, because MorrisL is a member of the sysadmin fixed server role, everything MorrisL cre-ates in any database is owned by the DBO, not MorrisL. Although this is technically possible, it's a poor method because it grants a great deal of administrative privilege over the server to people who don't need and/or shouldn't have such privilege.

A much better way to avoid broken ownership chains is to make all the users who need to create objects members of either the db_owner fixed database role or the db_ddladmin fixed database role. Then, if they need to create objects, they can specify the schema as needed (for example, CREATE TABLE schema.table_name). This way, the schema owns all objects in the database, and because the ownership never changes, SQL Server never needs to check any underlying permissions.

Don't forget that members of the db_owner role can do whatever they like with a database, whereas db_ddladmins have limited authority. Therefore, you may want to use db_ddladmin in most instances.

TAKE NOTE*

As discussed in Lesson 12, you may prefer to use the WITH EXECUTE clause for stored procedures and functions.

When a db_owner or db_ddladmin member creates an object as another user, it can be any database user, not just the DBO.

Now you have a good understanding of local security; but what if you have to access data on more than one server? The next section covers how to implement security in a distributed environment.

Introducing Linked Server Security

Let's return to the business analogy: your business is prospering, and you have expanded into two buildings. Your employees need access to resources in both buildings, which means you need to give your users a key to the new place.

You have the same concerns when your resources are spread across multiple SQL Servers; your users may need access to resources on multiple servers. This is especially true of something called a *distributed query*, which returns resultsets from databases on multiple servers; the remote servers in the query are called **linked servers**. Although you may wonder why you would want to perform distributed queries when you can replicate the data between servers (Lesson 23 discusses replication), you may have practical reasons for doing the former. Don't forget that because SQL Server is designed to store terabytes of data, some of your databases may grow to several hundred megabytes in size—and you don't want to replicate several hundred megabytes under normal circumstances.

The first step in configuring your server to perform distributed queries is to inform SQL Server that it will be talking to other database servers by running the sp_addlinkedserver stored procedure. The procedure to link to a server named AccountingSQL looks something like this:

```
sp_addlinkedserver @server='AccountingSQL', @provider='SQL
Server'
```

Your users can then run distributed queries by specifying two different servers in the query. The query:

```
SELECT * FROM
SQLServer.AdventureWorks.HumanResources.Employee, AccountingSQL.
AdventureWorks.HumanResources.Employee
```

X REF

For a discussion of replication, see Lesson 23.

accesses data from both the SQLServer server (the server the user is logged in to, or the sending server) and the AccountingSQL server (the remote server) in the same resultset.

The security issue here is that the sending server must log in to the remote server on behalf of the user to gain access to the data. SQL Server can use one of two methods to send this security information: security account delegation or linked server login mapping. If your users have logged in using Windows Authentication, and all the servers in the query are capable of understanding Windows domain security, you can use account delegation. Here's how it works:

1. If the servers are in different domains, you must make certain the appropriate Windows trust relationships are in place. The remote server's domain must trust the sending server's domain.
2. Add a Windows login to the sending server for the user to log in with.
3. Add the same account to the remote server.
4. Create a user account for the login in the remote server's database, and assign permissions.
5. When the user executes the distributed query, SQL Server sends the user's Windows security credentials to the remote server, allowing access.

If you have users who access SQL Server with standard logins, or if some of the servers don't participate in Windows domain security, you'll need to add a linked login. Here's how to do it:

1. On the remote server, create a standard login, and assign the necessary permissions.
2. On the sending server, map a local login to the remote login using the sp_addlinkedsrvlogin stored procedure. To map all local logins to the remote login RemUser, type the following:

   ```
   sp_addlinkedsrvlogin @rmtsrvname='AccountingSQL',
   @useself=FALSE, @locallogin=NULL, @rmtuser='RemUser',
   @rmtpassword='Pa$$w0rd'
   ```

3. When a user executes a distributed query, the sending server logs in to the AccountingSQL (remote) server as RemUser, with a password of Pa$$w0rd.

⊕ EXERCISE 16-15 REMOTELY ACCESSING ADVENTUREWORKS

1. Open **SSMS** → **Server Objects,** and right-click **Linked Servers.**
2. Select **New Linked Server...** from the context menu.
3. Enter the server name of someone else in the classroom. If your teacher has assigned partners, use your partner's server name.
4. For the Other Data Source select **SQL Native Client.**
5. Select the **Security** option in the tree view of **Select a page.**
6. Choose **Be made using the login's current security context.**
7. Accept **all** of the Server Options.
8. Click **OK** to accept this new linked server assignment.
9. Start a new query by clicking on the **New Query** button.
10. Enter the following code (substituting values appropriate to you where needed):

```
SELECT * FROM <YourPartner'sServerName>
.AdventureWorks.Person.Contact
```

11. Scan the results and note they did not come from your database.

Introducing Encryption

You can put another layer, *encryption*, on top of all this security. SQL Server 2005 encrypts data with hierarchical encryption and key management infrastructure. Each layer encrypts the layer below it by using a combination of certificates, asymmetric keys, and symmetric keys, in scopes that parallel the permissions hierarchy.

Thus far, you've seen how to protect your data from intruders by granting access and applying permissions to objects. But when someone legitimately accesses the server and starts transferring data, it travels over the network. If you need really robust security, you can go as far as to encrypt the data as it travels between the client and the server over the network at the server level. That way, if anyone is reading your network traffic, they will not be able to interpret the data.

To encrypt your connections to SQL Server, you first need to get a certificate. You can get one from one of the major vendors such as VeriSign, or you can install Windows Certificate services and supply your own. Once you have a certificate, you need to install it on the server. Here are the steps to do that:

1. If you run the SQL Server service as Local System, then log in to the server as an administrator. If you are using a service account, then log in to the server as the service account.
2. On the Start menu, click **Run;** then in the Open box, type **MMC,** and click **OK.**
3. In the Microsoft Management Console (MMC), on the File menu, click **Add/Remove Snap-in.**
4. In the Add/Remove Snap-in dialog box, click **Add.**
5. In the Add Standalone Snap-in dialog box, click **Certificates,** then click **Add.**
6. In the Certificates Snap-in dialog box, click **Computer account,** and then click **Finish.**
7. In the Add Standalone Snap-in dialog box, click **Close.**
8. In the Add/Remove Snap-in dialog box, click **OK.**
9. In the Certificates Snap-in dialog box, expand **Certificates,** expand **Personal,** and then right-click **Certificates;** then point to **All Tasks,** and, finally, click **Import.**
10. Complete the **Certificate Import Wizard** to add a certificate to the computer, and close the **MMC.**

After you have installed your certificate on the server, you need to configure the server to accept encrypted connections. Here is how to do that:

1. In SQL Server Configuration Manager, expand **SQL Server 2005 Network Configuration**, right-click **Protocols for <server instance>**, and then select **Properties**.
2. In the Protocols for <instance name> Properties dialog box, on the **Certificate** tab, select the desired certificate from the Certificate drop-down menu, then click **OK**.
3. On the Flags tab, in the ForceEncryption box, select **Yes**, then click **OK** to close the dialog box.
4. Restart the **SQL Server** service.

Finally, you need to configure the clients to request encrypted connections to the server. Here's how:

1. In SQL Server Configuration Manager, expand **SQL Server 2005 Network Configuration**, right-click **Protocols for <server instance>**, then select **Properties**.
2. In the Protocols for <instance name> Properties dialog box, on the **Certificate** tab, select the desired certificate from the Certificate drop-down menu, then click **OK**.
3. On the Flags tab, in the ForceEncryption box, select **Yes**, then click **OK** to close the dialog box.
4. Restart the **SQL Server** service.

The database-level cryptographic features in SQL Server rely on a database master key. This key is not generated automatically when the database is created; it must be created by the system administrator. It is only necessary to create the master key once per database. Learn how in Exercise 16-16.

EXERCISE 16-16 CREATING A DATABASE MASTER KEY

1. In Query Editor, connect to the database by executing the following Transact-SQL command:

```
USE AdventureWorks
GO
```

2. Choose a password for encrypting the copy of the master key that will be stored in the database.
3. Add this code snippet:

```
CREATE MASTER KEY ENCRYPTION BY PASSWORD = 'Pa$$w0rd'
```

4. Execute.

This prepares the master key for use in database objects. In your production environment, use a really complex password of, say, 56 or more letters. Be sure to write it down and store it in a secure location.

Creating a Security Plan

Suppose you have just been hired as database administrator for a small company that relies heavily on its SQL Server. A great deal of the data on the SQL Server is proprietary and, therefore, must be secured. You realize, however, that jumping right in and randomly applying permissions to databases is going to result in a mess—if not a disaster—so you take a more logical approach: you develop a security plan.

Creating a good security plan is always the first step in applying security to any type of system. Here are a few issues you should consider in your plan:

- **Type of users:** If all your users support trusted connections, you can use Windows accounts. If you have the authority to create groups in Windows, you may be able to

TAKE NOTE*

Lesson 17 introduces other security aspects. Consider taking a CompTIA Security + course or an ethical hacker course for a more complete understanding.

create Windows groups and then create logins for those groups, rather than creating individual accounts. If not all your users support trusted connections (such as Novell or Macintosh), you need to use Mixed mode authentication and create some standard logins.

- **Fixed server roles:** Once you have given users access to SQL Server, how much administrative power, if any, should they be given? If your users need administrative authority, add them to one of the fixed server roles; if not, you don't need to add them.

- **Database access:** Once your users are logged in, to which databases do they have access? It's highly unlikely that every user needs a user account in every database.

- **Type of access:** Once the users have a database user account, how much authority do they have in the database? For example, can all users read and write, or is a subset of users allowed only to read?

- **Group permissions:** It's usually best to apply permissions to database roles and then add users to those roles. Every system has exceptions, though; you may need to apply some permissions directly to users, especially those who should be denied access to a resource.

- **Object creation:** Figure out who needs the authority to create objects, such as tables and views, and group them in either the db_owner role or the db_ddladmin role. Doing this allows users to create objects as the DBO instead of as themselves. In this way, you can avoid broken ownership chains.

- **Public role permissions:** Remember that all database user accounts are members of the public role and can't be removed. Whatever permissions the public role has are given to your users, so limit the permissions on the Public group.

- **Guest access:** Do you want users with no database user account to be able to access databases through a guest account? For some databases, such as a catalog, this may be acceptable. In general, however, this may be considered a security risk and should not be used on all databases.

Table 16-5 shows the employees of your company and their security needs.

Table 16-5

Employees of Your Company

Name	Windows	Group Department	Network	Admin	Permissions
SmithB	N/A	Service	Novell	None	Read; no Write
GibsonH	N/A	Development	Novell	Server Configuration	Write, Create; no Read
RosmanD	None	Administration	Windows	None	Select, Insert, Update
MorrisL	None	IT	Windows	All	All
JohnsonK	Accounting	Accounting	Windows	None	Read, Write
JonesB	Accounting	Accounting	Windows	None	Read, Write
ChenJ	Sales	Sales	Windows	None	Read, Update
SamuelsR	Sales	Sales	Windows	None	Read, Update

You may notice that your company has two Novell network users. This means you need to create at least two standard logins and implement Mixed mode authentication.

Next notice that some of the users—specifically, Accounting and Sales—are already grouped together in Windows. Rather than create accounts for each member of these departments, you can instead add a Windows group login for the total membership of the group. Because RosmanD and MorrisL aren't members of a Windows group, they need Windows user logins.

Now look at the administrative rights that each user needs over the system. Because GibsonH needs to be able to configure server settings such as memory use, you should add him to the serveradmin fixed server role. Because MorrisL needs full administrative access to the entire system, you should add her to the sysadmin fixed server role.

To make this example easier to comprehend, consider these eight users as members of a company with only one database. Look at the permissions that everyone needs on that database. As a customer service rep, SmithB needs permission to read the data but not to write any data; the db_denydatawriter fixed database role fits those needs well. As a developer, GibsonH needs permission to create objects in the database, but he should not be able to read the data. Make GibsonH a member of the db_ddladmin role so he can create objects as DBO and avoid broken ownership chains. You could make GibsonH a member of the db_owner group and achieve the same effect, but then he would be able to do anything in the database, including read the data.

RosmanD needs to be able to select, insert, and update data, but she should not be able to delete any data. No fixed database role grants these three permissions together. You could apply all these permissions directly to RosmanD, but what if you hire more people who need the same permissions? It might be a better idea to create a custom database role; grant that role the Select, Insert, and Update permissions, and then make RosmanD a member of that role. The same is true of the Sales group, which needs permission to read and update; those members require a custom role.

For Accounting, it will be easiest just to add those members to the db_datareader and db_datawriter roles; this way, they will receive permissions to read and write to the database. MorrisL doesn't need to be a member of any role; because she is a member of the sysadmin fixed server role, she is automatically considered the DBO in every database on the server.

In the real world, of course, a security plan isn't going to be nearly this simple. You'll have hundreds, if not thousands, of users to deal with, from a variety of networks, and each user will need different permissions. In summary, although developing a security plan is probably more work than the actual implementation, you can't do without it.

SKILL SUMMARY

IN THIS LESSON YOU LEARNED:

SQL Server 2005 has a sophisticated security system that allows you to carefully implement your security plan. SQL Server can operate in Mixed security mode, which means Windows users and groups can be given access directly to SQL Server; or you can create separate, unique accounts that reside only in SQL Server. If SQL Server is running in Windows Authentication mode, every user must first connect with a preauthorized Windows account

This lesson examined the processes of creating and managing logins, groups, and users. You learned how to create a Standard login and a Windows user or group login using SQL Server Management Studio or T-SQL, and you learned when each type is appropriate. If you have a well-designed security plan that incorporates growth, managing your user base can be a painless task.

To limit administrative access to SQL Server at the server level, you learned you can add users to a fixed server role. To limit access in a specific database, you can add users to a database role; and if one of the fixed database roles isn't to your liking, you can create your own. You can even go as far as to limit access to specific applications by creating an application role.

Each database in SQL Server 2005 has its own independent permissions. We looked at the two types of user permissions: statement permissions, which are used to create or change the data structure, and object permissions, which manipulate data. Remember that statement permissions can't be granted to other users.

The next section in this lesson described the database hierarchy. We looked at the permissions available to the most powerful users—the sysadmins—down through the lower-level database users.

You then learned about chains of ownership. These are created when you grant permissions to others on objects you own. Adding more users who create dependent objects creates broken ownership chains, which can become complex and tricky to manage. You learned how to predict the permissions available to users at different locations within these ownership chains. You also learned that to avoid the broken ownership chains, you can add your users to either the db_owner database role or the db_ddladmin database role and have your users create objects as the DBO.

You can grant permissions to database users, as well as database roles. When users are added to a role, they inherit the permissions of the role, including the public role, of which everyone is a member. The only exception is when a user has been denied permission, because Deny takes precedence over any other right, no matter the level at which the permission was granted.

We then covered remote and linked servers and showed how you need to set up security needs to make remote queries work. We finished by taking a look at linked server security and applications.

For the certification examination:

- Know the differences in authentication modes. Know when to use Mixed mode versus Windows Authentication mode. Mixed mode allows users who do not have an Active Directory account, such as Novell or Unix users, to access the SQL Server. Windows Authentication mode allows only users with Active Directory accounts to access SQL Server.

- Understand roles. Be familiar with the various fixed server and database roles and what they can be used for in the real world. You also need to know when to create a custom database role instead of using the built-in roles. A good example is when you need to allow users to insert, update, and select on a table but not to delete. No built-in role allows this, so you would need a custom role.

- Understand permissions. Know what the permissions are, what they are for, as well as how to assign them. Don't forget that two types of permissions exist, object and statement. Object permissions control a user's ability to create or modify database objects, such as tables and views. Statement permissions control a user's ability to manipulate data using statements such as SELECT or INSERT.

■ Knowledge Assessment

Multiple Choice

Circle the letter or letters that correspond to the best answer or answers.

1. Jason is a member of a Windows group named Sales that has been granted access to SQL Server via a Windows group account in SQL Server. Jason should not have access to SQL Server, but he needs the permissions afforded the Sales group on other servers. How can you remedy this?
   a. Create a new Windows group named SQL_Sales and add everyone but Jason to the group. Next, grant access to the SQL_Sales group by creating a group account in SQL Server, then remove the Sales group account from SQL Server.
   b. Create a login on the SQL Server specifically for Jason, and deny the account access.
   c. Delete the Sales group login, and create separate accounts for everyone except Jason.
   d. Remove Jason from the Sales group in Windows, and grant him all the necessary permissions separately on all other servers on the network.

2. One of your users has created a table (John.table1) and granted Samantha Select permission on the table. Samantha, however, does not need to see all the data in the table so she creates a view (Samantha.view1). Thomas now wants access to Samantha's view, so Samantha grants Thomas Select permission on the view. What happens when Thomas tries to select from the view?

   a. Thomas can select from the view because he has been granted permissions on the view directly.

   b. Thomas cannot select from the view because he does not have permission on the underlying table, so the ownership chain is broken.

   c. Thomas can select from the view because Samantha granted him permission on the view and she has permission on the underlying table.

   d. Thomas can select, but he receives an error message stating that he does not have permission on the underlying table.

Table 16-6

Permissions for the Suppliers table

NAME	SELECT	INSERT	UPDATE	DELETE
Administration	Granted	Granted	Granted	Granted
Marketing	Granted	Denied	Denied	Denied
Joe	Granted	Granted	Granted	Granted
Public	Granted	Granted	Granted	Granted

3. Your SQL Server 2005 system stores information about suppliers in the Suppliers table. Table 16-6 shows the security for the table. Joe is a member of the Administration and Marketing roles in the database, and he needs to be able to perform inserts, updates, and deletes on the table. Which command should you use to give him these permissions?

   a. Use:

   ```
   sp_droprolemember 'Public', 'Joe'
   ```

   b. Use:

   ```
   sp_droprolemember 'Marketing', 'Joe'
   ```

   c. Use:

   ```
   sp_droprolemember 'Administration', 'Joe
   ```

   d. Do nothing; Joe already has these permissions.

4. You are the administrator of a SQL Server system that contains databases named Marketing and Sales. Amanda has a Windows account that has been granted a login to the SQL Server, and she has been given access to the Marketing database. Now she needs view and edit permissions on the Sales database as well. Which T-SQL statements should you execute?

   a. Use the following:

   ```
   GRANT ALL ON Sales TO 'Amanda'
   ```

   b. Use the following:

   ```
   EXEC sp_addrolemember 'db_datareader', 'Amanda'
   EXEC sp_addrolemember 'db_datawriter','Amanda'
   ```

   c. Use the following:

   ```
   GRANT SELECT ON Sales TO 'Amanda'
   GRANT INSERT ON Sales TO 'Amanda'
   GRANT UPDATE ON Sales TO 'Amanda'
   ```

d. Use the following:

```
EXEC sp_grantaccess 'Amanda', 'AmandaU'
GO
EXEC sp_addrolemember 'db_datareader', 'AmandaU'
EXEC sp_addrolemember 'db_datawriter','AmandaU'
```

Table 16-7

Current Security Settings

	SELECT	INSERT	UPDATE
Marketing	Revoked	Granted	Granted
Sales	Denied	Revoked	Revoked
Public	Granted	Revoked	Revoked

5. Andrea is a member of the Sales and Marketing roles in your database. She needs Select, Insert, and Update permissions on your table. With security configured as shown in Table 16-7, how can you grant her the necessary permissions?
   a. Add an account for Andrea, and grant it the necessary permissions.
   b. Grant Select permission to the marketing role.
   c. Grant Insert and Update permissions to the public role.
   d. Remove Andrea from the sales role.

6. Two developers named IversonB and JacksonT need to be able to create objects in the Inventory database as part of their regular duties. You need to give them the ability to create these objects without giving them too much authority on the server. What is the most secure way to do this?
   a. Add IversonB and JacksonT to the db_owner fixed database role, and instruct them to create objects as DBO.
   b. Add IversonB and JacksonT to the db_ddladmin fixed database role, and instruct them to create objects as DBO.
   c. Add IversonB and JacksonT to the sysadmin fixed server role, and instruct them to create objects as DBO.
   d. Grant IversonB and JacksonT the permission to create objects in the database separately, and instruct them to create objects as DBO.

7. You need to grant Robert permission to modify employee phone numbers in the Employees table, but you do not want him to be able to modify any other data in the table. What is the best way to accomplish this?
   a. Grant Robert Update permission on the Phone Number column of the table, but do not grant him permissions on any other column.
   b. Create a view that contains only the Phone Number column, and grant Robert Update permission on the view.
   c. Create a stored procedure to change the phone number, and grant Robert Execute permission on the stored procedure.
   d. Create triggers on the table that reject any updates from Robert on columns other than the Phone Number column.

8. You have spent a great deal of money and effort to create a custom accounting program in VisualBasic that is designed to meet some specific needs of your company. You find that some of your users are still accessing your database through other methods such as Microsoft Excel and Query Analyzer, and this is causing problems with the integrity of your database. How can you fix this problem?
   a. Create a filter in Profiler that will reject access by all programs except your custom program.
   b. Create an account for your new application, and have all your users log in to SQL using that account. Then remove permissions from any remaining user accounts in the database.

    c. Create an application role for the account, and grant it the necessary permissions. Then add all the users in the database to the application role.

    d. Create an application role, and grant it the necessary permissions in the database. Then remove any permissions for your users in the database, and hard-code the sp_setapprole stored procedure into your application to activate the role.

9. You have just created a new Windows account (Domain\BobH) for a new employee. You create a new SQL login for BobH using the following command:

```
sp_addlogin 'domain\BobH', 'password', 'accounting'
```

But Bob is now complaining he cannot access SQL Server when he logs in with his Windows account. Why not?

    a. You need to configure the SQL Server to allow trusted accounts by using the command:

```
sp_configure 'allow trusted connections', '1'
```

    b. The sp_addlogin command creates standard login accounts, not mapped login accounts. You need to map Bob's account to a SQL login with the sp_grantlogin stored procedure.

    c. Bob is not using the right network library to log in with a trusted account. Set the network library to Named Pipes, Multiprotocol, or TCP/IP.

    d. Bob's SQL Server account password does not match his Windows account password. Change one of the two so they match.

10. You are the administrator of a SQL Server system that contains a database named Accounting. To maintain strict security on the database, you want to make sure users do not have any default permissions when their account is first created. What should you do?

    a. Remove users from the public role, and add them back on an as-needed basis.

    b. In Management Studio, remove all of the permissions from the public role by clicking each box until it is cleared.

    c. Execute the REVOKE ALL FROM PUBLIC command in Query Editor while using your database.

    d. Do nothing; no default permissions are granted to users when they are first created.

11. You have the authority to create both Windows accounts and SQL logins and roles on your network. You have a Windows server that contains a shared folder called Administration and a shared folder called Marketing. On your SQL Server database you have a database called Marketing. Ten of your users will be working on a short-term project together; all of them require the same access to the Marketing database on the SQL Server and the Marketing folder on the Windows server, but only four of them are allowed access to the Administration folder on the Windows server. What is the best way to grant these users access to the database resources?

    a. Add all the users to a Windows group, and map a SQL Server login to the new group. Then grant permissions to the group login.

    b. Create separate Windows logins for each user, and add them to a custom database role. Then assign permissions to the database role.

    c. Create a separate Windows login for each user, and grant permissions on the database to each user login.

    d. Create one login for all the users to log in with, and grant that user account permissions on the database.

Table 16-8

Linked Server Permissions

SQL SERVER IN DOMAINA	LINKED SQL SERVER IN DOMAINB
Standard Account: BobH	
Windows Account:	
DomainA\ThomasQ	

12. You have several SQL Servers in your organization that participate in linked server queries, with security configured as shown in Table 16-8. BobH is complaining that the linked server queries are not working. Why can't BobH use linked server queries?

  a. The server was not added as a linked server with the sp_addlinkedserver stored procedure.

  b. The remote server has not been configured to accept incoming queries from other servers. You must configure it by setting the ALLOW LINKED QUERIES option to 1, using the sp_ configure stored procedure.

  c. BobH uses a standard account, so you need to map a linked server login for him by executing sp_addlinkedsrvlogin on the destination server.

  d. The users who cannot access the linked server use standard logins, so you need to map a linked server login by executing sp_addlinkedsrvlogin on the local server.

13. You have just installed a new SQL Server on your network, and you want to make sure no Windows administrator has administrative access on the SQL Server until receiving the proper training. What should you do to keep a Windows administrator from trying to administer the new SQL Server and possibly damaging it?

  a. Remove the BUILTIN\Administrators account from SQL Server. Then create a SQLAdmins group in Windows, and add all the SQL administrators to the new group. Finally, create a login mapped to the SQLAdmins group, and add it to the sysadmins role.

  b. Create a separate login for each of your Windows administrators, and deny access for each of their logins.

  c. Remove BUILTIN\Administrators from the sysadmins role, and create separate logins for each of the SQL administrators. Then add each separate login to the sysadmins role.

  d. Do nothing; by default, the Windows administrators do not have administrative access in SQL Server.

14. You are setting up a kiosk in a library that hundreds of people will access every month. You want to make sure visitors to the library have access to read data from the SQL Server, but they should not be able to change any of the data. You need to accomplish this with the least administrative overhead possible. What should you do?

  a. Create a Windows account named Kiosk, and map a SQL login to that account. Then create a database user account for Kiosk, and add it to the db_denydatawriter and db_datareader roles. Finally, have all the library patrons log in to the computer system as Kiosk.

  b. Enable the guest account in Windows, and map a SQL login to it. Then create a guest database user account, and add it to the db_denydatawriter and db_datareader roles.

  c. Enable the guest user account in Windows. No guest login or database accounts need to be created in SQL Server because they already exist. Add the guest account to the db_denydatawriter and db_datareader roles.

  d. Enable the guest user account in Windows, and map it to a SQL login. No database user account named guest will need to be created because it already exists in each database. Add the guest account to the db_denydatawriter and db_datareader roles.

15. You want to be able to use email, replication, and other interserver services with SQL Server. When you install SQL Server, which type of account should you use?

  a. The local server account

  b. A local account

  c. A domain account with administrative privileges

  d. A domain account with no administrative access

16. You need to create a new login account for one of your Unix users named WoodsJ. Which command would you use to do this?

  a. `sp_addlogin 'WoodsJ', 'Pa$$w0rd', 'AdventureWorks'`

  b. `sp_grantlogin 'WoodsJ', 'Pa$$w0rd', 'AdventureWorks'`

    c. `sp_createlogin 'WoodsJ', 'Pa$$w0rd', 'AdventureWorks'`

    d. `sp_makelogin 'WoodsJ', 'Pa$$w0rd', 'AdventureWorks'`

17. You have an HR database that all users will be allowed to read from to obtain information, but only the HR department should be able to read from and update the data in the database. What is the easiest and most secure way to ensure this?

    a. Add all the users who are not in the HR department to the db_datareader database role, and add all the users from the HR department to a custom database role that allows them all modification and selection permissions.

    b. Add all the users who are not in the HR department to the db_datareader and db_denydatawriter database roles, and add all the users from the HR department to the db_datareader and db_datawriter database roles.

    c. Add all the users who are not in the HR department to the db_datareader and db_denydatawriter database roles, and add all the users from the HR department to the db_datamodifier database role.

    d. Add all the users who are not in the HR department to the db_datareader and db_denydatawriter database roles, and add all the users from the HR department to the db_owner database role.

18. You have a number of users in your customer service department who need Select, Insert, and Update permissions, but they should not be able to delete—only managers should have the permission to delete data. How can you ensure that only managers can delete data and users can only perform the tasks listed?

    a. Add the users to the db_datareader and db_datawriter roles, and add the managers to the db_datadeleter role.

    b. Add the users to the db_datareader role and the managers to the db_datawriter role.

    c. Add the users to a custom role that allows only Select, Insert, and Update permissions; add the managers to a custom role that allows them to read and modify data.

    d. Add the users to a custom role that allows only Select, Insert, and Update permissions; add the managers to the db_datareader and db_datawriter roles.

19. You are the administrator of a SQL Server system that will be used only for development access; the server will have no production databases on the server whatsoever. All your developers need to be able to create databases and objects inside the databases, such as tables, views, and so on. To which roles should they be added at the server and database levels to accommodate these needs?

    a. sysadmins at the server level and db_owner at the database level

    b. sysadmins at the server level and db_ddladmins at the database level

    c. db_creator at the server level and db_ddladmin at the database level

    d. db_creator at the server level and db_owner at the database level

20. You are the administrator of a SQL Server system that will contain marketing, sales, and production data. Each of these departments is contained in a Windows group named after the department. Each of these departments should be able to read and modify its own data, but they should not be able to read or modify the data of other departments. You need to configure the server so it meets security requirements with minimal administrative overhead and resource consumption. What should you do? (Choose all that apply.)

    a. Create a single database for all the departments to share.

    b. Create a separate database for each department.

    c. Create a named instance of SQL Server for each department.

    d. Create a Windows Authenticated login for each department.

    e. Map each group to the sysadmin fixed server role.

    f. Map each user account to the db_datareader and db_datawriter database roles.

    g. Grant each of the database users Select, Insert, Update, and Delete permissions in the database.

    h. Create database user accounts for each department in the database.

Case Scenarios

Scenario 16-1: Setting Permissions

Add a classmate to your Windows Server 2003. Add that user to SQL Server 2005. Add that user access to the MSSQL_Training database. Pick a table and grant Select permissions and deny Write permissions for that user.

Ask one another how best to do this. Should access be via roles or explicitly applied? What other factors come into play?

Backing Up and Restoring

LESSON SKILL MATRIX

TECHNOLOGY SKILL	70-431 EXAM OBJECTIVE
Back up a database.	Foundational
Perform a full backup.	Foundational
Perform a differential backup.	Foundational
Perform a transaction log backup.	Foundational
Initialize a media set by using the FORMAT option.	Foundational
Append or overwrite an existing media set.	Foundational
Create a backup device.	Foundational
Back up filegroups.	Foundational
Restore a database.	Foundational
Identify which files are needed from the backup strategy.	Foundational
Restore a database from a single file and from multiple files.	Foundational
Choose an appropriate restore method.	Foundational

KEY TERMS

backup: A specialized copy of a database, filegroup, file, or transaction log that can be used by SQL Server to restore database data, typically after a serious database error or a system failure. Backups can be restored individually, or a set of backups can be restored in sequence.

mirrored media set: Physical mass storage units that contain two to four identical copies (mirrors) of each media family. Restore operations require only one mirror per family. This allows for a damaged media volume to be replaced by the corresponding volume from a mirror.

restore: A multiphase process that copies all the data and log pages from a specified backup to a specified database (the data copy phase) and rolls forward all the transactions that are logged in the backup (the redo phase). At this point, by default, a restore rolls back any incomplete transactions (the undo phase). This completes the recovery of the database and makes it available to users.

■ Maintaining Data Integrity

THE BOTTOM LINE

Maintaining data integrity is your most important responsibility. The first layer of defense is performing a backup of all data on a regular schedule. The time between the last backup and the moment of disaster could involve some data loss. You must work with your management to find the acceptable loss rate, combined with the investment rate, to maintain this goal.

You performed the backup. The disaster happened. Did you create a disaster recovery plan? Have you rehearsed that plan? Do the backup copies actually restore your databases to their original condition? If you didn't answer yes to everything, conduct drills. Know that you can restore your databases.

Enforcing Organizational Security Policies

The most important phase of maintaining data integrity, and the effort demanding your greatest attention, is the "watchdog" phase. You must constantly run baselines to check for performance degradation and potential data losses.

IDENTIFYING RISK

Identifying the risks that an organization faces is central to establishing security policies that will mitigate those risks. Risk identification usually involves four steps:

1. Asset identification determines the value of property, personnel, and ideas.
2. Risk assessment determines which events have the potential to damage assets and what the damage would cost.
3. Threat identification determines what actual or potential threats exist for each asset at risk and how likely those threats are to occur.
4. Vulnerability assessment determines the security weaknesses of each threatened asset and determines the cost of removing those vulnerabilities.

UNDERSTANDING FORENSIC REQUIREMENTS

Information security professionals must observe generally accepted forensic practices when investigating security incidents. Consider:

- **Evidence collection:** Following the correct procedure for collecting evidence from mass storage devices to ensure the integrity of the evidence and prevent tampering.
- **Evidence preservation:** Criminal cases and even internal security incidents can take months and even years to resolve. The legal agent must be able to preserve all gathered evidence in a proper manner for a potentially lengthy period of time.
- **Chain of custody:** Whoever gathers and preserves the evidence must also maintain a complete inventory that shows who has handled specific items and where they have been stored. If the chain of custody is broken, it might be impossible to prosecute a technology crime.
- **Jurisdiction:** Determining exactly who has the right to investigate and prosecute an information crime can be extremely difficult due to overlapping laws for copyright, computer fraud, mail tampering, and political boundaries.

IMPLEMENTING PHYSICAL SECURITY MEASURES

An organization's physical components have vulnerabilities that should be mitigated by employing appropriate physical security measures. Examine:

- **Buildings and grounds:** Have control access, fire risks, terrorism attacks, and electrical and other utility reliability been addressed?
- **Devices:** Are your computing devices of all types free from tampering? Are critical servers ready to be restored at a hot or a cold facility?
- **Communications:** Are the telecommunication links reliable?
- **Storage media:** Are backup copies stored off-site?

CREATING A BUSINESS CONTINUITY PLAN

Create a business continuity plan (BCP)—a policy—that defines how your enterprise will maintain normal day-to-day business operations in the event of a disruption or crisis. Test and review the BCP on a regular basis.

RECOVERING FROM A DISASTER

The disaster recovery plan (DRP) is a policy that defines how people and resources will be protected in the case of a natural or man-made disaster, and how the enterprise will recover from the disaster. The DRP might include a list of individuals responsible for recovery, an inventory of hardware and software, and a series of steps to take to respond to the disaster and rebuild affected systems.

EDUCATING USERS

The trusted user will likely prove to be your greatest threat. Be sure to have written governance policies, and make sure all employees read them. Conduct training sessions and drills at regular intervals to keep everyone aware of the importance of following those policies. Enforce your policies.

Implementing the First Layer of Defense

A backup and restoration process is your first line of defense against data loss.

A **backup** is a copy of your data stored somewhere other than on the mass storage devices supporting your database, usually on some type of tape media (a lot like audiocassette tapes); you can also store a backup on a hard drive on another computer connected over a local area network (LAN).

Why would you want to keep a copy of your data in two places? For many reasons, the first of which is the possibility of hardware failure. Computer hardware has a mean time between failures (MTBF) that is measured in hours. This means that every 40,000 hours or so, a piece of hardware is going to fail, and you can't do much about it. True, you could implement fault tolerance by providing duplicate hardware, but that isn't a complete guarantee against data loss. If you don't want to lose your data when a hard disk goes bad, it's best to create a backup.

Another reason for creating backups is the potential for a natural or man-made disaster. No matter how much redundant hardware you have in place, you can't assume it will survive the wrath of a tornado, hurricane, earthquake, flood, or fire. To thwart the wrath of the elements, you need to back up your data.

Finally, you need to create backups to guard against internally caused damage to your data. Sadly, today, a disgruntled employee who is angry with his or her boss or who is angry with the company in general may seek revenge by destroying or maliciously updating sensitive data. This is the worst kind of data loss, and the only way to recover from it is by having a viable backup.

Now that you understand the reasons to back up your data, you need to know how to do it. First, you'll learn how the backup process works, then you'll learn about the four types of backup you can perform to protect your data.

Understanding How Backups Work

Some features are common to all types of backup. For instance, you may wonder when you'll be able to get your users to stop using the database long enough to perform a backup. Stop wondering—all backups in SQL Server are online backups, which means your users can access the database while you're backing it up. How is this possible? Well, SQL Server uses transaction logs, which are a lot like a diary for the database. In a personal diary, you date everything that happens to you, such as:

3-21-08: Bought a car.

3-22-08: Drove new car to show off.

3-23-08: Drove car into tree.

3-24-08: Started looking for new car.

TAKE NOTE*

If you experience a database failure, use the NO_TRUNCATE option to back up the current transaction log file (this is known as the *tail log*). Together with your planned data and log backups, you can recover to the moment of failure.

Much like a diary, a transaction log puts a log sequence number (LSN) next to each line of the log. Every time SQL Server writes the data from the transaction log into the database, it creates a checkpoint in the log. SQL Server uses the checkpoint like a bookmark so it will remember where it left off the next time it copies from the log to the database. A transaction log might look as follows:

147 Begin Tran 1

148 Update Tran 1

149 Begin Tran 2

150 Update the first part of Tran 2

151 Commit Tran 1

152 Checkpoint

153 Update the second part of Tran 2

154 Commit Tran 2

When a data file backup starts, SQL Server records the current LSN from the log file. Once the backup completes, SQL Server backs up all the entries in the transaction log from the LSN it recorded at the start of the backup to the current LSN. Here's an example of how it works:

1. SQL Server checkpoints the data and records the LSN of the oldest open transaction (in this case, 149 Begin Tran 2, because it wasn't committed before the checkpoint).
2. SQL Server backs up all the pages of the database that contain data (no need to back up the empty ones).
3. SQL Server grabs all the parts of the transaction log that were recorded during the backup process—that is, all the lines of the transaction log with an LSN greater than the LSN recorded at the start of the backup session (in this case, 149 and greater). This way, your users can still do whatever they want with the database while it's being backed up.

X REF

For a discussion of replication, see Lesson 23.

To perform any type of backup, you need a place to store it. The medium you'll use to store a backup is called a *backup device*. You'll learn how to create one now.

CREATING A BACKUP DEVICE

Backups are stored on a physical backup medium, which can be a tape drive or a hard disk (local or accessed over a network connection). SQL Server isn't aware of the various forms of media attached to your server, so you must inform SQL Server where to store the backups. This is what a backup device is for; it's a representation of the backup medium. You can create two types of backup devices: permanent and temporary.

Temporary backup devices are created on the fly when you perform the backup. They're useful for making a copy of a database to send to another office so it has a complete copy of your data. Or, you may want to consider using a temporary backup device to copy your database for permanent off-site storage (usually for archiving).

CERTIFICATION READY?
Temporary devices are defined by specifying the physical file path. Permanent devices (also called logical devices) store defining criteria in a system table for future use.

Although it's true you can use replication (discussed in Lesson 23) to copy a database to a remote site, backing up to a temporary backup device can be faster than if your remote site is connected via a slow wide area network (WAN) link (such as 56K Frame Relay).

You can use permanent backup devices over and over again; you can even append data to them, making them perfect devices for regularly scheduled backups. You create permanent backup devices before performing the backup, and you can store them, like temporary devices, on a local hard disk, on a remote hard disk over a LAN, or on a local tape drive. You'll create a permanent backup device in Exercise 17-1.

EXERCISE 17-1 CREATING A PERMANENT BACKUP DEVICE

1. Open **SQL Server Management Studio** by selecting it from the SQL Server 2005 group under Programs on the Start menu. Expand **your server** and then **Server Objects**.
2. Right-click **Backup Devices** in Object Explorer, and select **New Backup Device**.
3. In the Device Name box of the Backup Device dialog box, enter **AdvWorksFull**. Notice that the filename and path are filled in for you; make sure you have enough free space on the drive SQL Server has selected.
4. Click **OK** to create the device.

If you go to Windows Explorer and search for a file named AdvWorksFull.bak right now, don't be too surprised if you don't find it. SQL Server hasn't created the file yet; it simply added a record representing the backup device to the sysdevices table in the master database telling SQL Server where to create the backup file the first time you perform a backup to the device.

If you're using a tape drive as a backup medium, it must be physically attached to the SQL Server machine. The only way around this requirement is to use a third-party backup solution.

PERFORMING FULL BACKUPS

Just as the name implies, a full backup is a backup of the entire database. It backs up the database files, the locations of those files, and portions of the transaction log (from the LSN recorded at the start of the backup to the LSN at the end of the backup). This is the first type of backup you need to perform in any backup strategy because all the other backup types depend on the existence of a full backup. This means you can't perform a differential or transaction log backup if you have never performed a full backup.

To create your baseline (which is what the full backup is called in a backup strategy) in this lesson's example, you need to back up the AdventureWorks database to the permanent backup device you created in the previous exercise. You'll do that in Exercise 17-2.

 EXERCISE 17-2 PERFORMING A FULL BACKUP

1. Open **SQL Server Management Studio**. Expand **your server** and then **Databases**.
2. Right-click **AdventureWorks**, and select **Properties**.
3. On the **Options** page, change Recovery Model to **Full** so you can perform a transaction log backup later.
4. Click **OK** to apply the changes.
5. Right-click **AdventureWorks** under Databases, point to **Tasks**, and click **Backup**.
6. In the Backup dialog box, make sure **AdventureWorks** is the selected database to backup and Backup Type is **Full**.
7. Leave the default name in the Name box. In the Description box, type **Full Backup of AdventureWorks**.
8. Under Destination, a disk device may already be listed. If so, select the **device**, and click **Remove**.
9. Under Destination, click **Add**.
10. In the Select Backup Destination box, click **Backup Device**, select **AdvWorksFull**, and click **OK**.
11. You should now have a backup device listed under Destination.
12. Switch to the **Options** page, and select **Overwrite All Existing Backup Sets**. This option initializes a new device or overwrites an existing one.
13. Select **Verify Backup When Finished** to check the actual database against the backup copy, and be sure they match after the backup is complete.
14. Click **OK** to start the backup.

15. When the backup is complete, you will get a notification; click **OK** to close it.

16. To verify the backup, you can look at the contents of the backup device, so expand **Backup Devices** under Server Objects in Object Explorer.

17. Right-click **AdvWorksFull**, and select **Properties**.

18. On the Media Contents page, you should see the full backup of AdventureWorks.

19. Click **OK** to return to SQL Server Management Studio.

Now that you have a full backup in place, you can start performing other types of backups. You'll learn about differential backups next.

PERFORMING DIFFERENTIAL BACKUPS

Differential backups record all the changes made to a database since the last full backup was performed. Thus, if you perform a full backup on Monday and a differential backup on Tuesday, the differential will record all the changes to the database since the full backup on Monday. Another differential backup on Wednesday will record all the changes made since the full backup on Monday. The differential backup gets a little bigger each time it's performed, but it's still a great deal smaller than the full backup; so, a differential is faster than a full backup.

SQL Server figures out which pages in the backup have recorded by reading the last LSN of the last full backup and comparing it with the data pages in the database. If SQL Server finds any updated data pages, it backs up the entire extent (eight contiguous pages) of data, rather than just the page that changed.

Performing a differential backup follows almost the same process as a full backup. In Exercise 17-3, you'll perform a differential backup on the AdventureWorks database to the permanent backup device you created earlier.

 EXERCISE 17-3 PERFORMING A DIFFERENTIAL BACKUP

1. Open **SQL Server Management Studio**. Expand your **server** and then **Databases**.

2. Right-click **AdventureWorks**, point to **Tasks**, and select **Backup**.

3. In the Backup dialog box, make sure **AdventureWorks** is the selected database to backup and Backup Type is **Differential**.

4. Leave the default name in the Name box. In the Description box, type **Differential Backup of AdventureWorks**.

5. Under Destination, make sure the **AdvWorksFull** device is listed.

6. On the Options page, make sure **Append to the Existing Backup Set** is selected so you don't overwrite your existing full backup.

7. On the Options tab, select **Verify Backup When Finished**.

8. Click **OK** to start the backup.

9. When the backup is complete, you will get a notification; click **OK** to close it.

10. To verify the backup, you can look at the contents of the backup device, so expand **Backup Devices** under Server Objects in Object Explorer.

11. Right-click **AdvWorksFull**, and select **Properties**.

12. On the Media Contents page, you should see the full backup of AdventureWorks.

13. Click **OK** to return to SQL Server Management Studio.

Performing only full and differential backups isn't enough. If you don't perform transaction log backups, your database could stop functioning.

PERFORMING TRANSACTION LOG BACKUPS

Although they rely on the existence of a full backup, transaction log backups don't back up the database itself. This type of backup records only sections of the transaction log, specifically since the last transaction log backup. It's easier to understand the role of the transaction log backup if you think of the transaction log the way SQL Server does: as a separate object. Then it makes sense that SQL Server requires a backup of the database, as well as the log.

The transaction log is an entity unto itself, but you should back it up for another important reason. When a database is configured to use the Full or Bulk-Logged recovery model, a transaction log backup is the only type of backup that clears old transactions from the transaction log. Therefore, if you performed only full and differential backups on most production databases, the transaction log would eventually fill to 100 percent capacity, and your users would be locked out of the database.

When a transaction log becomes 100 percent full, users are denied access to the database until an administrator clears the transaction log. The best way around this is to perform regular transaction log backups.

Performing a transaction log backup doesn't involve a lot of steps. In Exercise 17-4, you'll perform a transaction log backup on the AdventureWorks database using the backup device created earlier in this chapter.

 EXERCISE 17-4 PERFORMING A TRANSACTION LOG BACKUP

1. Open **SQL Server Management Studio**. Expand your **server** and then **Databases**.
2. Right-click **AdventureWorks**, point to **Tasks**, and select **Backup**.
3. In the Backup dialog box, make sure **AdventureWorks** is the selected database to back up and Backup Type is **Transaction Log**.
4. Leave the default name in the Name box. In the Description box, type **Transaction Log Backup of AdventureWorks**.
5. Under Destination, make sure the **AdvWorksFull** device is listed.
6. On the Options page, make sure **Append to the Existing Backup Set** is selected so you don't overwrite your existing full backup.
7. On the Options page, select **Verify Backup When Finished**.
8. Click **OK** to start the backup.
9. When the backup is complete, you will get a notification; click **OK** to close it.
10. To verify the backup, you can look at the contents of the backup device, so expand **Backup Devices** under Server Objects in Object Explorer.
11. Right-click **AdvWorksFull**, and select **Properties**.
12. On the Media Contents page, you should see the full backup of AdventureWorks.
13. Click **OK** to return to SQL Server Management Studio.

Full, differential, and transaction log backups are great for small to large databases, but another type of backup is specially designed for huge databases that are usually terabytes in size. In the next section you'll look into filegroup backups to see how you can use them to back up huge databases.

PERFORMING FILEGROUP BACKUPS

A growing number of companies have databases reaching the terabyte range. For good reason, these are known as *very large databases* (VLDBs). Imagine trying to perform a backup of a 2 TB database on a nightly, or even weekly, basis. Even if you have purchased the latest, greatest hardware, you're looking at a long backup time. Microsoft knows you don't want to wait that long for a backup to finish, so it gives you a way to back up small sections of the database at a time: a filegroup backup.

Filegroups were covered in Lesson 5. Essentially, a filegroup is a way of storing a database on more than one file, and it gives you the ability to control on which of those files your objects (such as tables or indexes) are stored. This way, a database isn't limited to being contained on one hard disk; it can be spread out across many hard disks and thus can grow quite large.

Using a filegroup backup, you can back up one or more of those files at a time rather than the entire database all at once.

However, you need to be aware of a caveat when using filegroup backups to accelerate the backup process for VLDBs. You can also use filegroups to expedite data access by placing tables on one file and the corresponding indexes on another file. Although this speeds up data access, it can slow the backup process because you must back up tables and indexes as a single unit. This means if the tables and indexes are stored on separate files, the files must be backed up as a single unit; you can't back up the tables one night and the associated indexes the next.

To perform a filegroup backup, you need to create a filegroup. In Exercise 17-5, you'll add one to the MSSQL_Training database you created in Lesson 5.

With a second filegroup in place that contains data, you can perform a filegroup backup in Exercise 17-6.

EXERCISE 17-5 PREPARING THE MSSQL_TRAINING DATABASE FOR A FILEGROUP BACKUP

1. Open **SQL Server Management Studio**. Expand your **server** and then **Databases**.
2. Right-click the **MSSQL_Training** database, and select **Properties**.
3. On the Filegroups page, click the **Add** button. In the Name text box, enter **Secondary.**
4. On the Files page, click the **Add** button, and enter this information:

   Name: MSSQL_Training_Data_3
   File Type: Data (Click the down button to see the options.)
   Filegroup: Secondary (Click the down button to see the options.)
   Initial Size: 3

5. Click **OK** to create the new file on the Secondary filegroup.
6. Now, to add a table to the new filegroup, expand **MSSQL_Training** in Object Explorer, right-click **Tables**, and select **New Table**.
7. Under Column Name in the first row, enter **Emp_Name.**
8. Next to Emp_Name, select **varchar** as the datatype. Leave the default length of 50.
9. Just below Emp_Name in the second row, enter **Emp_Number** as the column name with a type of varchar. Leave the default length of 50.
10. Select **View → Properties Window**.
11. Expand the **Regular Data Space Specification** section, and change the Filegroup or Partition Scheme Name property to Secondary.
12. Click the **Save** button (it looks like a floppy disk on the toolbar) to create the new table, and enter **Employees** for the table name.
13. Close the **Table Designer** by clicking the X in the upper-right corner of the window.
14. Now, to add some data to the new table, open a **new query**, and execute the following code (note that the second value is arbitrary):

    USE MSSQL_Training
    INSERT Employees
    VALUES('Tim Hsu', 'VA1765FR')
    INSERT Employees
    VALUES('Sue Hernandez', 'FQ9187GL')

15. Close the **query window**.

EXERCISE 17-6 PERFORMING A FILEGROUP BACKUP

1. Right-click the **MSSQL_Training** database in Object Explorer, point to **Tasks**, and select **Backup**.

2. In the Backup dialog box, make sure **MSSQL_Training** is the selected database to back up and Backup Type is **Full**.

3. Under Backup Component, select **Files and Filegroups**.

4. In the Select Files and Filegroups dialog box, check the **Secondary** box, and click **OK** (notice that the box next to MSSQL_Training_Data_3 is automatically checked).

5. Leave the default name in the Name box. In the Description box, type **Filegroup Backup of MSSQL_Training**.

6. Under Destination, make sure the **AdvWorksFull** device is the only one listed.

7. On the Options tab, make sure **Append to the Existing Backup Set** is selected so you don't overwrite your existing backups.

8. On the Options tab, select **Verify Backup When Finished**.

9. Click **OK** to start the backup.

10. When the backup is complete, you will get a notification; click **OK** to close it.

11. To verify the backup, you can look at the contents of the backup device, so expand **Backup Devices** under Server Objects in Object Explorer.

12. Right-click **AdvWorksFull**, and select **Properties**.

13. On the Media Contents page, you should see the full backup of MSSQL_Training.

14. Click **Close**, and then click **OK** to return to SQL Server Management Studio.

Note that you could have backed up the MSSQL_Training database to another backup device named MSSQL_Training, but we had you back it up to an existing device so the exercise would move along faster.

That takes care of the mechanics of all four types of backup. Next, you'll look at a technique to make the backups even faster—backing up to multiple devices.

BACKING UP TO MULTIPLE DEVICES

Thus far you've seen how to perform backups to a single backup device. If you really want to speed up the process, you can perform backups to multiple devices at the same time. You can perform this type of backup on the hard disk, network, or local tape drive, just like a normal backup.

If you want to do this with tape devices, you need more than one local tape drive in the SQL Server machine.

This type of backup uses multiple devices in parallel and writes the data in stripes across the media. What does that mean? You may expect that you fill one device to capacity and then move to the next, but that isn't what happens. The data is striped across all the media at the same time, which means all the devices are written to at once; this is why it's faster to use multiple devices for backup operations.

There is just one small drawback: Once you combine backup devices, you can't use them separately. If you back up AdventureWorks to three devices (BD1, BD2, and BD3), you can't back up another database to just BD3; you must use all three devices for the backup. The three devices are now considered part of a media set and can't be used separately without losing all the backups stored on the set.

To perform a backup with multiple devices, you need to create two more backup devices and then perform a backup. You'll do that in Exercise 17-7.

EXERCISE 17-7 BACKING UP TO MULTIPLE DEVICES

1. Open **SQL Server Management Studio** by selecting it from the SQL Server 2005 group under Programs on the Start menu. Expand **your server** and then **Server Objects**.

2. Right-click **Backup Devices** in Object Explorer, and select **New Backup Device**.

3. In the Name box of the Backup Device dialog box, enter **PSDev1**. Notice that the filename and path are filled in for you; make sure you have enough free space on the drive that SQL Server has selected.

4. Click **OK** to create the device.

5. Right-click **Backup Devices** in Object Explorer, and select **New Backup Device**.

6. In the Name box of the Backup Device dialog box, enter **PSDev2**. Again, notice that the filename and path are filled in for you.

7. Click **OK** to create the device.

8. To start the backup, right-click **Model** under System Databases, point to **Tasks**, and click **Backup**.

9. In the Backup dialog box, make sure **Model** is the selected database to back up and Backup Type is **Full**.

10. Leave the default name in the Name box. In the Description box, type **Full Backup of Model**.

11. Under Destination, a disk device may already be listed. If so, select the **device**, and click **Remove**.

12. Under Destination, click **Add**.

13. In the Select Backup Destination box, click **Backup Device**, select **PSDev1**, and click **OK**.

14. Under Destination, click **Add**.

15. In the Select Backup Destination box, click **Backup Device**, select **PSDev2**, and click **OK**.

16. On the Options page, select **Overwrite All Existing Backup Sets**. This option initializes a new device or overwrites an existing one.

17. Check **Verify Backup When Finished** to check the actual database against the backup copy and be sure they match after the backup is complete.

18. Click **OK** to start the backup.

19. When the backup is complete, you will get a notification; click **OK** to close it.

20. To verify the backup, you can look at the contents of the backup device, so expand **Backup Devices** under Server Objects in Object Explorer.

21. Right-click **PSDev1**, and select **Properties**.

22. On the Media Contents page, you should see the first half of the full backup of Model. You should also note that the Media Family Count property is 2, denoting this is part of a multiple-device backup.

23. Click **OK** to return to SQL Server Management Studio.

➕ MORE INFORMATION

You can use two slightly more advanced options to help with your database backups:

Copy-only backups. Sometimes you'll need to make a special backup of a database outside your normal backup scheme. For instance, you may need to send a copy of your database to an off-site archive for safekeeping. To do this without throwing off the rest of your backups, you can create a copy-only backup that backs up the database without affecting the logs or database. You do this using the COPY_ONLY option of the BACKUP statement.

Partial, full, and differential backups. A partial backup is a special type of backup that you can use only with filegroups. It backs up only the primary filegroup and all read-write filegroups. Read-only filegroups aren't backed up. You need to back up read-only filegroups only occasionally, because they don't change; thus, partial backups can make backups faster. To perform a partial backup, use the READ_WRITE_FILEGROUPS option of the BACKUP statement.

By using the T-SQL BACKUP statement, you can set a password for a backup set or media set to protect your data. If a password is set, users must have the password to back up and restore data from the protected backup or media set.

MAKING MULTIPLE BACKUP COPIES

Typically, backups are not part of a ***mirrored media set***, and BACKUP statements simply include a TO clause. However, a total of four mirrors are possible per media set. For a mirrored media set, you must have Enterprise Edition, and the backup operation must write to multiple groups of backup devices. Each group of backup devices comprises a single mirror within the mirrored media set. Every mirror must use the same quantity and type of physical backup devices, which must all have the same properties.

To back up to a mirrored media set, all of the mirrors must be present. To back up to a mirrored media set, specify the TO clause, to specify the first mirror; and specify a MIRROR TO clause for each additional mirror.

For a mirrored media set, each MIRROR TO clause must list the same number and type of devices as the TO clause.

 EXERCISE 17-8 CREATING MIRRORED BACKUP SETS

1. In Windows Explorer, create a new directory named **MirrorTest**.
2. Open a new **Query Editor** window.
3. Enter the following code:

```
BACKUP DATABASE AdventureWorks TO
DISK = 'c:\MirrorTest\AdventureWorks1A.bak',
DISK = 'c:\MirrorTest\AdventureWorks1B.bak',
DISK = 'c:\MirrorTest\AdventureWorks1C.bak'
MIRROR TO
DISK = 'c:\MirrorTest\AdventureWorks2A.bak',
DISK = 'c:\MirrorTest\AdventureWorks2B.bak',
DISK = 'c:\MirrorTest\AdventureWorks2C.bak'
GO
```

4. Go back to Windows Explorer and verify that you have six backup files in two media sets.

TAKE NOTE*

Backing up to multiple devices on the same drive degrades performance and eliminates the redundancy desired. In production, make sure you involve multiple spindles and perhaps multiple servers.

Knowing how to perform the various types of backups is extremely important, but it's useless if you don't know how to restore. You'll learn about the restoration process in the next section.

Restoring Databases

One of the most depressing sights you'll see as a database administrator is a downed database. Such a database is easy to spot in SQL Server Management Studio because you can't expand it in Object Explorer and it has no summary. This means something bad happened to the database; a corrupt disk is a likely culprit.

Suspect or corrupt databases aren't the only reasons to perform restores, though. You may, for example, need to send a copy of one of your databases to the home office or to a child office for synchronization. You may also need to recover from mistaken or malicious updates to the data. These reasons, and many others, make it important for you to know how to ***restore*** your databases.

The restore operation will likely miss recovering the last transactions entered by users, so be sure to alert your users of the need to restore. And train them how to verify that the last few entries are indeed there. Some corporations train users to maintain today's records until tomorrow in case a daily backup and subsequent restore misses all of yesterday's data entries.

PERFORMING STANDARD RESTORES

Restoring a database doesn't involve a lot of steps, but you need to understand one important setting before undertaking the task. The RECOVERY option, when set incorrectly, can thwart all your efforts to restore a database. The RECOVERY option tells SQL Server that you've finished restoring the database and that users should be allowed back in. Use this option *only* on the last file of the restore process.

For example, if you performed a full backup, then a differential backup, and then a transaction log backup, you would need to restore all three of them to bring the database back to a consistent state. If you specify the RECOVERY option when restoring the differential backup, SQL Server won't allow you to restore any other backups. In effect, you have told SQL Server that you're done restoring and it should let everyone start using the database again. If you have more than one file to restore, you need to specify NORECOVERY on all restores except the last one.

SQL Server also remembers where the original files were located when you backed them up. Thus, if you backed up files from the D drive, SQL Server will restore them to the D drive. This is fine unless your D drive has failed and you need to move your database to the E drive. You'll also run into this problem if you have backed up a database on a server at the home office and need to restore the database to a server at a child office. In this instance, you need to use the MOVE...TO option. MOVE...TO lets you back up a database in one location and move it to another location.

Finally, before allowing you to restore a database, SQL Server performs a safety check to make sure you aren't accidentally restoring the wrong database. The first step SQL Server takes is to compare the database name that is being restored to the name of the database recorded in the backup device. If the two are different, SQL Server won't perform the restore. Thus, if you have a database on the server named Accounting, and you're trying to restore from a backup device that has a backup of a database named Acctg, SQL Server won't perform the restore. This is a lifesaver, unless you're trying to overwrite the existing database with the database from the backup. If that is the case, you need to specify the REPLACE option, which is designed to override the safety check.

With all that said, you're ready to restore a database. You'll now make one of the databases suspect so you can see exactly what SQL Server does to restore it. Specifically, in Exercise 17-9 you'll blow away AdventureWorks and then restore it using the graphical user interface toolset in SQL Server Management Studio. Note that all T-SQL options (RECOVERY/ NORECOVERY/MOVE/REPLACE) have checkmarks or data entry equivalents.

 EXERCISE 17-9 RESTORING A DATABASE

1. Open the **SQL Server Configuration Manager** from the Start menu.
2. In the left pane, select **SQL Server 2005 Services**.
3. Right-click **SQL Server (MSSQLSERVER)** in the right pane, and click **Stop**. You'll be asked whether you want to stop the SQL Server Agent service as well; click **Yes**.
4. Find the file **AdventureWorks_Data.mdf** (usually in C:\Program Files\Microsoft SQL Server\MSSQL.1\MSSQL\Data\).
5. Rename the file as **AdventureWorks_Data.old**.
6. Find the file **AdventureWorks_Log.ldf**, and rename it as **AdventureWorks_Log.old**.
7. From the Configuration Manager, restart the **SQL Server Agent** and SQL Server services.
8. Open **SQL Server Management Studio**, and expand **Databases** under your server name. AdventureWorks cannot be expanded and has no summary; it is now inaccessible.

9. To restore the database, right-click **Databases**, and select **Restore Database**.

10. In the Restore Database dialog box, select AdventureWorks from the To Database drop-down list box.

11. Under Source for Restore, select From Device. Click the ellipsis (...) **button** next to the text box to select a device.

12. In the Specify Backup dialog box, select Backup Device from the Backup Media drop-down list box, and click **Add**.

13. In the Select Backup Device dialog box, select AdvWorksFull, and click **OK**.

14. Click OK to close the Specify Backup dialog box.

15. Under Select the Backup Sets to Restore, check all three backups (full, differential, and transaction log). Doing so returns the database to the most recent state.

16. On the Options page, make sure the RESTORE WITH RECOVERY option is selected, because you have no more backups to restore.

17. Click OK to begin the restore process.

18. In SQL Server Management Studio, right-click Database, and click **Refresh**.

19. Expand **Databases**, and you should see AdventureWorks back to normal.

You had to stop all the SQL Server services because while they're running, all the databases are considered open files—you wouldn't be able to work with them outside of SQL Server.

This type of restore is useful if the entire database becomes corrupt and you need to restore the whole database. However, what if only a few records are bad, and you need to return to the state the database was in just a few hours ago?

PERFORMING POINT-IN-TIME RESTORES

You'll usually get requests to return the data to a previous state at the end of the month, when accounting closes out the monthly books. Most often, the request sounds like this: "We forgot to carry a 1; can you bring the data back to yesterday at about 2:00 P.M.?" At this point, you remember that accounting signs your paycheck, so you're delighted to help them in any way you can; you tell them you can do it. "How is this possible?" you may ask. If you're performing transaction log backups, you can perform a point-in-time restore.

In addition to stamping each transaction in the transaction log with an LSN, SQL Server stamps them all with a time. That time, combined with the STOPAT clause of the RESTORE statement, makes it possible for you to return the data to a previous state. You need to keep two issues in mind while using this process. First, it doesn't work with full or differential backups, only with transaction log backups. Second, you'll lose any changes made to your entire database after the STOPAT time. For instance, if you restore your database to the state it was in yesterday at 2:00 P.M., everything that changed from yesterday at 2:00 P.M. until the time you restore the database will be lost and must be reinserted. Other than that, the point-in-time restore is a useful and powerful tool. You'll prepare to use it on AdventureWorks in Exercise 17-10. Look for the implementation of the T-SQL options in the GUI toolset.

CERTIFICATION READY?
When do you need to use the NORECOVERY switch?

EXERCISE 17-10 PREPARING FOR A POINT-IN-TIME RESTORE

1. You need to add a record that will survive the restore. Open a new SQL Server query in SQL Server Management Studio by clicking the **New Query** button on the toolbar.

2. To create a new record, enter and execute the following code:

```
USE AdventureWorks
INSERT HumanResources.Shift (Name, StartTime, EndTime,
ModifiedDate) VALUES('Test Shift 1', getdate() + 1, getdate()
+ 2, getdate () )
```

3. Note the time right now.

4. Wait two minutes, clear the query window, and then enter a new record using the following code:

```
USE AdventureWorks

INSERT HumanResources.Shift (Name, StartTime, EndTime, Modi-
fiedDate) VALUES('Test Shift 2', getdate() + 1, getdate() +
2, getdate () )
```

5. To see both records, clear the query window, and enter and execute the following code:

```
USE AdventureWorks

SELECT * FROM HumanResources.Shift
```

6. To perform a point-in-time restore, you must perform a transaction log backup. Open **SQL Server Management Studio**. Expand **your server** and then **Databases**.

7. In Object Explorer, right-click **AdventureWorks**, point to Tasks, and select Back Up.

8. In the Backup dialog box, make sure **AdventureWorks** is the selected database to back up and Backup Type is **Transaction Log**.

9. Leave the default name in the Name box. In the Description box, type **Point-in-time Backup of AdventureWorks**.

10. Under Destination, make sure the **AdvWorksFull** device is listed.

11. On the Options page, make sure **Append to the Existing Backup Set** is selected so you don't overwrite your existing full backup.

12. On the Options page, select **Verify Backup When Finished**.

13. Click **OK** to start the backup.

You have created two new records and performed a transaction log backup. In Exercise 17-11, you'll roll the database back to the point in time just before you added the second record so you can test the functionality of the point-in-time restore.

EXERCISE 17-11 PERFORMING A POINT-IN-TIME RESTORE

1. Open **SQL Server Management Studio**. Expand **your server** and then **Databases**.

2. Right-click **AdventureWorks**, point to **Tasks**, move to **Restore**, and select **Database**.

3. Click the **ellipsis (...) button** next to the Point in time restore text box.

4. In the Point in Time Restore dialog box, enter the time from step 3 of Exercise 17-9, and click **OK**.

5. Make sure you're restoring from the **AdvWorksFull** device, select **all available backups** in the device, and click OK to perform the restore.

6. To test the restore, open a **new SQL Server query** in SQL Server Management Studio, and enter and execute the following code:

```
USE AdventureWorks

SELECT * FROM HumanResources.Shift
```

7. Notice that Test Shift 2 is no longer there, but that Test Shift 1 remains.

Another type of restore will come in handy for VLDBs: piecemeal restores.

PERFORMING PIECEMEAL RESTORES

Piecemeal restores restore the primary filegroup and (optionally) some secondary filegroups and make them accessible to users. You can restore the remaining secondary filegroups later if needed.

Earlier in this lesson, you added a filegroup to the MSSQL_Training database; then you added a table to that filegroup, created some records in it, and backed up the secondary filegroup. You need to back up the primary filegroup before you can perform a piecemeal restore, though, so you'll perform another backup in Exercise 17-12.

The exercise demonstrates the capabilities of the piecemeal restore process. You can use it to restore the primary filegroup and, optionally, other filegroups to the same or another database to make the data accessible to users. You can restore the remaining filegroups later.

 EXERCISE 17-12 PERFORMING A PIECEMEAL RESTORE

1. Right-click the **MSSQL_Training** database in Object Explorer, point to **Tasks**, and select **Backup**.

2. In the Backup dialog box, make sure **MSSQL_Training** is the selected database to back up and Backup Type is Full.

3. Under Backup Component, select **Files and Filegroups**.

4. In the Select Files and Filegroups dialog box, check the **MSSQL_Training** box, and click OK (notice that all the other boxes in the list are automatically checked for you).

5. Leave the default name in the Name box. In the Description box, type **Piecemeal Backup of MSSQL_Training**.

6. Under Destination, make sure the **AdvWorksFull** device is the only one listed.

7. On the Options page, make sure **Append to the Existing Backup Set** is selected so you don't overwrite your existing backups.

8. On the Options tab, select **Verify Backup When Finished**.

9. Click **OK** to start the backup.

10. To perform a partial restore of the MSSQL_Training database to a new database named MSSQL_Training_part, execute the following code in a new query window:

```
RESTORE DATABASE MSSQL_Part
FILEGROUP = 'PRIMARY'
FROM DISK='C:\Program Files\
Microsoft SQL Server\MSSQL.1\MSSQL\
Backup\AdvWorksFull.bak'
WITH FILE=6, RECOVERY, PARTIAL,
MOVE 'MSSQL_Training_data' TO
'C:\MSSQL_Training_part_data.mdf',
MOVE 'MSSQL_Training_data2' TO
'C:\MSSQL_Training_part_data2.ndf',
MOVE 'MSSQL_Training_log' TO
'c:\MSSQL_Training_part_log.log'
```

11. To test the restore, enter and execute the following code:

```
USE MSSQL_Training_Part
SELECT * FROM Employees
```

12. This code should fail because the filegroup containing the Employees table wasn't restored. Enter and execute this code:

```
USE MSSQL_Training_Part
SELECT * FROM Customers
```

13. Close the query window.

With the mechanics of backing up and restoring under your belt, you're ready for a discussion of the theory behind backups. You need to know not only how but when to use each of these types of backups. In other words, you need to devise a viable backup strategy.

Devising a Backup Strategy

A backup strategy is a plan that details when to use which type of backup. For example, you could use only a full backup, a full with differential, or any other valid combination. Your challenge is to figure out which one is right for your environment. You'll now look at the pros and cons of each available strategy.

PLANNING FOR FULL BACKUPS ONLY

If you have a relatively small database, you can perform just full backups with no other type; but you need to understand what we mean by a "relatively small" database. When we're speaking of backups, the size of a database is relative to the speed of the backup medium. For example, a 200 MB database is fairly small, but if you have an older tape drive that isn't capable of backing up a 200 MB database overnight, you won't want to perform a full backup only on the tape drive every night. On the other hand, if you have a set of hardware capable of a 1 GB backup in a few hours, you can consider a full backup–only strategy. You must adapt to your situation. The following are the principles that govern what you should do.

The disadvantage of a full backup–only strategy is that it gives a comparatively slow backup when compared to other strategies. For example, if you perform a full backup every night on a 100 MB database, you're (obviously) backing up 100 MB every night. If you're using a differential backup with a full backup, you aren't backing up the entire 100 MB every night.

The major advantage of a full backup–only strategy is that the restore process is faster than with other strategies, because it uses only one tape. For instance, if you perform a full backup every night and the database fails on Thursday, all you need to restore is the full backup from Wednesday night, using only one tape or other medium. In the same scenario (as you'll see), the other strategies take more time because you have more media from which to restore.

One other disadvantage of a full backup–only strategy involves the transaction log. As we discussed earlier in this lesson, the transaction log is cleared only when a transaction log backup is performed. With a full-only strategy, your transaction log is in danger of filling up and locking your users out of the database. You can avoid this problem in two ways:

- First, you can set the recovery model for the database to Simple, which instructs SQL Server to completely empty the log every time it writes to the database from the log (a process called *checkpointing*). This isn't the best solution, though; you'll lose up-to-the-minute recoverability because the latest transactions will be deleted every time the server checkpoints. If your database crashes, you can restore it only to the time of the last full backup.

- Another option is to perform the full backup and, immediately afterward, perform a transaction log backup with the TRUNCATE_ONLY clause. This option frees space, but risks possible data loss. After the log is truncated by using either NO_LOG or TRUNCATE_ONLY, the changes recorded in the truncated portion of the log are not recoverable. Therefore, for recovery purposes, after using either of these options, you must immediately execute BACKUP DATABASE to take a full or differential database backup.

TAKE NOTE *

The NO_LOG or TRUNCATE_ONLY option will be removed in a future version of SQL Server, so avoid using it in new development work, and plan to modify applications that currently use it.

The first step you should take in the event of any database failure is to use the NO_TRUNCATE option with the transaction log backup to save the orphaned log. This last active log file is called the tail log.

Microsoft®

PLANNING FOR FULL BACKUPS WITH DIFFERENTIAL BACKUPS

If your database is too large to perform a full backup every night, you may want to consider adding differentials to the strategy. A full/differential strategy provides a faster backup than full alone. With a full-only backup strategy, you're backing up the entire database every time you perform a backup. With a full/differential strategy, you're backing up only the changes made to the database since the last full backup, which is faster than backing up the whole database.

The major disadvantage of the full/differential strategy is that the restore process is slower than with the full-only strategy, because full/differential requires you to restore more backups. Suppose you perform a full backup on Monday night and differentials the rest of the week, and your database crashes on Wednesday. To return the database to a consistent state, you'll need to restore the full backup from Monday and the differential from Tuesday. If your database crashes on Thursday, you'll need to restore the backups from Monday and Wednesday. If it crashes on Friday, you'll need to restore the full backup from Monday and the differential from Thursday.

The only other disadvantage to be aware of is that differential backups don't clear the transaction log. If you opt for this method, you should clear the transaction log manually by backing up the transaction log.

PLANNING FOR FULL WITH TRANSACTION LOG BACKUPS

Another method to consider, regardless of whether your database is huge, is full/transaction. This method offers several advantages. First, it's the best method to keep your transaction logs clean, because this is the only type of backup that purges old transactions from your transaction logs.

Second, this method makes for a fast backup process. For example, you can perform a full backup on Monday and transaction log backups three or four times a day during the week. This is possible because SQL Server performs online backups, and transaction log backups are usually small and quick (your users should barely notice).

A transaction log backup is also the only type of backup that gives you point-in-time restore capability. "How often will I use that?" you may ask. If you have any people in your company who aren't perfect, you'll probably use this capability quite a bit, so it's best to have it when you need it.

The disadvantage of this strategy is that the restore process is a little slower than full alone or full/differential. This is because you'll have more backups to restore, and any time you add more work to the process, it gets slower. For instance, suppose you perform a full backup on Monday and transaction log backups three times a day (at 10:00 A.M., 2:00 P.M., and 6:00 P.M.) throughout the week. If your database crashes on Tuesday at 3:00 P.M., you'll need to restore only the full backup from Monday and the transaction log backups from Tuesday at 10:00 A.M. and 2:00 P.M. However, if your database crashes on Thursday at 3:00 P.M., you'll need to restore the full backup from Monday, as well as all the transaction log backups made on Tuesday, Wednesday, and Thursday before the crash. So although this type of backup may have blinding speed, it involves a lengthy restore process. It may be better to combine all three types of backups.

PLANNING FOR FULL, DIFFERENTIAL, AND TRANSACTION LOG BACKUPS

If you combine all three types of backups, you get the best of all worlds. The backup and restore processes are still relatively fast, and you have the advantage of point-in-time restores as well. Suppose you perform a full backup on Monday, transaction log backups every four hours (10:00 A.M., 2:00 P.M., and 6:00 P.M.) throughout the day during the week, and differential backups every night. If your database crashes at any time during the week, all you need to restore is the full backup from Monday, the differential backup from the night before, and the transaction log backups up to the point of the crash. This approach is nice, fast, and simple. However, these combinations do not work well for a monstrous VLDB; for that you need a filegroup backup.

PLANNING FOR FILEGROUP BACKUPS

We discussed the mechanics of the filegroup backup earlier in this lesson, so you know they're designed to back up small chunks of the database at a time rather than the whole database all at once. This may come in handy, for example, with a 700 GB database contained in three files in three separate filegroups. You can perform a full backup once per month and then back up one filegroup per week during the week. Every day, you perform transaction log backups for maximum recoverability.

Suppose the disk containing the third file of your database crashes. With the other backup strategies, you would need to restore the full backup first and then the other backups. With filegroup backups, you don't need to restore the full backup first (thank goodness). All you need to restore is the backup of the filegroup that failed and the transaction log backups that occurred after the filegroup was backed up. If you backed up your third filegroup on Wednesday, and then it fails on Friday, you'll restore the filegroup backup from Wednesday and the transaction log backups from Thursday and Friday up to the point of the crash.

SQL Server is fully capable of determining which transactions belong to each filegroup. When you restore the transaction log, SQL Server applies only the transactions that belong to the failed group.

SKILL SUMMARY

IN THIS LESSON YOU LEARNED:

In this lesson, you learned how to back up and restore your databases. The first topic was backups. You have many reasons to back up data: natural disaster, hardware malfunction, and even people with malicious intent. If you perform regular backups, you can overcome these problems.

You can use four types of backups to help thwart the evils that could claim your data. First is the full backup, the basis of all other backups, which makes a copy of the entire database. Next, the differential backup grabs all the changes made to the database since the last full backup. The transaction log backup is useful for implementing a quick backup strategy, performing point-in-time restores, and clearing the transaction log on a periodic basis. Finally, the filegroup backup makes backups of small chunks of very large databases.

After learning how to back up data, you learned how to restore from those backups. First you performed a standard database restore, then you performed the more advanced point-in-time and piecemeal restores.

Finally, we discussed how to create a backup strategy so that you have a better idea of what to back up and when to do it.

For the certification examination:

- Understand backup devices. SQL Server can store backups on hard disk or tape drive; however, because SQL Server doesn't know about the hardware attached to your machine, you have to tell it, which is what a backup device does. Backup devices are SQL Server objects that represent the available backup media that SQL Server can use for storing backups. These can point to hard disk or tape drives and can be permanent or temporary.

- Know the backup types. Four backup types are available in SQL Server 2005. Full backups back up the entire database. You must perform a full backup before any other type. Differential backups record only the changes made to the database since the last full backup. Transaction log backups back up only the log, which is the only backup that will clear the transaction log. You can use filegroup backups to back up the contents of one or more filegroups.

- Know how to restore. Restoring a database is simple if you are using the standard restore method; you just need to remember which files to restore. If you want to return a database to the most recent content, then you restore the last full backup, the last differential (if any exist), and all the transaction log backups after the last full or differential backup. You can also perform a point-in-time backup that allows you to restore up to a specific point in time, but only if you have performed transaction log backups. You can also perform a piecemeal restore, which allows you to restore the primary and any secondary filegroups to a new database.

- Know how to devise a backup strategy. You need to know how to use all this technology to protect your data, and to effectively do that, you must have a backup strategy. You need to know when to use each type of backup and how to use those backups to restore your data after a disaster.

■ Knowledge Assessment

Multiple Choice

Circle the letter or letters that correspond to the best answer or answers.

1. One of your users has discovered some malicious updates to your data that occurred the day before at about 2:00 P.M. How can you return the database to the state it was in just before the update occurred?
   a. Perform a full database restoration with point-in-time recovery.
   b. Perform a differential database restoration with point-in-time recovery.
   c. Perform a transaction log restoration with point-in-time recovery.
   d. You cannot return the database to the previous state.

2. You have a huge database, several hundred gigabytes in size, with the recovery model set to Full. With your current hardware, a full backup of this database takes 15 hours. You cannot have the backup running during working hours because you do not have the system resources available to support users while performing a backup. Which backup strategy should you use?
   a. Perform a full backup every night.
   b. Perform a full backup and a transaction log backup every night.
   c. Perform a full backup every weekend and a differential backup every weeknight.
   d. Perform a full backup every weekend, a differential backup every weeknight, and a transaction log backup every night.

3. You have a VLDB with four filegroups (Primary, FG1, FG2, FG3), with the recovery model set to Full. You need to make sure the database is backed up in the shortest time possible while being able to restore in the shortest time possible. Which backup strategy should you use?
   a. Perform a full backup once a month, filegroup backups once a week, and transaction log backups throughout the week.
   b. Perform a full backup once a month, filegroup backups once a week, and differential backups throughout the week.
   c. Perform a full backup once a week and transaction log backups throughout the week.
   d. Perform a full backup every night.

4. You have a database named Sales that is set to use the Full recovery model. This is not a very big database—only about 200 MB—so you perform a full backup of this database every night and transaction log backups every two hours during the day starting at 8:00 A.M. At 12:30 P.M. on Tuesday you have a power surge, and the

Sales database becomes corrupted. How should you restore the database to get to the most current state?

   a. Restore the full backup from Monday night.
   b. Restore the full backup from Monday night, next restore the 12:00 P.M. transaction log backup, then restore the 10:00 A.M. transaction log backup, and finally restore the 8:00 A.M. transaction log backup.
   c. Restore the full backup from Monday night, next restore the 8:00 A.M. transaction log backup, then restore the 10:00 A.M. transaction log backup, and finally restore the 12:00 P.M. transaction log backup.
   d. Restore the 8:00 A.M. transaction log backup, next restore the 10:00 A.M. transaction log backup, and finally restore the 12:00 P.M. transaction log backup.

5. You have a medium-sized database named Sales that is set to use the Full recovery model. Your users insert, update, and delete data from this database frequently. You perform a full backup on this database every Saturday and differential backups Monday through Friday. One day your users start complaining they cannot update the database any longer. What should you do to get the database back up?

   a. Set the database to use the Simple recovery model.
   b. Set the database to use the Bulk-Logged recovery model.
   c. Back up the transaction log with NO RECOVERY.
   d. Back up the transaction log.

6. Your Sales database is very large, approximately 800 GB. You have split this database into four filegroups: Primary, OrdersFG, CatalogFG, and CustomersFG. Each filegroup contains tables and indexes for a group of data; for example, the CatalogFG filegroup contains all the tables and indexes used for storing product catalog data. One of your satellite offices also has a Sales database, but it is not an exact duplicate of yours. However, that office needs a copy of the product catalog tables. How can you send them the product catalog data?

   a. Send them the last full backup of the database, and have them restore it on their server. Then they can copy the product catalog tables from your database to theirs.
   b. Send them the last full backup of your database, and have them do a piecemeal restore of the CatalogFG filegroup. Then they can copy the data from the new database to the existing database.
   c. Send them the last backup of your Primary and CatalogFG filegroups, and have them do a piecemeal restore to a new database. Then they can copy the data from the new database to the existing database.
   d. Send them the last backup of your CatalogFG filegroup, and have them do a piecemeal restore of the CatalogFG filegroup. Then they can copy the data from the new database to the existing database.

7. You have three backup devices (BD1, BD2, and BD3) that point to tape drives locally installed on your server. You perform a full backup of your Manufacturing database every night on both of these devices using a parallel striped backup. You have recently created a new, smaller database named Production that you need to back up every night. What should you do?

   a. Back up the Production database to BD1, BD2, and BD3 in a parallel striped backup.
   b. Back up the Production database to BD1 only.
   c. Back up the Production database to BD2 only.
   d. Back up the Production database to BD3 only.

8. You have a large database named Ecommerce that is divided into four filegroups.
   - The Primary filegroup contains only system tables.
   - The OrderTablesFG filegroup contains order information tables.
   - The OrderIdxFG filegroup contains indexes associated with the order information tables.
   - The CatalogFG filegroup contains product catalog information tables and associated indexes.

You need to devise a backup strategy. Which filegroups need to be backed up as a unit?

a. They can all be backed up individually.

b. The Primary and OrderIdxFG filegroups must be backed up as a unit.

c. The Primary, CatalogFG, and OrderTablesFG filegroups must be backed up as a unit.

d. The OrderTablesFG and OrderIdxFG filegroups must be backed up as a unit.

9. You have a huge database that is split up into five filegroups. Two of these filegroups are for archive data, and they are marked as read-only so they cannot be changed accidentally. The other three filegroups are for system tables and current data. You want to perform a full backup of your current data once a week, but you need to back up your archived data only once a month. You want the weekly full backup to be as fast as possible. What should you do?

a. Make the weekly backup a copy-only backup.

b. Make the weekly backup a partial backup.

c. Make the weekly backup a differential backup.

d. Make the weekly backup a piecemeal backup.

10. Your developers are working on a new database on the development system. They do not want to lose the work they are doing on the database, so they need to have it backed up regularly. They are not interested in keeping the data from the database, because it is merely test data; they are interested only in the schema and other database objects. They need to be able to insert new data in the database at all times for testing purposes. This database will never exceed 200 MB in size. You also need to spend as little time as possible backing up this database. Which backup strategy should you use?

a. Set the recovery model to Full, perform a full backup every night, and then immediately perform a transaction log backup with the TRUNCATE ONLY option.

b. Set the recovery model to Simple, perform a full backup every night, and then immediately perform a transaction log backup with the TRUNCATE ONLY option.

c. Set the recovery model to Simple, and perform a full backup every night.

d. Set the recovery model to Full, and perform a full backup every night.

11. You have a database named Manufacturing that is set to use the Full recovery model. You perform a full backup of the entire database once a week on Saturday. You perform a differential backup every night, Monday through Friday, and perform transaction log backups every two hours starting at 6:00 A.M. until 6:00 P.M. On Wednesday at 11:15 A.M., your users start complaining they cannot get into the database. You verify the database is down. In what order should you restore each backup to bring the database back online? (Choose all that apply, and place them in order.)

a. Restore the differential backup from Tuesday.

b. Restore the 10:00 A.M. transaction log backup.

c. Restore the 6:00 A.M. transaction log backup.

d. Restore the 8:00 A.M. transaction log backup.

e. Restore the full backup from last Saturday.

f. Restore the differential backup from Monday.

12. You have an Accounting database that you use to store payroll and employee information. Your home office has requested you to send them a backup copy of this database so they can update their records. You need to send them this copy without affecting the backup strategy you are using. What should you do?

a. Make a full backup.

b. Make a copy-only backup.

c. Make a partial backup.

d. Make a differential backup.

13. You have a database named Ecommerce that contains product and order information for your company Web site, so it must be available at all times. How can you back the database up and still make it available to users?

a. Run the backups with the ONLINE option.

b. Run the backups using the ALLOW_ACCESS option.

    c. Create a copy-only backup every night, which allows users to access the database while it is being backed up.

    d. Just run your normal backups; nothing special is required.

14. You need to be able to back up your databases to a tape drive. The only tape drive you have is on another server on the network. How can you get SQL Server to use this remote tape drive as a backup device?

    a. Create the backup device using the NETWORKED option.

    b. Create the backup device using a Universal Naming Convention (UNC) path (\\server_ name\tape_drive).

    c. Purchase third-party backup software capable of backing up a SQL Server database.

    d. There is no way to use a remote tape drive.

15. You need to be able to restore your Accounting database to any point in time in case an accounting error is saved to the database before it is caught. To accomplish this, you decide to set the recovery model of the database to Simple and perform full backups of the database every night and transaction log backups every three hours during the day. Is this the correct solution?

    a. This is the correct solution.

    b. No; the recovery model should be set to Full.

    c. No; you need to perform differential backups to use a point-in-time restore.

    d. No; you need to back up the transaction logs at least once an hour to use point-in-time restores.

16. You have a database that is approximately 400 MB, and you need to be able to recover the database to a specific point in time. Which recovery model should you use for this database?

    a. Full

    b. Bulk-Logged

    c. Transactional

    d. Simple

17. You have a database, 350 MB in size, that contains sales data. You need to back up this database; however, you do not have enough hard disk space on your server to accommodate the backup device, you do not have a tape drive in the server, and you have no budget for new hardware. What can you do?

    a. Create a backup device on a remote server that has enough disk space to accommodate the device. Use the new backup device to back up your database.

    b. Create a backup device that points to a tape drive on a remote server. Use the new backup device to back up your database.

    c. Stop the SQL Server services, copy the data and log files to a remote server, and then restart the SQL Server services.

    d. There is nothing you can do; you must obtain more hardware.

18. Your developers are ready to create several new tables and modify several existing tables on your production SQL Server so they can accommodate a new application they are nearly ready to release. They have a lot of changes, so they need to do this after-hours, during the same time frame when your backups are scheduled to run. What can you do to allow the developers to modify the databases while the backups are running?

    a. You do not need to do anything special; database modifications are allowed during a backup.

    b. Run a full backup with the DDL_ALLOWED option so the developers can make changes to the database.

    c. Set the database to the Simple recovery model before running your backups that night to allow the developers to make changes.

    d. There is no way to allow schema changes to the database during a backup; you'll need to reschedule the backup.

19. You need to make sure your HumanResources database is available at all times; if it crashes, you need to be able to return it to the most current state. This is a small database that does not change much during the day, so you have decided to perform a full

backup every night. What should you do to keep the transaction log from filling to capacity?

a. Set the recovery model to Full, and perform a transaction log backup every night immediately after the full backup.

b. Set the recovery model to Simple, and perform a transaction log backup every night immediately after the full backup.

c. Set the recovery model to Bulk-Logged, and perform a transaction log backup every night immediately after the full backup.

d. Just set the recovery model to Simple; SQL Server will clear the log for you.

20. You have a database that is used to store customer information and is set to use the Full recovery model. You perform a full backup of the entire database once a week on Sunday. You perform a differential backup every night Monday through Saturday at 9:00 P.M. and transaction log backups every hour starting at 6:00 A.M. until 6:00 P.M. On Thursday at 8:00 A.M., as soon as you get to work, you find that the database has been down since 8:00 P.M. Wednesday night. In what order should you restore each backup to bring the database back online? (Choose all that apply, and place them in order.)

a. Restore the differential backup from Monday.

b. Restore the differential backup from Tuesday.

c. Restore the differential backup from Wednesday.

d. Restore each transaction log backup since the last differential backup.

e. Restore each transaction log backup since the last full backup.

f. Restore the full backup from last Sunday.

Case Scenarios

Scenario 17-1: Performing a Backup

Back up both the AdventureWorks database and log to C:\AdvWorksData.bak and C:\AdvWorksLog.bak using Transact-SQL code.

Scenario 17-2: Performing a Restore

Copy the Administration and Customers databases from your CD to C:\ProgramFiles\ Microsoft SQL Server\MSSQL.1\MSSQL\Backup. Create a database named Administration. Restore the database from SQL Server's default backup location. Do *not* create a database named Customers. Restore the database from SQL Server's default backup location.

Maintaining and Automating SQL Server

LESSON SKILL MATRIX

TECHNOLOGY SKILL	70-431 EXAM OBJECTIVE
Implement and maintain SQL Server Agent jobs.	Foundational
Set a job owner.	Foundational
Create a job schedule.	Foundational
Create job steps.	Foundational
Configure job steps.	Foundational
Disable a job.	Foundational
Create a maintenance job.	Foundational
Set up alerts.	Foundational
Configure operators.	Foundational
Modify a job.	Foundational
Delete a job.	Foundational
Manage a job.	Foundational
Manage databases by using Transact-SQL.	Foundational
Manage index fragmentation.	Foundational
Manage statistics.	Foundational
Shrink files.	Foundational
Perform database integrity checks by using DBCC CHECKDB.	Foundational
Configure SQL Server 2005 instances and databases	Foundational
Configure the SQL Server Database Mail subsystem for an instance.	Foundational
Gather performance and optimization data by using DMVs.	Foundational

KEY TERMS

job: A specified series of operations, called steps, performed sequentially by SQL Server Agent.

Database Mail: An enterprise solution for sending e-mail messages from the Microsoft SQL Server 2005 database engine, which can also include data or files from any resource on your network.

SQL Server Agent: A service that allows you to automate some administrative tasks; it controls anything timed or scheduled. SQL Server Agent service runs jobs, monitors SQL Server, and processes alerts. The service must be running before local and multiserver administrative jobs can run automatically.

■ Automating Administrative Activities

↓
THE BOTTOM LINE

Maintaining an efficient operation means you continually—as in all the time—watch for new bottlenecks. Reducing a bottleneck simply reveals a new bottleneck, so your job is to balance all bottlenecks equally so no one interferes more than another. Balancing bottlenecks requires a proactive program of regular maintenance. Maintenance functions are best performed during off-hours or minimal-use hours so as to cause the least interference to productivity. Automating these functions allows you to sleep well at night (the SWAN principle of time management).

Maintaining Indexes

You learned you need indexes on most SQL Server tables to speed up access to the data. Without these indexes, SQL Server would need to perform table scans, reading every record in the table, to find any amount of data. To keep your indexes running at peak efficiency, you must perform periodic maintenance on them.

TAKE NOTE *

sys.DM_*anything* are dynamic management functions or views that are new to SQL Server 2005. In general, dynamic management views and functions return server state information that can be used to monitor the health of a server instance, diagnose problems, and tune performance.

The primary issue to watch for in an index is page splitting. As described in Lesson 7, a page split is caused when a page of data fills to 100 percent and more data must be added to it. To make room for the new data, SQL Server must move half of the data from the full page to a new page.

Page splitting has a few disadvantages. First, the new page that is created is out of order. So instead of going right from one page to the next when looking for data, SQL Server has to jump around the database looking for the next page it needs. This is referred to as *fragmentation*. Not only that, but the server also has to take the time to delete half of the records on the full page and rewrite them on a new page.

Although page splitting has advantages in some scenarios, you will most often find you need to recover from the effects of page splitting by rebuilding the index. Before you do that, you need to ascertain whether your index is fragmented badly enough to warrant reconstruction. The way to determine this is by querying sys.DM_DB_INDEX_PHYSICAL_STATS.

UNDERSTANDING SYS.DM_DB_INDEX_PHYSICAL_STATS

To overcome the effects of fragmentation of the database, you need to either reorganize or completely rebuild the indexes on the tables. That is time-consuming, so you will want to do it only when needed. The best, and only, way to tell whether your indexes need reconstruction is to perform sys.DM_DB_INDEX_PHYSICAL_STATS.

You can get information from sys.DM_DB_INDEX_PHYSICAL_STATS using a simple SELECT query. Here is the schema for this view:

TAKE NOTE *

In previous versions of SQL Server, you would have used DBCC SHOWCONTIG to find index fragmentation, but that is now deprecated.

```
Sys.DM_DB_INDEX_PHYSICAL_STATS ( { database_id | NULL }
, { object_id | NULL }, { index_id | NULL | 0 }, {
partition_number | NULL }
, { mode | NULL | DEFAULT } )
```

The following list explains the arguments:

- database_id is the numeric ID of the database. You can substitute the DB_ID( ) function for this parameter.
- object_id is the numeric ID of the table or view to check. You can use the results of the Object_ID( ) function to get a specific object ID here.
- index_id is the numeric ID of the index to check. Use 0 for a heap or Object_ID( ) for a specific index. NULL returns all indexes.

- partition_number is the number of the partition you want to query if the database is partitioned. NULL or 0 returns all partitions; any other nonnegative value returns data for a specific partition.
- mode is the scan-level mode to use on the database. Valid values are DEFAULT, NULL, LIMITED, SAMPLED, and DETAILED. The default value is LIMITED.

When queried, DM_DB_INDEX_PHYSICAL_STATS returns a table with the columns explained in Books Online. Search for sys.DM_DB_INDEX_PHYSICAL_STATS.

Each scan mode has its own advantages and disadvantages, as listed in Table 18-1.

Table 18-1

Scan Modes

Mode	Description	Advantage	Disadvantage
Limited	Reads only parent-level pages.	This is the fastest mode; it is accurate, and it allows concurrent access during the scan.	Only a subset of statistics is calculated.
Sampled	Reads parent-level pages, and scans indexes with fewer than 10,000 pages at 100 percent. Otherwise, they are scanned at 1 percent and 2 percent simultaneously. If the difference between the two is close, then the 2 percent scan is reported; otherwise, a 10 percent sample is performed.	This is faster than a detailed scan; it calculates all statistics and allows concurrent access during the scan.	Calculated statistics may not be 100 percent accurate.
Detailed	Reads parent-level and every leaf-level page.	This calculates all statistics based on all available data.	This is the slowest mode, and data modification is prohibited during the scan.

So if you want to find the fragmentation on the Sales.SalesOrderDetail table in the AdventureWorks database, the query might look like this:

```
USE AdventureWorks;
SELECT INDEX_ID, AVG_FRAGMENTATION_IN_PERCENT
FROM sys.dm_db_index_physical_stats
(db_id(),Object_ID(N'Sales.SalesOrderDetail'),
NULL, NULL, 'DETAILED')
```

This would give you the index names in the Sales.SalesOrderDetail table and the corresponding amount of fragmentation. Using this data, you could then decide whether to reorganize or rebuild your indexes.

REORGANIZING AND REBUILDING INDEXES

If the amount of fragmentation on your index is less than 10 percent, you really don't need to do anything. When it's from 10 percent to 30 percent, you should reorganize your index; and anything higher requires a rebuild. To reorganize an index, use the ALTER INDEX REORGANIZE statement. Here is what it would look like if you wanted to reorganize the PK_Product_ProductPhotoID index on the Production.ProductPhoto table in the AdventureWorks database:

```
USE AdventureWorks
ALTER INDEX PK_ProductPhoto_ProductPhotoID
ON Production.ProductPhoto
REORGANIZE
```

You have two effective ways to rebuild indexes on a table. One way is to use the CREATE INDEX statement with the DROP_EXISTING option. The other way to reconstruct an index that is being used as a primary key is to use ALTER INDEX REBUILD, which is also used to repair corrupt indexes and rebuild multiple indexes at once. In Exercise 18-1, you will reconstruct the indexes on the Production.Product table in the AdventureWorks database.

As discussed in Lesson 7, the ONLINE option used in this lesson states whether the underlying tables and indexes are available for queries and data modification while indexing operations are taking place.

 EXERCISE 18-1 RECONSTRUCTING AN INDEX

1. Open a **new SQL Server query** in SQL Server Management Studio, and execute the following code to find the current amount of fragmentation on the Production. Product table:

```
USE AdventureWorks;
SELECT INDEX_ID, AVG_FRAGMENTATION_IN_PERCENT
FROM sys.dm_db_index_physical_stats (db_id(),
Object_ID(N'Production.Product'),
Default, Default, 'DETAILED');
```

2. Enter and execute the following code to reconstruct the index on the Orders table:

```
USE AdventureWorks;
ALTER INDEX ALL
ON Production.Product
REBUILD WITH (FILLFACTOR = 80, ONLINE = ON,
STATISTICS_NORECOMPUTE = ON);
```

3. Query the sys.DM_DB_INDEX_PHYSICAL_STATS statement to see whether the fragmentation is gone:

```
USE AdventureWorks;
SELECT INDEX_ID, AVG_FRAGMENTATION_IN_PERCENT
FROM sys.dm_db_index_physical_stats
(db_id(),Object_ID(N'Production.Product'),
Default, Default, 'DETAILED');
```

4. You should see 0 percent fragmentation.

MAINTAINING STATISTICS

Whenever you perform a query on your data, SQL Server creates a map of which tables and indexes to use to execute the query as fast as possible. This map is called an *execution plan*. To choose the fastest index for the query, SQL Server must know how much of the data in the index is applicable to the query being run. To get this information, SQL Server reads the index statistics, which tell the database engine what the index holds.

The problem is that indexes change when the data in the underlying table changes. When the index changes, the statistics become out of date. This isn't a problem if you created the index with the default value of STATISTICS_NORECOMPUTE OFF, because SQL Server will automatically update statistics for you. But if your server is low on resources and you had to turn this value on, then you will need to update your statistics manually. In Exercise 18-2, you will see how to update statistics manually using the UPDATE STATISTICS command.

EXERCISE 18-2 UPDATING INDEX STATISTICS

1. Open a **new SQL Server query** in SQL Server Management Studio.
2. Enter and execute the following code to reconstruct the index on the Sales.SalesOrderDetail table:

```
USE AdventureWorks
UPDATE STATISTICS Sales.SalesOrderDetail
```

Maintaining Databases

Database files are volatile; they are constantly being changed and updated, so just like any other volatile file on a system, they can become corrupt. Consequently, it is important to perform periodic maintenance on database files. You must perform two important tasks, the first of which is running DBCC CHECKDB.

UNDERSTANDING DBCC CHECKDB

You can use DBCC CHECKDB to check the allocation, logical, and structural integrity of objects in the database. This is necessary because databases are in a constant state of flux; in other words, data is always being inserted, updated, and deleted. So, it stands to reason that occasionally something is not going to be written to disk correctly and will need to be repaired.

The syntax of the command looks like this:

```
DBCC CHECKDB
[(
'database_name' | database_id | 0
[, NOINDEX
| { REPAIR_ALLOW_DATA_LOSS
| REPAIR_REBUILD
} ]
)]
[ WITH {
[ ALL_ERRORMSGS ]
[, [ NO_INFOMSGS ] ]
[, [ TABLOCK ] ]
[, [ ESTIMATEONLY ] ]
[, [ PHYSICAL_ONLY ] ] |
[, [ DATA_PURITY ] ]
}
]
```

The following list explains the options:

- **NOINDEX:** This specifies that intensive checks of nonclustered indexes should not be performed. This speeds up execution time. You can use this when you plan to rebuild indexes shortly after running DBCC CHECKDB.
- **REPAIR_REBUILD:** This tries to repair all reported errors as long as such repairs do not result in a loss of data; therefore, you incur no risk of losing data with this option.
- **REPAIR_ALLOW_DATA_LOSS:** This is the most comprehensive repair option. It performs all the checks the previous two options perform, and it adds the allocation and deallocation of rows for correcting allocation errors, correcting structural row and page errors, and deleting corrupted text objects. You incur a risk of losing data with this

option (as the name implies). To lessen that risk, you can perform this option as a transaction so you can roll back the changes.

- **ALL_ERRORMSGS:** If this is not used, then only the first 200 errors display. If this option is used, then all errors display. Error messages are sorted by object ID, except for those messages generated from tempdb.

- **NO_INFOMSGS:** This suppresses all informational messages.

- **TABLOCK:** By default, DBCC CHECKBD uses an internal database snapshot to perform its work. This allows users to access data while the command is being run, but it can be a little slow. TABLOCK causes DBCC CHECKDB to obtain locks instead of using a snapshot, which makes it run faster.

- **ESTIMATEONLY:** This displays the estimated amount of tempdb space needed to run DBCC CHECKDB with all the other specified options. The actual database check is not performed.

- **PHYSICAL_ONLY:** This tells DBCC to check only the physical structure of the database file. Using this, DBCC will check only the structure of the page and record headers and the physical structure of indexes, and it will make sure space inside the file is allocated correctly (that is, all pages have 8 kibibytes). This means DBCC can also detect torn pages, checksum failures, and common hardware failures, which can compromise a user's data. Using this option causes DBCC CHECKDB to run much faster than performing a full check, which makes it well suited for frequent use on production systems. PHYSICAL_ONLY always implies NO_INFOMSGS, and is not allowed with any of the repair options.

- **DATA_PURITY:** This causes DBCC CHECKDB to check the database for column values that are not valid or are out of range. For example, DBCC CHECKDB detects columns with date and time values that are larger than or less than the acceptable range for the date-time datatype; or DBCC CHECKDB detects decimal or approximate-numeric datatype columns with scale or precision values that are not valid. This is useful only for databases that have been upgraded from previous versions of SQL Server, because databases that are created in SQL Server 2005 have column-value integrity checks enabled by default.

In Exercise 18-3, you will try your hand at DBCC CHECKDB by running it on the AdventureWorks database.

 EXERCISE 18-3 USING DBCC CHECKDB ON ADVENTUREWORKS

1. Open a **new SQL Server query** in Management Studio.
2. Enter and execute the following code to check the AdventureWorks database for errors:

```
USE AdventureWorks
DBCC CHECKDB
```

3. You should see the results in the Messages pane.

SHRINKING FILES

When users enter new data into a database, SQL Server may have to expand the size of the data and log files on disk to accommodate the new data. When this happens, the size of the physical file on disk increases, so the hard drive has less space available for other files. When a user deletes data, though, the size of the physical file is not reduced; the file remains the same size. This condition can result in wasted system resources and possibly cause problems for other processes that need disk space.

To combat this problem, you need to occasionally shrink the data and log files so they do not take up too much space. Using SQL Server Management Studio, you can shrink the entire database or just a single file at a time. In Exercise 18-4, you will shrink the entire AdventureWorks database.

EXERCISE 18-4 SHRINKING THE ADVENTUREWORKS DATABASE

1. Open **SQL Server Management Studio**, and expand **your server** and then **Databases**.
2. You need to add some space to the database, so right-click **AdventureWorks**, and select **Properties**.
3. On the Files page, add **10 MB** to the size of the AdventureWorks_Data file.
4. Click **OK**.
5. Right-click **AdventureWorks**, go to **Tasks**, select **Shrink**, and finally click **Database**. You should see about 10 MB of free space.
6. Check the **Reorganize Files...** box, and click **OK**.
7. Right-click **AdventureWorks**, go to **Tasks**, select **Shrink**, and finally click **Database**. You should see very little free space.
8. Click **Cancel** to close the dialog box.

SQL Server also provides the DBCC Shrinkfile and DBCC ShrinkDatabase utilities to enable you to script these functions or include them in a job for scheduled processing.

DBCC Shrinkfile reduces the size of the specified data or log file for the current database, or empties a file by moving the data from the specified file to other files in the same filegroup, thereby allowing the file to be removed from the database. You can shrink a file to a size that is less than the size specified when it was created. This resets the minimum file size to the new value.

DBCC ShrinkDatabase reduces the size of the data and log files in the specified database, although the database cannot be made smaller than the minimum size specified when the database was originally created.

Check Books Online for the options for both of these routines.

Now you know how to keep your databases running at peak efficiency by performing regular maintenance, but you probably don't want to be there after-hours waiting for the best time to perform this maintenance. That is why you need to know how to automate these tasks. You'll start by looking into the basics of automation.

Understanding Automation Basics

You can automate nearly any administrative task you can think of through SQL Server. That may sound like an exaggeration, but look at the features you can automate:

- Any T-SQL code
- Scripting languages such as VBScript or JScript
- Operating system commands
- Replication tasks

This functionality is powerful, so before you start to use automation, you need to know how it works. At the heart of SQL Server's automation capability is the SQL Server Agent service (also referred to as "the agent"). Automation and replication are the sole functions of the service, which uses three subcomponents to accomplish its automation tasks:

- **Alerts:** An alert is an error message or event that occurs in SQL Server and is recorded in the Windows Application log. Alerts can be sent to users via e-mail, pager, or Net Send. If an error message isn't written to the Windows Application log, an alert is never fired.
- **Operators:** When an alert is fired, it can be sent to a user. Users who need to receive these messages are known in SQL Server as *operators*. Operators are used to configure who receives alerts and when they're available to receive these messages.
- **Jobs:** A job is a series of the steps defining the task to be automated. It also defines schedules, which dictate when the task is to be executed. Such tasks can be run one time or on a recurring basis.

These three components work together to complete the tapestry of administration. Here is an example of what may happen:

1. A user defines a job that is specified to run at a certain time.
2. When the job runs, it fails and thus writes an error message to the Windows Event log.
3. When the SQL Server Agent service reads the Windows Event log, the agent finds the error message that the failed job wrote and compares it to the sysalerts table in the MSDB database.
4. When the agent finds a match, it fires an alert.
5. The alert, when fired, can send an e-mail, pager message, or Net Send message to an operator.
6. The alert can also be configured to run another job designed to repair the problem that caused the alert.

For any of this to function, though, you must properly configure the SQL Server Agent service. To begin with, the agent must be running for automation to work. You can verify this in four ways.

- First, you can open SQL Server Management Studio and notice the SQL Server Agent icon: if it's a red circle with an X, the service is stopped; if it's a green arrow, the service is started. (You can start the service by right-clicking the icon and selecting Start.)
- Second, you can check and change the state of the service using the SQL Server Configuration Manager.
- Third, you can use the Services applet in the Control Panel.
- Fourth, you can use SQL Server Surface Area Configuration.

TAKE NOTE* SSMS won't even display SQL Server Agent unless the logged-in user is a member of SQLAgentOperatorRole, SQLAgentReaderRole, or SQLAgentUserRole associated with the MSDB database.

X REF

Replication is discussed in Lesson 23.

Not only should the agent be running, but it's also best to have it log in with a domain account, as opposed to a local system account, because using the local system account won't allow you to work with other SQL Servers on your network. This means you can't perform multiserver jobs, carry out replication (discussed in Lesson 23), or use SQL Server's e-mail capabilities. To make sure the agent is logging in with a domain account, open the **Services** applet in the Control Panel (if you're using Windows 2003, you'll find it in Administrative Tools under Programs on the Start menu), double-click the **SQL Server Agent** service, and select a domain account by clicking the **ellipsis** next to This Account.

Once all this is in place, you're nearly ready to begin working with automation. First, though, you should configure SQL Server to send e-mail using Database Mail.

Configuring Database Mail

You can use Database Mail to send e-mail for the SQL Server services using the standard Simple Mail Transfer Protocol (SMTP). It is actually a separate process that runs in the background (called SQLiMail90.exe), so if a problem occurs, SQL Server is unaffected. You can also specify more than one mail server, so if one mail server goes down, Database Mail can still process mail. Database Mail is also scalable because it uses the Service Broker queue, which allows the request to be handled asynchronously and even saves the request if the server goes down before it can be handled (see Lesson 21 for more about the Service Broker).

TAKE NOTE* SQL Mail is included for backward compatibility with SQL Server 2000. SQL Mail requires a MAPI client (such as Outlook) while Database Mail does not.

To top it off, Database Mail provides granular control so you can limit which users are allowed to send mail. You can also specify which file extensions are allowed and disallowed as attachments, as well as the maximum size of those attachments. Everything Database Mail does is logged in the Windows Application log, and sent messages are retained in the mailhost database for auditing.

This all sounds great, but how do you use it? First you need an SMTP mail server somewhere on the network, with a mail account configured for the SQL Server Agent service account. The topics of setting up and configuring an SMTP server are beyond the scope of this text, but if you have an e-mail account with your Internet service provider (ISP), you can use that. Then you can configure Database Mail using the Configuration Wizard. To send e-mail to operators, the MSDB database must be a mailhost, so you'll configure MSDB as a mailhost database in Exercise 18-5.

 EXERCISE 18-5 CONFIGURING A MAILHOST

1. Open **SQL Server Management Studio**, and connect to your server.
2. Expand **Management in Object Explorer**, right-click **Database Mail**, and select **Configure Database Mail**.
3. On the Select Configuration Task page, select **Set Up Database Mail by Performing the Following Tasks**, and click **Next**.
4. If a dialog box opens and asks you whether you would like to enable Database Mail, click **Yes**.
5. On the New Profile page, create a mail profile, and associate it with a mail server account:
   a. Enter **SQLAgentProfile** in the Profile Name box.
   b. Under SMTP Accounts, click **Add**.
   c. In the Account Name box, enter **Mail Provider Account 1**.
   d. In the Description box, enter **e-mail account information**.
   e. Fill in your outgoing mail server information using the information provided by your ISP or network administrator.
   f. If your e-mail server requires you to log in, check the **SMTP Server Requires Authentication** box, and enter your login information.
   g. Click **OK** to return to the wizard. Your account should now be listed under SMTP Accounts.
6. Click **Next**.
7. On the Manage Profiles Security page, check the **Public** box next to the mail profile you just created to make it accessible to all users. Set the Default Profile option to **Yes**, and click **Next**.
8. On the Configure System Parameters page, accept the defaults, and click **Next**.
9. On the Complete the Wizard page, review all your settings, and click **Finish**.
10. When the system is finished setting up Database Mail, click **Close**.

Now, in Exercise 18-6, you will configure the SQL Server Agent to use the mail profile you just created.

**EXERCISE 18-6 CONFIGURING THE SQL SERVER AGENT
TO USE THE MAILHOST**

1. In Object Explorer, right-click **SQL Server Agent**, and select **Properties**.
2. On the Alert System page, check the **Enable Mail Profile** box.
3. Select **Database Mail** from the Mail System drop-down list.

4. Select **SQLAgentProfile** from the Mail Profile drop-down list.

5. Click **OK**.

6. From SQL Computer Manager, stop and restart the **SQL Server Agent** service.

You can run the Configuration Wizard again at any time to make changes to the Database Mail configuration. For example, you may want to do the following:

- Create a new Database Mail database.
- Add or remove accounts or profiles.
- Manage profile security by marking them as public or private.
- View or change system parameters.
- Uninstall Database Mail.

With Database Mail successfully configured, you can create the operators who receive e-mail from SQL Server.

Internet Information Server comes with a built-in SMTP server that you can use with Database Mail.

Creating Operators

You need to configure several settings to enable SQL Server to contact the appropriate people when problems occur. Such settings include the names of the people to contact, when they are available, how they should be contacted (for example, via e-mail, pager, or Net Send), and which problems they should be called on to address. An operator is the object used in SQL Server to configure all these settings.

Net Send messages are messages sent from a source machine to a destination machine that pop up on the user's screen in a dialog box over all the open applications.

Suppose, for example, that several people in your company need to be alerted when a problem occurs with SQL Server, and that each of them needs to be alerted regarding different problems and in various ways. Your database administrator may need to be alerted about any administration issues (for example, a failed backup or full transaction log) via e-mail and pager. Your developers may need to be alerted to programming issues (for example, deadlocks) via e-mail. Managers in your company may need to know about other issues, such as a user deleting a customer from a customer database, and they prefer to receive Net Send messages. You can handle these types of users by creating separate operators for each and then configuring the desired settings.

To demonstrate, you'll configure an operator in Exercise 18-7.

 EXERCISE 18-7 CONFIGURING AN OPERATOR

1. Open **SQL Server Management Studio**.

2. In Object Explorer, expand **your server** and then **SQL Server Agent**.

3. Right-click **Operators**, and select New Operator.

4. In the Name box, enter **Administrator**.

5. If you configured your system to use Database Mail, enter your **e-mail address** as the e-mail name. If you didn't configure your system to use e-mail, skip this step.

6. Type the **name of your machine** in the Net Send Address box. You can find the name by right-clicking the My Computer icon on the Desktop, selecting **Properties**, and then clicking the **Network Identification** tab. The computer name is the first section of the full computer name (before the first period). For instance, if the full computer name is instructor.domain.com, the computer name is instructor.

7. If you carry a pager that is capable of receiving e-mail, you can enter your pager's e-mail address in the Pager E-mail Name box.

8. At the bottom of the page, you can select the days and times this operator is available for notification. If a day is checked, the operator will be notified on that day between the start and end times noted under Start Time and End Time. Check the box for each day, and leave the default workday times of 8:00 A.M. to 6:00 P.M.

9. We'll discuss the Notifications tab later; for now, click **OK** to create the operator.

Because you can make operators active at different times, it's possible to accidentally leave a small period of time uncovered. If an error occurs during that window of time, no operator will receive the alert, because no one is on duty. To avoid such a problem, you should create a fail-safe operator who will receive alerts when no one is scheduled to be on duty. You'll create one in Exercise 18-8.

With an operator in place, you're ready to start creating jobs to automate tasks.

 EXERCISE 18-8 CONFIGURING A FAIL-SAFE OPERATOR

1. In SQL Server Management Studio, right-click the **SQL Server Agent** icon in Object Explorer, and select **Properties**.

2. On the Alert System page, check the **Enable Fail-Safe Operator** box.

3. Select **Administrator** in the Operator drop-down list.

4. Check the box next to **Net Send** so you'll receive Net Send messages as a fail-safe operator.

5. Click **OK** to apply the changes.

Creating Jobs

A job is a series of tasks that can be automated to run whenever you need them to run. It may be easier to think of them in terms of cleaning your house. Most of us think of cleaning our house as one big job that needs to be done, but it's really a series of smaller tasks, such as dusting the furniture, vacuuming the carpet, doing the dishes, and so on. Some of these tasks need to be accomplished in succession (for example, dusting before vacuuming); others can happen at any time (for example, the dishes don't need to be done before you can wash the windows).

Any job for SQL Server works in much the same way. Take, for example, a job that creates a database. This isn't just one big job with one step to accomplish before you're finished; several steps need to be taken. The first step creates the database. The next step backs up the newly created database, because it's in a vulnerable state until it's backed up. After the database has been backed up, you can create tables in it and then, perhaps, import data into those tables from text files. Each of these tasks is a separate step that needs to be completed before you can start the next; but not all jobs are that way.

By controlling the flow of the steps, you can build error correction into your jobs. For example, in the create test database job, each step has simple logic that states, "On success, go to the next step; on failure, quit the job." If the hard disk turns out to be full, the job stops. If you create a step at the end of the job that is designed to clear up hard disk space, you can create logic that states, "If step 1 fails, go to step 5; if step 5 succeeds, go back to step 1." With the steps in place, you're ready to tell SQL Server when to start the job.

To tell SQL Server when to run a job, you need to create schedules, and you have a lot of flexibility in this regard. If a job creates a database, it wouldn't make much sense to run the job more than once, so you need to create a single schedule that activates the job after-hours. If you're creating a job that is designed to perform transaction log backups, you want a different schedule; you may, for example, want to perform these backups every two hours during the day (from 9:00 A.M. to 6:00 P.M.) and then every three hours at night (from 6:00 P.M. to 9:00 A.M.). In this instance, you need to create two schedules: one that is active from 9:00 A.M. to 6:00 P.M. and activates the job every two hours and another that is active from 6:00 P.M. to 9:00 A.M. and activates the job every three hours. If you think that's fancy, you'll love the next part.

Not only can you schedule jobs to activate at certain times of the day, but you can also schedule them to activate only on certain days of the week (for example, every Tuesday), or you can schedule them to run only on certain days of the month (for example, every third Monday). You can schedule jobs to run every time the SQL Server Agent service starts; you can even schedule them to run every time the processor becomes idle.

You can set schedules to expire after a certain amount of time, so if you know you're going to be done with a job after a few weeks, you can set it to expire—it will automatically be disabled (not deleted, just shut off).

You also can be notified about the outcome of a job. When you create a job, you can add an operator to the job that's notified on success, on failure, or on completion (regardless of whether the job failed or succeeded). This comes in handy when the job you're running is critical to your server or application.

With the ability to change the logical flow of steps, schedule jobs to run whenever you want, and have jobs notify you on completion, you can see how complex jobs can become. With this complexity in mind, it's always a good idea to sit down with a pencil and paper and plan your jobs before creating them; doing so will make your work easier in the long run.

To demonstrate this concept, you'll create a job in Exercise 18-9 that creates a new database and then backs it up.

 EXERCISE 18-9 CREATING A JOB

1. Open **SQL Server Management Studio** by selecting it from the SQL Server 2005 group under Programs on the Start menu.
2. Expand **your server** in Object Explorer, and then expand **SQL Server Agent**.
3. Right-click **Jobs**, and select **New Job**.
4. In the Name box, type **Create Test Database** (leave the rest of the boxes on this page with the default settings).
5. Go to the **Steps** page, and click the **New** button to create a new step.
6. In the Step Name box, type **Create Database**.
7. Leave Type as Transact-SQL, and enter the following code to create a database named Test on the C drive:

```
CREATE DATABASE TEST ON
PRIMARY (NAME=test_dat,
FILENAME='c:\test.mdf',
SIZE=10MB,
MAXSIZE=15,
FILEGROWTH=10%)
```

8. Click the **Parse** button to verify you entered the code correctly, and then move to the **Advanced** page.
9. On the Advanced page, verify that On Success Action is set to **Go to the Next Step** and that On Failure Action is set to **Quit the Job Reporting Failure**. Click **OK**.
10. To create the second step of the job, click the **New** button.

11. In the Name box, enter **Backup Test**.

12. Leave Type as Transact-SQL Script, and enter the following code to back up the database once it's created:

```
EXEC sp_addumpdevice 'disk', 'Test_Backup',
'c:\Test_Backup.dat' BACKUP DATABASE TEST TO Test_Backup
```

13. Click **OK** to create the step; you should now have two steps listed on the Steps page.

14. Move to the **Schedules** page, and click the **New** button to create a schedule that will instruct SQL Server when to fire the job.

15. In the Name box, type **Create and Backup Database**.

16. Select **One Time** from the Schedule Type drop-down list. Set the time to be five minutes from the time displayed in the system tray (usually, at the bottom-right corner of your screen).

17. Click **OK** to create the schedule and move to the Notifications tab.

18. On the Notifications tab, check the boxes next to **E-mail** (if you configured Database Mail earlier) and Net Send, choosing Administrator as the operator to notify. Next to each, select When the Job Completes from the list box (this will notify you no matter what the outcome of the job is).

19. Click **OK** to create the job. Wait until the time set in step 16 to verify completion. You should see a message pop up on your screen, notifying you of completion.

What just happened? You created a job with two steps; the first step created a new database named Test, and the second step backed up the database to a new backup device. This job was scheduled to run only one time and notify you of completion (whether or not it was a success).

The history of each job is stored in the MSDB database. By default, the database can store 1,000 lines of history, and each job can take up to 100 of those records.

It's not hard to see the value of creating jobs that run T-SQL code, but you can do more. Not only can you schedule T-SQL statements, but you can also schedule any active scripting language: VBScript, JScript, Perl, and so forth. This frees you from the boundaries of T-SQL, because scripting languages have features that SQL Server doesn't implement. For example, you can't directly access the file structure on the hard disk using T-SQL (to create a new text file, for example), but you can do so with a scripting language.

You can also create jobs that run on more than one server, which are called *multiserver jobs*. A multiserver job is a job that is created once, on one server, and downloaded to other servers over the network where the job is run. To create multiserver jobs, you must first designate two types of servers: a master and targets. The master server (or MSX) is where the multiserver jobs are created and managed. The target servers poll the master server at regular intervals for jobs, download those jobs, and then run them at the scheduled time.

Now that you know how to create jobs to automate tasks on SQL Server, you're ready to enhance your system even further. You'll learn about the process for creating alerts, which can automatically fix errors for you.

Creating Alerts

An alert is fired when an event (usually a problem) occurs on SQL Server; some examples are a full transaction log or incorrect syntax in a query. These alerts can then be sent to an operator so that they can be addressed. Alerts are based on one of three features: an error number, an error severity level, or a performance counter.

- All the errors that can occur in SQL Server are numbered (about 3,700 of them exist). Even with so many errors, there aren't enough. For example, suppose you want to fire an alert when a user deletes a customer from your Customers database. SQL Server doesn't have an alert with the structure of your database or your users' names; therefore, you have the ability to create new error numbers and generate an alert for such proprietary issues. You can create alerts to fire on any valid error number.

- Each error in SQL Server also has an associated severity level, stating how serious the error is. Alerts can be generated by severity level. Table 18-2 lists the common levels.

- Alerts can also be generated from performance counters. These are the same counters you would see in Performance Monitor, and they come in handy for correcting performance issues such as a full (or nearly full) transaction log. You can also generate alerts based on Windows Management Instrumentation (WMI) events. You'll see these in more detail later in this lesson. To start, you'll create some alerts using the errors and severity levels that are built into SQL Server.

Table 18-2

Severity Levels of Errors

LEVEL	DESCRIPTION
10	This is an informational message caused by mistakes in the information that was entered by the user. It isn't serious.
11–16	These are all errors that can be corrected by the user.
17	These errors are generated when the server runs out of resources, such as memory or hard disk space.
18	A nonfatal internal error has occurred. The statement will finish, and the user connection will be maintained.
19	A nonconfigurable internal limit has been reached. Any statement that causes this will be terminated.
20	A single process in the current database has suffered a problem, but the database itself is unscathed.
21	All processes in the current database are affected by the problem, but the database is undamaged.
22	The table or index that is being used is probably damaged. You should run DBCC to try to repair the object. (Alternatively, the problem may be in the data cache, which means a simple restart may suffice.)
23	This message usually means the entire database has been damaged somehow, and you should check the integrity of your hardware.
24	Your hardware has failed. You'll probably need to get new hardware and reload the database from a backup.

CREATING EVENT ALERTS BASED ON STANDARD ERRORS

Standard alerts are based on the error messages or severity levels that are built into SQL Server. To create an alert based on one of these events, the error must be written to the Windows Event log, because the SQL Server Agent reads errors from there. Once the SQL Server Agent has read the Event log and detected a new error, the agent searches through the MSDB database looking for a matching alert. When the agent finds one, the alert is fired; it can in turn notify an operator, execute a job, or both.

You'll create one of those alerts in this section—the one that fires from an error number (alerts based on severity work the same, except they're based on the severity of an error, not the number). Then, to fire that alert, you'll use the RAISERROR( ) command, which is designed specifically for the purpose of firing alerts. You'll begin in Exercise 18-10 by creating an alert based on error number 14599, which sends a Net Send notification to an operator.

→ **EXERCISE 18-10 CREATING AN ALERT FOR A STANDARD ERROR**

1. Open **SQL Server Management Studio**, expand **your server**, and then expand **SQL Server Agent**.
2. Right-click **Alerts**, and select New Alert.
3. In the Name box, enter **Number Alert**.
4. Select **SQL Server Event Alert** from the Type list.
5. Select **<all databases>** from the Database Name list.
6. Check the **Error Number** radio button, and enter **14599** in the text box.
7. On the Response page, check the **Notify Operators** box, and check the **Net Send** box next to Administrator.
8. On the Options page, check the **Net Send** box under Include Error Alert Text In, and click **OK**.

Now that you have an alert that is designed to fire whenever error number 14599 occurs, you'll generate error number 14599 using the RAISERROR( ) command in Exercise 18-11.

→ **EXERCISE 18-11 TESTING AN ALERT WITH RAISERROR( )**

1. Open a new SQL Server query by clicking the **New Query** button in SQL Server Management Studio.
2. Enter and execute the following code to fire the error (the WITH LOG option forces SQL Server to write the event to the Windows Application Event log):

   RAISERROR(14599,10,1) WITH LOG

3. When the Net Send message pops up, note the detail it gives you, including the error number, description, and additional text, and then click **OK**.

Look at this again, step by step. First you created an alert based on error number 14599. Then you configured the alert to notify an operator (you) via a Net Send message whenever the alert fires. After that, you used the RAISERROR( ) command with the WITH LOG option to make SQL Server write the error to the Windows Event log (if an error isn't written to the Event log, its alerts will never fire) to force the alert to fire and send you a notification.

Many alerts fire because of problems that can be repaired using minimal T-SQL code (a good example of this is a full transaction log). Because you would probably rather see a message that states, "There was a problem, and it's fixed" rather than "There's a problem; come and fix it yourself," you can configure alerts to execute jobs to fix the problems that caused the alerts to fire. You'll modify your existing alert to do just that in Exercise 18-12.

→ **EXERCISE 18-12 MODIFYING AN ALERT TO RUN A JOB**

1. First you need a job to run, so in Management Studio, expand **SQL Server Agent**, right-click **Jobs**, and select **New Job**.
2. Enter **Backup Test** in the Job name box.
3. On the Steps page, click the **New** button, and enter this information:
   a. Enter **Backup AdventureWorks** in the Step Name box.
   b. Enter this code in the Command box:

      BACKUP DATABASE AdventureWorks
      TO DISK='C:\AdventureWorks.bak'

   c. Click **OK**, and then click **OK** again to create the backup job.
4. To create the alert, expand **Alerts** under SQL Server Agent.

5. Right-click **Number Alert**, and select Properties.

6. Select the **Response** page.

7. Check the **Execute Job** box, and enter Backup Test in the Job name box.

8. Click OK to apply the changes.

9. To test the alert, open a new query, and execute this code:

```
RAISERROR(14599, 10, 1) WITH LOG
```

10. When the Net Send message pops up, note the message at the bottom stating that the Backup Test job has run, and then click **OK.**

Creating alerts based on built-in errors isn't so rough, is it? Even though SQL Server includes nearly 3,700 such errors, not nearly enough exist to cover all your needs. Therefore, you need to know how to create custom error messages on which to base your alerts.

CREATING EVENT ALERTS BASED ON CUSTOM ERRORS

Having 3,700 errors may seem like an awful lot, but they don't cover every situation for which you might need an alert. For example, suppose you have a sales department that allows customers to order on credit, and you need to keep track of those credit lines. Your sales managers probably want to be notified whenever a customer with good credit is deleted, or a customer's credit limit is decreased; or they may want to know when a customer's credit limit is raised to greater than $10,000. In any event, these error messages don't exist in SQL Server by default; you must create the error message before you can use it to fire an alert.

You're allowed to create as many error messages as you want in SQL Server, starting with error number 50,001 (this is the starting number for all user-defined errors). In Exercise 18-13 you'll create an alert based on a user-defined error and fire it with the RAISERROR( ) command.

 EXERCISE 18-13 CREATING AND FIRING AN ALERT BASED ON A CUSTOM ERROR

1. Open a new SQL Server query by clicking the **New Query** button in SQL Server Management Studio.

2. Enter and execute the following code to create the new error:

```
USE master
GO
EXEC sp_addmessage @msgnum=50001, @severity=10,
@msgtext=N' This is a custom error.', @with_log='TRUE'
GO
```

3. In Object Explorer, expand **your server**, and then expand **SQL Server Agent**.

4. Right-click **Alerts**, and select **New Alert**.

5. In the Name box, enter **Custom Alert**.

6. Select the **Error Number** radio button, and enter **50001** in the Error Number text box.

7. On the Response page, check the **Notify Operators** box, and check the **Net Send** box next to Administrator.

8. On the Options page, check the **Net Send** box, and click **OK** to create the alert.

9. To test the new alert, open a new query, and execute the following code (WITH LOG is not required because you specified that this event is always logged when you created it):

```
RAISERROR(50001,10,1)
```

10. When the Net Send message pops up, note the detail it gives you, and then click **OK.**

The alert you just created is good but isn't as useful as it could be. What if you need an alert to tell a manager in a customer service department that a customer has been deleted? If you employ the method used in the previous series of steps, you'll have a bland, slightly informative message stating that a customer has been deleted. If you use parameters in your error message, though, you can make the text much more meaningful.

A parameter is a placeholder for information that is supplied when the error is fired. For example, "A customer has been deleted" always displays the same static text every time the error occurs; but if you use a parameter such as "Customer %ls has been deleted," you can use the RAISERROR( ) command with a parameter that looks like this:

```
RAISERROR(50001,10,1,'Bob Smith')
```

to create the result "Customer Bob Smith has been deleted." Parameters can be more useful than static text; the parameters you can use are as follows:

- %ls and %s, for strings (such as 'Bob Smith')
- %ld and %d, for numbers

In Exercise 18-14 you'll modify your customer alert to use parameters and then fire it using the RAISERROR( ) command.

 EXERCISE 18-14 MODIFYING AN ERROR TO USE PARAMETERS

1. Open a new SQL Server query by clicking the **New Query** button in SQL Server Management Studio.

2. Enter and execute the following code to create the new error:

```
USE master
GO
EXEC sp_addmessage @msgnum=50001, @severity=10,
@msgtext=N' This is a custom error by %ls',
@with_log='TRUE',
@replace='replace'
GO
```

3. To fire the error, enter and execute the following code:

```
RAISERROR(50001,10,1,'SQL Guru')
```

4. When the Net Send message pops up, note that the description now mentions "SQL Guru," which replaced the %ls in the message text.

5. Click **OK** to close the Net Send message.

Now you have a better understanding of alerts that are based on error messages, both standard and custom, but you have more to learn. In SQL Server 2005, you can create alerts that are designed to repair problems before they even become problems; these are known as performance alerts.

CREATING PERFORMANCE ALERTS

Event alerts are great for tending to a problem after it has occurred, but not all problems can wait that long. You need to discover some problems before they cause damage to your system. You can do this using a performance alert.

Performance alerts are based on the same performance counters you may have seen in the Windows Performance Monitor program. These counters provide statistics about various components of SQL Server and then act on them. A good example of when to use such an alert is with a full transaction log error.

When a transaction log fills to 100 percent, no users can access the database, so they can't work. Some companies lose substantial amounts of money every hour their users aren't working, and it could take some time before you can bring the database to a usable state by clearing the transaction log. Therefore, you should find the problem before it happens by clearing the transaction log when it reaches a certain percentage, say 70 percent.

To see the capability of performance alerts in action, in Exercise 18-15, you'll create an alert that isn't something you're likely to see in the real world. In this exercise, you'll create an alert that fires when the transaction log for the AdventureWorks database is less than 100 percent full. On your own systems, you would want to set this to fire when the log is about 70 percent full, and then fire a job that will back up (and thus clear) the transaction log.

 EXERCISE 18-15 CREATING A PERFORMANCE ALERT

1. Open **SQL Server Management Studio**, expand **your server**, and then expand **SQL Server Agent**.
2. Right-click **Alerts**, and select **New Alert**.
3. In the Name box, enter **Performance Alert**.
4. In the Type list, select **SQL Server Performance Condition Alert**.
5. In the Object box, select **SQLServer:Databases**.
6. In the Counter box, select **Percent Log Used**.
7. In the Instance box, select **AdventureWorks**.
8. Make sure Alert If Counter is set to **Falls Below**.
9. In the Value box, type **100**.
10. Select the **Response** tab, check the **Notify Operators** box, and check the **Net Send** box next to your operator name.
11. Click **OK** to create the alert.
12. When the Net Send message pops up, note the detail that is provided, and click **OK** to close the message.

Because you probably don't want that error popping up every few minutes, you need to disable it, which you'll do in Exercise 18-16.

 EXERCISE 18-16 DISABLING AN ALERT

1. In SQL Server Management Studio, under Alerts in SQL Server Agent, double-click **Performance Alert** to expose its properties.
2. Uncheck the **Enable** box, and click **OK** to apply the changes.

Also, a new type of alert in SQL Server 2005 is sure to come in handy: WMI alerts.

CREATING WMI ALERTS

WMI is Microsoft's implementation of Web-based enterprise management, which is an industry initiative to make systems easier to manage by exposing managed components such as systems, applications, and networks as a set of common objects. SQL Server has been updated to work with WMI and respond to WMI events. But with all the techno-babble out of the way, what does this mean to you?

Using WMI alerts, you can respond to events that you couldn't even see before. For example, you can create an alert to fire when an ALTER LOGIN command is issued. This can be useful for managing security. In addition, you can create an alert to fire when a CREATE TABLE command is run so you can keep track of storage on your database. The only limitation is your imagination—and you need to know how to create WMI alerts. You'll create a WMI alert in Exercise 18-17 that fires when a DDL statement such as CREATE TABLE is issued on the AdventureWorks database.

EXERCISE 18-17 CREATING A WMI ALERT

1. Open **SQL Server Management Studio**, expand **your server**, and then expand **SQL Server Agent**.

2. Right-click **Alerts**, and select **New Alert**.

3. In the Name box, enter **WMI Alert**.

4. In the Type list, select **WMI Event Alert**.

5. Make sure Namespace is set to \\.\root\Microsoft\SqlServer\ServerEvents\ MSSQLSERVER.

6. Enter this query in the query box:

   ```
   SELECT * FROM DDL_DATABASE_LEVEL_EVENTS
   WHERE DatabaseName = 'AdventureWorks'
   ```

7. Select the **Response** tab, check the Notify Operators box, and check the **Net Send** box next to your operator name.

8. On the Options page, check the **Net Send** box under Include Alert Error Text In, and click **OK** to create the alert.

9. Open a new SQL Server query in SQL Server Management Studio by clicking the **New Query** button.

10. Enter and execute the following code to fire the new alert:

    ```
    USE AdventureWorks
    ALTER TABLE Person.Address
    ADD WMI_Test_Column VARCHAR(20) NULL
    ```

11. When the Net Send message pops up, note the detail that is provided, and click **OK** to close the message (it may take a few seconds for the message to open).

12. To return the AdventureWorks database to normal, execute the following command (note that the WMI alert will fire again):

    ```
    USE AdventureWorks
    ALTER TABLE Person.Address DROP COLUMN WMI_Test_Column
    ```

13. To disable the alert, open it, uncheck the **Enable** box, and click **OK**.

Now you've seen the importance of maintaining your database, and you've seen how to automate those administrative tasks using jobs, operators, and alerts. Wouldn't it be nice if you had a tool that would create these maintenance jobs for you? Microsoft knew you'd ask for that, so it created just such a tool: the Maintenance Plan Wizard.

Using the Maintenance Plan Wizard

You need to perform many tasks to keep your databases running at peak performance at all times. Such tasks as index reorganizations, database file size reductions, and database and transaction log backups all need to happen on a regular basis to keep your server running smoothly. The trick is that most of these tasks should happen off-hours. "No problem," you may respond. "I'll just create jobs for them." That is the proper response, but you'll have to create a number of jobs for each of your databases to keep them all up to par. To avoid all the labor of creating multiple jobs for multiple databases, use the Maintenance Plan Wizard.

You can use the wizard to create jobs for all the standard maintenance tasks discussed so far in this lesson. The best way to learn how to use it is to run it, so you'll do that in Exercise 18-18.

EXERCISE 18-18 RUNNING THE MAINTENANCE PLAN WIZARD

1. In SQL Server Management Studio, expand **Management**, right-click **Maintenance Plans**, and select **Maintenance Plan Wizard**.

2. On the first screen entitled Maintenance Plan Wizard, click the **Next** button.

3. On the Select Plan Properties page, enter **Maintenance Plan 1** in the Name box, enter a description if you'd like, select your local server, and click **Next**.

4. On the Select Maintenance Tasks page, check the boxes for all the available tasks, and click **Next**.

5. On the next page, you can set the order in which these tasks are performed. Leave the default, and click **Next**.

6. The next page allows you to select the databases you want to include in your maintenance plan. When you click the drop-down list, you're presented with several choices:

   - **All Databases:** This encompasses all databases on the server in the same plan.
   - **All System Databases:** This choice affects only the master, model, and MSDB databases.
   - **All User Databases:** This affects all databases (including AdventureWorks) except the system databases.
   - **These Databases:** This choice allows you to be selective about which databases to include in your plan.

7. For this exercise, select **All Databases**, and click **Next**.

8. On the Define Shrink Database Task page, select **All Databases**, and then click **Next**.

9. On the Define Reorganize Index Task page, select **All Databases** from the Databases drop-down list, and click **Next**.

10. The Define Rebuild Index Task page gives you a number of options for rebuilding your indexes, two of which are:

    - **Reorganize Pages with the Original Amount of Free Space:** This regenerates pages with their original fill factor.
    - **Change Free Space per Page Percentage To:** This creates a new fill factor. If you set this to 10, for example, your pages will contain 10 percent free space.

11. Again, select **All Databases**, accept the defaults, and click **Next**.

12. Next comes the Define Update Statistics Task page. Here, too, select **All Databases**, and click **Next**.

13. Next is the Define Cleanup History Task page. All the tasks performed by the maintenance plan are logged in the MSDB database. This list is referred to as the *history*, and it can become quite large if you don't "prune" it occasionally. On this page, you can set when and how the history is cleared from the database so you can keep it in check. Again, accept the defaults, and click **Next**.

14. On the Define Execute SQL Server Agent Job Task page, you can tell SQL Agent to run a job every time the maintenance plan runs. Because you have to select a job, check the **Backup Test** job, and click **Next**.

15. The next page allows you to control how full backups are performed. Select **All Databases** from the drop-down list, accept the defaults, and click **Next**.

16. The next page allows you to control how differential backups are performed. Select **All Databases** from the drop-down list, accept the defaults, and click **Next**.

17. The next page allows you to control how transaction log backups are performed. Select **All Databases** from the drop-down list, accept the defaults, and click **Next**.

18. On the Select Plan Properties page, click the **Change** button to create a schedule for the job.

19. Enter **Maintenance Plan 1 Schedule** for the schedule name, accept the rest of the defaults, and click OK to create the schedule.

20. Click **Next** to continue.

21. On the Select Report Options page, you can write a report to a text file every time the job runs, and you can e-mail the report to an operator. In this case, write a report to **C:**, and click **Next**.

22. On the next page, you can view a summary of the tasks to perform. Click **Finish** to create the maintenance plan.

23. Once SQL Server is finished creating the maintenance plan, you can click **Close**.

If you need to change the plan at any time after you've created it, all you need to do is expand **Maintenance Plans** (which is under Management), right-click the **plan**, and select **Modify**. From there you can change any aspect of your maintenance plan from the Properties dialog box. To view the plan's history, just right-click it and select **Maintenance Plan History**. This option displays everything the plan has accomplished recently.

As you can see, maintenance plans are helpful in keeping your database running smoothly and efficiently. Now you don't have to worry about staying late to run maintenance jobs or which task should be completed first. The plan does it all for you. One last tool helps automate administration, the Copy Database Wizard.

X REF

The Copy Database Wizard was introduced in Lesson 14.

■ Case Study: Automating Tasks

A company wanted to make sure all the databases on its server were running at peak efficiency at all times. The company wanted to perform the necessary maintenance after-hours, but it also wanted its DBA to be able to go home at night. So the company decided to automate the regular maintenance procedures.

This was simple and straightforward. All the staff had to do was run the Maintenance Plan Wizard for the databases. They created one maintenance plan for all the system databases (master, model, and MSDB) and one for each of the user databases. This way, if the plan failed for one database, they could get an e-mail letting them know which plan failed, and they could restart the plan for the database that failed.

After they created the maintenance plans, they found more to automate. It turns out that they also needed to download a file from one of its vendors via File Transfer Protocol (FTP) and import that file into a database every day. Initially, the DBA was downloading and importing this file manually—an unattractive prospect. If the DBA called in sick or went on vacation, the file sometimes did not get downloaded and imported, so the company's data was out of sync.

To fix this problem, they created a SQL Server Integration Services (SSIS) package that connected to the FTP server, downloaded the file, and imported it into the database. Then they created a job that runs the SSIS package every night. They configured the job to e-mail the DBA if it fails.

SKILL SUMMARY

IN THIS LESSON YOU LEARNED:

This lesson covered a lot of ground, but what you learned here will save you a lot of time and effort in server administration and reporting. First you learned about required maintenance—that you need to perform many tasks on your server to keep it running smoothly and efficiently. You must back up databases and transaction logs, reorganize index and data pages inside the database files, check for database integrity regularly, and keep statistics up to date.

You also learned that automation includes three main components: operators, jobs, and alerts. Operators are the individuals who are notified when a problem needs attention; they can be notified via e-mail, pager, or Net Send messages. Jobs are series of tasks and schedules that can be automated to activate at any time; they can include T-SQL code, command executive code, or scripting language code.

After that, you investigated mail support. To configure mail support, you learned you first need create a mailhost database and add a profile and an account. When these are in place, you can start sending e-mail. If you want to send mail to operators, you need to make MSDB a mailhost database.

Next you learned how to create operators and configure them to receive e-mail, pager, or Net Send messages. You can also configure them to be available only at certain times of the day by setting their availability.

In addition, you learned how to create jobs. You can configure jobs to run any type of code at any time, and you can configure them to inform an operator when they complete, when they succeed, or when they fail.

Next you set alerts, which are used to notify an operator when an error has occurred. Not all errors fire an event, though—only those that are written to the Windows Event log and have an alert configured will fire an alert that notifies someone. You learned how to create alerts that are based on the standard error messages that come with SQL Server, as well as how to create your own custom error messages that can be used for any purpose. We then discussed how to create and use performance alerts to stop problems before they start. You also learned how to create WMI alerts so you can be notified when server events occur, such as CREATE TABLE or other DDL statements.

After learning the importance of periodic maintenance and how to schedule jobs to run automatically, you learned how to tie all of that together by using the Maintenance Plan Wizard to automate these processes for you.

For the certification examination:

- Know how to find and fix index fragmentation. When users insert data in a table, SQL Server must make room for the new data in the table and any associated indexes. When an index page gets too full, SQL Server moves half of the data to a new page to make room for more data on the existing page. This is called a page split; when it occurs, the pages are no longer contiguous, and a condition called fragmentation occurs. You can use sys.DM_DB_ INDEX_PHYSICAL_STATS to find the amount of fragmentation on your indexes. If your index is less than 30 percent fragmented, you can reorganize it; anything higher than 30 percent requires a rebuild to bring the index back into shape.

- Know how to update statistics. SQL Server uses statistics to figure out which index, if any, you can use to speed up a SELECT query. If you created an index and told SQL Server not to automatically recompute statistics for you, then you will need to update them yourself using the UPDATE STATISTICS command.

- Know how to repair databases. Because databases are just files on the hard disk, they can become corrupted on occasion. You need to know how to use DBCC CHECKDB to find and fix imperfections in your databases.

- Understand Database Mail. New to SQL Server 2005, Database Mail is used for sending e-mail from SQL Server. This is especially useful for sending notifications for alerts and errors. Make sure you know how to set up a mailhost database and configure the SQL Server Agent to use a profile to send mail.

- Understand jobs, operators, and alerts. SQL Server automation is built on three primary features. Jobs are a series of steps that can be run on a set schedule. Operators are people or groups of people to be notified by e-mail, pager, or Net Send message when something happens on the server. Alerts are fired when something happens on the system, such as an error. Alerts can notify an operator and automatically run a job when fired.

- Know the Maintenance Plan Wizard and Copy Database Wizard. You can automate all the maintenance tasks discussed in this lesson by using the Maintenance Plan Wizard. Just run the wizard, and it will create all the appropriate jobs for you and then run them on a set schedule. The Copy Database Wizard is just as handy. When a developer needs to copy a database from development to production, for instance, or you need to copy a database from a satellite office to the home office, you can use this wizard to simplify the process.

■ Knowledge Assessment

Multiple Choice

Circle the letter or letters that correspond to the best answer or answers.

1. You have created an operator with an e-mail address and a Net Send address. You have also created several alerts for which the new operator should be notified. When any of the alerts fire, the operator gets the e-mail but never receives the Net Send message. What should you do to fix this?
   a. Start the Messenger service on the operator's computer.
   b. Start the alerter service on the operator's computer.
   c. Reinstall the SQL Server Agent on the SQL Server.
   d. Reconfigure the SQL Server Agent service to log in using the Network Service account.

2. You are performing maintenance on one of your databases, so you run this query against the database to find the index fragmentation:

   ```
   USE AdventureWorks;

   SELECT INDEX_ID, AVG_FRAGMENTATION_IN_PERCENT FROM
   sys.dm_db_index_physical_stats (db_id(),
   object_id('sales.SalesOrderDetail'), 1, null,
   'LIMITED');
   ```

   You receive this result:

   ```
   INDEX_ID AVG_FRAGMENTATION_IN_PERCENT 1 35.17
   ```

   Assuming that index 1 is named PK_IDX_Sales with a fill factor of 80 percent, what should you do to optimize this index?
   a. `ALTER INDEX ALL ON Sales.SalesOrderDetail REBUILD WITH (FILLFACTOR = 80, ONLINE = ON, STATISTICS_NORECOMPUTE = ON)`
   b. `ALTER INDEX PK_IDX_Sales ON Sales.SalesOrderDetail REORGANIZE`
   c. `ALTER INDEX PK_IDX_Sales ON Sales.SalesOrderDetail REBUILD WITH (FILLFACTOR = 80, ONLINE = ON, STATISTICS_NORECOMPUTE = ON)`
   d. `ALTER INDEX ALL ON Sales.SalesOrderDetail REORGANIZE`

3. You have just had a power surge at your office, and you are concerned that one of your databases may have been corrupted on the hard disk when the power surged. What can you run to find out whether the database's physical structure is still intact?
   a. `DBCC CHECKDB WITH ESTIMATEONLY`
   b. `DBCC CHECKDB WITH PHYSICAL_ONLY`
   c. `DBCC CHECKDB WITH DATA_PURITY`
   d. `DBCC CHECKDB WITH STRUCTURE_ONLY`

4. You want to be able to send e-mail to operators when alerts are fired or when a job fails. Which database needs to be a mailhost to allow this?
   a. Master
   b. Model
   c. MSDB
   d. Tempdb

5. Your customer service manager wants to be notified whenever a customer service representative adjusts a customer's credit limit to any amount greater than $10,000. How can you create an alert that will fire when a customer service representative adjusts a credit limit?

   a. `EXEC sp_addmessage @msgnum=50001, @severity=10, @msgtext=N'Credit increased', @with_log='TRUE'`

   b. `EXEC sp_addmessage @msgnum=50001, @severity=10, @msgtext=N' Credit increased ', @with_log='FALSE'`

   c. `EXEC sp_addmessage @msgnum=50001, @severity=19, @msgtext=N' Credit increased ', @with_log='TRUE'`

   d. `EXEC sp_addmessage @msgnum=50001, @severity=19, @msgtext=N' Credit increased ', @with_log='TRUE'`

6. You have a production database named Sales. As an administrator, it is your job to make sure all the tables in your production database do not get modified without a written request on file. You need to be notified whenever a table is modified in each database. What can you do?

   a. Create a performance alert based on the SQLServer:ObjectsModified counter, and set the threshold to any value greater than 1.

   b. Create a WMI alert with this query:

   ```
   SELECT * FROM DDL_DATABASE_LEVEL_EVENTS WHERE
   DatabaseName = 'Sales'
   ```

   c. Create a standard alert based on error number 14599.

   d. Create a custom error that fires an alert.

7. You have created several alerts and operators on your server. Each of your operators is configured to receive e-mail and Net Send messages. When the alerts occur, though, the operators are not receiving any notifications. What can you do to fix this?

   a. Make sure the SQL Server Agent service is running.
   b. Make sure the SQL Server Agent service is using a valid mail profile.
   c. Make sure the SQL Server Agent service is logging in as the Network Service account.
   d. Make sure the SQL Server Agent service is configured to log alerts to the Event log.

8. You are going to perform some standard maintenance on one of your servers that will take a couple of hours to complete. During this time, you have an alert based on a performance counter that will fire every few minutes until the maintenance is complete. You do not want this to happen, so what can you do to stop the alert from firing?

   a. Disable the custom error.
   b. Disable the alert.
   c. Delete the error, and re-create it when you are done with the maintenance.
   d. Delete the alert, and re-create it when you are done with the maintenance.

9. You are creating a job that copies a file from an FTP server and then imports the data in the file into a table in a database. You do not want the job to import old data if the FTP download fails, so what should you do?

   a. Make step 1 of the job the FTP download. Make step 2 of the job the import task. Have step 1 quit the job on failure.

   b. Make step 1 of the job the FTP download. Make step 2 of the job the import task. Have step 1 retry three times at an interval of five minutes. After the three retries, continue to step 2.

c. Make step 1 of the job the FTP download. Make step 2 of the job the import task. Make step 3 an ActiveX scripting task that creates a blank file. Have step 1 go to step 3 on failure; have step 3 go to step 2 on completion.

d. Make step 1 of the job the FTP download. Make step 2 of the job the import task. Have step 2 quit the job on failure.

10. You are performing maintenance on one of your databases, so you run the following query against the database to find the index fragmentation:

```
USE AdventureWorks;

SELECT INDEX_ID, AVG_FRAGMENTATION_IN_PERCENT FROM
sys.dm_db_index_physical_stats (db_id(),
object_id('Sales.SalesOrderDetail'), 1, null,
'LIMITED');
```

You receive this result:

```
INDEX_ID AVG_FRAGMENTATION_IN_PERCENT 1 29.36
```

Assuming that index 1 is named PK_IDX_Sales with a fill factor of 80 percent, what should you do to optimize this index?

a. `alter index all on Sales.SalesOrderDetail rebuild`
   `with fillfactor = 80, online = on,`
   `statistics_norecompute = on)`

b. `alter index pk_idx_Sales on Sales.SalesOrderDetail`
   `reorganize`

c. `alter index pk_idx_Sales on Sales.SalesOrderDetail`
   `rebuild with (fillfactor = 80, online = on,`
   `statistics_norecompute = on)`

11. One of the developers at your company has just completed development on a database and is ready to move it into production. What is the simplest way to copy the database from development to production?

a. Use the Maintenance Plan Wizard to copy the database from the development server to the production server.

b. Create a job that copies the database using T-SQL code.

c. Use the Copy Database Wizard to copy the database from the development server to the production server.

d. Use DBCC CHECKDB WITH COPY_ONLY to copy the database from the development server to the production server.

12. Your accounting database processes thousands of transactions per day, and you want to make sure it is always online. You need to be alerted whenever the log file reaches 75 percent full. What should you do?

a. Create a WMI alert with this query:

```
SELECT Percent_Log_Used FROM DDL_TLOG_LEVEL_EVENTS
WHERE DatabaseName = 'Sales'
```

b. Create a performance alert based on the Percent Log Used counter of the SQLServer: Databases object.

c. Create a job that runs the sp_spaceused stored procedure every 15 minutes.

d. Create a job that runs the DBCC CHECKLOG function every 15 minutes.

13. You have created a user-defined message that says, "Please call the help desk." It is numbered 50001, and it is configured to post to the Windows Application log. How can you fire the alert that is based on this custom error?

a. `ALERT(50001)`

b. `ALERT(50001, 10, 1)`

c. `RAISERROR (50001, 10, 1)`

d. `RAISERROR (50001, 10, 1) WITH LOG`

14. You want to make sure someone is always notified of errors when they occur. You have many operators who are all available at different times of the day throughout the week, but you want to make certain no time is left uncovered. What should you do?
    a. Make one of your operators available at all times.
    b. Create a last-resort operator.
    c. Create a fail-safe operator.
    d. Create an off-hours operator.

15. You have created an operator with an e-mail address and a Net Send address. You have also created several alerts for which the new operator should be notified. When any of the alerts fire, the operator gets the Net Send messages but never receives e-mails. You have verified that the MSDB database is a mailhost. What should you do to fix this?
    a. Make sure Outlook is installed on the server.
    b. Start the Messenger service on the server.
    c. Reconfigure the SQL Server Agent service to log in using the Network Service account.
    d. Make sure the SQL Server Agent service is configured to use a valid mail profile.

16. You had a systems failure over the weekend; everything seemed to come back up without major issues. However, your users are now complaining they are seeing some strange values in some of the queries they run against a database that was upgraded from SQL Server 2000. It looks like some of the columns now contain larger numbers than expected. What should you run to fix this?
    a. DBCC CHECKDB WITH ESTIMATEONLY
    b. DBCC CHECKDB WITH PHYSICAL_ONLY
    c. DBCC CHECKDB WITH DATA_PURITY
    d. DBCC CHECKDB WITH REPAIR_DATA

17. You have just bought a new server, and you need to start moving your databases from the old server to the new server. You cannot take the databases offline at any time because they are always in use. How can you move the databases to the new server while keeping them available?
    a. Use the Maintenance Plan Wizard to copy the databases.
    b. Use the Copy Database Wizard to copy the databases, and specify the SQL Management Object method for copying.
    c. Use the Copy Database Wizard to copy the databases, and specify the attach/detach method for copying.
    d. Run DBCC CHECKDB WITH COPY_ONLINE to copy the database.

18. You have a BugTracking database that your developers use to keep track of bugs in their custom software. Your development manager wants to be notified whenever a developer deletes a bug from the database. How can you create an error message that will fire an alert when a developer deletes a bug?
    a. EXEC sp_addmessage @msgnum=14599, @severity=10, @msgtext=N'Bug deleted', @with_log='TRUE'
    b. EXEC sp_addmessage @msgnum=14599, @severity=10, @msgtext=N'Bug deleted', @with_log='FALSE'
    c. EXEC sp_addmessage @msgnum=50001, @severity=10, @msgtext=N'Bug deleted', @with_log='TRUE'
    d. EXEC sp_addmessage @msgnum=50001, @severity=10, @msgtext=N'Bug deleted', @with_log='TRUE'

19. Your accounting manager wants to know whenever a record is deleted from the General Ledger database. She also needs to know the username of the person who deleted the record. How can you create an error message that will fire this alert?
    a. EXEC sp_addmessage @msgnum=50001, @severity=10, @msgtext=N'GL Record deleted by %d', @with_log='TRUE'
    b. EXEC sp_addmessage @msgnum=50001, @severity=10, @msgtext=N'GL Record deleted by %s', @with_log='TRUE'

    c. EXEC sp_addmessage @msgnum=50001, @severity=10,
        @msgtext=N'GL Record deleted by @d', @with_log='TRUE'

    d. EXEC sp_addmessage @msgnum=50001, @severity=10,
        @msgtext=N'GL Record deleted by @s', @with_log='TRUE'

20. You have an index named idx_SalesOrderDetail on the SalesOrderDetail table of your Sales database. The table is not used heavily, so there are not many changes on it throughout the day. Because it is so lightly used, you decided to save system resources by not having SQL Server automatically update the index statistics. What do you need to do to bring the index up to date?

    a. Run this: UPDATE STATISTICS Sales.SalesOrderDetail

    b. Run this: ALTER INDEX idx_SalesOrderDetail ON
        Sales.SalesOrderDetail REORGANIZE

    c. Run this: ALTER INDEX idx_SalesOrderDetail ON
        Sales.SalesOrderDetail UPDATE_STATS

    d. Run this: ALTER INDEX idx_SalesOrderDetail ON
        Sales.SalesOrderDetail REBUILD WITH (FILLFACTOR = 80,
        ONLINE = ON, STATISTICS_NORECOMPUTE = ON)

■ Case Scenarios

Scenario 18-1: Creating a Job

As a group, discuss how, and then actually create a job to back up master and then send a notification to an operator. What happens? What are the steps involved?

Monitoring and Optimizing SQL Server

LESSON SKILL MATRIX

TECHNOLOGY SKILL	70-431 EXAM OBJECTIVE
Gather performance and optimization data by using the SQL Server Profiler.	Foundational
Start a new trace.	Foundational
Save the trace logs.	Foundational
Configure SQL Server Profiler trace properties.	Foundational
Configure a System Monitor counter log.	Foundational
Correlate a SQL Server Profiler trace with System Monitor log data.	Foundational
Gather performance and optimization data by using the Database Engine Tuning Advisor.	Foundational
Build a workload file by using the SQL Server Profiler.	Foundational
Tune a workload file by using the Database Engine Tuning Advisor.	Foundational
Save recommended indexes.	Foundational
Monitor and resolve blocks and deadlocks.	Foundational
Configure SQL Server Profiler trace properties.	Foundational
Diagnose and resolve database server errors.	Foundational
Connect to a nonresponsive server by using the dedicated administrator connection (DAC).	Foundational
Review SQL Server startup logs.	Foundational
Review error messages in event logs.	Foundational
Monitor SQL Server Agent job history.	Foundational
Identify the cause of a failure.	Foundational
Identify outcome details.	Foundational
Find out when a job last ran.	Foundational

KEY TERMS

alert: A user-defined response to a SQL Server event. Alerts can either run a defined task or they can send an e-mail or pager message to a specified operator.

deadlock: A situation when two users, each having a lock on one piece of data, attempt to acquire a lock on the other's piece. Each user would wait indefinitely for the other to release the lock unless one of the user

processes is terminated. SQL Server detects deadlocks and terminates the least costly process.

error log: A text file that records system information.

log file: A file or set of files that contain records of the modifications made in a database.

trace file: A file used by SQL Server Profiler to record monitored events.

■ Monitoring and Optimizing Activities

THE BOTTOM LINE

It is your job to make sure the databases run smoothly, and that everything gets done efficiently. You will continue to tackle bottlenecks in this lesson, which presents more tools for maintaining data integrity and operating system efficiencies. Stay on top of all situations so little problems don't blossom into fire drills.

Using System Monitor

CERTIFICATION READY?
Test questions will pose a scenario and then ask you which of several utilities best resolves the problem even when several will do the job.

To ensure your company functions properly, you need to make certain the foundation of the company is doing its job. You need a management group that works well together and gets tasks done—a group where each member pulls his or her share of the load.

With SQL Server, this management group is the computer system itself. SQL Server cannot function properly if it does not have available system resources, such as ample memory, adequate processor power, fast disks, and a reliable network subsystem. If these systems do not work together, the overall system will not function properly. For example, if the memory is being overused, the disk subsystem will slow down, because the memory has to write to the pagefile (which is on the disk) far too often. To keep such things from happening, you need to get reports from the subsystems; you can do this using System Monitor.

System Monitor comes with Windows and is located in the Administrative Tools section of the Start menu (the tool is labeled "Performance"). Four views are available for your use:

Graph: This view displays a graph of system performance. As values change, the graph will spike or dip accordingly.

Report: The report view looks like what you might get on a piece of paper, except that the values here change with system use.

Alert: With *alert* view, you can tell System Monitor to warn you when something bad is looming on the horizon, perhaps when CPU use is almost—but not quite yet—too high. This type of warning gives you time to fix potential problems before they become actual problems.

Log: The log view is for record keeping. With log view, you can monitor your system over a time period and view the information later, as opposed to viewing it in realtime (the default).

With each of these views, you monitor objects and counters. An object is a part of the system, such as the processor or the physical memory. A counter displays the statistical information about how much that object is being used. For example, the % Processor Time counter under the Processor object will tell you how much time your processor spends working. Table 19-1 lists common counters and their recommended values.

Table 19-1

Common Counters and Values in System Monitor

Object	Counter	Recommended Value	Use	Recommendations
Processor	% Processor Time	Less than 75%	The amount of time the processor spends working	If this is too high, you should offload some processes to another server, or purchase a multiprocessor machine.
Memory	Pages/Sec	Fewer than 5	The number of times per second that data had to be moved from RAM to disk, and vice versa	If this is too high, it means your system is compensating for a lack of RAM by paging to disk. You should add more RAM if this is too high.
Memory	Available Bytes	More than 4 MB	The amount of physical RAM available	This number should be low, because Windows uses as much RAM as it can grab for file cache.
Memory	Committed Bytes	Less than physical RAM	The amount of RAM committed to use	If this is higher than the physical RAM, then you should consider adding more RAM.
PhysicalDisk	% Disk Time	Less than 50%	The amount of time the disk is busy reading or writing	If this is higher than 50%, you should consider offloading some processes to another machine or adding disks to your array.
Network Segment	% Network Utilization	Less than 30%	The amount of network bandwidth being used	If this is too high, you should consider segregating your network with a router or bridge to decrease broadcast traffic.

To see the Network Segment: % Network Utilization, you must install the Network Monitor Tools. Go to **Add/Remove Programs** in the Control Panel. Click on **Add/ Remove Windows Components.** Select **Management and Monitoring Tools,** click on **Details** and put a checkmark in front of **Network Monitor Tools**. Finish the install by following the on-screen instructions.

Now you'll get some practice with System Monitor in Exercise 19-1.

 EXERCISE 19-1 WORKING WITH SYSTEM MONITOR

1. Log on to **Windows** as **Administrator.**
2. From the Start menu, select **Programs → Administrative Tools → Performance.** Notice that the graph is already populated with counters.
3. On the toolbar, click the **Add** button (it looks like a plus sign) to open the Add Counters dialog box.
4. In the Performance Object box, select **Memory.**
5. In the Select Counters from List box, select **Available Bytes,** and click **Add.**
6. Click **Close,** and notice the graph being created on the screen.
7. Press **Ctrl+H,** and notice the current counter turns white. This makes the chart easier to read.
8. On the toolbar, click the **View Report** button (it looks like a sheet of paper), and notice how the same data appears in report view.

9. In the left pane, expand **Performance Logs and Alerts**, right-click **Alerts**, and select **New Alert Settings.**

10. Enter **Test Alert** in the Name box, and click **OK.**

11. In the Alert Settings dialog box, enter **Test Alert** in the Comment field.

12. Click **Add.**

13. Select the **Processor** object and the **% Processor Time** counter, and click **Add;** then click **Close.**

14. Select **Under** from the Alert When Value Is drop-down list, enter **70** for Limit, and click **OK.** This will generate an alert if the processor is not busy 70 percent of the time. In the real world, you would set this to more than 70 percent, thus warning you just before it becomes a serious problem.

15. Click **OK** to create the alert.

16. To view the alerts, open **Event Viewer,** and look for them in the Application log, then double-click the **event** to view its properties.

17. Watch the alerts generated for a short time, then select the **alert,** and finally press the **Delete** key. If asked whether you want to continue deleting a running alert; click **OK.**

18. Exit **System Monitor** and **Event Viewer.**

You can monitor SQL Server as well as Windows objects using System Monitor, because SQL Server provides its own objects and counters. The process for monitoring SQL Server is the same as it is with Windows—you just add different objects and counters. Table 19-2 describes the SQL Server counters you will be using most often.

Each machine is different. You will have to collect for yourself a baseline of data to compare against.

Table 19-2

Most Frequently Used SQL Server System Monitor Counters

OBJECT	COUNTER	USE	RECOMMENDATIONS
SQLServer: Buffer Manager	Buffer Cache Hit Ratio	How much data is being retrieved from cache instead of disk.	This should be in the high 90s. If it is too low, you may need to add more RAM to your system.
SQLServer: Buffer Manager	Page Reads/Sec	Number of data pages that are read from disk each second.	This should be as low as possible.
SQLServer: Buffer Manager	Page Writes/Sec	Number of data pages that are written to disk each second.	This should be as low as possible.
SQLServer: General Statistics	User Connections	Number of user connections. Each of these connections will take some RAM.	Use this to predict how much memory you will need for your system when you add new users.
SQLServer: Memory Manager	Total Server Memory (KB)	Total amount of memory that SQL Server has been dynamically assigned.	Use this when determining whether you have enough RAM to add more processes, such as replication, to a SQL Server.
SQLServer: SQL Statistics	SQL Compilations/Sec	Number of compiles per second.	This should be as high as possible.

Now that the system resources are working together, you need to make sure SQL Server is working the way you want it to work. To monitor SQL Server, you need to know how to use SQL Server Profiler.

Monitoring with SQL Profiler

When running a company, once you have the management team working in harmony, you can focus your attention on the rest of the workforce. As in any company, the employees need to be monitored to make sure they are doing their fair share of work. In this analogy, the queries that are run on SQL Server would be the employees that need to be monitored, and Profiler is the tool you need to do the work.

Profiler allows you to monitor and record what is happening inside the database engine. This is accomplished by performing a trace, which is a record of data that has been captured about events. Traces are stored in a table, a trace *log file*, or both, and they can be either shared (viewable by everyone) or private (viewable only by the owner).

The actions you will be monitoring, called events, are anything that happens to the database engine, such as a failed login or a completed query. These events are logically grouped into event classes in Profiler so that they will be easier for you to find and use. Some of these events are useful for maintaining security, and some are useful for troubleshooting problems, but most of these events are used for monitoring and optimizing. The following event categories are available:

Cursors: A cursor is an object that is used to work with multiple rows of data by moving through them one row at a time. This event class monitors events that are generated by cursor usage.

Database: This is a collection of events that monitor automatic changes in the size of data and log files.

Errors and Warnings: The events in this class monitor errors and warnings, such as a failed login or a syntax error.

Locks: When users access data, that data is locked so other users cannot modify data someone else is reading. This class of events monitors the locks placed on your data.

Objects: Monitor this class of events to see when objects (such as tables, views, or indexes) are opened, closed, or modified in some way.

Performance: This collection of events displays Showplan event classes as well as event classes produced by data manipulation operators.

Scans: Tables and indexes can be scanned, which means SQL Server must read through every single entry in the object to find the data you are looking for. The events in this class monitor these object scans.

Security Audit: These events monitor security. Such things as failed logins, password changes, and role changes are contained in this category.

Server: This category contains classes that monitor server control and memory change events.

Sessions: When a user connects to SQL Server, that user is said to have "started a session" with the server. This event class monitors user sessions.

Stored Procedures: A stored procedure is a collection of T-SQL code that is stored on the server, ready to be executed. This event class monitors events that are triggered by the use of stored procedures.

Transactions: A transaction is a group of T-SQL commands that are viewed as a unit, meaning either they must all be applied to the database together or all of them fail. This event class monitors SQL Server transactions (including anything that happens to a transaction log where transactions are recorded) as well as transactions that go through the DTC.

TSQL: This event class monitors any T-SQL commands that are passed from the client to the database server.

User Configurable: If the other events in Profiler do not meet your needs, you can create your own event to monitor with these user-configurable events. This is especially handy for custom applications you may create.

OLEDB: OLEDB is an interface that developers can use to connect to SQL Server. This event class monitors OLEDB-specific events.

Broker Service: Broker, a new component in SQL Server 2005, provides asynchronous message queuing and delivery. The Broker event class monitors events generated by the Service Broker.

Full Text: Full-text indexing gives you flexibility in querying SQL Server by letting you search for phrases, word variations, weighted results, and so on. These indexes are controlled by a separate service (msftesql.exe). Using this event class, you can monitor events generated by the full-text index service and its indexes.

Deprecation: Over the years, many commands have been deprecated in SQL Server. One such example is the DUMP statement, which was used in earlier versions of SQL Server to back up databases and logs but is no longer a valid command. The Deprecation event class helps you track down procedures and programs that are using deprecated functions and commands so you can update them.

Progress Report: This class of events helps you monitor the progress of long-running commands, such as online index operations.

When you create a trace, it is based on a trace template. A template is a predefined trace definition that can be used to create a trace out of the box, or you can modify it to fit your needs. You can choose from several templates:

Blank: This template has no configuration at all. It is a blank slate that you can use to create a completely unique trace definition.

SP_Counts: You can use this template to see how many stored procedures are started, which database ID they are called from, and which server process ID (SPID) called the stored procedure.

Standard: This template records logins and logouts, existing connections (at the time of the trace), completed remote procedure calls (RPCs), and completed T-SQL batches.

TSQL: This records the same events as the Standard template except that this template displays only the EventClass, TextData, SPID, and StartTime data columns. This is useful for tracking which queries are being run, when they are being run, and who is running them.

TSQL_Duration: This tracks which queries are being executed and how long those queries take. This is especially useful for finding queries and stored procedures with poor performance.

TSQL_Grouped: You can use this template to discover which applications are being used to connect to SQL Server and who is using those applications. This template tracks queries that are being run and groups them by application name, then Windows username, then SQL Server username, and then process ID.

TSQL_Replay: *Trace files* can be replayed against a server, meaning that every action in a trace file can be executed as if it were coming from a user. This template is especially useful for replaying against a server to find the cause of a crash or some other unexpected event.

TSQL_SPs: You can use this template to find out who is running stored procedures and what those stored procedures do.

Tuning: You can use this specifically for creating a trace file for the Database Tuning Advisor, which we will discuss later in this lesson.

In Exercise 19-2, you'll get some hands-on experience with Profiler by creating a trace that monitors the opening and closing of objects.

When the Server Processes Trace Data box is checked, SQL Server processes the trace. This can slow server performance, but no events are missed. If the box is unchecked, the client processes the trace data. This results in faster performance, but some events may be missed under a heavy server load.

 EXERCISE 19-2 CREATING A TRACE WITH PROFILER

1. From the Start menu, go to **Programs** → **Microsoft SQL Server 2005** → **Performance Tools** → **SQL Server Profiler.**

2. From the File menu, select **New Trace.**

3. Connect to your **default server instance** using the proper authentication; this opens the Trace Properties dialog box.

4. In the Trace Name box, type **Monitor.**

5. Use the TSQL_Replay template (we'll replay this later).

6. Check the **Save to File** box, and click **Save** to accept the default name and location. Leave the Enable File Rollover box checked and the Server Processes Trace Data box unchecked.

7. Check the **Save to Table** box, log on to your **default server instance**, and fill in the following:

   Database: AdventureWorks

   Owner: dbo

   Table: Monitor

8. Click the **Events Selection** tab, and check the **Show All Events** box toward the bottom of the tab.

9. In the Events grid, expand **Security Audit** (if it is not already expanded), and check the box to the left of Audit Schema Object Access Event. This will monitor the opening and closing of objects, such as tables.

10. Click **Run** to start the trace.

11. Leave Profiler running, and open a new **SQL Server query** in Management Studio.

12. Execute the following query:

    USE AdventureWorks

    SELECT * FROM Person.Contact

13. Switch to **Profiler**, and click the **Pause** button (double blue lines). In the Profiler, notice the amount of data that was collected.

14. Close **Profiler** and **Management Studio.**

If you look toward the end of the results in the trace, you should see the SELECT query you executed in step 12 in the previous exercise. Once a trace has been recorded, everything in the trace can be executed as if it were coming from a user. This is a process called *replaying*.

REPLAYING A TRACE FILE

When a detective is trying to solve a crime, one of the first steps is to re-create the action as closely as possible. This helps find specific clues that cannot be found any other way. In the same way, when something bad happens to SQL Server (such as a server crash), you need to be able to re-create the circumstances that led up to the event as closely as possible, which you can do with Profiler by replaying a trace.

Loading your saved traces into Profiler allows you to replay them against the server and, in this way, figure out exactly where the problem occurred. An especially nice touch is that you don't have to play the whole trace all at once; you can take it step by step to see exactly where the problem lies, and you can even play the saved traces against a different server so you don't crash your production server in the process. You'll try this in Exercise 19-3.

EXERCISE 19-3 REPLAYING A TRACE

1. Open **Profiler;** from the File menu, select **Open and Trace File.**
2. In the Open File dialog box, select **Monitor.trc**, and click **OK.**
3. On the toolbar in the trace window, click the **Execute One Step** button (a blue arrow pointing to a gray line). This will execute a single step at a time.
4. Log on to your default instance of SQL Server.
5. In the Replay dialog box that opens, you can choose to create an output file-name, which will store all error messages and output for later review. Leave this blank.
6. Under Replay Options, you can opt to enable debugging by replaying events in the order they were recorded, or disable debugging by replaying multiple events at the same time. Select the option to **Replay events in the order they were traced. This option enables debugging.** Click **OK.**
7. Scroll down, and select the first line you find that contains SQL:BatchCompleted.
8. On the toolbar, click the **Run to Cursor** button (an arrow pointing to double braces). This will execute all steps between the current position and the event you have selected.
9. Click the **Start Execution** button (a yellow arrow) to finish replaying the trace.
10. Close **Profiler.**

Profiler is a wonderful tool for monitoring database activity and reporting problems, but that is not all it can do. Profiler comes with yet another wizard that will help you even further improve the performance of your queries—the Database Engine Tuning Advisor.

Using the Database Engine Tuning Advisor

If one musical instrument in an orchestra is out of tune, the entire symphony sounds bad, and the performance is ruined. In the same way, if even one SQL Server database were out of tune, it could slow down the entire system. Perhaps an index was created using the wrong columns, or maybe users have started querying different data over time, which would require the creation of new indexes. If any of this is true, your databases need tuning. To do that, you need to use the Database Engine Tuning Advisor.

Before you can run the Database Engine Tuning Advisor, you need to create a workload. You do this by running and saving a trace in Profiler (usually by creating a trace with the Tuning template). It is best to get this workload during times of peak database activity to make sure you give the advisor an accurate load. First you need to create a workload file to use with the advisor, which you'll do in Exercise 19-4.

EXERCISE 19-4 CREATING A WORKLOAD FILE

1. First you need to remove the indexes from the test table, so open **Management Studio** and expand **Databases → AdventureWorks → Tables.**
2. Right-click **Monitor**, and select **Modify.**
3. Right-click the **key icon** by the RowNumber column, and select **Remove Primary Key.**
4. Click the **Save** button on the toolbar to remove the indexes from the table.
5. To stop any excess traffic on the server, right-click **SQL Server Agent** in Object Explorer, and select **Stop.**
6. From the Start menu, go to **Programs → Microsoft SQL Server 2005 → Performance Tools → Profiler.**
7. From the File menu, select **New Trace** to open the Trace Properties dialog box.

8. Connect to your **default server instance** using the proper authentication.

9. In the Trace Name box, type **Tuning**.

10. Use the **Tuning** template.

11. Check the **Save to File** box, and click **Save** to accept the default name and location. Leave the Enable File Rollover box checked and the Server Processes Trace Data box unchecked.

12. Click **Run** to start the trace.

13. Leave Profiler running, and open a new **SQL Server query** in Management Studio.

14. Execute the following query:

```
USE AdventureWorks
SELECT textdata FROM monitor
WHERE DatabaseName = 'AdventureWorks'
```

15. Switch to **Profiler,** click the **Stop** button (red box), and then close **Profiler.**

Exercise 19-5 will show you how to run the Database Engine Tuning Advisor using the workload file you just created.

➔ EXERCISE 19-5 USING THE DATABASE ENGINE TUNING ADVISOR

1. From the Start menu, go to **Programs → Microsoft SQL Server 2005 → Performance Tools → Database Engine Tuning Advisor.**

2. Connect to **your server** using the appropriate authentication method. This will create a new session in the advisor.

3. In the Session Name box, enter **Tuning Session.**

4. In the Workload section, click the **browse** button (it looks like a pair of binoculars), and locate the **Tuning.trc** trace file created earlier.

5. In the databases and tables grid, check the box next to AdventureWorks.

6. Switch to the **Tuning Options** tab. From here you can instruct the advisor which physical changes to make to the database; specifically, you can have the advisor create new indexes (clustered and nonclustered) and partition the database.

7. Leave the Limit Tuning Time option checked and set for the default time; this prevents the advisor from taking too many system resources.

8. Leave the default options for Physical Design Structures (PDS) Options to Use in Database, Partitioning Strategy to Employ, and Physical Design Structures (PDS) to Keep in Database.

9. Click the Advanced Options button. From here you can set these options:

   • Define Max. Space for Recommendations (MB) will set the maximum amount of space used by recommended physical performance structures.

   • All Recommendations Are Offline will generate recommendations that may require you to take the database offline to implement the change.

   • Generate Online Recommendations Where Possible will return online recommendations even if a faster offline method is possible. If there is no online method, then an offline method is recommended.

   • Generate Only Online Recommendations will return only online recommendations.

10. Click **Cancel** to return to the advisor.

11. Click the **Start Analysis** button on the toolbar.

12. You should see a progress status screen during the analysis phase.

13. After analysis is complete, you will be taken to the Recommendations screen; you should see a recommendation for creating an index on the monitor table.

14. You can also check the Reports screen for more detailed information on the analysis process.

15. To apply these recommendations, select **Apply Recommendations** from the Actions menu.

16. On the dialog box that pops up, click **Apply Now,** and click **OK.**

17. When the index has been created, click **Close.**

18. Close the **Database Engine Tuning Advisor.**

Troubleshooting SQL Server

Imagine the results if you were to randomly apply fixes to SQL Server in the hopes of solving a problem. This would cause chaos, and you would never solve the problem. Surprisingly, some people do this because they do not take the time, or do not know how, to find the actual cause of a problem. To fix a problem, the logical first step is to determine the cause of the problem, and the best way to do that is by reading the *error logs*.

READING ERROR AND EVENT LOGS

Error logs in SQL Server 2005 are stored in two places—the first is the SQL Server error logs. You'll access the SQL Server 2005 error logs in Exercise 19-6.

 EXERCISE 19-6 READING SQL SERVER ERROR LOGS

1. Open **Management Studio.**

2. In Object Explorer, expand **your server** and then expand **Management.**

3. Under Management, expand **SQL Server Logs.**

4. Under SQL Server Logs, you should see a current log and up to six archives; double-click the **current log** to open it.

5. In the Log File Viewer, you should see a number of messages. Many of these are informational, but some will be error messages. To find the errors, just read the description at the right of each error.

6. Click one of the errors to read more detail in the lower half of the right pane.

7. To view archive logs from here, check the box next to one of the logs.

8. To view Windows event logs, check the box next to an event log.

9. To filter the logs, click the **Filter** button on the toolbar, enter your filter criteria, and then click **OK.**

The second place you will find SQL Server error messages is in the Windows Application log, which you will access in Exercise 19-7.

 EXERCISE 19-7 READING WINDOWS EVENT LOGS

1. Select **Event Viewer** from the Administrative Tools group on the Start menu.

2. In Event Viewer, click the **Application Log** icon.

3. In the contents pane (on the right), you will see a number of messages. Some of these are for other applications, and a great deal of them are informational. You are primarily interested in yellow or red icons that mention SQL Server in the description.

4. Double-click **one of the messages** to get more details about it.

5. Close **Event Viewer.**

Once you have the information you need, you can begin the troubleshooting process. You'll start by looking at a common problem area: blocks.

TROUBLESHOOTING BLOCKS AND DEADLOCKS

Obviously, you do not want other users to be able to make changes to data while you are reading or modifying it yourself. This would cause confusion and inaccuracies in your database, and your system would soon go from being a database server to being a large paperweight. To keep this from happening, SQL Server automatically places locks on the data that is being accessed to limit what other users can do with that data at the same time. SQL Server has several types of locks; shared locks and exclusive locks are the most important to understand:

Shared locks are placed on data that is being accessed for read purposes. In other words, when a user executes a SELECT statement, SQL Server places a shared lock on the data requested. Shared locks allow other users to access the locked data for reading but not modification.

Exclusive locks are placed on data that is being modified. This means when a user executes an INSERT, UPDATE, or DELETE statement, SQL Server uses an exclusive lock to protect the data. Exclusive locks do not allow other users to access the locked data for any purpose; the data is exclusively available to the user who placed the lock.

You won't deal with other locks as often (if ever), but it is good to know they are there:

- Update locks indicate that a user may want to update data. This prevents a type of **deadlock** where two users are trying to update data but neither of them can get an exclusive lock because the other user has a shared lock on the data.
- Intent locks indicate SQL Server wants to place a lock lower in the database hierarchy, such as at the table level.
- Schema locks are used when executing data definition language statements, such as ALTER TABLE.
- Bulk update locks are used when bulk copy operations are in progress or when the TABLOCK hint is used on a query.

X REF

Query hints were introduced in Lesson 13.

SQL Server does a great job of dynamically setting these locks, so you don't need to be concerned with setting them yourself. What you do need to be concerned with is making sure your queries are properly written so SQL Server does not place locks that get in the users' way. The primary cause of this is deadlocks.

Deadlocks occur when users try to place exclusive locks on each other's objects. For example, User1 places an exclusive lock on Table1 and then tries to place an exclusive lock on Table2. User2 already has an exclusive lock on Table2, and User2 tries to put an exclusive lock on Table1. This condition could cause SQL Server to enter an endless loop of waiting for the locks to be released; but, fortunately, an algorithm built into SQL Server looks for and rectifies this problem. SQL Server picks one of the users (called the "victim" in SQL Server terminology) and kills his or her query. The user whose query was killed will receive an error message stating he or she is the victim of a deadlock and should try his or her query again later.

This can cause aggravation among the users because it slows their work. You can avoid deadlocks by monitoring SQL Server using one of three methods:

- Use Profiler to monitor the Locks: Deadlock and Locks:Deadlock Chain events in the Locks event category.
- Check the Current Activity folders under Management in Enterprise Manager.
- Use the sp_lock stored procedure to find out which locks are in place.

When you find the cause of the deadlock, you can have your developers rewrite the offending queries. Of course, that takes time, and you need to get your users running again right away. You can find which user is blocking other users by querying the sys.dm_exec_ requests system view. Once you find the offending session, you can terminate it with the KILL command. You'll see how to do that in Exercise 19-8.

EXERCISE 19-8 USING sys.dm_exec_requests and KILL

1. To start a locking session, open a **new query** in Management Studio, and execute this command:

```
BEGIN TRAN
SELECT * FROM monitor WITH (TABLOCKX, HOLDLOCK)
-- Note the use of query hints
```

2. Now, to create a blocked session, open a **new query,** and execute this code:

```
UPDATE monitor SET textdata = 'test'
WHERE rownumber = 1
```

3. Notice that the second query does not complete because the first query is holding an exclusive lock on the table. To find the session that is doing the blocking, open a **third query** window.

4. In the third query window, query the **sys.dm_exec_requests** system view for any session that is being blocked with this code:

```
SELECT session_id, status, blocking_session_id
FROM sys.dm_exec_requests
WHERE blocking_session_id > 0
```

5. The blocking_session_id is the session causing the problem. To end it, execute the **KILL** command with the **blocking_session_id** value. For example, if the blocking_session_id is 53, you would execute this:

```
KILL 53
```

6. Switch to the **second query** (from step 2); it should now be complete, with one row affected.

TROUBLESHOOTING JOBS

You can use jobs to automate tasks in SQL Server. Remember from Lesson 18 that jobs are actually a series of steps that occur, one after the other, to accomplish a task. If one or more of your jobs are not working, check the following:

- The SQL Server Agent service must be running for jobs to work. If it is not, start it.
- Make sure the job, each step of the job, and each schedule of the job is enabled.
- Make sure the owner of the job has all the necessary permissions to run the job.
- Check the logic of the job; that is, make sure all the steps fire in the correct order.

You can tell easily whether a job has run successfully by looking at the history to find out when the job last fired. You'll do that in Exercise 19-9.

EXERCISE 19-9 FIND OUT WHEN A JOB LAST FIRED

1. Open **Management Studio.**

2. Make sure your **SQL Server Agent** is started by right-clicking it in Object Explorer and selecting **Start**. Click **Yes** in the dialog box that opens.

3. To create a job to run, expand **SQL Server Agent**, right-click **Jobs**, and select **New Job**.

4. Enter **Test History** in the Name box.

5. Go to the **Steps** page, and click the **New** button.

6. Enter **History Step** in the Step Name box.

7. Select **AdventureWorks** from the database drop-down list.

8. Enter this code in the command box:

   SELECT * FROM Person.Contact

9. Click **OK**, and then click **OK** again to create the job.

10. When you return to Management Studio, right-click the **Test History** job, and click **Start Job**.

11. When the job has finished, click **Close**.

12. To find out when the job last ran, right-click the **Test History** job, and click **View History**.

13. In the Log File Viewer, expand the log file entry by clicking the **plus (+) sign**. This will show you when the job last ran and which step last completed.

14. Close the **Log File Viewer.**

Using the Dedicated Administrator Connection

It rarely happens, but SQL Server can stop responding to normal queries and appear to be frozen. How could this happen? Consider that when you bought the system that houses SQL Server, you likely planned for future growth and usage. No matter how much time and effort you put into this plan, however, some companies just outgrow their servers too quickly, and the servers can't handle the workload. In a scenario like this, it is possible that SQL Server might stop responding to normal queries. To troubleshoot this issue, or any kind of problem where SQL Server just isn't responding to normal calls, you need the Dedicated Administrator Connection (DAC).

The DAC is a special diagnostics connection that is always available for connection, even under normal operating circumstances. As the name implies, only administrators (members of the sysadmin server role) can connect to the DAC to run diagnostic queries and troubleshoot problems. How does it work?

By default, SQL Server listens for normal queries on TCP port 1433, so when a user runs a SELECT query, it is transmitted to the server over port 1433. The DAC listens, by default, on TCP port 1434, so it is not cluttered with user traffic. In other words, it is always free and available for connections. Because the DAC is always available provided SQL Server service is running, it always consumes some system resources, but these are kept to a minimum.

TAKE NOTE* SQL Server increments the port values for each new instance installed. Port 1433 is associated with the default instance only.

Because the DAC consumes minimal resources and is meant to be used only for diagnostic functions, some limitations exist on what you can do with it:

- To ensure available resources, only one DAC connection is allowed per server. If you try to open a DAC connection to a server that already has a DAC connection open, you will get error 17810, and the connection will be denied.

- You can't run any parallel commands or queries from within the DAC. For example, you cannot run BACKUP or RESTORE.

- Because of resource constraints, the DAC is not available in SQL Server 2005 Express Edition.

- Because of the limited resources available, you should not run complex queries in the DAC, such as large queries with complex joins.

- By default, you cannot access the DAC from a remote machine; you must be on the server. You can change this by setting the remote admin connections option to 1 by using the sp_configure stored procedure, like this:

```
sp_configure 'remote admin connections', 1
GO
RECONFIGURE
GO
```

That seems like a lot of restrictions, so you may be wondering what you are allowed to do. The DAC is especially good for these tasks:

- Querying dynamic management views:
  - You can query sys.dm_exec_requests to find blocking queries.
  - You can query sys.dm_os_memory_cache_counters to check the health of the system memory cache.
  - You can query sys.dm_exec_sessions for information about active sessions.
- Querying catalog views
- Running basic DBCC commands:
  - You can use DBCC FREEPROCCACHE to remove all elements from the procedure cache.
  - You can use DBCC FREESYSTEMCACHE to remove all unused entries from all caches.
  - You can use DBCC DROPCLEANBUFFERS to remove all clean buffers from the buffer pool.
  - You can use DBCC SQLPERF to retrieve statistics about how the transaction log space is used in all databases.
- Using the KILL command to end an errant session

You can see that this is a powerful weapon in your troubleshooting arsenal, but how do you use it? You'll fire up the DAC in Exercise 19-10.

EXERCISE 19-10 CONNECTING TO THE DAC

ANOTHER WAY

Open a new connection to your Database Engine and connect as admin: <YourServerName> in the Server name text box.

1. Open a **command prompt** on your server.
2. The following command connects to the server specified with the -S parameter using a trusted connection as specified by the -E parameter. The -A parameter specifies the DAC, or an administrative connection. Run the following command now:

   ```
   Sqlcmd -S (local) -A -E
   ```

3. You should see a 1> prompt. From here you can enter a query. Type the following, and hit **Enter**:

   ```
   SELECT session_id, status, blocking_session_id FROM
   sys.dm_exec_requests
   ```

4. You should now see a 2> prompt. Type **GO**, and hit **Enter** to execute the query.
5. You should now be back at the 1> prompt. Type **Exit**, and hit **Enter** to exit the DAC.

■ Case Study: Monitoring Counters

A company bought an excellent system when it first started using SQL Server. It was top of the line, with resources to spare. Over time, though, the company saw performance start to drop; it was a slow but steady decrease. After a few months of this, it seemed that the server wasn't responding at all.

The first information they needed to know was how many new users had been added since the server was first put in place. As it turns out, about 100 new users were added. That led to the next question: how heavily did they use SQL Server? It turns out that all the new users accessed the server regularly throughout the day.

First, they opened the Windows System Monitor and added a few counters:

> Processor:% Processor Time
>
> Memory:Committed Bytes
>
> Memory:Pages/Sec

The results were no real surprise. The Processor:% Processor Time counter was only about 15 percent maximum, well below the 75 percent upper limit. The Memory: Pages/Sec was at a sustained average value of 10, which is twice the acceptable limit. The Memory: Committed Bytes was about 300 MB higher than the installed physical RAM.

The solution here was simple: the processor was fine for the load on the server, but there was not enough RAM. The company forgot to consider that as new users were added to the system, more RAM would be consumed. They added more RAM to the system and performance returned to acceptable levels.

SKILL SUMMARY

IN THIS LESSON YOU LEARNED:

This lesson stressed the importance of monitoring and optimizing. Monitoring allows you to find potential problems before your users find them; without monitoring, you have no way of knowing how well your system is performing.

You can use System Monitor to monitor both Windows and SQL Server. Some of the more important counters to watch are Physical Disk:Average Disk Queue (which should be less than 2) and SQLServer:Buffer Manager: Buffer Cache Hit Ratio (which should be as high as possible).

You can use Profiler to monitor queries after they have been placed in general use; it is also useful for monitoring security and user activity. Once you have used Profiler to log information about query use to a trace file, you can run the Database Engine Tuning Advisor to optimize your indexes.

You also learned about troubleshooting problems, which is important because all systems will eventually have problems. You first learned where to find the SQL Server error logs in Management Studio and how to read them. You then saw how to find errors in Windows Event Viewer.

Next you learned about troubleshooting blocks using the sys.dm_exec_requests system view. This is a valuable skill because when a session is blocked, it will never execute, and your users will not be able to get their work done.

After that, you learned how to find out when a job last ran in Management Studio. It may seem simple, but this can save a lot of time when troubleshooting problem jobs.

Finally, you learned about a new tool in SQL Server 2005, the DAC. This is a special connection that is always open and listening on TCP port 1434. It allows a single member of the sysadmins server role to connect to an unresponsive SQL Server to run simple diagnostic queries.

For the certification examination:

- Know SQL Server counters, and understand how to use them. Know the counters available in SQL Server and the acceptable values for each of them. There are quite a few, so we won't rehash them here, but review Tables 19-1 and 19-2 to find the counters and values that are important to know.

- Familiarize yourself with Profiler. Profiler displays what is happening in the database engine by performing a trace, which is a record of data that has been captured about events that are logically grouped into event classes. There are a large number of events, most of which can be used in optimization.

- Get familiar with the DAC. The DAC is a special diagnostic connection that is always available for administrators to connect with. This special connection uses limited resources on the server and is useful for running simple diagnostic commands. You can use either sql-cmd with the -A switch, or Management Studio with admin: in front of the server name to connect to the DAC. Only one administrator at a time can connect.

- Know the error logs and locations. SQL Server logs errors in two places on the server: the SQL Server error logs and the Windows event logs. To find SQL Server errors in the Windows logs, you need to use Event Viewer and look in the Application log. The SQL Server error logs are best viewed in Management Studio.

- Know how to use sys.dm_exec_requests to troubleshoot blocks. Blocks occur when one session has an exclusive lock on an object that another session needs to use. If the blocking session does not let go of the lock, then the second session will never complete. This causes problems for your users, so to find the blocking session, you can query the sys.dm_exec_ requests system view and look specifically at the session_id, status, and blocking_session_id columns.

■ Knowledge Assessment

Multiple Choice

Circle the letter or letters that correspond to the best answer or answers.

1. You are the administrator of a SQL Server 2005 computer that has been running fine for some time. But now your users have started complaining of poor performance, which started when your company hired about 150 more people, each of them having access to the SQL Server computer. When you monitor the system, you notice that the Pages/Sec counter is consistently at 6 and the Buffer Cache Hit Ratio counter is sustained at 75. What should you do to increase performance?
   a. Add another SQL Server computer to the network, and replicate the database to the new server.
   b. Add another hard disk to the server, and implement RAID-5.
   c. Add more RAM to the server.
   d. Set the Query Governor to 2.

2. When performing routine maintenance on your server, you notice that the % Processor Time counter has been at 82 percent consistently since you added about 50 new users to the system. What should you do to remedy this without impacting the users?
   a. Nothing; 82 percent is an acceptable threshold for this counter.
   b. Purchase a faster processor.
   c. Move some of the users' databases to another SQL Server computer.
   d. Replace the current SQL Server computer with a faster server.

3. You are the administrator of a SQL Server 2005 computer that contains your company's inventory-tracking database. Each day more than 100 operators make approximately 5,000 changes to the database. Your accounting and sales departments generate monthly and daily reports against the database as well. Your developers need to analyze the activity against the database to see whether they can do anything

to accelerate the generation of these reports. What should you do to get a valid analysis?

a. Run Profiler on a client computer, configure it to monitor database activity, and log the data to a table in the inventory database.

b. Run Profiler on the server, configure it to monitor database activity, and log the data to a table in the inventory database.

c. Run Profiler on a client computer, configure it to monitor database activity, and log the data to a .trc file.

d. Run Profiler on the server, configure it to monitor database activity, and log the data to a .trc file.

4. One of your users is complaining that whenever she runs a certain query, she loses her connection to SQL Server and does not receive the results of the query. She is forced to reconnect to the server when this happens, and it is slowing her down in her work. What can you do to find the problem?

a. Run the query yourself on your own machine to see whether it crashes your system.

b. Run the query in Query Editor with the Set Statistics IO option set.

c. Run a trace while the user is performing the query, and replay the trace against a test server to find the exact step that is causing the problem.

d. Run a trace while the user is performing the query, and replay the trace against the production server to find the exact step that is causing the problem.

5. After adding about 100 new users to your server, you notice that the Average Disk Queue counter is at about 3 on a consistent basis. You need to fix this, so you decide to add more disks to the subsystem, but the counters are still too high. What should you do?

a. Add more RAM.

b. Add more disks to the array.

c. Purchase a faster processor.

d. Remove the users from the system, and add them to another SQL Server computer.

6. You are the administrator of a SQL Server 2005 system with an order-tracking database. You have about 325 users who are constantly updating this database. Shortly after updating the stored procedures that your users use to modify the data in the database, many of them started complaining they were getting errors and that their updates were not taking place. What should you do to correct this?

a. Run a trace, monitor the Locks:Deadlock object, and have the developers rewrite the offending query.

b. Rewrite your application so that the queries run from the client systems instead of the server.

c. Rewrite your application so that the queries run from the server instead of the client systems.

d. Increase the size of the tempdb database so that SQL Server has more room to perform any necessary calculations on the query.

7. You want to monitor the percent of network utilization because your users have been complaining about slow response times, but you cannot find the proper counter to do this. What do you need to do?

a. Run the command netcounters—install at the command prompt to start the network counters.

b. Start the Windows System Monitor in network monitor mode.

c. Install the Network Monitor Agent.

d. Install TCP/IP; the counter will be installed automatically.

8. Your users have been complaining about slow response times since your company hired some 125 people within the last two months. Not all of these users have access to the SQL Server computer, but they do all have access to the network. When you start

monitoring to find the problem, you notice that the network usage is at about 45 percent on a sustained basis. What should you do?

   a. Remove TCP/IP, and use NetBEUI instead.

   b. Remove TCP/IP, and use NWLink instead.

   c. Segment the network with a router or bridge.

   d. Nothing; 45 is an acceptable range for this counter.

9. You want to be warned when the processor reaches 70 percent utilization so you can monitor the system closely and make sure this does not develop into a more serious problem. What should you do?

   a. Create an alert that sends you a message whenever the % Processor Time value is greater than 70.

   b. Create an alert that sends you a message whenever the % Processor Time value is less than 100.

   c. Create a trace log that fires whenever the % Processor Time value is greater than 70.

   d. Create a Counter Log that fires whenever the % Processor Time value is greater than 70.

10. You have a SQL Server system that has been running fine for several months, but now the system does not seem to be responding to user queries. You need to troubleshoot the problem so your users can access the system again. What can you do?

   a. Reboot the server, and read the logs when it comes back up.

   b. Access the DAC, and run some diagnostic commands to find the problem.

   c. Run a trace in Profiler, and look for errors in the trace.

   d. Open Management Studio in debug mode, and run diagnostic commands to find the problem.

11. One of your users is complaining that an update query they are trying to run has been running for an excessively long time without completing. You suspect that the query may be blocked. How can you verify your suspicion?

   a. Query the sys.dm_blocked_sessions system view.

   b. Query the sys.dm_exec_sessions system view.

   c. Query the sys.dm_blocked_requests system view.

   d. Query the sys.dm_exec_requests system view.

12. One of your users is complaining that an update query he is trying to run has been running for an excessively long time without completing. You have investigated and found that the query is being blocked by session 135. Which command can you use to terminate the errant session?

   a. STOP 135

   b. END 135

   c. KILL 135

   d. TERMINATE 135

13. You are one of several SQL Server administrators in your company. One day you receive a complaint that one of your SQL Server machines does not seem to be responding to normal queries, so you try to connect to the DAC to troubleshoot the problem, but you are denied access and given error 17810. What is the problem?

   a. The server has stopped responding to DAC requests and must be rebooted.

   b. The DAC has not been enabled for the server to which you are trying to connect.

   c. The SQL Server Agent service is not running and must be started.

   d. Another administrator has already made a connection to the DAC, and only one connection is allowed at a time.

14. You created a database several weeks ago, and now users have really started putting it to use. You want to make sure it is running as fast as possible so you decide to run the Database Engine Tuning Advisor against it. What do you need to do first?

   a. Create a workload after-hours on the production system.

   b. Create a workload during working hours on the production system.

    c. Create a workload in a test environment using a duplicate of the production database.

    d. Create a workload in a test environment using a database filled with test data.

15. Your database server has suffered a serious problem and is no longer responding to normal commands. You connect via the DAC and find that one of your databases is now corrupt. You decide to restore the database using the RESTORE command to bring the database back online. Does your solution work?

    a. Yes; the solution works, and the database is restored.

    b. No; the RESTORE command cannot be run in the DAC because it modifies a database, which is not allowed.

    c. No; the RESTORE command cannot be run in the DAC because it runs in parallel, which is not allowed.

    d. No; the RESTORE command cannot be run in the DAC because it accesses the disk drive or tape drive to read the backup device, which is not allowed.

16. You need to be able to connect to the DAC from remote machines on your network. Which command should you run to configure this?

    a. None; you can access the DAC remotely by default.

    b. `sp_configure 'remote connections', 1`.

    c. `sp_configure 'remote admin connections', 0`.

    d. `sp_configure 'remote admin connections', 1`.

17. You have just configured your SQL Server to allow remote DAC connections, and you need to make sure your company firewall allows access through the correct port. Which port does your network administrator need to open to allow remote DAC access?

    a. 1433

    b. 1434

    c. 1435

    d. 1343

18. You have a Windows XP desktop machine running SQL Server 2005 Express Edition. The desktop has 1 GB of RAM and a 3 GHz processor. Can you access the DAC on the desktop machine?

    a. Yes; you can use the DAC.

    b. No; you cannot use the DAC because you do not have sufficient RAM.

    c. No; you cannot use the DAC because you are running Windows XP and the DAC requires a server operating system such as Windows Server 2003.

    d. No; you cannot use the DAC because you are running SQL Server Express Edition, which does not include the DAC.

19. You have a SQL Server with 4 GB of RAM, a 3 GHz processor, and a RAID-5 disk array with five disks. When looking at the Windows System Monitor you notice that the Memory:Committed Bytes counter is at 4.2 GB. What should you do to fix this?

    a. Nothing; this is an acceptable value for the Memory:Committed Bytes counter.

    b. You should add another disk to the RAID-5 disk array.

    c. You should consider adding more RAM.

    d. You should purchase a faster processor.

20. You are testing a new application and you need to be able to re-create any problems that may arise from the new code running against your SQL Server. You decide to run Profiler to capture all the activity on the server; but which template should you use to create the new trace?

    a. TSQL

    b. TSQL_SPs

    c. TSQL_Duration

    d. TSQL_Replay

    e. Tuning

■ Case Scenarios

Scenario 19-1: Using System Monitor

Select the counter that shows you the cost of counting the overhead of monitoring. Establish several repetitive queries to make quite a little bit of activity. Observe the impact of collecting data.

Scenario 19-2: Correcting Near Fatal Errors

Discuss the differences between starting SQL Server with sqlservr -m and sqlcmd -A.

High-Availability Methods

LESSON SKILL MATRIX

TECHNOLOGY SKILL	70-431 EXAM OBJECTIVE
Implement database mirroring.	Foundational
Prepare databases for database mirroring.	Foundational
Create endpoints.	Foundational
Specify database partners.	Foundational
Specify a witness server.	Foundational
Configure an operating mode.	Foundational
Implement log shipping.	Foundational
Initialize a secondary database.	Foundational
Configure log shipping options.	Foundational
Configure a log shipping mode.	Foundational
Configure monitoring.	Foundational
Managing database snapshots.	Foundational
Create a snapshot.	Foundational
Revert a database from a snapshot.	Foundational

KEY TERMS

database mirroring: A SQL Server 2005 high-availability technology configured between a principal and mirror database and an optional witness server. It maintains close synchronization of data and the database schema and offers the options of automatic failover. The process in which ownership of the principal role is switched from the principal server to the mirror server.

database snapshot: A read-only, static view of a database at the moment of snapshot creation.

distributed transaction: An atomic unit of work that spans multiple data sources. In a distributed transaction, all data modifications in all accessed data sources are either committed or terminated.

failover clustering: A process, implemented at the operating system level, of creating a shared data store and then putting from two to four servers (depending on the OS version) in one of two configurations whereby one server automatically takes over in the case of the other's failure.

log shipping: The process of copying, at set intervals, a log backup from a read/write database) on a primary server to one or more copies (the secondary databases) that reside on remote servers. The secondary servers are warm standbys for the primary server.

replication: A set of technologies for copying and distributing data and database objects from one database to another and then synchronizing among databases to maintain consistency.

■ Choosing the Redundancy Features You Need

THE BOTTOM LINE

Redundancy means having another copy of your database somewhere. This can be a backup copy. This can be a replicated copy. This can be a mirrored copy. The question you must ask yourself is: "How quickly must I recover from a disaster?" The options available to you range from seconds (high availability) to days; you must prearrange with your managers their risk tolerance, then pick the most cost-effective option.

Bill manages the database for an electrical parts distribution company in Westlake Village, California. He worked with his managers and they collectively decided that a full backup copy each night at midnight represented the greatest cost they were willing to expend for data integrity. All users are trained to keep yesterday's invoices ready for reentry in case of a massive system failure (which has never happened; Bill is good at his job). The company accepts the cost and delays of reentry as part of its disaster recovery plan.

SQL Server 2005 has the following features available, depending on the edition of SQL Server you're using. It is important to understand which features are available in specific editions of SQL Server before you decide to build a business technology around high availability.

You'll get the following high-availability features with Enterprise Edition:

- ***Replication***
- ***Distributed transactions***
- ***Failover clustering***
- Multiple instances (up to 50)
- Log shipping
- Database snapshots
- Database mirroring

You'll get the following high-availability features with Standard Edition:

- Replication
- Distributed transactions
- Failover clustering (maximum two nodes)
- Multiple instances (up to 16)
- Log shipping
- Database mirroring (synchronous with automatic failover only)

You'll get the following high-availability features with Workgroup Edition:

- Replication
- Distributed transactions
- Multiple instances (up to 16)
- Log shipping

You'll get the following high-availability features with Express Edition:

- Replication (subscriber only)
- Distributed transactions
- Multiple instances (up to 16)
- Log shipping
- Can be used as a witness

This lesson focuses on three techniques, but mentions others. Lesson 13 covers DTC and Lesson 23 covers replication, which rounds out your options in choosing the correct edition and the correct option for your organization.

TAKE NOTE*

Replication duplicates your data to another location, which can be a server sitting right beside your main server if you wish to use it for high availability. This is covered in Lesson 23.

Implementing Database Mirroring

Database mirroring allows you to create an exact copy of a database on a different server and implement high availability on the user database.

If you want to test database mirroring, you first need to enable database mirroring by setting the appropriate trace flags. Trace flag 1400 will enable you to use database mirroring. You can specify this using the following T-SQL statement:

```
DBCC TRACEON (1400)
```

Database mirroring is a software solution, implemented on a database-per-database basis, and involves two copies of a database, with only one accessible by the user. Since database mirroring does not require any additional hardware in terms of clustering support, you can use this as a cheaper implementation, instead of clustering a database. Keep in mind, however, that mirroring supports only user databases, and you might need additional requirements in a fault-tolerance scenario.

How does database mirroring work? Mirroring is a process that looks similar to log shipping; however, it involves a direct process between two separate instances of SQL Server. Updates made to a database on the first server, called the *principal*, are copied over, or are mirrored, to the target server, called the *mirror*. The process involves applying any transaction from the principal to the mirror.

When an application sends an update to the database, the database engine will also apply the transaction to the mirror and receive an acknowledgment that the transaction is committed, or hardened, into the target database, before the process will be returned to the user application. Figure 20-1 displays this process.

How do you configure database mirroring? Configuring database mirroring involves several steps, covered throughout the following sections. You have to configure the connection between servers, as well as which database you will mirror from one server to the other. You'll learn how to configure this in the "Preparing for Mirroring" section later in this lesson.

Figure 20-1

Database Mirroring

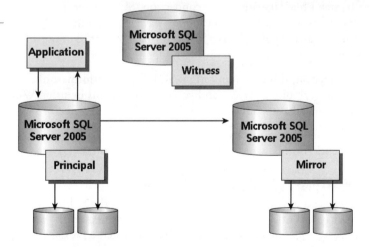

Understanding Database Mirroring Concepts

Mirroring, partners, witnesses—these are some basic concepts you need to understand thoroughly in order to start using database mirroring and comprehend where database mirroring fits into the fault-tolerance strategy of your business solutions.

Principal: The principal server is your primary database, and as such will be your starting point in a database-mirroring session. Every transaction that will be applied to this database will be transferred to the mirror using a process similar to distributed transactions. When a database mirroring session starts, the mirror server asks the principal server's transaction log for all transactions, based on the latest log sequence number.

Mirror: The mirror is the database that will receive the copies from the principal server; this assumes that a persistent connection between the mirror and the principal exists.

Standby server: The process of database mirroring is really one of maintaining a standby server (which means the mirrored database is not accessible by users) that you can easily switch over to in case of the principal server failing.

Synchronous/asynchronous: Database mirroring can work in two different ways: synchronous or asynchronous:

- **Synchronous mode:** In synchronous mode, every transaction applied to the principal will also be committed (or hardened) on the mirror server before another transaction can begin. You can consider this to be similar to distributed transactions, which means a transaction on the principal will be released only when it is also committed on the mirror. Once it receives an acknowledgment from the mirror server, the principal will notify the client that the statement has completed.

- **Asynchronous mode:** In asynchronous mode, the principal server sends log information to the mirror server, without waiting for an acknowledgment from the mirror server. This means transactions commit without waiting for the mirror server to commit, or harden, the log file. This mode allows the principal server to run with minimum transaction latency, and prohibits use of automatic failover.

PREPARING FOR MIRRORING

To prepare for database mirroring, you need to perform three configuration steps:

1. Configure the security and communication between the instances.
2. Create the mirror database.
3. Establish a mirror session.

CONFIGURING SECURITY AND COMMUNICATION BETWEEN INSTANCES

To establish a database mirror connection, SQL Server uses endpoints to specify the connection between servers. This means you have to create the endpoints for the database mirroring. And just as with SQL Server Service Broker, you have to use a CREATE ENDPOINT statement, as covered in the "Creating Endpoints" section.

Of course, in this communication, SQL Server performs authentication over the endpoints (mirror endpoint services), and you can achieve this by using Windows Authentication or certificate-based authentication.

If you are configuring a witness server, you also need to specify the communication and authentication between the principal and the witness and between the mirror and the witness.

CREATING THE MIRROR DATABASE

To create a mirror database, you have to restore the full backup of a principal, including all other types of backup (transaction logs) you created on the principal, before you can establish a session. It is important, however, that you use the NORECOVERY option when restoring from backup so the backup database will remain in a nonusable state. The mirror database needs to have the same name as the principal database.

ESTABLISHING A MIRROR SESSION

Your next step in setting up database mirroring is to set up the mirror session on the database by identifying the mirroring partners. On the principal database and on the mirror, you need to identify which partners are involved in database mirroring. You can do this from within SQL Server Management Studio; however, as a general rule in configuration, we recommend you script this using T-SQL syntax instead. Refer to the "Specifying Partners and Witnesses" section for more information.

CREATING ENDPOINTS

Endpoints are covered more completely in Lesson 22. Still, it won't be too difficult to configure endpoints for database mirroring. Database mirroring requires you to define TCP endpoints in the same way you will configure HTTP endpoints for Service Broker.

In an endpoint configuration, you identify TCP as the core protocol, and you specify the following options:

- Authentication
- Encryption
- Role

A typical configuration looks like this:

```
CREATE ENDPOINT Endpoint_Mirroring
STATE = STARTED
AS TCP ( LISTENER_PORT = 4099 )
FOR DATABASE_MIRRORING (
AUTHENTICATION = WINDOWS KERBEROS,
ENCRYPTION = SUPPORTED, ROLE = ALL);
```

SETTING THE AUTHENTICATION

Take a closer look at the authentication for database mirroring endpoints. Database mirroring supports Windows Authentication or certificate-based authentication.

Windows Authentication: The authentication mechanism is specified in the FOR_ DATABASE_ MIRRORING part of the CREATE ENDPOINT statement, as shown here, and has configurable options:

```
<FOR DATABASE_MIRRORING_language_specific_arguments.::=
FOR DATABASE_MIRRORING (
[ AUTHENTICATION = {
WINDOWS [ { NTLM | KERBEROS | NEGOTIATE } ]
| CERTIFICATE certificate_name } ]
[[, ] ENCRYPTION = { DISABLED|SUPPORTED|REQUIRED }
[ ALGORITHM { RC4|AES|AES RC4|RC4 AES } ] ]
[,] ROLE = { WITNESS | PARTNER | ALL } )
```

For your authentication options, you can specify WINDOWS authentication, and you need to choose the processing method (using NTLM or KERBEROS). By default, the NEGOTIATE option is set, which will cause the endpoint to negotiate between NTLM and Kerberos:

```
<authentication_options.::=
WINDOWS [ { NTLM | KERBEROS | NEGOTIATE } ]
```

However, if you specify a processing method, whether it is Kerberos or NTLM, that method will be used as the authentication protocol.

Certificate-based authentication: You can specify that the endpoint has to authenticate using a certificate by specifying the CERTIFICATE keyword and the name of the certificate, like this:

```
CERTIFICATE certificate_name
```

This means the endpoint must have the certificate, with the matching public key, in order to match the private key of the specified certificate. Using the CERTIFICATE option, you put the certificate as a mandatory requirement, and you can authenticate using certificates only.

The authentication options also allow you to specify that you first check certificate authentication, and if the certificate cannot be found, it should use Windows Authentication. You do this by using the CERTIFICATE keyword in combination with the WINDOWS keyword:

```
CERTIFICATE certificate_name
WINDOWS [ { NTLM | KERBEROS | NEGOTIATE } ]
```

If you prefer to first try Windows Authentication, and if that fails, to try with the certificate, you basically have to revert the keyword to the following syntax:

```
WINDOWS [ { NTLM | KERBEROS | NEGOTIATE } ] CERTIFICATE
certificate_name
```

SETTING THE ENCRYPTION

The next part of the mirror endpoint is the encryption you want to use when sending data over a connection. By default, database mirroring uses RC4 encryption:

```
[ , ] ENCRYPTION = { DISABLED |SUPPORTED | REQUIRED }
[ ALGORITHM { RC4 | AES | AES RC4 | RC4 AES } ]
```

Table 20-1 lists the possible encryption options you can use.

When specifying that you are using encryption, you can also specify which encryption mechanism to use, as listed in Table 20-2.

Table 20-1

Encryption Options When Mirroring Endpoints

OPTION	DESCRIPTION
DISABLED	The data sent over the connection is not encrypted.
SUPPORTED	The data is encrypted if the opposite endpoint is set to REQUIRED or SUPPORTED.
REQUIRED	The connections to this endpoint must use encryption.

Table 20-2

Encryption Algorithm Options When Mirroring Endpoints

OPTION	DESCRIPTION
RC4	The endpoint must use the RC4 algorithm (which is the default behavior).
AES	The endpoint must use the AES algorithm.
AES RC4	The endpoint will first negotiate for the AES algorithm.
RC4 AES	The endpoint will first negotiate for the RC4 algorithm.

SETTING THE ROLE

In the role part of the statement, you specify the endpoint's role:

- Partner
- Witness
- All

Using the ALL keyword as the role, you identify that the mirroring endpoint can be used for the witness as well as for a partner in a database-mirroring scenario.

Database mirroring can use only TCP (not HTTP) and does not have a predefined port number, which means you have to configure the port to anything you choose.

You must configure an endpoint on each of the partnering nodes in a database mirror. Also, the login you specify to authenticate needs to have GRANT CONNECT permission on the endpoint.

SPECIFYING PARTNERS AND WITNESSES

After specifying the endpoints, you need to establish the mirror session. You can do this by following these steps:

1. Configure the principal as a partner on the mirror.
2. Configure the mirror as a partner on the principal.
3. Optionally, configure a witness.

CONFIGURING THE PRINCIPAL AS A PARTNER ON THE MIRROR

You have to configure the mirror to point to the principal database. You have the ability to achieve this from within SQL Server Management Studio, but it is preferable to use the ALTER DATABASE syntax.

A typical configuration syntax looks like this:

```
ALTER DATABASE <database_name>
SET PARTNER = <server_network_address>
```

For example:

```
ALTER DATABASE MSSQL_Training
SET PARTNER =
'TCP://SQL.TRAINING.COM:4999'
```

CONFIGURING THE MIRROR AS A PARTNER ON THE PRINCIPAL

When you configure the mirror as a partner on the principal, you will initiate at that moment the database-mirroring session. Just like with specifying the principal as a partner in the previous step, you will use the ALTER DATABASE statement. A typical configuration syntax looks like this:

```
ALTER DATABASE <database_name>
SET PARTNER = <server_network_address>
```

For example:

```
ALTER DATABASE MSSQL_Training
SET PARTNER =
'TCP://REMOTE.TRAINING.COM:4999'
```

CONFIGURING A WITNESS

If you care about automatic failover, you should enable a witness server. The witness server does nothing but monitor the status of the participants. The good news is that you can have SQL Server Express Edition running on an old desktop computer participate as a witness in database mirroring.

To enable a witness, you merely need to set the witness option on the principal database and point to the already created witness server (that is, the endpoint, of course). Here's the syntax:

```
ALTER DATABASE <database_name>
SET WITNESS 5 <server_network_address>
```

For example:

```
ALTER DATABASE AdventureWorks
SET WITNESS = 'TCP://WITNESS.TRAINING.COM:4999'
```

In the previous examples, the TCP port we used was 4999. Keep in mind that this port number is not a requirement; you can essentially configure any port. Also be aware that, instead of using the IP address, it does make sense to configure a DNS name.

CONFIGURING THE OPERATING MODE

To support database mirroring, you have different operating modes for specifying a transaction safety level. The mode you use will impact how transactions are managed between the principal and mirror; also, you can choose whether to have automatic or manual failover with a potential loss of data. Specifically, database mirroring works in three modes:

High availability: In this mode, the database *transaction safety* is set to FULL, and you will use a witness server to monitor the availability of the principal and mirror. In this mode, every transaction applied to the principal will also be applied to the mirror. When the connection to the principal fails, clients will be reconnected to the mirror automatically, after an automatic role transfer occurs.

High protection: In the absence of a witness server, database mirroring will run in high protection mode, which still allows every transaction applied to the principal to be applied to the mirror. If the principal goes down, you can then manually force roles to switch, although a data loss can occur.

High performance: High-performance mode is also called *asynchronous mode*. The chance of data loss is high since it is not guaranteed that the transactions applied to the principal are also applied to the mirror at the moment the principal fails.

You can specify transaction safety to be FULL or OFF. When specifying transaction safety to FULL, you are running in synchronous mode, which of course will impact your transaction performance, but should be considered to be a low impact, given that you are implementing a nice failover method.

A synchronous operation implies that transactions will be committed and acknowledged after they are also committed and hardened on the mirrored server. So, having a reliable and high-performing network connection to the mirrored database is mandatory.

When switching transaction safety to OFF, you configure database mirroring to run, without waiting for the transaction to complete on the mirrored database, which causes potential data loss.

SWITCHING ROLES

A mirror database is a failover database for the principal, and that is what database mirroring is about. So, when the principal server fails, you want to switch roles over to the mirror, and from then on specify that the mirror should become the primary. This concept is called *role switching*. You have three options for role switching:

Automatic failover: When you're using a witness server, automatic failover will occur when the principal database is not available and when the witness server confirms this. At that moment, the mirror will be automatically promoted to the principal, and whenever the principal comes back on, it will automatically take the role of a mirror.

Manual failover: You can perform manual failover only if both the principal and the mirror are live and in a synchronized status. This is the operation you will use most frequently to perform maintenance tasks on the principal. You have to initiate the failover from the principal, and of course later you will again revert roles after you do database maintenance.

The statement used to switch database roles (manual failover) is an ALTER DATABASE statement, as shown here:

```
ALTER DATABASE MSSQL_Training SET PARTNER FAILOVER
```

Forced service: When you are not using a witness server, your principal might go down unexpectedly. In that case, you'll want to initiate manual failover to the mirror. Because at that time you have no idea whether the actual transactions that were committed on the principal have made it to the mirror (asynchronous mode), you'll want to switch roles, with

CERTIFICATION READY? Know these three modes. What are the differences?

the possibility of losing data. To achieve this, you need to invoke an ALTER DATABASE statement, as shown here:

```
ALTER DATABASE MSSQL_Training
SET PARTNER FORCE_SERVICE_ALLOW_DATA_LOSS
```

TAKE NOTE***

When forcing a service to switch the mirror to become the principal server, you may lose data.

Exercise 20-1 demonstrates how to set up a mirroring session. This exercise requires a default instance and two additional instances, which were created in Lesson 2. Also, the included scripts on your student CD need to be edited to reflect your actual server name every time you see the placeholder <YourServerName> for the default instance, Instance1, and Instance2. If your environment varies from this, adjust the instructions accordingly.

The exercise layout presumes the principal server to be the default instance. It also presumes the principal server to be located in the directory at MSSQL.1; the mirror server at MSSQL.2; and the witness server at MSSQL.3. If your environment varies from this, adjust the instructions accordingly.

Achieving success in this exercise requires that you pay strict attention to which instance you must work on at any given step. You will be constantly breaking a connection and making a new connection with a different instance. Pay close attention to where you must make each change.

This is a long exercise, and requires attention to detail to be successful. As always, failure is a learning experience. You will have learned even if unsuccessful; or, put another way, every effort is successful.

 EXERCISE 20-1 DATABASE MIRRORING

1. Log on to the operating system as **Administrator** with the password **Pa$$w0rd.** To complete this lab, you must start each instance of SQL Server running on your computer.

2. Open a **command prompt.**

3. Enter the following command:

   ECHO %COMPUTERNAME%

4. The name of your computer will be displayed on the screen. Note this name and use it whenever the placeholder text <YourComputerName> is used in this exercise.

5. Enter the following command to stop the default instance of SQL Server on your computer:

   NET STOP MSSQLSERVER

6. Enter the following command to start the default instance of SQL Server on your computer with trace flag 1400 on. Trace flags are used to start the server with nonstandard behavior. This flag enables the creation of the database mirroring endpoint, which is required for setting up and using database mirroring.

   NET START MSSQLSERVER /T1400

7. Enter the following command to start the INSTANCE1 instance of SQL Server on your computer with trace flag 1400 on.

   NET START MSSQL$INSTANCE1 /T1400

8. Enter the following command to start the INSTANCE2 instance of SQL Server on your computer with trace flag 1400 on.

   NET START MSSQL$INSTANCE2 /T1400

9. Close the **Command Prompt** window.

10. Open **SQL Server Management Studio.**

11. In the Connect to SQL Server dialog box, enter or confirm the following details, and then click **Connect.**

User Interface Element	Value
Server type	Database Engine
Server name	<YourServerName>
Authentication	Windows Authentication

12. Using Object Explorer, view the **properties** of the **AdventureWorks** database on the localhost server.

13. On the Options page of the Database Properties dialog box, set the recovery model of the database to **Full**. Click **OK** to implement the change.

14. Create a new **SQL Server query** (connecting to the localhost server using Windows Authentication), and add **Transact-SQL code** to back up the AdventureWorks database using the settings itemized in the following table.

Setting	Value
Database	AdventureWorks
Backup device	C:\DB_Mirror\AWBackup.bak
Options	CHECKSUM, NOFORMAT

15. It probably looks like this; if so, execute it:

```
USE master
GO
BACKUP DATABASE AdventureWorks TO DISK =
N'C:\DB_Mirror\AWBackup.bak' WITH CHECKSUM,
NOFORMAT
GO
```

16. When the backup has completed, view the contents of the **C:\DB_Mirror** folder and verify that a file named **AWBackup.bak** has been created.

17. Create a new **SQL Server query** (connecting to the <YourComputerName>\ INSTANCE1 server using Windows Authentication), and add a **RESTORE DATABASE** statement using the settings described in the following table. Check that the pathnames for the databases are correct for your instance configuration; for example, MSSQL.2, or MSSQL.3, or MSSQL.4.

Setting	Value
Database	AdventureWorks
Backup device	C:\DB_Mirror\AWBackup.bak
File	1
Move	C:\Program Files\Microsoft SQL Server\MSSQL.4\ MSSQL\DATA\ AdventureWorks_Data.NDF and C:\Program Files\Microsoft SQL Server\ MSSQL.4 \MSSQL\DATA\AdventureWorks_Log.NDF
Options	CHECKSUM, NORECOVERY, REPLACE (Note: The replace is in case AdventureWorks is already loaded; in this lesson, it's probably not needed.)

18. The code probably looks like this; if so, execute it to restore the database to the mirror server:

```
-- Restore database on mirror server
-- Run on Instance2
USE master
GO
RESTORE DATABASE AdventureWorks FROM DISK =
N'C:\DB_Mirror\AWBackup.bak' WITH FILE = 1,
MOVE N'AdventureWorks_Data' TO N'C:\Program
Files\Microsoft SQL Server
\MSSQL.4\MSSQL\DATA\AdventureWorks_Data.MDF',
MOVE N'dat1' TO N'C:\Program Files\Microsoft SQL
Server\MSSQL.4\MSSQL\DATA\dat1.ndf',
MOVE N'dat2' TO N'C:\Program Files\Microsoft SQL
Server\MSSQL.4\MSSQL\DATA\dat2.ndf',
MOVE N'AdventureWorks_Log' TO N'C:\Program Files\Microsoft SQL
Server\MSSQL.4\MSSQL\DATA\AdventureWorks_Log.LDF',
CHECKSUM, NORECOVERY
GO
```

TAKE NOTE *

When multiple instances of SOL Server are participating in mirroring sessions on the same computer, each instance requires an endpoint configured with a unique port. In this exercise, you will use port 5022 for the principal server, port 5023 for the mirror server, and port 5024 for the witness server. You should not use mirroring with multiple instances on the same computer in a production environment because this configuration does not provide adequate protection against hardware failure.

19. In the query window connected to the localhost instance, add **Transact-SQL code** to add a mirroring endpoint by using the settings listed in the following table.

SETTING	VALUE
Endpoint Name	AdvWorksEndpoint_1
State	STARTED
TCP Listener Port Role	5022
Role	PARTNER

20. Run the code that you just added, which probably looks like this:

```
USE master
GO
CREATE ENDPOINT AdvWorksEndpoint_1 STATE = STARTED
AS TCP ( LISTENER_PORT = 5022 ) FOR
DATABASE_MIRRORING (ROLE=PARTNER)
GO
```

21. In the query window connected to the <YourComputerName>\INSTANCE1 instance, add **Transact-SQL code** to add a mirroring endpoint by using the settings listed in the following table.

SETTING	VALUE
Endpoint Name	AdvWorksEndpoint_2
State	STARTED
TCP Listener Port	5023
Role	PARTNER

22. Run the code that you just added, which, again, probably looks like this:

```
USE master
GO
CREATE ENDPOINT AdvWorksEndpoint_2
STATE = STARTED
AS TCP ( LISTENER_PORT = 5023 )
FOR DATABASE_MIRRORING (ROLE=PARTNER)
GO
```

23. Create a new **SQL Server query** (connecting to the <YourComputerName>\ INSTANCE2 server by using Windows Authentication).

24. In the query window connected to the <YourComputerName>\INSTANCE2 instance, add **Transact-SQL code** to add a mirroring endpoint by using the settings shown in the following table.

SETTING	VALUE
Endpoint Name	AdvWorksEndpoint_3
State	STARTED
TCP Listener Port	5024
Role	WITNESS

25. Run the code you just added, which probably looks like this:

```
USE master
GO
CREATE ENDPOINT AdvWorksEndpoint_3
STATE = STARTED
AS TCP ( LISTENER_PORT = 5024 )
FOR DATABASE_MIRRORING (ROLE=WITNESS)
GO
```

26. In the query window connected to the <YourComputerName>\INSTANCE1 instance, add **Transact-SQL code** to identify the principal server (TCP:// <YourComputerName>:5022) as the mirror server's partner.

27. Run the script. It looks something like this, right?

```
USE master
GO
ALTER DATABASE AdventureWorks
SET PARTNER = 'TCP://<YourComputerName>:5022'
```

28. In the query window connected to the localhost instance, add **Transact-SQL code** to identify the mirror server (TCP://<YourComputerName>:5023) as the principal server's partner.

29. Run this script:

```
USE master
GO
ALTER DATABASE AdventureWorks
SET PARTNER = 'TCP://<YourComputerName>:5022'
```

30. In the query window connected to the localhost instance, add **Transact-SQL code** to retrieve the following columns from the sys.database_mirroring catalog view:
    - mirroring_state_desc
    - mirroring_partner_name
    - mirroring_witness_name
    - mirroring_witness_state_desc
    - mirroring_role_desc
    - mirroring_safety_level_desc

31. Run this script and review the results that describe the mirroring partnership:

```
-- Run on <YourComputerName> and <YourComputerName>\Instance1
SELECT mirroring_state_desc
, mirroring_partner_name
, mirroring_witness_name
, mirroring_witness_state_desc
, mirroring_role_desc
, mirroring_safety_level_desc
FROM sys.database_mirroring
```

32. In the query window connected to the localhost instance, add **Transact-SQL code** to specify TCP://<YourComputerName>:5024 as a witness server.

33. Execute this script:

```
USE master
GO
ALTER DATABASE AdventureWorks
SET WITNESS = 'TCP://<YourComputerName>:5024'
```

34. Create a new **SQL Server query** (connecting to the <YourComputerName>\INSTANCE2 server using Windows Authentication), and add **Transact-SQL code** to retrieve the following columns from the sys.database_mirroring_witnesses catalog view:
    - database name
    - principal_server_name
    - mirror_server_name
    - safety_level_desc

35. Run the script and review the results.

```
-- View session properties
-- Run on the third instance
SELECT database_name
, principal_server_name
, mirror_server_name
, safety_level_desc
FROM sys.database_mirroring_witnesses
```

36. Open the **Performance** tool from the Administrative Tools group on the Start menu.

37. Delete any performance counters that are currently displayed.

38. Click the **Add** button on the toolbar.

39. In the Add Counters dialog box, in the Performance object list, click **SQL Server:Database** Mirroring.

40. In the counters list, click Send/Receive Ack Time, and then click Add.

41. Click Close to close the dialog box.

42. In the query window connected to the localhost instance, add the following Transact-SQL code to update the AdventureWorks database:

```
USE AdventureWorks
UPDATE Person.Contact
SET LastName = 'Smith'
WHERE LastName = 'Abercrombie'
```

43. Execute the script.

44. Switch to the **Performance** tool.

45. Note the spike in the Send/Receive Ack counter.

46. Close the **Performance** tool.

47. In the query window connected to the <YourComputerName>\INSTANCE1 instance, add the following Transact-SQL code to query the Adventure Works database:

```
USE AdventureWorks
SELECT * FROM Person.Contact
```

48. Execute the script. Note the query cannot execute because the database is acting as a mirror database.

49. In the query window connected to the localhost instance, add **Transact-SQL code** to initiate manual failover to the mirror server. It should look something like this:

```
-- Run on <YourComputerName>
USE master
GO
ALTER DATABASE AdventureWorks
SET PARTNER FAILOVER
GO
```

50. Execute the script.

51. In the query window connected to <YourComputerName>\INSTANCE2 instance, add **Transact-SQL code** to retrieve the following columns from the sys.database_mirroring_witnesses catalog view:

- Database_name
- Principal_server_name
- Mirror_Server_name
- Safety_level_desc

52. Execute the script and review the results. Verify that the original mirror server (computer name:5023) is now the principal server, and vice versa.

```
-- View session properties
-- Run on <YourComputerName>\Instance2
SELECT database_name
, principal_server_name
```

```
, mirror_server_name
, safety_level_desc
FROM sys.database_mirroring_witnesses
```

53. In the query window connected to the <YourComputerName>\INSTANCE1 instance, add the following **Transact-SQL code** to query the Adventure Works database:

```
USE AdventureWorks
SELECT * FROM person.contact
```

54. Execute the script and verify that the data is available.

55. In the query window connected to the localhost instance, add the following **Transact-SQL code** to query the AdventureWorks database:

```
USE AdventureWorks
SELECT * FROM Person.Contact
```

56. Execute the script. Note that the query cannot be executed because the database is now acting as a mirror database.

57. In the query window connected to the localhost instance, add **Transact-SQL code** to terminate the mirror session.

58. Execute the following script:

```
-- Run on <YourComputerName>\Instance1
USE master
GO
ALTER DATABASE AdventureWorks
SET PARTNER OFF
```

59. In the query window connected to the <YourComputerName>\INSTANCE2 instance, add Transact-SQL code to retrieve the following columns from the sys.databases_mirroring_witnesses catalog view:
    - Database_name
    - Principal_server_name
    - Mirror_server_name
    - Safety _level- desc

60. Execute the script and review the results. Note that no rows exist because the database is no longer mirrored.

```
-- View session properties
-- Run on <YourComputerName>\Instance2
SELECT database_name
, principal_server_name
, mirror_server_name
, safety_level_desc
FROM sys.database_mirroring_witnesses
```

61. In Object Explorer, expand **Databases** and note that the AdventureWorks database is still in a restoring state.

62. In the query window connected to the localhost instance, add **Transact-SQL code** to recover the database.

63. Execute this script:

```
-- Run on ,YourComputerName.
RESTORE DATABASE AdventureWorks
WITH RECOVERY
```

64. Refresh the **Object Explorer** window to verify the new state of the database.

65. In the query window connected to the localhost instance, add **Transact-SQL code** to update the AdventureWorks database:

```
USE AdventureWorks
SELECT * FROM Person.Contact
```

66. Execute the script to confirm that the database is now accessible.

67. Close **SQL Server Management** Studio without saving changes.

68. Open a **command prompt.**

69. Enter the following command:

```
NET STOP MSSQL$INSTANCE1 /Y
```

This will stop the INSTANCE1 instance of SQL Server on your computer.

70. Enter the following command to stop the INSTANCE2 instance of SQL Server on your computer:

```
NET STOP MSSQL$INSTANCE2 /Y
```

71. Enter the following command to stop the default instance of SQL Server on your computer:

```
NET STOP MSSQLSERVER /Y
```

72. Enter the following command to start the default instance of SQL Server without trace flag 1400.

```
NET START MSSQLSERVER
```

73. Close the **Command Prompt** window.

More Information *

As the cost of bandwidth falls lower and lower, it could be interesting to combine a clustered environment with database mirroring on specific user databases.

In an ideal scenario, a company would then be able to keep its business running from a remote location when an entire region or area goes down. One of the key problems with clustering is that a company is limited to a geographical location that requires servers to be close to each other because of the cluster "heartbeat" and shared data store.

In previous editions of SQL Server, a lot of companies used a similar method via replication. They would replicate an entire user database to a remote server, which was hosted in an external data center that would allow them to switch over to the remote server in case of a server or database outage. This, however, caused a lot of implications once the "principal" server came up again, as they had to resynchronize and, essentially, break the replication.

Implementing Log Shipping

Log shipping has existed in several releases of SQL Server. It started as a manual process in SQL Server 7.0 and became an automated process in SQL Server 2000.

Log shipping is relatively easy: You take a backup of a transaction log and restore that onto another server, thus maintaining a standby server that can be used as a read-only server for different purposes, such as for Reporting Services or as your data engine to populate a data warehouse running SQL Server Analysis Services.

These are the steps involved in setting up log shipping:

1. Back up the transaction log on the primary database.

2. Copy the log files to the secondary database, which should reside on a separate server.

3. Restore that log file onto the secondary server.

It's as simple as that. Now, of course, we'll cover how to configure and initialize these servers and how to configure log shipping.

Log shipping consists of two servers:

- The *primary server* in a *log shipping* configuration has the primary database you want to back up and restore on another server. You configure the log shipping on the primary server/database.

- The *secondary server* hosts the database that maintains a copy of your primary database; and, of course, it is common that a server can maintain and host multiple copies of primary databases coming from multiple servers. A secondary database is usually initialized by taking a backup from the primary database.

MONITORING THE SERVER

Monitoring the server in log shipping is more or less similar to the process of using a witness server in database mirroring: You have to configure a monitor server that will keep track of when the last backup was taken and applied to the secondary server in order to have automatic failover.

In the next section, you will learn how to configure log shipping and monitor the log shipping process.

CONFIGURING LOG SHIPPING

You can configure log shipping from within SQL Server Management Studio or by using the corresponding stored procedures.

1. To initialize log shipping, right-click the database you want to use as the primary database, and from the Tasks menu, select the **Transaction Log Shipping** option.

2. Then, click the **Enable This As a Primary Database** in a Log Shipping Configuration at the top of this properties page.

3. The next step is to specify the transaction log backup location and backup settings.

After you configure the backup log and backup locations, you are then ready to create transaction log backups and configure the primary database for log shipping. The failover and redundancy between the primary database and the secondary database will be affected by the number of transaction log backups you take on the primary database and the frequency of the restore operations onto the secondary database.

As soon as you have specified the primary database, you have to specify the secondary server and database in order to initiate the failover database. Connect to an instance of SQL Server that you want to use as a secondary server by clicking the Add button under the Secondary Server Instances and Databases options. In this window, you have the option to specify a new database for log shipping, or you can pick an existing database and configure how the database needs to be initialized. If you create a new database, you also have the option to specify its file locations, as well the locations for the data file and log file.

After you select the target database, you will then specify the destination folder where the backup log files will be copied on the target server (secondary server). This means you have permission to both read from the primary and write to the target, which depends on the configuration of the SQL Server Agent account or proxy account.

By selecting the Copy Files tab, you can also specify the copy job schedule and how to retain or delete files.

The last step in configuring log shipping is to configure the recovery mode on the Restore Transaction Log tab of the Secondary Database Setting dialog box.

For this recovery option, you have two options:

No Recovery Mode: If you choose No Recovery Mode, you will not be able to read from the database, and it will be a hot standby server that you will switch to when an error occurs.

Standby Mode: If you choose the Standby Mode option, you will disconnect users from the secondary database while you perform a restore. In this mode, the database will return in a read-only mode after a restore operation is completed, and the database will then be accessible for you to, for example, populate your data warehouse environment or reporting services.

CHANGING ROLES

To perform a role change from the primary server to the secondary server, you need to perform an initial role change to be able to make future role changes. You can do this by following these steps:

1. Manually fail over from the primary server to the secondary server.
2. Disable the log shipping backup jobs on the initial primary server.
3. Configure log shipping on the secondary server (using the wizard).

In the configuration, it is advisable to use the same share and to verify that your initial database already exists.

After you perform these initial steps, you need to take the necessary actions to be able to implement the role swapping in a log shipping model.

To change roles and initiate failover, you have to perform the following steps:

1. Bring the secondary database online by using a RESTORE DATABASE statement and initiating recovery. This is something you would manually do by restoring the last transaction log from the primary server.
2. You will then disable the log shipping jobs on the primary server, and the copy and restore options on the secondary.
3. Enable the log shipping jobs on the secondary server (since that one is your primary now) and enable the copy and restore jobs on the former primary server.

Although log shipping is a fault-tolerant method, it can also be used just to create a standby or read-only server for reporting purposes, since in most database scenarios the process of creating a transaction log backup already exists.

MONITORING LOG SHIPPING

Log shipping creates a set of jobs that can be monitored from the history log in SQL Server Agent. If you configured your log shipping to use another server as a monitor server, then you can also view the status of the jobs and the execution of the backup tasks from that server.

You can review the status information and job execution information under the Agent Job Activity monitoring process, just like any other SQL Server Agent defined job.

Besides monitoring jobs in SQL Server Management Studio, you also have the ability to execute some stored procedures that provide you with information about the status of the SQL Server log shipping.

In SQL Server 2000, you can implement transaction log shipping as part of a database maintenance plan. But in SQL Server 2005, due to the many changes regarding the structure and definition of a database maintenance plan, the feature to perform log shipping no longer exists in the Maintenance Plan Wizard.

Managing Database Snapshots

How many times has a user made a mistake and you needed to recover from backup? One of the key problems of recovery is that SQL Server doesn't provide a way to back up a single table unless you force it to be created on its own filegroup. With a *database snapshot,* you have the ability to create a snapshot of your data, even before users start working with the data.

How does this work? When you create a snapshot of a database, it captures a moment in time, just as you do when you take a picture with your digital camera. And after you take that picture, you can look at the initial state when you snapped it and do comparisons with your current data.

Now, SQL Server is smart about this: It will record only the changes that occurred on a data page per data page level.

The cool features of database snapshots are the following:

- Recovering from dropped objects
- Recovering essentially any DML statement, such as insert/delete/update
- Performing data comparisons

We'll now cover how to create a database snapshot.

CREATING A SNAPSHOT

OK, it isn't all good news. There is no graphical interface for creating a database snapshot. This means you have to switch to a database query window to initiate a snapshot of a database.

The syntax to use is not much different from that in a CREATE DATABASE statement:

```
CREATE DATABASE SnapShotName ON
( NAME 5 Logicalfile, FILENAME 5
'Physicalfilename' )
AS SNAPSHOT OF SnapshotThisDatabase;
```

You use the AS SNAPSHOT keyword on the CREATE DATABASE statement, but that is not the only requirement. You also need to provide the same logical filename as given in the database used to create the snapshot.

The following statement should help you see the logical filename:

```
USE MSSQL_Training
SELECT name, physical_name from sys.database_files
WHERE type_desc = 'ROWS'
This results in something similar to this:
name physical_name
--------------------
MSSQL_Training C:\Program Files\ Microsoft SQL
Server\MSSQL.1\MSSQL\DATA\MSSQL_Training.mdf
```

The CREATE DATABASE snapshot created is as follows:

```
CREATE DATABASE MSSQL_Training_snapshot ON
( NAME = MSSQL_Training, FILENAME =
'C:\MSSQL_TrainingSnapshot.mdf' )
AS SNAPSHOT OF MSSQL_Training;
```

Please note that the CREATE DATABASE statement does not include, and should not include, a log file.

What does SQL Server do when you create a snapshot? It reserves the disk space on the hard disk, but it also uses much less space since it uses the sparse file system. As mentioned, only the changes to the actual data page are recorded, meaning that, initially, a snapshot will not take a lot of disk space.

As you review the file properties, you can see that the size on disk is definitely less than the size of the actual database. This is because no changes have occurred since creating the snapshot database.

SQL Server allows you to create multiple snapshots of a database. Of course, the snapshot database will reflect only the changes since the moment you took the snapshot. Think of this as taking a picture of a group of friends. If you take a picture of three people, that picture shows three people. When someone leaves and you take a new picture, the initial picture will still contain the three people, even though the situation has since changed. If, then, the group grows to 20 people, and you take another picture, this picture will contain the 20 people but will not alter what is shown your previous pictures.

REVERTING FROM A SNAPSHOT

The key benefit of working with snapshots is that you are able to compare a before and an after status of your data when you want to perform certain data-intensive actions. Another key benefit is that you can recover from malicious deletes. So, you have quite a few opportunities here.

The following are some of the key features of working with database snapshots:

Recovering from an update: When a database has a snapshot, the old value of the data will be stored in the snapshot database. Suppose you perform the following update in the MSSQL_Training database, on which you just created an initial snapshot:

```
UPDATE Countries
SET countryname = 'Canada'
WHERE countrycode = 'CA'
```

When selecting from the snapshot database, you will get the following:

```
SELECT * from MSSQL_Training_snapshot.dbo.Countries
countrycode countryname
------------------- ---------------------

BE Belgium
CA Canada
US USA
FR France
(4 row(s) affected)
```

To review your changed records, you can perform the following query:

```
SELECT new.countrycode, old.countryname,
NEW.countryname
FROM MSSQL_Training_snapshot.dbo.Countries old
JOIN MSSQL_Training.dbo.Countries new
ON new.countrycode = old.countrycode
AND new.countryname ,<> old.countryname
```

This will allow you to revert from the update by performing the following query:

```
UPDATE Countries
SET countryname = old.countryname
FROM MSSQL_Training_snapshot.dbo.Countries old
JOIN MSSQL_Training.dbo.Countries new
ON new.countrycode = old.countrycode
```

Recovering from a delete: Say someone accidentally deleted all your records in the countries table. You would be able to revert from the data loss by inserting from the old status that was saved in the snapshot database:

```
INSERT INTO Countries
SELECT * from MSSQL_Training_snapshot.dbo.Countries
```

X REF

The table, Countries, was created in Lesson 14.

Recovering from a dropped object: When you want to recover from a dropped object, the problem is that the object will no longer exist in the database; but it will still exist in the snapshot. Therefore, you will be able to script the object in the other database and then use one of the previous methods to recover from a delete.

As you can see, snapshots can be useful in a database recovery strategy. That said, you should not view them as a high-availability solution, but rather as a way to prevent human mistakes.

In Exercise 20-2 you will create a database snapshot, perform modifications to the actual database, compare those with the database snapshot, and recover from a deleted object.

EXERCISE 20-2 IMPLEMENTING DATABASE SNAPSHOTS

1. Connect to SQL **Server Management Studio,** and open a **new query** window.

2. In the new query window, type the following syntax to create a database snapshot. If you have multiple files, you need to list each logical name and filename separately. (See "How to Create a Database Snapshot in Books Online.")

   ```
   CREATE DATABASE MSSQL_Training_snapshot ON
   ( NAME = MSSQL_Training_data, FILENAME =
   'C:\MSSQL_TrainingSnapshot.mdf' )
   AS SNAPSHOT OF MSSQL_Training;
   ```

3. After you have created the snapshot, insert a record into the actual database:

   ```
   USE MSSQL_Training
   INSERT INTO Countries values ('ES', 'Spain')
   ```

4. Review the data stored in the snapshot:

   ```
   USE MSSQL_Training_SNAPSHOT
   SELECT * FROM Countries
   ```

5. This will result in the following:

   ```
   countrycode  countryname
   -------------------  ----------------------
   BE  Belgium
   CA  Canada
   US  USA
   FR  France
   (4 row(s) affected)
   ```

6. Update a record in the MSSQL_Training database:

   ```
   USE MSSQL_Training
   UPDATE Countries
   SET countryname = 'BelUSA'
   WHERE countrycode = 'BE'
   ```

7. Review the data stored in the snapshot:

   ```
   USE MSSQL_Training_SNAPSHOT
   SELECT * FROM Countries
   ```

8. This will result in the following:

   ```
   countrycode  countryname
   -------------------  ----------------------
   ```

```
BE  Belgium
CA  Canada
US  USA
FR  France
(4 row(s) affected)
```

9. Drop the table in the MSSQL_Training database:

```
USE MSSQL_Training
DROP TABLE Countries
```

10. Review the table existence in the Snapshot database.

```
USE MSSQL_Training_SNAPSHOT
SELECT * FROM Countries
```

11. This will result in the following:

```
countrycode  countryname
_____  _____

BE  Belgium
CA  Canada
US  USA
FR  France
(4 row(s) affected)
```

12. Perform a bulk insert to re-create the object in the MSSQL_Training database:

```
USE MSSQL_Training
SELECT * into Countries
FROM MSSQL_Training_snapshot.dbo.Countries
```

13. You have now successfully re-created a dropped object using database snapshots.

■ Case Study: Using Other High-Availability Methods

A company ships orders from pharmaceutical companies to customers all over the world. To provide fault tolerance on its production servers, the company decides to implement a clustered environment. However, the database administrator, as well as the company management, is concerned about potential data loss in case of a disaster, such as a plant explosion, earthquake, or flooding.

The general requirement is to not implement this recovery method on all databases, but to implement it generally for mission-critical databases.

To support the needs of the company, the network administrator and database department decide to use an external data center, to which they will implement database mirroring on their mission-critical databases. This will allow them to immediately switch over and keep their company running in case of a disaster at the local plant. And because of the highly secure environment the company runs in, they enforce encryption on the database mirror, and include certificate-based authentication.

Some of the processes the company runs invoke extensive manipulation of data. In case of a process failure, this company wants to be able to compare the status before initiating the process to the current status, because it was calculated and stored in the database. For this purpose, the company decides to implement database snapshots. And to minimize the creation of large snapshots, the company decides to create and manage multiple snapshots.

SKILL SUMMARY

IN THIS LESSON YOU LEARNED:

In this lesson, you learned about several high-availability options and how to implement them.

Database mirroring uses TCP communication so that you can create an exact copy of a database at a remote location. It also allows you to automatically switch over when implemented with a witness that monitors the connection and initiates the mirror to take over from the principal database.

You also learned how to work with log shipping, which takes a copy of the transaction log and "ships" it to a remote destination. To switch over to the remote standby server, you manually need to follow certain steps to perform the switch. The standby server, however, has the capability to be used as a read-only server that you can use to populate a data warehouse, for ad hoc querying, or for reporting capabilities.

Another effective method to implement is database snapshots. This takes a "picture" of data and saves only the changes to the snapshot from the moment you take the initial snapshot. Snapshots enable you to revert from user mistakes, but they do not provide fault tolerance.

For the certification examination:

- Familiarize yourself with the concept of database mirroring. Understand general terms, such as *principal*, *mirror*, and *witness server*. If you want to invoke automatic failover, you can achieve this only by having a witness. Database mirroring uses endpoints that communicate with each other using TCP. You also need to know how you can manually force a mirror to take over the role of the principal server.

- Understand log shipping. Know how to implement and use log shipping on a database—and keep in mind that this is implemented using transaction log backups. The ability to specify the schedule on the transaction log backup, and when to restore initially, determines the latency between the recovery and failover strategy. Log shipping is a manual failover process and allows you to have a hot standby server or read-only server that can be used for different purposes.

- Understand database snapshots. In a database snapshot, it is important to remember that the snapshot does not implement high availability; it only records data changes to a snapshot database. When retrieving data from a snapshot, the data will be partially read from the production database and so will get only the changed data pages from the snapshot.

■ Knowledge Assessment

Multiple Choice

Circle the letter or letters that correspond to the best answer or answers.

1. Which protocol is used by database mirroring endpoints?
   - **a.** HTTP
   - **b.** SMTP
   - **c.** TCP
   - **d.** SOAP

2. Which technologies help you to avoid user mistakes and prevent malicious deletes on a database? (Choose all that apply.)
   - **a.** Database mirroring
   - **b.** Clustering
   - **c.** DDL triggers
   - **d.** Database snapshots

3. You need to create a snapshot of the database TESTDB. What is the correct syntax to use?

   a. `CREATE DATABASE TESTDB_snapshot ON ( NAME = TESTDB_Data, FILENAME = 'C:\TestDB_Snapshot.sss' ) AS SNAPSHOT OF TestDB;`

   b. `CREATE DATABASE TESTDB_snapshot ON ( NAME = TESTDB_Data, FILENAME = 'C:\TestDB_Snapshot.sss' LOG ON 'C:\TestDB_Snapshot_log.sss') AS SNAPSHOT OF TestDB`

   c. `CREATE DATABASE SNAPSHOT TESTDB_snapshot AS SNAPSHOT OF TestDB`

   d. `CREATE DATABASE SNAPSHOT TESTDB_snapshot AS SNAPSHOT OF TestDB ON ( NAME = TESTDB_Data, FILENAME = 'C:\TestDB_Snapshot.sss' )`

4. A database snapshot has been created. Now, because of a user mistake, you need to restore a table and its indexes from the snapshot database. How can you achieve this with the least administrative effort?

   a. Use the Copy Database Wizard.

   b. Script the creation of the objects in the snapshot database, and run the script in the user database.

   c. Use a SELECT statement to reinsert the table.

   d. Rewrite the entire statement.

5. You have a database mirror in place without a witness server and notice that the principal database is down. Which statement should you execute to promote the mirror server to take the principal role?

   a. ALTER DATABASE databasename SET PARTNER FAILOVER

   b. ALTER DATABASE databasename SET PARTNER SWITCH_ROLE

   c. ALTER DATABASE databasename SET PARTNER FORCE_SERVICE_ALLOW_DATA_LOSS

   d. ALTER DATABASE databasename SET PARTNER FORCE_SERVICE_ALLOW_NO_DATA_LOSS

6. You are configuring an endpoint for database mirroring but are not sure about the correct syntax to use. Which lines would you insert on the following statement?

   ```
   CREATE ENDPOINT endpoint_mirroring STATE = STARTED ---
   insert line here ( AUTHENTICATION = WINDOWS KERBEROS,
   ENCRYPTION = SUPPORTED, ROLE5ALL);
   ```

   a. AS TCP (LISTENER_PORT = 5022) FOR DATABASE_MIRRORING

   b. AS HTTP (LISTENER_PORT = 5022) FOR SERVICE_BROKER

   c. AS HTTP (LISTENER_PORT = 5022) FOR DATABASE_MIRRORING

   d. AS HTTP (LISTENER_PORT = 5022) FOR SOAP

7. You implemented database mirroring; however, when a connection to the principal fails, you need to manually switch over to the mirror. What can you do to avoid this?

   a. Start SQL Server Agent.

   b. Review the Event log for error details.

   c. Break the mirror, and install a witness first.

   d. Configure a witness.

8. You configured database mirroring; however, the principal does not seem to be able to connect to the mirror. You verified that you created the mirroring endpoints on both the mirror and the principal using the following script on both the principal and the mirror:

   ```
   -- on principal and mirror you executed the script below
   CREATE ENDPOINT Endpoint_Mirroring STATE = STARTED AS TCP
   ( LISTENER_PORT = 5022 ) FOR DATABASE_MIRRORING
   ( AUTHENTICATION  = WINDOWS KERBEROS, ENCRYPTION = SUPPORTED,
   ROLE5ALL);

   -- on the mirror you executed the script below
   ```

```
ALTER DATABASE MSSQL_Training SET PARTNER = 'TCP://PRINCIPAL.
TRAINING.COM:4999'
-- on the principal you executed the script below ALTER DATABASE
MSSQL_Training SET PARTNER = 'TCP://MIRROR.TRAINING.COM:4999'
```

What might be the problem?

a. The mirror and principal communicate on the same port.

b. The mirror and principal endpoint have an incorrect port setting.

c. The mirror has the wrong port setting.

d. The principal should connect to port 5022.

9. You configured database mirroring; however, the principal does not seem to be able to connect to the mirror. You verified that you created the mirroring endpoints on both the mirror and the principal using the following script on both the principal and the mirror:

```
-- on principal you created the following endpoint

CREATE ENDPOINT endpoint_mirroring STATE = STARTED AS TCP
( LISTENER_PORT = 5022 ) FOR DATABASE_MIRRORING
( AUTHENTICATION = WINDOWS KERBEROS, ENCRYPTION = REQUIRED
ALGORITHM RC4, ROLE5PARTNER);

-- on mirror you created the following endpoint

CREATE ENDPOINT endpoint_mirroring STATE = STARTED AS TCP
( LISTENER_PORT = 5022 ) FOR DATABASE_MIRRORING
( AUTHENTICATION = WINDOWS KERBEROS, ENCRYPTION = REQUIRED
ALGORITHM RC4, ROLE5WITNESS);

-- on mirror you executed the script below

ALTER DATABASE MSSQL_Training SET PARTNER = 'TCP://PRINCIPAL.
TRAINING.COM:5022'

-- on principal you executed the script below

ALTER DATABASE MSSQL_Training SET PARTNER = 'TCP://MIRROR.
TRAINING.COM:5022'
```

What might be the problem?

a. You need to set SAFETY TO FULL on the database option.

b. You need to change the encryption mechanism to SUPPORTED.

c. You need to set the ROLE option on the principal to ALL or PARTNER.

d. You need to set the ROLE option on the mirror to ALL or PARTNER.

10. What should you do to centralize the results of a log shipping job to one server?

a. Centralize the location of the transaction log backup to that server.

b. Configure the server to be a monitoring server.

c. Open Windows Event Viewer to remotely review log shipping details.

d. You are unable to centralize log shipping details to one server.

11. When trying to implement log shipping, you notice that the backup jobs run successfully, but the secondary database fails to retrieve the transaction log files. What should you do?

a. Check the file permissions on the log backup location.

b. Reinitialize log shipping.

c. Start SQL Server Agent on the secondary database.

d. Check that SQL Server Agent runs in the same security context on the primary as on the secondary database.

12. After a primary database fails, you want to bring the secondary database online. What should be your first step?

a. Try to take a backup from the last transaction log on the primary database.

b. Restore the secondary with the RECOVERY option.

c. Stop the SQL Server Agent on the primary server.

d. Disable the log shipping jobs on the secondary server.

13. You created two database snapshots, one at 2:00 P.M. and one at 4:00 P.M. At 5:00 P.M., a user warns you he accidentally dropped an existing table. The user was certain that he dropped the table somewhere between 3:00 and 4:00 P.M. What should you do?
    a. Inform the user you cannot recover the table.
    b. Inform the user you can restore the table from the first snapshot.
    c. Inform the user you can restore the table from the second snapshot.
    d. Inform the user you will combine the 2:00 P.M. and 4:00 P.M. snapshots to recover both the table and data.

14. You created two database snapshots, one at 2:00 P.M. and one at 4:00 P.M. At 3:00 P.M., a user issued an UPDATE statement to a table without specifying a WHERE clause. What can you do to bring the data back to the state it was in before the user issued the statement? (Choose all that apply.)
    a. Update the database with the stored information in the 2:00 P.M. and 4:00 P.M. snapshots.
    b. Update the database with the stored information in the 2:00 P.M. snapshot.
    c. Drop the table, and retrieve all information from the 2:00 P.M. snapshot.
    d. Inform the user you will combine the 2:00 P.M. and 4:00 P.M. snapshots to recover both the table and data.

15. You created two database snapshots, one at 2:00 P.M. and one at 4:00 P.M. At 5:00 P.M. a user warns you he accidentally dropped a table he created around 3:00 P.M. The user was certain he dropped the table somewhere between 3:00 P.M. and 4:00 P.M. What should you do?
    a. Inform the user you cannot recover his table.
    b. Inform the user you can restore the table from the first snapshot.
    c. Inform the user you can restore the table from the second snapshot.
    d. Inform the user you will combine the 2:00 P.M. and 4:00 P.M. snapshots to recover both the data.

15. You are planning on integrating snapshots on an hourly basis. However, you want to perform maintenance and retain a snapshot only from the last eight hours. How can you accomplish this with the least administrative effort?
    a. Create a job that will automatically drop the database snapshots after eight hours.
    b. Manually drop database snapshots.
    c. When you create a new database snapshot, specify the WITH DROP_EXISTING option.
    d. You can create only one database snapshot at a time.

16. You have a SQL Server report server that is currently generating reports with data coming from your production database. The company has a log shipping database, and you also use database snapshots. Recently there has been a heavy workload on the production database. What can you do to minimize the impact of database querying on the production database?
    a. Point the report data sources to retrieve data from the snapshot.
    b. Point the report data sources to retrieve data from the secondary log shipped database.
    c. Set up replication to replicate data from the production database to the report server.
    d. Create another instance of SQL Server, and set up log shipping.

17. You need to implement a fault-tolerance method that will allow you to automatically switch over to a standby server when an error occurs with the primary production database. Which options can you choose to implement?
    a. Clustering
    b. Database snapshots
    c. Database mirroring
    d. Log shipping

18. You have only two servers in place and want to implement fault tolerance. What can you do to provide fault tolerance on two important user databases that you have?
    a. Implement a cluster.
    b. Implement database mirroring.
    c. Implement database snapshots.
    d. Implement log shipping.

19. What is one of the disadvantages of database mirroring?
    a. You need to have the same hardware.
    b. The database you mirror to will be in an unused standby state.
    c. You cannot have automatic failover.
    d. You need to have, at minimum, three servers.

■ Case Scenarios

Scenario 20-1: Maintaining Data Integrity

You support multiple servers in your facility. Your bosses agree to, at most, a 10-minute data loss under any circumstances in your security test and evaluation plan. They know the funding costs involved and accept this budget plan. Of the three options presented in this lesson, which best meets the need under a variety of circumstances. Discuss in class what you would do if you also had failover clustering and/or if you also had nightly backups with log file backups every five minutes.

21 LESSON

Service Broker

LESSON SKILL MATRIX

TECHNOLOGY SKILL	70-431 EXAM OBJECTIVE
Implement Service Broker components.	Foundational
Create services.	Foundational
Create queues.	Foundational
Create contracts.	Foundational
Create conversations.	Foundational
Create message types.	Foundational
Send messages to a service.	Foundational
Route a message to a service.	Foundational
Receive messages from a service.	Foundational

KEY TERMS

contract: A contract defines which message types an application uses to accomplish a particular task. A contract is an agreement between two services about which messages each service sends to accomplish a particular task. Contract definitions persist in the database where the type is created.

messages: Messages contain the information exchanged between applications that use Service Broker. Each message is part of a *conversation*.

queues: Queues store messages. Service Broker manages queues, and presents a view of a queue that is similar to a table.

route: Service Broker uses routes to determine where to deliver messages.

service: A service is a name for a specific business task or set of business tasks. Conversations occur between services.

Service Broker: Provides facilities for storing message queues in a SQL Server database.

■ Understanding the SQL Server Service Broker Architecture

THE BOTTOM LINE

Service Broker, a feature new to SQL Server 2005, provides a solution to common problems with *message* delivery and consistency that occur when transferring transactional messages or data from one server to another. The new technology in SQL Server 2005 allows SQL Server to implement its own architecture to create a *queue*-based message delivery system that guarantees delivery.

Before delving into the Service Broker architecture, you first need to understand why this technology is needed. Say you want to buy a conference ticket, but you don't want to line up at the ticket office, only to find that the tickets have sold out and that you can only be added to the standby list.

Wouldn't it be preferable if you could just use an application to formulate your ticket request and then receive a reply that tells you whether you have tickets or have been added to a standby list, even when the ticket office is closed and no one is there currently to process your request?

That is exactly what you can do with Service Broker. The Service Broker technology, which is part of the database engine, provides a message-based communication platform similar to this ticket scenario. The platform enables independent application components to perform as a whole.

Service Broker includes the infrastructure for asynchronous programming, which can be used for applications within a single database or a single instance, as well as for distributed applications.

Service Broker also makes it easy to scale your application up or down to accommodate the amount of traffic it receives. When a number of requests are queued up, you actually can implement more queue readers to process requests. Figure 21-1 shows you how SQL Server Service Broker works with messages, how messages are submitted to a queue, and how messages are processed from a queue.

The notable feature of this queue mechanism is that SQL Server will guarantee that messages will be submitted to and processed from the queue in the correct order. The same thing happens at a ticket desk: when the queue gets too busy, you can add service programs that will read from the queue and process it.

CERTIFICATION READY?
Service Broker provides a mechanism for implementing Service-Oriented Architecture concepts.

Figure 21-1

SQL Server Service Broker

BROKER ARCHITECTURE

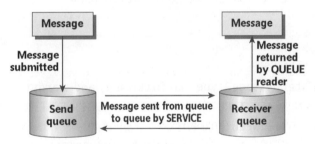

Working with Service Broker

Service Broker consists of various components that make up the entire architecture. It is important to understand all these components.

The first step you take when designing a broker architecture is to define which messages you need in the application. You can specify which message type can be sent by the initiator and what can be returned by the target or destination. The messages that are sent will be submitted to a queue and processed by a *service* program. To communicate from one service to the other, you also have to specify the route to get to that destination. What is the protocol you will use to route messages over servers? HTTP, of course; you will define HTTP endpoints and configure them to be used by the broker service. When defining which service can send and receive information from each other, you have to set up an agreement, called a *contract.*

It is important to understand the steps involved in configuring a broker architecture. We'll cover them in more depth in the following sections.

CREATING A MESSAGE TYPE

You can create a message type using the CREATE MESSAGE TYPE statement. In creating these message types, you can define different types, depending on how you structure the message body. Consider this to be the same as an e-mail message, for which you specify the subject and then define the body of the message. It's the same for a message type; the subject will be the message type, and you specify what the message body can contain. Sometimes, when you read an e-mail message, you know from the subject line what the content is about, and you don't need to type a body. The SQL Server Service Broker architecture supports the following message bodies:

None: No validation on the content takes place; you can send whatever you like in the body.

Header only: empty: This is the header only; you are sending a message with an empty body.

Well-formed XML: The data in the message body needs to be well-formed XML.

Schema-bound XML: The data in the message body needs to be schema-validated XML. This means the message-body XML schema must exist on the server. You learned in Lesson 15 how to work with the XML datatype and the XML Schema collection.

This leads to the following syntax:

```
CREATE MESSAGE TYPE message_type_name
[ AUTHORIZATION owner_name ]
[ VALIDATION = { NONE
| EMPTY
| WELL_FORMED_XML
| VALID_XML WITH
SCHEMA COLLECTION schema_collection_name
} ]
[ ; ]
```

Here is an example:

```
-- create message type on initiator and target
CREATE MESSAGE TYPE TicketRequest AUTHORIZATION dbo
VALIDATION = WELL_FORMED_XML
CREATE MESSAGE TYPE TicketStatus AUTHORIZATION dbo
VALIDATION = WELL_FORMED_XML
```

CREATING A QUEUE

The next step in configuring a broker architecture is creating the queue. You can specify what should happen to the queue when you submit a message, which you can do by configuring its status and activation properties.

In the following example, you will create the sender queue and the recipient queue that will process the send and received messages. Note that you are not putting any automatic activation on the queue so that you can see how to manually process a message from a queue. Here's the example:

```
-- Execute this statement on the sender
CREATE QUEUE SenderQUEUE
-- Execute this statement on the receiver
CREATE QUEUE ReceiverQUEUE
```

Later, you will use an ALTER QUEUE statement to specify you are automatically retrieving and processing messages from a queue.

The full syntax to create a queue is as follows:

```
CREATE QUEUE <object>
[ WITH
[ STATUS = { ON | OFF } [ , ] ]
[ RETENTION = { ON | OFF } [ , ] ]
[ ACTIVATION (
[ STATUS = { ON | OFF } , ]
PROCEDURE_NAME = <procedure>,
MAX_QUEUE_READERS = max_readers,
EXECUTE AS { SELF | 'user_name' | OWNER }
) ]
]
[ ON { filegroup | [ DEFAULT ] } ]
[ ; ]
object ::=
{
[ database_name. [ schema_name ]. | schema_name. ]
queue_name
}
procedure ::=
{
[ database_name. [ schema_name ] . | schema_name. ]
stored_procedure_name
}
```

CREATING A CONTRACT

In a contract, you set up the agreement between the sender of a message and the recipient. This contract defines which message type can be sent by the initiator and what can be returned by the target.

In the ticket service example, you will submit a ticket request from the initiator using a TicketRequest message, and receive a status update message from the sender in the form of a TicketStatus message.

The contract defines which messages can be sent to which queue; of course, it is absolutely possible to have various contracts submitting messages to the same queue.

The CREATE CONTRACT syntax is as follows:

```
CREATE CONTRACT contract_name
[ AUTHORIZATION owner_name ]
( { message_type_name
SENT BY { INITIATOR | TARGET | ANY }
| [ DEFAULT ] } [ ,...n] )
[ ; ]
```

Here's an example:

```
-- create the contract
CREATE CONTRACT TicketServicesContract
(TicketRequest SENT BY INITIATOR,
TicketStatus SENT BY TARGET)
```

CREATING A SERVICE

Now that you have configured queues, message types, and a contract, you can set up the service. A service references a contract. Service Broker uses the name of the service to route messages, deliver messages to the correct queue within a database, and enforce the contract for a conversation. If you are targeting multiple services to participate in the broker service, you need to create the routes between them.

You can assign multiple contracts to a service, as well. Service programs initiate conversations to this service using the contracts specified. If no contracts are specified, the service may only initiate conversations.

In the following example, you will set up the broker services that follow the TicketServicesContract:

```
-- create the service on the sender
CREATE SERVICE SendTicketingService ON
Queue SenderQUEUE
(TicketServicesContract)
-- create the service on the recipient
CREATE SERVICE ReceiveTicketingService ON
Queue ReceiverQUEUE
(TicketServicesContract)
```

Once the services are configured, you can specify the route between them if you communicate over multiple services. When not configured, you will use the local database service and default service route.

The CREATE SERVICE statement follows this syntax:

```
CREATE SERVICE service_name
[ AUTHORIZATION owner_name ]
ON QUEUE [ schema_name. ]queue_name
[ ( contract_name | [DEFAULT] [ ,...n ] ) ]
[ ; ]
```

You're almost ready to go now. But one last thing you need to check is whether the database has the broker service enabled. If not, no broker service communication is possible. You can check whether the database is broker service is enabled by querying the sys.databases view:

```
select name,service_broker_guid,is_broker_enabled
from sys.databases
```

If the broker service is enabled, it will return a value of 1; otherwise, you will have to enable the broker service by executing an ALTER DATABASE statement:

```
ALTER DATABASE MSSQL_Training
SET ENABLE_BROKER
```

After creating and configuring the broker service, you can proceed to the next level, performing a test message, and see whether you can get an item in the queue.

CREATING A ROUTE

For outgoing messages, Service Broker determines the routing by checking the routing table in the local database.

In a route, you specify the communication settings between services. Before creating a route, you should configure the HTTP endpoints by using the CREATE ENDPOINT statement, which is covered in Lesson 22.

One of the settings you need to determine is the broker instance identifier, which is expressed by a GUID. The broker instance you specify must be the identifier of the destination database; it can be determined by the following SELECT statement:

```
SELECT service_broker_guid
FROM sys.databases
WHERE database_id = DB_ID()
```

This is an example of how to specify the route:

```
CREATE ROUTE TicketingRoute
WITH
SERVICE_NAME = 'SendTicketingService',
BROKER_INSTANCE =
'D8D4D268-02A3-4C62-8F91-634B89C1E315',
ADDRESS = 'TCP://192.168.10.2:1234';
```

Here is the full syntax:

```
CREATE ROUTE route_name [ AUTHORIZATION owner_name ]
WITH
[ SERVICE_NAME = 'service_name', ]
[ BROKER_INSTANCE = 'broker_instance_identifier', ]
[ LIFETIME = route_lifetime, ]
ADDRESS = 'next_hop_address'
[ , MIRROR_ADDRESS = 'next_hop_mirror_address' ]
[ ; ]
```

In this example, however, you are using services that run on the same database, so you don't need to create a route.

Using Service Broker

After successfully configuring the broker service, you can start sending messages over the broker instance. Key components in this process are the queue and the service program.

On a queue, you have the ability to add an item to a queue and have the service program automatically pick up the message. You can configure this using the ACTIVATION option on the CREATE QUEUE statement.

What is so remarkable about a queue? Actually, you could consider this as a special system-created table with certain columns. (Table 21-1 displays the entire structure of a queue.) If you consider the queue to be a table, you can then think it possible to insert records (messages) into this table. However, the syntax you will be using is slightly different. Instead of inserting messages and selecting messages, you send and receive messages to and from a queue using SEND and RECEIVE statements.

Multiple messages can be *sent* together, which is expressed in a conversation. In the following section, you will learn how to submit messages to a queue. In the section after that, you will learn how to receive messages from the queue.

SENDING MESSAGES

You manage messages using a queue. To group messages, you initiate a dialog, in which you forward related messages. To identify a conversation, you use a unique identifier. You then have to end the conversation so the messages can be processed by the queue. The next sections show you how.

Table 21-1

Queue Description

Column Name	Datatype	Description
Status	Tinyint	Status of the message. For messages returned by the RECEIVE command, the status is always 1. Messages in the queue may contain one of the following values: 0=Received message, 1=Ready, 2=Not yet complete, and 3=Retained sent message.
queuing_order	Bigint	Message order number within the queue.
conversation_group_id	Uniqueidentifier	Identifier for the conversation group to which this message belongs.
conversation_handle	Uniqueidentifier	Handle for the conversation for which this message is a part.
Message_sequence_number	Bigint	Sequence number of the message within the conversation.
service_name	Nvarchar(512)	Name of the service to which the conversation belongs.
service_id	Int	SQL Server object identifier of the service to which the conversation belongs.
service_contract_name	Nvarchar(256)	Name of the contract that the conversation follows.
service_contract_id	Int	SQL Server object identifier of the contract that the conversation follows.
Message_type_name	Nvarchar(256)	Name of the message type that describes the message.
Message_type_id	Int	SQL Server object identifier of the message type that describes the message.
Validation	Nchar(2)	Validation used for the message (E=EmptyN=NoneX=XML).
Message_body	Varbinary(MAX)	Content of the message.
Message_id	Uniqueidentifier	Unique identifier for the message.

You begin a conversation from one service to another service like this:

```
BEGIN DIALOG [ CONVERSATION ] @dialog_handle
FROM SERVICE initiator_service_name
TO SERVICE 'target_service_name'
[ , { 'service_broker_guid' |
'CURRENT DATABASE' } ]
[ ON CONTRACT contract_name ]
[ WITH
[ { RELATED_CONVERSATION = related_conversation_handle
| RELATED_CONVERSATION_GROUP =
related_conversation_group_id } ]
[ [ , ] LIFETIME = dialog_lifetime ]
```

```
[ [ , ] ENCRYPTION = { ON | OFF } ] ]
[ ; ]
```

In this example, you will create an easy XML ticket request, wherein you provide the number of requested tickets and the e-mail address of the requestor:

```
-- test and submit an order to a queue
declare @message xml
declare @conversationhandle UNIQUEIDENTIFIER
set @message =
'<TICKETREQUEST><Requestor>student@training.com</Requestor>
<Requestednumber>5</Requestednumber>
<RequestedShow>SQL Server Seminar</RequestedShow>
</TICKETREQUEST>'
BEGIN DIALOG CONVERSATION @conversationHandle
FROM SERVICE SendTicketingService
TO SERVICE 'ReceiveTicketingService'
ON CONTRACT TicketServicesContract
WITH ENCRYPTION = OFF;
-- Send the message on the dialog.
SEND ON CONVERSATION @conversationHandle
MESSAGE TYPE TicketRequest
(@message);
END CONVERSATION @conversationHandle
-- End the conversation.
```

Now, let's delve more deeply into this example. Before sending a message, you need to initiate a conversation—consider this to be a normal conversation where you first say hi to someone before you start asking questions or chatting. This conversation handle is unique, which is why you declare it as a UNIQUEIDENTIFIER.

The type of message you'll send is XML; remember, you declared the message type to be a well-formed XML message.

In a conversation, you communicate from one service to the other over an existing contract. Within a conversation, it is possible to submit more than one message. Think about this as requesting some tickets for a show on Broadway at the same time you are requesting tickets for the U.S. Open Tennis final.

In the example, you are sending only one ticket request, which you do by using the SEND statement on the existing conversation. As soon as you submit the message, and have no additional messages to send within the same conversation, you end the conversation by using an END CONVERSATION statement. Of course, in a real-world scenario, you would create a stored procedure from this instead of repeating all the T-SQL syntax.

RECEIVING MESSAGES

Once you have the message submitted to the recipient, you have to retrieve it from the receiving queue. As already mentioned, if the queue is a table, this would be selecting from the table to process the message and, in a next step after processing, delete it from a table.

Retrieving a message from a queue, however, uses the RECEIVE statement, which will process every message. This message retrieval process may be complex, because you may want to retrieve messages from the queue one by one or all at once. When processing these messages, it is important to test on the message type and filter informational messages from the message you want to process.

The following example processes messages from a queue:

```
-- retrieve messages from a queue
DECLARE @conversation_handle UNIQUEIDENTIFIER,
@message_body XML,
@message_type_name NVARCHAR(128);
RECEIVE TOP(1)
@conversation_handle = conversation_handle,
@message_type_name = message_type_name,
@message_body = message_body
FROM [dbo].[ReceiverQUEUE]
-- DO SOMETHING with the message
IF @message_type_name = 'TicketRequest'
BEGIN
EXEC up_processticketrequest (@message_body)
END
END CONVERSATION @conversation_handle WITH CLEANUP;
END
```

In this example, again you declare a conversation handle to define a conversation handle. You also declare an XML datatype to retrieve the message body, and use a variable, to which you will assign the message type name.

The RECEIVE statement will process the message from the queue and store it in the variable. If the message type received is TicketRequest, you will proceed by executing a stored procedure, to which you pass the message. The procedure called will insert the ticket request into a stored procedure and submit an e-mail to the sender using SQL Database Mail. By the end of the processing, you conclude the conversation to delete the processed message from a queue. The full syntax for receiving messages from a queue is as follows:

```
[ WAITFOR ( ]
RECEIVE [ TOP ( n ) ]
<column_specifier> [ ,...n ]
FROM <queue>
[ INTO table_variable ]
[ WHERE { conversation_handle = conversation_handle
| conversation_group_id = conversation_group_id } ]
[ ) ] [ , TIMEOUT timeout ]
[ ; ]
<column_specifier> ::=
{ *
| { column_name | [ ] expression }
[ [ AS ] column_alias ]
| column_alias = expression
} [ ,...n ]
<queue> ::=
{
```

```
[ database_name.[ schema_name.| schema_name.]
queue_name
}
```

The WAITFOR statement waits until a message is received in the queue, while the RECEIVE statement with the TOP clause specifies how many messages you are processing at once. In a real-world scenario, you would process the messages in the queue using a stored procedure, meaning you would put the RECEIVE statement inside the stored procedure.

AUTOMATING THE QUEUE PROCESSING

To automate the queue processing, you can change the status of a queue (or specify this when you create the queue). When making changes to the queue, you execute the ALTER QUEUE statement, as shown here:

```
ALTER QUEUE ReceiverQUEUE
WITH ACTIVATION (STATUS = ON,
PROCEDURE_NAME = up_ProcessQUEUE,
EXECUTE AS OWNER)
```

In the example, you are activating the stored procedure up_ProcessQUEUE to fire when an item is submitted to a queue. The content of the stored procedure will, of course, check the messages submitted and take appropriate action.

In the ACTIVATION property, you specify which stored procedure needs to be called and in which security context the stored procedure will execute.

The stored procedure will look similar to the RECEIVE statement you issued:

```
CREATE PROCEDURE up_ProcessQueue
AS
BEGIN
DECLARE @conversation_handle UNIQUEIDENTIFIER,
@message_body XML,
@message_type_name NVARCHAR(128);
RECEIVE TOP(1)
@conversation_handle = conversation_handle,
@message_type_name = message_type_name,
@message_body = message_body
FROM [dbo].[ReceiverQUEUE]
-- DO SOMETHING with the message
IF @message_type_name = 'TicketRequest'
BEGIN
EXEC up_processticketrequest @message_body
END
END CONVERSATION @conversation_handle;
END
```

As soon as an item is submitted to the queue, the stored procedure will execute the statement and process it.

In Exercise 21-1, you will set up a broker architecture to send messages—a ticket request—from an initiator queue to a target queue. By the end of the exercise, you will have completed the entire process of setting up and configuring a broker architecture.

→ **EXERCISE 21-1 IMPLEMENTING A SERVICE BROKER ARCHITECTURE**

1. Open a **new query** window, and type the following syntax to enable the broker architecture in the MSSQL_Training database:

```
USE MASTER
GO
-- Enable the broker architecture
ALTER database MSSQL_Training
SET ENABLE_BROKER
GO
USE MSSQL_Training
GO
```

2. Execute the following code to create the message types:

```
-- define broker architecture
-- create message type on initiator and target
CREATE MESSAGE TYPE TicketRequest AUTHORIZATION dbo
VALIDATION = WELL_FORMED_XML
CREATE MESSAGE TYPE TicketStatus AUTHORIZATION dbo
VALIDATION = WELL_FORMED_XML
```

3. Execute the following code to create the sender and receiver queue:

```
-- CREATE QUEUES
-- Execute this statement on the sender
CREATE QUEUE SenderQUEUE
-- Execute this statement on the receiver
CREATE QUEUE ReceiverQUEUE
```

4. Execute the following code to create the contract:

```
-- create the contract
CREATE CONTRACT TicketServicesContract
(TicketRequest SENT BY INITIATOR,
TicketStatus SENT BY TARGET)
```

5. Execute the following code to initiate the services:

```
-- create the service on the sender
CREATE SERVICE SendTicketingService ON
Queue SenderQUEUE
(TicketServicesContract)
-- create the service on the recipient
CREATE SERVICE ReceiveTicketingService ON
Queue ReceiverQUEUE
(TicketServicesContract)
```

6. Execute the following code to submit a message to the queue:

```
-- test and submit an order to a queue
DECLARE @message xml
DECLARE @conversationhandle UNIQUEIDENTIFIER
SET @message =
```

```
'<TICKETREQUEST>
<Requestor>student@training.com</Requestor>
<Requestednumber>5</Requestednumber>
<RequestedShow>SQL Server Training</RequestedShow>
</TICKETREQUEST>' '
BEGIN DIALOG CONVERSATION @conversationHandle
FROM SERVICE SendTicketingService
TO SERVICE 'ReceiveTicketingService'
ON CONTRACT TicketServicesContract
WITH ENCRYPTION = OFF;
-- Send the message on the dialog.
SEND ON CONVERSATION @conversationHandle
MESSAGE TYPE TicketRequest
(@message);
END CONVERSATION @conversationHandle
-- End the conversation.
```

7. Execute the following SELECT statement to check whether this message is, and perhaps other messages are, in the queue:

```
-- check the content of the queue
SELECT * from ReceiverQUEUE
GO
```

8. Create a stored procedure to process the messages from the queue:

```
-- CREATE PROCEDURE TO RETRIEVE MESSAGES FROM THE QUEUE
CREATE PROCEDURE up_ProcessQueue
AS
BEGIN
DECLARE @conversation_handle UNIQUEIDENTIFIER,
@message_body XML,
@message_type_name NVARCHAR(128);
RECEIVE TOP(1)
@conversation_handle = conversation_handle,
@message_type_name = message_type_name,
@message_body = message_body
FROM [dbo].[ReceiverQUEUE]
-- DO SOMETHING with the message
IF @message_type_name = 'TicketRequest'
BEGIN
-- To process from the queue you would write a stored
procedure to handle the message
-- EXEC up_processticketrequest @message_body
--for exercise purposes you just select the message
SELECT @message_body
END
END CONVERSATION @conversation_handle;
END
GO
```

9. Alter the queue, and enable automatic activation:

```
-- alter the queue for automatic activation
ALTER QUEUE ReceiverQUEUE
WITH ACTIVATION (STATUS = ON,
PROCEDURE_NAME = up_ProcessQUEUE,
EXECUTE AS OWNER)
GO
```

10. Execute the stored procedure manually to check the queue processing:

```
-- EXECUTE the Stored Procedure Manually
EXEC up_ProcessQUEUE
```

As you probably noticed, a lot of syntax is required with the SQL Server Service Broker architecture, and SQL Server 2005 does not provide you a graphical interface to configure queues, and so on. However, you can review created queues and other related broker service objects in Object Explorer.

■ Case Study: Implementing a Broker Architecture

A company wanted to automate its process to submit orders to suppliers and to inform distributors about orders that need to be shipped to their customers. Prior to installing SQL Server 2005, the company had been manually submitting an order by e-mail in the form of an Excel spreadsheet, which was then imported by a supplier into an order-entry system. The complaint of this company was that it took too long before suppliers confirmed the delivery of a certain order. Since all the suppliers had already implemented SQL Server 2005, the company's technology design team decided to work out a new solution.

The result of this two-phase design translates to SQL Server Service Broker architecture.

1. When an article reaches its minimum stock, a message for purchase is submitted to a queue. The service program submits a purchase request to the supplier, which is verified by a confirmation that the order is currently processing.

2. The company is planning on extending this automated service beyond its suppliers to also inform distributors about orders that need to be delivered. Also, the team is investigating how it can integrate the service on its own delivery trucks, so that as soon as an order is delivered to the customer, the company automatically sends a delivery confirmation to the central database.

The design group decided to implement this strategy because it will allow the company to integrate with future customers, and it will give the company the ability to deliver queued messages to BizTalk Server 2006 by using a data connector that allows BizTalk Server to read from a SQL Server Service Broker service queue.

SKILL SUMMARY

IN THIS LESSON YOU LEARNED:

In this lesson, you learned how to configure a Service Broker architecture. A Service Broker architecture is useful in an environment where you need a message-based system or a queue-based system.

Since SQL Server 2005 is secure out of the box, you need to enable Service Broker on the database level before you can start using it, which is something people frequently forget to do.

Because of security reasons, Service Broker, by default, is capable of communicating only on local servers. If you want to allow external access, you need to configure an endpoint for Service Broker. You learned how to do this in this lesson. HTTP can use endpoints for SOAP requests, and endpoints can provide access to the database from any client that can explore and use a Web service.

Service Broker works with message types, contracts, queues, and service programs. On a queue, you can specify how an endpoint should be activated. The entire configuration of the Web service, including the permissions and IP restrictions, are managed within SQL Server. Users will need to be granted permissions before they can connect to an endpoint.

For the certification examination:

- Know how to configure and work with the Service Broker. Understand the Service Broker architecture and the components it consists of in terms of services, service programs, contracts, message types, and routing.

- Understand how to create a service. Know how a service is created by identifying which contract is used, and be able to configure and identify the CREATE SERVICE syntax.

- Understand how to create a queue. On a queue, you have the possibility to initiate the activation of the queue and specify the service program to use (stored procedure).

- Understand how to create a contract. In a contract, you identify what message types the initiator can send and what can be returned by the sender.

- Understand how to create a message type. Message type bodies can be empty (i.e., header-only messages), or they may need to be well-formed XML or match an XML schema collection.

- Know how to initiate a conversation. When submitting messages to a queue, you need to create a conversation. Within a conversation, you can submit multiple messages that relate to each other.

- Understand how to send and receive messages. When sending and receiving messages, you use the SEND and RECEIVE keywords. You need to fully understand the syntax, how to retrieve messages from a queue, and how to close the conversation when it has concluded.

- Understand how to create and secure HTTP endpoints. When creating endpoints, you need to identify the virtual directory or path on the server, as well as configure the methods that can be used by the endpoint. You need to know that all security is managed within the endpoint configuration and that a user must have the appropriate permissions to connect to an endpoint.

■ Knowledge Assessment

Multiple Choice

Circle the letter or letters that correspond to the best answer or answers.

1. You need to create a message type TicketIssued that will have an empty message body. What is the syntax you use to accomplish this?
   a. CREATE MESSAGE TYPE TicketIssued VALIDATION = NONE
   b. CREATE MESSAGE TYPE TicketIssued VALIDATION = EMPTY
   c. CREATE MESSAGE TYPE TicketIssued BODY = NONE
   d. CREATE MESSAGE TYPE TicketIssued BODY = EMPTY

2. You need to insert a message in a queue and execute the following statements, but for some reason the message was not submitted to the queue. Identify the problem.

```
declare @message xml
declare @conversationhandle UNIQUEIDENTIFIER
set @message = '<TICKETREQUEST>
<Requestor>student@training.com</Requestor>
<Requestednumber>5</Requestednumber>
<RequestedShow>SQL Server
Training</RequestedShow></TICKETREQUEST>'
BEGIN DIALOG CONVERSATION @conversationHandle
FROM SERVICE SendTicketingService
TO SERVICE 'ReceiveTicketingService'
ON CONTRACT TicketServicesContract
WITH ENCRYPTION = OFF;
END CONVERSATION @conversationHandle
-- End the conversation.
```

   a. You need to commit the transaction by the end of the statement.
   b. You forgot to insert the record in the queue table using the INSERT statement.
   c. You forgot to send the message on the conversation.
   d. You cannot close the conversation at the end of a conversation message.

3. You need to create the infrastructure for a service. One of the tasks is to create a queue. You don't want the queue to allow the receipt of messages until you complete all work. Which code can you use?
   a. CREATE QUEUE SalesQueue
   b. CREATE QUEUE SalesQueue WITH STATUS=ON
   c. CREATE QUEUE SalesQueue WITH STATUS=OFF
   d. CREATE QUEUE SalesQueue WITH RETENTION=OFF

4. For auditing purposes for a certain queue you want to retain messages sent or received on conversations until the conversations have ended. Which method can you use?
   a. CREATE QUEUE SalesAuditQueue WITH RETENTION=OFF.
   b. CREATE QUEUE SalesAuditQueue WITH RETENTION=ON.
   c. CREATE QUEUE SalesAuditQueue.
   d. SELECT statement instead of RECEIVE.

5. You are building the infrastructure for a service. You create a queue, and you need to have the queue active. Service Broker will activate a stored procedure to handle messages. Currently, the stored procedure is not finished, and you want to prevent its activation. Which method can you use?
   a. CREATE QUEUE SalesQueue WITH STATUS = ON, ACTIVATION (STATUS=OFF, PROCEDURE_NAME = sales_procedure, MAX_QUEUE_READERS = 10, EXECUTE AS SELF)
   b. CREATE QUEUE SalesQueue WITH STATUS = OFF, ACTIVATION (STATUS=OFF, PROCEDURE_NAME = sales_procedure, MAX_QUEUE_READERS = 10, EXECUTE AS SELF)
   c. CREATE QUEUE SalesQueue WITH STATUS = OFF, ACTIVATION (STATUS=ON, PROCEDURE_NAME = sales_procedure, MAX_QUEUE_READERS = 10, EXECUTE AS SELF)
   d. CREATE QUEUE SalesQueue WITH ACTIVATION (STATUS=ON, PROCEDURE_NAME = sales_procedure, MAX_QUEUE_READERS = 10, EXECUTE AS SELF)

6. You need to create a contract to send and receive ticket requests and status. Both types can be sent from both ends of the conversation. Which method can you use?
   a. CREATE CONTRACT TicketServicesContract (TicketRequest SENT BY INITIATOR, TicketStatus SENT BY TARGET)

   b. CREATE CONTRACT TicketServicesContract (TicketRequest
      SENT BY ANY, TicketStatus SENT BY ANY)
   c. CREATE CONTRACT TicketServicesContract (TicketRequest
      SENT BY INITIATOR, TicketStatus SENT BY INITIATOR)
   d. CREATE CONTRACT TicketServicesContract (TicketRequest
      SENT BY TARGET, TicketStatus SENT BY TARGET)

7. You need to create a contract to send and receive ticket requests and status. Both types can be sent from both ends of the conversation. Additionally, you want to be able to send messages of the default message type. Which method can you use?
   a. CREATE CONTRACT TicketServicesContract (TicketRequest SENT BY
      ANY, TicketStatus SENT BY ANY)
   b. CREATE CONTRACT TicketServicesContract (TicketRequest SENT BY
      INITIATOR, TicketStatus SENT BY TARGET)
   c. CREATE CONTRACT TicketServicesContract (DEFAULT SENT BY ANY,
      TicketRequest SENT BY ANY, TicketStatus SENT BY ANY)
   d. CREATE CONTRACT TicketServicesContract ([DEFAULT] SENT BY ANY,
      TicketRequest SENT BY ANY, TicketStatus SENT BY ANY)

8. You need to change the authorization for an existing contract. How can you accomplish that?
   a. Use the DROP CONTRACT statement,
      followed by a CREATE CONTRACT statement.
   b. Alter the contract using ALTER CONTRACT.
   c. Use the ALTER AUTHORIZATION statement.
   d. Use the DROP CONTRACT statement.

9. Which of the following is not true regarding services?
   a. You can have multiple contracts for a service.
   b. You can use the DEFAULT contract for creating a service.
   c. You cannot create a service without a contract.
   d. You can add and remove contracts from an existing service.

10. You need to modify an existing service. You want to use a new queue and move the existing messages from the old queue to the new one. How can you accomplish that?
   a. Use the ALTER SERVICE statement and the ON QUEUE option.
   b. You cannot move existing messages to a new queue.
   c. Drop the existing service and re-create it using the new queue.
   d. Move the messages manually.

11. You want to create a service that will use the DEFAULT contract and a contract named SalesContract. How can you accomplish that?
   a. CREATE SERVICE SalesService ON QUEUE SalesQueue
   b. CREATE SERVICE SalesService ON QUEUE SalesQueue ([DEFAULT])
   c. CREATE SERVICE SalesService ON QUEUE SalesQueue ([DEFAULT],
      SalesContract)
   d. CREATE SERVICE SalesService ON QUEUE SalesQueue (SalesContract)

12. Which of the following is true about conversations and encryption? (Choose all that apply.)
   a. Messages exchanged within services are always encrypted.
   b. Messages exchanged with services in the same instance of SQL Server 2005 are not encrypted.
   c. When the services are in different databases, a database master key is not required.
   d. The ENCRYPTION setting of the BEGIN DIALOG statement specifies whether messages sent and received must be encrypted.

13. You create a conversation between two services. You want to specify 30 minutes as the maximum amount of time that the conversation will remain open. How can you accomplish that?
   a. DECLARE @dialog_handle UNIQUEIDENTIFIER BEGIN DIALOG
      CONVERSATION @dialog_handle FROM SERVICE
      SalesClientService TO SERVICE 'SalesService' ON
      CONTRACT SalesContract WITH LIFETIME = 1800;

    b. DECLARE @dialog_handle UNIQUEIDENTIFIER BEGIN DIALOG
       CONVERSATION @dialog_handle FROM SERVICE
       SalesClientService TO SERVICE 'SalesService' ON
       CONTRACT SalesContract WITH LIFETIME = 1800000;

    c. DECLARE @dialog_handle UNIQUEIDENTIFIER BEGIN DIALOG
       CONVERSATION @dialog_handle FROM SERVICE
       SalesClientService TO SERVICE 'SalesService' ON
       CONTRACT SalesContract WITH LIFETIME = 30;

    d. DECLARE @dialog_handle UNIQUEIDENTIFIER BEGIN DIALOG
       CONVERSATION @dialog_handle FROM SERVICE
       SalesClientService TO SERVICE 'SalesService' ON
       CONTRACT SalesContract;

14. You need to remove all messages from one side of an existing conversation. The remote services are owned by another company and have been completely removed. How can you complete your task?

    a. END CONVERSATION @conversation_handle;

    b. END CONVERSATION @conversation_handle WITH ERROR = 1
       DESCRIPTION = 'Remote service is unavailable';

    c. END CONVERSATION @conversation_handle WITH CLEANUP;

    d. Do nothing; SQL Server will clean up automatically.

15. Which of the following are true about the SEND statement? (Choose all that apply.)

    a. To send a message, you need a valid conversation identifier.

    b. It's mandatory to specify a message type.

    c. You can send a message with the message body empty.

    d. You can specify NULL for the message_body_expression argument.

16. You retrieve a message using the RECEIVE statement from queue that has the RETENTION setting ON. What is the effect of the RECEIVE statement on the message in this particular case?

    a. The RECEIVE statement will remove the message from the queue.

    b. The RECEIVE statement will have no effect on the message.

    c. The RECEIVE statement will update the status column of the queue for the retrieved message and leave the message in the queue.

    d. The RECEIVE statement will update the queuing_order column of the queue.

17. You want to receive all available messages from a specified conversation group. You do not need all columns from the queue, just the message body. Which code can you use?

    a. RECEIVE * FROM SalesQueue WHERE conversation_group_id
       = @conversation_group;

    b. RECEIVE * FROM SalesQueue WHERE
       conversation_handle = @conversation_group;

    c. RECEIVE message_body FROM SalesQueue WHERE
       conversation_ group_id = @conversation_group;

    d. RECEIVE message_type FROM SalesQueue WHERE
       conversation_ group_id = @conversation_group;

■ Case Scenarios

Scenario 21-1: Understanding Service-Oriented Architecture (SOA)

You and your classmates are on the Joint Application Design team for your company. The company hired a contractor to facilitate meetings of your subject matters experts—those people in each department who know the business best. The facilitator explains to you during a briefing that SOA is all about *doing* work for users rather than just supplying them with the data to do their jobs.

Brainstorm with your classmates. Where else can you use this technology? Consider:

- Actually printing a label for the shipping clerk?
- Printing a service ticket for the IT help desk technician?

Endpoints

LESSON SKILL MATRIX

TECHNOLOGY SKILL	70-431 EXAM OBJECTIVE
Implement an HTTP endpoint.	Foundational
Create an HTTP endpoint.	Foundational
Secure and HTTP endpoint.	Foundational

KEY TERMS

HTTP endpoint: An endpoint is the connecting point for two services in the communication architecture, and is addressed by a protocol and an IP port number.

SOAP: The Simple Object Access Protocol (or Service-Oriented Architecture Protocol, or just plain SOAP) is a lightweight XML-based protocol that is designed to exchange structured and typed information on the Web. SOAP can be used in combination with a variety of existing Internet protocols and formats, including HTTP (Hypertext Transfer Protocol), SMTP (Simple Mail Transfer Protocol), and MIME (Multipurpose Internet Mail Extensions), and can support a wide range of applications from messaging systems to remote procedure calls (RPCs).

■ Introducing HTTP Endpoints

THE BOTTOM LINE Endpoints provide a reliable, securable, scalable messaging system that enables SQL Server to communicate over the network.

You already know you'll need to specify endpoints when setting up the communication between two broker services. Recall from Lesson 21 that Service Broker uses HTTP.

Here you'll learn you have many more options with endpoints. One of the great features is that you can create endpoints to provide the user with access to the database objects using a Web service; endpoints are also used as configuration points for database mirroring. These are the types of endpoints you can use:

Service Broker endpoint: SQL Server uses Service Broker endpoints for Service Broker communication outside the SQL Server instance. An endpoint is a SQL Server object that represents the capability for SQL Server to communicate over the network, so a Service Broker endpoint configures SQL Server to send and receive Service Broker messages over the network.

Service Broker endpoints provide options for transport security and message forwarding. A Service Broker endpoint listens on a specific TCP port number.

By default, an instance of SQL Server does not contain a Service Broker endpoint. You must create a Service Broker endpoint to send or receive messages outside the SQL Server instance. You must also enable Service Broker as you did in Exercise 21-1, step 1.

Mirror endpoints: For database mirroring, a server instance requires its own dedicated database mirroring endpoint. Mirror endpoints are special-purpose endpoints used exclusively to receive database-mirroring connections from other server instances.

The same as broker instance endpoints, database-mirroring endpoints use TCP to send and receive messages between the server instances in database-mirroring sessions. Each configured database mirror endpoint uses a TCP-specific port number exclusively. You did this in Exercise 20-1, step 25, for example.

HTTP endpoints: SQL Server exposes native XML Web services through the database engine by configuring and creating *HTTP endpoints*. To enable native HTTP *SOAP* requests, SQL Server registers with the HTTP listener http.sys, which is available only on Windows Server 2003, Windows XP Service Pack 2, and Vista. This means SQL Server uses XML and HTTP to access services and objects, without the need for client software. You don't need to have Internet Information Services (IIS) running and configured for this service.

SQL Server uses SOAP (formerly, the Service-Oriented Architecture Protocol but now simply SOAP) message requests to an instance of SQL Server over HTTP to provide the following:

- Access to T-SQL batch statements, with or without parameters
- Access to stored procedures, extended stored procedures, and scalar-valued user-defined functions

The key point to remember is that SQL Server does not use IIS; instead, it directly registers with http.sys. When setting up a Web service that can listen natively for an HTTP SOAP request, you have to configure this endpoint using the CREATE ENDPOINT statement.

In the following sections, you will learn how to configure endpoints for the various usages. Also, you will learn how to configure endpoint security.

Configuring HTTP Endpoints

HTTP endpoints can listen and receive requests on any TCP port, regardless of the URL you specified.

Since endpoints register with http.sys, the request will first go to the server identified in the URL; then the http.sys layer will forward the URL to the instance of SQL Server while bypassing IIS, even if installed.

To configure an endpoint, you use the CREATE ENDPOINT statement. You can break this statement into two parts to describe its functionality. The following is the full syntax:

```
CREATE ENDPOINT endPointName [ AUTHORIZATION login ]
STATE = { STARTED | STOPPED | DISABLED }
AS { HTTP | TCP } (
<protocol_specific_arguments>
)
FOR { SOAP | TSQL |
SERVICE_BROKER | DATABASE_MIRRORING } (
<language_specific_arguments>
)
<AS HTTP_protocol_specific_arguments>::=
AS HTTP (
PATH = 'url'
, AUTHENTICATION =( { BASIC | DIGEST |
```

```
INTEGRATED | NTLM | KERBEROS } [,...n ] )
, PORTS = ( { CLEAR | SSL} [... n ] )
[ SITE = {'*' | '+' | 'webSite' },]
[, CLEAR_PORT = clearPort ]
[, SSL_PORT = SSLPort ]
[, AUTH_REALM = { 'realm' | NONE } ]
[, DEFAULT_LOGON_DOMAIN = { 'domain' | NONE } ]
[, COMPRESSION = { ENABLED | DISABLED } ]
)
<AS TCP_protocol_specific_arguments>::=AS TCP (
LISTENER_PORT = listenerPort
[, LISTENER_IP = ALL |
(<4-part-ip> | <ip_address_v6> ) ]
)
<FOR SOAP_language_specific_arguments>::=
FOR SOAP(
[ { WEBMETHOD [ 'namespace'.] 'method_alias'
( NAME = 'database.owner.name'
[, SCHEMA = { NONE | STANDARD | DEFAULT } ]
[, FORMAT = { ALL_RESULTS | ROWSETS_ONLY } ]
)
} [,...n ] ]
[ BATCHES = { ENABLED | DISABLED } ]
[, WSDL = { NONE | DEFAULT | 'sp_name' } ]
[, SESSIONS = { ENABLED | DISABLED } ]
[, LOGIN_TYPE = { MIXED | WINDOWS } ]
[, SESSION_TIMEOUT = timeoutInterval | NEVER ]
[, DATABASE = { 'database_name' | DEFAULT }
[, NAMESPACE = { 'namespace' | DEFAULT } ]
[, SCHEMA = { NONE | STANDARD } ]
[, CHARACTER_SET = { SQL | XML }]
[, HEADER_LIMIT = int ]
)
<FOR SERVICE_BROKER_language_specific_arguments>::=
FOR SERVICE_BROKER (
[ AUTHENTICATION = {
WINDOWS [ { NTLM | KERBEROS | NEGOTIATE } ]
| CERTIFICATE certificate_name
| WINDOWS [ { NTLM | KERBEROS
| NEGOTIATE } ] CERTIFICATE certificate_name
| CERTIFICATE certificate_name WINDOWS
[ { NTLM | KERBEROS | NEGOTIATE } ]
} ]
[, ENCRYPTION = { DISABLED | SUPPORTED | REQUIRED }
[ ALGORITHM { RC4 | AES | AES RC4 | RC4 AES } ]
]
```

```
[, MESSAGE_FORWARDING = { ENABLED | DISABLED* } ]
[, MESSAGE_FORWARD_SIZE = forward_size ]
)
<FOR DATABASE_MIRRORING_language_specific_arguments>::=
FOR DATABASE_MIRRORING (
[ AUTHENTICATION = {
WINDOWS [ { NTLM | KERBEROS | NEGOTIATE } ]
| CERTIFICATE certificate_name
} ]
[ [, ] ENCRYPTION = { DISABLED |SUPPORTED | REQUIRED }
[ ALGORITHM { RC4 | AES | AES RC4 | RC4 AES } ]
]
[,] ROLE = { WITNESS | PARTNER | ALL }
)
```

This is quite a syntax, isn't it? Now we'll break it down to make it more readable.

CONFIGURING THE PROTOCOL AND ENDPOINT

This is the protocol and endpoint configuration:

```
CREATE ENDPOINT .. AS

...

FOR
```

In this part, you provide information specific to the protocol being used, which will be TCP or HTTP, depending on whether you use the endpoint for database mirroring and Service Broker or for XML Web services.

In this configuration, you also specify the method of authentication and the list of IP addresses you want to permit or restrict connecting to the endpoint.

This is an example of specifying the first part of the CREATE block:

```
CREATE ENDPOINT sql_endpoint
STATE = STARTED
AS HTTP(
PATH = '/sql',
AUTHENTICATION = (INTEGRATED ),
PORTS = ( CLEAR ),
SITE = 'LOCALHOST'
)
```

This statement will create an endpoint with the initial state started, using integrated security on port 80 with the virtual path http://localhost/sql.

USING THE FOR CLAUSE

After the FOR clause, you specify the payload for the endpoint, which can consist of several supported types:

HTTP SOAP: When using HTTP SOAP, you specify the stored procedures you want to expose in the endpoint as Web methods. You can specify a corresponding stored procedure or a user-defined function.

When a client application sends an HTTP SOAP request, the client can call all these exposed methods.

The configuration allows you to provide SOAP configuration information such as the following:

- The allowance of ad hoc queries
- Whether to return the XSD schema for the resultset
- The endpoint namespace

A typical FOR clause looks like this:

```
FOR SOAP (
WEBMETHOD 'CheckTicketStatus'
(name='MSSQL_Training.dbo.up_CheckTicketStatus',
SCHEMA=STANDARD ),
WSDL = DEFAULT,
SCHEMA = STANDARD,
DATABASE = 'MSSQL_Training',
NAMESPACE = 'http://localhost/'
);
```

Service Broker: Configuring an endpoint for the broker allows you to specify the endpoint to which the broker service can connect. A typical configuration looks like this:

```
CREATE ENDPOINT BrokerEndpoint
STATE = STARTED
AS TCP ( LISTENER_PORT = 4037 )
FOR SERVICE_BROKER ( AUTHENTICATION = WINDOWS );
GO
```

Database mirroring: Database mirroring, covered in Lesson 20, is one of the high-availability features you can use with SQL Server 2005. You can configure the endpoint for database mirroring. A typical configuration looks like this:

```
CREATE ENDPOINT endpoint_mirroring
STATE = STARTED
AS TCP ( LISTENER_PORT = 5022 )
FOR DATABASE_MIRRORING (
AUTHENTICATION = WINDOWS KERBEROS,
ENCRYPTION = SUPPORTED,
ROLE=ALL);
```

When registering endpoints, the endpoint will be known by http.sys only when the SQL Server instance is running. To reserve the necessary namespaces in http.sys, and prevent them from being overwritten by an IIS configuration when the SQL Server instance is not running, it is advisable to register the endpoint using the sp_reserve_http_namespace stored procedure.

Securing HTTP Endpoints

An endpoint is a securable object, and to be able to connect/create or alter an endpoint, you need to have appropriate permissions.

The following are the most common permissions that can be granted:

```
ALTER
CONNECT
CONTROL
TAKE OWNERSHIP
VIEW DEFINITION
```

You have the possibility to GRANT/REVOKE/DENY permission on the endpoint in order to provide a database user or role access to the endpoint configuration.

The GRANT permission you have to specify follows this syntax:

```
GRANT permission ON ENDPOINT::endpointname TO user or role
```

Thus, when you want to allow endpoint access to every user connecting to SQL, a typical configuration looks like this:

```
GRANT CONNECT ON ENDPOINT::sqlendpoint TO public
```

Before a user can connect to an endpoint, CONNECT permissions have to be granted.

SKILL SUMMARY

IN THIS LESSON YOU LEARNED:

In this lesson, you learned about and how to configure endpoints. Endpoints are not only used by SOAP requests; they are also the configurable network addresses for Server Broker and database mirroring. Together with the endpoint, you will specify the authentication of the endpoint.

For the certification examination:

- Understand how to create and secure HTTP endpoints. When creating endpoints, you need to identify the virtual directory or path on the server, as well as configure the methods that can be used by the endpoint. You need to know that all security is managed within the endpoint configuration, and that a user needs to have the appropriate permissions in order to connect to an endpoint.

■ Knowledge Assessment

Multiple Choice

Circle the letter or letters that correspond to the best answer or answers.

1. You want to expose the sp_who stored procedure as a Web method on a Windows XP machine with IIS installed and running. You run the following code:

```
1.  CREATE ENDPOINT sql_endpoint
2.  STATE = STARTED
3.  AS HTTP(
4.  PATH = '/sql',
5.  AUTHENTICATION = (INTEGRATED ),
6.  PORTS = ( CLEAR ),
7.  SITE = 'MySERVER'
8.  )
9.  FOR SOAP (
10. WEBMETHOD 'ConnectionsInfo'
11. (name='master.sys.sp_who'),
12. WSDL = DEFAULT,
13. SCHEMA = STANDARD,
```

```
14. DATABASE = 'master',
15. NAMESPACE = 'http://tempUri.org/'
16. );
17. GO
```

However, running the code, you get the following error message: "An error occurred while attempting to register the endpoint 'sql_endpoint'. One or more of the ports specified in the CREATE ENDPOINT statement may be bound to another process. Attempt the statement again with a different port or use netstat to find the application currently using the port and resolve the conflict." How can you solve the problem? (Select the best option.)

a. Add the following line of code between line 6 and line 7, specifying any free port:

```
CLEAR_PORT = 7200.
```

b. Uninstall IIS.

c. Use Basic Authentication.

d. Change the PORTS argument to SSL instead of CLEAR.

2. You expose the sp_who stored procedure as a Web method using the following code:

```
1. CREATE ENDPOINT sql_endpoint
2. AS HTTP(
3. PATH = '/sql',
4. AUTHENTICATION = (INTEGRATED ),
5. PORTS = ( CLEAR ),
6. CLEAR_PORT = 7200,
7. SITE = 'YUKON'
8. )
9. FOR SOAP (
10. WEBMETHOD 'ConnectionsInfo'
11. (name='master.sys.sp_who'),
12. WSDL = DEFAULT,
13. SCHEMA = STANDARD,
14. DATABASE = 'master',
15. NAMESPACE = 'http://tempUri.org/'
16. );
```

The query completed successfully. However, your client application receives a "Service Unavailable" error. How can you fix the problem? (Choose all that apply.)

a. Use ALTER ENDPOINT, and specify the STATE attribute with the STARTED value.

b. Use the SQL Server 2005 Surface Area Configuration tool to start the endpoint.

c. Change line 9 to FOR SERVICE_BROKER.

d. Change line 9 to FOR DATABASE_MIRRORING.

3. You create a database-mirroring endpoint that will support both the partner and witness role. You use the CREATE ENDPOINT statement for that. Which attribute will allow both mirroring roles?

a. The AUTH_REALM attribute.

b. The FORMAT attribute. Use the SQL Server 2005 Surface Area Configuration tool to start the endpoint.

c. The MESSAGE_FORWARDING attribute. Change line 9 with FOR SERVICE_ BROKER.

d. The ROLE attribute.

■ Case Scenarios

Scenario 22-2: Using Endpoints

You and your classmates design Web interfaces to several SQL Server databases. Discuss the value of endpoints. They are now objects in the database: What does this imply? They are now securable: How does this differ from SQL Server 2000? They are now universal: Which other applications can use this feature?

Replication

LESSON SKILL MATRIX

TECHNOLOGY SKILL	70-431 EXAM OBJECTIVE
Manage replication.	
Distinguish between replication types.	Foundational
Configure a publisher, a distributor, and a subscriber.	Foundational
Configure replication security.	Foundational
Configure conflict resolution settings for merge replication.	Foundational
Monitor replication.	Foundational
Improve replication performance.	Foundational
Plan for, stop, and restart recovery procedures.	Foundational

KEY TERMS

distributor: A database instance that acts as a store for replication-specific data associated with one or more publishers. Each publisher is associated with a single database (known as a *distribution database*) at the distributor.

latency: The amount of time that elapses between when a data change is completed at one server and when that change appears at another (for example, the time between when a change is made at the publisher and when it appears at the subscriber.

replication: A set of technologies for copying and distributing data and database objects from one database to another, and then synchronizing among databases to maintain consistency.

publisher: A database instance that makes data available to other locations through replication. The

publisher can have one or more publications, each defining a logically related set of objects and data to replicate.

pull subscription: A subscription created and administered at the publisher. The distribution agent or merge agent for the subscription runs at the distributor.

push subscription: A subscription created and administered at the publisher. The distribution agent or merge agent for the subscription run at the distributor.

subscriber: A database instance that receives replicated data. A subscriber can receive data from multiple publishers and publications. Depending on the type of replications chosen, the subscriber can also pass data changes back to the publisher, or republish the data to other subscribers.

■ Introducing Replication

THE BOTTOM LINE

Replication allows you to move a selected copy of your data from one location to another; from an Oracle server and back; from a DB2 server and back; to London and back at night when the communication costs are the lowest. Replication breaks the cardinal rule in database design of storing data once. As always, rules should be broken only when a good business reason justifies doing so.

You use *replication* to put copies of the same data at different locations throughout the enterprise. You might want to replicate your data for several reasons, but the following are among the most common:

- To move data closer to the user.
- To reduce locking conflicts when multiple sites want to work with the same data.
- To allow site autonomy so each location can set up its own rules and procedures for working with its copy of the data.
- To preclude the impact of read-intensive operations, such as report generation and ad hoc query processing from the OLTP database.

SQL Server 2005 uses two strategies for replication: replication itself and distributed transactions. Whichever strategy you use, the copies of the data are current and consistent. You can also use both strategies in the same environment.

The main difference between replication and distributed transactions is in the timing. With distributed transactions, your data is 100 percent synchronized 100 percent of the time. When you use replication, some *latency* is involved. It may be as little as a few seconds or as long as several days or even weeks. Distributed transactions require that the replicated databases be connected at all times. If they are not, then the distributed transactions will fail. Replication does not have this requirement.

INTRODUCING THE PUBLISHER/SUBSCRIBER METAPHOR

SQL Server 2005 uses a publisher/subscriber metaphor to describe and implement replication. Your database can play different roles as part of the replication scenario: it can be a publisher, subscriber, distributor, or any combination of these. When you publish data, you do it in the form of an article, which is stored in a publication. Here are the key terms used as part of the publisher/subscriber metaphor:

Publisher: The *publisher* is the source database where replication begins. It makes data available for replication.

Subscriber: The *subscriber* is the destination database where replication ends. It either receives a snapshot of all the published data or applies transactions that have been replicated to itself.

Distributor: The *distributor* is the intermediary between the publisher and subscriber. It receives published transactions or snapshots and then stores and forwards these publications to the subscribers.

Publication: The publication is the storage container for different articles. A subscriber can subscribe to an individual article or an entire publication.

Article: An article is the data, transactions, or stored procedures that are stored within a publication. This is the actual information that is going to be replicated.

Two-phase commit: Two-phase commit (sometimes referred to as 2PC) is a form of real-time distribution in which modifications are made to all involved databases at the same time. This is handled through the use of distributed transactions. As with any transaction, either all statements commit successfully or all modifications are rolled back. Two-phase commit uses the Microsoft DTC to accomplish its tasks. The DTC implements the functionality of a portion of the Microsoft Transaction Server. In this lesson, we will focus on replication, as opposed to two-phase commits.

A publisher can publish data to one or more distributors. A subscriber can subscribe through one or more distributors. A distributor can have one or more publishers and subscribers.

INTRODUCING ARTICLES

An article is data in a table. The data can be the entire table or just a subset of the data in the table. Your articles need to be bundled into one or more publications in order for them to be distributed to the subscribers. When you want to publish a subset of data in a table, you must specify some type of partitioning, either vertical or horizontal.

With a vertical partition, you select specific columns from your table. In a horizontal partition, you select specific rows of data from the table. Table 23-1 shows an example of both a vertical partition and a horizontal partition. Here, the horizontal partition might be when you want to make specific rows of data available to different regions. More specifically, you could create three separate articles. One article would be horizontally partitioned based on region 1; the next article would be horizontally partitioned on region 2; and the third would be horizontally partitioned on region 3. Each region could then subscribe to only its regional data.

Table 23-1

Vertical and Horizontal Partitions

Horizontal Partition

ReCode	EmpID	Q1	Q2	Q3
1	5	40.1	39.8	37.7
1	7	28.7	33.5	38.2
1	8	39.9	42.2	48.1
1	13	28.8	32.8	33.7

Vertical Partition

ReCode	EmpID	Q1	Q2	Q3
2	2		44.6	
1	5		39.8	
2	3		41.7	
3	11		28.8	
1	7		33.5	
1	8		42.2	
3	22		45.5	
1	13		32.8	

INTRODUCING PUBLICATIONS

Articles must be stored in a publication, which is the basis for your subscriptions. When you create a subscription, you are actually subscribing to an entire publication; however, you can read individual articles. Referential integrity is maintained within your publication because all articles in a publication are updated at the same time. In SQL Server 2005, you can publish to non–Microsoft SQL Server computers. The replicated data does not need to be in the same sort order or be of the same datatype.

Understanding Replication Factors and Distribution Types

Before you can choose a distribution type, you should need to be aware of all the factors that will influence your decision. The three main items to consider are autonomy, latency, and transactional consistency.

Autonomy: This refers to how much independence you want to give each subscriber with regard to the replicated data. Will the replicated data be considered read-only? How long will the data at a subscriber be valid? How often do you need to connect to the distributor to download more data?

Latency: Latency refers to the time lag between updates on the subscriber. Does your subscriber need to be in synchronization at all times? Is every minute enough? What if you are a salesperson on the road who dials in to the office once a day to update your data? Is this good enough?

Transactional consistency: Although several types of replication exist, the most common method is to move transactions from the publisher through the distributor and on to the subscriber. Transactional consistency comes into play here. Do all the transactions that are stored need to be applied at the same time, and in order? What happens if there is a delay in the processing?

Once you understand these factors, you need to start asking yourself the following questions, after which you can decide on a distribution type:

- What am I going to publish? Will it be all the data in a table, or will I partition information?
- Who has access to my publications? Are these subscribers connected or dial-up users?
- Will subscribers be able to update my data, or is their information considered read-only?
- How often should I synchronize my publishers and subscribers?
- How fast is my network? Can subscribers be connected at all times? How much traffic is there on my network?

Each of the several types of distribution you can use has different levels of autonomy, transactional consistency, and latency involved. You can choose from three basic types: snapshot replication, transactional replication, and merge replication.

When you factor in latency, autonomy, and consistency, you end up with seven different distribution types:

- Distributed transactions
- Transactional replication
- Transactional replication with immediate updating subscribers
- Snapshot replication
- Snapshot replication with immediate updating subscribers
- Merge replication
- Queued updating

As shown in Figure 23-1, distributed transactions have the least amount of latency and autonomy, but they have the highest level of consistency. Merge replication has the highest amount of latency and autonomy and a lower level of consistency.

USING DISTRIBUTED TRANSACTIONS

When you use distributed transactions (also called *two-phase commit*, or 2PC) to replicate your data, you have almost no autonomy or latency, but you do have guaranteed transactional consistency. With 2PC, either all changes are made at the same time or none of the changes

Figure 23-1

Distribution Types

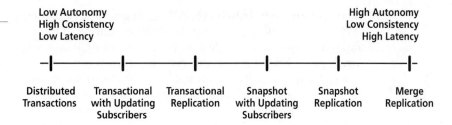

| Low Autonomy
High Consistency
Low Latency | | | | | High Autonomy
Low Consistency
High Latency |

| Distributed
Transactions | Transactional
with Updating
Subscribers | Transactional
Replication | Snapshot
with Updating
Subscribers | Snapshot
Replication | Merge
Replication |

is made. Remember that all the affected subscribers must be in contact with the publisher at all times. This type of distribution is most useful when subscribers must have realtime data, such as in a reservation system.

For example, think of a cruise line that has only so many rooms of a particular type available. If someone in Dallas wants the captain's suite and someone in California wants the same suite, the first one to book the room will get it. The other booking won't be allowed because that location will immediately show that the room is already booked.

USING TRANSACTIONAL REPLICATION

When you use the transactional replication distribution method, transactions are gathered from the publishers and stored in the distribution database. Subscribers then receive these transactions and must work with the data as if it were read-only. This is because any changes made to their local copy of the data might prohibit new transactions from being applied properly, which would destroy the transactional consistency.

Each site, however, has limited autonomy. You can introduce some latency because the subscribers don't have to be in contact at all times. Transactional consistency can be maintained as long as the subscribed data remains unchanged by the subscribers.

One of the main advantages to this approach is that transactions are relatively small items to move through the system (unlike snapshot replication, which we will look at shortly). The main disadvantage of using transactional replication is that subscribers must treat the data as read-only.

Use this distribution method when subscribers can treat their data as read-only and need the updated information with a minimal amount of latency.

This type of replication would be useful in an order-processing/distribution system with several locations where orders are taken. Each of the order locations would be a publisher, and the published orders could then be replicated to a subscription database at your central warehouse. The central warehouse could then accept the orders, fill them, and ship them.

USING TRANSACTIONAL REPLICATION WITH IMMEDIATE UPDATING SUBSCRIBERS

When you use transactional replication with immediate updating subscribers, you are gaining site autonomy, minimizing latency, and keeping transactional consistency. This (in most cases) would be considered the best possible solution.

When you implement transactional replication with immediate updating subscribers, you are essentially working with all the tenets of transactional replication. The major difference is that when you change the subscription data, 2PC changes the publishing database as well. In this fashion, your local subscriber is updated at the same time as the publisher. Other subscribers will have your changes downloaded to them at their next synchronization.

This scenario can be useful for a reservation system that needs to be updated frequently but does not need total synchronization. Let's use a library as an example here. Say you want to reserve a book about SQL Server 2005. You go to the computer, look up the book you want to reserve, and find that one copy is currently available at the library. When you try to reserve the book, however, you might find that the data isn't 100 percent up to date and the book has already been checked out. In this example, when you try to reserve your book, the subscriber automatically runs a 2PC to the publisher. At the publisher, someone has already checked out the last copy, and therefore the update fails. At the next synchronization, your subscriber will be updated with the news that the last copy has been checked out.

USING SNAPSHOT REPLICATION

When you use snapshot replication as your distribution method, you are actually moving an entire copy of the published items through the distributor and on to the subscribers. This type of replication allows for a high level of both site autonomy and transactional consistency because all records are going to be copied from the publisher and because the local copy of the data will be overwritten at the next synchronization. Latency may be a bit higher because you probably will not move an entire snapshot every few minutes.

Online Analytical Processing (OLAP) servers are prime candidates for this type of replication. The data at each subscriber is considered read-only and doesn't have to be 100 percent in synchronization all the time. This allows your IT departments to run their reporting and ad hoc queries on reasonably fresh data without affecting the OLTP server (which is doing all of the order-processing work).

Keep in mind that most people who run ad hoc queries generally don't modify the data. They are looking for historical information, such as how many widgets they sold, so the data that is a few hours or even a few days old will generally not make a difference to the results returned by the queries.

USING SNAPSHOT REPLICATION WITH IMMEDIATE UPDATING SUBSCRIBERS

The initial portion of this distribution style works just as in snapshot replication, plus it gives the subscriber the ability to update the publisher with new information. The updates use the 2PC protocol, as described previously.

This maintains a high level of site autonomy, a high level of transactional consistency, and a moderate level of latency. The data may be downloaded to the subscriber only once a day, but the publisher must first approve any updates the subscriber tries to make to the data.

This type of distribution is useful when you have read-only data that needs to be updated infrequently. If your data needs to be updated often, we suggest you use transactional replication with immediate updating subscribers.

Snapshot replication might be useful when auditing your database, downloading portions of the data, and then double-checking that everything is being updated properly. You could then quickly fix the occasional mistake, and auditing could continue.

USING MERGE REPLICATION

Merge replication provides the highest amount of site autonomy, the highest latency, and the lowest level of transactional consistency. Merge replication allows each subscriber to make changes to his or her local copy of the data. At some point, these changes are merged with those made by other subscribers, as well as changes made at the publisher. Ultimately, all sites receive the updates from all other sites. This is known as *convergence*; that is, all changes from all sites converge and are redistributed so that all sites have the same changes.

Transactional consistency is nearly nonexistent here because different sites may all be making changes to the same data, resulting in conflicts. SQL Server 2005 will automatically choose a particular change over another change and then converge that data. To simplify, sooner or later, all sites will have the same copy of the data, but that data may not necessarily be what you want. For example, subscriber A makes changes to record 100. Subscriber B also makes changes to record 100. Although this doesn't sound too bad, suppose the changes that subscriber A made to record 100 are because of changes that were made to record 50. If subscriber B doesn't have the same data in record 50, then subscriber B will make a different decision. Obviously, this can be incredibly complex.

You might wonder why anyone would want to use merge replication. There are many reasons, and with some careful planning you can make merge replication work to your advantage. You can modify triggers to determine which record is the correct record to use. When records are changed at multiple sites, the default rule is to take the changes based on a site priority, converge the results, and then send them. The exception to this general rule occurs when the main database, as well as all the user databases, are changed. In this case, the user changes are applied first, and then the main database changes are applied. For example, say you have a central server that you call Main, and you have 20 salespeople who are using merge replication. If one of your salespeople modifies record 25, and you modify record 25 at the Main server, when the records are converged, the user changes will first be placed in the Main server, and then the Main server changes will overwrite them.

If you design your publishers and subscribers to minimize conflicts, merge replication can be advantageous. Look at the highway patrol, for example. A patrol car might pull over a car and write the driver a ticket for speeding. At the end of the day, that data is merged with data from other officers who have also written tickets. The data is then converged back to all the different squad cars' computers, and now all the police know who to watch for on the roads.

USING QUEUED UPDATING

With transactional and snapshot replication, you can also configure queued updating. Like the immediate updating subscribers option, this gives your users the ability to make changes to the subscription database; but unlike immediate updating subscribers, queued updating will store changes until the publisher can be contacted. This can be extremely useful in networks where you have subscribers who are not always connected or the connection is unreliable. Here is how it works:

1. Updates made on the subscribers are captured by triggers on the subscribing tables and stored in the storage queue.
2. The updates are stored in a table named MSreplication_queue in the subscription database. These messages are automatically sent to the distributor when it becomes available.
3. The queue reader agent applies the changes to the publication.
4. Any conflicts are detected and resolved according to a conflict resolution policy that is defined when the publication is created.
5. Changes made at the publisher are applied to all remaining subscribers.

Here are some things to keep in mind if you plan to use queued updating:

- INSERT statements must include a column list.
- Subscribers using immediate or queued updating cannot republish at the subscriber.
- Once a publication is configured to use queued updating, the option cannot be removed (though subscribers do not need to use it). To remove the option, you must delete and re-create the publication.
- You cannot use transformable subscriptions with queued updating. The Transform Published Data page of the Create Publication Wizard will not be displayed.
- Only SQL Server 2000 and higher servers can subscribe using queued updating.

Understanding Replication Internals

Understanding how the transactions or snapshots are handled is essential to a full understanding of how SQL Server 2005 implements replication.

When you set up your subscribers, you can create either pull or push subscriptions:

Push subscriptions help centralize your administrative duties because the subscription itself is stored on the distribution server. This allows the publisher to determine what data is in the subscription and when that subscription will be synchronized. In other words, the data can be pushed to the subscribers based on the publisher's schedule. Push subscriptions are most useful if a subscriber needs to be updated whenever a change occurs at the publisher. The publisher knows when the modification takes place, so it can immediately push those changes to the subscribers.

Pull subscriptions are configured and maintained at each subscriber. The subscribers will administer the synchronization schedules and can pull changes whenever they consider it necessary. This type of subscriber also relieves the distribution server of some of the overhead of processing. Pull subscriptions are also useful in situations in which security is not a primary issue. In fact, you can set up pull subscriptions to allow anonymous connections, including pull subscribers residing on the Internet.

Ordinarily, non–SQL Server databases such as DB2 must use *push subscriptions.* If you have a real need to pull with another database system, you can write your own custom program using the Replication Management Objects (RMO) programming interface.

In either a push environment or a pull environment, five replication agents handle the tasks of moving data from the publisher to the distributor on to the subscribers. The location of the particular agent depends on the type of replication (push or pull) you are using:

Logreader agent: Located on the distribution server, the logreader's job is to monitor the transaction logs of published databases that are using this distributor. When the logreader agent finds a transaction, it moves the transaction to the distribution database on the distributor; transactions are stored and then forwarded to the subscribers by the distribution agent for transactional and snapshot replication, or by the merge agent for merge replication.

Distribution agent: The distribution agent is responsible for moving the stored transactions from the distributor to the subscribers.

Snapshot agent: This agent, which is also used for snapshot replication, is responsible for copying the schema and data from the publisher to the subscriber. Before any type of replication can begin, a copy of the data must reside on each subscriber. With this baseline established, transactions can then be applied at each subscriber, and transactional consistency can be maintained.

Merge agent: The merge agent is responsible for converging records from multiple sites and then redistributing the converged records back to the subscribers.

Queue reader agent: The queue reader agent runs on the distributor and is responsible for reading messages from the queue on the subscribers and applying them to the appropriate publication. It is used only with queued updating publications and subscribers.

You will now see how these different agents work in concert to create the different distribution types.

Remote Agent Activation allows you to run a distribution or merge agent on one machine and activate it from another. It can save resources on your servers in a heavy replication environment.

Understanding Merge Replication

When you use merge replication, the merge agent can be centrally located on the distributor, or it can reside on every subscriber involved in the merge replication process. When you have implemented push replication, the merge agent will reside on the distributor. In a pull scenario, the merge agent is on every subscriber.

Figure 23-2

The Merge Replication Process

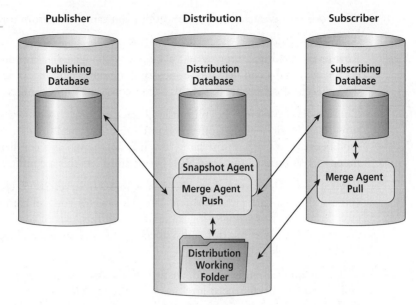

WALKING THROUGH THE MERGE PROCESS

The following steps outline the merge process and how each agent interacts with the other agents:

1. As shown in Figure 23-2, the snapshot agent that resides on the distribution server takes an initial snapshot of the data and moves it to the subscribers. This move takes place through the Distribution working folder. The folder is just a holding area for the snapshot data before it is moved to the subscriber. As stated earlier, you must do this first so you can apply later transactions. Subscribers must have the appropriate permissions to access the Distribution working folder on the distribution server.

2. Replication can now begin.

3. The merge agent (wherever it resides) will take modifications from the publishers and apply them to the subscribers.

4. The merge agent will also take modifications from the subscribers and apply them to the publishers.

5. The merge agent will gather any merge conflicts and resolve them by using triggers. Merge information will be stored in tables at the distributor. This allows you to track data lineage.

To track these changes, SQL Server adds some new tables to the publication and subscription databases. The most important of these is the MSmerge_contents table, which is used to track changes to the replicated table, as well as possible conflicts. SQL Server also creates triggers on the publishing and subscription servers used for merge replication. These triggers are automatically invoked when changes are made at either of these locations. Information about the changes is stored in the database system tables on the distribution server. With this change information, SQL Server can track the lineage or history of changes made to a particular row of data.

Merge replication is most useful in situations in which there will be few conflicts. A horizontally partitioned table based on a region code or some other ID is best suited to merge replication.

PERFORMING CONFLICT RESOLUTION IN MERGE REPLICATION

Performing updates to the same records at multiple locations causes conflicts. To resolve these conflicts, SQL Server 2005 uses the MSmerge_contents table and some settings from the publication itself.

When you first create a merge publication, you can choose from three levels of conflict resolution tracking in a merge publication:

Row-level tracking: In row-level tracking, any change to an entire row on multiple subscribers is considered a conflict. If one subscriber modifies data in ColA, and another modifies data in ColB on the same row, SQL Server considers this a conflict.

Column-level tracking: In column-level tracking, any change to a single column on multiple subscribers is considered a conflict. If one subscriber modifies data in ColA, and another modifies data in ColB on the same row, it is not viewed as a conflict. However, if they both modify ColA on the same row, SQL Server considers this a conflict.

Logical record-level tracking: This is new to SQL Server 2005. Using a JOIN statement, you can create logical records to replicate. This means you can combine data from multiple tables to replicate as a single, logical table. Using this level of conflict tracking tells SQL Server that if users at multiple subscribers modify the same data in any of the joined tables, there is a possible conflict.

When the publication is created, changes to the data are tracked in the MSmerge_contents table. If you are using record-level tracking, the metadata about the changes are stored in the lineage column; if you are using column-level tracking, the COLV1 column is also used. Using this lineage, the merge agent evaluates the current values for a record or column and the new values to determine whether a conflict exists. If a conflict does exist, SQL Server considers two more important factors before resolving it.

First, when you create a subscription to the publication, you can also set the priority for the subscription. When there is a conflict, subscribers with higher priority win out over subscribers with lower priority, and the higher-priority change is replicated to all subscribers. The lower-priority change is logged to the MSmerge_conflicts_info table and, if there is an INSERT or UPDATE conflict, the MSMerge_conflict_publication_article table.

Second, you have a choice of resolvers to use when creating a new publication. If you use the default resolver, SQL Server will automatically resolve the conflict, apply the winning changes to all subscribers, and notify you of a conflict. If you choose a manual resolver, you will have to manually choose the winning changes and apply them yourself. The manual option works best only if you have a complex merge replication scenario that requires complex business logic.

When you begin to customize the conflict resolution process, we suggest you store both the record that is converged and the conflicting records that were not converged. This allows you to manually test and optimize your triggers.

Understanding Snapshot Replication

When you use snapshot replication, an entire copy of the publication is moved from the publisher to the subscriber. Everything on the subscriber database is overwritten, allowing for autonomy, as well as transactional consistency because all changes are made at once. Latency can be high for this type of replication if you want it to be. You can schedule your refreshes when and as often as you want (we have found that this normally occurs once a day, at off-peak hours). Keep in mind that snapshot replication occurs on demand. This means no data is transferred from the publisher to the distributor until a subscriber is ready to receive it. The snapshot then moves straight through. Status information is stored in the distribution database; however, the snapshot agent and the distribution agent do all their work at the time the snapshot is initiated.

When you use snapshot replication, there is no merge agent. Snapshot replication uses the distribution agent. If you are using a pull replication, the distribution agent resides on the subscription server. If you are doing a push replication, the agent resides on the distributor.

Figure 23-3

The Snapshot Replication
Process

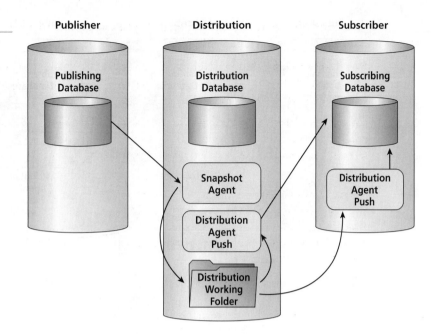

When used in a push scenario, snapshot replication consumes a large amount of overhead on the distribution server. We suggest that most snapshot subscribers use a pull scenario at regularly scheduled intervals. The following steps (see Figure 23-3) outline the snapshot replication process:

1. The snapshot agent reads the published article and then creates the table schema and data in the Distribution working folder.

2. The distribution agent creates the schema on the subscriber.

3. The distribution agent moves the data into the newly created tables on the subscriber.

4. Any indexes that were used are re-created on the newly synchronized subscription database.

This works in the same fashion when you are using snapshot replication with immediate updating subscribers. The only difference is that the subscriber will use a two-phase commit to update both the subscription database and the publishing database at the same time. During the next refresh, all subscribers will receive a copy of the modified data.

Understanding Transactional Replication

When you use transactional replication, only the changes (transactions) made to the data are moved. Before these transactions can be applied at a subscriber, however, the subscriber must have a copy of the data as a base. Because of its speed and relatively low overhead on the distribution server, transactional replication is currently the most often-used form of replication. Generally, data on the subscriber is treated as read-only, unless you are implementing transactional replication with immediate updating subscribers. Because the transactions are so small, this type of replication is often set up to run continuously. Every time a change is made at the publisher, it is automatically applied to the subscriber, generally within one minute.

When you use transactional replication, you don't need the merge agent. The snapshot agent must still run at least once; it uses the distribution agent to move the initial snapshot from the publisher to the subscriber. You also use the logreader agent when using transactional replication. The logreader agent looks for transactions in published databases and moves those

Figure 23-4

The Transactional Replication Process

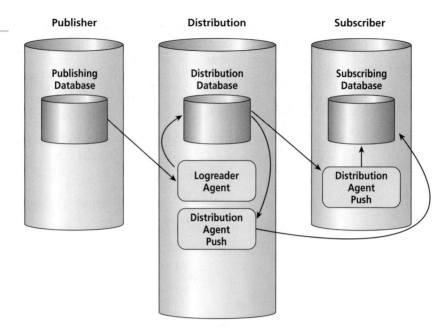

transactions to the distribution database. The following steps (see Figure 23-4) outline the transactional replication process:

1. The logreader agent reads the published article and then creates the schema on the subscriber and bulk-copies the snapshot over to the subscriber. (This happens only when the subscription is created or re-created.)

2. The logreader agent scans the transaction logs of databases marked for publishing. When it finds an appropriate transaction, it copies the transaction to the distribution database. The distribution database will store the transaction for a configurable length of time.

3. The distribution agent will then apply those transactions to the subscribers at the next synchronization. The subscriber next runs the sp_repldone system stored procedure on the distribution database. This marks the newly replicated transactions stored on the distributor in the MSrepl_commands table as completed.

4. When the next distribution cleanup task executes, the marked transactions are truncated from the distribution server.

CONSIDERING PUBLICATION ISSUES

Before you start your replication process, you should consider a few more topics, including data definition issues, IDENTITY column issues, and some general rules involved when publishing. Keep the following data definition items in mind when you are preparing to publish data:

Timestamp datatypes: A timestamp datatype is different from a date time datatype. Timestamps are automatically updated to the current date and time whenever the record is inserted or updated. When they are replicated, they are changed to a binary datatype to ensure that the data from the publisher matches the data at the subscriber. If it was not altered, the timestamp will automatically update itself when the transaction is applied at the subscriber. This is the opposite of merge replication, where the timestamp datatype is replicated but the data is not. This allows the timestamp to be regenerated at the subscriber and used in conflict resolution.

Identity values: SQL Server 2005 has the capability to replicate identity values. To do this, you must assign a range of identity values to each server involved in the replication at the time the publication is created (for example, the publisher gets 1,000–2,005; subscriber A gets 2,001–3,000; and subscriber B gets 3,001–4,000). When each server runs out of identity values, a new range is automatically assigned.

User-defined datatypes: If you have created your own user-defined datatypes on the publishing server, you must also create those same datatypes on the subscriptions servers if you want to replicate that particular column of data.

Not for replication: Most objects in the database can be created using the NOT FOR REPLICATION option, which prevents the object from being replicated. For example, if you have a constraint on a table that you do not want to be replicated to subscribers, then you would create the constraint using NOT FOR REPLICATION, and it would never be replicated.

You should keep the following publishing restrictions in mind, as well:

- If you are not using snapshot replication, your replicated tables must have a primary key to ensure transactional integrity.
- Publications cannot span multiple databases. All articles in a publication must be derived from a single database.
- Varchar(max), nvarchar(max), and varbinary(max) binary large objects (BLOBs) are not replicated when you use transactional or merge replication. Because of their size, these objects must be refreshed by running a snapshot. What will be replicated is the 16-byte pointer to their storage location within the publishing database.
- You cannot replicate from the master, model, MSDB, or tempdb databases.

CONSIDERING DISTRIBUTOR ISSUES

Here are some tips to keep in mind when selecting a machine to be the distributor:

- Ensure you have enough hard disk space for the Distribution working folder and the distribution database.
- You must manage the distribution database's transaction log carefully. If that log fills to capacity, replication will no longer run, which can adversely affect your publishing databases as well.
- The distribution database will store all transactions from the publisher to the subscriber. It will also track when those transactions were applied.
- Snapshots and merge data are stored in the Distribution working folder.
- Be aware of the size and number of articles being published.
- Text, ntext, and image datatypes are replicated only when you use a snapshot.
- A higher degree of latency can significantly increase your storage space requirements.
- Know how many transactions per synchronization cycle there are. For example, if you modify 8,000 records between synchronizations, you will have 8,000 rows of data stored on the distributor.

Understanding Replication Models

You can use one of several models when you implement replication:

CERTIFICATION READY?
SQL Server 2005 adds peer-to-peer transactional replication that might read or modify the data at any of the databases participating in data sharing.

- Central publisher/central distributor
- Remote distribution
- Central subscriber/multiple publishers
- Multiple publishers/multiple subscribers

You'll now look more closely at each of these and see which business situations they most accurately represent.

INTRODUCING CENTRAL PUBLISHER/CENTRAL DISTRIBUTOR

As shown in Figure 23-5, both the publishing database and the distribution database are on the same SQL Server system. This configuration is useful when modeling replication strategies for the following business scenarios:

Figure 23-5

Central Publisher Model

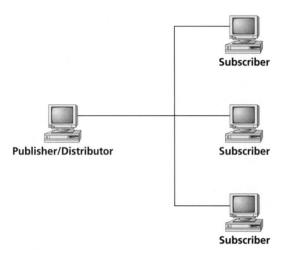

- Asynchronous order processing during communication outages
- Distribution of price lists, customer lists, vendor lists, and so on
- Removal of administrative activities from the OLTP environment
- Establishment of executive information systems

One of the most important aspects of the central publisher model is the ability to move data to a separate SQL Server system. This allows the publishing server to continue handling online transaction processing duties without having to absorb the impact of the ad hoc queries generally found in IT departments.

You can use any type of replication here—transactional, merge, or snapshot. If you do not have to update BLOB objects such as text, ntext, and image datatypes, we suggest you use transactional replication. IT departments generally don't need to make changes to the subscribed data.

You can further reduce the impact of replication on your OLTP server by implementing pull subscriptions. This will force the distribution agent to run on each subscriber rather than on the OLTP publishing server.

INTRODUCING REMOTE DISTRIBUTION

In this model, you remove the impact of the distribution process from your OLTP server, which gives you the best possible speed on the OLTP server. This model is useful in situations in which you need the optimal performance from your OLTP server. As discussed earlier, a single distribution server can work with multiple distributors and multiple subscribers. Figure 23-6 shows a representation of this strategy.

This calls for transactional replication and minimizing the impact of replication on the publishing database. By moving just transactions rather than moving snapshots or attempting to merge data at the publisher, you can gain the most possible speed and have the lowest impact on the publisher.

Figure 23-6

Remote Distribution Model

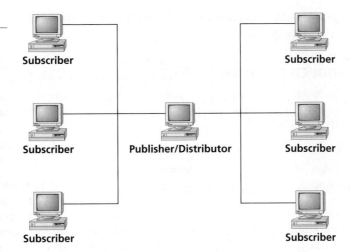

INTRODUCING CENTRAL SUBSCRIBER/MULTIPLE PUBLISHERS

The central subscriber model shown in Figure 23-7 is useful in the following situations:

- Roll-up reporting
- Local warehouse inventory management
- Local customer order processing

You need to keep several issues in mind when you attempt to use this model. Because multiple publishers are writing to a single table in the database, you must take some precautions to ensure that referential integrity is maintained. If, say, your New York office sent an order with a key of 1000, and your Milwaukee office also sent an order with a key of 1000, you would have two records with the same primary key. You could get bad data in your Denver headquarters database because the primary key is designed to guarantee the uniqueness of each record. In this situation, only one of those records would post.

To make sure this doesn't become a problem, you would implement a composite primary key using the original order ID number, along with a location-specific code. You could, for example, give New York a location code of NY and the Milwaukee branch a location code of MW. This way, the new composite keys would be NY1000 and MW1000. There would be no more conflicting records, and both orders would be filled from the Denver office.

This scenario is especially suited to transactional replication because the data at the Denver site is really read-only. Snapshot replication wouldn't work here because that would overwrite

Figure 23-7

Central Subscriber Model

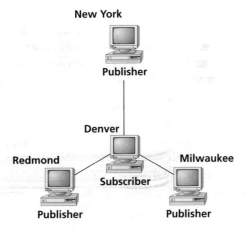

everyone else's data. You could use merge replication if the other locations needed to be able to see all the orders placed.

INTRODUCING MULTIPLE PUBLISHERS/MULTIPLE SUBSCRIBERS

Use this model when you need to maintain a single table on multiple servers. Each server subscribes to the table and also publishes the table to other servers. This model can be particularly useful in the following business situations:

- Reservations systems
- Regional order-processing systems
- Multiple warehouse implementations

Think of a regional order-processing system, as shown in Figure 23-8. Suppose you place an order on Monday and want to check on that order on Tuesday. When you call the company, you may be routed to any of several regional order-processing centers. Each of these centers should have a copy of your order so that you can go over the order with a salesperson wherever he or she is.

We suggest you use transactional replication for this scenario, using some type of region code (as described in the central subscriber/multiple publishers scenario). Each order-processing center should publish only its own data, but it should subscribe to data being published by the other publishers. In addition, each location should update only the data it owns. This scenario is also a good candidate for the transactional replication with an updating subscriber model. In this case, each center could update data owned by another center; however, this update would take place at both servers and, therefore, maintain transactional consistency.

A variation of this would be central publisher/multiple subscribers where you have only one publisher with a number of subscribers.

Replicating over the Internet and to Heterogeneous Database Servers

In addition to the replication scenarios already discussed, it is possible to replicate data to non-Microsoft database servers. This is known as *heterogeneous database replication*. You can also replicate to databases across the Internet.

USING HETEROGENEOUS REPLICATION

Heterogeneous replication occurs when you publish to other databases through an OLE DB connection. In special cases, you can even use SQL Server 2005 to subscribe to these OLE DB databases. Currently, SQL Server supports replication to Oracle and IBM databases that

Figure 23-8

Multiple Publishers of One Table Model

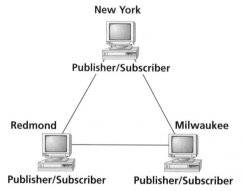

conform to the IBM Distributed Relational Database Architecture (DRDA) data protocol. When you publish to these non–SQL Server subscribers, you need to keep the following rules in mind:

- Only push subscriptions are supported.
- You can publish index views as tables; they cannot be replicated as an indexed view.
- Snapshot data will be sent using bulk copy's character format.
- Datatypes will be mapped as closely as possible.
- The account under which the distribution agent runs must have read access to the install directory of the OLE DB provider.
- If an article is added to or deleted from a publication, subscriptions to non–SQL Server subscribers must be reinitialized.
- NULL and NOT NULL are the only constraints supported for all non–SQL Server subscribers.
- Primary key constraints are replicated as unique indexes.

USING INTERNET REPLICATION

If you want to enable SQL Server to publish to the Internet, you must make some additional configuration changes to your SQL Server 2005 computer. For either a push style or a pull style of replication, you must configure the following:

- TCP/IP must be installed on the computers where the merge agent and distribution agents are running.
- The publishing server and the distribution server should be on the same side of the firewall.
- The publishing server and the distribution server should have a direct network connection to each other (rather than a connection across the Internet). This is to address both security and latency concerns.

You need to make some additional configuration changes if you are going to allow pull subscriptions:

- Your distribution server must have Microsoft IIS installed and running.
- Both the merge and distribution agents must be configured with the correct FTP address. You do this through the distribution agent or from a command prompt.
- The working folder must be available to your subscription servers.
- The FTP home folder on your IIS computer should be set to the Distribution working folder. This is normally *ServerName*\C$\Program Files\Microsoft SQL Server\ MSSQL\ REPLDATA\FTP.

For additional information on how to set up replication for the Internet, refer to the SQL Server Books Online.

> **TAKE NOTE** *
>
> In previous versions of SQL Server, you could replicate using ODBC; this is no longer supported. Replication to Microsoft Access is no longer supported either.

Installing and Using Replication

In the following sections, you will learn how to configure your servers for replication. You will then walk through the process of installing a distribution database, a publishing database, and a subscription database. You will finish up this topic by creating and then subscribing to an article and a publication.

To successfully install and enable replication, you must install a distribution server, create your publications, and then subscribe to them. Before any of this can take place, you must first configure SQL Server.

To install your replication scenario, you must be a member of the sysadmins fixed server role.

CONFIGURING SQL SERVER FOR REPLICATION

Before you can configure your SQL Server for replication, the computer itself must meet the following requirements:

- All servers involved with replication must be registered in Management Studio.
- If the servers are from different domains, trust relationships must be established before replication can occur.
- Any account you use must have access rights to the Distribution working folder on the distribution server.

You must enable access to the Distribution working folder on the distribution server. For a Windows server, the default location is C:\Program Files\Microsoft SQL Server\MSSQL\ MSSQL.X\Data. Create a new folder named repldata. Share this folder and set permission for the agents as appropriate. For example, for Snapshot replication you will probably set the repl_snapshot agent to full control, the repl_distribution agent to read, and the repl_merge agent to read.

TAKE NOTE *

Search for Replication Tutorials in Books Online for specific instructions for your circumstances.

Use a single Windows domain account for all your SQL Server Agents. Do not use a LocalSystem account because this account has no network capabilities and will not, therefore, allow replication. Also, you need to make the account a member of the Domain Administrators group because only administrators have access to the hidden shares.

INSTALLING A DISTRIBUTION SERVER

Before you can start replicating data, you need to install a distribution server. You'll do that in Exercise 23-1.

Before you can enable a publication database, you must be a member of the sysadmin fixed server role. Once you have enabled publishing, any member of that database's db_owner role can create and manage publications.

EXERCISE 23-1 INSTALLING A DISTRIBUTION SERVER

1. Open **Management Studio,** and connect to **your server.**
2. Right-click **Replication,** and click **Configure Distribution**.
3. You are presented with a welcome page; click **Next** to continue.
4. The Select Distributor page appears. Select the server that will act as its own distributor option, and click **Next**.
5. You are now asked to specify the snapshot folder. The only reason to change this is if you are replicating over the Internet and need to specify a folder that is accessible via FTP. Accept the **defaults,** and click **Next**.
6. The Distribution Database page appears next. You can supply a name for the distribution database, as well as location information for its database file and transaction log. Keep the defaults, and click **Next** to continue.
7. Now you are on the Publishers page, where you can choose which servers you want to configure as publishers. The ellipsis (...) button allows you to specify security credentials such as login ID and password, as well as the location of the snapshot folder. Be sure to place a checkmark next to your local **SQL Server** system, and then click **Next** to continue.
8. On the Wizard Actions page, you can have the wizard configure distribution, write a script to configure distribution that you can run later, or both. Leave the Configure distribution box checked, and click **Next** to continue.
9. On the Complete the Wizard page, review your selections, and click **Finish**.
10. When the wizard is finished, click **Close**.

ADDING A PUBLICATION

Now you can add a publication and articles to your server. When you add a new publication, you need to determine the type of replication that will be used, the snapshot requirements, and the subscriber options such as updating subscribers. You can also partition your data and decide whether you will allow push or pull subscriptions.

The Create Publication Wizard allows you to specify the following options:

- Number of articles
- Schedule for the snapshot agent
- Whether to maintain the snapshot on the distributor
- Tables and stored procedures you want to publish
- Publications that will share agents
- Whether to allow updating subscribers
- Whether to allow pull subscriptions

Each publication will use a separate publishing agent by default, but you can override this option.

In Exercise 23-2 you will create a new publication based on the Production.ProductCategory table in the AdventureWorks database.

 ### EXERCISE 23-2 CREATING A PUBLICATION

1. Connect to your **SQL Server** system in Management Studio.
2. Expand **Replication,** right-click **Local Publications,** and click **New Publication.** This brings you to the New Publication Wizard welcome page.
3. Click **Next** to continue.
4. On the Publication Database page, highlight **AdventureWorks,** and click Next to continue.
5. On the Publication Type page, you can choose the type of publication to create. For this exercise, choose **Transactional Publication,** and click **Next** to continue.
6. On the articles page, you can select the data and objects you want to replicate. Expand **Tables,** and check the **ProductCategory** box.
7. You can also set the properties for an article from this page. Make sure **Product-Category** is highlighted, click **Article Properties,** and then click **Set Properties of Highlighted Table Article.**
8. In the Destination Object section, change the Destination Object name to **ReplicatedCategory,** change the Destination Object Owner to **dbo,** and click **OK.**
9. Back at the Articles page, click **Next** to continue.
10. On the next page, you can filter the data that is replicated. You do not want to filter the data in this case, so click **Next** to continue.
11. On the Snapshot Agent page, check the box to create a snapshot immediately, and click **Next.**
12. On the Agent Security page, you are asked how the agents should log on and access data. To set this for the snapshot agent, click the **Security Settings** button next to Snapshot Agent.
13. Ordinarily, you would create an account for the agent to run under, but to make the exercise simpler, you will run the agent using the **SQL Server Agent** account, so select the radio button for that option, and click **OK.**
14. Back at the Agent Security page, click **Next** to continue.
15. On the Wizard Actions page, you can have the wizard create the publication, write a script to create the publication that you can run later, or both. Leave the **Create the Publication** box checked, and click **Next** to continue.

16. On the Complete the Wizard page, you need to enter a name for the new publication, so enter **CategoryPub**, and click Finish.

17. When the wizard is finished, click **Close**.

Now that you have a distributor and a publication, you are ready to create a subscription.

CREATING A SUBSCRIPTION

As part of the process of creating a subscription, you will be able to specify the publishers you
want to subscribe to and a destination database to receive the published data, verify your security
credentials, and set up a default schedule. You will create a pull subscription in Exercise 23-3.

 EXERCISE 23-3 CREATING A SUBSCRIPTION

1. Connect to your **SQL Server** system in Management Studio.

2. Expand **Replication**, right-click **Local Subscriptions**, and click **New Subscription**.
This brings you to the New Subscription Wizard welcome page.

3. On the Publication page, select **your server** from the Publisher drop-down list, select
CategoryPub from the Databases and Publications list, and click **Next** to continue.

4. On the Distribution Agent Location page, you are asked which machine should run
the replication agents, at the distributor or at the subscriber. Because you want
to create a pull subscription, select the **Run Each Agent at Its Subscriber** option,
and click **Next.**

5. On the Subscribers page, you can choose a subscriber for the publication. Check
the box next to **your server.**

6. The drop-down list is populated with all the available databases on the subscriber.
Select the **MSSQL_Training** database (created in Lessons 5 and 6), and click **Next**.

7. On the next page, you need to set the distribution agent security. To do so, click
the **ellipsis (...)** button in the Subscription Properties list.

8. Ordinarily, you would create an account for the agent to run under, but to make
the exercise simpler, you will run the agent using the **SQL Server Agent** account,
so select the radio button for that option, and click **OK.**

9. Back at the Distribution Agent Security page, click **Next** to continue.

10. The next step is to set the synchronization schedule. For snapshots, it might be
wise to set up some type of regular schedule. For merge replication, you will most
likely use a manual form of synchronization called *on demand.* Because you are
using transactional replication, select **Run Continuously**, and click **Next** to continue.

11. On the next page, you can tell SQL Server when to initialize subscription, if at all.
If you have already created the schema on the subscriber, you do not need to initialize the subscription. In this case, you should select **Immediately** from the drop-
down list, make sure the **Initialize** box is checked, and click **Next** to continue.

12. On the Wizard Actions page, you can have the wizard create the subscription,
write a script to create the subscription that you can run later, or both. Leave
the **Create the Subscription** box checked, and click Next to continue.

13. On the Complete the Wizard page, you can review your options and click **Finish** to
create the subscription.

14. When the wizard is finished, click **Close.**

Now, with a subscription in place, you can test replication to make sure it is working as expected.

TESTING REPLICATION

You can now verify that replication is running properly. In Exercise 23-4 you will check for
the initial snapshot synchronization. You will then add some data to the ProductCategory
table and review the data in the ReplicatedCategory table to make sure it was replicated.

EXERCISE 23-4 TESTING REPLICATION

1. You should have four records in the ReplicatedCategory table. To verify that, open a **new query,** and execute the following code:

```
USE MSSQL_Training
SELECT * FROM ReplicatedCategory
GO
```

2. Now add a new record to the ProductCategory table in the AdventureWorks database. Run the following code to add a new record:

```
USE AdventureWorks
INSERT INTO Production.ProductCategory (Name)
VALUES('Tools')
GO
```

3. You should get the message that one row was added. Give the server about a minute to replicate the transaction; then run the following query:

```
USE MSSQL_Training
SELECT * FROM ReplicatedCategory
GO
```

4. You should get five records back. The last record should be the new Tools record.

Managing Replication

Managing and maintaining replication can be intensive work for an administrator. Microsoft SQL Server 2005 has included many tools in the Replication Monitor to make this job a lot easier. Before you look at the various tools and methodologies, you'll see some of the administrative issues you should consider.

CONSIDERING ADMINISTRATIVE ISSUES

This section provides some tips for optimizing your replication, along with some tips for minimizing your administrative duties:

- Use a remote distributor to minimize the impact of replication on your publishing servers.
- Use pull subscriptions to offload the work from the distributors to each subscriber.
- Use immediate updating subscribers rather than merge replication if possible.
- Replicate only the data you need. Use filters to partition your data.
- Keep in mind that replication increases network traffic. Make sure your network, especially your WAN links, can handle it.
- Use primary keys on replicated tables to ensure entity integrity.
- Use the same SQL Server Agent domain account for all servers involved in replication to minimize the impact of administering security issues.
- Ensure that replication jobs and their agents are running smoothly. Check the agent histories and logs periodically.
- Create and monitor replication alerts.
- Ensure that the distribution database and the Distribution working folder have enough space, and that they have the appropriate permissions assigned to them.
- Develop a recovery and resynchronization plan. You can use replication scripts for version control as well as a huge part of the recovery process.
- Keep a valid backup of the distribution database, and make sure the database and log do not fill to capacity.

It is essential that the distribution database and log do not fill to capacity. When this database or log fills to capacity, it can no longer receive publication information. When this occurs, the logged transactions at the publisher cannot be removed from the log (unless you disable publishing). Over time, your publishing database's transaction log will also fill to capacity, and you will no longer be able to make data modifications.

CONSIDERING REPLICATION BACKUP ISSUES

When you perform backups of your replication scenario, you can make backups of just the publisher, the publisher and distributor, the publisher and subscriber, or all three. Each of the strategies has its advantages and disadvantages. The following list highlights these distinctions:

Publisher only: This strategy requires the least amount of resources and computing time because the backup of the publisher does not have to be coordinated with any other server backups to stay synchronized. The disadvantage is that restoring a publisher or distributor is a slow and time-consuming process.

Publisher and distributor: This strategy accurately preserves the publication, as well as the errors, history, and replication agent information from the distributor. You can recover quickly because there is no need to reestablish replication. The disadvantages of this strategy are the coordination of the backups and the amount of storage and computing time necessary to perform a simultaneous backup.

Publisher and subscriber(s): This strategy significantly reduces the recovery time by removing the initialization process (running a snapshot). The main disadvantages of this strategy manifest when you have multiple subscribers. Every subscriber will have to be backed up and restored.

Publisher, distributor, and subscriber(s): This strategy preserves all of the complexity of your replication model. The disadvantages are storage space and computing time. This scenario also requires the most time for recovery.

USING THE REPLICATION MONITOR

You can administer your publishers, subscribers, and publications, as well as the different replication agents through the Replication Monitor utility. You can also look at agent properties and histories, and even set replication alerts with this utility.

The Replication Monitor gathers replication information about the different replication agents. This includes the agent history, with information about inserts, updates, deletes, and any other transactions that were processed. Through the Replication Monitor, you can also edit the various schedules and properties of the replication agents.

In Exercise 23-5 you'll use the Replication Monitor.

 EXERCISE 23-5 USING REPLICATION MONITOR

1. Open the **Management Studio** on the distribution server.
2. Right-click **Replication**, and select **Launch Replication Monitor**.
3. Expand **your server** to view the publications available.
4. Switch to the **Subscription Watch List** tab. From here you can view reports about the performance of all publications and subscriptions that this distributor handles.
5. Switch to the **Common Jobs** tab. On this tab you can view the status of replication jobs that affect all publications and subscriptions handled by this distributor.
6. Select the **CategoryPub** publication in the left pane.
7. On the All Subscriptions tab, you can view reports about all of the subscriptions for this particular publication.
8. Switch to the **Tracer Token** tab. From here you can insert a special record called a *tracer token* that is used to measure performance for this subscription.

9. To test it, click the **Insert Tracer** button, and wait for the results.

10. Switch to the **Warnings and Agents** tab. From here you can change settings for agents and configure replication alerts.

11. Click the **Configure Alerts** button, select **Replication: Agent Failure**, and click **Configure**.

12. Notice that this opens a new alert dialog box (alerts were discussed in Lesson 19). Check the **Enable** box, and click OK to enable this alert.

13. Click **Close** to return to Replication Monitor.

14. Close **Replication Monitor**.

WORKING WITH REPLICATION SCRIPTS

Now that you have replication set up and working properly, you may want to save all your hard work in the form of a replication script. Scripting your replication scenario has the following advantages:

- You can use the scripts to track different versions of your replication implementation.
- You can use the scripts (with some minor tweaking) to create additional subscribers and publishers with the same basic options.
- You can quickly customize your environment by modifying the script and then rerunning it.
- You can use the scripts as part of your database recovery process.

Scripting replication is so simple that it requires only two clicks: right-click **Replication**, and then select **Generate Scripts**. That's it.

From here you can script the distributor and publications for the various replication items stored with this distribution server. You can also script the options for any subscribers and even the replication jobs. When you have made your choices, just click the **Script to File** button, and save the script wherever you like.

ENHANCING REPLICATION PERFORMANCE

Replication requires considerable memory and processor resources. You can perform a number of tweaks to increase the performance of your replication scheme, though. Here are a few suggestions:

- **Set a minimum memory allocation limit:** By default, SQL Server dynamically configures the amount of RAM it uses while it is running. The problem is that it may release too much memory and then not have enough when replication starts. True, SQL Server will just allocate more memory, but now that you have configured replication, it is faster if you simply tell SQL Server to always allocate more memory. In that light, consider allocating an additional 16 MB of RAM to SQL Server if the server is a remote distributor or a combined published and distributor.
- **Use a separate hard disk for all the databases used in replication:** You should add hard disk arrays for the publication, distribution, and subscription databases, if you can.
- **Use multiple processors:** All the agents involved in replication are multithreaded, which means they can take advantage of multiple processors. Therefore, more CPUs equal faster replication.

■ Case Study: Deciding on a Replication Model and Type

A company began doing business in California, and when it grew big enough, opened a regional branch office on the East Coast. Everyone at the new East Coast office had access to the inventory data so they could make sales without having to call the home office to find out whether the parts were in stock. They also needed the capability to update their local copy of the data and have those changes reflected at the home office.

Before anything else, they had to assess the network connections between the offices to make sure they were reliable. If the network was not reliable, they would not have been able to use immediate updating subscribers, so that would be out of the picture. Fortunately, they found that the network was fast and reliable, so they could consider using all the available types of replication.

When it came to the type of replication, they needed to know how much and how often the data would change. If the entire database changed every day, and it was a small database, then they might have been able to get away with snapshot replication. But if the database was large, snapshot would not be the answer because it takes too much bandwidth, and transactional replication would be better. In this case, the company's data was too big for snapshot replication, so they opted for transactional with immediate updating subscribers.

Next they needed to consider the model. In this instance, they had one publisher in California and one subscriber that was quite some distance away. Because there was only one subscriber, they decided to use the central publisher/central distributor model.

One more question popped up: Should the subscription be push or pull? The staff at this company's headquarters in California wanted to control when data was replicated, so they made this a push subscription so they could have that control.

- **Publish only the amount of data required:** This may seem like common sense, but it is one of the biggest culprits of slow replication. You should publish only the columns you need to publish. Publishing too many columns adds time at every step of the process and slows down the entire process. Ergo, use vertical partitioning whenever possible.

- **Place the snapshot folder on a drive that does not have database or log files:** This does not have to be a dedicated disk, mind you; it can have other things on it if necessary. The data and log files are constantly written to and read from, which means if you put the snapshot folder on a disk containing these files, it will have to compete for disk time. If you move it to a disk that is relatively empty, though, it will not need to compete, and snapshots will move faster.

- **Be sparing with horizontal partitioning:** When you horizontally partition a publication, the logreader agent has to apply the filter to every single row that is affected by the update as it scans the transaction log. This takes extra CPU time that can slow your system down, so if it is not necessary, don't use it.

- **Use a fast network:** Again, this is common sense. Because replication occurs between two or more database servers, a network is involved at some point. The faster the network, the faster replication will be.

- **Run agents continuously instead of frequently:** Running agents on frequent schedules, such as every minute, is actually more work for the server than if you just turn on the agent and leave it on. This is because the server has to expend CPU and memory to stop and start the agent regularly. It's better to just leave it on.

Replication also exposes many new and useful performance counters that can be used in your optimization efforts. Recall that performance counters are grouped into performance objects and are used in the SQL Server Performance Monitor. With all of these new performance counters, you can track how effective your replication strategies are and then fine-tune your scenario.

SKILL SUMMARY

IN THIS LESSON YOU LEARNED:

Replication is a powerful tool used to distribute data to other database engines in your enterprise, which you need to do so your data will be closer to your users and, therefore, faster and easier for them to access.

Microsoft uses a publisher/subscriber metaphor to explain replication. The publisher contains the data that needs to be copied. The subscribers get a copy of the data from the publisher, and the distributor moves the data from the publisher to the subscribers. The data is published in groups called *publications*; a publication can contain several *articles*, which are the actual data being replicated.

You can choose from three main types of replication: merge, transactional, and snapshot. Each has pros and cons, but you should consider three main issues when picking a replication type: autonomy, latency, and consistency. In other words, you need to know whether the data has to be replicated right away or whether it can be late (latency); you need to know whether subscribers can update the data (autonomy); and you need to know whether the transactions need to be applied all at the same time and in a specific order (consistency).

When you have picked the right type of replication, you have a number of physical models to choose from:

- Central publisher/central distributor

- Remote distribution

- Central subscriber/multiple publishers

- Multiple publishers/multiple subscribers

- Heterogeneous replication

Once you have implemented a replication solution, you need to back it up. You should back up all the databases involved in replication, but especially the distributor, because if you do not, the transaction log in the distribution database will fill up and replication will stop.

You should also generate replication scripts so that if your server ever suffers a catastrophic failure, you will be able to rebuild the replication solution much faster.

Also keep in mind all the points for enhancing replication performance. Once you have implemented replication, your users will come to depend on it, and if it doesn't move fast enough, it will not be dependable, and your users will not be happy. If you keep it in top shape, though, users will be able to take full advantage of the power of replication.

For the certification examination:

- Know the publisher/subscriber metaphor: Publishers contain the original copy of the data where changes are made. Subscribers receive copies of the data from the publishers. The data is disseminated to the subscribers through the distributor.

- Know the types of replication: Three basic types of replication exist: snapshot, transactional, and merge. In transactional replication, transactions are read right from the transaction log and copied from the publisher to the subscribers. In snapshot replication, the entire publication is copied every time the publication is replicated. In merge replication, data from the publisher is merged with data from the subscribers, which are allowed to update. With the immediate updating subscribers and queued updating options, subscribers can make changes to data that has been replicated with transactional and snapshot data as well.

- Know the replication models: You need to be familiar with the various models—that is, who publishes, who subscribes, and who distributes:

  - In the central publisher/central distributor model, a single server is both the publisher and distributor, and there are multiple subscribers.

  - The remote distribution model has one publishing server, a separate distributor, and multiple subscribers.

- In the central subscriber/multiple publishers model, multiple publishers all publish to a single subscribing server.

- The multiple publishers/multiple subscribers model contains multiple publishing servers and multiple subscribing servers. The number of distributors is undefined.

- Heterogeneous replication describes replication to a third-party database engine, such as DB2 or Oracle.

- Understand how publications and articles work: A publication comprises articles that contain the data being replicated. An article is actually a representation of a table. The article can be partitioned either vertically or horizontally, and it can be transformed.

Knowledge Assessment

Multiple Choice

Circle the letter or letters that correspond to the best answer or answers.

1. You are the administrator of a SQL Server 2005 server located in New York City. That server contains a sales database that needs to be replicated to your satellite offices in Berlin, London, and Moscow, which are connected via a partial T1 connection that consistently runs at 80 percent capacity. Your sales associates make changes to the database regularly throughout the day, but the users in the satellite offices do not need to see the changes immediately. Which type of replication should you use?
   a. Merge
   b. Transactional
   c. Snapshot
   d. Transactional with updating subscribers
   e. Snapshot with updating subscribers

2. You are the administrator of a SQL Server 2005 server located in New York City. That server contains a sales database that needs to be replicated to your satellite offices in Berlin, London, and Moscow, which are connected via a partial T1 connection that consistently runs at 80 percent capacity. Your sales associates make changes to the database regularly throughout the day, but the users in the satellite offices do not need to see the changes immediately. Which replication model should you use?
   a. Central subscriber/multiple publishers
   b. Multiple publishers/multiple subscribers
   c. Central publisher/central distributor
   d. Remote distribution

3. You are the administrator of several SQL Server computers that are configured to use replication in a remote distribution configuration with several subscribers. All of the subscribers require the ability to update the data they receive, so you implement transactional replication with the immediate updating subscribers option. After several weeks, replication starts to fail intermittently. What is the most likely cause?
   a. The SQL Server Agent has stopped.
   b. The Distributed Transaction Coordinator has stopped.
   c. The network connection is down intermittently.
   d. The distribution database transaction log is full.

4. You are the administrator of a SQL Server 2005 server, and you have just installed a new accounting application that stores its data in a database named Accounting. Users in your satellite office need to access the Accounting database to run reports regularly, but they are connected by a very slow network connection. Most of the reports they run will

require data that is accurate up to the last working day. You cannot make any changes to the database. What should you do? (Choose all that apply.)

    a. Implement merge replication.

    b. Implement snapshot replication.

    c. Implement transactional replication.

    d. Schedule replication to run continuously.

    e. Schedule replication to run at off-peak hours.

5. You work for a multinational company where each branch office has its own accounting department. The network connections between the branch offices are reliable, but they are consistently at 80 percent usage during the day. All of your branch office accounting departments need a copy of the accounting database that they can update locally, and they need it to be as current as possible. Which replication type best suits your needs?

    a. Merge

    b. Transactional

    c. Snapshot

    d. Transactional with updating subscribers

    e. Snapshot with updating subscribers

6. You have successfully installed and configured replication on your SQL Server 2005 computer. After you create a publication and add a push subscriber to the publication, you notice that the subscriber is not receiving the data. On further investigation you find that the snapshot agent is failing. What is the most likely cause?

    a. The snapshot agent is frozen. Stop and restart it.

    b. A push subscription is being used instead of a pull subscription, so the snapshot agent is running on the distributor instead of the subscriber.

    c. The snapshot agent does not have access to the Distribution working folder.

    d. The transaction log for the distribution database needs to be cleared.

7. You have a company with several sales offices located throughout the country. Headquarters needs an up-to-date copy of the sales offices' databases. When headquarters sends new inventory to the sales offices, they want to update the database at headquarters and have the new data replicated to the respective sales offices. How could you make sure the sales offices are getting only the data that pertains to their particular office?

    a. Create multiple horizontally partitioned articles at headquarters.

    b. Create multiple vertically partitioned articles at headquarters.

    c. Create a single horizontally partitioned article at headquarters.

    d. Create a single vertically partitioned article at headquarters.

8. You have a company with several sales offices located throughout the country. Headquarters needs an up-to-date copy of the sales offices' databases. When headquarters sends new inventory to the sales offices, they want to update the database at headquarters and have the new data replicated to the respective sales offices. Which replication type should you use?

    a. Merge

    b. Transactional

    c. Snapshot

    d. Transactional with updating subscribers

    e. Snapshot with updating subscribers

9. You have a company with several sales offices located throughout the country. Headquarters needs an up-to-date copy of the sales offices databases. When headquarters sends new inventory to the sales offices, they want to update the database at headquarters and have the new data replicated to the respective sales offices. Which replication model should you use?

    a. Central subscriber/multiple publishers

    b. Multiple publishers/multiple subscribers

    c. Central publisher/central distributor

    d. Remote distribution

10. A small automotive parts company has four shops, each with its own inventory database to maintain. The owner wants the shops to be able to share inventory so that employees can pick up a part from another nearby store rather than waiting for a shipment from the manufacturer. To do this, employees at each shop should be able to update their local copy of the inventory database, decrement the other store's inventory, and then go pick up the part. This way, the other store won't sell its part because it will have already been taken out of stock. Which replication type should you use to accomplish this?
    a. Merge
    b. Transactional
    c. Snapshot
    d. Transactional with updating subscribers
    e. Snapshot with updating subscribers

11. A small automotive parts company has four shops, each with its own inventory database to maintain. The owner wants the shops to be able to share inventory so that employees can pick up a part from another nearby store rather than waiting for a shipment from the manufacturer. To do this, employees at each shop should be able to update their local copy of the inventory database, decrement the other store's inventory, and then go pick up the part. This way, the other store won't sell its part because it will have already been taken out of stock. Which replication model should you use to accomplish this?
    a. Central subscriber/multiple publishers
    b. Multiple publishers/multiple subscribers
    c. Central publisher/central distributor
    d. Remote distribution

12. You have just set up a merge replication subscription between three SQL Server machines using a multiple publishers/multiple subscriber topology. The article looks like this:

    ```
    ProdID ProdName ProdPrice Updated Int varchar(200) money timestamp
    ```

    You soon start getting complaints that the updated column is not being replicated correctly. You can change any part of this that you need in order to fix the problem. What can you do to fix this?
    a. Alter the Updated column using the NOT FOR REPLICATION option.
    b. Alter the Updated column using the REPLICATE AS TIMESTAMP option.
    c. Change to a remote distributor topology.
    d. Change to transactional replication.

13. You are the administrator of several SQL Server systems. Your main server is located in the home office in Denver, and you have servers in satellite offices in Orlando, Nashville, San Francisco, and Portland. You have configured the server in Denver as a publisher and distributor, and you need to configure each of the satellite servers as subscribers as quickly as possible with minimal administrative overhead. What should you do?
    a. Run the Pull Subscription Wizard on each subscriber.
    b. Push the subscription from the publisher to each subscriber.
    c. Run the Pull Subscription Wizard on one subscriber, generate replication scripts on that subscriber, and modify and run the scripts on the remaining subscribers.
    d. Run the Pull Subscription Wizard on one subscriber, and use DTS to copy the database to the remaining subscribers.

14. When checking the subscriber database in a transactional replication scenario, you notice that updates are no longer happening. When you check the publisher, you notice that the database is working properly but the transaction log seems to be filling up even though you are performing regular backups. What is the most likely cause?
    a. The subscriber database does not have access to the Distribution working folder.
    b. The distribution database transaction log has filled to capacity.

    c. The publisher has lost its network connection to the distributor.

    d. The logreader agent has been stopped on the distributor.

15. You are configuring a snapshot replication scenario with a single publisher and almost 100 subscribers. You want to remove as much burden from the distributor as possible. How should you create the subscriptions?

    a. Create push subscriptions so that the snapshot agent runs on the distributor.

    b. Create pull subscriptions so that the snapshot agent runs on the subscriber.

    c. Create push subscriptions so that the distribution agent runs on the distributor.

    d. Create pull subscriptions so that the distribution agent runs on the subscriber.

16. You are the administrator of a SQL Server 2005 computer, and you want to set up snapshot replication on the server. You will be publishing 4 GB to 5 GB of data, and that amount is expected to increase over time. Each of your subscribers will receive a new snapshot every month, so you need to minimize the workload on the publisher/distributor. What should you do? (Choose all that apply.)

    a. Store the snapshot in its default folder on the distributor.

    b. Store the snapshot in a shared folder on a file server.

    c. Create push subscriptions.

    d. Create pull subscriptions.

    e. Separate the publisher and distributor, each one on its own server.

    f. Use heterogeneous replication.

17. You are the SQL Server administrator for a large bank. The bank's customers can access their accounts at the headquarters or at any of the bank's regional offices. The server at headquarters maintains a master copy of the database, so when a customer withdraws funds or makes a deposit at any of the regional offices, the data must be copied to the database at headquarters. The data at headquarters must, in turn, be replicated to all the regional offices. All of this must happen as quickly as possible. What should you do?

    a. Implement snapshot replication, and set the snapshot agent to run continuously.

    b. Implement merge replication, and configure the conflict resolver to keep transactions from the subscriber.

    c. Implement transactional replication with immediate updating subscribers, and configure the logreader agent to run continuously.

    d. Implement transactional replication with queued updating subscribers, and configure the logreader agent to run continuously.

18. You are using a transactional replication scenario, and you notice that your varchar(max) type fields are not being updated regularly. Changes are made to the text fields on a weekly basis, but the changes to the text fields are showing up at the subscribers only once a month. Why is this?

    a. The varchar(max) fields were created with the NOT FOR REPLICATION option.

    b. The publication schedule was set to replicate the varchar(max) fields only on a monthly basis.

    c. The subscribers are refreshed with a snapshot on a monthly basis.

    d. The subscribers are configured to pull the varchar(max) fields only once a month.

19. You are using a multiple publishers/multiple subscribers scenario with transactional replication in which you do not want users to be able to modify data that comes from another database. To do this, you create a constraint that does not allow users to modify data that does not use their own location code. If this constraint gets replicated, it would prevent users from modifying their own local data. How do you prevent the constraint from being replicated?

    a. Create the constraint with the NOT FOR REPLICATION option.

    b. Use snapshot instead of transactional replication because it does not replicate constraints, triggers, or stored procedures.

    c. Configure the publisher to drop and re-create the constraints when replicating data.

    d. Do nothing; constraints are not replicated.

20. To use the Replication Monitor to check the status of replication, which server would you connect to?
    a. The publisher
    b. The subscriber
    c. The distributor
    d. Any of the above

■ Case Scenarios

Scenario 23-1: Using Distributed Transactions versus Replication

Your main office is in Los Angeles. You have five warehouses, one each in Los Angeles, New York, Atlanta, Portland, and Denver. Each needs to know the inventory on-hand at the other sites.

Discuss the pros and cons of implementing remote-site copies of your databases using distributed queries and replication. What are the advantages and disadvantages of each? Which replication scenario best fits for this topography?

■ Section 1: Getting Started in Database Management

THE BOTTOM LINE

What is a database? In the simplest of terms a database is any resource that stores information and makes the retrieval by the user easy. By this definition a telephone directory is a database: it holds the data and makes retrieval easy. A dictionary is a database: it holds data and makes retrieval easy.

In today's world data output is usually preceded by an electronic database. Data is collected by some means, stored in an electronic database management system (DBMS) and printed (as the telephone directory) or made available online (as company catalogs).

Evolving Database Development

IBM started the modern database movement with their Information Management System (IMS) in 1968/69 with a hierarchical data model. This was followed in 1973 with the Committee on Data System Languages (CODASYL) with a network data model along with a record-at-a-time data manipulation language. Current develop really got started, though, with the publishing of E. F. "Ted" Codd's seminal contributions to the theory of relational databases in 1970. Dr. Codd proposed storing data in simple data structures (tables); access data through a high level set-at-a-time data manipulation language; and without the need for a defined physical storage structure. This resulted, after a slow start, in IBM creating the System R project. This, in turn, proved to be the genesis of Larry Ellison, Bob Miner and Ed Oates of the Software Development Laboratories first issuing, in 1977, what is now known as Oracle and later Mark Hoffman and Bob Epstein, in 1985, Sybase.

In 1987, Sybase implemented the concept of a client/server model, triggers and stored procedures and immediately became a dominant force in the marketplace. Microsoft struck an agreement with Sybase on March 27, 1987 to develop a desktop version for use with the then not-yet-released OS/2 and all other operating systems. In 1988, Microsoft announced a new Ashton-Tate/Microsoft SQL Server product to meet the needs of desktop users needing a more robust offering then Microsoft's Database Manager or Ashton-Tate's dBASE III (and promised dBase IV) on OS/2. This cooperation disintegrated and in May 1990 Microsoft shipped SQL Server 1.1 for Windows 3.0. On April 12, 1994 the Sybase/Microsoft agreement ended and on June 14, 1995 Microsoft SQL Server 6.0 was released to manufacturing. Microsoft has matured SQL Server from version 6.0, 6.5, 7.0, 8.0 (known as SQL Server 2000) and, now, 9.0 (known as SQL Server 2005).

Optimizing Databases

You use databases for two distinct purposes: putting data in and getting data out. Two separate architectures have evolved to optimize these two needs: online transactional processing and online analytical processing. Table A-1 compares the features of each.

Table A-1

Comparison of OLTP and OLAP Features

OLTP	OLAP
Atomic data	Aggregated data
True for a moment in time	Used to examine trends
Few indexes	Lots of indexes
Used to process transactions	Used to make reports
Lots of tables	Few tables
Highly normalized	Highly denormalized
Short transaction times	Long search times
Designed once	Constantly evolving
Fixed storage requirement	Constantly growing
Completed transactions archived	Historical data saved
Used by operations specialists	Used by decision makers

Notice that the features of each are almost diametrically opposed. An OLTP, good for putting data in, has lots of tables; an OLAP, good for getting data out, has few tables. An OLTP works best with few indexes (ideally none) while OLAP works best with lots of indexes (the more the better). Trying to use one structure or the other for both putting data in and getting data out compromises the efficiency of a single design. Too many designers try to make the OLTP serve both purposes to the detriment of both.

This course, though, concentrates on the OLTP architecture. Please follow this course with another focused on reporting methods. Microsoft includes Analysis Services with your license to support just this need. When you study this additional technique you will learn about star and snow flake schemas, cubes, data warehousing, decision support systems, data mining, data marts, executive information systems, data farmers, and a host of other topics all focused on efficiently retrieving information.

Applying Database Management Systems in Your Environment

You are taking a course on how to manage SQL Server. This appendix introduces you to background tasks and information to put your choice of a DBMS in context. The next section delves into the program, planning, and budgeting aspects of creating an initial or changing your database system.

■ Section 2: Planning for Database Management

 THE BOTTOM LINE

You've probably heard it before: measure twice; cut once. In this environment: plan, plan, plan. The 80-20 rule applies here, too. Eighty percent of the development effort should be planning; anticipate *everything*.

Develop an Enterprise model. This is a number of separate models that, when properly integrated, provide a coherent picture of the enterprise and its information needs.

A database management system (DBMS) supports the enterprise in meeting its business requirements. Imagine, if you can, how an airline might manage all of the ticket sales, seat assignments, flight schedules, staffing assignments and the myriad of other details needed to keep citizens willing to fly without an electronic database management system. The shear enormity of the information flow precludes returning to times past when travel agents communicated by telephone to a booking agent to reserve a flight.

Justifying a Business Investment

To add a database or improve information management capabilities you must make your decisions based on business needs. Start by identifying (1) anticipated benefits and (2) likely costs. When the Return on Investment (ROI—the anticipated revenue divided by the budgeted costs) exceeds one for a stipulated time period, you have met the initial requirements. Remember that not all requirements justify an electronic database—the iPhone in your pocket not withstanding—because the clipboard and notepad still work.

If you have gotten this far you must sell the project to the funding authority; generally upper management. There are three perspectives from which to argue for the project: facts, faith, and fear. Most financial managers like cold, hard facts. Approach your CFO in this manner. You have a great working relationship with your CIO. The CIO might simply believe. The CEO, though, fears a loss of market share, declining revenues, or obsolescence. Approach this person with how a database management system might relieve him or her of all that pent up tension.

If you survive the initial foray into the business aspects of database management and you get a provisional go ahead, it's time to prepare a more detailed presentation.

Performing a Readiness Assessment

The most significant managers must whole heartedly approve the Readiness Assessment and agree to a project time frame, funding levels, and participation by business subject matter experts. You must have strong management sponsorship: it is perhaps the most important factor. The CEO must recognize the loss of productivity by his key employees during the modeling effort.

You are presenting a compelling business motivation for continuing with the modeling phase. The value of automated data applications is what it does for the business.

You are assessing the culture of your organization: How many will lose their jobs? How much training or re-training will be required? How will people react to doing their job differently? If your future users won't accept the new business processes, don't start.

Assess the project feasibility. Are current data sources accurate and standardized enough to make an automated system feasible? Can you complete the project on time and on budget?

Sometimes the IT group are considered drones; someone to do desktop support and network maintenance. Database management requires that this team be considered as part of business management. Your IT group can't be outsiders and still help everyone else meet business goals. The IT groups needs to be a central part of the business, to attend staff meetings, and to participate in retreats.

The project plan must include:

- Staffing issues
- The formal plan
- Modeling approaches
- Critical success factors

You're successful, so far. Right? You have the green light to proceed.

Modeling the Enterprise

You have the green light to do some more planning. The bosses like the concepts you've presented. Now you must start turning ideas into realities. Start by discovering everything needed by the business.

MODELING BUSINESS PROCESSES

Fifteen years ago, the buzz phrase was functional decomposition. This is the process of determining why and how business requirements get accomplished. IDEF modeling tools (among others) came in to play to capture the knowledge of subject matter experts. This is graphically displayed as an ICOM (input, constraints, output, and mechanisms). Input can be a request for product or service, a constraint can be an environmental regulation or other limiting factor, the output can be the finished product or completed service while a mechanism can be an enabler such as sufficient budget to hire and train employees. The top level ICOM gets progressively decomposed into more and more functions until the most basic tasks are discovered.

This information is only known to the skilled people who perform these functions. These are the people most needed in a daily way to keep the enterprise running smoothly. The time they devote to this project will be noticed—probably by everyone.

Today the buzz phrase is Service Oriented Architecture (SOA). Slightly different modeling tools meet essentially the same requirements but with a slightly different emphasis: functional decomposition focused on information flow requirements between ICOMs while SOA focuses how services can be delivered by the DBMS. For a simple example consider your shipping clerk. Functional decomposition would provide that person with a workstation to look up delivery and invoice requirements. SOA could directly print shipping labels and invoices on a local printer. No longer is there a need for computer training for the clerk or a rugged computer in the warehouse.

Let your imagination run wild. What can you do in your environment to produce a useful output rather than deliver just information? That invoice you printed for the shipping clerk could just as easily be delivered (perhaps by email) directly to the customer together with a shipping tracking number.

SQL Server 2005 comes with new features called Service Broker and Notification Services to make these ideas a much simpler reality.

MODELING THE DATA

You've finished facilitating meetings of the subject matter experts. Let them go back to work.

Now it's time for planners, architects and database designers to start looking at what information needs to be collected to support all of the functions and services uncovered during your business analysis phase.

Some are so intuitively obvious you didn't need the subject matter experts: first name, last name, telephone number, address, city, state, and ZIP, right? But you also discovered little known or appreciated people doing mundane but critically important tasks. You now start detailing the full gamut of your information requirements.

You will probably choose to create an entity relationship model. Here are a few terms to get you started:

- **Entities:** Entities are the principal data objects about which information is to be collected; they usually denote a person, place, thing, or event of informational interest. A particular occurrence of an entity is called an *entity instance* or, sometimes, an *entity occurrence*.

- **Relationships:** Relationships represent real-world associations among one or more entities and, as such, have no physical or conceptual existence other than that which depends upon their entity associations. A particular occurrence of a relationship is called a *relationship instance* or, sometimes, *relationship occurrence*.

- **Roles:** A role is the name of one end of a relationship when each end needs a distinct name for clarity of the relationship.

- **Attributes:** Attributes are characteristics of entities that provide descriptive detail about them. A particular occurrence of an attribute within an entity or relationship is called an *attribute value*. There are two types of attributes: identifiers and descriptors. An identifier, or key, is used to uniquely determine an instance of an entity (such as a social security number); a descriptor, or nonkey attribute, is used to specify a repetitive characteristic of a particular entity instance (such as male or female). Both identifiers and descriptors may consist of either a single attribute or some composite of attributes.

A relationship is indicated between entity occurrences as one-to-one; one-to-zero, one or many; and many-to-many. The modeling notations (examples include Chen, crows-feet, UML, and IDEF) map entities and relationships in a graphical manner.

The relationship between the Book table and the Author table is a many-to-many situation: a book can have more than one author and an author can write more than one book. To represent a many-to-many relationship in a DBMS a third table linking the two is required. This is also known as a *junction table*.

Certain data entities have an affinity due to being involved in similar business processes. For example, the entities CustomerID and CustAcctNo have an affinity because they are usually used in the same processes. Similarly, certain business processes group logically together. This affinity or grouping is referred to as clustering. *Affinity Analysis* is a technique to identify the logical clustering of data and processes.

There are software tools to help with these tasks such as Embarcadero's ERStudio and Computer Associate's ERWIN. These are entity relationship modeling software packages to perform analysis, capture table layouts, and create data dictionaries. Once complete, these tools will build the database for you.

DECIDING TO BUILD OR BUY

You have come the point of business process understanding that permits you to evaluate commercial-off-the-shelf software packages. Can you purchase a customer relation management package, for example, cheaper than you can develop a database and the needed client software?

It's time to go back to management with a proposal for the next phase. You need time to estimate the requirements and a budget for an in-house effort to compare with the expected purchase price. Consider using Software Life Cycle Processes, IEEE/EIA 12207, to guide you in examining total costs. For example, your CRM vendor will provide support for a subscription fee but if you develop in-house you will still need support staff. In this option *you* must hire, train, and equip them to work with your users. You may need a larger, air-conditioned, secure server room.

BUILDING IT YOUR SELF

You have modeled the total task and chosen an in-house development solution. To keep momentum most projects require early successes. Therefore, your project might include a phased approach that considers several factors in developing the initial scope:

- It should be a joint project between IT and other business functions
- The initial scope should be meaningful and manageable
- The initial focus should be a single business requirement from a single process.
- The number of initial users should be limited.
- Success criteria should be developed at the start, along with the scope.

To keep management interested you must present continuing benefits. Economic feasibility considerations include:

- Tangible benefits are either cost reductions or revenue increase.
- Tangible development costs include salaries, consultant fees, hardware and software purchases, and data conversion.
- Tangible operating costs include annual licenses, upgrades, repairs, user training, and depreciation.
- Intangible benefits include improved morale, increase product quality, decrease in time to market, reduction in turnover, increase competitive advantage, and more timely information.
- Intangible costs include disruption to environment, loss of goodwill, reduction in morale, and diversion of attention to daily responsibilities.

Complete your plan in yet more detail. Construction activities must include:

- Entity identification: What are the building blocks?
- ER diagramming: How do entities relate to others?
- Process identification: What is the workflow?
- Entity life cycle analysis: Does work modify entities?
- Event analysis: How do events cluster to processes?
- Association diagramming: How do objects interact?
- Critical factor analysis: What is needed for success?
- SWOT analysis: What are strengths, weaknesses, opportunities and threats?
- Information needs analysis: What data does each business area need most? What data is currently available?
- Systems evaluation: Are current networks, servers, and other infrastructure sufficient?

You don't yet have the data in the database. It must exist somewhere in some form. How do you get it from where it is to where it needs to be? The data staging process includes:

- Extraction of data from multiple sources
- Transformation and cleansing

- Loading the data often to multiple targets
- Security access and encryption policies
- Job control which includes scheduling, monitoring, and notification

Critical success factors include:

- Having a strong project sponsor
- Generating user buy-in
- Identifying business needs
- Starting with a narrow scope
- Understanding the organizational culture
- Creating clear requirements documents
- Defining all data and communication requirements
- Prototyping often

NORMALIZING YOUR DATABASE

In 1985, Ted Codd published his twelve rules to define what is required from a database management system (DBMS) in order for it to be considered relational (RDBMS). Out of this has evolved what is now known as normalization. Normalization involves a seemingly simple two step process: (1) put the data into tabular form (by removing repeating groups) and (2) remove duplicated data to separate tables.

Most implementations may stop at the third normal form as this is considered the maximum needed for "business sensitive" data. Indeed, many references stipulate the 3NF as "completely" normalized. There are, however, four more for specialized circumstances: Boyce-Codd, 4NF, 5NF, and 6NF—for a total of seven normal forms. Boyce-Codd focuses on candidate keys, 4NF addresses multivalued dependencies, 5NF deals with splitting tables, and 6NF has been proposed to deal with time-dependent data.

OK. You decided to build your own system. You used an entity relationship software tool. You have proposed tables. You're almost ready to create your database.

The cardinal rule of OLTP database design: **store data once**. Examine the table layout and its data as shown Table A-2 below:

Table A-2

Table layout not yet normalized

Order Number	Order Date	Customer Number	Customer Name	Customer Address	Items Ordered
100	10/1/2007	54545	Acme Co	1234 First St;Oxnard, CA 93030	1, A4536, Flange, 7 lbs, $75;4, R2400, Injector, 0.5 lbs, $108;4, R2403, Injector, 0.5 lbs, $116;1, L5436, Head, 63 lbs, $750;
101	10/1/2007	12000	Top Dog Inc	555 Main Ave;Fresno, CA 95051	1, X9567, Pump, 5 lbs, $62.50;
102	10/1/2007	A6651	Pinnacle Corp	4242 SW 2nd;Seattle, WA 97123	7, G9200, Fan, 3 lbs, $15;1, G5437, Fan, 3 lbs, $15;1, H6250, Control, 5 lbs, $32;
103	10/1/2007	54546	Acme Co	1234 First St; Oxnard, CA 93030	40, G9200, Fan, 3 lbs, $480;1, P5523, Housing, 1 lbs, $165;1, X9567, Pump, 5 lbs, $42;

Note the repetitive data. Acme Co is stored twice; the customer number is stored twice. As a corollary, only one data value should be stored in a field. The customer address and items ordered columns each have comma-separated values. The solution: normalize.

■ Section 3: Understanding Process Models and Hardware Architectures

THE BOTTOM LINE

Database Management Systems (DBMSs) are complex, mission-critical pieces of software. Today's DBMSs are based on decades of academic and industrial research, and intense corporate software development. Database systems were among the earliest widely-deployed online server systems, and as such have pioneered design issues spanning not only data management, but also applications, operating systems, and networked services.

The electronic database has four main components: a process manager that encapsulates and schedules the various tasks in the system; a statement-at-a-time query processing engine; a shared transactional storage subsystem that knits together storage, buffer management, concurrency control and recovery; and a set of shared utilities including memory management, disk space management, replication, and various batch utilities used for administration.

No one database management system meets all enterprise business needs. Literally hundreds of database management systems exist on the market and each focuses on some specific need. This section introduces you to some to the technical considerations involved.

You need to decide which of the many offerings best meets your business needs. SQL Server is one of the top three systems (along with Oracle and DB2). Each has distinctions making each more attractive under specific circumstances. You are taking a SQL Server course and, therefore, SQL Server features are emphasized.

Introducing the Page Concept

During the 1970s, IBM dominated the automated data processing market. They built their architecture around a central computer, a network and, what are now called, dumb terminals. The System Network Architecture, created in 1974, polled individual terminals asking the question: "Do you need to be serviced now?" If the operator had hit the Execute key on the terminal, the answer was "Yes".

The terminals had no internal intelligence. The display was eighty characters wide by 25 lines high. Quick math tells you that this is 2,000 characters total. Some more inference reveals that 2^{11} equals 2,048 bytes and that this amount of data could refresh the screen (with the needed overhead control bytes) exactly. This delivery and receipt method became known as a *page*. The server delivered a page-worth of data to the terminal and the user's terminal sent a page-worth of data back to the server. All of the processing occurred on the mainframe.

TAKE NOTE*

8 KB equals 8,000 bytes.

The page concept still exists. Some DBMSs allow you to select the page size desired; typically 2 KiB, 4 KiB, 8 KiB, or 16 KiB. SQL Server has a fixed page size of 8 KiB—8,096 Bytes. This page concept pervades throughout SQL Server management. For example, eight pages equals an extent. Extents govern all input/output file retrievals (64 KiB blocks).

Understanding Uniprocessors and OS Threads

Most systems (e.g., Oracle) are designed to be portable, but not all. Notable examples of OS-specific DBMSs are DB2 for MVS, and Microsoft SQL Server. These systems can exploit (and sometimes add) special OS features, rather than using DBMS-level workarounds.

PASSING DATA ACROSS PROCESSORS

In a simplified context, there are three process model options for a DBMS. From simplest to most sophisticated, these are:

1. **Process per Connection:** This was the model used in early DBMS implementations on UNIX. In this model, users run a client tool, typically on a machine across a network from the DBMS server. They use a database connectivity protocol (e.g., ODBC or JDBC) that connects to a main dispatcher process at the database server machine, which forks a separate process (not a thread) to serve that connection. This is relatively easy to implement in UNIX-like systems, because it maps DBMS units of work directly onto OS processes. The OS scheduler manages timesharing of user queries, and the DBMS programmer can rely on OS protection facilities to isolate standard bugs like memory overruns. Moreover, various programming tools like debuggers and memory checkers are well-suited to this process model. A complication of programming in this model regards the data structures that are shared across connections in a DBMS, including the lock table and buffer pool. These must be explicitly allocated in OS-supported "shared memory" accessible across processes, which requires a bit of special-case coding in the DBMS.

   In terms of performance, this architecture is not attractive. It does not scale very well in terms of the number of concurrent connections, since processes are heavy-weight entities with sizable memory overheads and high context-switch times. Hence this architecture is inappropriate for one of the bread-and-butter applications of commercial DBMSs: high-concurrency transaction processing. This architecture was replaced in the commercial DBMS vendors long ago, though it is still a compatibility option in many systems (and in fact the default option on installation of Oracle for UNIX).

2. **Server Process:** This is the most natural architecture for efficiency today. In this architecture, a single multithreaded process hosts all the main activity of the DBMS. A dispatcher thread (or perhaps a small handful of such threads) listens for SQL commands. Typically the process keeps a pool of idle worker threads available, and the dispatcher assigns incoming SQL commands to idle worker threads, so that each command runs in its own thread. When a command is completed, it clears its state and returns its worker thread to the thread pool. Shared data structures like the lock table and buffer pool simply reside in the process' heap space, where they are accessible to all threads.

   The usual multithreaded programming challenges arise in this architecture: the OS does not protect threads from each other's memory overruns and stray pointers, debugging is tricky especially with race conditions, and the software can be difficult to port across operating systems due to differences in threading interfaces and multi-threaded performance. Although thread API differences across operating systems have been minimized in recent years, subtle distinctions across platforms still cause hassles in debugging and tuning.

3. **Server Process plus I/O Processes:** The Server Process model makes the important assumption that asynchronous I/O is provided by the operating system. This feature allows the DBMS to issue a read or write request, and work on other things while the disk device works to satisfy the request. Asynchronous I/O can also allow the DBMS to schedule an I/O request to each of multiple disk devices; and have the devices all working in parallel; this is possible even on a uniprocessor system, since the disk devices themselves work autonomously, and in fact have their own microprocessors on board. Some time after a disk request is issued, the OS interrupts the DBMS with a notification the request has completed. Because of the separation of requests from responses, this is sometimes called a split-phase programming model.

   Asynchronous I/O support in the operating system is a fairly recent development: Linux only included asynchronous disk I/O support in the standard kernel in 2002.

Without asynchronous I/O, all threads of a process must block while waiting for any I/O request to complete, which can unacceptably limit both system throughput and per-transaction latency. To work around this issue on older OS versions, a minor modification to the Server Process model is used. Additional I/O Processes are introduced to provide asynchronous I/O features outside the OS. The main Server threads queue I/O requests to an I/O Process via shared memory or network sockets, and the I/O Process queues responses back to the main Server Process in a similar fashion. There is typically about one I/O Process per disk in this environment, to ensure that the system can handle multiple requests to separate devices in parallel.

The integration of SQL Server with the Windows Server operating system makes this the model of choice by Microsoft.

PASSING DATA ACROSS THREADS

A good Server Process architecture provides non-blocking, asynchronous I/O. It also has dispatcher threads connecting client requests to worker threads. This design begs the question of how data is passed across these thread or process boundaries. The short answer is that various buffers are used

- **Disk I/O buffers:** The most common asynchronous interaction in a database is for disk I/O: a thread issues an asynchronous disk I/O request, and engages in other tasks pending a response. There are two separate I/O scenarios to consider:

- **DB I/O requests: The Buffer Pool.** All database data is staged through the DBMS buffer pool. In Server Process architectures, this is simply a heap-resident data structure. To flush a buffer pool page to disk, a thread generates an I/O request that includes the page's current location in the buffer pool (the frame), and its destination address on disk. When a thread needs a page to be read in from the database, it generates an I/O request specifying the disk address, and a handle to a free frame in the buffer pool where the result can be placed. The actual reading and writing and pages into and out of frames are done asynchronously.

- **Log I/O Requests: The Log Tail.** The database log is an array of entries stored on a set of disks. As log entries are generated during transaction processing, they are staged in a memory queue that is usually called the log tail, which is periodically flushed to the log disk(s) in FIFO order. In many systems, a separate thread is responsible for periodically flushing the log tail to the disk.

  The most important log flushes are those that commit transactions. A transaction cannot be reported as successfully committed until a commit log record is flushed to the log device. This means both that client code waits until the commit log record is flushed, and that DBMS server code must hold resources (e.g. locks) until that time as well. In order to amortize the costs of log writes, most systems defer them until enough are queued up, and then do a "group commit" by flushing the log tail. Policies for group commit are a balance between keeping commit latency low (which favors flushing the log tail more often), and maximizing log throughput (which favors postponing log flushes until the I/O can be amortized over many bytes of log tail).

- **Client communication buffers:** SQL typically is used in a "pull" model: clients consume result tuples from a query cursor by repeatedly issuing the SQL FETCH request, which may retrieve one or more tuples per request. Most DBMSs try to work ahead of the stream of FETCH requests, enqueuing results in advance of client requests.

In order to support this work-ahead behavior, the DBMS worker thread for a query contains a pointer to a location for enqueuing results. A simple option is to assign each client to a network socket. In this case, the worker thread can use the socket as a queue for the tuples it produces. An alternative is to multiplex a network socket across multiple clients. In this case, the server process must (a) maintain its own state per client, including a communication queue for each client's SQL results, and (b) have a "coordinator agent" thread (or set of threads) available to respond to client FETCH requests by pulling data off of the communication queue.

Using DBMS Threads and OS Threads

Most modern operating systems support reasonable threads packages. They may not provide the degree of concurrency needed by the DBMS (Linux threads were very heavyweight until recently), but they are almost certainly more efficient than using multiple processes.

Since most database systems evolved along with their host operating systems, they were originally architected for single-threaded processes. As OS threads matured, a natural form of evolution was to modify the DBMS to be a single process, using an OS thread for each unit that was formerly an OS process. This approach continues to use the DBMS threads, but maps them into OS threads rather than OS processes. This evolution is relatively easy to code, and leverages the code investment in efficient DBMS threads, minimizing the dependency on high-end multithreading in the OS.

In fact, most of today's DBMSs are written in this manner, and can be run over either processes or threads. They abstract the choice between processes and threads in the code, mapping DBMS threads to OS-provided "dispatchable units" (to use DB2 terminology), be they processes or threads.

Current hardware provides one reason to stick with processes such as the "dispatchable unit". On many architectures today, the addressable memory per process is not as large as available physical memory—for example, on Linux for ×86 only 3 GB of RAM is available per process. It is certainly possible to equip a modern PC with more physical memory than that, but no individual process can address all of the memory. Using multiple processes alleviates this problem in a simple fashion.

There are variations in the threading models in today's leading systems. Oracle on UNIX is configured by default to run in Process-Per-User mode, but for better performance can run in the Server Process fashion: DBMS threads multiplexed across a set of OS processes. On Windows, Oracle uses a single OS process with multiple threads as dispatchable units: DBMS threads are multiplexed across a set of OS threads. DB2 does not provide its own DBMS threads. On UNIX platforms DB2 works in a Process-per-User mode: each user's session has its own agent process that executes the session logic. DB2 on Windows uses OS threads as the dispatchable unit, rather than multiple processes. Microsoft SQL Server only runs on Windows; it runs an OS thread per session by default, but can be configured to multiplex various "DBMS threads" across a single OS thread; in the case of SQL Server the "DBMS threads" package is actually a Windows-provided feature known as fibers.

Understanding Parallelism, Process Models, and Memory Coordination

Parallel hardware is a fact of life in modern server situations, and comes in a variety of configurations.

USING A SHARED MEMORY MODEL

A *shared-memory* parallel machine is one in which all processors can access the same RAM and disk with about the same performance. This architecture is fairly standard today—most server hardware ships with between two and eight processors. On shared-memory machines, the OS typically supports the transparent assignment of dispatchable units (processes or threads) across the processors, and the shared data structures continue to be accessible to all. Hence the Server Process architecture parallelizes to shared-memory machines with minimal effort.

USING A SHARED NOTHING MODEL

A *shared-nothing* parallel machine is made up of a cluster of single-processor machines that communicate over a high-speed network interconnect. There is no way for a given processor to directly access the memory or disk of another processor. This architecture is also fairly standard today, and has unbeatable scalability and cost characteristics. It is mostly used at the extreme high end, typically for decision-support applications on data warehouses. Shared nothing machines can be cobbled together from individual PCs, but for database server purposes they are typically sold as packages including specialized network interconnects (e.g. the IBM SP2 or the NCR WorldMark machines.) In the OS community, these platforms have been dubbed "clusters", and the component PCs are sometimes called "blade servers".

Shared nothing systems provide no hardware sharing abstractions, leaving coordination of the various machines entirely in the hands of the DBMS. In these systems, each machine runs its own Server Process, but allows an individual query's execution to be parallelized across multiple machines. The basic architecture of these systems is to use horizontal data partitioning to allow each processor to execute independently of the others. For storage purposes, each tuple in the database is assigned to an individual machine, and hence each table is sliced "horizontally" and spread across the machines (typical data partitioning schemes include hash-based partitioning by tuple attribute, range-based partitioning by tuple attribute, or round-robin). Each individual machine is responsible for the access, locking and logging of the data on its local disks. During query execution, the query planner chooses how to horizontally repartition tables across the machines to satisfy the query, assigning each machine a logical partition of the work. The query executors on the various machines ship data requests and tuples to each other, but do not need to transfer any thread state or other low-level information. As a result of this value-based partitioning of the database tuples, minimal coordination is required in these systems. However, good partitioning of the data is required for good performance, which places a significant burden on the DBA to layout tables intelligently, and on the query optimizer to do a good job partitioning the workload.

This simple partitioning solution does not handle all issues in the DBMS. For example, there has to be explicit cross-processor coordination to handle transaction completion, to provide load balancing, and to support certain mundane maintenance tasks. For example, the processors must exchange explicit control messages for issues like distributed deadlock detection and two-phase commit. This requires additional logic, and can be a performance bottleneck if not done carefully.

Also, partial failure is a possibility that has to be managed in a shared-nothing system. In a shared-memory system, the failure of a processor typically results in a hardware shutdown of the entire parallel computing machine. In a shared-nothing system, the failure of a single node will not necessarily affect other nodes, but will certainly affect the overall behavior of the DBMS, since the failed node hosts some fraction of the data in the database. There are three possible approaches in this scenario. The first is to bring down all nodes if any node fails; this in essence emulates what would happen in a shared memory system. The second approach, which Informix dubbed "Data Skip", allows queries to be executed on any nodes that are up, "skipping" the data on the failed node. This is of use in scenarios where availability trumps consistency, but the best effort results generated do not have any well-defined semantics. The third approach is to employ redundancy schemes like chained declustering, which spread copies of tuples across multiple nodes in the cluster. These techniques are designed to tolerate a number of failures without losing data. In practice, however, these techniques are not provided; commercial vendors offer coarser-grained redundancy solutions like database replication, which maintain a copy of the entire database in a separate "standby" system.

USING A SHARED DISK MODEL

A *shared-disk* parallel machine is one in which all processors can access the same disks with about the same performance, but are unable to access each other's RAM. This architecture is quite common in the very largest "single-box" (non-cluster) multiprocessors, and hence is important for very large installations—especially for Oracle, which does not sell a shared-nothing software platform. Shared disk has become an increasingly attractive approach in recent years, with the advent of Network Attached Storage devices (NAS), which allow a storage device on a network to be mounted by a set of nodes.

One key advantage of shared-disk systems over shared-nothing is in usability, since DBAs of shared-disk systems do not have to consider partitioning tables across machines. Another feature of a shared-disk architecture is that the failure of a single DBMS processing node does not affect the other nodes' ability to access the full database. This is in contrast to both shared-memory systems that fail as a unit, and shared-nothing systems that lose at least some data upon a node failure. Of course, this puts more emphasis on the reliability of the storage nodes.

Because there is no partitioning of the data in a shared disk system, data can be copied into RAM and modified on multiple machines. Unlike shared-memory systems there is no natural place to coordinate this sharing of the data—each machine has its own local memory for locks and buffer pool pages. Hence there is a need to explicitly coordinate data sharing across the machines. Shared-disk systems come with a distributed lock manager facility, and a cache-coherency protocol for managing the distributed buffer pools. These are complex pieces of code, and can be bottlenecks for workloads with significant contention.

Understanding Admission Control

As the workload is increased in any multi-user system, performance will increase up to some maximum, and then begin to decrease radically as the system starts to "thrash". As in operating system settings, thrashing is often the result of memory pressure: the DBMS cannot keep the "working set" of database pages in the buffer pool, and spends all its time replacing pages. In DBMSs, this is particularly a problem with query processing techniques like sorting and hash joins, which like to use large amounts of main memory. In some cases, DBMS thrashing can also occur due to contention for locks; transactions continually deadlock with each other and need to be restarted. Hence any good multi-user system has an admission control policy, which does not admit new clients unless the workload will stay safely below the maximum that can be handled without thrashing. With a good admission controller, a system will display graceful degradation under overload: transactions latencies will increase proportionally to their arrival rate, but throughput will remain at peak.

Admission control for a DBMS can be done in two tiers. First, there may be a simple admission control policy in the dispatcher process to ensure that the number of client connections is kept below a threshold. This serves to prevent overconsumption of basic resources like network connections, and minimizes unnecessary invocations of the query parser and optimizer. In some DBMSs this control is not provided, under the assumption that it is handled by some other piece of software interposed between clients and the DBMS: e.g., an application server, transaction processing monitor, or web server.

The second layer of admission control must be implemented directly within the core DBMS query processor. This execution admission controller runs after the query is parsed and optimized, and determines whether a query is postponed or begins execution. The execution admission controller is aided by information provided by the query optimizer, which can estimate the resources that a query will require. In particular, the optimizer's query plan can specify (a) the disk devices that the query will access, and an estimate of the number of random and sequential I/Os per device (b) estimates of the CPO load of the query, based on the operators in the query plan and the number of tuples to be processed, and most importantly (c) estimates about the memory footprint of the query data structures, including space for sorting and hashing tables. As noted above, this last metric is often the key for an admission controller, since memory pressure is often the main cause of thrashing. Hence many DBMSs use memory footprint as the main criterion for admission control.

■ Section 4: Understanding Storage Models

THE BOTTOM LINE

In addition to the process model, another basic consideration when designing a DBMS is the choice of the persistent storage interface to use.

There are basically two storage model options: the DBMS can interact directly with the device drivers for the disks, or the DBMS can use the typical OS file system facilities. This decision has impacts on the DBMS's ability to control storage in both space and time. You need to consider these two dimensions in turn, and proceed to consider the use of the storage hierarchy in more detail.

Introducing Spatial Control

Sequential access to disk blocks is between 10 and 100 times faster than random access.

This gap is increasing quickly. Disk density—and hence sequential bandwidth—improves following Moore's Law, doubling every 18 months. Disk arm movement is improving at a much slower rate. As a result, it is critical for the DBMS storage manager to place blocks on the disk so that important queries can access data sequentially. Since the DBMS can understand its workload more deeply than the underlying OS, it makes sense for DBMS architects to exercise full control over the spatial positioning of database blocks on disk.

The best way for the DBMS to control spatial locality of its data is to issue low-level storage requests directly to the "raw" disk device interface, since disk device addresses typically correspond closely to physical proximity of storage locations. Most commercial database systems offer this functionality for peak performance. Although quite effective, this technique has some drawbacks. First, it requires the DBA to devote entire disks to the DBMS; this used to be frustrating when disks were very expensive, but it has become far less of a concern today. Second, "raw disk" access interfaces are often OS-specific, which can make the DBMS more difficult to port. However, this is a hurdle that most commercial DBMS vendors chose to overcome years ago. Finally, developments in the storage industry like RAID, Storage Area Networks (SAN), and Network-Attached Storage (NAS) have become popular, to the point where "virtual" disk devices are the norm in many scenarios today—the "raw" device interface is actually being intercepted by appliances or software that reposition data aggressively on one or more physical disks. As a result, the benefits of explicit physical control by the DBMS have been diluted over time.

An alternative to raw disk access is for the DBMS to create a very large file in the OS file system, and then manage positioning of data in the offsets of that file. This offers reasonably good performance. In most popular file systems, if you allocate a very large file on an empty disk, the offsets in that file will correspond fairly well to physical proximity of storage regions. Hence this is a good approximation to raw disk access, without the need to go directly to the device interface. Most virtualized storage systems are also designed to place close offsets in a file in nearby physical locations. Hence the relative control lost when using large files rather than raw disks is becoming less significant over time. However, using the file system interface has other ramifications.

Note that in either of these schemes, the size of a database page might be a tunable parameter that can be set at the time of database generation; it should be a multiple of the sized offered by typical disk devices. If the file system is being used, special interfaces may be required to write pages of a different size than the file system default; the POSIX mmap/msync calls provide this facility. SQL Server does not permit tunable database page sizes but note also that the fixed 8 KiB page is the same size as the allocation unit to the physical disk.

Introducing SQL Server File Management Mechanisms

You may know that Microsoft used a Control-Z character to denote the end of a file back in DOS days. You would properly infer that the file system locates a file and reads it in total into memory for processing. The file could be as large as 2 GiB because virtual memory would put what could not be contained in RAM off to the paging system file.

Now imagine how that would work in SQL Server that scales to terabytes of data. The file system cannot be read as a total—there isn't room anywhere but the original disk drive from which the data was retrieved. The solution? Read data in 64 KiB chunks known as extents from anywhere within the physical file.

SQL Server accomplishes this by using four mapping schemes and dividing the entire file into pages each 8 KiB in size. Here's how:

- **The File Header:** Page 0 of the physical file contains the File Header.

- **Page Free Space:** Page 1 and each 80,000 pages later of the physical file contains a page recording the allocation status of each page, whether an individual page has been allocated and the amount of free space on each page. The PFS has one byte for each page, recording whether the page is allocated, and if so, whether it is empty, 1 to 50 percent full, 51 to 80 percent full, 81 to 95 percent full, or 96 to 100 percent full.

  After an extent has been allocated to an object, the Database Engine uses the PFS pages to record which pages in the extent are allocated or free. This information is used when the Database Engine has to allocate a new page. The amount of free space in a page is only maintained for heap and text/image pages. It is used when the Database Engine has to find a page with free space available to hold a newly inserted row. Indexes do not require that the page free space be tracked because the point at which to insert a new row is set by the index key values.

- **Global Allocation Map:** Page 2 and each 64,000 pages of the physical file later, GAM pages record what extents have been allocated. Each GAM covers 64,000 extents, or almost 4 GB of data. The GAM has one bit for each extent in the interval it covers. If the bit is 1, the extent is free; if the bit is 0, the extent is allocated.

- **Shared Global Allocation Map:** Page 3 and each 64,000 pages of the physical file later, SGAM pages record which extents are currently being used as mixed extents and also have at least one unused page. Each SGAM covers 64,000 extents, or almost 4 GB of data. The SGAM has one bit for each extent it covers. If the bit is 1, the extent is being used as a mixed extent and all its pages are being used.

- **Index Allocation Map:** An IAM page maps the extents in a 4 GiB part of a database file used by an allocation unit. An IAM page covers a 4 GiB range in a file and is the same coverage as a GAM or SGAM page. If the allocation unit contains extents from more than one file or more than one 4 GiB range of a file, there will be multiple IAM pages linked in an IAM chain. Therefore, each allocation unit has a least one IAM page for each file on which it has extents. There may also be more than one IAM page on a file if the range of the extents on the file allocated to the allocation unit exceeds the range that a single IAM page can record.

  IAM pages are allocated as required for each allocation unit and are located randomly in the file.

All of this means that when you CREATE a database, you must specify the file size needed. SQL Server allocates the file of the desired size, builds the various maps and stores empty space ready to be used. You also must specify whether or not you want this file size to grow and whether by size or percent. This further means that as records are deleted new empty space occurs. Regular maintenance using the Maintenance Wizard, DBCC ShrinkDatabase, DBCC ShrinkFile and other utilities become important tasks to defragment your physical file rather than constantly consuming more disk real estate.

Introducing Temporal Control: Buffering

In addition to controlling where on the disk data should be, a DBMS must control when data gets physically written to the disk. A DBMS contains critical logic that reasons about when to write blocks to disk. Most OS file systems also provide built-in I/O buffering mechanisms to decide when to do reads and writes of file blocks. If the DBMS uses standard file system interfaces for writing, the OS buffering can confound the intention of the DBMS logic by silently postponing or reordering writes. This can cause major problems for the DBMS.

The first set of problems regard the correctness of the database: the DBMS cannot ensure correct transactional semantics without explicitly controlling the timing of disk writes. Writes to the log device must precede corresponding writes to the database device, and commit requests cannot return to users until commit log records have been reliably written to the log device.

The second set of problems with OS buffering concern performance, but have no implications on correctness. Modern OS file systems typically have some built-in support for read-ahead (speculative reads) and write-behind (postponed, batched writes), and these are often poorly-suited to DBMS access patterns. File system logic depends on the contiguity of physical byte offsets in files to make decisions about reads and writes. DBMS-level I/O facilities can support logical decisions based on the DBMS' behavior. For example, the stream of reads in a query is often predictable to the DBMS, but not physically contiguous on the disk, and hence not visible via the OS read/write API. Logical DBMS-level read-ahead can occur when scanning the leaves of a B+-tree, for example. Logical read-aheads are easily achieved in DBMS logic by a query thread issuing I/Os in advance of its needs—the query plan contains the relevant information about data access algorithms, and has full information about future access patterns for the query. Similarly, the DBMS may want to make its own decisions about when to flush the log buffer (often called the log "tail"), based on considerations that mix issues like lock contention with I/O throughput. This mix of information is available to the DBMS but not to the OS file system.

The final performance issues are "double buffering" and the extreme CPU overhead of memory copies. Given that the DBMS has to do its own buffering carefully for correctness, any additional buffering by the OS is redundant. This redundancy results in two costs. First, it wastes system memory, effectively limiting the memory available for doing useful work. Second, it wastes time, by causing an additional copying step: on reads, data is first copied from the disk to the OS buffer, and then copied again to the DBMS buffer pool. On writes, both of these copies are required in reverse. Copying data in memory can be a serious bottleneck in DBMS software today. Main-memory operations are not "free" compared to disk I/O. In practice, a well-tuned database installation is typically not I/O-bound. This is achieved in high-end installations by purchasing the right mix of disks and RAM so that repeated page requests are absorbed by the buffer pool, and disk I/Os are shared across the disk arms at a rate that can feed the appetite of all the processors in the system. Once this kind of "system balance" is achieved, I/O latencies cease to be a bottleneck, and the remaining main memory bottlenecks become the limiting factors in the system. Memory copies are becoming a dominant bottleneck in computer architectures: this is due to the gap in performance evolution between raw CPU cycles per second (which follows Moore's law) and RAM access speed (which trails Moore's law significantly).

Introducing Buffer Management

In order to provide efficient access to database pages, every DBMS implements a large shared buffer pool in its own memory space. The buffer pool is organized as an array of frames, each frame being a region of memory the size of a database disk block. Blocks are copied in native format from disk directly into frames, manipulated in memory in native format, and written back. This translation-free approach avoids CPU bottlenecks in "marshalling" and "unmarshalling" data to/from disk; perhaps more importantly, the fixed-sized frames sidestep complexities of external memory fragmentation and compaction that are associated with generic memory management.

Associated with the array of frames is an array of metadata called a page table, with one entry for each frame. The page table contains the disk location for the page currently in each frame, a dirty bit to indicate whether the page has changed since it was read from disk, and any information needed by the page replacement policy used for choosing pages to evict on overflow. It also contains a pin count for the page in the frame; the page is not candidate for page replacement unless the pin count is 0. This allows tasks to (hopefully briefly) "pin" pages into the buffer pool by incrementing the pin count before manipulating the page, and decrementing it thereafter.

■ Section 5: Understanding the Query Processor

A relational query engine takes a declarative SQL statement, validates it, optimizes it into a procedural dataflow implementation plan, and (subject to admission control) executes that dataflow on behalf of a client program, which fetches ("pulls") the result tuples, typically one at a time or in small batches.

In general, relational query processing can be viewed as a single-user, single-threaded task. Concurrency control is managed transparently by lower layers of the system. The only exception to this rule is that the query processor must explicitly pin and unpin buffer pool pages when manipulating them. In this section you focus on the common case SQL commands: "DML" statements including SELECT, INSERT, UPDATE and DELETE.

Parsing and Authorizing

Given a SQL DML SELECT statement, the main tasks for the parser are to check that the query is correctly specified, to convert it into an internal format, and to check that the user is authorized to execute the query. Syntax checking is done naturally as part of the parsing process, during which time the parser generates an internal representation for the query.

The parser handles queries one "SELECT" block at a time. First, it considers each of the table references in the FROM clause. It canonicalizes each table name into a schema.tablename format; users have default schemas which are often omitted from the query specification. It then invokes the catalog manager to check that the table is registered in the system catalog; while so checking it may also cache metadata about the table in internal query data structures. Based on information about the table, it then uses the catalog to check that attribute references are correct. The data types of attributes are used to drive the (rather intricate) disambiguation logic for overloaded functional expressions, comparison operators, and constant expressions. For example, in the expression "(EMP.salary * 1.15) < 75000", the code for the multiplication function and comparison operator—and the assumed data type and internal format of the strings "1.15" and "75000"—will depend upon the data type of the EMP.salary attribute, which may be an integer, a floating-point number, or a "money" value. Additional standard SQL syntax checks are also applied, including the usage of tuple variables, the compatibility of tables combined via set operators (UNION/INTERSECT/EXCEPT), the usage of attributes in the SELECT list of aggregation queries, the nesting of subqueries, and so on.

If the query parses correctly, the next phase is to check authorization. Again, the catalog manager is invoked to ensure that the user has the appropriate permissions (SELECT/DELETE/ INSERT/UPDATE) on the tables in the query. Additionally, integrity constraints are consulted to ensure that any constant expressions in the query do not result in constraint violations. For example, an UPDATE command may have a clause of the form "SET EMP.salary = −1". If there is an integrity constraint specifying positive values for salaries, the query will not be authorized for execution.

If a query parses and passes authorization checks, then the internal format of the query is passed on to the query rewrite module for further processing.

MANAGING CATALOGS

The database catalog is a form of metadata: information about the data in the system. The catalog is itself stored as a set of tables in the database, recording the names of basic entities in the system (users, schemas, tables, columns, indexes, etc.) and their relationships. By keeping the metadata in the same format as the data, the system is made both more compact and simpler to use: users can employ the same language and tools to investigate the metadata that they use for other data, and the internal system code for managing the metadata is largely the same as the code for managing other tables. This code and language reuse is an important lesson that is often overlooked in early stage implementations, typically to the significant regret of developers later on.

For efficiency, basic catalog data is treated somewhat differently from normal tables. High-traffic portions of the catalog are often materialized in main memory at bootstrap time, typically in data structures that "denormalize" the flat relational structure of the catalogs into a main-memory network of objects. This lack of data independence in memory is acceptable because the in-memory data structures are used in a stylized fashion only by the query parser and optimizer. Additional catalog data is cached in query plans at parsing time, again often in a denormalized form suited to the query. Moreover, catalog tables are often subject to special-case transactional tricks to minimize "hot spots" in transaction processing.

Rewriting Queries

The query rewrite module is responsible for a number of tasks related to simplifying and optimizing the query, typically without changing its semantics. The key in all these tasks is that they can be carried out without accessing the data in the tables—all of these techniques rely only on the query and on metadata in the catalog. Most rewrite systems operate on internal representations of the query, rather than on the actual text of a SQL statement.

- **View rewriting:** The most significant role in rewriting is to handle views. The rewriter takes each view reference that appeared in the FROM clause, and gets the view definition from the catalog manager. It then rewrites the query to remove the view, replacing it with the tables and predicates referenced by the view, and rewriting any predicates that reference the view to instead reference columns from the tables in the view. This process is applied recursively until the query is expressed exclusively over base tables. This view expansion technique, first proposed for the set-based QUEL language in INGRES, requires some care in SQL to correctly handle duplicate elimination, nested queries, NULLs, and other tricky details.

- **Constant arithmetic evaluation:** Query rewrite can simplify any arithmetic expressions that do not contain tuple variables: e.g., "R.x < 10+2" is rewritten as "R.x < 12",

- **Logical rewriting of predicates:** Logical rewrites are applied based on the predicates and constants in the WHERE clause. Simple Boolean logic is often applied to improve the match between expressions and the capabilities of index-based access methods: for example, a predicate like "NOT Emp.Salary > 1000000" may be rewritten as "Emp. Salary <= 1000000". These logical rewrites can even short-circuit query execution, via simple satisfiability tests: for example, the expression "Emp.salary < 75000 AND Emp. salary > 1000000" can be replaced with FALSE, possibly allowing the system to return an empty query result without any accesses to the database. Unsatisfiable queries may seem implausible, but recall that predicates may be "hidden" inside view definitions, and unknown to the writer of the outer query—e.g., the query above may have resulted from a query for low-paid employees over a view called "Executives".

  An additional, important logical rewrite uses the transitivity of predicates to induce new predicates: e.g., "R.x < 10 AND R.x = S.y" suggests adding the additional predicate "AND S.y < 10". Adding these transitive predicates increases the ability of the optimizer to choose plans that filter data early in execution, especially through the use of index-based access methods.

- **Semantic optimization:** In many cases, integrity constraints on the schema are stored in the catalog, and can be used to help rewrite some queries. An important example of such optimization is redundant join elimination. This arises when there are foreign key constraints from a column of one table (e.g., Emp.deptno) to another table (Dept). Given such a foreign key constraint, it is known that there is exactly one Dept for each Emp. Consider a query that joins the two tables but does not make use of the Dept columns:

are assumed by the optimizer to have some "typical" values. Query preparation is especially useful for form-driven, canned queries: the query is prepared when the application is written, and when the application goes live, users do not experience the overhead of parsing, rewriting, and optimizing. In practice, this feature is used far more heavily than ad-hoc queries that are optimized at runtime.

As a database evolves, it often becomes necessary to re-optimize prepared plans. At a minimum, when an index is dropped, any plan that used that index must be removed from the catalog of stored plans, so a new plan will be chosen upon the next invocation.

Other decisions about re-optimizing plans are more subtle, and expose philosophical distinctions among the vendors. Some vendors (e.g., IBM) work very hard to provide predictable performance. As a result, they will not reoptimize a plan unless it will no longer execute, as in the case of dropped indexes. Other vendors (e.g., Microsoft) work very hard to make their systems self-tuning, and will reoptimize plans quite aggressively: they may even reoptimize, for example, if the value distribution of a column changes significantly, since this may affect the selectivity estimates, and hence the choice of the best plan. A self-tuning system is arguably less predictable, but more efficient in a dynamic environment.

This philosophical distinction arises from differences in the historical customer base for these products, and is in some sense self-reinforcing. IBM traditionally focused on high end customers with skilled DBAs and application programmers. In these kinds of high budget IT shops, predictable performance from the database is of paramount importance—after spending months tuning the database design and settings, the DBA does not want the optimizer to change its mind unpredictably. By contrast, Microsoft strategically entered the database market at the low end; as a result, their customers tend to have lower IT budgets and expertise, and want the DBMS to "tune itself" as much as possible.

Over time these companies' business strategies and customer bases have converged so that they compete directly. But the original philosophies tend to peek out in the system architecture, and in the way that the architecture affects the use of the systems by DBAs and database programmers.

Executing the Query

A query executor is given a fully-specified query plan, which is a fixed, directed dataflow graph connecting operators that encapsulate base-table access and various query execution algorithms. In some systems this dataflow graph is already compiled into opcodes by the optimizer, in which case the query executor is basically a runtime interpreter. In other systems a representation of the dataflow graph is passed to the query executor, which recursively invokes procedures for the operators based on the graph layout. Focus on this latter case; the op-code approach essentially compiles the logic described here into a program.

INTRODUCING THE ITERATOR

Essentially all modern query executors employ the iterator model, which was used in the earliest relational systems. Iterators are most simply described in an object-oriented fashion. All operators in a query plan—the nodes in the dataflow graph—are implemented as objects from the superclass iterator. Each iterator specifies its inputs, which define the edges in the dataflow graph. Each query execution operator is implemented as a subclass of the iterator class: the set of subclasses in a typical system might include filescan, index scan, nested-loops join, sort, merge-join, hash-join, duplicate-elimination, and grouped aggregation. An important feature of the iterator model is that any subclass of iterator can be used as input to any other—hence each iterator's logic is independent of its children and parents in the graph, and there is no need to write special-case code for particular combinations of iterators.

An important property of iterators is that they couple dataflow with controlflow. The get_next ( ) call is a standard procedure call, returning a tuple reference to the callee via the call stack. Hence a tuple is returned to a parent in the graph exactly when control is returned.

This implies that only a single DBMS thread is needed to execute an entire query graph, and there is no need for queues or rate-matching between iterators. This makes relational query executors clean to implement and easy to debug, and is a contrast with dataflow architectures in other environments, e.g., networks, which rely on various protocols for queuing and feedback between concurrent producers and consumers.

The single-threaded iterator architecture is also quite efficient for single-site query execution. In most database applications, the performance metric of merit is time to query completion. In a single-processor environment, time to completion for a given query plan is achieved when resources are fully utilized. In an iterator model, since one of the iterators is always active, resource utilization is maximized. (This assumes that iterators never block waiting for I/O requests. As noted, I/O prefetching is typically handled by a separate thread. In the cases where prefetching is ineffective, there can indeed be inefficiencies in the iterator model. This is typically not a big problem in single-site databases, though it arises frequently when executing queries over remote tables.)

Support for parallel query execution is standard in most modern DBMSs. Fortunately, this support can be provided with essentially no changes to the iterator model or a query execution architecture, by encapsulating parallelism and network communication within special exchange iterators.

LOCATING THE DATA

This discussion of iterators has conveniently sidestepped any questions of memory allocation for in-progress data; you never learned how tuples were stored in memory, or how they were passed from iterator to iterator. In practice, each iterator has a fixed number of tuple descriptors pre-allocated: one for each of its inputs, and one for its output. A tuple descriptor is typically an array of column references, where each column reference is composed of a reference to a tuple somewhere else in memory, and a column offset in that tuple. The basic iterator "superclass" logic never dynamically allocates memory, which raises the question of where the actual tuples being referenced are stored in memory.

There are two alternative answers to this question. The first possibility is that base-table tuples can reside in pages in the buffer pool; call these BP-tuples. If an iterator constructs a tuple descriptor referencing a BP-tuple, it must increment the pin count of the tuple's page; it decrements the pin count when the tuple descriptor is cleared. The second possibility is that an iterator implementation may allocate space for a tuple on the memory heap; call this an M-tuple. It may construct an M-tuple by copying columns from the buffer pool (the copy bracketed by a pin/unpin pair), and/or by evaluating expressions (e.g., arithmetic expressions like "EMP.sal * 0.1") in the query specification.

An attractive design pitfall is to always copy data out of the buffer pool immediately into M-tuples. This design uses M-tuples as the only in-progress tuple structure, which simplifies the executor code. It also circumvents bugs that can result from having buffer-pool pin and unpin calls separated by long periods of execution (and many lines of code)—one common bug of this sort is to forget to unpin the page altogether (a "buffer leak"). Unfortunately, exclusive use of M-tuples can be a major performance problem, since memory copies are often a serious bottleneck in high-performance systems.

On the other hand, there are cases where constructing an M-tuple makes sense. It is sometimes beneficial to copy a tuple out of the buffer pool if it will be referenced for a long period of time. As long as a BP-tuple is directly referenced by an iterator, the page on which the BP-tuple resides must remain pinned in the buffer pool. This consumes a page worth of buffer pool memory, and ties the hands of the buffer replacement policy. It is most efficient to support tuple descriptors that can reference both BP-tuples and M-tuples.

CHANGING DATA MODIFICATION STATEMENTS

Another class of DML statements modify data: INSERT, DELETE and UPDATE statements. Typically, execution plans for these statements look like simple straight-line query plans, with a single access method as the source, and a data modification operator at the end of the pipeline.

In some cases, however, these plans are complicated by the fact that they both query and modify the same data. This mix of reading and writing the same table (possibly multiple times) raises some complications. A simple example is the notorious "Halloween problem", so called because it was discovered on October 31st by the System R group. The Halloween problem arises from a particular execution strategy for statements like "give everyone whose salary is under $20K a 10% raise". A naive plan for this query pipelines an index scan iterator over the Emp.salary field into an update iterator; the pipelining provides good I/O locality, because it modifies tuples just after they are fetched from the B1-tree. However, this pipe lining can also result in the index scan "rediscovering" a previously-modified tuple that moved rightward in the tree after modification—resulting in multiple raises for each employee. In our example, all low-paid employees will receive repeated raises until they earn more than $20K; this is not the intention of the statement.

SQL semantics forbid this behavior: a SQL statement is not allowed to "see" its own updates. Some care is needed to ensure that this visibility rule is observed. A simple, safe implementation has the query optimizer choose plans that avoid indexes on the updated column, but this can be quite inefficient in some cases. Another technique is to use a batch read-then-write scheme, which interposes Record-ID materialization and fetching operators between the index scan and the data modification operators in the dataflow. This materialization operator receives the IDs of all tuples to be modified and stores them in temporary file; it then scans the temporary file and fetches each physical tuple ID by RID, feeding the resulting tuple to the data modification operator. In most cases if an index was chosen by the optimizer, it implies that only a few tuples are being changed, and hence the apparent inefficiency of this technique may be acceptable, since the temporary table is likely to remain entirely in the buffer pool. Pipe lined update schemes are also possible, but require (somewhat exotic) multiversion support from the storage engine.

Accessing Methods

The access methods are the routines for managing access to the various disk-based data structures supported by the system, which typically included unordered files ("heaps") of tuples, and various kinds of indexes. All commercial database systems include B1-tree indexes and heap files. Most systems are beginning to introduce some rudimentary support for multidimensional indexes like R-trees. Systems targeted at read-mostly data warehousing workloads usually include specialized bitmap variants of indexes as well.

The basic API provided by an access method is an iterator API, with the init ( ) routine expanded to take a "search predicate" (or in the terminology of System R, a "search argument", or SARG) of the form column operator constant. A NULL SARG is treated as a request to scan all tuples in the table. The get_next ( ) call at the access method layer returns NULL when there are no more tuples satisfying the search argument.

There are two reasons to pass SARGs into the access method layer. The first reason should be clear: index access methods like B1-trees require SARGs in order to function efficiently. The second reason is a more subtle performance issue, but one that applies to heap scans as well as index scans. Assume that the SARG is checked by the routine that calls the access method layer. Then each time the access method returns from get_next ( ), it must either (a) return a handle to a tuple residing in a frame in the buffer pool, and pin the page in that frame to avoid replacement or (b) make a copy of the tuple. If the caller finds that the SARG is not satisfied, it is responsible for either (a) decrementing the pin count on the page, or (b) deleting the copied tuple. It must then try the next tuple on the page by reinvoking get_next ( ). This logic involves a number of CPU cycles simply doing function call/return pairs, and will either pin pages in the buffer pool unnecessarily (generating unnecessary contention for buffer frames) or create and destroy copies of tuples unnecessarily. Note that a typical heap scan will access all of the tuples on a given page, resulting in multiple iterations of this interaction per page. By contrast, if all this logic is done in the access method layer, the repeated pairs of call/return and either pin/unpin or copy/delete can be avoided by testing the SARGs a page at a time, and only returning from a get_next ( ) call for a tuple that satisfies the SARG.

A special SARG is available in all access methods to FETCH a tuple directly by its physical Record ID (RID). FETCH-by-RID is required to support secondary indexes and other schemes that "point" to tuples, and subsequently need to dereference those pointers.

In contrast to all other iterators, access methods have deep interactions with the concurrency and recovery logic surrounding transactions. You learn these issues next.

■ Section 6: Understanding Transactions: Concurrency Control and Recovery

 THE BOTTOM LINE

Database systems are often accused of being enormous, monolithic pieces of software that cannot be split into reusable components. In practice, database systems—and the development teams that implement and maintain them—do break down into independent components with narrow interfaces in between. This is particularly true of the various components of query processing described in the previous section. The parser, rewrite engine, optimizer, executor, and access methods all represent fairly independent pieces of code with well-defined, narrow interfaces that are "published" internally between development groups.

The truly monolithic piece of a DBMS is the transactional storage manager, which typically encompasses four deeply intertwined components:

1. A lock manager for concurrency control
2. A log manager for recovery
3. A buffer pool for staging database I/Os
4. Access methods for organizing data on disk.

Introducing ACID

ACID stands for Atomicity, Consistency, Isolation, and Durability. These terms are not formally defined. These are not mathematical axioms that combine to guarantee transactional consistency. Despite the informal nature, the ACID acronym is useful to organize a discussion of transaction systems.

- Atomicity is the "all or nothing" guarantee for transactions—either all of a transaction's actions are visible to another transaction, or none are.
- Consistency is an application-specific guarantee, which is typically captured in a DBMS by SQL integrity constraints. Given a definition of consistency provided by a set of constraints, a transaction can only commit if it leaves the database in a consistent state.
- Isolation is a guarantee to application writers that two concurrent transactions will not see each other's in-progress updates. As a result, applications need not be coded "defensively" to worry about the "dirty data" of other concurrent transactions.
- Durability is a guarantee that the updates of a committed transaction will be visible in the database to subsequent transactions, until such time as they are overwritten by another committed transaction.

Roughly speaking, modern DBMSs implement Isolation via locking and Durability via logging; Atomicity is guaranteed by a combination of locking (to prevent visibility of transient database states) and logging (to ensure correctness of data that is visible). Consistency is managed by runtime checks in the query executor: if a transaction's actions will violate a SQL integrity constraint, the transaction is aborted and an error code returned.

Introducing Lock Manager and Latches

Every commercial relational DBMS implements serializability via strict two-phase locking (2PL): transactions acquire locks on objects before reading or writing them, and release all locks at the time of transactional commit or abort. The lock manager is the code module responsible for providing the facilities for 2PL. As an auxiliary to database locks, lighter-weight latches are also provided for mutual exclusion.

Database locks are simply names used by convention within the system to represent either physical items (e.g., disk pages) or logical items (e.g., tuples, files, volumes) that are managed by the DBMS. Note that any name can have a lock associated with it—even if that name represents an abstract concept. The locking mechanism simply provides a place to register and check for these names. Locks come in different lock "modes", and these modes are associated with a lock-mode compatibility table.

The lock manager supports two basic calls; lock (lockname, transactionID, mode), and remove_transaction (transactionID). Note that because of the strict 2PL protocol, there need not be an individual call to unlock resources individually—the remove transaction call will unlock all resources associated with a transaction. However, the SQL standard allows for lower degrees of consistency than serializability, and hence there is a need for an unlock (lockname, transactionID) call as well. There is also a lock_upgrade (lockname, transactionID, newmode) call to allow transactions to "upgrade" to higher lock modes (e.g., from shared to exclusive mode) in a two-phase manner, without dropping and reacquiring locks. Additionally, some systems also support a conditional_lock (lockname, transactionID, mode) call. The conditional_lock call always returns immediately, and indicates whether it succeeded in acquiring the lock. If it did not succeed, the calling DBMS thread is not enqueued waiting for the lock.

To support these calls, the lock manager maintains two data structures. A global lock table is maintained to hold locknames and their associated information. The lock table is a dynamic hash table keyed by (a hash function of) lock names. Associated with each lock is a current_mode flag to indicate the lock mode, and a waitqueue of lock request pairs (transactionID, mode). In addition, it maintains a transaction table keyed by transactionID, which contains two items for each transaction T: (a) a pointer to T's DBMS thread state, to allow T's DBMS thread to be rescheduled when it acquires any locks it is waiting on, and (b) a list of pointers to all of T's lock requests in the lock table, to facilitate the removal of all locks associated with a particular transaction (e.g., upon transaction commit or abort).

Internally, the lock manager makes use of a deadlock detector DBMS thread that periodically examines the lock table to look for waits-for cycles. Upon detection of a deadlock, the deadlock detector aborts one of the deadlocked transaction. In shared-nothing and shared-disk systems, distributed deadlock detection facilities are required as well.

In addition to two-phase locks, every DBMS also supports a lighter-weight mutual exclusion mechanism, typically called a latch. Latches are more akin to monitors than locks; they are used to provide exclusive access to internal DBMS data structures. As an example, the buffer pool page table has a latch associated with each frame, to guarantee that only one DBMS thread is replacing a given frame at any time. Latches differ from locks in a number of ways:

- Locks are kept in the lock table and located via hash tables; latches reside in memory near the resources they protect, and are accessed via direct addressing.

- Locks are subject to the strict 2PL protocol. Latches may be acquired or dropped during a transaction based on special-case internal logic.

- Lock acquisition is entirely driven by data access, and hence the order and lifetime of lock acquisitions is largely in the hands of applications and the query optimizer. Latches are acquired by specialized code inside the DBMS, and the DBMS internal code issues latch requests and releases strategically.

- Locks are allowed to produce deadlock, and lock deadlocks are detected and resolved via transactional restart. Latch deadlock must be avoided; the occurrence of a latch deadlock represents a bug in the DBMS code.
- Latch calls take a few dozen CPU cycles, lock requests take hundreds of CPU cycles.

The latch API supports the routines latch (object, mode), unlatch (object), and conditional_latch (object, mode). In most DBMSs, the choices of latch modes include only Shared or eXclusive. Latches maintain a current_mode, and a waitqueue of DBMS threads waiting on the latch. The latch and unlatch calls work as one might expect. The conditional_latch call is analogous to the conditional_lock call described above, and is also used for index concurrency.

INTRODUCING ISOLATION LEVELS

Very early in the development of the transaction concept, there were attempts to provide more concurrency by providing "weaker" semantics than serializability. The challenge was to provide robust definitions of the semantics in these cases. The ANSI SQL standard defines four "Isolation Levels":

1. **READ UNCOMMITTED:** A transaction may read any version of data, committed or not. This is achieved in a locking implementation by read requests proceeding without acquiring any locks. (In all isolation levels, write requests are preceded by write locks that are held until end of transaction.)
2. **READ COMMITTED:** A transaction may read any committed version of data. Repeated reads of an object may result in different (committed) versions. This is achieved by read requests acquiring a read lock before accessing an object, and unlocking it immediately after access.
3. **REPEATABLE READ:** A transaction will read only one version of committed data; once the transaction reads an object, it will always read the same version of that object. This is achieved by read requests acquiring a read lock before accessing an object, and holding the lock until end-of-transaction.
4. **SERIALIZABLE:** Fully serializable access is guaranteed.

At first blush, REPEATABLE READ seems to provide full serializability, but this is not the case. Early in the System R project, a problem arose that was dubbed the "phantom problem". In the phantom problem, a transaction accesses a relation more than once with the same predicate, but sees new "phantom" tuples on re-access that were not seen on the first access. (Despite the spooky similarity in names, the phantom problem has nothing to do with the Halloween problem.) This is because two-phase locking at tuple-level granularity does not prevent the insertion of new tuples into a table. Two-phase locking of tables prevents phantoms, but table-level locking can be restrictive in cases where transactions access only a few tuples via an index.

Commercial systems provide the four isolation levels above via locking-based implementations of concurrency control. Unfortunately, the ANSI standard failed to achieve the goal of providing truly declarative definitions. Both rely in subtle ways on an assumption that a locking scheme is used for concurrency control, as opposed to an optimistic or multi-version concurrency scheme.

In addition to the standard ANSI SQL isolation levels, various vendors provide additional levels that have proven popular in various cases.

- **CURSOR STABILITY:** This level is intended to solve the "lost update" problem of READ COMMITTED. Consider two transactions T1 and T2. T1 runs in READ COMMITTED mode, reads an object X (say the value of a bank account), remembers its value, and subsequently writes object X based on the remembered value (say adding $100 to the original account value). T2 reads and writes X as well (say subtracting $300 from the account). If T2's actions happen between T1's read and T1's write, then the effect of T2's update will be lost—the final value of the account in our example will be up by $100, instead of being down by $200 as desired. A transaction in CURSOR STABILITY mode holds a lock on the most recently-read item on a query cursor; the lock is automatically dropped when the cursor is moved (e.g., via another FETCH) or the transaction terminates. CURSOR STABILITY allows the transaction to do read-think-write sequences on individual items without intervening updates from other transactions.

- **SNAPSHOT ISOLATION:** A transaction running in SNAPSHOT ISOLATION mode operates on a version of the database as it existed at the time the transaction began; subsequent updates by other transactions are invisible to the transaction. When the transaction starts, it gets a unique start-timestamp from a monotonically increasing counter; when it commits it gets a unique end-timestamp from the counter. The transaction commits only if there is no other transaction with an overlapping start/end-transaction pair that wrote data that this transaction also wrote. This isolation mode depends upon a multi-version concurrency implementation, rather than locking (though these schemes typically coexist in systems that support SNAPSHOT ISOLATION.)

- **READ CONSISTENCY:** This is a scheme defined by Oracle; it is subtly different from SNAPSHOT ISOLATION. In the Oracle scheme, each SQL statement (of which there may be many in a single transaction) sees the most recently committed values as of the start of the statement. For statements that FETCH from cursors, the cursor set is based on the values as of the time it is opened. This is implemented by maintaining multiple versions of individual tuples, with a single transaction possibly referencing multiple versions of a single tuple. Modifications are maintained via long-term write locks, so when two transactions want to write the same object the first writer "wins", whereas in SNAPSHOT ISOLATION the first committer "wins".

Weak isolation schemes provide higher concurrency than serializability. As a result, some systems even use weak consistency as the default; Oracle defaults to READ COMMITTED, for example. The downside is that Isolation (in the ACID sense) is not guaranteed. Hence application writers need to reason about the subtleties of the schemes to ensure that their transactions run correctly. This is tricky given the operationally defined semantics of the schemes.

Introducing the Log Manager

The log manager is responsible for maintaining the durability of committed transactions, and for facilitating the rollback of aborted transactions to ensure atomicity. It provides these features by maintaining a sequence of log records on disk, and a set of data structures in memory. In order to support correct behavior after crash, the memory resident data structures obviously need to be re-createable from persistent data in the log and the database.

The standard theme of database recovery is to use a Write-Ahead Logging (WAL) protocol. The WAL protocol consists of three very simple rules:

1. Each modification to a database page should generate a log record, and the log record must be flushed to the log device before the database page is flushed.

2. Database log records must be flushed in order; log record r cannot be flushed until all log records preceding r are flushed.

3. Upon a transaction commit request, a COMMIT log record must be flushed to the log device before the commit request returns successfully.

Many people only remember the first of these rules, but all three are required for correct behavior.

The first rule ensures that the actions of incomplete transactions can be undone in the event of a transaction abort, to ensure atomicity. The combination of rules (2) and (3) ensure durability: the actions of a committed transaction can be redone after a system crash if they are not yet reflected in the database.

Given these simple principles, it is surprising that efficient database logging is as subtle and detailed as it is. In practice, however, the simple story above is complicated by the need for extreme performance. The challenge is to guarantee efficiency in the "fast path" for transactions that commit, while also providing high-performance rollback for aborted transactions, and quick recovery after crashes. Logging gets even more baroque when application-specific optimizations are added, e.g., to support improved performance for fields that can only be incremented or decremented ("escrow transactions".)

In order to maximize the speed of the fast path, every commercial database system operates in a mode called "DIRECT, STEAL/NOT-FORCE": (a) data objects are updated in place, (b) unpinned buffer pool frames can be "stolen" (and the modified data pages written back to disk) even if they contain uncommitted data, and (c) buffer pool pages need not be "forced" (flushed) to the database before a commit request returns to the user. These policies keep the data in the location chosen by the DBA, and they give the buffer manager and disk schedulers full latitude to decide on memory management and I/O policies without consideration for transactional correctness. These features can have major performance benefits, but require that the log manager efficiently handle all the subtleties of undoing the flushes of stolen pages from aborted transactions, and redoing the changes to not-forced pages of committed transactions that are lost on crash.

Another fast-path challenge in logging is to keep log records as small as possible, in order to increase the throughput of log I/O activity. A natural optimization is to log logical operations (e.g., "insert (Bob, $25000) into EMP") rather than physical operations (e.g., the after-images for all byte ranges modified via the tuple insertion, including bytes on both heap file and index blocks.) The tradeoff is that the logic to redo and undo logical operations becomes quite involved, which can severely degrade performance during transaction abort and database recovery. (Note also that logical log records must always have well-known inverse if they need to participate in undo processing.) In practice, a mixture of physical and logical logging (so-called "physiological" logging) is used. In ARIES, physical logging is generally used to support REDO, and logical logging is used to support UNDO—this is part of the ARIES rule of "repeating history" during recovery to reach the crash state, and then rolling back transactions from that point.

Crash recovery performance is greatly enhanced by the presence of database checkpoints— consistent versions of the database from the recent past. A checkpoint limits the amount of log that the recovery process needs to consult and process. However, the naive generation of checkpoints is too expensive to do during regular processing, so some more efficient "fuzzy" scheme for check pointing is required, along with logic to correctly bring the checkpoint up to the most recent consistent state by processing as little of the log as possible. ARIES uses a very clever scheme in which the actual checkpoint records are quite tiny, containing just enough information to initiate the log analysis process and to enable the recreation of main-memory data structures lost at crash time.

Finally, the task of logging and recovery is further complicated by the fact that a database is not merely a set of user data tuples on disk pages; it also includes a variety of "physical" information that allows it to manage its internal disk-based data structures.

Locking and Logging in Indexes

Indexes are physical storage structures for accessing data in the database. The indexes themselves are invisible to database users, except inasmuch as they improve performance. Users cannot directly read or modify indexes, and hence user code need not be isolated (in the ACID sense) from changes to the index. This allows indexes to be managed via more efficient (and complex) transactional schemes than database data. The only invariant that index concurrency and recovery needs to preserve is that the index always returns transactionally consistent tuples from the database.

LATCHING IN B+-TREES

B+-trees consist of database disk pages that are accessed via the buffer pool, just like data pages. Hence one scheme for index concurrency control is to use two-phase locks on index pages. This means that every transaction that touches the index needs to lock the root of the B+-tree until commit time—a recipe for limited concurrency. A variety of latch-based schemes have been developed to work around this problem without setting any transactional locks on index pages. The key insight in these schemes is that modifications to the tree's physical structure (e.g., splitting pages) can be made in a non-transactional manner as long as all concurrent transactions continue to find the correct data at the leaves. There are roughly three approaches to this:

- Conservative schemes, which allow multiple transactions to access the same pages only if they can be guaranteed not to conflict in their use of a page's content. One such conflict is that a reading transaction wants to traverse a fully packed internal page of the tree, and a concurrent inserting transaction is operating below that page, and hence might need to split it. These conservative schemes sacrifice too much concurrency compared with the more recent ideas below.

- Latch-coupling schemes, in which the tree traversal logic latches each node before it is visited, only unlatching a node when the next node to be visited has been success-fully latched. This scheme is sometimes called latch "crabbing", because of the crablike movement of "holding" a node in the tree, "grabbing" its child, releasing the parent, and repeating. Latch coupling is used in some commercial systems; IBM's ARIES-1M version is well described. ARIES-1M includes some fairly intricate details and corner cases—on occasion it has to restart traversals after splits, and even set (very short-term) tree-wide latches.

- Right-link schemes, which add some simple additional structure to the B1-tree to mini-mize the requirement for latches and retraversals. In particular, a link is added from each node to its right-hand neighbor. During traversal, right-link schemes do no latch coupling—each node is latched, read, and unlatched. The main intuition in right-link schemes is that if a traversing transaction follows a pointer to a node n and finds that n was split in the interim, the traversing transaction can detect this fact, and "move right" via the rightlinks to find the new correct location in the tree.

LOGGING FOR PHYSICAL STRUCTURES

In addition to special-case concurrency logic, indexes employ special-case logging logic. This logic makes logging and recovery much more efficient, at the expense of more complexity in the code. The main idea is that structural index changes need not be undone when the associ-ated transaction is aborted; such changes may have no effect on the database tuples seen by other transactions. For example, if a B+-tree page is split during an inserting transaction that subsequently aborts, there is no pressing need to undo the split during the abort processing.

This raises the challenge of labeling some log records "redo-only"—during any undo process-ing of the log, these changes should be left in place. ARIES provides an elegant mechanism for these scenarios called nested top actions, which allows the recovery process to "jump over" log records for physical structure modifications without any special case code during recovery.

This same idea is used in other contexts, including in heap files. An insertion into a heap file may require the file to be extended on disk. To capture this, changes must be made to the file's "extent map", a data structure on disk that points to the runs of contiguous blocks that constitute the file. These changes to the extent map need not be undone if the inserting trans-action aborts—the fact that the file has become larger is a transactionally invisible side-effect, and may be in fact be useful for absorbing future insert traffic.

USING NEXT-KEY LOCKING

The challenge is to provide full serializability (including phantom protection) while allowing for tuple-level locks and the use of indexes.

The phantom problem arises when a transaction accesses tuples via an index: in such cases, the transaction typically does not lock the entire table, just the tuples in the table that are accessed via the index (e.g., "Name BETWEEN 'Bob' AND 'Bobby'"). In the absence of a table-level lock, other transactions are free to insert new tuples into the table (e.g., Name='Bobbie'). When these new inserts fall within the value-range of a query predicate, they will appear in subsequent accesses via that predicate. Note that the phantom problem relates to visibility of database tuples, and hence is a problem with locks, not just latches. In principle, what is needed is the ability to somehow lock the logical space represented by the original query's search predicate. Unfortunately, it is well known that predicate locking is expensive, since it requires a way to compare arbitrary predicates for overlap—something that cannot be done with a hash-based lock table.

The standard solution to the phantom problem in B+-trees is called "next-key locking". In next-key locking, the index insertion code is modified so that an insertion of a tuple with index key k is required to allocate an exclusive lock on the "next-key" tuple that exists in the index: the tuple with the lowest key greater than k. This protocol ensures that subsequent insertions cannot appear "in between" two tuples that were returned previously to an active transaction; it also ensures that tuples cannot be inserted just below the lowest-keyed tuple previously returned (e.g., if there were no 'Bob' on the 1st access, there should be no 'Bob' on subsequent accesses). One corner case remains: the insertion of tuples just above the highest-keyed tuple previously returned. To protect against this case, the next-key locking protocol requires read transactions to be modified as well, so that they must get a shared lock on the "next-key" tuple in the index as well: the minimum-keyed tuple that does not satisfy the query predicate. An implementation of next-key locking is described for ARIES.

Understanding Interdependencies of Transactional Storage

Transactional storage systems are monolithic that include concurrency control, recovery management, and access methods. Write-ahead logging makes implicit assumptions about the locking protocol—it requires strict two-phase locking, and will not operate correctly with non-strict two-phase locking. To see this, consider what happens during the rollback of an aborted transaction. The recovery code begins processing the log records of the aborted transaction, undoing its modifications. Typically this requires changing pages or tuples that were previously modified by the transaction. In order to make these changes, the transaction needs to have locks on those pages or tuples. In a non-strict 2PL scheme, if the transaction drops any locks before aborting, it is unable to acquire the new locks it needs to complete the rollback process!

Access methods complicate things yet further. Most DBMSs still only implement heap files and B+-trees as native, transactionally protected access methods. As illustrated above for B1-trees, high-performance implementations of transactional indexes include intricate protocols for latching, locking, and logging. The B+-trees in serious DBMSs are riddled with calls to the concurrency and recovery code. Even simple access methods like heap files have some tricky concurrency and recovery issues surrounding the data structures that describe their contents (e.g., extent maps). This logic is not generic to all access methods—it is very much customized to the specific logic of the access method, and its particular implementation.

Concurrency control in access methods has been well-developed only for locking oriented schemes. Other concurrency schemes (e.g., Optimistic or Multiversion concurrency control) do not usually consider access methods at all, or if they do mention them it is only in an offhanded and impractical fashion. Hence it is unlikely that one can mix and match different concurrency mechanisms for a given access method implementation.

Recovery logic in access methods is particularly system-specific: the timing and contents of access method log records depend upon fine details of the recovery protocol, including the handling of structure modifications (e.g., whether they get undone upon transaction rollback, and if not how that is avoided), and the use of physical and logical logging.

Even for a specific access method, the recovery and concurrency logic are intertwined. In one direction, the recovery logic depends upon the concurrency protocol: if the recovery manager has to restore a physically consistent state of the tree, then it needs to know what inconsistent states could possibly arise, to bracket those states appropriately with log records (e.g., via nested top actions). In the opposite direction, the concurrency protocol for an access method may be dependent on the recovery logic: for example, the right link scheme for B+-trees assumes that pages in the tree never "re-merge" after they split, an assumption that requires the recovery scheme to use a scheme like nested top actions to avoid undoing splits generated by aborted transactions.

The buffer management is relatively well-isolated from the rest of the components of the storage manager. As long as pages are pinned correctly, the buffer manager is free to encapsulate the rest of its logic and reimplement it as needed, e.g., the choice of pages to replace (because of the STEAL property), and the scheduling of page flushes (thanks to the NOT FORCE property).

■ Section 7: Understanding Shared Components

THE BOTTOM LINE

Database systems allocate significant amounts of memory for other tasks as well, and the correct management of this memory is both a programming burden and a performance issue. Query optimization can use a great deal of memory, for example, to build up state during dynamic programming. Query operators like hash joins and sorts allocate significant memory for private space at runtime. In commercial systems, memory allocation is made more efficient and easier to debug via the use of a context-based memory allocator.

Introducing the Memory Allocator

A memory context is an in-memory data structure that maintains a list of regions of contiguous virtual memory, with each region possibly having a small header containing a context label or a pointer to the context header structure.

The basic API for memory contexts includes calls to:

- **Create a context with a given name or type.** The type of the context might advise the allocator how to efficiently handle memory allocation: for example, the contexts for the query optimizer grow via small increments, while contexts for hash joins allocate their memory in a few large batches. Based on such knowledge, the allocator can choose to allocate bigger or smaller regions at a time.
- **Allocate a chunk of memory within a context.** This allocation will return a pointer to memory (much like the traditional malloc( ) call). That memory may come from an existing region in the context; if no such space exists in any region, the allocator will ask the operating system for a new region of memory, label it, and link it into the context.
- **Delete a chunk of memory within a context.** This may or may not cause the context to delete the corresponding region. Deletion from memory contexts is somewhat unusual—a more typical behavior is to delete an entire context.
- **Delete a context.** This first frees all of the regions associated with the context, and then deletes the context header.
- **Reset a context.** This retains the context, but returns it to the state of original creation—typically by deallocating all previously-allocated regions of memory.

Memory contexts provide important software engineering advantages. The most important is that they serve as a lower-level, programmer-controllable alternative to garbage collection. For example, the developers writing the optimizer can allocate memory in an optimizer context for a particular query, without worrying about how to free the memory later on. When the optimizer has picked the best plan, it can make a copy of the plan in memory from a separate executor context for the query, and then simply delete the query's optimizer context—this saves the trouble of writing code to carefully walk all the optimizer data structures and delete their components. It also avoids tricky memory leaks that can arise from bugs in such code. This feature is very useful for the naturally "phased" behavior of query execution, which proceeds from parser to optimizer to executor, typically doing a number of allocations in each context, followed by a context deletion.

Note that memory contexts actually provide more control than most garbage collectors: developers can control both spatial and temporal locality of deallocation. Spatial control is provided by the context mechanism itself, which allows the programmer to separate memory into logical units. Temporal control is given by allowing programmers to issue context deletions when appropriate. By contrast, garbage collectors typically work on all of a program's memory, and make their own decisions about when to run. This is one of the frustrations of attempting to write server-quality code in Java.

Memory contexts also provide performance advantages in some cases, due to the relatively high overhead for malloc( ) and free( ) on many platforms. In particular, memory contexts can use semantic knowledge (via the context type) of how memory will be allocated and deallocated, and may call malloc( ) and free( ) accordingly to minimize OS overheads. In particular, some pieces of a database system (e.g., the parser and optimizer) allocate a large number of small objects, and then free them all at once via a context deletion. On most platforms it is rather expensive to call free( ) on many small objects, so a memory allocator can instead malloc( ) large regions, and apportion the resulting memory to its callers. The relative lack of memory deallocations means that there is no need for the kind of compaction logic used by malloc( ) and free( ). And when the context is deleted, only a few free( ) calls are required to remove the large regions.

Introducing Memory Allocation for Query Operators

A philosophical design difference among vendors can be seen in the allocation of memory for space-intensive operators like hash joins and sorts. Some systems (e.g., DB2) allow the DBA to control the amount of RAM that will be used by such operations, and guarantee that each query gets that amount of RAM when executed; this guarantee is ensured by the admission control policy. In such systems, the operators allocate their memory off of the heap via the memory allocator. These systems provide good performance stability, but force the DBA to (statically!) decide how to balance physical memory across various subsystems like the buffer pool and the query operators.

Other systems (e.g., MS SQL Server) try to manage these issues automatically, taking the memory allocation task out of the DBA's hands. These systems attempt to do intelligent memory allocation across the various pieces of query execution, including caching of pages in the buffer pool and the use of memory by query operators. The pool of memory used for all of these tasks is the buffer pool itself, and hence in these systems the query operators take memory from the buffer pool, bypassing the memory allocator.

The former class of systems assumes that the DBA is engaged in sophisticated tuning, and that the workload for the system will be amenable to one carefully-chosen setting of the DBA's memory "knobs". Under these conditions, these systems should always perform predictably well. The latter class assumes that DBAs either do not or cannot correctly set these knobs, and attempts to replace the DBA wisdom with software logic. They also retain the right to change their relative allocations adaptively, providing the possibility for better performance on changing workloads. This distinction says something about how these vendors expect their products to be used, and about the administrative expertise (and financial resources) of their customers.

Introducing Disk Management Subsystems

Disk drives are complex and heterogeneous pieces of hardware, varying widely in capacity and bandwidth. Hence every DBMS has a disk management subsystem that deals with these issues, managing the allocation of tables and other units of storage across multiple devices.

One aspect of this module is to manage the mapping of tables to devices and or files. One-to-one mappings of tables to files sound natural, but raised problems in early file systems. First, OS files traditionally could not be larger than a disk, while database tables may need to span multiple disks. Second, it was traditionally bad form to allocate too many OS files, since the OS typically only allowed a few open file descriptors, and many OS utilities for directory management and backup did not scale to very large numbers of files. Hence in many cases a single file is used to hold multiple tables. Over time, most file systems have overcome these limitations, but it is typical today for OS files to simply be treated by the DBMS as abstract storage units, with arbitrary mappings to database tables.

More complex is the code to handle device-specific details for maintaining temporal and spatial control. There is a large and vibrant industry today based on complex storage devices that "pretend" to be disk drives, but are in fact large hardware/software systems whose API is a legacy disk drive interface like SCSI. These systems, which include RAID boxes and Network Attached Storage (NAS) devices, tend to have very large capacities, and complex performance characteristics. Users like these systems because they are easy to install, and often provide easily-managed, bit-level reliability with quick or instantaneous failover. These features provide a significant sense of comfort to customers, above and beyond the promises of DBMS recovery subsystems. It is very common to find DBMS installations on RAID boxes, for example.

Unfortunately, these systems complicate DBMS implementations. As an example, RAID systems perform very differently after a fault than they do when all the disks are good, potentially complicating the I/O cost models for the DBMS. Also, these system—like file systems before them—tend to want to exercise temporal control over writes by managing their own caching policies, possibly subverting the write-ahead logging protocol. In the case of power failures, this can lead to consistency at the per-bit granularity (storage-oriented consistency), without transactional consistency. It is uncomfortable for the DBMS vendors to point their fingers at the disk vendors in such cases; at the end of the day, DBMS vendors are expected to provide transactional consistency on any popular storage device. Hence DBMSs must understand the ins and outs of the leading storage devices, and manage them accordingly.

RAID systems also frustrate database administrators by underperforming for database tasks. RAID was conceived for byte stream-oriented storage (a la UNIX files), rather than the tuple-oriented storage used by database systems. Hence RAID devices do not tend to perform as well as database-specific solutions for partitioning and replicating data across multiple physical devices. Most databases provide DBA commands to control the partitioning of data across multiple devices, but RAID boxes subvert these commands by hiding the multiple devices behind a single interface.

Moreover, many users configure their RAID boxes to minimize space overheads ("RAID level 5"), when the database would perform far, far better via simpler schemes like disk mirroring (a.k.a. "RAID level 1"). A particularly unpleasant feature of RAID level 5 is that writes are much more expensive than reads; this can cause surprising bottlenecks for users, and the DBMS vendors are often on the hook to explain or provide workarounds for these bottlenecks. For better or worse, the use (and misuse) of RAID devices is a fact that commercial systems must take into account, and most vendors spend significant energy tuning their DBMSs to work well on the leading RAID boxes.

Introducing Replication Services

It is often desirable to replicate databases across a network via periodic updates. This is frequently used for an extra degree of reliability—the replicated database serves as a slightly-out-of-date "warm standby" in case the main system goes down. It is advantageous to keep the warm standby in a physically different location, to be able to continue functioning after a fire or other catastrophe. Replication is also often used to provide a pragmatic form of distributed database functionality for large, geographically distributed enterprises. Most such enterprises partition their databases into large geographic regions (e.g., nations or continents), and run all updates locally on the primary copies of the data. Queries are executed locally as well, but can run on a mix of fresh data from their local operations, and slightly-out-of-date data replicated from remote sites regions.

There are three typical schemes for replication, but only the third provides the performance and scalability needed for high-end settings. It is, of course, the most difficult to implement.

1. **Physical Replication:** The simplest scheme is to physically duplicate the entire database every replication period. This scheme does not scale up to large databases, because of the bandwidth for shipping the data, and the cost for reinstalling it at the remote site. Moreover, it is tricky to guarantee a transactionally consistent snapshot of the database; doing so typically requires the unacceptable step of quiescing the source system during the replication process. Physical replication is therefore mostly used as a special case need using backup at the source and restore at the destination.

2. **Trigger-Based Replication:** In this scheme, triggers are placed on the database tables so that upon any insert, delete, or update to the table, a "difference" record is installed in special replication table. This replication table is shipped to the remote site, and the modifications are "replayed" there. This scheme solves the problems mentioned above for physical replication, but has a number of performance problems. First, most database vendors provide very limited trigger facilities—often only a single trigger is allowed per table (unlike SQL Server). In such scenarios, it is often not possible to install triggers for replication. Second, database trigger systems cannot usually keep up with the performance of transaction systems. At a minimum, the execution of triggering logic adds approximately 100% more I/Os to each transaction that modifies a database, and in practice even the testing of trigger conditions is quite slow in many systems. Hence this scheme is not desirable in practice, though it is used with some regularity in the field.

3. **Log-Based Replication:** Log-based replication is the replication solution of choice when feasible. In log-based replication, a log "sniffer" process intercepts log writes and ships them to the remote site, where they are "played forward" in REDO mode. This scheme overcomes all of the problems of the previous alternatives. It is low-overhead, providing minimal or invisible performance burdens on the running system. It provides incremental updates, and hence scales gracefully with the database size and the update rate. It reuses the built-in mechanisms of the DBMS without significant additional logic. Finally, it naturally provides transactionally consistent replicas via the log's built-in logic.

Most of the major vendors provide log-based replication for their own systems. Providing log-based replication that works across vendors is much more difficult—it requires understanding another vendor's log formats, and driving the vendors replay logic at the remote end.

Introducing Batch Utilities

Every system provides a set of utilities for managing their system. These utilities are rarely benchmarked, but often dictate the manageability of the system. A technically challenging and especially important feature is to make these utilities run online, i.e. while user queries and transactions are in flight. This is important in 24x7 operations, which have become much more common in recent years due to the global reach of ecommerce: the traditional "reorg window" in the wee hours is often no-longer available. Hence most vendors have invested significant energy in recent years in providing online utilities:

• **Optimizer Statistics Gathering:** Every DBMS has a process that sweeps the tables and builds optimizer statistics of one sort or another. Some statistics like histograms are non-trivial to build in one pass without flooding memory.

- **Physical Reorganization and Index Construction:** Over time, access methods can become inefficient due to patterns of insertions and deletions leaving unused space. Also, users may occasionally request that tables be reorganized in the background—e.g., to recluster (sort) them on different columns, or to repartition them across multiple disks. Online reorganization of files and indexes can be tricky, since it must avoid holding locks for any length of time, but still needs to maintain physical consistency. In this sense it bears some analogies to the logging and locking protocols used for indexes.

- **Backup/Export:** All DBMSs support the ability to physically dump the database to backup storage. Again, since this is a long-running process, it cannot naively set locks. Instead, most systems perform some kind of "fuzzy" dump, and augment it with logging logic to ensure transactional consistency. Similar schemes can be used to export the database to an interchange format.

■ Section 8: Understanding Database Objects

THE BOTTOM LINE

The organization of a database involves many different objects. All objects of a database can be physical or logical. The physical objects are related to the organization of the data on the physical device (mass storage unit). SQL Server's physical objects are files and filegroups. Logical objects represent a user's view of a database. Databases, tables, columns, and views (virtual tables) are examples of logical objects.

If, in the creation of a new item in SQL Server, it requires a name, it's an object. If it has a name, even if system generated, it's an object. SQL Server exposes all of these objects in Management Studio.

Introducing Primary Database Objects

Each DBMS consists of a large number of objects. SQL Server is no exception. Here are some of the most important:

- **Aggregate Function:** A function that performs a calculation on a column in a set of rows and returns a single value.

- **Check Constraint:** A property assigned to a table column that prevents certain types of invalid data values from being placed in the column. For example, a UNIQUE or PRIMARY KEY constraint prevents you from inserting a value that is a duplicate of an existing value, a CHECK constraint prevents you from inserting a value that does not match a specified condition, and NOT NULL prevents you from inserting a NULL value.

  A check constraint also defines which data values are acceptable in a column. You can apply CHECK constraints to multiple columns, and you can apply multiple CHECK constraints to a single column. When a table is dropped, CHECK constraints are also dropped.

- **CLR Scalar Function:** A function that is created by referencing a SQL Server assembly. The implementation of the CLR function is defined in an assembly that is created in the .NET Framework common language runtime (CLR).

- **CLR Stored Procedure:** A stored procedure that is created by referencing a SQL Server assembly. The implementation of the CLR stored procedure is defined in an assembly that is created in the .NET Framework common language runtime (CLR).

- **CLR Table Valued Function:** A user defined function that is created by referencing a SQL Server assembly. The implementation of the CLR user defined function is defined in an assembly that is created in the .NET Framework common language runtime (CLR).

- **CLR Trigger:** A DML trigger or DDL trigger that is created by referencing a SQL Server assembly. The implementation of the CLR trigger is defined in an assembly that is created in the .NET Framework common language runtime (CLR).

- **Columns:** In an SQL table, the area in each row that stores the data value for some attribute of the object modeled by the table. For example, the Employee table in the AdventureWorks sample database models the employees of the Adventure Works Cycles company. The Title column in each row of the Employee table stores the job title of the employee represented by that row, the same way a Job Title field in a window or form would contain a job title.

- **Database:** A collection of information, tables, and other objects organized and presented to serve a specific purpose, such as searching, sorting, and recombining data. Databases are stored in files.

- **Default Constraints:** A property defined for a table column that specifies a constant to be used as the default value for the column. If any subsequent INSERT or UPDATE statement specifies a value of NULL for the column, or does not specify a value for the column, the constant value defined in the DEFAULT constraint is placed in the column.

- **Extended Stored Procedure:** A function in a dynamic link library (DLL) that is coded using the SQL Server Extended Stored Procedure API. The function can then be invoked from Transact-SQL using the same statements that are used to execute Transact-SQL stored procedures. Extended stored procedures can be built to perform functionality not possible with Transact-SQL stored procedures.

- **Foreign Key Constraint:** The column or combination of columns whose values match the primary key (PK) or unique key in the same or another table. Also referred to as the referencing key.

- **Indexes:** In a relational database, a database object that provides fast access to data in the rows of a table, based on key values. Indexes can also enforce uniqueness on the rows in a table. SQL Server supports clustered and nonclustered indexes. The primary key of a table is automatically indexed. In full-text search, a full-text index stores information about significant words and their location within a given column.

- **Primary Key Constraint:** A column or set of columns that uniquely identify all the rows in a table. Primary keys do not allow null values. No two rows can have the same primary key value; therefore, a primary key value always uniquely identifies a single row. More than one key can uniquely identify rows in a table. Each of these keys is called a candidate key. Only one candidate can be chosen as the primary key of a table; all other candidate keys are known as alternate keys. Although tables are not required to have primary keys, it is good practice to define them. In a normalized table, all the data values in each row are fully dependent on the primary key. For example, in a normalized employee table that has EmployeeID as the primary key, all the columns should contain data related to a specific employee. This table does not have the column DepartmentName because the name of the department is dependent on a department ID, not on an employee ID.

- **Scalar Function:** User-defined scalar functions return a single data value of the type defined in the RETURNS clause. For an inline scalar function, there is no function body; the scalar value is the result of a single statement. For a multistatement scalar function, the function body, defined in a BEGIN...END block, contains a series of Transact-SQL statements that return the single value. The return type can be any data type except **text, ntext, image, cursor,** and **timestamp.**

- **Stored procedures:** A precompiled collection of Transact-SQL statements that are stored under a name and processed as a unit. SQL Server supplies stored procedures for managing SQL Server and displaying information about databases and users. SQL Server-supplied stored procedures are called system stored procedures.

- **Table Valued Function:** User-defined table-valued functions return a **table** data type. For an inline table-valued function, there is no function body; the table is the result set of a single SELECT statement.

- **Tables:** A two-dimensional object, which consists of rows and columns, that stores data about an entity modeled in a relational database.
- **Triggers:** A stored procedure that executes in response to a data manipulation language (DML) or data definition language (DDL) event.
- **User defined data types:** A more meaningful name given to a system data type by the developer for repetitive use in one or more databases. For example:

```
CREATE TYPE ZIP FROM CHAR(5) NOT NULL;
```

- **User defined functions:** In SQL Server, a Transact-SQL function defined by a user. Functions encapsulate frequently performed logic in a named entity that can be called by Transact-SQL statements instead of recoding the logic in each statement
- **Variables:** Defined entities that are assigned values. A local variable is defined with a DECLARE @localvariable statement and assigned an initial value within the statement batch where it is declared with either a SELECT or SET @localvariable statement.
- **Views:** A presentation of the data from one or more columns from one or more tables. Because each view can have specific permissions user access can be controlled to what they need to know or change very specifically.

Appendix B
SQL DML Constructs

■ Section 1: Introducing SQL

THE BOTTOM LINE

Most relational databases use a common set-based language known as the Structured Query Language. Administrators and developers alike use this language in their daily efforts.

This appendix provides an abbreviated introduction to the Data Manipulation Language syntax to help you successfully complete the remainder of the course and get you started—but just started—in grasping the power of this RDBMS interface tool.

International standards define Structured Query Language constructs and syntax. The American National Standards Institute that sponsored the creation of SQL originally defined three levels of compliance. Every vendor meets the entry level criteria. Each vendor also supplements the standard with their own enhancements. SQL Server calls theirs Transact-SQL; other vendors have different designators.

As an administrator working with multiple vendor RDBMSs (Oracle, IBM, Sybase, many others) you must focus your syntax development at the entry level for consistent results from the multiple platforms.

All implementations of SQL break the syntax into three groups:

- Data Definition Language (DDL) constructs
- Data Control Language (DCL) constructs
- Data Manipulation Language (DML) constructs

DDL statements create objects in your database and consist of just three key words:

- CREATE to initiate a new object
- ALTER to change an existing object
- DROP to eliminate an existing object

DCL statements provide access control to objects and consist of just three key words:

- GRANT to allow user access to an object
- DENY to disallow user access to an object
- REVOKE to remove a GRANT or a DENY. This is state where control must come from another action as from membership in a role.

DML statements provide interaction with the data in your RDBMS and consist of just four key words:

- SELECT to retrieve data
- INSERT to add data
- UPDATE to change data
- DELETE to remove data

■ Section 2: Using the SELECT Statement

THE BOTTOM LINE

The SELECT statement proves to be the most used SQL command. This statement retrieves data from your tables and is composed of just six key words that must be in this order:

- SELECT
- FROM
- WHERE
- GROUP BY
- HAVING
- ORDER BY

All but the key word SELECT are optional.

Understanding the SELECT statement

Use the following parts of the SELECT statement to specify the columns and rows that you want returned from a table:

- The select list specifies the columns to be returned.
- The FROM clause specifies the table from which columns and rows are returned.
- The WHERE clause specifies the rows to return. The search condition in the WHERE clause restricts the rows that are retrieved by using conditional and logical operators.

Examine the partial syntax:

```
SELECT [ALL | DISTINCT] <select_list>
FROM [[database_name.][owner_name].]{ table_name }
[AS] alias
WHERE <search_condition>
```

Here's an example:

```
USE AdventureWorks;
GO
SELECT *
FROM Production.Product;
GO
```

SPECIFYING COLUMNS

You can retrieve particular columns from a table by listing them in the select list. The select list contains the columns, expressions, or keywords to select.

When you specify columns to retrieve, understand the following rules and advice:

- The select list retrieves and displays the columns in the specified order.
- Separate the column names with commas. Do not place a comma after the last column name.
- Use an asterisk (*) in the select list to retrieve all columns from a table.

Examine the syntax:

```
<select_list>:: =
{ *
| { table_name | table_alias }.*
| [{ table_name | table_alias }.]
{ column_name | expression | IDENTITYCOL |
ROWGUIDCOL }
[ [AS] column_alias ]
| column_alias = expression
} [,...n]
```

Here's an example:

```
USE AdventureWorks;
GO
SELECT Title
FROM HumanResources.Employee;
GO
```

USING THE WHERE CLAUSE TO SPECIFY ROWS

The WHERE clause of the SELECT statement restricts the number of rows that are returned.

Using the WHERE clause, you can also retrieve specific rows based on a given search condition. Only rows that match the search condition in the WHERE clause are returned by the SELECT statement. The search condition in the WHERE clause can contain an unlimited list of predicates (expressions that return a value of TRUE, FALSE or UNKNOWN).

When you specify rows with the WHERE clause, understand the following rules and advice:

- Place single quotation marks around all char, nchar, varchar, nvarchar, text, datetime, and smalldatetime data.
- Use positive rather than negative predicates because negative predicates slow the speed of data retrieval.
- Whenever possible, use a WHERE clause to limit the number of rows that are returned, rather than returning all rows from a table. Returning fewer rows of data improves performance, especially when you use the SELECT * statement.

The following syntax shows how multiple predicates are combined with the AND or OR logical operators:

```
<search_condition>::=
[NOT] <predicate> [{AND | OR} [NOT] <predicate>]
[,...n]
```

The following syntax shows the expressions that can be used in the predicates:

```
<predicate>::=
{
expression { = | <> | != | > | >= | !> | < | <= |
```

```
    !< }expression
    | string_expression [NOT] LIKE string_expression
    [ESCAPE 'escape_character']
    | expression [NOT] BETWEEN expression AND expression
    | expression [NOT] IN (expression [,...n])
    | expression IS [NOT] NULL
    }
```

Here's an example:

```
    USE AdventureWorks;
    GO
    SELECT Title, FirstName, LastName
    FROM Person.Contact
    WHERE LastName = 'Abercrombie';
    GO
```

USING STRING COMPARISONS

You can use the LIKE operator in combination with wildcard characters to select rows by comparing character values from the rows to a pattern string specified with the LIKE operator. When you use the LIKE operator, consider the following rules and advice:

- If you want to do an exact string comparison, use a comparison operator rather than the LIKE operator; for example, use Country = 'USA' rather than Country LIKE 'USA'.
- All characters in the pattern string are significant, including leading and trailing blank spaces.
- LIKE can be used only with data of the char, nchar, varchar, nvarchar, or datetime data types.

Here's an example:

```
    SELECT name
    FROM sys.objects
    WHERE name LIKE 'sys%';
    GO
```

Types of Wildcard Characters: Use the following four wildcard characters to form your character string search criteria:

Wildcard	Description
% (percent)	Any string of zero or more characters
_ (underscore)	Any single character
[ ] (bracket)	Any single character within the specified range (for example, [s-w]) or set (for example [aeiou])
[^] (caret)	Any single character *not* within the specified range (for example, [^s-w]) or set (for example [^aeiou])

USING THE BETWEEN OPERATOR

Use the BETWEEN operator in the WHERE clause to retrieve rows that are within a specified range of values. When you use the BETWEEN operator, understand the following rules and advice:

- SQL Server includes the end values in the resultset.
- Use the BETWEEN operator, rather than a predicate that includes the AND operator, with two comparison operators (> = x AND < = y). However, to search for an exclusive

range in which the returned rows do not contain the end values, use a predicate that includes the AND operator with two comparison operators (> x AND < y).

- Use the NOT BETWEEN operator to retrieve rows outside of the specified range. Be aware, however, that negative conditions slow data retrieval.
- Be careful when using the BETWEEN operator with date and time values because midnight is the endpoint for the ending date value. No data with a time after midnight on the ending date will be returned.

Here's an example:

```
USE AdventureWorks;
GO
SELECT Name FROM Production.Product
WHERE ProductID BETWEEN 319 AND 342;
GO
```

USING THE IN OPERATOR

Use the IN operator in the WHERE clause to retrieve rows that match a specified list of values. When you use the IN operator, understand the following rules and advice:

- Use either the IN operator or a series of predicates that are connected with an OR operator; SQL Server resolves them in the same way, returning identical resultsets at the same processing cost.
- Do not include the NULL value in the list. A NULL value in the list evaluates to the comparison, = NULL. This may return unpredictable resultsets.
- Use the NOT IN operator to retrieve rows that are not in your list of values. Be aware, however, that negative conditions slow data retrieval as it forces the query optimizer to perform a table scan.

Here's an example:

```
SELECT ProductModelID, Name
INTO dbo.Gloves
FROM Production.ProductModel
WHERE ProductModelID IN (3, 4);
GO
```

USING THE IS NULL OPERATOR

Use the IS NULL operator to retrieve rows for which information is missing from a specified column. When you retrieve rows that contain unknown values, understand the following rules and advice:

- Null values fail all comparisons because they do not evaluate equally with one another.
- You define whether columns allow null values in the CREATE TABLE statement.
- Use the IS NOT NULL operator to retrieve rows that have known values in the specified columns.

Here's an example:

```
USE tempdb;
GO
IF OBJECT_ID (N'#Bicycles',N'U') IS NOT NULL
DROP TABLE #Bicycles;
GO
```

USING LOGICAL OPERATORS

Use the logical operators AND and OR to combine a series of predicates and to refine query processing. Use the logical NOT operator to negate the value of a predicate. The results of a query may vary depending on the grouping and ordering of the predicates.

When you use logical operators, understand the following rules and advice:

- Use the AND operator to retrieve rows that meet all of the search criteria.
- Use the OR operator to retrieve rows that meet any of the search criteria.
- Use the NOT operator to negate the expression that follows the operator.

ORDERING OF PREDICATES

When you use more than one logical operator in a statement, understand the following rules and advice:

- SQL Server evaluates the NOT operator first, followed by the AND operator, and then the OR operator.
- The precedence order is from left to right if all operators in an expression are of the same level.

USING PARENTHESES

Use parentheses when you have two or more expressions as the search criteria. Using parentheses allows you to:

- Group expressions
- Change the order of evaluation
- Make expressions more readable

USING THE ORDER BY CLAUSE

Use the ORDER BY clause to sort rows in the resultset in ascending or descending order. When you use the ORDER BY clause, understand the following rules and advice:

- When SQL Server is installed, a sort order is specified. The sort order is a set of rules that determines how SQL Server sorts and compares character data. Different sort orders are available and different sort orders can be applied to different objects. Execute the sp_helpsort system stored procedure or SERVERPROPERTY ('Collation') to determine the sort order that is in use on your SQL Server.
- SQL Server does not guarantee an order in the resultset unless the order is specified with an ORDER BY clause.
- SQL Server sorts in ascending order by default.
- Columns that are included in the ORDER BY clause do not have to appear in the select list.
- The total size of the columns specified in the ORDER BY clause cannot exceed 8,060 bytes.
- You can sort by column names, computed values, or expressions.
- In the ORDER BY clause, you can refer to columns by their names, aliases, or positions in the select list. The columns are evaluated in the same way and return the same resultset.
- To sort the values of a column in descending order, specify the DESC keyword after the column reference in the column list of the ORDER BY clause. You can specify the ASC keyword to sort the values of a column in ascending order, but it is not necessary because ASC is the default.
- Do not use an ORDER BY clause on text or image columns.

Here's an example:

```
SELECT ProductModelID, Name
FROM Production.ProductModel
```

```
WHERE ProductModelID NOT IN (3, 4)
UNION
SELECT ProductModelID, Name
FROM dbo.Gloves
ORDER BY Name;
GO
```

ELIMINATING DUPLICATES

If you require a list of unique values, use the DISTINCT clause to eliminate duplicate rows in the resultset. When you use the DISTINCT clause, consider the following rules and advice:

- All rows that meet the search condition specified in the WHERE clause of the SELECT statement are returned in the resultset, unless you have specified the DISTINCT clause.
- The combination of values in the select list determines distinctiveness.
- Rows that contain any unique combination of values are retrieved and returned in the resultset.
- The DISTINCT clause presents the resultset in random order unless you have included an ORDER BY clause.
- If you specify a DISTINCT clause, the ORDER BY clause may include only the columns listed in the select list of the SELECT statement.

Here's an example:

```
USE AdventureWorks;
GO
SELECT DISTINCT Title
FROM HumanResources.Employee;
GO
```

CHANGING COLUMN NAMES

Create more readable column names by using the AS keyword to replace default column names with aliases in the select list.

When you change column names, understand the following rules and advice:

- By default, columns that are based on expressions do not have column names. Use column aliases to give names to columns that are based on expressions.
- Place single quotation marks around column aliases that contain blank spaces or that do not conform to SQL Server object naming conventions.
- You can include up to 128 characters in a column alias.
- You can use column aliases in the ORDER BY clause of the SELECT statement but you cannot use column aliases in the WHERE, GROUP BY or HAVING clauses of the SELECT statement.

Examine the partial syntax

```
{ column_name | expression } [AS] column_alias
```

Here's an example:

```
USE AdventureWorks;
GO
SELECT Title AS 'Job Title'
FROM HumanResources.Employee;
GO
```

■ Section 3: Using the Insert Statement

THE BOTTOM LINE   Use the INSERT statement to add new records (rows) to a table.

The INSERT statement adds rows to a table.

Use the INSERT statement with the VALUES clause to add rows to a table. When you insert rows, understand the following rules and advice:

- Use the *column_list* to specify columns that will store each incoming value. You must enclose the *column_list* in parentheses and delimit column names in the list with commas. If you are supplying values for all columns, using the *column_list* is optional.
- Specify the data that you want to insert by using the VALUES clause. The VALUES clause is required. The VALUES clause must specify a value for every column in the table or for every column in the *column_list*, if a *column_list* was specified. Values in the VALUES clause must be enclosed in parentheses and delimited with commas.

  The order of the values in the VALUES clause must be the same as the column order in the table or in the *column_list*. The data types of new data must correspond to the data types of the columns in the table. Many data types have an associated entry format. For example, character data and dates must be enclosed in single quotation marks.

- An INSERT statement fails if the data values violate a constraint or rule.
- To make your script clearer, you should always specify a *column_list*.

Examine the partial syntax

```
INSERT [INTO] table_name[(column_list)]
{VALUES ({DEFAULT | NULL | expression}[,...n])}
|DEFAULT VALUES
```

Here's an example:

```
INSERT dbo.CubeExample (ProductName,
CustomerName, Orders)
VALUES ('Filo Mix', 'Romero y tomillo', 10);
GO
```

USING THE DEFAULT KEYWORD

When a table has default constraints, or when a column has a default value, use the DEFAULT keyword in the INSERT statement to have SQL Server supply the default value for you.

When you use the DEFAULT keyword, understand the following rules and advice:

- SQL Server inserts a null value for columns that allow null values and do not have default values.
- If you use the DEFAULT keyword, and the columns do not have default values or allow null values, the INSERT statement fails.
- Enter a null value explicitly by typing NULL without single quotation marks.
- You cannot use the DEFAULT keyword with a column that has the IDENTITY property (an automatically assigned, incremented value). Therefore, do not list columns with an IDENTITY property in the *column_list* or VALUES clause.
- SQL Server inserts the next appropriate value for columns that are defined with the timestamp data type.

Here's an example:

```
INSERT dbo.CubeExample (ProductName, CustomerName,
Orders)
```

```
VALUES ('Outback Lager', 'Wilman Kala', DEFAULT);
GO
```

USING THE DEFAULT VALUES KEYWORD

Use the DEFAULT VALUES keyword to insert an entire row into a table without specifying values for any columns.

Inserting a row with the DEFAULT VALUES keyword is useful in an application in which you want to show a new identity number to a user while they are adding a new record. Using this technique, you are able to show the identity number before the user has added the new row, because the row is actually added in advance with default values. After adding the new row, you can display the new identity number and other default values to the user when they begin editing the values for the new row. When the user has finished entering the new values, use the UPDATE statement to update the row with the new values.

When you use the DEFAULT VALUES keyword, understand the following rules and advice:

- SQL Server inserts a null value for columns that allow null values and do not have a default value.
- If you use the DEFAULT VALUES keyword, and the columns do not have default values or allow null values, the INSERT statement fails.
- SQL Server inserts the next appropriate value for columns with an IDENTITY property or a timestamp data type.
- Use the DEFAULT VALUES keyword to generate sample data and populate tables with default values.

Here's an example:

```
INSERT INTO Table1 DEFAULT VALUES;
GO
```

INSERTING PARTIAL DATA

If a column has a default value or accepts null values, you can omit the column from an INSERT statement, rather than specify the DEFAULT keyword. SQL Server automatically inserts the values.

When you insert partial data, understand the following rules and advice:

- Specify the columns for which you are providing a value in the column_list. The data in the VALUES clause corresponds to the specified columns. Unnamed columns are filled in as if they had been named and a default value had been supplied. If an unnamed column does not have a default value, a null value is inserted if the column allows null values.
- Do not specify columns in the *column_list* that have an IDENTITY property or that allow default or null values.

■ Section 4: Using the DELETE Statement

THE BOTTOM LINE Use the DELETE statement to remove records (rows) from a table.

Use the DELETE statement to remove one or more rows from a table.

When you use the DELETE statement, consider the following rules and advice:

- SQL Server deletes all rows from the table that match the WHERE clause search condition.

- SQL Server deletes all rows from a table if you do not include a WHERE clause in the DELETE statement.
- Each deleted row is logged in the transaction log.

Examine the partial syntax

```
DELETE [FROM] table_name
WHERE <search_condition>
```

USING THE TRUNCATE TABLE STATEMENT

Use the TRUNCATE TABLE statement to delete all rows from a table.

When you use the TRUNCATE TABLE statement, consider the following facts:

- SQL Server deletes all rows but retains the table structure and its associated objects such as indexes and constraints.
- The TRUNCATE TABLE statement executes more quickly than the DELETE statement because SQL Server logs only the deallocation of data pages, not the deletion of each row.
- If a table has an IDENTITY column, the TRUNCATE TABLE statement resets the IDENTITY seed value. If you delete all rows from a table that has an IDENTITY column using the DELETE statement, the IDENTITY seed value is not reset.

Examine the syntax

```
TRUNCATE TABLE table_name
```

Section 5: The UPDATE Statement

THE BOTTOM LINE   Use the UPDATE statement to modify records (rows) in a table.

The UPDATE statement modifies existing data.

Use the UPDATE statement to change single rows, groups of rows, or all of the rows in a table. When you update rows, understand the following rules and advice:

- Specify which rows to update with the WHERE clause.
- Specify the new values with the SET clause. In the SET clause, list one or more assignments delimited by commas, setting a column name from the table equal to a new value.
- The data types of the input values must be the same as the data types that are defined for the columns.
- SQL Server does not update rows that violate any integrity constraints. The changes do not occur, and the statement is rolled back.
- You can change the data in only one table at a time.
- You can assign the value of an expression to a column. For example, an expression can be a calculation like (UnitPrice * 2) or the addition of two values from columns like (Amount + Tax).

Examine the partial syntax

```
UPDATE table_name
SET {column_name = {expression |DEFAULT}}[,...n]
[WHERE <search_condition>]
```

Here's an example:

```
UPDATE Sales.SalesPerson
SET Bonus = 6000, CommissionPct = 0.10,
SalesQuota = NULL;
GO
```

■ Section 6: Introducing Joins

THE BOTTOM LINE Use the JOIN statement to retrieve data from two or more tables in one SELECT statement where each pair of tables is (usually) linked together on a column in each table containing a common datatype.

You join tables to produce a single resultset that incorporates rows and columns from two or more tables. When you join tables, Microsoft SQL Server 2005 uses the values in the join column(s) from one table to select rows from another table. Rows with matching join column values are combined into new rows, which make up the resultset.

For example, in a properly normalized database, only a product identifier will be stored in an orders table. If you need to retrieve a list of orders that includes product descriptions, you will join the orders table and the products table on the product identifier. The product description and the other columns from the product table may then be used in the select list of the query. In this case, the join performs a lookup function to retrieve the product description for each order.

Examine the partial syntax

```
SELECT {column_name} [,…n]
FROM {table_or_view_name}
[
[ INNER | {{LEFT | RIGHT | FULL} [OUTER] }]
JOIN
table_or_view_name ON search_conditions]
] […n]
```

Here's an example:

```
SELECT c.LastName, c.FirstName, e.Title
INTO EmployeeTwo
FROM Person.Contact c
JOIN HumanResources.Employee e
ON e.ContactID = c.ContactID
WHERE ManagerID = 66;
GO
```

SELECTING SPECIFIC COLUMNS FROM MULTIPLE TABLES

A join allows you to select columns from multiple tables by expanding on the FROM clause of the SELECT statement. Two additional keywords are included in the FROM clause—JOIN and ON:

- The JOIN keyword and its options specify which tables are to be joined and how to join them.
- The ON keyword specifies the columns that the tables have in common.

QUERYING TWO OR MORE TABLES TO PRODUCE A RESULTSET

A join allows you to query two or more tables to produce a single resultset. When you implement joins, understand the following rules and advice:

- Most join conditions are based on the primary key of one table and the foreign key of another table.
- If a table has a composite primary key, you must reference the entire key in the ON clause when you join tables.

- Use columns common to the specified tables to join the tables. These columns should have the same or similar data types, but do not have to have the same names.
- Qualify each column name using the *table_name.column_name* format if the column names are the same.
- Try to limit the number of tables in a join because queries that join a large number of tables are slower than queries that join fewer tables.

Using Inner Joins

Inner joins combine tables by comparing values in columns that are common to both tables. SQL Server returns only rows that match the join conditions.

When to Use Inner Joins: Use inner joins to obtain information from two separate tables and combine that information into one resultset. When you use inner joins, understand the following rules and advice:

- Inner joins are the SQL Server default. You can abbreviate the INNER JOIN clause to JOIN.
- Specify the columns that you want to display in your resultset by including the column names in the select list.
- Include a WHERE clause to restrict the rows that are returned in the resultset.
- The columns used as the join condition need not have the same column name but must share a common datatype.
- Do not use a null value as a join condition because null values do not evaluate equally with one another.
- SQL Server does not guarantee an order in the resultset unless one is specified with an ORDER BY clause.
- You can use multiple JOIN clauses and join more than two tables in the same query.

USING OUTER JOINS

Like inner joins, outer joins return combined rows that match the join condition. However, in addition to the rows that match the join condition, left and right outer joins return unmatched rows from one of the tables and full outer joins return unmatched rows from both of the tables. Columns from the source table of the unmatched rows contain data, but columns from the other table contain null values.

When to Use Left or Right Outer Joins: Use left or right outer joins when you require a complete list of data from one of the joined tables—for example, if you generate a query of product sales by joining a products table and a sales table. An inner join will only return rows for products that were sold. If you use a left outer join and specify the products table as the left table, rows will be returned for every product. Sales columns will contain data for products that were sold and null for products that were not sold.

When you use left or right outer joins, understand the following rules and advice:

- Use a left outer join to display all rows from the first-named table (the table on the left of the JOIN clause).
- Use a right outer join to display all rows from the second-named table (the table on the right of the JOIN clause).
- Do not use a null value as a join condition because null values do not evaluate equally with one another.
- You can abbreviate the LEFT OUTER JOIN or RIGHT OUTER JOIN clause as LEFT JOIN or RIGHT JOIN.

USING CROSS JOINS

Cross joins display every combination of all rows in the joined tables. A common column is not required, and the ON clause is not used for cross joins.

When to Use Cross Joins: Cross joins are rarely used on a normalized database, but you can use them to generate test data for a database or lists of all possible combinations for checklists or business templates.

When you use cross joins, SQL Server produces a Cartesian product in which the number of rows in the result set is equal to the number of rows in the first table, multiplied by the number of rows in the second table. For example, if there are 8 rows in one table and 9 rows in the other table, SQL Server returns a total of 72 rows.

■ Section 7: Using Cross Joins

 SQL Server 2005 allows up to 256 tables in a single query.

When you use multiple joins, it is easier to consider each join independently—for example, if tables A, B, and C are joined. The first join combines table A and B to produce a resultset; this resultset is combined with table C in the second join to produce the final resultset. Columns from any of the tables can be specified in the other clauses of the SELECT statement. If two tables have a column with the same name, qualify each column name using the *table_name.column_name* format.

Using Cross Joins

If you want to find rows that have values in common with other rows in the same table, you can join a table to another instance of itself; this is known as a *self-join*.

When to Use Self-Joins: Self-joins are used to represent hierarchies or tree structures. For example, a company employment structure is typically hierarchical. Each employee has a manager who is also an employee. In an employee table, the primary key is the employee ID and the manager ID column is the foreign key that relates the employee table to itself.

Self-joins are also useful for finding matching data in a table. For example, in the pubs database you can create a query on the authors table that lists for each author the other authors that live in the same city.

When you use self-joins, understand the following rules and advice:

- Table aliases are required to reference two copies of the table. Remember that table aliases are different from column aliases. A table alias is specified in the FROM clause after the table name.
- It may be necessary to use conditions in the WHERE clause to filter out duplicate matching rows if the same column is used more than once in the select list.

■ Section 8: Combining Multiple Resultsets

 The UNION operator combines the result of two or more SELECT statements into a single resultset.

Unlike joins, which combine rows from the base tables into single rows, UNION appends rows from resultsets after each other.

Use the UNION operator when the data that you want to retrieve cannot be accessed with a single query. UNION is often used to recombine tables that have been partitioned. For example, old rows from an orders table can be moved to archive tables that each hold orders from a three-month period. To retrieve a single resultset from more than one of these tables, create individual SELECT statements and combine them with the UNION operator.

When you use the UNION operator, understand the following rules and advice:

- The resultsets must have matching columns. The columns do not have to have the same names, but there must be the same number of columns in each resultset and the columns must have compatible data types and be in the same order.
- SQL Server removes duplicate rows from the resultset. However, if you use the ALL option, all rows (including duplicates) are included in the resultset.
- The column names in the resultset are taken from the first SELECT statement. Therefore, if you want to define new column headings for the resultset, you must create the column aliases in the first SELECT statement.
- If you want the entire resultset to be returned in a specific order, you must specify a sort order by including an ORDER BY clause after the last SELECT statement. Otherwise, the resultset may not be returned in the order that you want. SQL Server generates an error if you specify an ORDER BY clause for any of the other SELECT statements in the query.
- An ORDER BY clause used with the UNION operator can only use items that appear in the select list of the first SELECT statement.
- You may experience better performance if you break a complex query into multiple SELECT statements and then use the UNION operator to combine them.

Examine the Syntax

```
select_statement
UNION [ALL]
select_statement
[,...n]
```

Here's an example:

```
SELECT LastName, FirstName
FROM EmployeeOne
UNION ALL
SELECT LastName, FirstName
FROM EmployeeTwo
UNION ALL
SELECT LastName, FirstName
FROM EmployeeThree;
GO
```

Section 9: Creating a Table from a Resultset

 THE BOTTOM LINE   You can place the resultset of any query into a new table with the SELECT INTO statement.

You may use the SELECT INTO statement to create and populate new tables and to create temporary tables and break down complex problems that require a data set from various sources. If you first create a temporary table, the queries that you execute on it may be simpler than those you would execute on multiple tables or databases.

When you use the SELECT INTO statement, understand the following rules and advice:

- SQL Server creates a table and inserts a resultset into the table. Ensure that the table name that is specified in the SELECT INTO statement is unique. If a table exists with the same name, the SELECT INTO statement fails.

- You can create a local or global temporary table. Create a local temporary table by preceding the table name with a number sign (#) or create a global temporary table by preceding the table name with a double number sign (##). A local temporary table is available only to the connection that created it, while a global temporary table is available to all connections:

  - A local temporary table is deleted when the user closes the connection.
  - A global temporary table is deleted when the table is no longer used by any connections.
  - Set the select into/bulkcopy database option on in order to create a permanent table.
  - You must create column aliases for calculated columns in the select list. You may use aliases to rename other columns; otherwise, the column name will be used.

Examine the Syntax

```
SELECT select_list
INTO new_table_name
FROM table_source
[WHERE search_condition]
```

Here's an example:

```
SELECT * -- The dash-dash indicates a comment
INTO #Bicycles -- #Bicycles is a temporary table
FROM Production.Product
WHERE ProductNumber LIKE 'BK%';
GO
```

■ Section 10: Using Subqueries

THE BOTTOM LINE   A subquery is a SELECT statement nested inside a SELECT, INSERT, UPDATE, or DELETE statement or inside another subquery.

Subqueries can be nested or correlated; nested subqueries execute once when the outer query is executed, and correlated subqueries execute once for every row that is returned when the outer query is executed.

When to Use Subqueries: Use subqueries to break down a complex query into a series of logical steps and solve a problem with a single statement. Subqueries are useful when your query relies on the results of another query.

When to Use Joins Rather Than Subqueries: Often, a query that contains subqueries can be written as a join. Query performance may be similar with a join and a subquery. The difference is that a subquery may require the query optimizer to perform additional steps, such as sorting, which may influence the processing strategy.

Using joins typically allows the query optimizer to retrieve data in the most efficient way. If a query does not require multiple steps, it may not be necessary to use a subquery.

USING SUBQUERIES

When you decide to use subqueries, understand the following rules and advice:

- You must enclose subqueries in parentheses.
- You can only use one expression or column name in the select list of a subquery that returns a value.

- You can use subqueries in place of an expression as long as a single value or list of values is returned.
- You cannot use subqueries on columns that contain text and image data types.
- You can have as many levels of subqueries as you need—there is no limit.
- The query that contains the subquery is usually called the *outer query* and a subquery is called an *inner query*.

Nested Subqueries: Nested subqueries return either a single value or a list of values. SQL Server evaluates a nested subquery once and then uses the value or list returned by the subquery in the outer query.

Single Value Subqueries: Use a nested subquery that returns a single value to compare to a value in the outer query. When you use nested subqueries to return a single value, understand the following rules and advice:

- Single-value subqueries can be used anywhere that an expression can be used.
- In a WHERE clause, use the nested subquery with a comparison operator.
- If a nested subquery returns more than one value when the outer query expects only one value, SQL Server displays an error message.
- You can use an aggregate function or specify an expression or column name to return a single value.
- Each nested subquery is evaluated only once.

Correlated Subqueries: For correlated subqueries, the inner query uses information from the outer query and executes once for every row in the outer query.

When you use correlated subqueries, understand the following rules and advice:

- You must use aliases to distinguish table names.
- Correlated subqueries can usually be rephrased as joins. Using joins rather than correlated subqueries enables SQL Server query optimizer to determine how to correlate the data in the most efficient way.

Here's an example:

```
USE AdventureWorks;
GO
SELECT DISTINCT Name
FROM Production.Product
WHERE ProductModelID IN
(SELECT ProductModelID
FROM Production.ProductModel
WHERE Name = 'Long-sleeve logo jersey');
GO
```

USING CORRELATED SUBQUERIES

Use the EXISTS and NOT EXISTS keywords with correlated subqueries to restrict the resultset of an outer query to rows that satisfy the subquery. The EXISTS and NOT EXISTS keywords return TRUE or FALSE, based on whether rows are returned by the subquery. The subquery is tested to see if it will return rows; it does not return any data. Use * (asterisk) in the select list of the subquery as there is no reason to use column names.

Here's an example:

```
USE AdventureWorks;
GO
```

```
SELECT DISTINCT Name
FROM Production.Product p
WHERE EXISTS
(SELECT *
FROM Production.ProductModel pm
WHERE p.ProductModelID = pm.ProductModelID
AND pm.Name = 'Long-sleeve logo jersey');
GO
```

■ Section 11: Using Cursors

THE BOTTOM LINE
Cursors (CURrent Set Of ResultS) offer the ability to navigate forward and backward through a resultset one row at a time in order to view or process data. Think of a cursor as a pointer to a current position or a specific row within a resultset.

Cursors extend standard resultset processing by:

- Allowing positioning at a specific row in the resultset.
- Retrieving and modifying one row or block of rows from the current position in the resultset.
- Supporting different levels of sensitivity to changes to the data underlying the resultset.

REQUESTING CURSORS

Microsoft SQL Server supports two methods for requesting a cursor:

- Transact-SQL
- Application programming interface (API) cursor functions

SQL Server supports the cursor functionality of the following database APIs and object interfaces:

- ADO (ActiveX Data Object)
- OLE DB
- ODBC (Open Database Connectivity)

All cursors require temporary resources to cache data. These resources can be in the form of RAM, a paging file (such as the virtual memory feature of Microsoft Windows), temporary files, or databases. You should not create large cursors or use cursors unnecessarily because excessive use of these temporary resources may degrade the performance of SQL Server and user applications.

Cursors are cached on the client or the server under the following circumstances:

- When you request a client cursor, SQL Server sends the entire resultset across the network to the client.
- When you request a server cursor, SQL Server uses its own resources to manage temporary objects. Only rows that are selected within the cursor are returned to the client over the network.

API cursors may be cached on the client or the server. Transact-SQL cursors are always cached on the server.

Using Transact-SQL Cursors

Use Transact-SQL cursors for complex, row-oriented functionality.

Build a Command String for Execution: You can use Transact-SQL cursors to build command strings that include parameters such as database object names or data from user tables. You might use a cursor in a stored procedure to execute a Transact-SQL statement (such as UPDATE STATISTICS) on many related objects in a database.

Increase Script Readability: Using a cursor rather than a nested SELECT statement can sometimes improve the readability of a stored procedure. If this is the case and if the performance of the two queries is comparable, using a Transact-SQL cursor is appropriate.

Perform Multiple Unrelated Manipulations with Data: You can pass local cursors between stored procedures when you want to generate a resultset once and perform unrelated manipulations on the resultset. For example, you can use a cursor to offer users multiple ways to view the data in a resultset.

Compensate for Database and Application Limitations: You also can use cursors to compensate for database and application limitations. An example of this is the sp_helptext system stored procedure. This system stored procedure uses a Transact-SQL cursor to break down the text of a database object into multiple rows because previous versions of SQL Server had a 255-character limit on the char data type.

UNDERSTANDING HOW TRANSACT-SQL CURSORS WORK

1. Declare the cursor. This includes the SELECT statement that generates a resultset and defines the characteristics of the cursor, such as whether the rows in the cursor can be updated.

2. Execute the OPEN statement to generate the resultset and populate the cursor.

3. Retrieve rows from the cursor resultset. The operation to retrieve one row or one block of rows from a cursor is called a *fetch*. Performing a series of fetches is called *scrolling*.

4. Use values from or perform operations on the row at the current position of the cursor.

5. Close and deallocate the cursor.

KNOWING THE TYPES OF TRANSACT-SQL CURSORS

SQL Server supports five types of cursors: fast-forward, forward-only, static, dynamic, and keyset-driven. The different types of cursors vary in their ability to detect changes to the resultset and in the resources, such as memory and space in the tempdb database, that they use.

If you have a cursor open and the data in the underlying table, on which the cursor is based, is changed by other connections, different cursor types may or may not reflect those changes. The following table shows how the cursor type that you choose determines whether your cursor resultset reflects changes that are made to the membership, order, or values of the data in the underlying table:

Cursor type	Membership	Order	Values
Forward-only	Dynamic	Dynamic	Dynamic
Static	Fixed	Fixed	Fixed
Dynamic	Dynamic	Dynamic	Dynamic
Keyset-driven	Fixed	Fixed	Dynamic

Fast-forward: A *fast*-forward cursor is auto-fetch, auto-closed, read-only.

Forward-only: A *forward-only* cursor only supports fetching rows serially from the first to the last row of the cursor. It does not retrieve rows from the database until the rows are fetched from the cursor. The effects of all INSERT, UPDATE, and DELETE statements that any other connection makes before a row is fetched are visible when the row is fetched.

Static: A *static* cursor fixes a resultset when the cursor is opened and the resultset is always read-only. Thus, it is not possible to update the underlying tables of a static cursor through the cursor. The resultset is stored in tempdb when the static cursor is opened. Changes made by other connections after the cursor is opened are never reflected by the cursor. Static cursors are also called *insensitive* or *snapshot cursors*.

Dynamic: Dynamic cursors are the opposite of static cursors. A *dynamic* cursor reflects all changes that are made to the data values, order, and membership of rows in the resultset when you scroll through a cursor resultset. The effects of all UPDATE, INSERT, and DELETE statements that any user makes are visible as rows are fetched through the cursor. You can fetch rows randomly from anywhere in the cursor. Dynamic cursors are also called *sensitive cursors*.

Keyset-driven: The membership and order of rows in a keyset-driven cursor are fixed when the cursor is opened. *Keyset-driven* cursors are controlled by a unique set of identifiers (keys), known as a *keyset*. The keys are built from a set of columns that uniquely identify a set of rows in the resultset. The keyset is the set of key values from all the rows that qualified for the SELECT statement when the cursor was opened, and the membership and order of rows is never updated.

Inserts and updates that the user makes through the cursor are visible, as are changes that other connections make to data values in nonkeyset columns. The keyset for a keyset-driven cursor is stored in tempdb when it is the cursor opened.

Consider the following facts when you determine which type of cursor to use:

- Dynamic cursors open faster than static or keyset-driven cursors.
- In joins, keyset-driven and static cursors can be faster than dynamic cursors.
- Static and keyset-driven cursors increase the use of the tempdb database. Static server cursors build the entire cursor in tempdb; keyset-driven cursors build the keyset in tempdb. For this reason, if a large number of users each open a static or keyset-driven cursor, tempdb may run out of space.

TAKE NOTE*

Cursors with fixed characteristics of membership, order, and values perform faster than cursors with dynamic characteristics, although they may be slower to open initially.

Understanding Cursor Characteristics

You can define the behavior and locking characteristics of cursors. Transact-SQL cursors and ODBC API cursors support specifying scrollability and sensitivity. Not all API cursors support specifying behaviors. All cursors support varying levels of locking.

Scrollability: *Scrollability* defines the fetch options that the cursor supports. Cursors can be scrollable or forward-only. A scrollable cursor supports all fetch options; a forward-only cursor supports only the fetch next option.

Sensitivity: *Sensitivity* defines whether updates that are made against the base rows are visible through the cursor. Sensitivity also defines whether you can make updates through the cursor. If you make an update to the current row of a cursor, the actual update is made to the underlying table; this is called a *positioned update*.

A sensitive cursor reflects data modifications that anyone makes. Positioned updates can be made through the cursor, except when a read-only sensitive cursor is used. An insensitive cursor is read-only and does not support updates.

Locking: Because SQL Server must acquire an exclusive lock before it can update a row, updates that are made through a cursor can be blocked by other connections that hold a shared lock on a row. The transaction isolation level of a cursor allows a programmer to determine the full locking behavior of a specific cursor environment.

When any row in a cursor is updated, SQL Server locks it with an exclusive lock. Locks are held for varying lengths of time, depending on the situation:

- If the update is performed within a transaction, the exclusive lock is held until the transaction is terminated.
- If the update is performed outside of a transaction, the update is committed automatically and when it is complete, the exclusive lock is freed.

EXAMINING TRANSACT-SQL CURSOR SYNTAX

You use five statements when you work with Transact-SQL cursors. The following table summarizes these five statements:

Statement	Description
DECLARE CURSOR	Defines cursor structure and allocates resources
OPEN	Populates a declared cursor with a resultset
FETCH	Navigates within a cursor resultset
CLOSE	Releases the current resultset and frees any cursor locks held on the rows on which the cursor is positioned
DEALLOCATE	Removes the cursor definition and deallocates resources

DECLARE CURSOR: The *DECLARE CURSOR* statement defines the characteristics of the cursor, the query that the cursor uses, and any variables that the cursor uses.

Consider the following rules and advice when you declare cursors:

- The *select_statement* is a standard SELECT statement. Certain keywords, such as DISTINCT and UNION, force the cursor type to static.
- LOCAL or GLOBAL specifies the scope of the cursor. The cursor can be local to a stored procedure, trigger, or Transact-SQL script in which case it can be used only by that code and is removed when the code is finished executing. If the cursor is global, then it may be used by subsequent stored procedures, triggers or Transact-SQL scripts, executed on the connection, and is not removed until the connection is closed or until the cursor is closed and deallocated. The default is global.
- The current user must have SELECT permission on the table and the columns that are used in the cursor.

There are two forms of the DECLARE CURSOR syntax. The first form of the DECLARE CURSOR statement uses the ANSI SQL-92 syntax. The second form uses the extended Transact-SQL cursor syntax.

Examine the ANSI SQL-92 Syntax

```
DECLARE cursor_name [INSENSITIVE] [SCROLL] CURSOR
FOR select_statement
[FOR {READ ONLY | UPDATE [OF column_name
[,...n]]}]
```

Examine the Transact-SQL Syntax

```
DECLARE cursor_name CURSOR
[LOCAL | GLOBAL]
```

```
[FORWARD_ONLY | SCROLL]
[STATIC | KEYSET | DYNAMIC | FAST_FORWARD]
[READ_ONLY | SCROLL_LOCKS | OPTIMISTIC]
[TYPE_WARNING]
FOR select_statement
[FOR UPDATE [OF column_name [,…n]]]
```

OPEN: The *OPEN* statement opens and populates the cursor by executing the SELECT statement. If the cursor is declared with the INSENSITIVE or STATIC options, OPEN creates a temporary table to hold the rows of the cursor. If the cursor is declared with the KEYSET option, the OPEN statement creates a temporary table to hold the keyset.

Examine the Syntax

```
OPEN{ {[GLOBAL] cursor_name} |
@cursor_variable_name}
```

FETCH: The *FETCH* statement retrieves a specific row from the cursor.

Examine the Syntax:

```
FETCH
[ [NEXT | PRIOR | FIRST | LAST
| ABSOLUTE {n | @ nvar}
| RELATIVE {n | @ nvar}]
FROM ]
{{[GLOBAL] cursor_name} | @cursor_variable_name}
[INTO @variable_name[,...n]]
```

Consider the following rules and advice when you use the FETCH statement:

- The type of FETCH option that is supported within a cursor depends on the type of declared cursor.
- The @@FETCH_STATUS function is updated at every execution of the FETCH statement. Use @@FETCH_STATUS before you attempt to operate on the data to determine whether a fetch was a success or a failure.

CLOSE: The *CLOSE* statement releases the current resultset. It releases any locks that are held on the row on which the cursor is positioned but leaves the data structures accessible for reopening. Modifications and fetches are not allowed until the cursor is reopened. Closed cursors may be reopened.

Examine the Syntax:

```
CLOSE {{[GLOBAL] cursor_name} |
@cursor_variable_name}
```

DEALLOCATE: The *DEALLOCATE* statement removes the association between a cursor and a cursor name or cursor variable that references the cursor. If the cursor name or cursor variable is the last reference to the cursor, the data structures used by the cursor are released.

Examine the Syntax:

```
DEALLOCATE {{[GLOBAL] cursor_name} |
@cursor_variable_name}
```

Here are two examples:

A. Use simple cursor and syntax

The resultset generated at the opening of this cursor includes all rows and all columns in the table. This cursor can be updated, and all updates and deletes are represented in fetches made

---

TAKE NOTE *

The *@cursor_variable_name* option allows you to reference a cursor that has been associated with a cursor variable. This is generally used in stored procedures.

against this cursor. FETCH NEXT is the only fetch available because the SCROLL option has not been specified.

```
DECLARE vend_cursor CURSOR
FOR SELECT * FROM Purchasing.Vendor
OPEN vend_cursor
FETCH NEXT FROM vend_cursor;
GO
```

B. Use nested cursors to produce report output

This example shows how cursors can be nested to produce complex reports. The inner cursor is declared for each vendor.

```
SET NOCOUNT ON
DECLARE @vendor_id int, @vendor_name nvarchar(50),
@message varchar(80), @product nvarchar(50)
PRINT '---- Vendor Products Report ----'
DECLARE vendor_cursor CURSOR FOR
SELECT VendorID, Name
FROM Purchasing.Vendor
WHERE PreferredVendorStatus = 1
ORDER BY VendorID
OPEN vendor_cursor
FETCH NEXT FROM vendor_cursor
INTO @vendor_id, @vendor_name
WHILE @@FETCH_STATUS = 0
BEGIN
PRINT ' '
SELECT @message = '--- Products From Vendor: ' +
@vendor_name
PRINT @message
-- Declare an inner cursor based
-- on vendor_id from the outer cursor.
DECLARE product_cursor CURSOR FOR
SELECT v.Name
FROM Purchasing.ProductVendor pv, Production.Product v
WHERE pv.ProductID = v.ProductID AND
pv.VendorID = @vendor_id- Variable value from the outer cursor
OPEN product_cursor
FETCH NEXT FROM product_cursor INTO @product
IF @@FETCH_STATUS = 0
PRINT '    <<None>>'
WHILE @@FETCH_STATUS = 0
BEGIN
SELECT @message = '    ' + @product
PRINT @message
FETCH NEXT FROM product_cursor INTO @product
END
```

```
CLOSE product_cursor
DEALLOCATE product_cursor
-- Get the next vendor.
FETCH NEXT FROM vendor_cursor
INTO @vendor_id, @vendor_name
END
CLOSE vendor_cursor
DEALLOCATE vendor_cursor
```

Working with Data from Cursors

In addition to navigating through data in cursors, you can modify data through a cursor or share the data.

Modify Data through Cursors: You can modify data through local and global Transact-SQL cursors. You must declare the cursor as updateable and you must not declare it as read-only. In an updateable cursor, you can use UPDATE or DELETE statements with the WHERE CURRENT OF *cursor_name* clause to modify the current row.

Pass Local Cursors between Stored Procedures: Stored procedures that declare and open local cursors can pass the cursors out for use by the calling stored procedure, trigger, or batch. Passing a cursor is done by declaring a variable with the cursor varying data type as an output parameter. Variables that are used to pass cursors are called *cursor variables*.

Consider the following rules and advice about cursor variables:

- Cursor variables can only be used as output parameters; they cannot be used as input parameters.
- Local variables can also be declared with the cursor data type to hold a reference to a local cursor.

Pass local cursors between stored procedures when you want to generate a resultset once and perform unrelated manipulations on the resultset. For example, you could pass a local cursor to allow users to choose from a list of manipulations to perform on the cursor resultset.

Get Cursor Information: Various system stored procedures and functions provide information about cursors.

System Stored Procedures: When a cursor has been declared, you can use the following system stored procedures to determine the characteristics of the cursor. These system stored procedures do not return a standard resultset. They all report their output as an output cursor, so you have to declare a cursor variable and then fetch the rows from the cursor in order to use them.

System stored procedure	Description
sp_cursor_list	Returns a list of cursors that are currently opened by the connection and the attributes of the cursors
sp_describe_cursor	Describes the attributes of a cursor, such as whether it is forward-only or scrolling
sp_describe_cursor_columns	Describes the attributes of the columns in the cursor resultset
sp_describe_cursor_tables	Describes the base tables that the cursor accesses

Functions: Many functions return information about the status of a cursor. The following table describes three of the more commonly used functions:

Global variable	Description
@@FETCH_STATUS	Returns the status of the last cursor FETCH statement that was issued against any cursor that is currently opened on the connection
@@CURSOR_ROWS	Returns the number of qualifying rows in the last cursor that is opened on the connection
CURSOR_STATUS	After calling a stored procedure that returns a cursor as an output parameter, the function allows you to determine the status of the cursor that was returned.

■ Section 12: Using the INSERT...SELECT Statement

THE BOTTOM LINE
The INSERT...SELECT statement adds rows to an existing table by inserting the result set of a SELECT statement into the table.

Using the INSERT...SELECT statement is more efficient than writing multiple, single-row INSERT statements. When you use the INSERT...SELECT statement, understand the following rules and advice:

- All rows that satisfy the SELECT statement are inserted into the outermost table of the query.
- The table that receives the new rows must already exist in the database.
- The columns of the table that receives the new rows must have data types that are compatible with the columns of the table source.
- Determine whether a default value exists or whether a null value is allowed for any columns that are omitted from the SELECT statement. If there is no default and null values are not allowed, you must provide values for these columns.

Examine the syntax:

```
INSERT [INTO] table_name
SELECT select_list
FROM table_list
WHERE search_conditions
```

Here's an example:

```
INSERT dbo.EmployeeSales
SELECT 'SELECT', e.EmployeeID,
c.LastName, sp.SalesYTD
FROM HumanResources.Employee AS e
INNER JOIN Sales.SalesPerson AS sp
ON e.EmployeeID = sp.SalesPersonID
INNER JOIN Person.Contact AS c
ON e.ContactID = c.ContactID
WHERE e.EmployeeID LIKE '2%'
ORDER BY e.EmployeeID, c.LastName;
GO
```

■ Section 13: Deleting Rows Based on Other Tables

THE BOTTOM LINE

Use the DELETE statement with joins or subqueries to remove rows from a table based on data stored in other tables. This is more efficient than writing multiple, single-row DELETE statements.

USING AN ADDITIONAL FROM CLAUSE

In a DELETE statement, the WHERE clause references values in the table itself and is used to decide which rows to delete. If you use a FROM clause, you can reference other tables to make this decision. When you use the DELETE statement with a FROM clause, consider the following facts:

You can use the optional FROM keyword before the table name from which the rows are deleted. Do not confuse this keyword with the FROM clause.

The FROM clause may introduce a join and acts as the restricting criteria for the DELETE statement.

Examine the partial syntax:

```
DELETE [FROM] {table_name | view_name}
[FROM {table_or_view | joined_table}[,...n]]
[WHERE {search_condition | CURRENT OF
cursor_name}]
```

Here's an example:

```
DELETE FROM Sales.SalesPersonQuotaHistory
FROM Sales.SalesPersonQuotaHistory AS spqh
INNER JOIN Sales.SalesPerson AS sp
ON spqh.SalesPersonID = sp.SalesPersonID
WHERE sp.SalesYTD > 2500000.00;
GO
```

SPECIFYING CONDITIONS IN THE WHERE CLAUSE

You also can use subqueries to determine which rows to delete from a table based on rows of another table. You can specify the conditions in the WHERE clause rather than using an additional FROM clause. Use a nested or correlated subquery in the WHERE clause to determine which rows to delete.

■ Section 14: Updating Rows Based on Other Tables

THE BOTTOM LINE

Use the UPDATE statement with a FROM clause or a subquery to modify a table based on values from other tables.

Using the UPDATE Statement

When you use joins and subqueries with the UPDATE statement, understand the following rules and advice:

- SQL Server never updates the same row twice in a single UPDATE statement. This built-in restriction minimizes the amount of logging that occurs during updates.

- Use the SET keyword to introduce the list of columns or variable names to be updated. Any column prefix that is specified in the SET clause must match the table or view name that is specified after the UPDATE keyword.

- Tables introduced by subqueries or the FROM clause cannot be updated in the UPDATE statement.

Examine the partial syntax:

```
UPDATE {table_name | view_name}
SET column_name={expression | DEFAULT | NULL}
[, ...n]
{[FROM {table_or_view |
joined_table}[,...n]]
[WHERE search_conditions ]}
WHERE CURRENT OF cursor_name
```

Here's an example:

```
UPDATE dbo.Table2
SET dbo.Table2.ColB = dbo.Table2.ColB +
dbo.Table1.ColB
FROM dbo.Table2
INNER JOIN dbo.Table1
ON (dbo.Table2.ColA = dbo.Table1.ColA);
GO
```

Using Joins: Use the FROM clause to specify tables and joins that are used to provide the criteria for the UPDATE statement.

Using Subqueries: When you use subqueries to update rows, understand the following rules and advice:

- SQL Server executes the subquery once for each row in the table to be updated. Therefore, the subquery must return a single value for each row.

- If the subquery does not return a single value, the results are unspecified.

- Consider using aggregate functions with subqueries because SQL Server never updates the same row twice in a single UPDATE statement.

■ Section 15: Using Aggregate Functions

THE BOTTOM LINE

Functions that calculate summary values such as an average or a sum are called aggregate functions. SQL Server provides a rich set of aggregate functions for quickly calculating summary values on columns of a table using a single statement.

When an aggregate function is executed, Microsoft SQL Server 2005 summarizes the values in a particular column for an entire table or for groups of rows within the table. A single aggregate value is produced for the entire table or for each group of rows. Use aggregate functions with the SELECT statement to summarize the values for an entire table. Add the GROUP BY clause to the SELECT statement to summarize values for groups of rows.

Introducing Aggregate Functions

The following table briefly describes some of the Transact-SQL aggregate functions:

Aggregate function	Description
AVG	The average of all the values
COUNT	The number of non-null values
COUNT(*)	The number of rows in the table or group including null values and duplicates
MAX	The maximum value from all the values
MIN	The minimum value from all the values
SUM	The sum of all the values
STDEV	The statistical deviation of all values
STDEVP	The statistical deviation for the population of all values
VAR	The statistical variance of all values
VARP	The statistical variance for the population of all values

All aggregate functions, except for the COUNT(*) function, return NULL if no rows satisfy the WHERE clause of the SELECT statement. The COUNT(*) function returns a value of zero if no rows satisfy the WHERE clause.

The data type of a column determines the functions that you can use with it. The following table describes the relationships between functions and data types.

Function	Supported data types
COUNT	Any type except uniqueidentifier, text, image, or ntext
MIN and MAX	Char, varchar, datetime, and all numeric data types except the bit data type
SUM, AVG, STDEV, STDEVP, VAR and VARP	All numeric types except the bit data type

> **TAKE NOTE** *
>
> Index frequently aggregated columns to improve query performance. For example, if you frequently use aggregate functions on the quantity column when querying a sales table, indexing the quantity column will improve the performance of these queries.

When you use aggregate functions in the select list of a SELECT statement, you cannot use column names in the same statement because an aggregate function returns a single value and a column reference returns a value for each row. In the next lesson, you will learn how to group rows on columns that have common values in many rows.

Examine the partial syntax:

```
SELECT {{AVG | COUNT | MAX | MIN | SUM
| STDEV | STDEVP | VAR | VARP}(expression | *)
} [,...n]
FROM table_list
[ WHERE search_conditions ]
```

Here's an example:

```
USE AdventureWorks;
GO
SELECT ProductID, AVG(OrderQty) AS
AverageQuantity, SUM(LineTotal) AS Total
FROM Sales.SalesOrderDetail
GROUP BY ProductID
```

```
HAVING SUM(LineTotal) > $1000000.00
AND AVG(OrderQty) < 3;
GO
```

Section 16: Using Aggregate Functions with Null Values

THE BOTTOM LINE   Null values can cause aggregate functions to produce unexpected results.

If you execute a SELECT statement that includes a COUNT function on a column that contains 18 rows, two of which contain null values, the COUNT function returns a result of 16. SQL Server ignores the two rows that contain null values.

Therefore, use caution when using aggregate functions on columns that contain null values, because the resultset may not be representative of your data. However, if you decide to use aggregate functions with null values, consider the following facts:

- All SQL Server aggregate functions, with the exception of the COUNT(*) function, ignore null values in columns.
- The COUNT(*) function counts all rows, even if every column contains a null value. For example, if you execute a SELECT statement that includes the COUNT(*) function on a column that contains 18 rows, two of which contain null values, the COUNT(*) function returns a result of 18.

Section 17: Using Other Clauses

THE BOTTOM LINE   Use the GROUP BY clause on columns or expressions to organize rows into groups and to summarize those groups. Use the GROUPING, COMPUTE, COMPUTE BY, and TOP clauses to achieve specialized resultsets.

When you use the GROUP BY clause, understand the following rules and advice:

- SQL Server produces a row of values for each defined group.
- SQL Server returns only single rows for each group that you specify; it does not return detail information.
- All columns that are specified in the select list must be included in the GROUP BY clause. Columns included in the GROUP BY clause do not need to be specified in the select list.
- If you include a WHERE clause, SQL Server groups only the rows that satisfy the WHERE clause conditions.
- The total size of the columns listed in the GROUP BY clause can be up to 8,060 bytes.
- If you use the GROUP BY clause on columns that contain null values, the null values are processed as a group. To exclude the rows with null values, use the IS [NOT] NULL comparison operator in the WHERE clause of the SELECT statement.
- Use the ALL keyword with the GROUP BY clause to display summary rows for every group, regardless of whether the rows satisfy the WHERE clause. For groups for which no rows satisfy the WHERE clause, NULL is returned in the summary columns.

Examine the partial syntax:

```
SELECT select_list
FROM table_source
[ WHERE search_condition ]
```

```
[ GROUP BY [ALL] group_by_expression [,...n]]
[HAVING search_condition ]
```

Here's an example:

```
USE AdventureWorks;
GO
SELECT SalesOrderID, SUM(LineTotal) AS SubTotal
FROM Sales.SalesOrderDetail sod
GROUP BY SalesOrderID
ORDER BY SalesOrderID;
GO
```

USING THE GROUP BY CLAUSE WITH THE HAVING CLAUSES

Use the HAVING clause on columns or expressions to set conditions on the groups included in a resultset. The HAVING clause sets conditions on the GROUP BY clause in much the same way that the WHERE clause sets conditions for the rows returned by the SELECT statement.

The WHERE clause determines which rows are grouped. The HAVING clause determines which groups are returned.

When you use the HAVING clause, understand the following rules and advice:

- Use the HAVING clause only with the GROUP BY clause to restrict the grouping. Using the HAVING clause without the GROUP BY clause is not meaningful.
- You can have up to 128 conditions in a HAVING clause. When you have multiple conditions, combine them with logical operators (AND, OR, or NOT).
- In the HAVING clause, you can reference any of the columns that appear in the select list, including the aggregate functions. You cannot reference aggregate functions in the WHERE clause.
- The HAVING clause is applied after the ALL keyword so the HAVING clause overrides the ALL keyword and only returns groups that satisfy the HAVING clause.

USING THE GROUP BY CLAUSE WITH THE ROLLUP OPERATOR

Use the GROUP BY clause with the ROLLUP operator to summarize group values. The GROUP BY clause with the ROLLUP operator provides data in a standard relational format.

When you use the GROUP BY clause with the ROLLUP operator, understand the following rules and advice:

- The ROLLUP operator adds extra summary rows to the resultset by grouping rows based on the columns in the GROUP BY clause but successively excluding the rightmost columns. The row of the resultset that excludes all the columns is therefore a summary of all the rows in the resultset. The added rows have null values in the excluded columns.
- The aggregate values in extra rows in the resultset are subtotals for the groups represented by the leftmost columns in the GROUP BY clause.
- You can have up to 10 grouping expressions when you use the ROLLUP operator.
- You cannot use the ALL keyword with the ROLLUP operator.
- When you use the ROLLUP operator, ensure that the columns that follow the GROUP BY clause have a relationship that is meaningful in your business environment.

Examine the partial syntax:

```
SELECT select_list
FROM table_source
[ WHERE search_condition ]
[ [ GROUP BY [ALL] group_by_expression [, ...n]]
```

```
[ WITH { CUBE | ROLLUP } ]
]
[HAVING search_condition ]
```

Here's an example:

```
USE AdventureWorks;
GO
SELECT ProductName, CustomerName, SUM(Orders)
AS 'Sum orders'
FROM dbo.CubeExample
GROUP BY ProductName, CustomerName
WITH ROLLUP;
GO
```

USING THE GROUP BY CLAUSE WITH THE CUBE OPERATOR

The CUBE operator is similar to the ROLLUP operator but adds summary rows for all possible column combinations in the GROUP BY clause. The GROUP BY clause with the CUBE operator provides data in a standard relational format.

When you use the GROUP BY clause with the CUBE operator, understand the following rules and advice:

- If you have n columns or expressions in the GROUP BY clause, SQL Server returns $2^n - 1$ possible combinations in the resultset.
- You can include up to 10 grouping expressions when you use the CUBE operator.
- You cannot use the ALL keyword with the CUBE operator.
- When you use the CUBE operator, ensure that the columns that follow the GROUP BY clause have a relationship that is meaningful in your business environment.

Here's an example:

```
USE AdventureWorks;
GO
SELECT ProductID, SUM(LineTotal) AS Total
FROM Sales.SalesOrderDetail
WHERE UnitPrice < $5.00
GROUP BY ProductID, OrderQty
WITH CUBE
ORDER BY ProductID;
GO
```

USING THE GROUPING FUNCTION

Use the GROUPING function with either the ROLLUP or CUBE operator to distinguish between the standard rows and the rows that are generated by the ROLLUP or CUBE operator in your resultset. Using the GROUPING function helps to determine whether the NULLs that appear in your resultset are actual null values in the base tables or null values generated by the ROLLUP or CUBE operator. A 1 in a GROUPING column means that the row was generated by the CUBE operator and a 0 means that the row is a standard GROUP BY summary row.

When you use the GROUPING function, understand the following rules and advice:

- The GROUPING function is used like any expression in the select list. SQL Server returns a column for the GROUPING function values in the resultset.

- The GROUPING function returns a value of 1 for any row in the resultset that is a ROLLUP or CUBE summary and has a null value in the column specified in the GROUPING function.

- The GROUPING function returns a value of 0 for any row in the resultset that does not have a null value in the column specified by the GROUPING function. The row could still be a row generated by the ROLLUP or CUBE operator, but it may have a null value in a different column from the GROUP BY list.

- You can specify the GROUPING function only for columns that exist in the GROUP BY clause.

- Use the GROUPING function to assist in referencing your resultsets programmatically.

Here's an example:

```
USE AdventureWorks;
GO
SELECT ProductModelID, GROUPING(ProductModelID),
p.Name AS ProductName, GROUPING(p.Name),
SUM(OrderQty)
FROM Production.Product p
INNER JOIN Sales.SalesOrderDetail sod
ON p.ProductID = sod.ProductID
GROUP BY ProductModelID, p.Name
WITH CUBE;
GO
```

USING THE COMPUTE AND COMPUTE BY CLAUSES

The COMPUTE and COMPUTE BY clauses allow you to add aggregate function values to a SELECT statement in a nonrelational format that is not ANSI-standard. These clauses add subtotals to standard resultsets for queries that do not have a GROUP BY clause.

The COMPUTE clause combines the results of a standard SELECT statement and the result of a SELECT statement that specifies an aggregate function. The COMPUTE BY clause combines the results of a standard SELECT statement, the result of a SELECT statement that specifies an aggregate function, and the results of a SELECT statement that has a GROUP BY clause.

The COMPUTE and COMPUTE BY clauses are useful for quickly generating summary data but the output is not well suited for generating resultsets to use with other applications as the text word "Sum" is automatically added (Excel, for one, doesn't like nonnumeral characters). For example, you may want to use the clauses to print basic reports quickly or to verify results of applications that you are writing. However, other tools, such as Microsoft Access or Microsoft Reporting Services, offer richer reporting capabilities.

If you use the COMPUTE and COMPUTE BY clauses, consider the following facts:

- Columns used in the aggregate functions in the COMPUTE list must be listed in the select list.

- You cannot include text, ntext, or image data types in a COMPUTE or COMPUTE BY clause.

- You cannot use the COUNT(*) aggregate function with COMPUTE.

- You cannot use the GROUP BY clause and the COMPUTE or COMPUTE BY clauses in the same statement.

- You cannot adjust the format of your resultset. For example, if you use the SUM aggregate function, SQL Server displays the word *sum* in your resultset; you cannot change it to another string such as Grand Total.

- You cannot use the SELECT INTO statement in the same statement as a COMPUTE clause because statements that include COMPUTE do not generate relational output.
- COMPUTE and COMPUTE BY cannot be used with cursors. ROLLUP and CUBE can be used with cursors.
- The ORDER BY clause must precede the COMPUTE [BY] clause.

Examine the partial syntax:

```
SELECT select_list
FROM table_source
[ WHERE search_condition ]
[ COMPUTE {{ AVG | COUNT | MAX | MIN | SUM
| STDEV | STDEVP | VAR | VARP }
(expression) }[,…n]
[ BY expression [,…n] ]
]
```

Here's an example:

```
USE AdventureWorks;
GO
SELECT ProductID, LineTotal
FROM Sales.SalesOrderDetail
WHERE UnitPrice < $5.00
ORDER BY ProductID, LineTotal
COMPUTE SUM(LineTotal) BY ProductID;
GO
```

LISTING THE TOP *n* VALUES

Use the TOP *n* clause to list only the first *n* rows or *n* percent of a resultset. Although the TOP *n* clause is not ANSI-standard, it is useful, for example, to list a company's top selling products.

When you use the TOP *n* or TOP *n* PERCENT clause, understand the following rules and advice:

- You should always specify an ORDER BY clause when using the TOP *n* clause. If you do not use an ORDER BY clause, SQL Server returns the top n rows that satisfy the WHERE clause in no particular order.
- Use an unsigned integer following the TOP keyword.
- If the TOP *n* PERCENT keyword yields a fractional number of rows, SQL Server rounds the number of rows up to the next integer value.
- Use the WITH TIES keyword to include "ties" in the resultset. Ties result when two or more rows have the same values in columns specified in the ORDER BY clause. The resultset may therefore include more rows than specified in the TOP *n* clause.

Here's an example:

```
USE AdventureWorks;
GO
DECLARE @p AS int
SET @p='10'
SELECT TOP(@p)*
FROM HumanResources.Employee;
GO
```

Glossary

A

alert A user-defined response to a SQL Server event. Alerts can either run a defined task or they can send an e-mail or pager message to a specified operator.

alias datatype A user-defined datatype based on existing built-in datatypes—for example, ZipCode based on Char(5). Formerly known as user-defined datatypes.

B

backup A specialized copy of a database, filegroup, file, or transaction log that can be used by SQL Server to restore database data, typically after a serious database error or a system failure. Backups can be restored individually, or a set of backups can be restored in sequence.

built-in datatype Microsoft-supplied options for storing data in a table; in the table creation, the datatype for an attribute must always be specified.

bulk export To copy a large set of data rows from a SQL Server table into a data file.

bulk import To load a large set of data rows from a data file into a SQL Server table. The database engine applies logging and locking optimizations when possible.

C

cache An allocated section of system memory (RAM); commonly used to hold the compiled code of a stored procedure for fast, efficient processing.

catalog The ANSI-compliant term for a database; fully synonymous with database.

check constraint Specifies data values that are acceptable in a column; it can be based on columns in other tables or columns in the same table.

CLR Common language runtime; database objects created in Visual Basic, C#, Python, Perl, and many other procedural languages.

clustered index An index that physically arranges the records in ascending order and stores the records in the leaf level of the index.

code page For character data, a definition of the bit patterns that represent specific letters, numbers, or symbols. ASCII characters use 1 byte per character; each byte can have 1 to 256 bit patterns. Unicode data uses 2 bytes per character and have 1 to 65,536 bit patterns.

code point The Universal Character Set (UCS) encodes characters. The UCS contains more than 100,000 abstract characters, each identified by an unambiguous name and an integer number called its code point. The UCS facilitates ordering and keeping localities such as Japan and China distinct in sorted results.

collation A set of rules that determines how data is compared, ordered, and presented. Character data is sorted using collation information that includes locale, sort order, and case sensitivity.

compile The act of converting high-level code (such as T-SQL) to machine language code by the Query Optimizer.

computed column When you use the CREATE TABLE syntax, you may create a column that is derived from other columns in the table. For example, the Unit Sales column times the Unit Price column provides the Total Sales column. Normalization techniques prohibit storing aggregated values (total sales), yet such a column can reduce the need for JOINs and thus decrease overhead processing when delivering a resultset. Values are stored in the index—not in the data column itself.

contract A contract defines which message types an application uses to accomplish a particular task. A contract is an agreement between two services about which messages each service sends to accomplish a particular task. Contract definitions persist in the database where the type is created.

D

database A catalog of tables and entities describing a solution for collecting and reporting data and information.

Database Mail An enterprise solution for sending e-mail messages from the Microsoft SQL Server 2005 database engine, which can also include data or files from any resource on your network.

database mirroring A SQL Server 2005 high-availability technology configured between a principal and mirror database and an optional witness server. It maintains close synchronization of data and the database schema and offers the options of automatic failover. The process in which ownership of the principal role is switched from the principal server to the mirror server.

database snapshot A read-only, static view of a database at the moment of snapshot creation.

datatype A specification for the way SQL Server stores data in a table; data formats failing the enumerated requirement will fail to be loaded into the table and generate an error.

DDL Data Definition Language; CREATE, ALTER, and/or DROP statements that change the architecture (the schema) of the database.

deadlock A situation when two users, each having a lock on one piece of data, attempt to acquire a lock on the other's piece. Each user would wait indefinitely for the other to release the lock unless one of the user processes is terminated. SQL Server detects deadlocks and terminates the least costly process.

default constraint Specifies the value for the column when an INSERT statement does not provide a value.

deterministic function A deterministic process returns the same value each time it is invoked. The square root of 4 is 2, every time.

direct recursion Direct recursion occurs when a trigger fires and performs an action on the same table that causes the same trigger to fire again.

distributed transaction An atomic unit of work that spans multiple data sources. In a distributed transaction, all data modifications in all accessed data sources are either committed or terminated.

distributed transaction A transaction spanning multiple data sources. In a distributed transaction, all data modifications in all accessed data sources are either committed or terminated.

distributor A database instance that acts as a store for replication-specific data associated with one or more publishers. Each publisher is associated with a single database (known as a distribution database) at the distributor.

DML Data Manipulation Language; SELECT, INSERT, UPDATE, and/or DELETE actions against data in tables.

domain A centrally managed server to which users must authenticate (log on with an identification phrase and password) that applies uniform security rules to everyone.

E

encryption A method for keeping sensitive information confidential by changing data into an unreadable form.

error log A text file that records system information.

ETL Extraction, transformation, and loading; the complex process of copying and cleaning data from heterogeneous sources.

event notification A method of monitoring events using the Service Broker to reliably deliver the message.

explicit transaction A group of SQL statements enclosed within transaction delimiters that define both the start and end of the transaction.

extent Eight 8 KB pages; the unit of disk I/O.

extent Eight pages; 64 KB of data; the physical disk input/output unit of transfer.

F

failover clustering A process, implemented at the operating system level, of creating a shared data store and then putting from two to four servers (depending on the OS version) in one of two configurations whereby one server automatically takes over in the case of the other's failure.

fill factor The percentage to which index pages are filled on initial creation or rebuild; they are not maintained at this level. You must perform regular maintenance on indexes to recover the desired fill factor.

foreign key constraint Specifies the data values that are acceptable to update, based on values in another column or table.

forest Domains that share a common Active Directory database schema; that is, the Active Directory components are the same; are in common with every domain.

H

heap A data store without an index.

HTTP endpoint An endpoint is the connecting point for two services in the communication architecture, and is addressed by a protocol and an IP port number.

I

implicit transaction A connection option in which each SQL Statement executed by the connection is considered a separate transaction.

index allocation map A means by which SQL Server finds all database pages; SQL Server walks the map; the output order is unpredictable—not necessarily the order in which entered.

indexed view An arrangement of rows and column in which data from one or more columns from one or more base tables are materialized; that is, data is stored in a clustered indexed view.

indirect recursion Indirect recursion occurs when a trigger fires and performs an action that causes another trigger in the same or a different table to fire, and, subsequently, causes an update to occur on the original table. This then causes the original trigger to fire again.

inline table-valued function An inline routine returns a dataset (rows and columns) based on internal Transact-SQL logic between BEGIN and END statements.

J

job A specified series of operations, called steps, performed sequentially by SQL Server Agent.

L

latency The amount of time that elapses between when a data change is completed at one server and when that change appears at another (for example, the time between when a change is made at the publisher and when it appears at the subscriber.

lazywriter The lazywriter is a system process that ensures free buffers are available by removing infrequently used pages from the buffer cache. "Dirty" pages are first written to disk.

linked server A definition of an OLE DB data source used by SQL Server-distributed queries. The linked server definition specifies the OLE DB provider required to access the data and includes enough addressing information for the OLE DB provider to connect to the data. Any rowsets exposed by the OLEDB data source can then be referenced as tables, called linked tables, in SQL Server distributed queries.

lock A restriction on access to a resource in a multiuser environment. SQL Server locks users out of specific database objects automatically to maintain security or prevent concurrent data modification problems.

log file A file or set of files that contain records of the modifications made in a database.

log shipping The process of copying, at set intervals, a log backup from a read/write database) on a primary server to one or more copies (the secondary databases) that reside on remote servers. The secondary servers are warm standbys for the primary server.

M

messages Messages contain the information exchanged between applications that use Service Broker. Each message is part of a conversation.

mirrored media set Physical mass storage units that contain two to four identical copies (mirrors) of each media family. Restore operations require only one mirror per family. This allows for a damaged media volume to be replaced by the corresponding volume from a mirror.

multistatement table-valued function A table-valued routine returns a data set (row and columns) based on an included SELECT statement.

N

nesting Any trigger can contain an INSERT, UPDATE, and/or DELETE statement that affects another table. Triggers are nested when a trigger performs an action that initiates another trigger.

nonclustered index An index in which the logical order of the index key values is different from the physical order of the corresponding rows in a table. The index contains row locators that point to the storage location of the table data.

nondeterministic function A nondeterministic process returns a different value each time it is run. The system time changes with each check.

NULL Specifies whether the column value may be void or the column must have a value (NOT NULL).

O

OLTP Online transaction processing; as distinct from OLAP, which stands for online analytical processing. OLTP is optimized for data entry, whereas OLAP is optimized for data analysis.

P

page 8 KB; the basic storage unit of SQL Server 2005. Except under special circumstances, a row in a database cannot exceed 8,096 bytes in size.

page A unit of storage and processing; in SQL Server, this is fixed as 8 KB in size, or 8,192 bytes. Page sizes vary in other RDBMSs, and are selectable in some.

partition A unit of a partitioned table, index or view; a part of a total dataset that may be across multiple servers; a mechanism allowing federated servers.

partition function A tool to define how the rows of a partitioned table or index are spread across a set of partitions based on the values of specific columns.

partition scheme A database object that maps the partitions of a partition function to a set of filegroups.

partitioned view A view whose base tables may be from one or more servers; a technique for implementing federated servers.

permission Any one of many access tokens created to enable a principal to access a securable.

primary key constraint Identifies each row uniquely. Null values are not allowed.

principal Any type of authenticated user logged in to SQL Server.

publisher A database instance that makes data available to other locations through replication. The publisher can have one or more publications, each defining a logically related set of objects and data to replicate.

pull subscription A subscription created and administered at the publisher. The distribution agent or merge agent for the subscription runs at the distributor.

push subscription A subscription created and administered at the publisher. The distribution agent or merge agent for the subscription run at the distributor.

Q

queues Queues store messages. Service Broker manages queues, and presents a view of a queue that is similar to a table.

R

RAID Redundant Array of Independent Disks; in the original paper presented before the ACM, this was entitled "Redundant Array of Inexpensive Disks." Both terms are in use today, although to most people "inexpensive" is relative.

RDBMS Relational database management system; a system that organizes data into related rows and columns; distinguished from flat-file database systems; SQL Server is a relational database management system (RDBMS); Oracle, DB2, MySQL, Sybase, and many, many others are RDBMSs.

recompile Conditions always change; when statistics become out of date, a recompile may improve performance by giving the Query Optimizer a chance to reoptimize the execution plan.

replication A set of technologies for copying and distributing data and database objects from one database to another and then synchronizing among databases to maintain consistency.

restore A multiphase process that copies all the data and log pages from a specified backup to a specified database (the data copy phase) and rolls forward all the transactions that are logged in the backup (the redo phase). At this point, by default, a restore rolls back any incomplete transactions (the undo phase). This completes the recovery of the database and makes it available to users.

route Service Broker uses routes to determine where to deliver messages.

rule A constraint defined once and applied to potentially many tables; not encouraged for use in SQL Server 2005.

S

scalar function A scalar code segment returns a single data value as defined by the RETURN statement.

securable An object that can have a security descriptor.

selectivity The uniqueness of data entries. The gender column has low selectivity—approximately 50 percent are male and 50 percent are female. The Query Optimizer may not use an index unless the selectivity is in the 5 to 7 percent range.

service A service is a name for a specific business task or set of business tasks. Conversations occur between services.

Service Broker Provides facilities for storing message queues in a SQL Server database.

SOAP The Simple Object Access Protocol (or Service-Oriented Architecture Protocol, or just plain SOAP) is a lightweight XML-based protocol that is designed to exchange structured and typed information on the Web. SOAP can be used in combination with a variety of existing Internet protocols and formats, including HTTP (Hypertext Transfer Protocol), SMTP (Simple Mail Transfer Protocol), and MIME (Multipurpose Internet Mail Extensions), and can support a wide range of applications from messaging systems to remote procedure calls (RPCs).

sort order The set of rules in a collation that define how characters are evaluated in comparison operations and the sequence in which they are sorted.

spindle A physical disk drive; distinct from partition, which may be one or more per spindle.

SQL Structured Query Language; a means of defining, controlling, and manipulating RDBMS data.

SQL Server Agent A service that allows you to automate some administrative tasks; it controls anything timed or scheduled. SQL Server Agent service runs jobs, monitors SQL Server, and processes alerts. The service must be running before local and multiserver administrative jobs can run automatically.

SQL Server Books Online The reference required for all aspects of SQL Server. BOL includes T-SQL syntax, tutorials, and how-to's; it is the definitive guide to solving SQL Server issues.

SQL Server Configuration Manager Enable or disable services and protocols, again, to minimize your vulnerability to attack.

SQL Server Management Studio The primary tool for managing objects in your database.

SQL Server Surface Area Configuration Enable or disable various features you need or don't need specifically. Reduce your hacker attack vulnerability by presenting the minimum features possible.

stored procedure A precompiled collection of Transact-SQL statements or CLR code segments that are stored under a name and processed as a unit. SQL Server supplies stored procedures for managing SQL Server and displaying information about databases and users. SQL Server-supplied procedures are called system stored procedures.

subscriber A database instance that receives replicated data. A subscriber can receive data from multiple publishers and publications. Depending on the type of replications chosen, the subscriber can also pass data changes back to the publisher, or republish the data to other subscribers.

T

table A two-dimensional database object that consists of rows and columns and stores data about an entity modeled in a relational database.

trace file A file used by SQL Server Profiler to record monitored events.

transaction A group of database operations combined into a logical unit of work that is either wholly committed or totally rolled back.

transaction log A database file in which all changes to the database are recorded. SQL Server uses transaction logs during recovery to assure data integrity.

transaction rollback Recovery of a user-specified transaction to the last savepoint inside a transaction or to the beginning of transaction; used to restore data to a known and correct state.

tree Contiguous name space in a network. MSN.COM and MICROSOFT.COM must necessarily be two trees even though in the same forest, as they represent different names. Research. Microsoft.Com and Marketing.Microsoft.com, in contrast, are in the same tree.

trigger A collection of Transact-SQL or common language runtime code that automatically executes when an INSERT, UPDATE, and/or DELETE statement is run.

trigger A stored procedure implemented to fire automatically during an insert, update, and/or delete action against a table.

typed XML XML that is validated by an XML schema.

U

Unicode Unicode defines a set of letters, numbers, and symbols that SQL Server recognizes in the nchar, navarchar, and ntext datatypes. It is related to but separate from character sets. Unicode has 65,536 possible values, compared to the ASCII character set's 256, and takes twice as much space to store. Unicode includes characters for most languages.

unique constraint Prevents duplication of alternative (not primary key) values in columns. Null values are allowed.

untyped XML Allows storing of any form of XML data inside the database without verifying it and matching the data with an XML schema.

user-defined datatype The terminology used to describe a named object for use as a datatype in a table; now known as an alias datatype.

V

view A filter through which one or more columns from one or more base tables are displayed.

VLDB A very large database—many gibibytes or tebibytes.

VPC Virtual Personal Computer; an application that runs an operating system on your host operating system;

a means of isolating one computer environment from another running in the same operating system.

W

workgroup An arrangement of clients that each stands alone; each must be administered individually; there is no central domain controller.

X

XSD XML Schema Definition Language. An XML schema defines the elements, attributes, and datatypes that conform to the World Wide Web Consortium (W3C) XML Schema Part 1: Structures Recommendation for the SML Schema Definition Language. The W3C XML Schema Part 2: Datatypes Recommendation is the guidance for defining datatypes used in XML schemas. The XML schema definition language enables you to define the structure and datatypes for XML messages.

XSL Extensible Stylesheet Language; an XML vocabulary that is used to transform XML data to another form, such as HTML, by means of a style sheet that defines presentation rules.

XSLT Extensible Stylesheet Language Transformations. This evolved from the early Extensible Stylesheet Language (XSL) standard. XSL specifies a language definition for XML data presentation and data transformations. Data presentation means displaying data in some format and/or medium, and concerns style. Data transformation refers to parsing an input XML document into a tree of nodes and then converting the source tree into a result tree; transformation concerns data exchange.